A HISTORY OF WESTERN SOCIETY

Volume I: From Antiquity to the Enlightenment

A HISTORY OF WESTERN SOCIETY

Second Edition

Volume I: From Antiquity to the Enlightenment

John P. McKay

Bennett D. Hill

John Buckler

University of Illinois, Urbana

Houghton Mifflin Company

Boston

Dallas   Geneva, Illinois
Hopewell, New Jersey   Palo Alto
London

About the Authors

John P. McKay A native of St. Louis, Missouri, John P. McKay received his B.A. from Wesleyan University (1961), his M.A. from the Fletcher School of Law and Diplomacy (1962), and his Ph.D. from the University of California, Berkeley (1968). He began teaching history at the University of Illinois in 1966 and became a professor there in 1976. John won the Herbert Baxter Adams Prize for his book *Pioneers for Profit: Foreign Entrepreneurship and Russian Industrialization, 1885–1913* (1970). He has also written *Tramways and Trolleys: The Rise of Urban Mass Transport in Europe* (1976) and has translated Jules Michelet's *The People* (1973). His research has been supported by fellowships from the Ford Foundation, the Guggenheim Foundation, and IREX. Recently named general editor of *Industrial Development and the Social Fabric: An International Series of Historical Monographs,* John continues to serve on the editorial board of the *Journal of Economic History.*

Bennett D. Hill A native of Philadelphia, Bennett D. Hill earned an A.B. at Princeton (1956) and advanced degrees from Harvard (A.M., 1958) and Princeton (Ph.D., 1963). He is a professor of history at the University of Illinois at Urbana, where he served as chairman of the department from 1978 to 1981. He has published *English Cistercian Monasteries and Their Patrons in the Twelfth Century* (1968) and *Church and State in the Middle Ages* (1970); and articles in *Analecta Cisterciensia, The New Catholic Encyclopaedia, The American Benedictine Review,* and *The Dictionary of the Middle Ages.* His reviews have appeared in *The American Historical Review, Speculum, The Historian, The Catholic Historical Review,* and *Library Journal.* He has been a fellow of the American Council of Learned Societies, served on numerous committees for the National Endowment for the Humanities and the Woodrow Wilson Foundation, and is an associate editor of the *American Benedictine Review.*

John Buckler Born in Louisville, Kentucky, John Buckler received his B.A. from the University of Louisville in 1967. Harvard University awarded him the Ph.D. in 1973. He is currently an associate professor at the University of Illinois, and is serving on the Subcommittee on Cartography of the American Philological Association. In 1980 Harvard University Press published his *The Theban Hegemony, 371–362 B.C.* His articles have appeared in journals both here and abroad, including the *American Journal of Ancient History, Classical Philology, Rheinisches Museum für Philologie, Classical Quarterly, Wiener Studien,* and *Symbolae Osloenses.*

Text Credits

Excerpts from S. N. Kramer, *The Sumerians* (Chicago: University of Chicago Press, 1964), copyright © by the University of Chicago. Reprinted by permission. Excerpts from "Sumerian Myths and Epic Tales," trans. S. N. Kramer; "Akkadian Myths and Epics," trans. E. Z. Speiser; "Laws from Mesopotamia and Asia Minor," trans. S. N. Kramer; and "Summarian Wisdom Text," trans. S. N. Kramer, in *Ancient Near Eastern Texts Relating to the Old Testament* by James B. Pritchard (ed.), 3rd ed. with Supplement (copyright © 1969 by Princeton University Press), pp. 44–590 (passim). Reprinted by permission of Princeton University Press. Excerpts from *Greek Elegy and Iambus,* trans. by J. M. Edmonds, Harvard University Press, 1931, reprinted by permission of the publisher and the Loeb Classical Library. Excerpts from Sappho reprinted by permission of Schocken Books Inc. from *Greek Lyric Poetry* edited by Willis Barnstone. Copyright © 1962, 1967 by Willis Barnstone. Excerpts from J. T. McNeil and H. Gamer, trans., *Medieval Handbooks of Penance,* Octagon Books, New York, 1965. Reprinted by permission of Columbia University Press. Riddle No. 44 from Michael Alexander, trans., *The Earliest English Poems* (London: Penguin Books Ltd, 1966), p. 99. Copyright © Michael Alexander, 1966. Reprinted by permission of Penguin Books Ltd. Excerpts from "Richard II," Act II, Scene I, and "Hamlet," Act III, Scene I, in *The Complete Plays and Poems of William Shakespeare* (edited by William A. Neilson and C. J. Hill). Copyright © 1942 by Houghton Mifflin Company. Copyright renewed, 1969.

Cover: Winter Scene on a Frozen Canal Oil on wood by Hendrick Avercamp (c. 1585/6–1634). From the Collection of Mr. & Mrs. Edward William Carter.

Printed in the U.S.A.

Library of Congress Catalog Card Number: 82-81320

ISBN: 0-395-32798-9

CONTENTS

MAPS

PREFACE

A HISTORY OF WESTERN SOCIETY grew out of the authors' desire to infuse new life into the study of Western civilization. As we wrote in the preface to the first edition, "History is the study of change over time and historians have seen many changes in their own discipline in recent years. Imaginative questions and innovative research have opened up vast new areas of interest and increased historical knowledge rapidly." We noted that the pushing back of the frontiers of knowledge had been especially dramatic in European social history, but that similar advances had characterized economic and intellectual history, while new research and fresh interpretations were simultaneously revitalizing the study of the traditional mainstream of political, diplomatic, and religious development. Yet it seemed to us that although new discoveries and controversies were stimulating professional historians, both the broad public and the intelligentsia often appeared to be losing interest in the past. The distinguished mathematical economist of our acquaintance who smugly quipped "What's new in history?" – confident that the answer was nothing and that historians were as dead as the events they examine – was not alone.

It was our conviction, based on considerable experience introducing large numbers of students to the broad sweep of Western civilization, that a book reflecting current trends could excite readers and inspire a new interest in history and a heightened curiosity about our Western heritage. Our strategy was twofold. First, we made social history the core element of our work. Not only did we incorporate recent research by social historians, but also we sought to re-create the life of ordinary people in appealing human terms. At the same time we were determined to give the great economic, political, intellectual, and cultural developments the attention they unquestionably deserve. We wanted to give individual readers and instructors a balanced, integrated perspective, so that they could pursue on their own or in the classroom those themes and questions that they found particularly exciting and significant.

In preparing the second edition we have worked hard to build upon the favorable response to our efforts. Social history remains the core element of our work, and once again important recent research on such subjects as population, diet, women, and the family has been integrated into the text. At the same time we have expanded somewhat our treatment of major intellectual and cultural developments in order to realize fully the promise of the balanced approach of the first edition. Thus the discussion of such topics as Judaism, Islam, medieval philosophy, the baroque, romanticism, and nineteenth-century science has been substantially expanded, for example, while new material on ancient Egypt, medieval drama, Renaissance literature, French classicism, Descartes, Darwin, and realism has been woven into the work. Finally, every chapter of the book has been painstakingly reviewed for content and clarity, resulting in a wholly new chapter on the ancient Near East and in many small improvements, notably in the discussion of feudalism, the English Reformation, and the French Revolution. In all our endeavors the encouraging, constructive comments and suggestions of many readers have been greatly appreciated.

Other distinctive features from the first edition remain in the second. To help guide the reader toward historical understanding we have posed specific historical questions at the beginning of each chapter. These questions are then answered in the course of the chapter, each of which now concludes with a concise summary of the chapter's findings. Timelines, which students find useful, have been added in many chapters.

We have also tried to suggest how historians actually work and think. We have quoted rather extensively from a wide variety of primary sources and have demonstrated in our use of these quotations how historians sift and weigh evidence. We want the reader to realize that history is neither a list of cut-and-dried facts nor a senseless jumble of conflicting opinions. It is our further hope that the primary quotations, so carefully fitted into their historical context, will give the reader a sense that even in the earliest and most remote periods of human experience history has been shaped by individual men and women, some of them great aristocrats, others ordinary folk.

Each chapter concludes with several carefully selected suggestions for further reading. These suggestions are briefly described, in order to help readers know where to go to continue thinking and learning about the Western world. The chapter bibliographies have been expanded in order to keep them current with the vast and complex new work being done in many fields. In a number of areas each new journal or monograph may present fresh perspectives or challenge accepted views, and the best of these recent works have been singled out for citation.

The second edition has many new illustrations and all the illustrations in *A History of Western Society* have been carefully selected to re-enforce both the book's social theme and its balanced treatment of all aspects of Western history. Artwork is an integral part of our book, for the past can speak in pictures as well as words. Maps and line drawings are also a fundamental part of the book and, as with illustrations, they carry captions to enhance their value.

Western civilization courses differ widely in chronological structure from one campus to another. To accommodate the various divisions of historical time into intervals that fit a two-quarter, three-quarter, or two-semester period, *A History of Western Society* is being published in three versions, each set embracing the complete work:

One-volume hardcover edition, A HISTORY OF WESTERN SOCIETY; two-volume paperback, A HISTORY OF WESTERN SOCIETY *Volume I: From Antiquity to the Enlightenment* (Chapters 1-17), *Volume II: From Absolutism to the Present* (Chapters 16-31); three-volume paperback, A HISTORY OF WESTERN SOCIETY *Volume A: From Antiquity to the Reformation* (Chapters 1-13), *Volume B: From the Renaissance to 1815* (Chapters 12-21), *Volume C: From the Revolutionary Era to the Present* (Chapters 21-31).

Note that overlapping chapters in both the two- and the three-volume sets permit still wider flexibility in matching the appropriate volume with the opening and closing dates of a course term. Furthermore, for courses beginning with the Renaissance rather than antiquity or the medieval period, the reader can begin study with Volume B.

A History of Western Society also has a study guide for students, as well as an instructor's manual. Both of these excellent aids have been written primarily by Professor James Schmiechen of Central Michigan University. Professor Schmiechen read all our drafts, from the first prospectus to the final typescript of the second edition, and he gave us many valuable suggestions in addition to his enthusiastic and warmly appreciated support. His *Study Guide* contains chapter summaries, chapter outlines, study questions, self-check lists of important concepts and events, and a variety of study aids and suggestions. An innovation in this revision of the *Study Guide* – one that we feel will be extremely useful to the student – is our step-by-step Reading with Understanding exercises, which take the reader by ostensive example through reading and studying activities like underlining, summarizing, identifying main points, classifying information according to sequence, and making historical comparisons. To enable both students and instructors to use the *Study Guide* with the greatest possible flexibility, the guide is available in two volumes, with considerable overlapping of chapters. Instructors and students who use only Volumes A and B of the text have all the pertinent study materials in a single volume, *Study Guide, Volume* 1 (Chapters 1–21); likewise, those who use only Volumes B and C of the text also have all the necessary materials in one volume, *Study Guide, Volume* 2 (Chapters 12–31).

It is also a pleasure to thank Roger Schlesinger, Washington State University; Charles Rearick, University of Massachusetts at Amherst; Donald Buck, DeAnza College; James Powell, Syracuse University; John M. Riddle, North Carolina State University; Laurence Lee Howe, University of Louisville; and Archibald Lewis, University of Massachusetts at Amherst, Jack R. Harlan, University of Illinois; Marc Cooper, Southwestern Missouri State University; and Lowell L. Blaisdell, Texas Tech University; Kevin K. Carroll, Arizona State University; Robert G. Clouse, Indiana State University; Albert A. Hayden, Wittenberg University; Harry M. Hutson, University of Tennessee at Martin; Dorothy Vogel Krupnik, Indiana University of Pennsylvania; Charles A. Le Guin, Portland State University; Carolyn C. Lougee, Stanford University; Paul J. Pinckney, University of Tennessee-Knoxville; C. Mary Taney, Glassboro State College; William M. Welch, Jr., Troy State University; and John C. White, University of Alabama-Huntsville, who read and critiqued the manuscript through its development.

Many of our colleagues at the University of Illinois kindly provided information and stimulation for our book, often without even knowing it. N. Frederick Nash, Rare Book Librarian, gave freely of his time and made many helpful suggestions for illustrations. Barbara Bohen, Director of the World Heritage Museum at the University, allowed us complete access to the sizable holdings of the museum. James Dengate kindly supplied information on objects from the museum's collection. Caroline Buckler took many excellent photographs of the museum's objects and generously helped us at crucial moments in production. Such wide-ranging expertise was a great asset for which we are very appreciative. Bennett Hill wishes to express his sincere appreciation to the Rt. Rev. James A. Wiseman, Abbot of St. Anselm's Abbey, Washington, D.C. for his support and understanding in the preparation of this second edition; and to William McKane for help with the maps.

Each of us has benefited from the generous criticism of his co-authors, although each of us assumes responsibility for what he has written. John Buckler has written the first six chapters; Bennett Hill has continued the narrative through Chapter 16; and John McKay has written Chapters 17 through 31. Finally, we warmly welcome any comments or suggestions for improvements from our readers.

JOHN P. MCKAY
BENNETT D. HILL
JOHN BUCKLER

CHAPTER 1

NEAR EASTERN ORIGINS

THE CULTURE of the modern Western world has its origins in places as far away as modern Iraq, Iran, and Egypt. In these areas human beings abandoned their life of roaming and hunting to settle in stable agricultural communities. From these communities grew cities and civilizations, societies that invented concepts and techniques that have become integral parts of contemporary life. Fundamental is the development of writing by the Sumerians in Mesopotamia, an invention that enables knowledge of the past to be preserved and facilitates the spread and accumulation of learning, lore, literature, and science. Mathematics, astronomy, and architecture were all innovations of the ancient Near Eastern civilizations. So too were the first law codes and religious concepts that still permeate daily life.

How did wild hunters become urban dwellers? How did the roots of Western culture establish themselves in far-off Mesopotamia, and what caused Mesopotamian culture to become predominant throughout most of the ancient Near East? What part did the Egyptians play in this vast story? Lastly, what did the arrival of the Hittites on the fringes of Mesopotamia and Egypt mean to the superior cultures of their new neighbors? These are the questions this chapter will explore.

On December 27, 1831, young Charles Darwin stepped aboard the H.M.S. *Beagle* to begin a voyage to South America and the Pacific Ocean. In the course of that five-year voyage he became convinced that species of animals and human beings had evolved from lower forms. At first Darwin was reluctant to make public his theories because they ran counter to the biblical account of creation, which claimed that God had made Adam in one day. Finally, however, in 1859 he published *On the Origin of Species.* In 1871 he fol-

lowed it with *The Descent of Man,* in which he argued that human beings and apes are descended from a common ancestor. Even before Darwin had proclaimed his theories, evidence to support them had come to light. In 1856, the fossilized bones of an early form of man were discovered in the Neander valley of Germany. Called Neanderthal Man after the place of his discovery, he was physically more primitive than and anatomically a bit different from modern man (*Homo sapiens,* or thinking man). But he was clearly a human being and not an ape. He offered proof of Darwin's theory that *Homo sapiens* had evolved from less-developed forms.

The theories of Darwin, supported by the evidence of fossilized remains, ushered in a new scientific era, an era in which scientists and scholars have re-examined the very nature of human beings and their history. Men and women of the twentieth century have made new discoveries, solved some old problems, and raised many new ones. Since 1959, the anthropologists Louis and Mary Leakey and their son Richard, working in the Olduvai Gorge in East Africa, have uncovered fossilized bones of several very early types of human beings as well as species of advanced apes. The work of the Leakeys alone demonstrates how complex the course of human evolution has been.

Why did some human types become extinct while others thrived? More importantly, what are the links among the fossilized remains? The answers to these questions lie in the future. For the moment, perhaps the wisest and most humble answer is the observation of Loren Eiseley, a noted American anthropologist: "The human interminglings of hundreds of thousands of years of prehistory are not to be clarified by a single generation of archaeologists."[1]

Despite the enormous uncertainty surrounding human development, a reasonably clear picture can be had of two important early periods: the Paleolithic or Old Stone Age, and the Neolithic or New Stone Age. The immensely long Paleolithic Age, which lasted from about 400,000 B.C. until about 7000 B.C., takes its name from the crude stone tools the earliest hunters chipped from flint and obsidian, a black volcanic rock. During the much shorter Neolithic Age, which lasted from about 7000 B.C. to about 3000 B.C., human beings began using new types of stone tools and pursuing agriculture.

THE PALEOLITHIC AGE

Life in the Paleolithic Age was perilous and uncertain at best. Survival depended largely on the success of the hunt, but the hunt often brought sudden and violent death. Paleolithic peoples hunted in a variety of ways, depending on the climate and the environment. Often the hunters stationed themselves at river fords and waterholes and waited for their prey to come to them. Paleolithic hunters were thoroughly familiar with the habits of the animals they relied upon, and paid close attention to their migratory habits. Other hunters trapped their quarry, and those who lived in open areas stalked and pursued game. Paleolithic peoples hunted a huge variety of animals, ranging from elephants in Spain to deer in China.

Success in the hunt often depended more on the quality and effectiveness of the hunters' social organization than on their bravery. Paleolithic hunters were organized — they hunted in groups. They used their knowledge of the animal world and their power of thinking to plan how to down their prey. The ability to think and to act as an organized social group meant that Paleolithic hunters could successfully feed on animals that were bigger, faster, and stronger than themselves.

Paleolithic peoples also nourished themselves by gathering nuts, berries, and seeds. Just as they knew the habits of animals, so they had vast knowledge of the plant kingdom. Some Paleolithic peoples even knew how to plant wild seeds to supplement their food supply. Thus, they relied on every part of the environment for their survival.

Home for Paleolithic folk also varied according to climate and environment. Particularly in cold regions, they sought refuge in caves from the weather, predatory animals, and other people. In warmer climates and in open country they built shelters, some of them no more elaborate than temporary huts or sunscreens.

The basic social unit of Paleolithic societies was probably the family, but family bonds were no doubt stronger and more extensive than those of families in modern, urban, and industrialized societies. It is likely that the bonds of kinship were strong not just within the nuclear family of father, mother, and children, but throughout the extended family of uncles, aunts, cousins, nephews, and nieces. People in nomadic societies typically depend on the extended family for cooperative work and mutual protection. The ties of kinship probably also extended beyond the family to the tribe. A *tribe* was a group of families, led by a patriarch, who considered themselves to be descended from a common ancestor. Most tribes probably consisted of from thirty to fifty people.

As in the hunt, so too in other aspects of life — the members of the group had to cooperate in order to survive. The adult males normally hunted, and between hunts made their stone weapons. The realm of the women was probably the camp. There they made utensils, and were probably responsible for the invention of weaving. They fashioned skins into cloths, tents, and footwear. They left the camp to gather nuts, grains, and fruits to supplement the group's diet. Their unique function was the bearing of children, who were essential to the continuation of the group.

Women also had to tend the children, especially in their earliest and most helpless days. Part of women's work was tending the fire, which served for warmth and cooking and also for protection against wild animals.

Paleolithic peoples were also world travelers. Before the dawn of history bands of *Homo sapiens* flourished in Europe, Africa, and Asia, and had crossed into the continents of North and South America and Australia. By the end of the Paleolithic Age, there were very few "undiscovered" areas left in the world.

Some of the most striking accomplishments of Paleolithic peoples were intellectual. The development of the human brain made thought possible. Unlike animals, whose behavior is the result of instinct, Paleolithic peoples used reason to govern their actions. Thought and language permitted the lore and experience of the old to be passed on to the young. An invisible world also opened up to *Homo sapiens*. The Neanderthalers developed the custom of burying their dead and of leaving offerings with the body, perhaps in the belief that in some way life continued after death.

Paleolithic peoples produced the first art. They decorated the walls of their caves with paintings of animals and scenes of the hunt. They also began to fashion clay models of pregnant women and of animals. Many of the surviving paintings, such as those at Altamira in Spain and Lascaux in France, are located deep in the caves, in areas not easily accessible.

These areas were probably places of ritual and initiation, where young men were taken when they joined the ranks of the hunters. They were also places of magic. The animals depicted on the walls were either those hunted for food or those feared as predators. Many are shown wounded by spears or arrows; others are pregnant. The early artists may have been expressing the hope that the hunt would be successful and game plentiful. By portraying the animals as realistically as possible, the artists and hunters may have hoped to gain power over them. The statuettes of pregnant women seem to express a wish for fertile women to have babies and thus ensure the group's survival. The wall paintings and statuettes express human beings' earliest yearnings to control their environment.

Despite their many achievements, Paleolithic peoples were sometimes their own worst enemies. At times they fought each other for control of hunting grounds, and some early hunters wiped out less aggressive peoples. On occasion Paleolithic peoples seem to have preyed on one another, probably under the threat of starvation. One of the grimmest indications that Neanderthal Man was at times cannibalistic comes from a cave in Yugoslavia, where investigators found human bones burned and split open. Even so, cannibalism appears to have been rare. The overriding struggle of the Paleolithic Age was with an uncompromising environment.

THE NEOLITHIC AGE

Hunting is at best a precarious way of life, even when the diet is supplemented with seeds and fruits. If the climate changed even slightly, the all-important herds might move to new areas. As recently as the late 1950s the

Caribou Eskimos of the Canadian Northwest Territories suffered a severe famine when the caribou herds, their only source of food and bone for weapons, changed their migration route. Paleolithic tribes either moved with the herds, and adapted themselves to new circumstances, or – like the Caribou Eskimos – perished. Several long ice ages – periods when huge glaciers covered vast parts of Europe – subjected small bands of Paleolithic hunters to extreme hardship.

Not long after the last Ice Age, around 7000 B.C., some hunters and gatherers began to rely chiefly on agriculture for their sustenance. This development has traditionally been called "the Agricultural Revolution." Yet the work of Jack R. Harlan, a leading scientist in the field of agronomy, has caused scholars to reappraise the origins of agriculture:

Agriculture is not an invention or a discovery and is not as revolutionary as we had thought; furthermore, it was adopted slowly and with reluctance. The current evidence indicates that agriculture evolved through an extension and intensification of what people had already been doing for a long time.[2]

Striking support for Harlan's view came in 1981 from an American archaeological expedition to the Nile valley in Egypt. Investigators found that for thousands of years nomads had planted wheat and barley in the silt left by the flooding of the Nile. These people, however, never shifted to a life of settled farming. Instead, the crops they grew were just another, though important, source of their food. In short, hunters and gatherers apparently long knew how to grow crops, but did not base their existence on them.

The real transformation of human life occurred when hunters and gatherers gave up their nomadic way of life to depend primarily on the grain they grew and the animals they domesticated. Agriculture made for a more stable and secure life. Neolithic peoples thus flourished, fashioning an energetic and creative era. They were responsible for many fundamental inventions and innovations that the modern world takes for granted. First, obviously, is systematic agriculture, the primary economic activity of the entire ancient world and the basis of all modern life. The settled routine of Neolithic farmers led to the evolution of towns and eventually cities. Neolithic farmers usually raised more food than they could consume, and their surpluses permitted larger and healthier populations. Since surpluses of food could also be bartered for other commodities, the Neolithic era witnessed the beginnings of large-scale trade. In time the increasing complexity of Neolithic societies led to the development of writing, prompted by the need to keep records and later by the urge to chronicle experiences, learning, and beliefs.

The transition to settled life also had a profound impact on the family. The shared needs and pressures that make for strong extended-family ties in nomadic societies are less prominent in settled societies. Bonds to the extended family weakened. In towns and cities, the nuclear family – father, mother, and children – was more dependent on its immediate neighbors than on kinfolk.

Meanwhile, however, the nomadic way of life and the family relationships it nurtured continued to flourish alongside settled agriculture. Even nomadic life changed. Neolithic nomads traveled with flocks of domesticated animals, which were their main source of wealth and food. Often farmers and nomads bartered peaceably with one another, each group trading its surpluses for those of the other. Although nomadic peoples continued

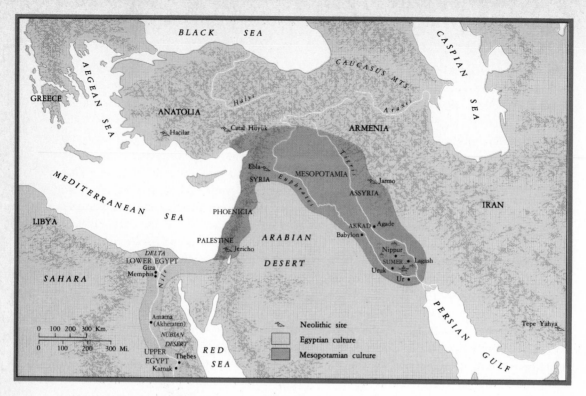

MAP 1.1 SPREAD OF CULTURES *This map illustrates the spread of Mesopotamian and Egyptian culture through a semicircular stretch of land often called the "Fertile Crescent."*

to exist throughout the Neolithic period and into modern times, the future belonged to the Neolithic farmers and their descendants. While the development of agriculture may not have been revolutionary, the changes that it ushered in certainly were.

Until recently, scholars thought that agriculture originated in the ancient Near East and gradually spread elsewhere. Contemporary work, however, points to a more complex pattern of development. For unknown reasons people in various parts of the world all seem to have begun domesticating plants and animals at roughly the same time, around 7000 B.C. Four main points of origin have been identified. In the Near East, sites as far apart as Tepe Yahya in modern Iran, Jarmo in Iraq, Jericho in Palestine, and Hacilar in modern

Turkey (see Map 1.1) raised wheat, barley, peas, and lentils. They also kept herds of sheep, pigs, and possibly goats. In western Africa, Neolithic farmers domesticated many plants, including millet, sorghum, and yams. In northeastern China, peoples of the Yangshao culture developed techniques of field agriculture, animal husbandry, potterymaking, and bronze metallurgy. Innovations in the New World were equally striking. Indians in Central and South America domesticated a host of plants, among them corn, beans, and squash. From these far-flung areas, knowledge of farming techniques spread to still other regions.

The first farmers gathered and planted the seeds of wild wheat, barley, and other plants. Later farmers learned to improve their crops.

The excavators of Tepe Yahya demonstrated in 1976 how specialization in farming could have led to a new species of grain: the Neolithic farmers of Tepe Yahya, preferring a particular species of wheat to others, planted only that species; when nearby wild grasses fertilized the wheat naturally, a new hybrid species resulted.

The deliberate planting of crops itself led to changes in their genetic structure. The plants and animals cultivated by Neolithic farmers gradually evolved to the point where most of them could no longer survive in the wild. Thus human beings and the plants and animals they domesticated depended on each other for survival. Contemporary work on the origins of farming has led to a chilling revelation: the genetic base of most modern domesticated plants, like wheat and corn, is so narrow that a new pest or plant disease could destroy much of it. The result would be widespread famine. Human society is depending on a precarious food base.

Once people began to rely on farming for their livelihood, they settled in permanent villages and built houses. The location of the village was crucial. Early farmers chose places where the water supply was constant and adequate for their crops and flocks. At first, villages were small, consisting of a few households. As the population expanded and prospered, villages usually developed into towns. Between 8000 and 7000 B.C., the community at Jericho grew to at least two thousand people. Jericho's inhabitants lived in mud-brick houses built on stone foundations, and they surrounded their town with a massive fortification wall. The Neolithic site of Catal Hüyük in Anatolia (modern Turkey) covered thirty-two acres. The outer houses of the settlement formed a solid wall of mud brick, which served as a bulwark against attack. At Tepe Yahya, too, the Neolithic farmers surrounded their town with a wall.

Walls offered protection and permitted a more secure and stable way of life than that of the nomad. They also prove that towns grew in size, population, and wealth, for these fortifications were so large that they could have been raised only by a large labor force. They also indicate that towns were developing social and political organization. The fortifications were the work of the whole community, and they would have been impossible without central planning.

One of the major effects of the advent of agriculture and settled life was a dramatic increase in population. No census figures exist for this period, but the number and size of the towns prove that Neolithic society was expanding. Early farmers found that agriculture provided a larger and much more dependable food supply than had hunting and gathering. No longer did the long winter months mean the immediate threat of starvation. Farmers raised more food than they could consume, and they learned to store the surplus for the winter. Because the farming community was better fed than ever before, it was also more resistant to diseases that kill people who are suffering from malnutrition. Thus Neolithic farmers were healthier and longer-lived than their predecessors. All these factors explain the growth of towns like Jericho and Jarmo.

The surplus of food had two other momentous consequences. First, grain became an article of commerce. The farming community traded surplus grain for items it could not produce itself. The community thus obtained raw materials such as precious gems and metals. In Mesopotamia the early towns imported copper from the north, and eventually copper replaced stone for tools and weapons. Trade also brought Neolithic communities

TOWER AT JERICHO *Photographed during excavation, this tower is a good example of the strong fortifications of Neolithic towns. The sheer size of the walls amply illustrates the huge amount of labor and central planning necessary to build them. (Consulate General of Israel)*

particular crafts produced more and better goods than any single individual could.

Prosperity and stable conditions nurtured other innovations and discoveries. Neolithic farmers improved their tools and agricultural techniques. They domesticated bigger, stronger animals, such as the bull and the horse, to work for them. To harness the power of these animals they invented tools like the plow, which came into use by 3000 B.C. The first plows had wooden shares and could break only light soils, but they were far more efficient than stone hoes. By 3000 B.C. the wheel had been invented, and farmers devised ways of hitching bulls and horses to wagons. These developments enabled Neolithic farmers to raise more food more efficiently and easily than ever before, simply because animals and machines were doing a greater proportion of the actual work.

In arid regions like Mesopotamia and Egypt, farmers learned to irrigate their land. By diverting water from rivers, they were able to open new land to cultivation. River waters flooding the fields deposited layers of rich mud, which increased the fertility of the soil. Thus the rivers, together with the manure of domesticated animals, kept replenishing the land. One result was a further increase in population and wealth. Irrigation, especially on a large scale, demanded group effort. The entire community had to plan which land to irrigate and how to lay out the canals. Then everyone had to help dig the canals. The demands of irrigation underscored the need for strong central authority within the community. Successful irrigation projects in turn strengthened such central authority by proving it effective and beneficial. Towns evolved corporate spirit and governments, to which individuals were subordinate. Here were the makings of urban life.

The development of systematic agriculture

into touch with one another, making possible the spread of ideas and techniques.

Second, agricultural surplus made possible the division of labor. It freed some members of the community from the necessity of raising food. Artisans and craftsmen devoted their attention to making the new stone tools farming demanded — hoes and sickles for fieldwork and mortars and pestles for grinding the grain. Other artisans began to shape clay into pottery vessels, which were used to store grain, wine, and oil, and which served as kitchen utensils. Still other artisans wove baskets and cloth. People who could specialize in

was a fundamental turning-point in the history of civilization. Farming gave rise to stable settled societies, which enjoyed considerable prosperity. It made possible an enormous increase in population. Some inhabitants of the budding towns turned their attention to the production of goods that made life more comfortable. Settled circumstances and a certain amount of leisure made the accumulation and spread of knowledge easier. Finally, sustained farming prepared the way for urban life.

MESOPOTAMIAN CIVILIZATION

Mesopotamia is the Greek name for the land between the Euphrates and Tigris rivers. Both rivers have their headwaters in the mountains of Armenia in modern Turkey. Both are fed by numerous tributaries, and the entire river system drains a vast mountainous region. Overland routes in Mesopotamia usually follow the Euphrates, because the banks of the Tigris are frequently steep and difficult. North of the ancient city of Babylon, the land levels out into a barren expanse. In 401 B.C., the Greek writer and adventurer Xenophon gave a vivid description of this area:

In this area the land is a level plain just like the sea, full of wormwood. If there was any brush or reed there, it was invariably fragrant, like spices. Trees there were none, but wild animals of all sorts — a great many wild asses and many ostriches. There were also bustards and gazelles.[3]

The desert continues south of Babylon, and in 1857 the English geologist and traveler W. K. Loftus depicted it in grim terms:

There is no life for miles around. No river glides in grandeur at the base of its [the ancient city of Uruk] mounds; no green date groves flourish near its ruins. The jackal and the hyena appear to shun the dull aspect of its tombs. The king of birds never hovers over the deserted waste. A blade of grass or an insect finds no existence there. The shrivelled lichen alone, clinging to the weathered surface of the broken brick, seems to glory in its universal dominion upon those barren walls.[4]

Farther south the desert gives way to a six-thousand square-mile region of marshes, lagoons, mudflats, and reed banks. At last, in the extreme south the Euphrates and the Tigris unite and empty into the Persian Gulf.

This forbidding area became the home of many folk and the land of the first cities. Bands of Semitic nomads occupied the region around Akkad (modern Baghdad). Into the south came the Sumerians, a people who probably migrated from the east. The Sumerians were farmers and city builders. By 3000 B.C. they had established a number of cities in the southernmost part of Mesopotamia, a region that became known as Sumer. As the Sumerians pushed north, they came into contact with the Semites, who readily adopted Sumerian culture, and turned to urban life. The Sumerians soon changed the face of the land and made Mesopotamia the "cradle of civilization" (see Map 1.1).

ENVIRONMENT AND MESOPOTAMIAN CULTURE

From the outset geography had a profound effect on the evolution of Mesopotamian civilization. In this region agriculture is possible only with irrigation. Consequently, the Sumerians and later the Akkadians built their cities along the Tigris and Euphrates and their branches. The rivers supplied fish, a major element of the city dwellers' diet. The rivers also provided reeds and clay, which they used

MAP OF NIPPUR *The oldest map in the world, dating to ca 1500 B.C., shows the layout of the Mesopotamian city of Nippur. Inscribed on a clay tablet, the map has enabled archaeologists to locate ruined buildings: (A) the ziggurat, (B) canal, (C) enclosure and gardens, (D) city gates, and (E) the Euphrates River. (From the photographic collections of the University Museum, The University of Pennsylvania)*

as building materials. Since this entire area lacks stone, mud-brick became the primary building-block of Mesopotamian architecture.

Although the rivers sustained life, they acted simultaneously as a powerful restraining force, especially on Sumerian political development. They made Sumer a geographical maze. Between the rivers, streams, and irrigation canals stretched open desert or swamp, where nomadic tribes roamed. Communication between cities was difficult and at times dangerous. City was isolated from city, each in its own locale. Thus each Sumerian city became a state, independent of the others and protective of its independence. Any city that tried to unify the country was resisted by the other cities. As a result, the political history of Sumer is one of almost constant warfare.

The experience of the city of Nippur is an example of how bad conditions could become. At one point in its history Nippur was conquered eighteen times in twenty-four years. Although Sumer was eventually unified, unification came late and was always tenuous.

The harsh environment fostered a grim, even pessimistic, spirit among the Mesopotamians. They especially feared the ravages of flood. The Tigris can bring quick devastation, as it did to Baghdad in 1831, when floodwaters destroyed seven thousand homes in a single night. The same tragedy occurred often in antiquity. The chronicle of King Hammurabi recorded years when floods wiped out whole cities. Vulnerability to natural disaster deeply influenced Mesopotamian religious beliefs.

The Mesopotamians considered natural catastrophes the work of the gods. At times the Sumerians described their chief god, Enlil, as "the raging flood which has no rival." The gods, they believed, even used nature to punish the Mesopotamians. According to the myth of the Deluge, which gave rise to the biblical story of Noah, the god Enki warned Ziusudra, the Sumerian Noah:

A flood will sweep over the cult-centers;
To destroy the seed of mankind . . .
Is the decision, the word of the assembly of
*   the gods.*[5]

The myth of Atrahasis describes the gods' annoyance at the prosperity of mankind and tells how Enlil complained to the other gods:

Oppressive has become the clamor of mankind.
By their uproar they prevent sleep.
Let the flour be cut off for the people,
In their bellies let the greens be too few.[6]

Enlil and the other gods decide to send a drought and then a flood to destroy human life. In the face of harsh conditions, the Mesopotamians considered themselves weak and insignificant as compared to the gods. This feeling was particularly strong among the Sumerians.

The Mesopotamians did not worship their deities because the gods were holy. Human beings were too insignificant to pass judgment on the conduct of the gods, and the gods were too superior to honor human morals. Rather, the Mesopotamians worshiped the gods because they were mighty. Likewise, it was not the place of men and women to understand the gods. The Sumerian Job once complained to his god:

The man of deceit has conspired against me,
And you, my god, do not thwart him,
You carry off my understanding.[7]

The motives of the gods were not always clear. In times of affliction one could only pray and offer sacrifices to appease them.

SUMERIAN SOCIETY

The Sumerians sought to please and calm the gods, especially the patron deity of the city. In the center of each city the people erected a shrine and then built their houses around it. The best way to honor the god was to make the shrine as grand and as impressive as possible, for a god who had a splendid temple might think twice about sending floods to destroy the city.

The temple had to be worthy of the god, a symbol of his power, and it had to last. Special skills and materials were needed to build it. Only stone was suitable for its foundations and precious metals for its decoration. Since the Mesopotamians had to import both stone and metals, temple construction encouraged trade. Architects, engineers, craftsmen, and workers had to devote a great deal of thought, effort, and time to build the temple. By 2000

B.C. the result was Mesopotamia's first monumental architecture – the ziggurat, a massive stepped tower that dominated the city.

Once the ziggurat was built, a professional priesthood was needed to run it and to perform the god's rituals. The people of the city met the expenses of building and maintaining the temple and its priesthood by setting aside extensive tracts of land for that purpose. The priests took charge of the produce of the temple lands and the sacred flocks. Part of the yield went to the feeding and clothing of the priests and the temple staff, and for offerings to the gods. Part was sold or bartered to obtain goods, such as precious metals or stone, needed for construction, maintenance, and ritual.

Until recently, the dominant position and wealth of the temple had led historians to consider the Sumerian city-state an absolute theocracy, or government by an established priesthood. According to this view, the temple and its priests owned the city's land and controlled its economy. Newly discovered documents and recent works, however, have resulted in new ideas about the Sumerian city and its society. It is now known that the temple owned a large fraction, but not all, of the city's territory, and did not govern the city. A king, or *lugal,* exercised political power, and most of the city's land was the property of individual citizens.

Sumerian society was a complex arrangement of freedom and dependence and was divided into four categories: nobles, free clients of the nobility, commoners, and slaves. The nobility consisted of the king and his family, the chief priests, and high palace officials. The king originally rose to power as a war leader, elected by the citizenry, who established a regular army, trained it and led it into battle. The might of the king and the frequency of warfare in Mesopotamia quickly made him the supreme figure in the city, and kingship soon became hereditary. The symbol of his status was the palace, which rivaled the temple in grandeur.

The king and the lesser nobility held extensive tracts of land that were, like the estates of the temple, worked by slaves and clients. Clients were free men and women who were dependent on the nobility. In return for their labor the clients received small plots of land to work for themselves. Although this arrangement assured the clients of a livelihood, the land they worked remained the possession of the nobility or the temple. Thus, not only did the nobility control most – and probably the best – land, they also commanded the obedience of a huge segment of society. They were the dominant force in Mesopotamian society.

Commoners were free citizens. They were independent of the nobility; however, they could not rival the nobility in social status and political power. Commoners belonged to large patriarchal families that owned land in their own right. Commoners could sell their land, if the family approved, but even the king could not legally take their land without their approval. Commoners had a voice in the political affairs of the city and full protection under the law.

Until comparatively recent times, slavery has been a fact of life throughout the history of Western society. Some Sumerian slaves were foreigners and prisoners of war. Some were criminals, who had lost their freedom as punishment for their crimes. Still others served as slaves in repayment of debts. These were more fortunate than the others, because the law required that they be freed after three years. But all slaves were subject to whatever treatment their owners might mete out. They could be beaten and even branded. Yet they were not considered dumb beasts. Slaves engaged in trade and made profits. Indeed, many slaves bought their freedom. They could borrow money, and they received at least some protection under the law.

THE SPREAD OF MESOPOTAMIAN CULTURE

The Sumerians established the basic social, economic, and intellectual patterns of Mesopotamia, but the Semites played a large part in spreading Sumerian culture far beyond the boundaries of Mesopotamia. Despite the cultural ascendancy of the Sumerians, their unending wars wasted their strength. In 2331 B.C., the Semitic chieftain Sargon conquered Sumer and created a new empire. The symbol of his triumph was a new capital, the city of Agade. Sargon, the first "world conqueror," led his armies to the Mediterranean Sea. Although his empire lasted only a few generations, it spread Mesopotamian culture throughout the Fertile Crescent, the belt of rich farmland that extends from Mesopotamia in the east up through Syria in the north and down to Egypt in the west (see Map 1.1).

Sargon's impact and the extent of Mesopotamian influence even at this early period have been dramatically revealed at Ebla in modern Syria. In 1964, archaeologists unearthed there a once-flourishing Semitic civilization that had assimilated political, intellectual, and artistic aspects of Mesopotamian culture. In 1975, the excavators uncovered thousands of clay tablets, which proved that the people of Ebla had learned the art of writing from the Mesopotamians. Eblaite artists borrowed heavily from Mesopotamian art but developed their own style, which in turn influenced Mesopotamian artists. The Eblaites transmitted the heritage of Mesopotamia to other Semitic centers in

Syria. In the process, a universal culture developed in the ancient Near East, a culture basically Mesopotamian but fertilized by the traditions, genius, and ways of many other peoples.

When the clay tablets of Ebla were discovered, many scholars confidently predicted that they would shed fresh light on the Bible. Some even claimed to recognize in them biblical names like Jerusalem and the "Five Cities of the Plain," which included Sodom and Gomorrah. Careful study since then suggests that these claims were more often optimistic than accurate: so far the Ebla tablets have added very little to biblical scholarship. Yet they are a goldmine of data on the ancient history of northern Syria. Some of them deal with Ebla's relations with neighboring peoples, while others provide detailed information on local agricultural production and the weaving industry. All confirm the existence and importance of direct contact between Mesopotamia and Syria as early as the third millennium B.C. Moreover, they demonstrate the early and widespread influence of Mesopotamian civilization far beyond its own borders.

SARGON OF AKKAD   This bronze head, with elaborately worked hair and beard, portrays the great conqueror Sargon of Akkad. Originally the eyes were probably precious jewels, which have subsequently been gouged out. This head was found in the ruins of the Assyrian capital of Nineveh, where it had been taken as loot. (Directorate General of Antiquities, Baghdad, Iraq)

THE TRIUMPH OF BABYLON

Although the empire of Sargon was extensive, it was also short-lived. It was left to the Babylonians to unite Mesopotamia politically as well as culturally. The Babylonians were Amorites, a Semitic people who had migrated from Arabia and settled in the Sumerian city of Babylon. Babylon enjoyed an excellent geographical position, and it was ideally suited to be the capital of Mesopotamia. It dominated trade on the Tigris and Euphrates rivers: all commerce to and from Sumer and Akkad had to pass by its walls. It also looked beyond Mesopotamia. Babylonian merchants followed the Tigris north to Assyria and An-

atolia. The Euphrates led merchants to Syria, Palestine, and the Mediterranean. The city grew great because of its commercial importance and its power being soundly based.

Babylon was also fortunate in its far-seeing and able king Hammurabi (1792–1750 B.C.). Hammurabi set out to do three things: to make Babylon secure, to unify Mesopotamia, and to win for the Babylonians a place in Mesopotamian civilization. The first two he accomplished by conquering Assyria in the north and Sumer and Akkad in the south. Then he turned to his third goal.

Politically, Hammurabi joined in his kingship the Semitic concept of the tribal chieftain

Meaning	Pictograph	Ideogram	Phonetic sign
A	Star			
B	Woman			
C	Mountain			
D	Slave woman			
E	Water In			

FIGURE 1.1 SUMERIAN WRITING (Excerpted from S. N. Kramer, The Sumerians: Their History, Culture and Character, *University of Chicago Press, Chicago, 1963, pp. 302–306*)

and the Sumerian idea of urban kingship. Culturally, he encouraged the spread of myths that explained how Marduk, the god of Babylon, had been elected king of the gods by the other Mesopotamian deities. Hammurabi's success in making Marduk the god of all Mesopotamians made Babylon the religious center of Mesopotamia. Through Hammurabi's genius the Babylonians made their own contribution to Mesopotamian culture — a culture vibrant enough to maintain its identity even while assimilating new influences. Hammurabi's conquests and the activity of Babylonian merchants spread this enriched culture north to Anatolia and west to Syria and Palestine.

THE INVENTION OF WRITING AND THE FIRST SCHOOLS

Mesopotamian culture spread as rapidly as it did largely because of the invention and evolution of writing. Until recently, scholars have credited the Sumerians with the invention of writing. Recent work, however, suggests that the Sumerian achievement, a form of writing called cuneiform — from the Latin for wedge-shaped, which describes the strokes of the stylus — may have been a comparatively late stage in the development of writing. The origins of writing probably go back thousands of years earlier than previously thought. As early as the ninth millennium B.C., Near Eastern peoples used clay tokens as counters for recordkeeping. By the fourth millennium B.C., people had realized that drawing pictures of the tokens on clay was simpler than making tokens. This breakthrough in turn suggested that more information could be conveyed by adding pictures of still other objects. The result was a complex system of pictographs, in which each sign was a picture of an object. Pictographs were the forerunners of cuneiform writing.

How did this pictographic system work and how did it evolve into cuneiform writing? At first, if a scribe wanted to indicate a star, he simply drew a picture of it on a wet clay tablet (see line A of Figure 1.1), which became rock-hard when baked. Anyone looking at the picture would know what it meant and would think of the word for star. This complicated and laborious system had serious limitations. It would not represent abstract ideas or combinations of ideas. For instance, how could it depict a slave woman?

The solution appeared when the scribe discovered that he could combine signs to express meaning. To refer to a slave woman he used the sign for woman (line B) and the sign for mountain (line C) — literally, "mountain woman" (line D). Since the Sumerians regularly obtained their slave women from the mountains, this combination of signs was easily understandable.

The next step was to simplify the system. Instead of drawing pictures, the scribe made conventionalized signs. Thus, the signs became ideograms: they symbolized ideas. The sign for star could also be used to indicate heaven, sky, or even god.

The real breakthrough came when the scribe learned to use signs to represent sounds. For instance, the scribe drew two parallel wavy lines to indicate the word *a,* or "water" (line E). Besides water, the word *a* in Sumerian also meant "in." The word *in* expresses a relationship that is very difficult to represent pictorially. Instead of trying to invent a sign to mean *in,* some clever scribe used the sign for water, because the two words sounded alike. This phonetic use of signs made possible the combining of signs to convey abstract ideas. The use of writing enabled merchants to keep complicated business records, inventories, and bills of lading. More important, the learning, lore, history, and philosophy of a culture could be recorded and preserved for unborn generations.

The Sumerian system of writing was so complicated that only professional scribes mastered it, and even they had to study it for many years. By 2500 B.C., scribal schools flourished throughout Sumer. Most students came from wealthy families, and it was largely a male profession. Each school had a master, teachers, and monitors. Discipline was strict, and students were caned for sloppy work and misbehavior. One graduate of a scribal school had few fond memories of the joy of learning. He described a typical day:

My headmaster read my tablet, said:
"There is something missing," caned me.
. . . .
The fellow in charge of silence said:
"Why did you talk without permission," caned me.
The fellow in charge of the assembly said:
"Why did you stand at ease without permission,"
*   caned me.*[8]

The boy was so lax at his work that he was expelled. Only when his father wined and dined the headmaster was he allowed to return to school.

The Sumerian system of schooling set the educational standards of Mesopotamian culture, and the Akkadians and Babylonians adopted its practices and techniques. Students began by learning how to prepare clay tablets and make signs. They studied grammar and word lists, and they solved simple mathematical problems. Mesopotamian education always had a practical side, because of the economic and administrative importance of scribes. Most scribes took administrative positions in the temple or palace, where they kept records of business transactions, accounts, and inventories. But scribal schools did not limit their curriculum to business affairs. They were also centers of culture and learning. Topics of study included mathematics, botany, and linguistics. Advanced students copied and studied the classics of Mesopotamian literature. Talented students and learned scribes wrote compositions of their own. As a result of this work many literary, mathematical, and religious texts survive today, giving a surprisingly full picture of Mesopotamian intellectual and spiritual life.

MESOPOTAMIAN THOUGHT AND RELIGION

The Mesopotamians made significant and sophisticated advances in mathematics, using a numerical system based on units of sixty. For practical purposes they also used factors of ten and six. They developed the concept of place value — that the value of a number depends on where it stands in relation to other numbers. Mesopotamian mathematical texts are of two kinds: tables and problems. Scribes compiled tables of squares and square roots, cubes and cube roots, and reciprocals. They wrote texts of problems, which dealt not only with equations and pure mathematics but also with concrete problems, such as how to plan irrigation ditches. The Mesopotamians did not consider mathematics a purely theoretical science. The building of cities, palaces, temples, and canals demanded knowledge of geometry and trigonometry. The Mesopotamians solved the practical problems involved, but they did not turn their knowledge into theories. In this respect, they were quite different from the Greeks, who enjoyed theorizing.

Mesopotamian medicine was a combination of magic, prescriptions, and surgery. Mesopotamians believed that demons and evil spirits caused sickness and that incantations and magic spells could drive them out. Or, they believed, the physician could force the demon out by giving the patient a foul-tasting prescription. As medical knowledge grew, some prescriptions were found to work and thus were true medicines. The physician relied heavily on plants, animals, and minerals for his recipes, and he often mixed them with beer to cover their unpleasant taste. Surgeons practiced a dangerous occupation, and the penalties for failure were severe. One section of Hammurabi's law code decreed: "If a physician performed a major operation on a seignior with a bronze lancet and has caused the seignior's death, or he opened up the eye-socket of a seignior and has destroyed the seignior's eye, they shall cut off his hand."[9] No wonder that one medical text warned physicians to have nothing to do with a dying person.

Mesopotamian thought had its profoundest impact in theology and religion. The Sumerians originated many beliefs, and the Akkadians and Babylonians added to them. The American journalist H. L. Mencken once suggested that "the theory that the universe is run by a single God must be abandoned and . . . in place of it we must set up the theory that it is actually ruled by a board of gods all of equal puissance and authority."[10] The Mesopotamians would have agreed that many gods run the world, but they did not consider all gods and goddesses equal to one another. Some deities had very important jobs, such as taking care of music, law, sex, and victory, while others had lesser tasks, such as overseeing leatherworking and basketweaving. The god in charge of metalworking was hardly the equal of the god of wisdom.

Divine society was a hierarchy. According to the Sumerians the air-god Enlil was the king of the gods, and he laid down the rules by which the universe was to be run. Enki, the god of wisdom, put Enlil's plans into effect. The Babylonians believed that the gods elected Marduk as their king, after which he assigned the lesser gods various duties to perform. Once the gods received their tasks, they carried them out forever.

Mesopotamian gods lived their lives much as human beings lived theirs. The gods were anthropomorphic, or human in form. Unlike men and women, they were powerful and immortal and could make themselves invisible. Otherwise, Mesopotamian gods and goddesses were very human: they celebrated with food and drink, and they raised families. They enjoyed their own "Garden of Eden," a green and fertile place. They could be irritable, and they were not always holy. Even Enlil was punished by other gods because he had once raped the goddess Ninlil.

The Mesopotamians had many myths and epics to account for the creation of the universe. According to one Sumerian myth, only the primeval sea existed at first. Genesis, the first book of the Old Testament, says precisely the same thing. The sea produced heaven and earth, which were united. Heaven and earth gave birth to Enlil, who separated them and made possible the creation of the other gods.

Babylonian beliefs were similar. In the beginning was the primeval sea, the goddess Tiamat, who gave birth to the gods. When Tiamat tried to destroy the gods, Marduk killed her and divided her body:

He split her like a shellfish into two parts:
Half of her he set up and ceiled as sky,
Pulled down the bar and posted guards.
He bade them not to let her waters escape.[11]

These myths are the earliest known attempts to answer the question "how did it all begin?" The Mesopotamians obviously thought about these matters, as about the gods, in human terms. They never organized their beliefs into a philosophy, but their myths offered understandable explanations of natural phenomena. They were emotionally satisfying, and that was their greatest appeal.

Mesopotamian myths also explained the origin of human beings. In one myth the gods decided to make their lives easier by creating servants, whom they wanted made in their own image. Nammu, the goddess of the watery deep, brought the matter to Enki. After some thought, Enki instructed Nammu and the others:

Mix the heart of the clay that is over the abyss.
The good and princely fashioners will thicken the clay.
You, do you bring the limbs into existence.[12]

In Mesopotamian myth, as in Genesis, men and women were made in the divine image. However, human beings lacked godlike powers. The myth "The Creation of the Pickax" gives an excellent idea of their insignificance. According to this myth, Enlil drove his pickax into the ground, and out of the hole crawled the Sumerians, the first people.

As Enlil stood looking at them, some of his fellow gods approached him. They were so pleased with Enlil's work that they asked him to give them some people to serve them. Consequently, the Mesopotamians believed it their duty to supply the gods with sacrifices of food and drink and to house them in fine temples. In return, they hoped that the gods would be kind.

These ideas about the creation of the universe and of human beings are part of the Mesopotamian legacy to Western civilization. They spread throughout the ancient Near East and found a home among the Hebrews, who adopted much of Mesopotamian religious thought and made it part of their own beliefs. Biblical parallels to Mesopotamian literary and religious themes are many. Such stories as the creation of Adam, the Deluge, the Garden of Eden, and the tale of Job can be traced back to Mesopotamian originals. Through the Bible, Mesopotamian as well as Jewish religious concepts influenced Christianity and Islam. Thus these first attempts by women and men to understand themselves and their world are still alive today.

DAILY LIFE IN MESOPOTAMIA

The law code of King Hammurabi offers a wealth of information about daily life in Mesopotamia. Hammurabi issued his code to "establish law and justice in the language of the land, thereby promoting the welfare of the people." His code may seem harsh, but it was no more harsh than the Mosaic law of the Hebrews, which it heavily influenced. Hammurabi's code inflicted such penalties as mutilation, whipping, and burning. Today in parts of the Islamic world these punishments are still in use. Despite its severity, a spirit of justice and a sense of responsibility pervade the code. Hammurabi genuinely felt that his

LAW CODE OF HAMMURABI Hammurabi ordered his code to be inscribed on a stone pillar and set up in public. At the top of the pillar Hammurabi is depicted receiving the scepter of authority from the god Shamash. (Clichés des Musées Nationaux, Paris)

duty was to govern the Mesopotamians as righteously as possible. He tried to regulate the relations of his people so that they could live together in harmony.

Hammurabi's code has two striking characteristics. First, the law differed according to the social status of the offender. Aristocrats were not punished as harshly as commoners, nor commoners as harshly as slaves. Even slaves had rights, however, and received some protection under the law. Second, the code demanded that the punishment fit the crime. Like the Mosaic law of the Hebrews, it called for "an eye for an eye, and a tooth for a tooth," at least among equals. However, an aristocrat who destroyed the eye of a commoner or slave could pay a fine instead of los-

ing his own eye. Otherwise, as long as the criminal and the victim shared the same social status, the victim could demand exact vengeance for his injury.

Hammurabi's code began with legal procedure. There were no public prosecutors or district attorneys, so individuals brought their own complaints before the court. Each side had to produce written documents or witnesses to support its case. In cases of murder, the accuser had to prove the defendant guilty: any accuser who failed to do so was put to death. This strict law was designed to prevent people from lodging groundless charges. The Mesopotamians were very worried about witchcraft and sorcery. Anyone accused of witchcraft, even if the charges were not proved, underwent an ordeal by water. The gods themselves would decide the case. The defendant was thrown into the Euphrates, which was considered the instrument of the gods. A defendant who sank was guilty; a defendant who floated was innocent. (In medieval Europe and colonial America accused witches also underwent ordeals by water, but they were considered innocent only if they sank.) Another procedural regulation covered the conduct of judges. Once a judge had rendered a verdict, he could not change it. Any judge who did so was fined heavily and deposed from his position. In short, the code tried to guarantee a fair trial and a just verdict.

Hammurabi expected his officials to do their duty and to protect his subjects. Governors and city officials were required to wipe out crime, and they paid personally for their failures to protect the innocent. If a person was robbed and the robber was not caught, the officials had to repay the victim. This law encouraged officials to keep order. Soldiers either carried out the king's commands or faced dire consequences. Any officer or private who tried to shirk his duty by hiring a substitute was put to death, as was any officer who illegally forced men to serve in the army. The law protected soldiers from abuse by their officers. Any officer who wronged a soldier or stole his property was put to death.

Consumer protection is not a modern idea; it goes back to Hammurabi's day. Merchants and businessmen had to guarantee the quality of their goods and services. A boatbuilder who did sloppy work had to repair the boat at his own expense. A boatman who lost the owner's boat or sank someone else's boat replaced it and its cargo. Housebuilders guaranteed their work with their lives. Careless work could result in the collapse of a house and the death of its inhabitants. If that happened, the builder himself was put to death. A merchant who tried to increase the interest rate on a loan forfeited the entire amount. A farmer who hired an overseer to cultivate his land had the right to order an incompetent overseer to be dragged through the fields. Hammurabi's laws tried to ensure that consumers got what they paid for and paid a just price.

Crime was a feature of Mesopotamian urban life just as it is in modern cities. Burglary was a serious problem, hard to control. Because houses were built of mud-brick, it was easy for an intruder to dig through the walls. Hammurabi's punishment for burglary matched the crime. A burglar caught in the act was put to death on the spot, and his body was walled into the breach he had made. The penalty for looting was also grim: anyone caught looting a burning house was thrown into the fire.

Mesopotamian cities had breeding places of crime. Taverns were notorious for being the haunts of criminals, especially since they often met at taverns to make their plans. Tavernkeepers were expected to keep order and arrest anyone overheard planning a crime.

Taverns were normally run by women, and they also served as houses of prostitution. Prostitution was disreputable but not illegal, and the law did not regulate it. Despite their social stigma, taverns were popular places, for Mesopotamians were fond of beer and wine. Tavernkeepers made a nice profit, but if they were caught increasing their profits by watering drinks, they were drowned.

The aim of all these statutes was to punish the criminal. Exact retribution gave the victim or the victim's family legal satisfaction and was intended to end the matter. To some degree the code protected society by eliminating people who had committed serious crimes. Beyond that it did not go.

Because farming was essential to Mesopotamian life, Hammurabi's code dealt extensively with agriculture. Tenant farming was widespread, and tenants rented land on a yearly basis. Instead of money they paid a proportion of their crops as rent. Unless the land was carefully cultivated, it quickly reverted to wasteland. Therefore tenants faced severe penalties for neglecting the land or not working it at all. Since irrigation was essential to grow crops, tenants had to keep the canals and ditches in good repair. Otherwise, the land would be subject to floods and farmers to crippling losses. Anyone whose neglect of the canals resulted in damaged crops had to bear all the expense of the lost crops. If the tenant could not pay the costs, he was sold into slavery.

The oxen farmers used for plowing and threshing grain were ordinarily allowed to roam the streets. If an ox gored a passer-by, its owner had to pad its horns, tie it up, or else bear the responsibility for future damages. Sheep raising was very lucrative because textile production was a major Mesopotamian industry. (Mesopotamian cloth was famous throughout the Near East.) The shepherd was a hired man with considerable responsibility. He was expected to protect the flock from wild animals, which were a standing problem, and to keep the sheep out of the crops. Since date palms were the only source of wood in Mesopotamia, wanton destruction of trees was a serious offense. This strict regulation of agriculture paid rich dividends. The Mesopotamians often enjoyed bumper crops, which fostered a large and thriving population.

Hammurabi gave careful attention to marriage and the family. As elsewhere in the Near East, marriage had aspects of a business agreement. The prospective groom and the father of the future bride arranged everything. The man offered the father a bridal gift, usually a sum of money. If the man and his bridal gift were acceptable, the father provided his daughter with a dowry. After marriage the dowry belonged to the woman (although the husband normally administered it) and was a means of protecting her rights and status. Once the two men agreed upon financial matters, they drew up a contract; no marriage was considered legal without one. Either party could break off the marriage, but not without paying a stiff penalty. Fathers often contracted marriages while their children were still young. The girl either continued to live in her father's house until she reached maturity or she went to live in the house of her father-in-law. During this time she was legally considered a wife. Once she and her husband became of age, they set up their own house.

The wife was expected to be rigorously faithful. The penalty for adultery was death. According to Hammurabi's code: "If the wife of a man has been caught while lying with another man, they shall bind them and throw them into the water."[13] The husband had the power to spare his wife by obtaining a pardon for her from the king. He could, however, accuse his wife of adultery even if he had not caught her in the act. In such a case she could try to clear herself before the city council, which investigated. If she was found innocent, she could take her dowry and leave her husband. If a woman decided to take the direct approach and kill her husband, she was impaled.

The husband had virtually absolute power over his household. Like the later Roman *paterfamilias* (Chapter 5), he could even sell his wife and children into slavery to pay his debts. Sons did not lightly oppose their fathers, and any son who struck his father could have his hand cut off. A father was free to adopt children and include them in his will. Artisans sometimes adopted children to teach them the family trade. Although the father's power was great, he could not disinherit a son without just cause. Cases of disinheritance became matters for the city to decide, and the code ordered the courts to forgive a son for his first offense. Only if a son wronged his father a second time could he be disinherited.

Law codes are preoccupied with the problems of society, and provide a bleak view of things. Other Mesopotamian documents give a happier glimpse of life. Although Hammurabi's code dealt with marriage shekel by shekel, a Mesopotamian poem tells of two people meeting secretly in the city. Their parting is delightfully modern:

Come now, set me free, I must go home,
Kuli-Enlil . . . set me free, I must go home.
What can I say to deceive my mother?[14]

Countless wills and testaments show that husbands habitually left their estates to their wives, who in turn willed the property to their children. All this suggests happy family life. Hammurabi's code restricted married women from commercial pursuits, but financial documents prove that many women engaged in business without hindrance. Some carried on the family business, while others became wealthy landowners in their own right. Mesopotamians found their lives lightened by holidays and religious festivals. Traveling merchants brought news of the outside world, and swapped marvelous tales. Despite their pessimism, the Mesopotamians enjoyed a vibrant and creative culture, a culture that left its mark on the entire Near East.

EGYPT, THE LAND OF THE PHARAOHS (3100–1200 B.C.)

The Greek historian and traveler Herodotus in the fifth century B.C. called Egypt the gift of the Nile River. No other single geographical factor had such a fundamental and profound impact on the shaping of Egyptian life, society, and history as the Nile. Unlike the rivers of Mesopotamia it rarely brought death and destruction. Its waters, even in flood times, seem almost tame when compared to the rampaging Tigris. The river was primarily a creative force. The Egyptians never feared the Nile in the way the Mesopotamians feared their rivers. Instead, they sang its praises:

Hail to thee, O Nile, that issues from the earth
*   and comes to keep Egypt alive! . . .*
He that waters the meadows which Re created,
He that makes to drink the desert . . .
He who makes barley and brings emmer [wheat]
*   into being . . .*
He who brings grass into being for the cattle . . .
He who makes every beloved tree to grow . . .
O Nile, verdant art thou, who makest man and
*   cattle to live.*[15]

In the mind of the Egyptians the Nile was the supreme fertilizer and renewer of the land. Each September the Nile floods its valley,

transforming it into a huge area of marsh or lagoon. By the end of November the water retreats, leaving behind a thin covering of fertile mud ready to be planted with crops.

The annual flood made the growing of abundant crops almost effortless, especially in southern Egypt. Herodotus, who was used to the rigors of Greek agriculture, was amazed by the ease with which the Egyptians raised their crops:

For indeed without trouble they obtain crops from the land more easily than all other men. . . . They do not labor to dig furrows with the plough or hoe or do the work which other men do to raise grain. But when the river by itself inundates the fields and the water recedes, then each man, having sown his field, sends pigs into it. When the pigs trample down the seed, he waits for the harvest. Then when the pigs thresh the grain, he gets his crop.[16]

As late as 1822, John Burckhardt, an English traveler, watched nomads sowing grain by digging large holes in the mud and throwing in seeds. The extraordinary fertility of the Nile valley made it easy to produce an annual agricultural surplus, which in turn sustained a growing and prosperous population.

Whereas the Tigris and Euphrates and their many tributaries carved up Mesopotamia into isolated areas, the Nile served to unify Egypt. The river was the principal highway, and promoted easy communication throughout the valley. As individual bands of settlers moved into the Nile valley, they created stable agricultural communities. By about 3100 B.C., there were some forty of these communities, which were in constant contact with one another. This contact, encouraged and facilitated by the Nile, virtually assured the early political unification of the country.

Egypt was fortunate in that it was nearly self-sufficient. Besides the fertility of its soil, Egypt possessed enormous quantities of stone,

PERIODS OF EGYPTIAN HISTORY

PERIOD	DATES	SIGNIFICANT EVENTS
Archaic	3100–2660 B.C.	Unification of Egypt
Old Kingdom	2660–2180 B.C.	Construction of the pyramids
First Intermediate	2180–2080 B.C.	Political chaos
Middle Kingdom	2080–1640 B.C.	Recovery and political stability
Second Intermediate	1640–1570 B.C.	Hyksos "invasion"
New Kingdom	1570–1075 B.C.	Creation of an Egyptian empire
		Akhenaten's religious policy

which served as the raw material of architecture and sculpture. Abundant clay was available for pottery, as was gold for jewelry and ornaments. The raw materials that Egypt lacked were close at hand. The Egyptians could obtain copper from Sinai and timber from Lebanon. They had little cause to look to the outside world for their essential needs, which helps to explain the insular quality of Egyptian life.

Geography further encouraged isolation by closing Egypt off from the outside world. To the east and west of the Nile valley stretch grim deserts. The Nubian Desert and the cataracts of the Nile discourage penetration from the south. Only in the north did the Mediterranean Sea leave Egypt exposed. Thus geography shielded Egypt from invasion and from extensive immigration. Unlike the Mesopotamians, the Egyptians enjoyed centuries of peace and tranquillity, during which they could devote most of their resources to peaceful development of their distinctive civilization.

Yet Egypt was not completely sealed off. As early as 3250 B.C. Mesopotamian influences,

notably architectural techniques and materials and perhaps even writing, made themselves felt in Egyptian life. Still later, from 1680 to 1580 B.C., northern Egypt was ruled by foreign invaders, the Hyksos. Infrequent though they were, such periods of foreign influence fertilized Egyptian culture without changing it in any fundamental way.

THE GOD-KING OF EGYPT

The geographic unity of Egypt quickly gave rise to political unification of the country under the authority of a king, whom the Egyptians called pharaoh. The details of this process have been lost, though some archaeologists recently made a startling suggestion. Tomb finds from the ancient region of Nubia, in modern Sudan, indicate that monarchy may have developed there earlier than in Egypt. If so, Egyptians may have developed the concept of kingship from their neighbors to the south.

The Egyptians themselves told of a great king, Menes, who united Egypt into a single kingdom around 3100 B.C. Thereafter the

Egyptians divided their history into dynasties, or families of kings. For modern historical purposes, however, it is more useful to divide Egyptian history into periods. The political unification of Egypt ushered in the period known as the Old Kingdom, an era remarkable for its prosperity and artistic flowering, and for the evolution of religious beliefs.

In the realm of religion, the Egyptians developed complex and often contradictory ideas about an afterlife. These beliefs were all rooted in the environment of Egypt itself. The climate of Egypt is so stable that change is cyclical and dependable: though the heat of summer bakes the land, the Nile always floods and replenishes it. The dry air preserves much that would decay in other climates. Thus there was an air of permanence about Egypt; the old lived on and became part of the present.

This cyclical rhythm permeated Egyptian religious beliefs. According to the Egyptians, the god Osiris, a fertility god associated with the Nile, dies each year, and each year his wife Isis brings him back to life. Osiris eventually became king of the dead, a god who weighed the hearts of human beings to determine whether they had lived justly enough to deserve everlasting life. Osiris's care for the dead was shared by Anubis, the jackal-headed god who annually helped Isis resuscitate Osiris. Anubis was the god of mummification, which was essential to Egyptian funerary rites.

The focal point of religious and political life in the Old Kingdom was the pharaoh, who commanded the wealth, resources, and the people of all Egypt. The pharaoh's power was such that the Egyptians considered him to be the falcon-god Horus in human form. He was a guarantee to his people, a pledge that the gods of Egypt (strikingly unlike those of Mesopotamia) cared for their people. The king's surroundings had to be worthy of

THE PYRAMIDS AT GIZA *Giza was the burial place of the pharaohs of the Old Kingdom and of their aristocracy, whose rectangular tombs are visible behind the middle pyramid. The small pyramids at the foot of the foremost pyramid probably belong to the pharaoh's wives. (Courtesy, Museum of Fine Arts, Boston)*

a god. Only a magnificent palace was suitable for his home; in fact, the very word *pharaoh* means "great house." The king's tomb also had to reflect his might and exalted status. To this day the great pyramids at Giza near Cairo bear silent but magnificent testimony to the god-kings of Egypt. The pharaoh's ability to command the resources and labor necessary to build a huge pyramid amply demonstrates that the god-king was an absolute ruler.

The religious significance of the pyramid is as awesome as the political. The pharaoh as a god was the earthly sun, and the pyramid, which towered to the sky, helped him ascend

EGYPTIAN FARM WORK This tomb depicts the cycle of the agricultural year from ploughing to reaping. (Metropolitan Museum of Art, New York)

the heavens after death. The pyramid provided the dead king with everything that he would need in the afterlife. His body had to be preserved from decay if his *ka,* an invisible counterpart of the body, was to live on. So the Egyptians developed an elaborate process of embalming the dead pharaoh and wrapping his corpse in cloth. As an added precaution, they carved a statue of the pharaoh out of hard stone; if anything happened to the fragile mummy, the pharaoh's statue would help keep his ka alive. The need for an authentic likeness accounts for the naturalism of Egyptian portraiture. Artistic renderings of the pharaohs combine accuracy and the abstract in the effort to capture the essence of the living person. This approach produced that haunting quality of Egyptian sculpture – portraits of lifelike people imbued with a solemn, ageless, and serene spirit.

To survive in the spirit world the ka needed

everything that the pharaoh needed in life: food and drink, servants and armed retainers, costly ornaments, and herds of animals. In Egypt's prehistoric period, the king's servants and herdsmen and their flocks were slaughtered at the tomb to provide for the ka. By the time of the Old Kingdom, artists had substituted statues of scribes, officials, soldiers, and servants for their living counterparts. To remind the ka of daily life, artists covered the walls of the tomb with scenes of ordinary life, ranging from agricultural routines to banquets and religious festivities, from hunting parties to gardens and ponds. Designed to give joy to the ka, these paintings, models of furniture, and statuettes today provide an intimate glimpse of Egyptian life 4,500 years ago.

The humor and vivacity of Egyptian tomb paintings are striking, especially when they depict everyday scenes. The scene above, which dates only to about 1300 B.C. is remarkable chiefly because it is typical. This tomb painting shows an Egyptian couple at work in the fields. In the top band the couple reap wheat, while in the second band they harvest flax. To the right in the second band the couple is seen ploughing for the next year's crop. In the bottom two bands are an orchard of date palms and a garden filled with flowers and herbs. The wavy bands represent irrigation canals. The simple agricultural implements include a metal sickle and a light plough drawn by two oxen. Unfortunately, however, research published in 1982 suggests that many Egyptian farmers suffered from various parasites that thrived in the warm, stagnant water of the irrigation canals. Nonetheless, tomb scenes like this one preferred warmth to harsh realities. Other sources of information give a gloomier view of daily life.

THE PHARAOH'S PEOPLE

Because the common folk stood at the bottom of the social and economic scale, they were always at the mercy of grasping officials. The arrival of the tax collector was never a happy occasion. One Egyptian scribe described the worst that could happen:

And now the scribe lands on the river-bank and is about to register the harvest-tax. The janitors carry staves and the Nubians rods of palm, and they say, Hand over the corn, though there is none. The cultivator is beaten all over, he is bound and thrown into a well, soused and dipped head downwards. His wife has been bound in his presence and his children are in fetters.[17]

That was an extreme situation. Nonetheless, taxes might amount to 20 percent of the harvest, and the collection of taxes could often be brutal.

On the other hand, everyone, no matter how lowly, had the right of appeal, and the account of one such appeal, "The Tale of the Eloquent Peasant," was a favorite Egyptian story. The hero of the tale, Khunanup, was robbed by the servant of the high steward, and Khunanup had to bring his case before the steward himself. When the steward delayed his decision, Khunanup openly accused him of neglecting his duty, saying, "The arbitrator is a spoiler; the peace-maker is a creator of sorrow; the smoother over of differences is a creator of soreness."[18] The pharaoh himself ordered the steward to give Khunanup justice, and the case was decided in the peasant's favor.

Egyptian society seems to have been a curious mixture of freedom and constraint. Slavery did not become widespread until the New Kingdom. There was neither a caste system nor a color bar, and humble people could rise to the highest positions if they possessed talent. The most famous example of social mobility (which, however, dates to the New Kingdom) is the biblical story of Joseph, who came to Egypt as a slave and rose to be second only to the pharaoh. On the other hand, most ordinary folk were probably little more than serfs, who could not easily leave the land of their own free will. Peasants were also subject to forced labor, just as they were in early modern France, and this labor included work on the pyramids and canals. Young men were drafted into the pharaoh's army, which served both as a fighting force and as a labor corps.

The vision of thousands of people straining to build the pyramids and countless artists adorning the pharaoh's tomb brings to the modern mind a distasteful picture of oriental despotism. Yet H. Frankfort, one of the most perceptive historians of ancient Egypt, has treated the matter in a purely Egyptian context:

Nothing would be more misleading than to picture the Egyptians in abject submission to their absolute ruler. . . . Their polity was not imposed but evolved from immemorial predilections and was adhered to, without protest, for almost three thousand years. . . . If a god had consented to guide the nation, society held a pledge that the unaccountable forces of nature would be well disposed and bring prosperity and peace. . . . Truth, justice, were "that by which the gods live," an essential element in the established order. Hence, Pharaoh's rule was not tyranny, or his service slavery.[19]

The Egyptian view of life and society is alien to those raised on the Western concepts of individual freedom and human rights. To the ancient Egyptians the pharaoh embodied justice and order – harmony among men and women, nature, and the divine. If the pharaoh was weak, or if he allowed anyone to challenge his unique position, he opened the way to chaos. Twice in Egyptian history the pharaoh failed to maintain rigid centralization. During those two eras, known as the First and Second Intermediate periods, Egypt was exposed to civil war and invasion. Yet even in the darkest times the monarchy survived, and in each period a strong pharaoh arose to crush the rebels or expel the invaders and restore order.

THE HYKSOS IN EGYPT (1640–1570 B.C.)

While Egyptian civilization flourished behind its bulwark of sand and sea, momentous changes were taking place in the ancient Near East, changes that would leave their mark even on rich and insular Egypt. These changes involved enormous and remarkable movements of peoples, especially peoples who spoke Semitic languages.

The original home of the Semites was probably the Arabian peninsula. Some tribes

moved into northern Mesopotamia, others into Syria and Palestine, and still others into Egypt. Shortly after 1800 B.C., people whom the Egyptians called Hyksos, which means "Rulers of the Uplands," began to settle in the Delta. Egyptian tradition, as later recorded by the priest Manetho in the third century B.C., depicted the coming of the Hyksos as a brutal invasion:

In the reign of Toutimaios – I do not know why – the wind of god blew against us. Unexpectedly from the regions of the east men of obscure race, looking forward confidently to victory, invaded our land, and without a battle easily seized it all by sheer force. Having subdued those in authority in the land, they then barbarously burned our cities and razed to the ground the temples of the gods. They fell upon all the natives in an entirely hateful fashion, slaughtering them and leading both their children and wives into slavery. At last they made one of their people king, whose name was Salitis. This man resided at Memphis, leaving in Upper and Lower Egypt tax collectors and garrisons in strategic places.[20]

Although the Egyptians portrayed the Hyksos as a conquering horde, they were probably no more than nomads looking for good land. Their entry into the delta was probably gradual and generally peaceful, much like that of the Hebrews, who did not arrive until around 1500 B.C. Indeed, the Hebrews are typical of the Semitic movement. They were a pastoral people, organized in large tribes whose chiefs and patriarchs directed the life of the community.

The Hyksos "invasion" was one of the fertilizing periods of Egyptian history; it introduced new ideas and techniques into Egyptian life. The Hyksos brought with them the method of making bronze and casting it into tools and weapons. They thereby brought Egypt fully into the Bronze Age culture of the

Mediterranean world, a culture in which the production and use of bronze implements became basic to society. Bronze tools made farming more efficient than ever before because they were sharper and more durable than the copper tools they replaced. The Hyksos' use of bronze armor and weapons as well as horse-drawn chariots and the composite bow, made of laminated wood and horn and far more powerful than the simple wooden bow, revolutionized Egyptian warfare. However much the Egyptians learned from the Hyksos, Egyptian culture eventually absorbed the newcomers. The Hyksos came to worship Egyptian gods and modelled their monarchy on the pharaoh's.

THE NEW KINGDOM: REVIVAL AND EMPIRE (1570–1200 B.C.)

Politically, Egypt was only in eclipse. The Egyptian sun shone again when a remarkable line of kings, the pharaohs of the Eighteenth Dynasty, arose to challenge the Hyksos. The pharaoh Ahmose (1558–1533 B.C.) pushed the Hyksos out of the Delta. Thutmose I (1512–1500 B.C.) subdued Nubia in the south, and Thutmose III (1490–1436 B.C.) conquered Palestine and Syria and fought inconclusively with the Hurrians' new kingdom of Mitanni on the upper Euphrates. These warrior-pharaohs inaugurated the New Kingdom – a period in Egyptian history characterized by enormous wealth and conscious imperialism. During this period, probably for the first time, widespread slavery became a feature of Egyptian life. The pharaoh's armies returned home leading hordes of slaves, who constituted a new labor force for imperial building projects. The Jews, who according to the Old Testament migrated into Egypt during this period to escape a drought, were soon enslaved and put to work on imperial construction projects.

The kings of the Eighteenth Dynasty created the first Egyptian empire. They ruled Palestine and Syria through their officers, and they incorporated the African region of Nubia. Egyptian religion and customs flourished in Nubia, making a huge impact on African culture there and in neighboring areas. These warrior-kings celebrated their success with monuments on a scale unparalleled since the pharaohs of the Old Kingdom had built the pyramids. Even today the colossal granite statues of these pharaohs and the rich tomb objects of Tutankhamen ("King Tut") testify to the might, wealth, and splendor of the New Kingdom.

AKHENATEN AND MONOTHEISM

One of the most extraordinary of this unusual line of kings was Akhenaten (1367–1350 B.C.), a pharaoh more concerned with religion than conquest. Nefertiti, his wife and queen, encouraged his religious bent. Akhenaten and Nefertiti were monotheists: that is, they believed that the sun-god Aton, whom they worshiped, was universal, the only god. They considered all other Egyptian gods and goddesses frauds, and forbade their worship.

The religious notions and actions of Akhenaten and Nefertiti were in direct opposition to traditional Egyptian beliefs. The Egyptians had long worshiped a host of gods, chief among whom was Amon-Re. Originally Amon and Re had been two distinct sun-gods, but the Egyptians merged them and worshiped Amon-Re as the king of the gods. Besides Amon-Re, the Egyptians honored such other deities as Osiris, Osiris's wife Isis, and his son Horus. Indeed, Egyptian religion had room for many gods and an easy tolerance for new gods.

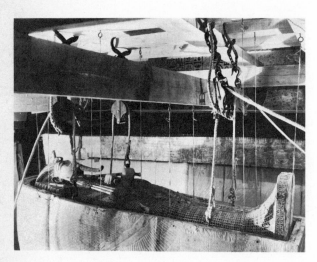

THE TOMB OF "KING TUT" *The pharaoh Tutankhamun was buried in three coffins, one inside the other. Shown here is the removal of the second coffin from the other coffin. The innermost coffin was made of gold. (The Metropolitan Museum of Art. Photograph by Harry Burton)*

THE PHARAOH'S COFFIN *This magnificent coffin from the tomb of "King Tut" depicts the pharaoh in all of his glory. Crossed over his chest are a crook and a flail, which were the emblems of the god Osiris. Richly engraved on the coffin are figures representing both Lower and Upper Egypt. (Metropolitan Museum of Art, New York)*

Herodotus once remarked that the Egyptians "are excessively religious, more so than other men." Akhenaten's attack on the old gods threatened all Egyptians, for the old gods were crucial to the afterlife. Naturally, then, many Egyptians viewed Akhenaten's attack on Osiris, Isis, Anubis, and other gods as a threat to their own chances for immortality. Others were sincerely devoted to the old gods for different reasons. After all, had not Amon-Re driven out the Hyksos and brought Egypt a new era of happiness? To these genuine religious sentiments were added the motives of the traditional priesthood. Although many priests were genuinely scandalized by Akhenaten's monotheism, many others were more concerned about their own welfare. What were the priests of the outlawed gods to do? Akhenaten had destroyed their livelihood and their reason for existence. On grounds of pure self-interest, the established priesthood opposed Akhenaten. Opposition in turn drove the pharaoh to intolerance and persecution. With a vengeance he tried to root out the old gods and their rituals.

Akhenaten celebrated his break with the past by building a new capital, Akhetaten, the modern El-Amarna. There Aton was honored with an immense temple and proper worship. Worship of Aton focused on "truth" (as Akhenaten defined it) and a desire for the natural. The pharaoh and his queen demanded that the "truth" be carried over into art. Unlike Old Kingdom painting and sculpture, which blended the actual and the abstract, the art of this period became relentlessly realistic. Sculptors molded exact likenesses of Akhenaten, despite his ugly features and misshapen body. Artists portrayed the pharaoh in intimate family scenes, playing with his infant daughter or expressing affection to members of his family. On one relief Akhenaten appears gnawing a cutlet of meat, while on another he lolls in a chair. Akhenaten was being portrayed as a mortal man, not as the dignified pharaoh of Egypt.

Akhenaten's monotheism was imposed from above, and failed to find a place among the people. The prime reason for Akhenaten's failure is that his god had no connection with the past of the Egyptian people, who trusted the old gods and felt comfortable praying to them. Average Egyptians were no doubt distressed and disheartened when their familiar gods were outlawed, for they were the heavenly powers that had made Egypt powerful and unique. The fanaticism and persecution that accompanied the new monotheism were in complete defiance of the Egyptian tradition of tolerant polytheism, or worship of several gods. Thus, when Akhenaten died, his religion died with him.

THE HITTITE EMPIRE

At about the time of the Hyksos entry into the Nile Delta, other parts of the Near East were also troubled by the arrival of newcomers. Two new groups of peoples, the Hurrians and Kassites, carved out kingdoms for themselves. Meanwhile the Hittites, who had long been settled in Anatolia (modern Turkey), became a major power in that region and began to expand eastward. Around 1595 B.C., a century and a half after Hammurabi's death, the Hittites and the Kassites brought down the Babylonian kingdom and established Kassite rule there. The Hurrians created the kingdom of Mitanni on the upper reaches of the Euphrates and Tigris.

The Hittites were an Indo-European people. The term *Indo-European* refers to a large family of languages that includes English, most of the languages of modern Europe,

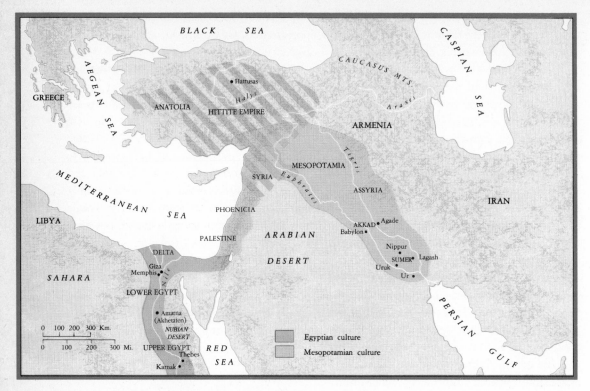

MAP 1.2 BALANCE OF POWER IN THE NEAR EAST *This map shows the areas controlled by the Hittites and Egyptians at the height of their power.*

Greek, Latin, Persian, and Sanskrit, the sacred tongue of ancient India. During the eighteenth and nineteenth centuries, European scholars learned that peoples who spoke related languages had spread as far west as Ireland and as far east as central Asia. In the twentieth century, linguists deciphered the language of the Hittites, and the Linear B script of Mycenaean Greece. When both languages proved to be Indo-European, scholars were able to form a clearer picture of these vast movements. Archaeologists were able to date them roughly and put them into their historical context.

The original home of the Indo-Europeans remains to be identified. Judging primarily from the spread of the languages, linguists have suggested that the migrations started from central Europe. Although two great waves began around 2000 B.C. and 1200 B.C., these migrations were typically sporadic and gradual. For instance, the Celtic-speaking Gauls did not move into modern France, Belgium, and Germany until the seventh century B.C., long after most Indo-Europeans had found new homes.

Around 2000 B.C., however, Indo-Europeans were on the move on a massive scale. Peoples speaking the ancestor of Latin pushed into Italy, and Greek-speaking Mycenaeans settled in Greece. The Hittites came into prominence in Anatolia, and other folk thrust into Iran, India, and central Asia. At first the waves of Indo-Europeans and others disrupted existing states, but in time the newcomers settled down.

THE RISE OF THE HITTITES

Until recently, scholars thought that as part of these vast movements the Hittites entered Anatolia only around 1800 B.C. Current archaeological work and new documents, however, prove that Hittites had settled there at least as early as 2700 B.C. Nor did they overrun the country in a sweeping invasion, burning, looting, and destroying as they advanced. Their arrival and diffusion seems in fact to have been rather peaceful, accompanied by intermarriage and alliance with the native population. So well did the Hittites integrate themselves into the local culture of central Anatolia that they even adopted the worship of several native deities.

Although much uncertainty still surrounds the earliest history of the Hittites, their rise to prominence in Anatolia is quite well documented. During the nineteenth century B.C. the native kingdoms in the area engaged in suicidal warfare that left most of Anatolia's once-flourishing towns in ashes and rubble. In this climate of exhaustion the Hittite king Hattusilis I built a hill citadel at Hattusas, the modern Boghazköy, from which he led his Hittites against neighboring kingdoms. Hittite tradition recorded Hattusilis' achievements:

And on whatever campaign he went, he also by his strength kept the hostile country in subjection. And he kept devastating countries, and he made the countries tremble; and he made them boundaries of the sea.[21]

Hattusilis' grandson and successor Mursilis I extended the Hittite arms as far as Babylon. With help from the Kassites, Mursilis captured the city and snuffed out the dynasty of Hammurabi. While the Hittites carried off Babylonian loot, the Kassites took control of the territory. Upon his return home, the victorious Mursilis was assassinated by members of his own family, plunging the kingdom into confusion and opening the door to foreign invasion. The Hittites quickly lost substantial tracts of land in the east and south, and Hattusas itself prepared for attack. Mursilis' career is representative of the success and weakness of the Hittites. They were extremely vulnerable to attack by vigilant and tenacious enemies. Yet once united behind a strong king, they were a power to be reckoned with.

HITTITE SOCIETY

The geography of central Anatolia encouraged the rise of self-contained agricultural communities. Each was probably originally ruled by a petty king, but under the Hittites a group of local officials known as the Elders handled community affairs. Besides the farming population, a well-defined group of artisans fashioned the pottery, cloth, leather goods, and metal tools needed by society. Documents also report that traveling merchants peddled goods and gossip, reminding individual communities that they were part of a larger world. Like many other societies, ancient and modern, the Hittites held slaves, who nonetheless enjoyed certain rights under the law.

At the top of Hittite society was the aristocracy, among whom the relatives of the king constituted a privileged group. The king's relations were a mighty and often unruly group who served as the chief royal administrators. The royal family was often a threat to the king, for some of them, like the assassin of Mursilis I, readily resorted to murder as a method of seizing power. Sons of the king traditionally served as governors of conquered provinces.

THE HITTITE GOD ATARLUHAS *This statue of the god Atarluhas, with two lions at his feet, was set up near the gateway of the Hittite city of Carchemish. A bird-headed demon holds the lions. In 1920 this statue was destroyed in a war between Turkey and Syria. (The British Museum)*

Just as the aristocracy stood at the head of society, so the king and queen stood above the aristocracy. The king was supreme commander of the army, chief judge, and supreme priest. He carried on all diplomatic dealings with foreign powers, and in times of war personally led the Hittite army into the field. The queen, who was highly regarded, held a strong, independent position. She had important religious duties to perform, and some queens even engaged in diplomatic correspondence with foreign queens.

The Hittites are typical of many newcomers

to the ancient Near East in that they readily assimilated the cultures that they found. On arriving in Anatolia, they adopted much of the local culture. Soon they fell under the far more powerful spell of the superior Mesopotamian culture. The Hittites adopted the cuneiform script for their own language. Hittite kings published law codes, just as Hammurabi had done. Royal correspondence followed Mesopotamian forms. The Hittites delighted in Mesopotamian myths, legends, and epics. Of Hittite art, one scholar has observed that "there is hardly a single Hittite monument which somewhere does not show traces of Mesopotamian influence."[22] To the credit of the Hittites, one must add that they used these Mesopotamian borrowings to create something of their own. Nonetheless, the huge debt of the Hittites and other invaders brilliantly illustrates the great attraction and strength of Mesopotamian culture.

THE ERA OF HITTITE GREATNESS
(CA 1475–CA 1200 B.C.)

The Hittites, like the Egyptians of the New Kingdom, eventually produced an energetic and capable line of kings who restored order and rebuilt Hittite power. Once Telepinus (1525–1500 B.C.) had brought the aristocracy under control, Suppiluliumas I (1380–1346 B.C.) secured central Anatolia and Mursilis II (1345–1315 B.C.) regained Syria. Around 1300 B.C. Mursilis' son stopped the Egyptian army of Rameses II at the battle of Kadesh in Syria. Having fought each other to a standstill, the Hittites and Egyptians first made peace, then an alliance. Alliance was followed by friendship, and friendship by active cooperation. The two greatest powers of the early Near East tried to make war between them impossible.

The Hittites exercised remarkable political

wisdom and flexibility in the organization and administration of their empire. Some states they turned into vassal-kingdoms, ruled by the sons of the Hittite king; the king and his sons promised each other mutual support in times of crisis. Still other kingdoms were turned into protectorates, whose native kings were allowed to rule their populations with considerable freedom. The native kings swore obedience to the Hittite king, and had to contribute military contingents to the Hittite army. Although they also sent tribute to the Hittites, the financial burden was moderate. The common people of these lands probably felt Hittite overlordship little if at all.

While the Hittites were often at war, owing to the sheer number of enemies surrounding them, they often sought diplomatic and political solutions to their problems. They were realistic enough to recognize the limits of their power and far-sighted enough to appreciate the value of peace and alliance with Egypt. Together the two kingdoms provided much of the ancient Near East with a precious interlude of peace.

THE FALL OF EMPIRES (1200 B.C.)

This stable and generally peaceful situation endured until the cataclysm of the thirteenth century B.C., when both the Hittite and Egyptian empires were destroyed by invaders. The most famous of these marauders, called the "Sea Peoples" by the Egyptians, remain one of the puzzles of ancient history. Despite much new work, modern archaeology is still unable to identify the Sea Peoples satisfactorily. It is known, however, that they were part of a larger movement of peoples. Although there is serious doubt about whether the Sea Peoples alone overthrew the Hittites, they did

deal both the Hittites and the Egyptians a hard blow, making the Hittites vulnerable to overland invasion from the north and driving the Egyptians back to the Nile Delta. The Hittites fell under the external blows, but the Egyptians, shaken and battered, retreated to the Delta and held on.

In 1200 B.C., as earlier, both Indo-European and Semitic-speaking peoples were on the move. They brought down the old centers of power and won new homes for themselves. In Mesopotamia the Assyrians destroyed the kingdom of Mitanni and struggled with the Kassites; the Hebrews moved into Palestine; and another wave of Indo-Europeans penetrated Anatolia. But once again these victories were political and military, not cultural. The old cultures — especially that of Mesopotamia — impressed their ideas, values, and ideals on the newcomers. Although the chaos of the thirteenth century B.C. caused a serious material decline throughout the ancient Near East, the old cultures lived on through a dark age.

———◆———

In the long span of years covered by this chapter, human beings made astonishing strides, advancing from primitive hunters to builders of complex and sophisticated civilizations. By harnessing the plant and animal worlds for their welfare, human beings prospered dramatically. With their basic bodily needs more than satisfied, they realized even greater achievements, including more complex social groupings, metal technology, and long-distance trade. The intellectual achievements of these centuries were equally impressive. Ancient Near Eastern peoples created advanced mathematics, monumental architecture, and engaging literature. Although the societies of the Near East suffered stunning blows in the thirteenth century B.C., more persisted than perished. The great achievements of Mesopotamia and Egypt survived to improve and sustain the lives of those who came after.

NOTES

1. L. Eiseley, *The Unexpected Universe,* Harcourt Brace Jovanovich, New York, 1969, p. 102.

2. J. R. Harlan, "The Plants and Animals That Nourish Man," *Scientific American* 235 (September 1976): 89.

3. Xenophon *Anabasis* 1.5.1.

4. W. K. Loftus, *Travels and Researches in Chaldaea and Susiana,* R. Carter & Brothers, New York, 1857, p. 163.

5. J. B. Pritchard, ed., *Ancient Near Eastern Texts,* 3rd ed., Princeton University Press, Princeton, 1969, p. 44. Hereafter called *ANET.*

6. Ibid., p. 104.

7. *ANET,* p. 590.

8. Quoted in S. N. Kramer, *The Sumerians,* University of Chicago Press, Chicago, 1964, p. 238.

9. *ANET,* p. 175.

10. H.L. Mencken, *A Mencken Chrestomathy,* Knopf, New York, 1949, p. 67.

11. *ANET,* p. 67.

12. Kramer, p. 150.

13. *ANET,* p. 171.

14. Kramer, p. 251.

15. *ANET,* p. 372.

16. Herodotus *The Histories* 2.14.

17. Quoted in A. H. Gardiner, "Ramesside Texts Relating to the Taxation and Transport of Corn," *Journal of Egyptian Archaeology* 27 (1941): 19-20.

18. A. H. Gardiner, "The Eloquent Peasant," *Journal of Egyptian Archaeology* 9 (1923): 17.

19. H. Frankfort, *The Birth of Civilization in the Near East,* Doubleday, New York, 1956, pp. 119-120.

20. Manetho *History of Egypt* fr. 42.75-77.

21. E. H. Sturtevant and G. Bechtel, *A Hittite Chrestomathy,* Linguistic Society of America, Philadelphia, 1935, p. 183.

22. M. Vieyra, *Hittite Art* 2300-750 B.C., Alec Tiranti, London, 1955, p. 12.

SUGGESTED READING

The continuing research on the evolution of mankind makes any book quickly outdated, but a commendable exception is R. Leakey and R. Lewin, *Origins* (1977). G. Clark, *Archaeology and Society: Reconstructing the Prehistoric Past,* 3rd ed. (1957), is a study in methodology, and his *The Stone Age Hunters* (1967) describes life and society in the Paleolithic Age. A convenient general treatment is G. Clark and S. Piggott, *Prehistoric Societies* (1965). F. Dahlberg, *Woman the Gatherer* (1981), demonstrates the importance to primitive society of women's role in gathering.

As the text suggests, the origins of agriculture and the Neolithic period have recently received a great deal of attention. Professor Harlan's conclusions, besides the article cited in note 2, are set out in a series of works including "Agricultural Origins: Centers and Noncenters," *Science* 174 (1971): 468-474, and *Crops and Man* (1975). The 1981 Egyptian expedition mentioned in the text is described by F. Wendorf and R. Schild, "The Earliest Food Producers," *Archaeology* 34 (September/October 1981): 30-36. A broad survey of the problem is M. N. Cohen, *The Food Crisis in Prehistory* (1977).

For the societies of Mesopotamia, see A. Leo Oppenheim, *Ancient Mesopotamia,* rev. ed. (1977); M. E. L. Mallowan, *Early Mesopotamia and Iran* (1965); and H. W. F. Saggs, *The Greatness That Was Babylon* (1962). E. Chiera, *They Wrote on Clay* (1938), offers a delightful glimpse of Mesopotamian life, as does H. W. F. Saggs, *Everyday Life in Babylonia and Assyria* (1965).

C. Aldred, *The Egyptians* (1961), provides a good, readable survey of Egyptian developments. More detailed is A. Gardiner, *Egypt of the Pharaohs*

(1961). A. Nibbi, *Ancient Egypt and Some Eastern Neighbors* (1981) looks at Egyptian history in a broad context. See also J. M. White, *Everyday Life in Ancient Egypt* (1963).

Recent general introductions to problems and developments shared by several Near Eastern societies come from D. H. Trump, *The Prehistory of the Mediterranean* (1980), and a series of studies edited by T. A. Wertime and J. D. Muhly, *The Coming of the Age of Iron* (1980). J. B. Pritchard, *The Ancient Near East,* 2 vols. (1958, 1976) is a fine synthesis by one of the world's leading Near Eastern specialists. A sweeping survey is C. Burney, *The Ancient Near East* (1977). Pioneering new work on the origins of writing appears in a series of pieces by D. Schmandt-Besserat, notably "An Archaic Recording System and the Origin of Writing," *Syro-Mesopotamian Studies* 1/2 (1977): 1–32, and "Reckoning before Writing," *Archaeology* 32 (May/June, 1979): 23–31.

O. R. Gurney, *The Hittites,* 2nd ed. (1954) is still a fine introduction by an eminent scholar. Good also is J. G. MacQueen, *The Hittites and Their Contemporaries in Asia Minor* (1975). The 1960s were prolific years for archaeology in Turkey. A brief survey by one of the masters of the field is J. Mellaart, *The Archaeology of Modern Turkey*

(1978), which also tests a great number of widely-held historical interpretations. The Sea Peoples have been the subject of two recent studies: A. Nibbi, *The Sea Peoples and Egypt* (1975), and N. K. Sandars, *The Sea Peoples* (1978).

For Near Eastern religion and mythology, good introductions are S. N. Kramer, ed., *Mythologies of the Ancient World* (1961); E. O. James, *The Ancient Gods: The History and Diffusion of Religion in the Ancient Near East and the Eastern Mediterranean* (1960); and J. Gray, *Near Eastern Mythology* (1969). A survey of Mesopotamian religion by one of the foremost scholars in the field is T. Jacobsen, *The Treasures of Darkness: A History of Mesopotamian Religion* (1976).

Surveys of Near Eastern art include H. Frankfort, *The Art and Architecture of the Ancient Orient* (1954), old but still very useful; R. D. Barnett and D. J. Wiseman, *Fifty Masterpieces of Ancient Near Eastern Art* (1969); and J. B. Pritchard's delightful *The Ancient Near East in Pictures,* 2nd ed. (1969). For literature, see S. Fiore, *Voices from the Clay: The Development of Assyro-Babylonian Literature* (1965); W. K. Simpson, ed., *The Literature of Ancient Egypt* (1973); and, above all, J. B. Pritchard, ed., *Ancient Near Eastern Texts* cited frequently in the Notes.

CHAPTER 2

SMALL KINGDOMS AND MIGHTY
EMPIRES IN THE NEAR EAST

THE MIGRATORY INVASIONS that brought down the Hittites and stunned the Egyptians in the thirteenth century B.C. ushered in an era of confusion and weakness. Although much was lost in the chaos, the old cultures of the ancient Near East survived to nurture new societies. In the absence of powerful empires, the Phoenicians, Syrians, Hebrews, and many other peoples carved out small independent kingdoms, until the Near East was a patchwork of them. During this period Hebrew culture and religion evolved under the influence of urbanism, kings, and prophets.

In the ninth century B.C. this jumble of small states gave way to an empire that for the first time embraced the entire Near East. Yet the very ferocity of the Assyrian Empire led to its downfall only two hundred years later. In 550 B.C. the Persians and Medes, who had migrated into Iran, created a "world empire" stretching from Anatolia in the west to the Indus valley in the east. For over two hundred years the Persians gave the ancient Near East peace and stability.

How did Egypt, its political greatness behind it, pass on its cultural heritage to its African neighbors? How did the Jewish state evolve, and what was daily life like in Jewish society? What forces helped to shape Jewish religious thought, still powerfully influential in today's world? What enabled the Assyrians to overrun their neighbors, and how did their cruelty finally cause their undoing? Lastly, how did Iranian nomads create the Persian Empire? This chapter will seek answers to these questions.

EGYPT, A SHATTERED KINGDOM

The invasions of the Sea Peoples ended the great days of Egyptian power. One scribe left behind a somber portrait of Egypt stunned and leaderless:

The land of Egypt was abandoned and every man was a law to himself. During many years there was no leader who could speak for others. Central government lapsed, small officials and headmen took over the whole land. Any man, great or small, might kill his neighbor. In the distress and vacuum that followed ... men banded together to plunder one another. They treated the gods no better than men, and cut off the temple revenues.[1]

No longer able to dream of foreign conquests, Egypt looked to its own security from foreign invasion. Egyptians suffered a four-hundred-year period of political fragmentation, a new dark age known to Egyptian specialists as the Third Intermediate Period (eleventh–seventh centuries B.C.).

The decline of Egypt was especially sharp in foreign affairs. Whereas the pharaohs of the Eighteenth Dynasty had held sway as far abroad as Syria, their weak successors found it unsafe to venture far from home. In the wake of the Sea Peoples, numerous small kingdoms sprang up in the Near East, each fiercely protective of its own independence. To them Egypt was a memory, and foreign princes often greeted Egyptian officials with suspicion or downright contempt. One Egyptian official, Wen-Amon, left a lively report of his reception in Phoenicia, on an official mission to buy wood. Instead of the respect and deference Wen-Amon expected, he was greeted by the thundering of the king of Byblos:

If the ruler of Egypt were the lord of mine, and I were his servant also, he would not have to send silver and gold, saying: "Carry out the commission of Amon!" There would be no carrying of a royal-gift, such as they used to do for my father. As for me — me also — I am not your servant! I am not the servant of him who sent you either![2]

In the days of Egypt's greatness, no mere king of Byblos would have dared to speak so insolently to an Egyptian official.

Disrupted at home and powerless abroad, Egypt fell prey to invasion by its African neighbors. Libyans from North Africa filtered into the Nile Delta, where they established independent dynasties. Indeed, from 950 to 730 B.C. northern Egypt was ruled by Libyan pharaohs. The Libyans built cities, and for the first time a sturdy urban life grew up in the Delta. Although the coming of the Libyans changed the face of the Delta, the Libyans genuinely admired Egyptian culture, and eagerly adopted Egypt's religion and way of life.

In southern Egypt, meanwhile, the pharaoh's decline opened the way to the energetic Africans of Nubia, who extended their authority northward throughout the Nile valley. Nubian influence in these years, though pervasive, was not destructive. Since the imperial days of the Eighteenth Dynasty (see pages 29–31), the Nubians too had adopted many features of Egyptian culture. Now Nubian kings and aristocrats embraced Egyptian culture wholesale. The thought of destroying the heritage of the pharaohs would have struck them as stupid and barbaric. Thus the Nubians and the Libyans repeated an old Near Eastern phenomenon: new peoples conquered old centers of political and military power, but were themselves assimilated into the older culture.

The reunification of Egypt occurred late and unexpectedly. With Egypt distracted and disorganized by foreign invasions, an independent African state, the Kingdom of Kush, grew up in modern Sudan with its capital at Nepata. These Africans too worshiped Egyptian gods and used Egyptian hieroglyphs to write their language. In the eighth century B.C. their king Piankhy swept through the entire Nile valley from Nepata in the south to the Delta in the north. United once again, Egypt enjoyed a brief period of peace during which Egyptians continued to assimilate their African conquerors. In the Kingdom of Kush, Egyptian methods of administration and bookkeeping, Egyptian arts and crafts, and Egyptian economic practices became common, especially among the aristocracy. Nonetheless, reunification of the realm did not lead to a new Egyptian empire. In the centuries between the fall of the New Kingdom and the recovery of Egypt, several small but vigorous kingdoms had taken root and grown to maturity in the ancient Near East. By 700 B.C. Egypt was once again a strong kingdom, but no longer a mighty empire.

Yet Egypt's legacy to its African neighbors remained vibrant and rich. By trading and exploring southward along the coast of the Red Sea, the Egyptians introduced their goods and ideas as far south as the land of Punt, probably a region on the Somali coast. As early as the New Kingdom Egyptian pharaohs had exchanged gifts with the monarchs of Punt, and contact between the two areas persisted. Egypt was the primary civilizing force in Nubia, which became an African version of the pharaoh's realm, complete with royal pyramids and Egyptian deities, governmental procedures, and language. Egyptian religious beliefs penetrated as far south as Ethiopia. Just as Mesopotamian culture enjoyed wide appeal throughout the Near East, so Egyptian culture had a massive impact on northeastern Africa.

THE CHILDREN OF ISRAEL

The fall of the Hittite Empire and Egypt's collapse created a vacuum of power in the western Near East that allowed for the rise of

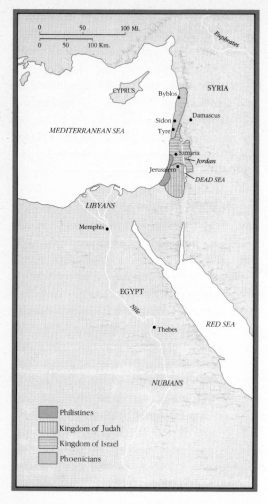

MAP 2.1   SMALL KINGDOMS IN THE NEAR
EAST   *This map illustrates the political fragmenta-*
tion of the Near East after the great wave of thir-
teenth-century invasions.

numerous small states. No longer crushed between the Hittites in the north and the Egyptians in the south, various peoples — some of
them newcomers — created homes and petty
kingdoms in Syria, Phoenicia, and Palestine.
After the Sea Peoples had raided Egypt, a
branch of them, known in the Bible as Philis-

tines, settled along the coast of modern Israel
(see Map 2.1). Establishing themselves in five
cities somewhat inland from the sea, the Philistines set about farming and raising flocks.

Another sturdy new culture was that of the
Phoenicians, a Semitic-speaking people who
had long inhabited several cities along the
coast of modern Lebanon. They had lived
under the shadow of the Hittites and Egyptians, but in this period the Phoenicians enjoyed full independence. (It was one of their
princes, the king of Byblos, who had given
Wen-Amon an unpleasant taste of the Phoenicians' newly found sense of freedom.) Unlike the Philistine newcomers, who turned
from seafaring to farming, the Phoenicians
took to the sea. They became outstanding
merchants and explorers. In their trading
ventures they sailed as far west as modern
Tunisia, where in 813 B.C. they founded the
city of Carthage, which would one day struggle with Rome for domination of the western
Mediterranean. Phoenician culture was urban,
based on the prosperous commercial centers
of Tyre, Sidon, and Byblos. The Phoenicians'
overwhelming cultural achievement was the
development of an alphabet, which they
handed on to the Greeks sometime in the late
eighth century B.C.

South of Phoenicia arose another small
kingdom, that of the Hebrews or ancient
Jews. Although smaller, poorer, less important, and less powerful than neighboring
kingdoms, the realm of the Hebrews was to
nourish religious ideas that underlie all of
Western civilization. Who were the Jewish
people, and what brought them to this new
land? Earlier Mesopotamian and Egyptian
sources refer to people called Habiru or Ha-
piru, which seems to mean a class of homeless, independent nomads. One such group of
Habiru were the biblical Hebrews. The original homeland of the Hebrews was probably

PHOENICIAN CARGO VESSELS An Assyrian artist has captured all of the energy and vivacity of the seafaring Phoenicians. The sea is filled with Phoenician cargo ships, which ranged the entire Mediterranean.

These ships are transporting cedar from Lebanon, some of it stowed on board, while other logs float in their wake. (Giraudon/Louvre)

northern Mesopotamia, and the most crucial event in their historical development was their enslavement in Egypt. According to the Old Testament, the Hebrews had followed their patriarch Abraham out of Mesopotamia into Canaan, and from there had migrated into the Nile Delta to escape a drought. Arriving during the imperial days of the Eighteenth Dynasty, the Hebrews were soon enslaved and forced to labor on building projects. The passing of Egypt's greatness was the Hebrews' opportunity.

The agent of the Hebrews' deliverance from slavery was Moses, a figure so towering in legendary stature that his actual existence has been doubted. According to the Old Testament, Yahweh – called Jehovah in the Bible – appeared in a burning bush and commanded Moses to lead the Hebrews out of Egypt into Canaan. Thus Moses, in obedience to the injunctions of Yahweh, directed his people to undertake a political act in the name of their god. The biblical book of Exodus depicts Moses leading the liberated Hebrews from Egypt into Canaan, which was to be their new homeland.

Today archaeologists are trying to ascertain precisely what happened around the time of the Hebrew exodus, and in the process to assess the accuracy of the biblical account. The archaeological record indicates that the thirteenth century B.C. was a time of warfare, disruption, and destruction, and seems to confirm the biblical portrayal of the exodus as a long period of conflict and turmoil. Apparently, nomadic Hebrew tribes filtered into Palestine from Egypt. According to Exodus, the Hebrews at this time consisted of a loose political confederation of twelve disunited tribes, which they believed to be descended from the twelve great-grandsons of Abraham.

In a series of vicious wars and savage slaughters they slowly won a place for themselves in Palestine (see Map 2.1). Success was not automatic, and the Hebrews suffered defeats and setbacks, but gradually they spread their power northward. In some cases they assimilated themselves to the culture of the natives, even going so far as to worship Baal, an ancient Semitic fertility god. In other instances, they carved out little strongholds and enslaved the natives. Even after the conquest, nearly constant fighting was required to consolidate the Hebrews' position.

The greatest danger to the Hebrews came from the Philistines, whose superior technology and military organization at first made them invincible. In Saul (ca 1000 B.C.), a farmer of the tribe of Benjamin, the Hebrews found a champion and a spirited leader. Saul carried the war to the Philistines, often without success. Yet in the meantime he established a monarchy over the twelve Hebrew tribes. Thus, under the peril of the Philistines, the Hebrew tribes evolved from scattered independent units into a centralized political organization in which the king directed the energies of the people.

Saul's work was carried on by David of Bethlehem, who in his youth had followed Saul into battle against the Philistines. Through courage and cunning David became king of Judah, hurled back the Philistines, and waged war against his other neighbors. To give his kingdom a capital he captured the city of Jerusalem, which he enlarged, fortified, and made the religious and political center of his realm. David's military successes won the Hebrews unprecedented security, and his forty-year reign was a period of vitality and political consolidation. David spent his last days dawdling in his harem, and letting the reins of power slip from his hands. Yet his ruin was not Israel's ruin. His work in consolidating the monarchy and enlarging the kingdom paved the way for his son Solomon.

Solomon (ca 965-925 B.C.) applied his energies to creating a nation out of a collection of tribes ruled by a king. He divided the kingdom, for purposes of effective administration, into twelve territorial districts cutting across the old tribal borders. To Solomon the twelve tribes of Israel were far less important than the Hebrew nation. He also yearned to bring his kingdom up to the level of its more sophisticated neighbors, and set about a building program to make Israel a respectable Near Eastern state. Work was begun on a magnificent temple in Jerusalem, on cities, palaces, fortresses, and roads. Solomon worked to bring Israel into the commercial mainstream of the world around it, and kept up good relations with Phoenician cities to the north. To pay for all this activity he imposed taxes far greater than any levied before, much to the displeasure of his subjects.

Solomon dedicated the temple in grand style, and made it the home of the Ark of the Covenant, the cherished chest that contained the holiest of Hebrew religious articles. As is recorded in the Old Testament:

And they [the priests] brought up the ark of the lord, and the tabernacle of the congregation, and all the holy vessels that were in the tabernacle, even these did the priests and the Levites bring up. And king Solomon, and all the congregation of Israel, that were assembled unto him, were with him before the ark, sacrificing sheep and oxen, that could not be told nor numbered for multitude. And the priests brought in the ark of the lord unto his place, into the oracle of the house, to the most holy place.[3]

The temple in Jerusalem was to be the religious heart of the kingdom and the symbol of

Hebrew unity. It also became the stronghold of the priesthood, for a legion of priests was needed to conduct religious sacrifices, ceremonies, and prayers. Yet Solomon's efforts were crowned with strife. He was too liberal in his ways, especially when it came to religion, to please some people, and the financial demands of his building program drained the resources of his people. His use of forced labor for his building projects further fanned popular resentment. However, Solomon had turned a rude kingdom into a state with broad commercial horizons and greater knowledge of the outside world. At his death, the Hebrews broke into two political halves (see Map 2.1). The northern part of the kingdom of David and Solomon became Israel, with its capital at Samaria. The southern half was Judah, and Solomon's city of Jerusalem remained its center. With political division went a religious rift: Israel, the northern kingdom, established rival sanctuaries to gods other than Yahweh. The Hebrew nation was divided, but at least it was divided into two far more sophisticated political units than before the time of Solomon. The Hebrews had taken their place in the increasingly cosmopolitan world of the Near East.

THE EVOLUTION OF JEWISH RELIGION

Hand in hand with their political evolution from fierce nomads to urban dwellers, the Hebrews were evolving spiritual ideas that still permeate Western society. Their chief literary product, the Old Testament, has fundamentally influenced both Christianity and Islam and still exerts a compelling force on the modern world.

It was Moses, the man who led the Hebrews to the promised land, who declared to the Hebrews Yahweh's covenant with them. According to the Old Testament, Yahweh appeared to Moses during the Exodus from Egypt, and ordered Moses to tell the Hebrews that he would watch over them, his chosen people. In return the Jews were to obey the Ten Commandments, which enjoined them to worship Yahweh and no other god.

Yahweh was unique because he was a lone god. Unlike the gods of Mesopotamia and Egypt, Yahweh was not the son of another god, nor did he have a divine wife or family. Initially an anthropomorphic god, Yahweh gradually lost his human form and became totally spiritual. Although Yahweh could assume human form, he was not to be depicted in any form. Consequently, the Jews considered graven images – statues and other representations – idolatrous.

At first Yahweh was probably conceived of as no more than the god of the Jews, a god who sometimes faced competition from Baal and other gods in Palestine. Enlil, Marduk, Amon-Re, and the others sufficed for foreigners. In time, however, the Jews came to regard Yahweh as the only god who existed. This was the beginning of true monotheism.

Yahweh was considered the creator of all things; his name means "he causes to be." He governed the cosmic forces of nature, including the movements of the sun, moon, and stars. His presence filled the universe. At the same time Yahweh was a personal god. Despite his awesome power, he was not too mighty or aloof to care for the individual. The Jews even believed that he intervened in human affairs.

Unlike Akhenaten's monotheism, Jewish monotheism was not an unpopular religion imposed from above. It was the religion of a whole people, deeply felt and cherished. Yet the Jews did not consider it their duty to spread the belief in the one god. The Jews rarely proselytized, as later the Christians did. As the chosen people, the chief duty of the

Jews was to maintain the worship of Yahweh as he demanded.

The original form of Yahweh's covenant with the Jews, the Ten Commandments, embodied an ethical code of conduct. It forbade the Jews to steal, murder, lie, and commit adultery. The covenant was a constant force in Jewish life, and the Old Testament records one occasion when the entire nation formally reaffirmed it:

And the king [of the Jews] stood by a pillar, and made a covenant before the lord, to walk after the lord, and to keep his commandments and his testimonies and his statutes with all their heart and all their soul, to perform the words of this covenant that were written in this book [Deuteronomy]. And all the people stood to the covenant.[4]

From the Ten Commandments evolved Jewish law, a code of law and custom originating with Moses and built upon by priests and prophets. The earliest part of this code, the Torah or Mosaic law, was often as harsh as Hammurabi's code, which had a powerful impact upon it. Later tradition, largely the work of prophets who lived from the eleventh to the fifth centuries B.C., was more humanitarian. The work of the prophet Jeremiah (ca 626 B.C.) exemplifies this gentler spirit. According to Jeremiah, Yahweh demanded righteousness from his people and protection for the weak and helpless:

For if ye thoroughly amend your ways and your doings; if ye thoroughly execute judgment between a man and his neighbor; if ye oppress not the stranger, the fatherless, and the widow, and shed not innocent blood in this place, neither walk after other gods to your hurt: then I will cause you to dwell in this place, in the land that I gave your fathers, for ever and ever.[5]

Here the emphasis is on mercy and justice, on avoiding wrongdoing to others because it is

displeasing to Yahweh. These precepts replaced the old law's demand for "an eye for an eye." Thus this passage is representative of a subtle and positive shift in Jewish thinking. Jeremiah proclaimed that the god of anger was also the god of forgiveness: "Return, thou backsliding Israel, saith the lord; and I will not cause mine anger to fall upon you; for I am merciful, saith the lord, and I will not keep anger forever."[6] Although Yahweh would punish wrongdoing, he would not destroy those who repented. One generation might be punished for its misdeeds, but Yahweh's mercy was a promise of hope for future generations.

The uniqueness of this phenomenon can be seen by comparing the essence of Hebrew monotheism with the religious outlook of the Mesopotamians. Whereas the Mesopotamians considered their gods capricious, the Jews knew what Yahweh expected of them. The Jews believed that their god would protect them and make them prosper if they obeyed his commandments. The Mesopotamians thought human beings insignificant as compared to the gods, so insignificant that the gods might even be indifferent to them. The Jews too considered themselves puny in comparison to Yahweh. Yet they were Yahweh's chosen people, and he had promised never to abandon them. Finally, though the Mesopotamians believed that the gods generally preferred good to evil, their religion did not demand ethical conduct. The Jews could please their god only by living up to high moral standards in addition to worshiping him.

The evolution of Hebrew monotheism resulted in one of the world's greatest religions, which deeply influenced the development of two others. Many parts of the Old Testament show obvious debts to Mesopotamian culture. Nonetheless, to the Jews goes the credit for developing a religion so emotionally satisfying and ethically grand that it has not only flourished but also profoundly influenced Christianity and Islam. Without Moses there could not have been Jesus or Mohammed. The religious standards of the modern West are deeply rooted in Judaism.

DAILY LIFE IN ISRAEL

Historians generally know far more about the daily life of the aristocracy and the wealthy in ancient societies than about the conditions of the common people. Jewish society is an exception, simply because the Old Testament, which lays down laws for all Jews, has much to say about peasants and princes alike. Comparisons with the social conditions of Israel's ancient neighbors and modern anthropological work among Palestinian Arabs shed additional light on biblical practices. Thus the life of the common people in ancient Israel is better known than, for instance, the lives of ordinary Romans or ancient Chinese.

The nomadic Hebrews first entered Palestine as tribes, consisting of numerous families who thought of themselves as all related to one another. As the Jews consolidated their hold on Palestine, and as the concept of one Jewish nation gained a hold, the importance of the tribes declined.

At first good farm land, pasture land, and watering-spots were held in common by the tribe. Common use of land was — and still is — characteristic of nomadic peoples. Typically each family or group of families in the tribe drew lots every year to determine who worked what fields. But as formerly nomadic peoples turned increasingly to settled agriculture, communal use of land gave way to family ownership. In this respect the experience of the ancient Hebrews seems typical of many early peoples. Slowly but inevitably the shift from nomad to farmer affected far more than just how people fed themselves. Family relationships reflected evolving circumstances. The extended family, organized in tribes, is even today typical of nomads. With the transition to settled agriculture, the tribe gradually becomes less important than the extended family. With the advent of village life, and finally full-blown urban life, the extended family in turn gives way to the nuclear family.

The family — people related to one another, all living in the same place — was the primary social institution among the Jews. At its head, stood the father, who like the Mesopotamian father held great powers. The father was the master of his wife and children, with power of life and death over his family. By the eighth century B.C., the advent of full-blown urban life began to change the shape of family life again. The father's power and the overall strength of family ties relaxed. Much of the father's power passed to the elders of the town, especially the power of life and death over his children. One result of this general development was the liberation of the individual person from the tight control of the family.

Marriage was one of the most important and joyous events in the life of the Hebrew family. When the Jews were still nomads, a man could have only one lawful wife but any number of concubines. Settled life changed marriage customs and later Jewish law allowed men to be polygamous. Not only did kings David and Solomon have harems, but rich men might also have several wives. The chief reason for this custom, as in Mesopotamia, was the desire for children. Given the absence of medical knowledge and the rough conditions of life, women faced barrenness, high infant mortality, and rapid aging. Several women in the family led to some quarrelsome households; and the legal wife, if she were barren, could be scorned and ridiculed by her husband's concubines.

The common man was too poor to afford the luxury of several women in the home. The typical marriage in ancient Israel was monogamous, and a virtuous wife was revered and honored. Perhaps the finest and most fervent song of praise to the good wife comes from the book of Proverbs in the Old Testament:

Who can find a virtuous woman? for her price is far above rubies ... Strength and honour are her clothing; and she shall rejoice in time to come. She openeth her mouth with wisdom; and in her tongue is the law of kindness. She looketh well to the ways of her household, and eateth not the bread of idleness. Her children arise up, and call her blessed; her husband also, and he praiseth her ... Favour is deceitful, and beauty is vain: but a woman that feareth the lord, she shall be praised.[7]

The commandment "honor thy father and thy mother" was fundamental to the Mosaic law. The wife was a pillar of the family, and her work and wisdom were respected and treasured.

Betrothal and marriage were serious matters in ancient Israel. As in Mesopotamia, they were left largely in the hands of the parents. Boys and girls were often married when they were little more than children, and their parents naturally made the marriage arrangements. Rarely were the prospective bride and groom consulted. Marriages were often contracted within the extended family, and commonly among first cousins – a custom still found among Palestinian Arabs today. Although early Jewish custom permitted marriage with foreigners, the fear of alien religions soon led to restrictions against mixed marriages.

The father of the groom offered a bridal gift to the bride's father. This custom, the marriage price, also existed among the Mesopotamians and still survives among modern Palestinian Arabs. The gift was ordinarily money, the amount depending on the social status and wealth of the two families. In other instances, the groom could work off the marriage price by performing manual labor, as Jacob did for Leah and Rachel. At the time of the wedding the man gave his bride and her family wedding presents; unlike Mesopotamian custom, the bride's father did not provide her with a dowry.

As in Mesopotamia, marriage was a legal contract, not a religious ceremony. At marriage a woman left her family and joined the family and clan of her husband. The occasion when the bride joined her husband's household was festive. The groom wore a crown and his best clothes. Accompanied by his friends, also dressed in their finest and carrying musical instruments, the bridegroom walked to the bride's house, where she awaited him in her richest clothes, jewels, and a veil which she removed only later when the couple was alone. The bride's friends joined the group, and together they all marched in procession to the groom's house, their way marked by music and songs honoring the newlyweds. Though the wedding feast might last for days, the couple consummated their marriage on the first night; the next day the bloody linen was displayed to prove the bride's virginity.

Divorce was available only to the husband. He could normally end the marriage very simply and for any of a number of reasons:

When a man hath taken a wife, and married her, and it come to pass that she find no favour in his eyes, because he hath found some uncleanness in her: then let him write her a bill of divorcement, and give it in her hand, and send her out of his house. And when she is departed out of his house, she may go and be another man's wife.[8]

The right to initiate a divorce was denied the wife. Even adultery by the husband was not necessarily grounds for divorce. Jewish law, like the Code of Hammurabi, generally punished adultery with death. Generally speaking, Jewish custom frowned on divorce, and the typical couple entered into marriage fully expecting to spend the rest of their lives together.

The newly married couple was expected to begin a family at once. Children, according to the book of Psalms, "are an heritage of the lord: and the fruit of the womb is his reward."[9] The desire for children to perpetuate the family was so strong that if a man died before he could sire a son, his brother was legally obliged to marry the widow. The son born of the brother was thereafter considered the offspring and heir of the dead man. If the brother refused, the widow had her revenge by denouncing him to the elders in public:

Then shall his brother's wife come unto him in the presence of the elders, and loose his shoe from off his foot, and spit in his face, and shall answer and say, So shall it be done unto that man that will not build up his brother's house.[10]

Sons were especially desired because they maintained the family bloodline and kept the ancestral property within the family. The first-born son had special rights, honor, and responsibilities. At his father's death he became the head of the household, and received a larger inheritance than his younger brothers. Daughters were less highly valued because they would eventually marry and leave the family. Yet in Jewish society, unlike other cultures, infanticide was illegal; Yahweh had forbidden it.

The Old Testament often speaks of the pain of childbirth. Professional midwives frequently assisted at deliveries. The newborn infant was washed, rubbed with salt, and wrapped in swaddling-clothes – bands of cloth that were wrapped around the baby. Normally the mother nursed the baby herself,

and weaned the infant at about the age of three. The mother customarily named the baby immediately after birth, but children were free to change names after they grew up. Eight days after the birth of a son, the ceremony of circumcision – removal of the foreskin of the penis – took place. Circumcision signified that the boy belonged to the Jewish community, and according to Genesis was the symbol of Yahweh's covenant with Abraham.

As in most other societies, so in ancient Israel the early education of children was in the hands of the mother. It was she who taught her children right from wrong and gave them their first instruction in the moral values of their society. As boys grew older, they received more of their education from their fathers. Fathers instructed their sons in religion and the history of their people. Many children were taught to read and write, and the head of each family was probably able to write. Fathers also taught their sons the family craft or trade. Boys soon learned that inattention could be painful, for Jewish custom advised fathers to be strict: "He that spareth his rod hateth his son: but he that loveth him chasteneth him betimes."[11]

Once children grew to adulthood, they entered fully into economic and social life. For most that meant a life on the farm, whose demands and rhythm changed very little over time. Young people began with the lighter tasks. Girls traditionally tended flocks of sheep and drew water from the well for household use. The well was a popular meeting spot, where girls could meet other young people and even travelers passing through the country with camel caravans. After the harvest, young girls followed behind the reapers to glean the fields. Even this work was governed by law and custom: once the girls had gone through the fields, they were not to return, for Yahweh had declared that anything left behind belonged to the needy:

THE SEASONS OF THE YEAR *The Hebrew agricultural year, like that of other peoples, was tied to the sun, seasons, and stars. The center of this mosaic floor shows the sun in its chariot, pulled by four horses. In the outer circle are the signs of the zodiac, while the four seasons of the year peer at the viewer from the corners of the panel. (Consulate General of Israel)*

When thou cuttest down thine harvest in thy field, and hast forgot a sheaf in the field, thou shalt not go again to fetch it: it shall be for the stranger, for the fatherless, and for the widow: that the lord thy God may bless thee in all the work of thine hands.[12]

Boys also tended flocks, especially in wild areas. Like the young David, they practiced their marksmanship with slings and entertained themselves with music. They shared the lighter work, such as harvesting grapes and beating the limbs of olive trees to shake the fruit loose. Only when they grew to full strength did they perform the hard work of harrowing, ploughing, and harvesting.

The land was precious to the family, not simply because it provided a living, but also because it was a link to the past. It was the land of the family's forebears, and held their tombs. The family's feeling for its land was so strong that in times of hardship when land had to be sold, the nearest kin had first right to buy it. Thus the land might at least remain within the extended family.

Ironically, the success of the first Hebrew kings endangered the future of many family farms. With peace, more settled conditions, and increasing prosperity, some Jews began to amass larger holdings by buying out poor and struggling farmers. Far from discouraging this development, the kings created their own huge estates. In many cases slaves, both Jewish and foreign, worked these large farms and estates shoulder-to-shoulder with paid free men. Although the Old Testament called upon the royal and the rich to treat the slave and the laborer with justice and charity, there is no reason to think that Hebrew slavery was different from any other slavery. The prophet Jeremiah thundered against the exploiters:

Woe unto him that buildeth his house by unrighteousness, and his chambers by wrong; that useth his neighbor's service without wages, and giveth him not for his work.[13]

In still later times, rich landowners rented plots of land to poor, free families; the landowners provided the renters with seed and livestock, and normally took half the yield as rent. Although many Old Testament prophets denounced the destruction of the family farm, as the Gracchi were later to condemn the destruction of small Roman farms (Chapter 5), the trend continued toward large estates worked by slaves and hired free men.

The development of urban life among the Jews created new economic opportunities, especially in crafts and trades. People specialized in particular occupations, like milling flour, baking bread, making pottery, weaving cloth, and carpentry. All these crafts were family trades. Sons worked with their father; if the business prospered, they might be assisted by a few paid workers or slaves. The practitioners of a particular craft usually lived in a particular street or section of the town, a custom that is still prevalent in the Middle East today. By the sixth century B.C. craftsmen had formed guilds, intended like European guilds in the Middle Ages (Chapter 9) to protect their interests and aid their members. By banding together, craftsmen gained a corporate status within the community.

Commerce and trade developed later than crafts. In the time of Solomon, foreign trade was in the king's domain. Aided by the Phoenicians, who ranked among the leading merchants of the Near East, Solomon built a fleet to trade with ports on the Red Sea. Solomon also participated in the overland caravan trade. Otherwise, trade with neighboring countries was handled by foreigners, usually Phoenicians. Jews dealt mainly in local trade, and in most instances craftsmen and farmers sold directly to their customers. Only much later, after the great Exile – the period in the sixth century B.C., known as the Babylonian Captivity, when the Babylonians resettled the Jews in Mesopotamia – did Jews become merchants in large numbers. Many of Israel's wise men disapproved of commerce, and like the ancient Chinese, they considered it unseemly to profit from others' work.

Between the eclipse of the Hittites and Egyptians and the rise of the Assyrians, the Hebrews moved from nomadism to urban life and full participation in the mainstream of ancient Near Eastern culture. Retaining their unique religion and customs, they drew from the practices of other peoples and contributed to the lives of their neighbors.

ASSYRIA, THE MILITARY MONARCHY

Small kingdoms like those of the Phoenicians and the Hebrews could exist only in the absence of a major power. The beginning of the ninth century B.C. saw the rise of such a power: the Assyrians of northern Mesopotamia, whose chief capital was at Nineveh on the Tigris river. The Assyrians were a Semitic-speaking people heavily influenced, like so many other peoples of the Near East, by the Mesopotamian culture of Babylon to the south. They were also one of the most warlike peoples in history, largely because throughout their history they were threatened by neighboring folk. Living in an open and exposed land, the Assyrians experienced frequent and devastating attacks by the wild war-loving tribes to their north and east and by the Babylonians to the south. The constant threat to the Assyrians' survival promoted political cohesion and military might.

For over two hundred years the Assyrians labored to dominate the Near East. In 859 B.C. the new Assyrian king Shalmaneser unleashed the first of a long series of attacks on the peoples of Syria and Palestine. Year after relentless year, Assyrian armies hammered at the peoples of the west. These ominous events inaugurated two turbulent centuries marked by Assyrian military campaigns, constant efforts by Syria and the two Jewish kingdoms to maintain or recover their independence, eventual Assyrian conquest of Babylonia and northern Egypt, and periodic political instability in Assyria itself, which prompted stirrings of freedom throughout the Near East.

Under the Assyrian kings Tiglath-pileser III (744–727 B.C.) and Sargon II (721–705 B.C.), both mighty warriors, the Near East trembled as never before under the blows of

Assyrian armies. The Assyrians stepped up their attacks in Anatolia, Syria, and Palestine. The kingdom of Israel and many other states fell; others, like the kingdom of Judah, became subservient to the warriors from the Tigris. In 717–716 B.C. Sargon led his army in a sweeping attack along the Philistine coast into Egypt. He defeated the pharaoh, who suffered the further ignominy of paying tribute to the foreign conquerors. Sargon also lashed out at Assyria's traditional enemies to the north, and then turned south against a renewed threat in Babylonia. By means of almost constant warfare, Tiglath-pileser III and Sargon carved out an Assyrian empire that stretched from east and north of the Tigris river to central Egypt (see Map 2.2).

An empire forged with so much blood and effort was vulnerable to revolt, and revolt provoked brutal retaliation. The Assyrian king Ashurbanipal (668–633 B.C.) left a grisly account of how he dealt with the Babylonians, who had conspired against him and perhaps earlier against his grandfather, King Sennacherib:

I tore out the tongues of these whose slanderous mouths had uttered blasphemies against my god Ashur and had plotted against me, his god-fearing prince; I defeated them completely. The others, I smashed alive with the very same statues of protective deities with which they had smashed my own grandfather Sennacherib – now finally as a belated burial sacrifice for his soul. I fed their corpses, cut into small pieces, to dogs, pigs, zibu-birds, vultures, the birds of the sky and also to the fish of the ocean. After I had performed this and thus made quiet again the hearts of the great gods, my lords, I removed the corpses of those whom the pestilence had felled, whose leftovers after the dogs and pigs had fed on them were obstructing the streets, filling the places of Babylon, and of those who had lost their lives through the horrible famine.[14]

Revolt against the Assyrians inevitably promised the rebels bloody battles, prolonged sieges accompanied by starvation, plague, and sometimes even cannibalism, and finally surrender followed by systematic torture and slaughter.

Though atrocity and terrorism struck unspeakable fear into Assyria's subjects, Assyria's success was actually due to sophisti-

THE KING OF ASSYRIA ON THE MARCH *The might of the Assyrian king and his retinue shines clearly in this relief. With almost photographic precision the artist has captured the details of the chariot's* *construction, the harness of the horses, and the weapons and equipment of the accompanying infantrymen. (Metropolitan Museum of Art, New York)*

cated, far-sighted, and effective military organization. By Sargon's time the Assyrians had invented the mightiest military machine the ancient Near East had ever seen. The mainstay of the Assyrian army, the soldier who ordinarily decided the outcome of battles, was the infantryman, armed with a spear and sword and protected by helmet and armor. The Assyrian army also featured archers, some on foot, others on horseback, still others in chariots — the latter ready to wield lances once they had expended their supply of arrows. Some infantry archers wore heavy armor, strikingly similar to the armor worn much later by William the Conqueror's Normans. These soldiers served as a primitive field artillery, whose job was to sweep the enemy's walls of defenders so that others could storm the defenses. Slingers also served as artillery in pitched battles. For mobility on the battlefield, the Assyrians organized a corps of chariots.

Assyrian military genius was remarkable for the development of a wide variety of siege machinery and techniques, including excavation to undermine city walls and battering-rams to knock down walls and gates. Never

before in the Near East had anyone applied such technical knowledge to warfare. The Assyrians even invented the concept of a corps of engineers, who bridged rivers with pontoons or provided soldiers with inflatable skins for swimming. Furthermore, the Assyrians knew how to coordinate their efforts, both in open battle and in siege warfare. Sennacherib's account of his siege of Jerusalem in 701 B.C. is a vivid portrait of the Assyrian war machine in action:

As to Hezekiah, the Jew, he did not submit to my yoke, I laid siege to 46 of his strong cities, walled forts and to the countless small villages in their vicinity, and conquered them by means of well-stamped earth-ramps, and battering rams brought thus near to the walls combined with the attack by foot soldiers, using mines, breaches as well as sapper work ... Himself I made prisoner in Jerusalem, his royal residence, like a bird in a cage. I surrounded him with earthwork in order to molest those who were leaving his city's gate ... Hezekiah himself, whom the terror-inspiring splendor of my lordship had overwhelmed and whose irregular and elite troops which he had brought into Jerusalem, his royal residence, in order to strengthen it, had deserted him, did send me, later, to Nineveh,

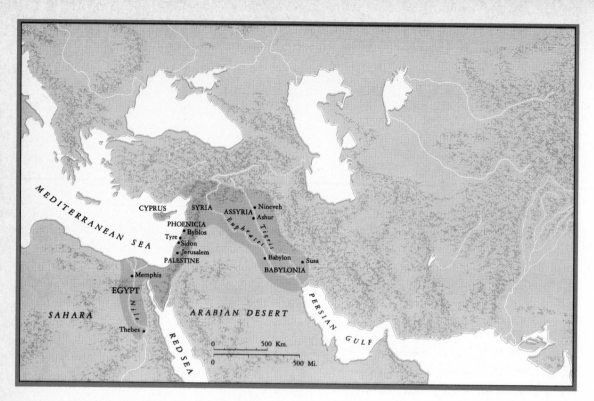

MAP 2.2 THE ASSYRIAN EMPIRE *The Assyrian Empire at its height included almost all of the old centers of power in the ancient Near East.*

my lordly city, together with 30 talents of gold, 800 talents of silver . . . and all kinds of valuable treasures.[15]

Hezekiah and Jerusalem shared the fate of many a rebellious king and capital, and were indeed lucky to escape severe reprisals. The Assyrians were too powerful and well organized and far too tenacious to be turned back by isolated strongholds, no matter how well situated or defended.

ASSYRIAN RULE

Not only did the Assyrians know how to win battles; they also knew how to use their victories. As early as the reign of Tiglath-pileser III, the Assyrian kings began to organize their conquered territories into an empire. The lands closest to Assyria became provinces governed by Assyrian officials. Kingdoms beyond the provinces were not annexed, but became dependent states that followed Assyria's lead. The Assyrian king chose their rulers, either by regulating the succession of native kings or by supporting native kings who appealed to him. The Old Testament recounts how Ahaz, king of Judah, called for help from Tiglath-pileser, and in return for Assyrian support became his vassal:

So Ahaz sent messengers to Tiglath-pileser king of Assyria, saying, I am thy servant and thy son: come up, and save me out of the hand of the king of Syria, and out of the hand of the king of Israel, which rise up against me. And Ahaz took the

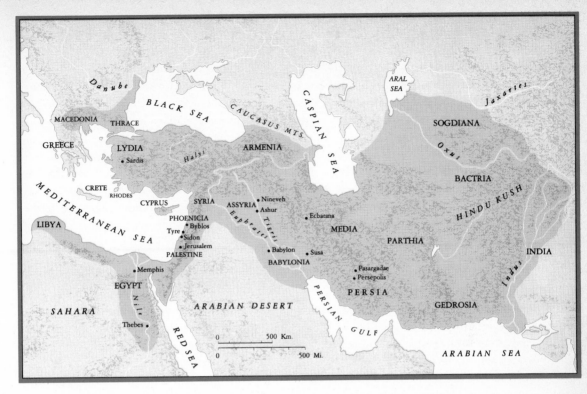

MAP 2.3 THE PERSIAN EMPIRE *The Persian Empire not only included more of the ancient Near East than had the Assyrian Empire, but it also extended as far east as western India.*

silver and gold that was found in the house of the lord, and in the treasures of the king's house, and sent it for a present to the king of Assyria.[16]

Against still more distant states the kings waged frequent war in order to conquer them outright or to make their dependent states secure.

Royal roads and swift mounted messengers linked the Assyrian empire, and Assyrian records describe how these royal messengers brought the king immediate word of unrest or rebellion within the empire. Because of good communications, Assyrian kings could generally move against rebels at a moment's notice. Thus, though rebellion was common in the Assyrian empire, it rarely got off the ground before the king struck back hard.

In the seventh century B.C. Assyrian power seemed secure. From their capitals at Nineveh, Kalah, and Ashur on the Tigris river, the Assyrians ruled a vast empire. Good communications, an efficient army, and calculated terrorism easily kept down the conquered population. With grim efficiency they sacked rebellious cities, leaving forests of impaled prisoners or piles of severed heads to signal their victory. Their ferocity horrified their subjects and bred a vast hatred among them.

Yet the downfall of Assyria was swift and complete. Babylon finally won its independence in 626 B.C. and joined forces with a new people, the Medes, an Indo-European-speaking folk from Iran. Together the Babylonians and the Medes destroyed the Assyrian empire in 612 B.C., paving the way for the rise of the

Persians. The Hebrew prophet Nahum spoke for many when he proclaimed: "Nineveh is laid waste: who will bemoan her?".[17] Their cities destroyed and their power shattered, the Assyrians disappeared from history, remembered only as a cruel people of the Old Testament who oppressed the Hebrews. Two hundred years later, when the Greek adventurer and historian Xenophon passed by the ruins of Nineveh, he marvelled at their extent but knew nothing of the Assyrians. The glory of their empire was forgotten.

Yet modern archaeology has brought the Assyrians out of obscurity. In 1839 the intrepid English archaeologist and traveler A. H. Layard began to excavate Nineveh, then a mound of debris beside the Tigris. His findings electrified the world. In the course of a few years Layard's discoveries shed remarkable new light on Assyrian history. His excavations had an equally stunning impact on the history of art. Layard's workers unearthed masterpieces, including monumental sculpted figures — huge winged bulls, human-headed lions, and sphinxes — as well as brilliantly sculpted friezes. Equally valuable were the numerous Assyrian cuneiform documents, which ranged from royal accounts of mighty military campaigns to simple letters by common people.

Among the most renowned of Layard's finds were the Assyrian palace reliefs, whose number has been increased by the discoveries of twentieth-century archaeologists. Assyrian kings delighted in scenes of war, which their artists depicted in graphic detail. By the time of Ashurbanipal, Assyrian artists had hit upon the idea of portraying a series of episodes — in fact, a visual narrative — of events that had actually taken place. Scene followed scene in a continuous frieze, so the viewer could follow the progress of a military campaign from the time that the army marched out until the enemy was conquered. So too with another theme of the palace reliefs — the lion hunt. Hunting lions was probably a royal sport, although some scholars have suggested a magical significance. They argue that the hunting scenes depict the king as the protector of his people, the one who wards off evil. In any case, here too the viewer proceeds in sequence, from preparations for the chase through the hunting itself to the killing of the lions. These reliefs, like those depicting warfare, tell a story in pictures, an artistic technique novel in the ancient Near East.

Assyrian art, like much of Egyptian art, was realistic, but the warmth and humor of the Egyptian scenes are absent from the Assyrian reliefs. Assyrian art is stark and often brutal in subject matter, yet marked by an undeniable strength and sophistication of composition. Assyrian realism is well represented by the illustration on page 57, a scene which portrays the climax of the royal lion hunt. The scene is like a photograph, snapped at the height of the action. The king, mounted on horseback, has already fired his arrows into two lions, who nonetheless are still full of fight. The wounded lion on the left has just pounced on a riderless horse, which in a moment will fall mortally wounded. Meanwhile, the king thrusts his spear into another lion, which has begun its spring. The artistic rendering of the figures is exciting and technically flawless. The figures are anatomically correct and in proper proportion and perspective. The whole composition conveys both action and tension. Assyrian art fared better than Assyrian military power. The techniques of Assyrian artists influenced the Persians, who adapted them to gentler scenes.

In fact, many Assyrian innovations, military and political as well as artistic, were taken over wholesale by the Persians. Although the memory of Assyria was hateful throughout

ROYAL LION HUNT   This relief from the palace of Ashurbanipal at Nineveh shows the king fighting two lions, and it is typical of the energy and artistic brilliance of Assyrian sculptors. (Reproduced by Courtesy of the Trustees of the British Museum)

the Near East, the fruits of Assyrian organizational genius helped enable the Persians to bring peace and stability to the same regions where Assyrian armies had spread terror.

THE EMPIRE OF THE PERSIAN KINGS

Like the Hittites before them, the Iranians were Indo-Europeans from central Europe and southern Russia who migrated into a land inhabited by more primitive peoples. Once settled in the area between the Caspian Sea and the Persian Gulf, the Iranians, like the Hittites, fell under the spell of the more sophisticated cultures of their Mesopotamian neighbors. Yet the Iranians went on to create one of the greatest empires of antiquity, one that encompassed hundreds of peoples and cultures. The Persians, the most important of the Iranian peoples, had a far-sighted conception of empire. They respected their subjects

and allowed them to practice their native customs and religions. Thus, the Persians gave the Near East political unity coupled with cultural diversity. Never before had any Near Eastern people viewed empire in such intelligent and humane terms.

THE LAND OF MOUNTAINS AND PLATEAU

Persia – the modern country of Iran – is a stark land of towering mountains and flaming deserts, with a broad central plateau in the heart of the country (see Map 2.3). Iran stretches from the Caspian Sea in the north to the Persian Gulf in the south. Between the Tigris-Euphrates valley in the west and the Indus valley in the east rises an immense plateau, surrounded on all sides by lofty mountains that cut off the interior from the sea.

The central plateau is very high, a landscape of broad plains, scattered oases, and two vast deserts. The high mountains, which catch the moisture coming from the sea, generate ample rainfall for the plain. This semi-tropical area is very fertile, in marked contrast to the aridity of most of Iran. The mountains surrounding the central plateau are dotted with numerous oases, often very fertile, which have from time immemorial served as havens for small groups of people.

At the center of the plateau lies an enormous depression – a forbidding region devoid of water and vegetation, so glowing hot in summer that it is virtually impossible to cross. This depression forms two distinct grim and burning salt deserts, perhaps the most desolate spots on earth. These two deserts form a barrier between east and west.

Iran's geographical position and topography explain its traditional role as the highway between East and West. Throughout history wild, nomadic people migrating from the broad steppes of Russia and Central Asia have streamed into Iran. Confronting the uncrossable salt deserts, most have turned either eastward or westward, moving on until they reached the advanced and wealthy urban centers of Mesopotamia and India. When cities emerged along the natural lines of east-west communication, Iran became the area where nomads met urban dwellers, a meeting-ground of unique significance for the civilizations of both East and West.

THE COMING OF THE MEDES AND THE PERSIANS

The history of human habitation in Iran is long and rich: traces of prehistoric peoples date back as far as 15,000–10,000 B.C. About the prehistoric period, historians and archaeologists still have much to learn. Perhaps the best recent account of prehistoric developments comes from one of the world's foremost experts on ancient Iran, the French scholar Roman Ghirshman:

The arrival of the Iranians in the plateau was preceded by a long period of several millennia, during which there slowly developed the civilization of prehistoric man, who, coming down from his caves, established himself in the plains and valleys. Over the course of more than thirty centuries man acquired the knowledge of and developed agriculture, domesticated animals, took the first steps in metallurgy. His art of painted pottery, doubtless born in the plateau, underwent a rapid rise and extensive diffusion. Man organized his social life by creating villages, and, never remaining isolated, he established and enlarged his contacts with other human groups.[18]

The Iranians entered this land around 1000 B.C. The most historically important of them were the Medes and the Persians, related peoples who settled in different areas. Both groups were part of the vast movement of Indo-European-speaking peoples whose wanderings led them into Europe, the Near East, and India in many successive waves (page 31). These Iranians were nomads, who migrated with their flocks and herds. Like their kinsmen the Aryans, who moved into India, they were also horse-breeders, and the horse gave them a decisive military advantage over the prehistoric peoples of Iran. The Iranians rode into battle in horse-drawn chariots or on horseback, and easily swept the natives before them. Yet because the influx of Iranians went on for centuries, there continued to be constant cultural interchange between conquering newcomers and conquered natives.

Excavations at Siyalk, some 125 miles south of present-day Tehran, provide a valuable glimpse of the encounter of Iranian and native. The village of Siyalk had been inhabited since prehistoric times before falling to the Iranians. The new lords fought all comers: natives, rival Iranians, and even the Assyrians, who often raided far east of the

Tigris. Under the newly-arrived Iranians, Siyalk became a fortified town with a palace and perhaps a temple, all enclosed by a circuit wall strengthened by towers and ramparts. The town was surrounded by fields and farms, for agriculture was the basis of this evolving society.

The Iranians initially created a patchwork of tiny kingdoms, of which Siyalk was one. The chieftain or petty king was basically a warlord who depended on his fellow warriors for aid and support. This band of noble warriors, like the Greek heroes of the *Iliad,* formed the fighting strength of the army. The king owned estates that supported him and his nobles; for additional income the king levied taxes, which were paid in kind and not in cash. He also demanded labor services from the peasants. Below the king and his warrior nobles were free people who held land and others who owned nothing. Artisans produced the various goods needed to keep society running. At the bottom of the social scale were slaves – probably both natives and newcomers – to whom fell the drudgery of hard labor and household service to the king and his nobles.

This early period saw some significant economic developments. The use of iron increased. By the seventh century B.C. iron farm implements had become widespread, leading to increased productivity, greater overall prosperity, and higher standards of living. At the same time Iranian agriculture saw the development of the small estate. Farmers worked small plots of land, and the general prosperity of the period bred a sturdy and free peasantry, who enjoyed greater freedom than their contemporaries in Egypt and Mesopotamia.

Kings exploited Iran's considerable mineral wealth, and Iranian iron, copper, and lapis lazuli attracted Assyrian raiding parties. Even more important, mineral wealth and Iranian horse-breeding stimulated brisk trade with the outside world. Kings found that merchants, who were not usually Iranians, produced large profits to help fill the kings' coffers. Overland trade also put the Iranians in direct contact with their Near Eastern neighbors.

Gradually two groups of Iranians began coalescing into larger units. The Persians had settled in Persis, the modern region of Fars, in southern Iran. Their kinsmen the Medes occupied Media, the modern area of Hamádan in the north, with their capital at Ecbatana. The Medes were exposed to attack by nomads from the north, but their greatest threat was the frequent raids of the Assyrian army. Even though distracted by grave pressures from their neighbors, the Medes united under one king around 710 B.C., and extended their control over the Persians in the south. In 612 B.C. the Medes were strong enough to join the Babylonians in overthrowing the Assyrian Empire. With the rise of the Medes, the balance of power in the Near East shifted for the first time east of Mesopotamia.

THE CREATION OF THE PERSIAN EMPIRE

In 550 B.C. Cyrus the Great (559–530 B.C.), king of the Persians and one of the most remarkable statesmen of antiquity, threw off the yoke of the Medes by conquering them and turning their country into his first satrapy, or province. In the short space of a single lifetime, Cyrus created one of the greatest empires of antiquity. Two characteristics lift Cyrus above the common level of warrior-kings. First, he thought of Iran, not just Persia and Media, as a state. His concept has survived a long, complex, and often turbulent history to play its part in the contemporary world.

Second, Cyrus held an enlightened view of

TOMB OF CYRUS *For all of his greatness Cyrus retained a sense of perspective. His tomb, though monumental in size, is rather simple and unostentatious. Greek writers reported that it bore the following epitaph: "O man, I am Cyrus the son of Cambyses. I established the Persian Empire and was king of Asia. Do not begrudge me my memorial." (Oriental Institute, University of Chicago)*

empire. Many of the civilizations and cultures that fell to his armies were, he realized, far older, more advanced, and more sophisticated than his. Free of the narrow-minded snobbery of the Egyptians, the religious exclusiveness of the Hebrews, and the calculated cruelty of the Assyrians, Cyrus gave Near Eastern peoples and their cultures his respect, toleration, and protection. Conquered peoples continued to enjoy their institutions, religion, language, and way of life under the Persians. The Persian Empire, which Cyrus created, became a political organization sheltering many different civilizations. To rule such a vast area and so many diverse peoples demanded talent, intelligence, sensitivity, and a cosmopolitan view of the world. These qualities Cyrus and many of his successors possessed in abundance. Consequently, the Persians gave the

ancient Near East over two hundred years of peace, prosperity, and security.

Cyrus showed his magnanimity at the outset of his career. Once the Medes had fallen to him, Cyrus united them with his Persians. Ecbatana, the Median capital, became a Persian seat of power. Medes were honored with important military and political posts, and thenceforth helped the Persians to rule the expanding empire. Cyrus' conquest of the Medes resulted not in slavery and slaughter, but in the union of Iranian peoples.

With Iran united, Cyrus looked at the broader world. He set out to achieve two goals: first, to win control of the west, and thus of the terminal ports of the great trade routes that crossed Iran and Anatolia. Secondly, Cyrus strove to secure eastern Iran from the pressure of nomadic invaders. In 550 B.C. neither goal was easy. To the northwest was the young kingdom of Lydia in Anatolia, whose king Croesus was proverbial for his wealth. To the west was Babylonia, enjoying a new period of power now that the Assyrian Empire had been crushed. To the southwest was Egypt, still weak but sheltered behind its bulwark of sand and sea. To the east ranged tough, mobile nomads, capable of massive and destructive incursions deep into Iranian territory.

Cyrus turned first to Croesus' Lydian kingdom, which fell to him around 546 B.C. He established a garrison at Sardis, the capital of Lydia, and ordered his generals to subdue the Greek cities along the coast of Anatolia. Cyrus had thus gained the important ports that looked out to the Mediterranean world. And for the first time the Persians came into direct contact with the Greeks, a people with whom their later history was to be intimately connected.

From Lydia, Cyrus next marched to the far eastern corners of Iran. In a brilliant campaign he conquered the regions of Parthia, Bactria, and even the most westerly part of India. All of Iran was now Persian, from Mesopotamia in the west to the western slopes of the Hindu Kush in the east.

In 540 B.C. Cyrus moved against Babylonia, now isolated from outside help. When Persian soldiers marched quietly into Babylon the next year, the Babylonians welcomed Cyrus as a liberator. Cyrus described the event himself thus:

When I made my gracious entry into Babylon, with rejoicing and pleasure I took up my lordly residence in the royal palace. Marduk, the great lord, turned the noble race of the Babylonians toward me, and I gave daily care to his worship. My numerous troops marched peacefully into Babylon. In all Sumer and Akkad I permitted no unfriendly treatment. The dishonoring yoke was removed from them. Their fallen dwellings I restored; I cleared out the ruins.[19]

Cyrus won the hearts of the Babylonians with toleration of and adherence to Babylonian religion, humane treatment, and support of their efforts to refurbish their capital.

Cyrus was equally generous toward the Jews. He allowed them to return to Palestine, from which they had been deported by the Babylonians. He protected them, gave them back the sacred items they used in worship, and rebuilt the temple of Yahweh in Jerusalem. The Old Testament sings the praises of Cyrus, whom the Jews considered the shepherd of Yahweh, the lord's anointed:

[Yahweh] that saith of Cyrus, he is my shepherd, and shall perform all my pleasure: even saying to Jerusalem, thou shalt be built; and to the temple, thy foundation shall be laid. Thus saith the lord to his anointed, to Cyrus, whose right hand I have holden, to subdue nations before him.[20]

Rarely have conquered people shown such gratitude to their conquerors. Cyrus's benev-olent policy created a Persian Empire in which the cultures and religions of its members were respected and honored. Seldom have conquerors been as wise, sensitive, and far-sighted as Cyrus and his Persians.

THUS SPAKE ZARATHUSTRA

Iranian religion was originally simple and primitive. Ahuramazda, the chief god, was the creator and benefactor of all living creatures. Yet unlike Yahweh, he was not a lone god. The Iranians were polytheistic. Mithra the sun god, whose cult would later spread throughout the Roman Empire (page 187), saw to justice and redemption. Other Iranian deities personified the natural elements: moon, earth, water, and wind. As in ancient India, fire was a particularly important god. The sacred fire consumed the blood sacrifices that the early Iranians offered to all of their deities.

Early Iranian religion was close to nature and unencumbered by ponderous theological beliefs. A priestly class, the Magi, developed among the Medes to officiate at sacrifices, chant prayers to the gods, and tend the sacred flame. A fine, concise description of this early worship comes from the great German historian Eduard Meyer:

Iranian religion knew neither divine images nor temples. On a hilltop one called upon god and his manifestations — sun and moon, earth and fire, water and wind — and erected altars with their eternal fire. But in other appropriate places one could, without further preparation, pray to the deity and bring him his offerings, with the assistance of the Magi, who in addition chanted the holy formulas.[21]

In time the Iranians built fire temples for these sacrifices. As late as the nineteenth century, fire was still worshiped in Baku, a major city on the Russian-Iranian border.

Around 600 B.C. the prophet Zarathustra — or Zoroaster, as he is more generally known — breathed new meaning into Iranian religion. Of Zoroaster the man, as little is known as of Moses; like his Jewish counterpart, Zoroaster is remembered for his work, which long outlived him. Like Moses, Zoroaster preached a novel concept of divinity and human life. Life, he taught, is a constant battleground between two opposing forces, good and evil. Ahuramazda embodied good and truth but was opposed by Ahriman, a hateful spirit who stood for evil and falsehood. Ahuramazda and Ahriman were locked together in a cosmic battle for the human race, a battle that stretched over thousands of years. But, according to Zoroaster, people were not mere pawns in this struggle. Each person had to choose which side to join — whether to lead a life characterized by good behavior and truthful dealings with others or by wickedness and lies.

Zoroaster emphasized the responsibility of the individual in this decision. He taught that people possessed the free will to decide between Ahuramazda and Ahriman, and that people must rely on their own consciences to guide them through life. Their decisions were crucial, Zoroaster warned, for there would be a time of reckoning. He promised that Ahuramazda would eventually triumph over evil and lies, and that at death each person would stand before the tribunal of good. Ahuramazda, like the Egyptian god Osiris, would judge whether the dead had lived righteously and on that basis would weigh their lives in the balance. Then good and truth would conquer evil and lies. In short, Zoroaster taught the concept of a Last Judgment at which Ahuramazda would decide each person's eternal fate on the basis of that person's deeds in life.

In Zoroaster's thought the Last Judgment was linked to the notion of a divine kingdom after death for those who had lived according to good and truth. They would accompany Ahuramazda to a life of eternal truth in what Zoroaster called "the House of Song" and "the Abode of Good Thought." There they would dwell with Ahuramazda forever. Liars and the wicked, denied this blessed immortality, would be condemned to eternal pain, darkness, and punishment. Thus, Zoroaster preached a Last Judgment that led to a heaven or a hell.

Although tradition has it that Zoroaster met with opposition and coldness, his thought converted Darius (521–486 B.C.), one of the most energetic men ever to sit on the Persian throne. The Persian royal family adopted Zoroastrianism, though without trying to impose it on others. Under the protection of the Persian kings, Zoroastrianism swept through Iran, winning converts and sinking roots that sustained healthy growth for centuries. Zoroastrianism survived the fall of the Persian Empire to influence religious thought in the age of Jesus and to make a vital contribution to Manicheanism, a theology that was to spread through the Byzantine Empire and pose a significant challenge to Christianity. A handful of the faithful still follow the teachings of Zoroaster, whose vision of divinity and human life has transcended the centuries.

PERSIA'S WORLD EMPIRE

Cyrus' successors rounded out the Persian conquest of the ancient Near East. In 525 B.C. Cyrus's son Cambyses (530–522 B.C.) subdued Egypt. Darius (521–486 B.C.) and his son Xerxes (486–464 B.C.) invaded Greece, but were fought to a standstill and forced to retreat (Chapter 3); the Persians never won a permanent foothold in Europe. Yet Darius

DARIUS AND XERXES   This relief from the Persian capital of Persepolis shows King Darius and Crown Prince Xerxes in state. Behind them the royal bodyguard stands at attention, as the royal pair receives the guard's commander. (Oriental Institute, University of Chicago)

carried Persian arms into India. Around 513 B.C. western India became the Persian satrapy, or province, of Hindush, which included the valley of the Indus river. Thus, within thirty-seven years the Persians transformed themselves from a subject people to the rulers of an empire that included Anatolia, Egypt, Mesopotamia, Iran, and western India. They had created a "world empire" encompassing all of the oldest and most honored kingdoms and peoples of the ancient Near East. Never before had the Near East been united in one such vast political organization (see Map 2.3).

The Persians knew how to use the peace that they had won on the battlefield. Unlike the Assyrians, they did not resort to royal terrorism to keep order. Like the Assyrians, however, they employed a number of bureaucratic techniques to bind the empire together. The sheer size of the empire made it impossible for one man to rule it effectively. Consequently the Persians divided the empire into some twenty huge satrapies – provinces measuring hundreds of square miles, many of

them kingdoms in themselves. Each satrapy had a governor, drawn from the Median and Persian nobility and often a relative of the king; the governor or satrap was directly responsible to the king. An army officer, also responsible to the king, commanded the military forces stationed in the satrapy. Still another official collected the royal taxes. Moreover, the king sent out royal inspectors to watch the satraps and other officials, a method of royal surveillance later used by the medieval king Charlemagne (Chapter 8).

Effective rule of the empire demanded good communications. To meet this need the Persians established a network of roads. The main highway, known as the Royal Road, spanned some 1677 miles from the Greek city of Ephesus on the coast of Asia Minor to Susa in western Iran. The distance was broken into 111 post-stations, each equipped with fresh horses for the king's messengers. Other roads branched out to link all parts of the empire, from the coast of Asia Minor to the valley of the Indus river. Along these roads royal

THE ROYAL PALACE AT PERSEPOLIS King Darius began and King Xerxes finished building a grand palace worthy of the glory of the Persian Empire. Pictured here is the monumental audience hall, where the king dealt with ministers of state and foreign envoys. (Oriental Institute, University of Chicago)

couriers sped so quickly that the Greek historian and traveler Herodotus marvelled at them:

There is nothing which is mortal that arrives faster than these couriers ... For they say that as many days as the whole journey takes that many horses and men stand at intervals, a horse and man stationed at each daily segment of road. These neither snow nor rain nor heat nor night prevents from traversing their appointed run as fast as possible. The first courier hands over the dispatch to the second, the second to the third. Thereafter from one to another the dispatch passes on.[22]

This system of communications enabled the Persian king to keep in intimate touch with his subjects and officials. He was able to rule efficiently, keep his ministers in line, and protect the rights of the peoples under his control. How effective Persian rule could be, even in small matters, is apparent in a letter from King Darius to the satrap of Ionia, the Greek region of Anatolia. The satrap had transplanted Syrian fruit trees in his province, an experiment Darius praised. Yet the king also learned that his governor had infringed on the rights granted to the sanctuary of the Greek god Apollo, an act that provoked the king to anger:

The King of Kings, Darius the son of Hystaspes says this to Gadatas, his slave [satrap]. I learn that you are not obeying my command in every particular. Because you are tilling my land, transplanting fruit trees from across the Euphrates [Syria] to Asia Minor, I praise your project, and there will be laid up for you great favor in the king's house. But because you mar my dispositions towards the gods, I shall give you, unless you change your ways, proof of my anger when wronged. For you exacted payment from the sacred gardeners of the temple of Apollo, and you ordered them to dig up secular land, failing to understand the attitude of my forefathers towards the god, who told the Persians the truth.[23]

Fruit trees and foreign gods — even such small matters as these were important to the man whom the world called "The King of Kings, the King of Persia, the King of the Provinces."[24] This document alone suggests the efficiency of Persian rule and the compassion of Persian kings. Conquered peoples, left free to enjoy their traditional ways of life, found in the Persian king a capable protector. No wonder that many Near Eastern peoples were, like the Jews, grateful for the long period of peace they enjoyed as the subjects of the Persian Empire.

———◆———

Between around 1200 and 500 B.C. the Near East passed from fragmentation to political unification under the Persian Empire. On the road from chaos to order, from widespread warfare to general peace, peoples in many areas wrought vast and enduring achievements. The Egyptians survived invasion to share their heritage with their African neighbors and later with the Greeks. The homeless Hebrews laboriously built a state and entered the broader world of their neighbors. Simultaneously, they evolved religious and ethical beliefs that permeate the modern West.

Although the Assyrians made the Near East tremble in terror of their armies, they too contributed to the heritage of these long years. Their military and, particularly, political abilities gave the Persians the tools they needed to govern a host of different peoples. Those tools were to be well used. For over two hundred years Persian kings offered their subjects enlightened rule. The Persians gave the ancient Near East a period of peace and stability in which peoples enjoyed their native traditions and lived in concord with their neighbors.

Meanwhile to the west, another people — the Greeks — were slowly shaping cultural and political ideals that were to have an even greater impact on the future. Although Greece and the Near East would eventually become locked in a mighty conflict, the heritage of the East would blend with that of Greece to influence Western civilization in a fundamental way.

NOTES

1. James H. Breasted, *Ancient Records of Egypt,* University of Chicago Press, Chicago, 1907, IV, paragraph 398.

2. J. B. Pritchard, ed., *Ancient Near Eastern Texts,* Princeton University Press, Princeton, 1950, p. 27.

3. 1 Kings 8:4–6.

4. 2 Kings 23:3.

5. Jeremiah 7:5–7.

6. Ibid. 3:12.

7. Proverbs 31:10, 25–30.

8. Deuteronomy 24:1–2.

9. Psalms 128:3.

10. Deuteronomy 25:9.

11. Proverbs 13:24.

12. Deuteronomy 24:19.

13. Jeremiah 23:13.

14. Pritchard, *op. cit.*, p. 288.

15. Ibid.

16. 2 Kings 16:7–8.

17. Nahum 3:7.

18. R. Ghirshman, *L'Iran des origines à l'Islam,* Albin Michel, Paris, 1976, p. 343.

19. Quoted from A. T. Olmstead, *A History of the Persian Empire,* University of Chicago Press, Chicago, 1963, p. 53.

20. Isaiah 44:28–45:1.

21. E. Meyer, *Geschichte des Altertums,* 7th ed., Vol. IV, Part I, Wissenchaftliche Buchgesellschaft, Darmstadt, 1975, pp. 114–115.

22. Herodotus 8.98.

23. R. Meiggs and D. M. Lewis, *A Selection of Greek Historical Inscriptions,* Clarendon Press, Oxford, 1969, no. 12.

24. Behistun Inscription col. 1.1.

SUGGESTED READING

Although late Egyptian history is still largely a specialist's field, K. A. Kitchen, *The Third Intermediate Period in Egypt (1100–650 B.C.)* (1973) is a good synthesis of the period. Valuable too is M. L. Bierbrier's monograph, *Late New Kingdom in Egypt, c. 1300–664 B.C.* (1975). More general is R. David, *The Egyptian Kingdoms* (1975). H. S. Smith, *A Visit to Ancient Egypt: Life at Memphis and Saqqara (c. 500–30 B.C.* (1974) gives a picture of life during the period, and P. L. Shinnie, *Meroe: A Civilization of the Sudan* (1967), does the same for one of Egypt's most important southern neighbors. Those interested in the whole story of Wen-Amon's adventures should read H. Goedicke, *The Report of Wenamun* (1975). Sir A. H. Gardiner, ed., *Late Egyptian Stories* (1973) contains other pieces of late Egyptian literature.

D. Harden, *The Phoenicians,* 2nd ed. (1971) gives a good account of Phoenician history and life. More recently, G. Herm, *The Phoenicians: The Purple Empire of the Ancient World* (1975), treats Phoenician seafaring and commercial enterprises. A more general treatment of the entire area is R. Fedden, *Syria and Lebanon,* 3rd ed. (1965). Those interested in individual Phoenician cities should see N. Jidejian, *Byblos through the Ages,* 2nd ed. (1971), *Tyre through the Ages* (1969), and *Sidon through the Ages* (1971). For a history of Phoenicia written at the time of the Roman Empire, see A. I. Baumgarten, *The Phoenician History of Philo of Byblos* (1981).

The Jews have been one of the best studied people in the ancient world, and the reader can easily find many good treatments of Jewish history and society. A readable and balanced book is J. Bright, *A History of Israel,* 2nd ed. (1972). Somewhat older is A. S. Kapelrud, *Israel from Earliest Times to the Birth of Christ* (1966). Other useful general books include G. W. Anderson, *The History and Religion of Israel* (1966), which is a solid scholarly treatment of the subject. The archaeological exploration of ancient Israel is so fast-paced that nearly any book is quickly outdated. Nonetheless, A. Negev, *Archaeological Encyclopedia of the Holy Land* (1973), which is illustrated, is still a good place to start.

S. Yeivin, *The Israelite Conquest of Canaan* (1971), though a bit dated, is a good survey of the Jewish entry into Palestine. M. Pearlman, *In the Footsteps of Moses* (1974), a more popular account, also treats the period. R. de Vaux, *Ancient Israel, Its Life and Institutions,* 2nd ed. (1965), ranges across all eras of Jewish history, and is especially recommended because of its solid base in the ancient sources. The period of Jewish kingship has elicited a good deal of attention. Most recent is B. Halpern, *The Constitution of the Monarchy in Israel* (1981), which makes the significant point that the Jews are the only ancient Near Eastern people to have recorded the decision to adopt monarchy as a form of government. Also valuable in this connection is A. R. Johnson, *Sacral Kingship in Ancient Israel,* 2nd ed. (1967). Solomon's importance as a strong king and an innovator is underlined by a series of studies, especially T. N. Mettinger, *Solomonic State Officials: A Study of the Civil Service Officials of the Israelite Monarchy* (1971); E. W. Heaton, *Solomon's New Men: The*

Emergence of Ancient Israel as a National State (1974); and lastly J. Gutmann, *The Temple of Solomon* (1975).

More specific than de Vaux' splendid general work on Hebrew society is P. A. H. de Boer, *Fatherhood and Motherhood in Israelite and Judean Piety* (1974), which treats a fundamental aspect of Jewish religion and society. A fascinating and ambitious new study of myth and religion is J. O'Brien and W. Major, *In the Beginning: Creation Myths from Ancient Mesopotamia, Israel and Greece* (1981). Lastly, P. R. Ackroyd, *Israel under Babylon and Persia* (1970), gives an informative account of Jewish inability to resist expansion of the great monarchies.

The Assyrians, despite their achievements, have not attracted the scholarly attention that the ancient Jews and other Near Eastern peoples have. Even though outdated, A. T. Olmstead, *History of Assyria* (1928), still possesses the merit of being soundly based in the original sources. Olmstead was a rare scholar who attempted to understand the entire development of the ancient Near East. More recent and more difficult is J. A. Brinkman, *A Political History of Post-Kassite Babylonia, 1158–722 B.C.* (1968), which treats the Babylonian response to the rise of Assyria. M. Cogan, *Imperialism and Religion: Assyria, Judah and Israel in the Eighth and Seventh Centuries B.C.E.* (1973), traces the various effects of Assyrian expansion on the two Jewish kingdoms.

An informative look at the Assyrians themselves comes from J. Laessoe, *People of Ancient Assyria: Their Inscriptions and Correspondence* (1963). Those who appreciate the vitality of Assyrian art should start with the masterful work of R. D. Barnett and W. Forman, *Assyrian Palace Reliefs,* 2nd ed. (1970), an exemplary combination of fine photographs and learned, though not difficult, discussion.

In addition to the works on Iran cited in the Notes, G. C. Cameron, *History of Early Iran* (1969); W. Culican, *The Medes and the Persians* (1965); and J. A. deGobineau, *The World of the Persians* (1971), which is illustrated with color plates, all provide introductions to Persian history. Vastly informative but difficult is E. Herzfeld, *The Persian Empire: Studies in the Geography and Ethnology of the Ancient Near East* (1968), a posthumous work by one of the world's leading authorities on the Persians. Very useful is J. D. Pearson, ed., *A Bibliography of Pre-Islamic Persia* (1975). S. A. Matheson, *Persia: An Archaeological Guide* (1972), is a good guide to Persian monuments. A good brief account of Cyrus the Great's career can be found in M. E. L. Mallowan, "Cyrus the Great (558–529 B.C.)," *Iran* 10 (1972), 1–17.

J. H. Moulton, *Early Zoroastrianism: The Origins, the Prophet, and the Magi* (1972), is a sound treatment of the beginnings and early spread of Zoroastrianism. R. C. Zaehner, *The Dawn and Twilight of Zoroastrianism* (1961) discusses the whole course of Zoroastrianism's history. Zaehner also provides a good introduction to the basic teachings of Zoroastrianism in his *Teachings of the Magi: A Compendium of Zoroastrian Beliefs* (1975).

Chapter 3

The Legacy of Greece

THE ANCIENT NEAR EAST was the seat of old cultures and rich empires, but the rocky peninsula of Greece was the home of the civilization that fundamentally shaped Western civilization. The Greeks were the first to explore most of the questions that continue to concern Western thinkers to this day. Going beyond mythmaking and religion, the Greeks strove to understand, in logical, rational terms, the universe and the position of men and women in it. The result was the birth of philosophy and science, which were far more important to most Greek thinkers than religion. The Greeks speculated on human beings and society and created the very concept of politics.

While the scribes of the ancient Near East produced king lists, the Greeks invented history to record, analyze, and understand how people and states functioned in time and space. In poetry, the Greeks spoke as individuals. In drama, they dealt with the grandeur and weakness of humanity and with the demands of society on the individual. The greatest monuments of the Greeks were not temples, statues, or tombs, but profound thoughts set down in terms as fresh and immediate today as they were some 2,400 years ago.

The history of the Greeks is divided into two broad periods: the Hellenic (the subject of this chapter), roughly the time between the arrival of the Greeks and the triumph of Philip of Macedon, and the Hellenistic, the age beginning with Alexander the Great and ending with the Roman conquest (the subject of Chapter 4).

What geographical factors helped to mold the evolution of the city-state and to shape the course of the Greek experience? How did the Greeks develop basic political forms — forms as different as democracy and tyranny — that have influenced all of later Western history?

MAP 3.1 ANCIENT GREECE *In antiquity the home of the Greeks included the islands of the Aegean and the western shore of Turkey as well as the Greek peninsula itself.*

What did the Greek intellectual triumph entail? And, lastly, how and why did the Greek genius eventually fail? These profound questions, which can never be fully answered, are the themes of this chapter.

THE LAND AND THE POLIS

Hellas, as the ancient Greeks called their land, encompassed the Aegean Sea and its islands as well as the Greek peninsula (see Map 3.1). The Greek peninsula itself is an extension of the Balkan system of mountains, stretching in the direction of Egypt and the Near East. Greece is mountainous; its rivers are never more than creeks, and most of them go dry in the summer. It is, however, a land blessed with good harbors, the most important of which look to the east. The islands of the Aegean continue to sweep to the east, and serve as steppingstones between the peninsula and Anatolia. As early as 1000 B.C., Greeks from the peninsula had settled along the coastline of Anatolia (Asia Minor); the heartland of these eastern Greeks was in Ionia. Thus, geography alone encouraged the Greeks to turn their attention to the old civilizations of Asia Minor and Egypt.

Despite the poverty of its soil, Greece is strikingly beautiful, as the eminent German historian K. J. Beloch has written:

Greece is an alpine land, which rises from the waters of the Mediterranean sea, scenically probably the most beautiful region in southern Europe. The noble contours of the mountains, the bare,

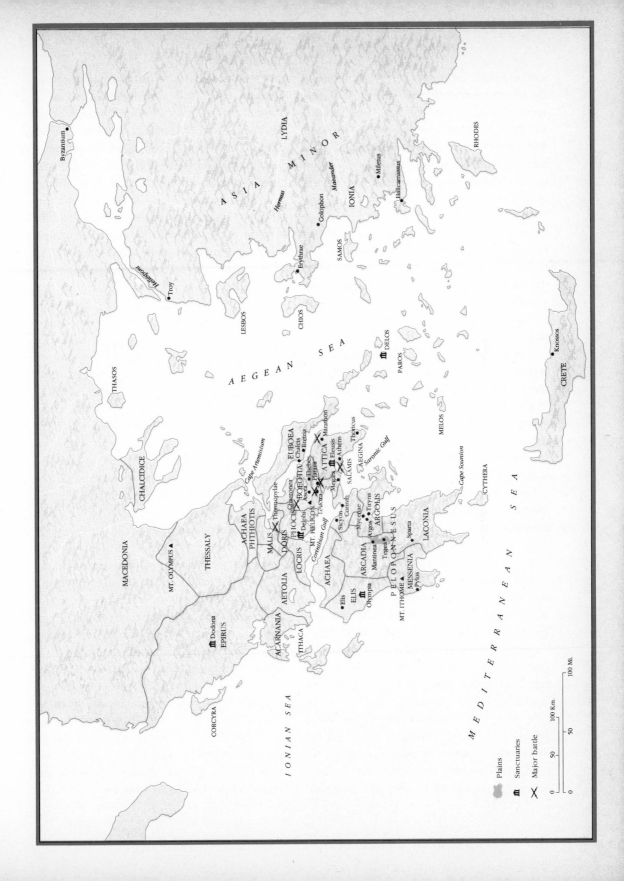

MACEDONIA

MT. OLYMPUS ▲

THESSALY

ACHAEA PHTHIOTIS

AETOLIA

ACARNANIA

EPIRUS ☖ Dodona

ITHACA

CORCYRA

I O N I A N   S E A

CHALCIDICE

THASOS

Cape Artemisium

MALIS
DORIS
✕ Thermopylae
PHOCIS Chaeronea
LOCRIS ✕
Delphi ☖ MT. HELICON
Corinthian Gulf

ACHAEA

ELIS
● Elis
Olympia ☖

ARCADIA
Mantinea ●
● Tegea

MESSENIA
MT. ITHOME ▲
● Pylos

P E L O P O N N E S U S

LACONIA
Sparta ●

EUBOEA
Chalcis ●
● Eretria
BOEOTIA ✕
Thebes ●
Plataea ✕
Leuctra ●

ATTICA
Marathon
✕
☖ Eleusis
Megara ● Athens ●
SALAMIS Thoricus
✕

AEGINA
Saronic Gulf

Cape Sounion

Sicyon ●
Corinth ●
Mycenae ●
Tiryns ●
Argos ● ARGOLIS

CYTHERA

LESBOS

CHIOS

SAMOS

☖ DELOS

PAROS

MELOS

A E G E A N   S E A

Byzantium ●

Hellespont
● Troy

ASIA   MINOR

LYDIA

Hermus

Maeander

● Colophon

Erythrae ●

IONIA
● Miletus

Halicarnassus ●

RHODES

Knossos ●

CRETE

M E D I T E R R A N E A N   S E A

Plains
Sanctuaries   ☖
Major battle   ✕

100 Mi.
50
0

100 Km.
50
0

rocky slopes, the dusty green of the conifer forests, the white cover of snow which envelops the higher summits for the greatest part of the year, added to which is the profound blue surface of the sea below, and above everything the diffused brightness of the southern sun; this gives a total picture, the charm of which impresses itself unforgettably on the soul of the observer.[1]

The Greeks gloried in their land, and its beauty was one of the factors that elicited their loyalty to the soil of this hard peninsula. The climate of Greece is mild; though hot in summer, the air is dry and stirred by breezes. In winter snow may blanket the mountain slopes, but rarely covers the lowlands.

Simultaneously, geography acted as an enormously divisive force in Greek life. The mountains of Greece dominate the landscape. They cut the land into many small pockets, and isolate areas of inhabitation from one another. Innumerable peninsulas open to the sea, which is dotted with islands, most of them small and many uninhabitable. The geographical fragmentation of Greece encouraged political fragmentation. Furthermore, communications were extraordinarily poor. Rocky tracks were far more common than roads, and the few roads were unpaved. Usually they were nothing more than a pair of ruts cut into the rock to accommodate the wheels of vehicles. The small physical units of Greece discouraged the growth of great empires.

As in Sumer, the typical Greek political unit was the city-state, which the Greeks called the polis. Rarely did there occur the combination of extensive territory and political unity that allowed one polis to rise above others. Only three city-states were able to muster the resources of an entire region behind them (see Map 3.2): Sparta, which dominated the regions of Laconia and Messenia; Athens, which united the large peninsula of Attica under its rule; and Thebes, which in several periods marshaled the resources of the fertile region of Boeotia. Otherwise, the political pattern of ancient Greece was one of many small city-states, few of which were much stronger or richer than their neighbors.

Physically, the term *polis* designated a city or town and its surrounding countryside. The typical polis consisted of people living in a compact group of houses within the city. The city's water supply came from public fountains and cisterns. By the fifth century B.C., the city was generally surrounded by a wall. The city contained a point, usually elevated, called the acropolis, and a public square or marketplace (agora). On the acropolis, which in the early period was a place of refuge, stood the temples, altars, public monuments, and various dedications to the gods of the polis. The agora was originally the place where the warrior assembly met, but it became the political center of the polis. In the agora were porticoes, shops, and public buildings, such as council and administrative buildings and courts.

The unsettled territory of the polis was typically the source of its wealth. This territory consisted of arable land, pastureland, and wasteland. Farmers left the city each morning to work their fields or tend their flocks of sheep and goats, and they returned to the city at night. On the wasteland men often quarried stone, mined for precious metals, or at certain times of the year obtained small amounts of fodder. Thus, the polis encompassed a combination of urban and agrarian life.

Regardless of its size or wealth, the polis was fundamental to Greek life. Aristotle, perhaps Greece's greatest thinker, could not envisage civilized life apart from the polis. "The

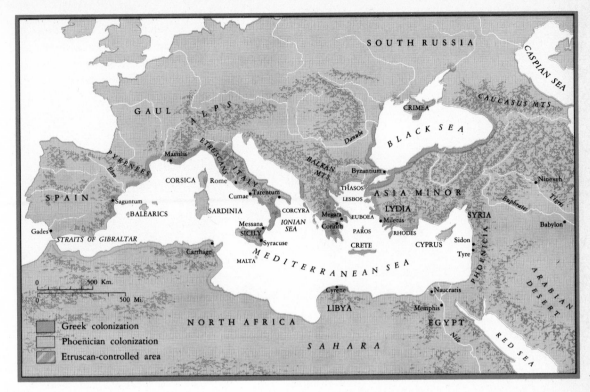

MAP 3.2 COLONIZATION OF THE MEDITER-
RANEAN *Although both the Greeks and Phoenicians colonized the Mediterranean basin at roughly
the same time, the Greeks spread over far greater
areas.*

polis," he wrote, "exists by nature, and man is
by nature a being of the polis."[2] Aristotle was
summing up the Greek view that the life of
men and women in the polis was the only way
to live according to nature.

The polis was far more than a political institution. Above all, it was a community of
citizens, and the affairs of the community
were the concern of all citizens. The intimacy
of the polis was an important factor, and one
hard for modern city dwellers to imagine. The
philosopher Plato thought that five thousand
citizens constituted the right population for
an ideal polis. Though utopian, Plato was not

in this case being unrealistic. Although population figures for Greece are mostly guess-
work, because most city-states were small
enough not to need a census, the polis of
Thebes in Boeotia is a useful illustration of
how small a Greek state was. When Alexander the Great destroyed Thebes in 335 B.C.,
he sold thirty thousand people into slavery.
Some six thousand people had died in the
fighting, and many others he spared. Thus the
free population of Thebes had numbered between thirty and forty thousand at most, and
Thebes was a large polis, a major power. Most
city-states were far smaller.

THE SHAPE OF THE ATHENIAN POLIS   This quaint print, which depicts the Athenian acropolis and surrounding area, shows clearly the basic geographical requirements of the polis. Early Greeks desired an elevated spot, or acropolis, as a place of refuge. Later, in more secure times, the acropolis often became the main seat of the polis' temples. At the foot of the citadel spread the agora, public buildings, and private homes. (Photo: Caroline Buckler)

The mild climate of Greece meant that much of Greek life was spent outdoors. In a polis, as in a modern Greek village, a person might easily see most other citizens in the course of the day. Nearly everything that happened within the polis was known immediately and discussed at length. Any stranger who arrived with news from abroad found a large and talkative audience at once. Similarly, the citizen would normally see the public buildings and the temples of the polis daily. The monuments of past victories, the tombs of dead warriors, all these would be personal and familiar. In short, life in the polis was very public. The smallness of the polis enabled Greeks to see how the individual fitted into the overall system — how the human parts made up the social whole.

The customs of the community were at the same time the laws of the polis. Rome later created a single magnificent body of law, but the Greeks had as many law codes as they had city-states. Though the laws of one polis might be roughly similar to those of another polis, the law of any given polis was unique simply because the customs and the experience of each polis had been unique.

The polis also had a religious aspect. Although all Greeks customarily worshiped the great deities — Zeus, Hera, Apollo, Athena, and others, who supposedly lived on Mount Olympus — the citizens of each polis had their own particular cults for these gods. Besides the Olympian gods, each polis had its own minor deities, each with his or her own local cult. Participation in the cults and rituals was a civic duty. By honoring the gods and goddesses of the polis, the citizens honored the polis itself. But this civic religion, unlike the religion of the Hebrews, did not entail religious belief. What individuals believed was their own business. Citizens could be total atheists, but they were still expected to participate in the religion of the polis. Their participation did not brand them as hypocrites, but rather as loyal citizens.

The polis could be governed in any of several ways. First, it could be a monarchy, a term derived from the Greek for "the rule of one man." A king could represent the community, reigning according to law and respecting the rights of the citizens. Second, the aristocracy – those who owed their position to birth – could govern the state. Third, the running of the polis could be the duty and prerogative of an oligarchy, which literally means "the rule of a few" – a small group of wealthy citizens, regardless of their status at birth. Or the polis could be governed by a democracy, the rule of the people, which in Greece meant that all the citizens, without respect to birth or wealth, administered the workings of government. How a polis was governed depended on who had the upper hand. When the wealthy held power, they usually instituted oligarchies; when the people could break the hold of the rich, they established democracies. In any case, no polis ever had an iron-clad and unchangeable constitution.

Still another form of Greek government was tyranny. Under tyranny the polis was ruled by a tyrant, a man who had seized power by unconstitutional means. The Greeks did not in theory consider tyranny a legitimate form of government, but in practice it flourished from the seventh century B.C. to the end of the Classical Period. Although the earliest tyrants may have been popular figures, abuses of tyranny soon gave this type of government a bad name. One lasting effect of tyranny, nevertheless, was to break the exclusive hold of the aristocracy on Greek government. Even so, the Greeks always considered tyranny a political perversion.

Ironically, the very integration of the polis proved to be one of its weaknesses. Because the bonds that held the polis together were so intimate, Greeks were extremely reluctant to allow foreigners to share fully in its life. An alien, even someone Greek by birth, could almost never expect to be made a citizen. Nor could women play a political role in the polis. Women participated in the civic cults, and they served as priestesses, but the polis had no room for them in state affairs. Thus, the exclusiveness of the polis doomed it to a limited horizon.

The individualism of the polis proved to be another serious weakness. The citizens of each polis were determined to remain free and autonomous. Rarely were the Greeks willing to unite in larger political bodies. When they did, they preferred leagues or confederations in which each polis insisted on its autonomy. The political result in Greece, as in Sumer, was almost constant warfare. The polis could dominate, but unlike Rome it could not incorporate.

THE BRONZE AGE (2000 – 1100 B.C.)

Greek-speaking peoples did not enter the peninsula of Greece until the Bronze Age. Of these early years the ancient Greeks themselves remembered almost nothing. One of the sterling achievements of modern archaeology is the discovery of this lost past. In the nineteenth century, Heinrich Schliemann, a German businessman turned archaeologist, excavated the site of Mycenae in Greece and

PERIOD	SIGNIFICANT EVENTS	MAJOR WRITERS
Bronze Age 2000–1100 B.C.	Arrival of the Greeks in Greece Rise and fall of the Mycenaean kingdoms	
Dark Age 1100–800 B.C.	Greek migrations within the Aegean basin Social and political recovery Evolution of the polis Rebirth of literacy	Homer Hesiod
Lyric Age 800–500 B.C.	Rise of Sparta and Athens Colonization of the Mediterranean basin Flowering of lyric poetry Development of philosophy and science in Ionia	Archilochus Sappho Tyrtaeus Solon Anaximander Heraclitus
Classical Age 500–338 B.C.	Persian wars Growth of the Athenian empire Peloponnesian War Rise of drama and historical writing Flowering of Greek philosophy Spartan and Theban hegemonies Conquest of Greece by Philip of Macedon	Herodotus Thucydides Aeschylus Sophocles Euripides Aristophanes Plato Aristotle

the site of Troy in Asia Minor. He discovered the lost past of the Greek people, and to this past he gave the name Mycenaean.

The Mycenaeans entered Greece around 2000 B.C. and settled in central Greece and the Peloponnesus, the peninsula that forms the southernmost part of Greece (see Map 3.1). Mycenaean civilization was utterly unlike anything the later Greeks evolved. The political unit of the Mycenaeans was the kingdom, not the polis. The king and his warrior-aristocracy stood at the top of society. The symbol of the king's power and wealth was the palace, which was also the economic center of the kingdom. Within its walls royal craftsmen fashioned jewelry and rich ornaments, made and decorated fine pottery, forged weapons,

prepared hides and wool for clothing, and manufactured the goods needed by the king and his retainers. Palace scribes kept account of taxes and drew up inventories of the king's possessions. From the palace the king directed the lives of his subjects, and he tightly controlled society. About the king's subjects, almost nothing is known.

The Mycenaean kingdoms were in touch with each other and with the Bronze Age culture of the Minoans in Crete, but these contacts were often violent. The Minoans had established a vibrant and artistically gifted civilization, from which the Mycenaeans derived much of their art. The wealth of the Minoans tempted Mycenaean greed and ambition, and in about 1450 B.C. a band of Mycenaean raiders conquered Cnossus, the most important and the richest Minoan site. This attack was typical of the Mycenaeans, who were consistently a warlike and restless people.

Indeed, the entire history of Mycenaean Greece is a dreary tale of warfare. During the years 1300–1100 B.C., kingdom after kingdom suffered attack and destruction. But not one alien artifact has been found on any of these sites. There are no traces of invading peoples, nothing to suggest that these kingdoms fell to foreign invaders. Instead, the legends preserved by later Greeks told of grim wars between Mycenaean kingdoms and of the fall of great royal families. Apparently Mycenaean Greece destroyed itself in a long series of internecine wars, a pattern that would be repeated by Greeks of later ages.

The fall of the Mycenaean kingdoms ushered in a period of such poverty, disruption, and backwardness that historians usually call it the Dark Age of Greece (1100–800 B.C.). Even literacy was a casualty of the chaos. Yet even this period was important to the development of Greek civilization. It was a time of widespread movements of Greek-speaking peoples. Some Greeks sailed to Crete, where they established new communities. A great wave of Greeks spread eastward through the Aegean to the coast of Asia Minor. These immigrations turned the Aegean into a Greek lake. The people who stayed behind gradually rebuilt Greek society. They thus provided an element of continuity, a link between the Mycenaean period and the Greek culture that emerged from the Dark Age.

The movement of Greek-speaking peoples was not confined to the descendants of the Mycenaeans. During the Dark Age the last peoples who would help create Greek civilization of the historical period moved into Greece. The Boeotians entered Greece from

MINOAN SNAKE GODDESS   *This elegant statuette in many ways represents all of the difficulty of interpreting Minoan civilization. Although the Minoans left behind many brilliant pieces of art, they left no history or literature as guides for the understanding of them. Consequently, it is impossible to know what this goddess meant to the Minoans. (Museum of Fine Arts, Boston. Gift of Mrs. W. Scott Fitz)*

THE RETURN OF ODYSSEUS *This fine fifth-century relief portrays one of the most popular episodes from the* Odyssey: *the return of Odysseus from the Trojan War. Although his faithful wife, Penelope,* *and some poor retainers welcomed him eagerly (as this scene suggests), he had singlehandedly to defeat neighboring lords who coveted his kingdom. (Metropolitan Museum of Art, Fletcher Fund, 1930)*

Thessaly and settled in Boeotia. The Dorians, who were nomads, followed the Boeotians and settled in the Peloponnesus. Although the Dorians have traditionally been accused of overthrowing the Mycenaean kingdoms, recent archaeological work has proved that they entered Greece long afterwards. The common language of all these peoples, newcomers and survivors alike, was a bond between them.

HOMER, HESIOD, AND THE HEROIC PAST (1100 – 800 B.C.)

The Greeks, unlike the Hebrews, had no sacred book that chronicled their past. Instead, they had the *Iliad* and the *Odyssey,* the epic poems created by Homer (eighth century B.C.) to describe a time when gods still walked the earth. And they learned the origin and the descent of the gods from the *Theogony,* an epic poem by Hesiod (ca 700 B.C.). For all their importance to Greek thought and literature, Homer and Hesiod were shadowy figures. Later Greeks knew little about them and were not even certain when they had lived. Although some later Greeks thought they had flourished in the tenth century B.C., the historian Herodotus (484–425 B.C.) gave a more accurate date:

It seems to me that the age of Hesiod and Homer was no more than 400 years earlier than my time.

They are the poets who gave the Greeks the genealogy of the gods, and they distributed to the gods their honors and acts, and they declared their forms.[3]

This uncertainty over the poets' dates is significant. It indicates that the Greeks remembered very little of their own past, especially the time before they entered Greece. They had also forgotten a great deal about the Bronze and Dark Ages.

Instead of authentic history the poems of Homer and Hesiod offered the Greeks an ideal past, a largely legendary Heroic Age. In terms of pure history these poems contain scraps of information about the Bronze Age, much about the early Dark Age, and some about the poets' own era. Chronologically, then, the Heroic Age falls mainly in the period between the collapse of the Mycenaean world and the rebirth of literacy. Yet it is a mistake to treat the *Iliad* and the *Odyssey* as history; they are magnificent blendings of legends, myth, and a little authentic tradition.

The *Iliad* recounts an expedition of Mycenaeans, whom Homer called Achaeans, to besiege the city of Troy in Asia Minor. The heart of the *Iliad,* however, is the quarrel between Agamemnon, the king of Mycenae, and Achilles, the tragic hero of the poem, and how their quarrel brought suffering to the Achaeans. Only when Achilles put away his anger and pride did he consent to come forward, face, and kill the Trojan hero Hector. The *Odyssey* narrates the adventures of Odysseus, one of the Achaean heroes who fought at Troy, during his voyage home from the fighting.

The splendor of these poems does not lie in their plots, though the *Odyssey* is a marvelous adventure story. Rather, both poems portray engaging but often flawed characters who are larger than life and yet typically human.

Achilles, the hero of the *Iliad,* is capable of mastering Trojan warriors but can barely control his own anger. Agamemnon commands kings, yet is a man beset by worries. Hector, the hero of the Trojans, is a formidable, noble, and likable foe. Odysseus, the hero of the *Odyssey,* trusts more to his wisdom and good sense than to his strength. Odysseus' wife Penelope faithfully endures the long years of war and separation, patiently waiting for her beloved husband to return from Troy.

Homer was strikingly successful in depicting the deeds of the great gods, who sit on Mount Olympus and watch the fighting at Troy as though they were spectators at a modern baseball game. Sometimes they even participate in the action. Homer's deities are reminiscent of the Mesopotamian gods and goddesses. Hardly a decorous lot, the Olympians are raucous, petty, deceitful, and splendid. In short, they are human. Zeus, the king of the gods, favors the Trojans, but Hera, his wife and queen of the gods, supports the Achaeans. To distract Zeus so that she can aid her favorites, Hera seduces him with wine and sex. Athena, the gray-eyed goddess of wisdom, squabbles with human beings as though she were a fishwife. In the *Odyssey,* Hephaestus, the god of fire, uses an invisible net to catch his wife, Aphrodite, the goddess of love, sleeping with Ares, the god of war. When Hephaestus summons the other gods to witness the scene, they laugh and joke about his catch. One god even wishes that someday he could be as unlucky as Ares.

Homer at times portrayed the gods in a serious vein, but he never treated them in a systematic fashion, as did Hesiod. Hesiod's epic poem, the *Theogony,* traces the descent of Zeus. Hesiod was influenced by Mesopotamian myths, which the Hittites had adopted and spread to the Aegean. Hesiod's poem claims that in the beginning there was chaos, the "yawning deep." From chaos came Gaea (Earth), who gave birth to Uranus (Heaven). Gaea and Uranus then gave birth to Cronus and Ocean (the deep-swelling waters). Cronus, the son of Earth and Heaven, like the Mesopotamian Enlil, separated the two and became king of the gods.

Like the Hebrews, Hesiod envisaged his cosmogony – that is, his account of the way the universe developed – in moral terms. Zeus, the son of Cronus, defeated his evil father and took his place as the king of the gods. He then sired Lawfulness, Right, Peace, and other powers of light and beauty. Thus, in Hesiod's conception, Zeus was the god of righteousness, a god who loved justice and hated wrongdoing.

In another epic poem, *Works and Days,* Hesiod wrote of his own time. He lived in the village of Ascra in Boeotia, a scenic place set between beautiful mountains and fertile plains, but Hesiod was a grim pessimist and did not think highly of his village: "Ascra, bad in winter, uncomfortable in summer, never good." Although sometimes portrayed as a common man, Hesiod was a wealthy farmer. He may not, however, have been an aristocrat. The matter of his social standing sets him apart, for all the other great writers of Greece – and, later, Rome – were members of the aristocracy, for only they had the wealth, leisure, and education to create literature. Naturally, then, ancient Greek and Roman literature always reflected the values, cares, and ambitions of the aristocracy. For this reason alone, the common people in Greco-Roman culture are largely unknown to the modern world. Hesiod opens a window to the other side of life.

Hesiod was the victim of injustice. In his will, Hesiod's father had divided his lands between Hesiod and his brother Perses. Perses bribed the aristocratic authorities to give him the larger part of the inheritance and then squandered his wealth. Undaunted by the injustice of the powerful, Hesiod thundered back in a voice reminiscent of Khunanup, the "Eloquent Peasant" (see page 27):

Bribe-devouring lords, make straight
your decisions,
Forget entirely crooked judgments.
He who causes evil to another harms himself.
Evil designs are most evil to the plotter.[4]

The similarities are striking between the fictional Khunanup and Hesiod, both of whom were oppressed by the rich and powerful. Yet the differences are even more significant. Hesiod, unlike Khunanup, did not receive justice from the political authorities of the day, but he fully expected divine vindication. Hesiod's call for justice has gone ringing through the centuries, its appeal as fresh today as when he first uttered it more than two millennia ago. Hesiod spoke of Zeus as Jeremiah had spoken of Yahweh, warning that Zeus would see that justice was done and injustice punished. He cautioned his readers that Zeus was angered by those who committed adultery and those who harmed orphans and offended the aged. Hesiod's ethical concepts and his faith in divine justice were the product of his belief that the world was governed by the power of good.

Hesiod went on to advise Perses how to become a prosperous farmer. Hesiod's agricultural year was determined by the stars and the seasons. He advised Perses to plow when the constellation Pleiades set and to harvest when it rose. Wood was best cut in autumn, and the farmer should then begin building his plows and wagons and fashioning his tools. When the star Arcturus rose at dusk, it was time to prune the vines. Hesiod warned against doing field work during the time of biting cold, when

all the immense wood roars;
Wild animals shiver and put their tails
    between their legs,
Even those whose hide is covered with fur.
For now the cold wind blows through animals
    even though they be shaggy-breasted.[5]

In the heat of the summer, however, when the crops were stored in the barn, the farmer rested, sitting in the shade and sipping wine.

In *Works and Days* Hesiod also offered some hardheaded advice on how to live. Although his pessimism was pervasive, his advice was very practical. Hesiod was not theorizing; he was giving his readers tips on how to survive in a hard world. He recommended that a man get a house, an ox, and a slave woman to help with the field work. A man should not take a wife until he was around thirty years old. Then he should be very careful about his prospective bride: "He who trusts women trusts deceivers." Beware of the flirt because "she wants your barn." Marry, he advised, a fine maiden, "for a man gains nothing better than a good wife." Hesiod warned that a couple should have only one son; but if they have a second, they should do so late in life. He insisted upon the importance of good neighbors, because neighbors will help each other in times of trouble. The constant theme of Hesiod's philosophy is to live justly and uprightly, but never trust anyone.

THE LYRIC AGE (800–500 B.C.)

Hesiod stood on the threshold of one of the most vibrant periods of Greek history, an era of extraordinary expansion geographically, ar-

tistically, and politically. Greeks ventured as far east as the Black Sea and as far west as Spain (see Map 3.2). With the rebirth of literacy, this period also witnessed a tremendous literary flowering as poets broke away from the heroic tradition and wrote about their own lives. The individualism of the poets typifies this age of adventure and exploration, and the term "Lyric Age" strikingly conveys the spirit of these years. Politically, these were the years when Sparta and Athens – the two poles of the Greek experience – rose to prominence.

OVERSEAS EXPANSION

During the years 1100–800 B.C., the Greeks not only recovered from the breakdown of the Mycenaean world, but also grew in wealth and numbers. This new prosperity brought with it new problems. Greece is a small and not especially fertile country. The increase in population meant that many men and their families had very little land or none at all. Land hunger drove many Greeks to seek new homes outside of Greece. Other factors, largely intangible, played their part as well: the desire for a new start, a love of excitement and adventure, and natural curiosity about what lay beyond the horizon.

The Mediterranean offered the Greeks an escape valve, for they were always a seafaring people. To them the sea was a highway, not a barrier. Through their commercial ventures they had long been familiar with the rich areas of the western Mediterranean. Moreover, the geography of the Mediterranean basin favored colonization. The land and the climate of the Mediterranean region are remarkably uniform. Greeks could travel to new areas, whether to Cyprus in the east or to Malta in the west, and establish the kind of settlement they had had in Greece. They could also raise the same crops that they had raised in Greece. The move to a new home was not a move into totally unknown conditions. Once the colonists had established themselves in their new homes, they continued life essentially as they had lived it in Greece.

From about 750 to 550 B.C., Greeks from the mainland and from Asia Minor poured onto the coasts of the northern Aegean, the Ionian Sea, and the Black Sea, and into North Africa, Sicily, southern Italy, southern France, and Spain (see Map 3.2). Just as the migrations of the Dark Age had turned the Aegean into a Greek lake, this later wave of colonization spread the Greeks and their culture throughout the Mediterranean. Colonization on this scale had a profound impact on the course of Western civilization. It meant that the prevailing culture of the Mediterranean basin would be Greek, and to this heritage Rome would later fall heir.

One man can in many ways stand as the symbol of the vital and robust era of colonization. Archilochus was born on the island of Paros, the bastard son of an aristocrat. He knew that because of his illegitimacy he would never inherit his father's land, and this knowledge seems to have made him self-reliant. He was also a poet of genius, the first of the lyric poets who left an indelible mark on this age. Unlike the epic poets, who portrayed the deeds of heroes, Archilochus sang of himself. He knew the sea, the dangers of sailing, and the price that the sea often exacted. He spoke of one shipwreck in grim terms and even treated the god of the sea with irony: "Of fifty men gentle Poseidon left one, Koiranos, to be saved from shipwreck."

Together with others from Paros he took part in the colonization of Thasos in the northern Aegean. He described the island in less than glowing terms: "Like the spine of an ass it stands, crowned to the brim with a wild forest." His opinion of his fellow colonists was hardly kinder; about them he commented: "So the misery of all Greece came together in Thasos." Yet at Thasos he fell in love with a woman named Neoboule. They did not marry because her father opposed the match. In revenge, Archilochus seduced Neoboule's younger sister, railed at the entire family, and left Thasos to live the life of a mercenary.

His hired lance took him to Euboea, and he left a striking picture of the fighting there:

Not many bows will be strung, nor slings be slung
When Ares begins battle in the plain.
There will be the mournful work of the sword:
For in this kind of battle are the spear-famed
Lords of Euboea experienced.[6]

Through it all, however, Archilochus kept his sardonic humor. Commenting on the death of a relative, for example, he remarked, "I won't cure anything by weeping or make it worse by pursuing pleasures and festivities." For Archilochus the adventure of colonization had a happy, if unusual, ending. The people of Paros, overlooking his waywardness because of his poetic genius, welcomed him back. Later he was killed defending his homeland.

Archilochus exemplifies the energy, restlessness, self-reliance, and sense of adventure that characterizes this epoch. People like him broke old ties, faced homelessness and danger, and built new homes for themselves. They made the Mediterranean Greek.

LYRIC POETS

Archilochus the colonist and adventurer is not nearly as important as Archilochus the lyric poet, whose individualism set a new tone in Greek literature. For the first time in Western civilization, men and women began to write of their own experiences. Their poetry reflected their belief that they had something precious to say about themselves. To them poetry did not belong only to the gods or to the great heroes on the plain of Troy. Some lyric poets used their literary talents for the good of their city-states. They stood forth as individuals and in their poetry urged their countrymen to be patriotic and just.

One of the most unforgettable of these writers is the poet Sappho. Unlike Archilochus, she neither braved the wilds nor pushed into the unknown, yet she was no less individual than he. Sappho was born in the seventh century B.C. on the island of Lesbos, a place of sun, sea, and rustic beauty. Her marriage produced a daughter, to whom she wrote some of her poems. Sappho's poetry is personal and intense. She delighted in her surroundings, which were those of aristocratic women, and she celebrated the little things around her. Hers was a world of natural beauty, of sacred groves, religious festivals, wedding celebrations, and noble companions. Sappho fondly remembered walks with a girlfriend:

There was neither a hill nor a sanctuary
Nor a stream of running water
Which we failed to visit;
Nor when spring began any grove
Filled with the noise of nightingales.[7]

The rising of Hesperus, the evening star, prompted her to welcome it:

Hesperus, bringing back all things
*   Which light-giving dawn disperses,*
You bring back the sheep, you bring back the goat,
*   You bring the child back to its mother.*[8]

Sappho is best known for erotic poetry, for she expressed her love frankly and without shame. She was bisexual, and much of her poetry dealt with her homosexual love affairs.

MOSAIC PORTRAIT OF SAPPHO   *The Greek letters in the upper left corner identify this idealized portrait as that of Sappho. The mosaic, which was found at Sparta, dates to the late Roman Empire and testifies to Sappho's popularity in antiquity. (Photo: Caroline Buckler)*

In one of her poems she remembered the words of her lover:

Sappho, if you don't come out,
Surely I will no longer love you.
O come to us and free your lovely
Strength from your bed.
Lifting off your Chian robe,
Bathe in the waters like a
Pure lily beside a spring.[9]

In another poem Sappho described Aphrodite appearing to her in answer to her prayers. The goddess advised her to be patient: the girl she loved would return her love soon enough.

In antiquity Sappho's name became linked with female homosexual love. Today, the English word *lesbian* is derived from Sappho's island home. Yet to see Sappho as licentious is to misunderstand her and her world completely. The Greeks accepted bisexuality — that men and women could enjoy both ho-

STATUE OF "LEONIDAS" *Found at Sparta, this statue is thought by some to represent Leonidas, the Spartan king who was killed at Thermopylae. The statue, with its careful rendering of the muscles and the face, reflects the Spartan ideal of the strong, intelligent, and brave warrior. (Photo: Caroline Buckler)*

mosexual and heterosexual lovemaking. Homosexual relationships normally carried no social stigma. In her mature years Sappho was courted by a younger man who wanted to marry her. By then she had already proclaimed her love for several girls, yet the young man was not troubled by these affairs. As it turned out, Sappho refused to marry because she was past child-bearing age.

In their poetry Archilochus and Sappho reveal two sides of Greek life in this period.

Archilochus exemplifies the energy and adventure of the age, while Sappho expresses the intensely personal side of life. The common link is their individualism, their faith in themselves, and their desire to reach out to other men and women in order to share their experiences, thoughts, and wisdom.

THE GROWTH OF SPARTA

During the Lyric Age the Spartans expanded the boundaries of their polis and made it the leading power in Greece. Like other Greeks, the Spartans faced the problems of overpopulation and land hunger. Unlike other Greeks, the Spartans solved these problems by conquest, not by colonization. To gain more land the Spartans set out in about 735 B.C. to conquer Messenia, a rich and fertile region in the southwestern Peloponnesus. This conflict, known as the First Messenian War, lasted for twenty years and ended in a Spartan triumph. The Spartans appropriated Messenian land and turned the Messenians into helots, or state serfs.

In about 650 B.C., Spartan exploitation and oppression of the Messenian helots led to a helot revolt so massive and stubborn that it became known as the Second Messenian War. The Spartan poet Tyrtaeus, a contemporary of these events, vividly portrayed the ferocity of the fighting:

For it is a shameful thing indeed
When with the foremost fighters
An elder falling in front of the young men
Lies outstretched,
Having white hair and grey beard,
Breathing forth his stout soul in the dust,
Holding in his hands his genitals
stained with blood.[10]

Confronted with horrors such as this, Spartan enthusiasm for the war waned. To rally his countrymen Tyrtaeus urged the warriors to face the Messenians:

And let each man coming near
*   with his great spear or sword,*
Wounding his man cut him down and take him;
And putting foot against foot and leaning shield
*   against shield,*
Crest upon crest and helmet upon helmet,
And chest to chest, drawing near,
*   let him fight his man,*
Taking him with the hilt of his sword
*   or with his great spear.*[11]

Finally, after some thirty years of fighting, the Spartans put down the revolt. Nevertheless, the political and social strain caused by this war led to a transformation of the Spartan polis.

It took the full might of the Spartan people, aristocrat and commoner alike, to win the Second Messenian War. After the victory the nonnobles, who had done much of the fighting, demanded rights equal to those of the nobility. Their agitation disrupted society, until the aristocrats agreed to remodel the state. Although the Spartans later claimed that the changes brought about by this compromise were the work of Lycurgus, a legendary, semidivine lawgiver, they were really the work of the entire Spartan people.

The Lycurgan regimen, as these reforms were called, was a new political, economic, and social system. Political distinctions among the Spartans were eliminated, and all citizens became equal to one another. In effect, the Lycurgan regimen abolished the aristocracy and made the government an oligarchy. Actual governance of the polis was in the hands of two kings, who were primarily military leaders. The kings and twenty-eight elders made up a council that deliberated on foreign and domestic matters and prepared legislation for the assembly,

which consisted of all Spartan citizens. The real executive power of the polis was in the hands of five *ephors,* or overseers. The ephors were elected from and by all the people.

To provide for their economic needs the Spartans divided the land of Messenia among all citizens. Helots worked the land, raised the crops, provided the Spartans with their living, and occasionally served in the army. The Spartans kept the helots in line by means of systematic terrorism, hoping to to beat them down and keep them quiet. Spartan citizens were supposed to devote their time exclusively to military training.

In the Lycurgan system every citizen owed primary allegiance to Sparta. Suppression of the individual, together with emphasis on military prowess, led to a barracks state. Family life itself was sacrificed to the polis. If an infant was deformed or handicapped at birth, the polis could demand that the parents put it out to die. In this respect the Spartans were no better or worse than other Greeks. Infanticide was common in ancient Greece and Rome, and many people resorted to it as a way of keeping population down. The difference is that in other Greek states the decision to kill a child belonged to the parents, not to the polis.

Once a Spartan boy reached the age of seven, he lived in barracks with other boys his age. Spartan youth all underwent rugged physical and military training until they reached twenty-four, when they became front-line soldiers. For the rest of their lives, Spartan men kept themselves prepared for combat. Their military training never ceased, and the older men were expected to be models of endurance, frugality, and sturdiness to the younger men. In battle Spartans were supposed to stand and die rather than retreat. An anecdote about one Spartan mother sums up Spartan military values. As her son was setting off to battle, the mother handed him his shield and advised him to come back either victorious carrying the shield or dead being carried upon it. In short, in the Lycurgan regimen Spartans were expected to train vigorously, disdain luxury and wealth, do with little and like it.

THE EVOLUTION OF ATHENS

Like Sparta, Athens too faced pressing social and economic problems during the Lyric Age, but the Athenian response to them was far different from that of the Spartans. Instead of creating an oligarchy, the Athenians extended to all citizens the right and duty of governing the polis. Indeed, the Athenian democracy was one of the most thoroughgoing in Greece.

In the seventh century B.C., however, the aristocracy still governed Athens, as oppressively as the "bribe-devouring lords" against whom Hesiod had railed. The aristocrats owned the best land, met in an assembly to govern the polis, and interpreted the law. Noble landowners were forcing small farmers into economic dependence. Many families were being sold into slavery; others were exiled and their land pledged to the rich. Poor farmers who borrowed from their wealthy neighbors put up their land as collateral. If a farmer was unable to repay the loan, his creditor put a stone on the borrower's field to signify his indebtedness and thereafter took one-sixth of the annual yield until the debt was paid. If the farmer had to borrow again, he pledged himself and at times his family. If he was again unable to repay the loan, he became the slave of his creditor. Because the harvests of the poor farmer were generally small, he normally raised enough to live on but not enough to repay his loan.

The peasants, however, were strong in numbers, and they demanded reforms. They wanted the law to be published so that everyone would know its contents. Under pressure, the aristocrats relented and turned to Draco, a fellow aristocrat, to codify the law. In 621 B.C., Draco published the first law code of the Athenian polis. His code was thought harsh, but it nonetheless embodied the ideal that the law belonged to all citizens. The aristocrats hoped in vain that Draco's law code would satisfy the peasants. Many of the poor began demanding redistribution of the land, and it was obvious that broader reform was needed. Unrest among the peasants continued.

In many other city-states conditions such as those in Athens led to the rise of tyrants. The word *tyrant* brings to mind a cruel and bloody dictator, but the Greeks seem at first to have used the word to denote a leader who seized power without legal right. Many of the first tyrants, though personally ambitious, were men who kept the welfare of the polis in mind. They usually enjoyed the support of the peasants because they reduced the power of the aristocrats. Later tyrants were often harsh and arbitrary – hence the Greeks began to use the word in the modern sense – and when they were, peasants and aristocrats alike suffered.

Only one person in Athens had the respect of both aristocrats and peasants: Solon, himself an aristocrat and poet, but a man opposed to tyrants. Like Hesiod, Solon used his poetry to condemn the aristocrats for their greed and dishonesty. He stormed against

those citizens who are persuaded
to destroy this great city
because they desire reckless wealth.[12]

Solon recited his poems in the Athenian agora, where everyone could hear his relentless call for justice and fairness. The aristocrats realized that Solon was no crazed revolutionary, and the common people trusted him. Around 594 B.C., the aristocrats elected him *archon,* chief magistrate of the Athenian polis, and gave him extraordinary power to reform the state.

Solon immediately freed all people enslaved for debt, recalled all exiles, canceled all debts on land, and made enslavement for debt illegal. He also divided society into four legal groups on the basis of wealth. In the most influential group were the wealthiest citizens, but even the poorest and least powerful group enjoyed certain rights. Solon allowed them into the old aristocratic assembly, where they could take part in the election of magistrates.

In all his work, Solon gave thought to the rights of the poor as well as the rich. He gave the commoners a place in government and a voice in the political affairs of Athens. His work done, Solon insisted that all swear to uphold his reforms. Then, since many were clamoring for him to become tyrant, he left Athens to travel.

Although Solon's reforms solved some immediate problems, they did not bring peace to Athens. Some aristocrats attempted to make themselves tyrants, while others banded together to oppose them. In 546 B.C., Pisistratus, an exiled aristocrat, returned to Athens, defeated his opponents, and became tyrant. Pisistratus reduced the power of the aristocracy while supporting the common people. Under his rule Athens prospered, and his building program began to transform it into one of the splendors of Greece. His reign as tyrant promoted the growth of democratic ideas by arousing in the Athenians rudimentary feelings of equality.

Athenian acceptance of tyranny did not long outlive Pisistratus, for his son Hippias ruled harshly, and his excesses led to his overthrow. After a brief period of turmoil between factions of the nobility, Cleisthenes, a wealthy and prominent aristocrat, emerged triumphant in 508 B.C., largely because he won the support of the people. Cleisthenes created the Athenian democracy, and he did so with the full knowledge and approval of the Athenian people. He reorganized the state completely, but he presented every innovation to the assembly for discussion and ratification. All Athenian citizens had a voice in Cleisthenes' work.

Cleisthenes created a new local unit, the deme, to serve as the basis of his political system. Citizenship was tightly linked to the deme, for each deme kept the roll of those within its jurisdiction who were admitted to citizenship. Cleisthenes also created ten new tribes as administrative units. All the demes were grouped in tribes, which thus formed the link between the demes and the central government. The central government included an assembly of all citizens and a new council of five hundred members. The council prepared legislation for the assembly to consider, and it handled diplomatic affairs. The result of Cleisthenes' work was to make Athens a democracy with a government efficient enough to permit effective popular rule.

Athenian democracy was to prove an inspiring ideal in Western civilization. It demonstrated that a large group of people, not just a few, could efficiently run the affairs of state. By heeding the opinions, suggestions, and wisdom of all its citizens, the state enjoyed the maximum amount of good counsel. Since all citizens could speak their minds, they did not have to resort to rebellion or conspiracy to express their desires.

Athenian democracy must not, however, be thought of in modern terms. In Athens democracy meant a form of government in which poor men as well as rich enjoyed political power and responsibility. In practice, though, most important offices were held by aristocrats. Furthermore, Athenian democracy denied political rights to many people, including women and slaves. Foreigners were seldom admitted to citizenship. Unlike modern democracies, Athenian democracy did not mean that the citizen would merely vote for others who would then run the state. Instead, every citizen was expected to be able to perform the duties of most magistrates. In Athens citizens voted and served. The people were the government. It is this union of the individual and the state — the view that the state exists for the good of the citizen and that the duty of the citizen is to serve it well — that has made Athenian democracy so compelling an ideal.

THE CLASSICAL PERIOD
(500–338 B.C.)

In the years 500–338 B.C., Greek civilization reached its highest peak in politics, thought, and art. In this period the Greeks beat back the armies of the Persian Empire. Then, turning their spears against one another, they destroyed their own civilization in a century of warfare. Some thoughtful Greeks felt prompted to record and analyze these momentous events; the result was the creation of history. This era saw the flowering of philosophy, as thinkers in Ionia and on the Greek mainland began to ponder the nature and meaning of the universe and human experience. Not content to ask "why," they used their intellects to explain the world around them and to determine humanity's place in it.

The Greeks invented drama, and the Athenian tragedians Aeschylus, Sophocles, and Euripides explored themes that still inspire audiences today. Greek architects reached the zenith of their art and created buildings whose very ruins still inspire awe. Because Greek intellectual and artistic efforts attained their fullest and finest expression in these years, this age is called the Classical Period. Few periods in the history of Western society can match it in sheer dynamism and achievement.

THE DEADLY CONFLICTS (499–404 B.C.)

One of the hallmarks of the Classical Period was warfare. In 499 B.C. the Ionian Greeks, with the feeble help of Athens, rebelled against the Persian Empire. In 490 B.C., the Persians struck back at Athens but were beaten off at the Battle of Marathon, a small plain in Attica. This failure only prompted the Persians to try again. In 480 B.C., the Persian king Xerxes led a mighty invasion force into Greece. In the face of this emergency the Greeks united and pooled their resources to resist the invaders. The Spartans provided the overall leadership and commanded the Greek armies. The Athenians, led by the wily Themistocles, provided the heart of the naval forces.

The first confrontation between the Persians and the Greeks occurred at the pass of Thermopylae and in the waters off Artemisium in northern Greece. At Thermopylae the Greek hoplites — the heavily armed troops — showed their mettle. Before the fighting began, a report came in that when the Persian archers shot their bows the arrows darkened the sky. One gruff Spartan merely replied, "Fine, then we'll fight in the shade." The Greeks at Thermopylae fought to the last man, but the Persians took the position. In their next two battles, the Greeks fared better. In 480 B.C., the Greek fleet smashed the Persian navy at Salamis, an island south of Athens. The following year, the Greek army destroyed the Persian forces at Plataea, a small polis at Boeotia.

The significance of these Greek victories is nearly incalculable. By defeating the Persians, the Greeks ensured that oriental monarchy would not stifle the Greek achievement. The Greeks were thus able to develop their particular genius in freedom. These decisive victories meant that Greek political forms and intellectual concepts would be the heritage of the West.

After turning back the invasion, the Greeks took the fight to the Persian Empire. In 478 B.C., the Greeks decided to continue hostilities until they had liberated the Ionians from Persian rule. To achieve that goal a strong navy was essential. The Greeks turned to Athens, the leading naval power in the Aegean, for leadership. Athens and other states, especially those in the Aegean, responded by establishing the Delian League. Athens controlled the Delian League, providing most of the warships for operations and determining how much money each member should contribute to the league's treasury.

Over the next twenty years Athens drove the Persians out of the Aegean and turned the Delian League into an Athenian empire. Athenian rule became severe, and the Athenian polis became openly imperialistic. Although all members of the Delian League were supposed to be free and independent states, Athens reduced them to the status of subjects. A sense of the harshness of Athenian rule can be gained from the regulations the Athenians imposed on their subject allies. After the Athenians had suppressed a revolt in Euboea, they imposed an oath on the people:

I will not revolt from the people of Athens either by any means or devices whatsoever or by word or deed, nor will I be persuaded by anyone who does revolt. And I will pay the tribute to the Athenians that I can persuade the Athenians [to levy]. I will be to them the best and truest ally possible. I will help and defend the people of Athens if anyone wrongs them, and I will obey the people of Athens.[13]

The Athenians dictated to the people of Erythrae, a polis on the coast of Asia Minor, their form of government:

There will be a council of 120 men chosen by lot. ... The [Athenian] overseers and garrison commander will choose the current council by lot and establish it in office. Henceforth the council and the [Athenian] garrison commander will do these things thirty days before the council goes out of office.[14]

The Athenians also interfered with the economic affairs of the allies and decreed that they use Athenian coins, weights, and measures. The lengths to which the Athenians could go are exemplified in the oath they forced on the people of Colophon, another polis in Asia Minor: "And I will love the Athenian people, and will not desert them . . ." The Athenians were willing to enforce their demands by armed might, and they were ready both to punish violations and to suppress discontent.

The expansion of Athenian power and the aggressiveness of Athenian rule alarmed Sparta and its allies. While relations between Athens and Sparta cooled, Pericles (ca 494–429 B.C.) became the leading statesman in Athens. An aristocrat of solid intellectual ability, he turned Athens into the wonder of Greece. But like the democracy he led, Pericles was aggressive and imperialistic. He made

MAP 3.3 THE PELOPONNESIAN WAR *This map, which shows the alignment of states during the Peloponnesian War, vividly illustrates the large scale of the war and its divisive impact.*

no effort to allay Spartan fear and instead continued Athenian expansion. At last, in 459 B.C., Sparta and Athens went to war over conflicts between Athens and some of Sparta's allies. The war ended fourteen years later with no serious damage to either side and nothing settled. But this war had divided the Greek world between two great powers.

During the 440s and 430s, Athens continued its severe policies toward its subject allies and came into conflict with Corinth, one of Sparta's leading allies (see Map 3.3). Once

again Athens and Sparta were drifting toward war. In 432 B.C., the Spartans convened a meeting of their allies, who complained of Athenian aggression and demanded that Athens be stopped. With a show of reluctance, the Spartans agreed to declare war. The real reason for war, according to the Athenian historian Thucydides, was very simple:

The truest explanation, though the one least mentioned, was the great growth of Athenian power and the fear it caused the Lakedaimonians [Spartans], which drove them to war.[15]

At the outbreak of this, the Peloponnesian War, a Spartan ambassador warned the Athenians: "This day will be the beginning of great evils for the Greeks." Few men have ever spoken more prophetically. The Peloponnesian War lasted a generation (431–404 B.C.) and brought in its wake fearful plagues, famine, civil wars, widespread destruction, and huge loss of life. Thucydides, the historian who also fought as a general in the war, described its cataclysmic effects:

For never had so many cities been captured and destroyed, whether by the barbarians or by the Greeks who were fighting each other. . . . Never had so many men been exiled or slaughtered, whether in the war or because of civil conflicts.[16]

As the war dragged on, old leaders like Pericles died and were replaced by men of the war generation. In Athens the most prominent of this new breed of politicians was Alcibiades (ca 450–404 B.C.), an aristocrat, a kinsman of Pericles, and a student of the philosopher Socrates. Alcibiades was brilliant, handsome, charming, and popular with the people. He was also self-seeking and egotistical; a shameless opportunist, his first thoughts were always for himself.

Alcibiades' schemes helped bring Athens down to defeat. Having planned an invasion of Sicily that ended in disaster, he deserted to the Spartans and plotted with the Persians, who had sided with Sparta, against his homeland. When his treachery had brought the Athenians to the brink of defeat, he struck a bargain with them. He promised to persuade Persia to throw its support to Athens, if the Athenians would allow him to return home. When they agreed, Alcibiades cheerfully double-crossed the Spartans and led the Athenians against Sparta's forces.

In the end, all of Alcibiades' intrigues failed. The Spartans defeated the Athenian

MOSAIC PORTRAIT OF ALCIBIADES *The artist has caught all the craftiness, intelligence, and quickness of Alcibiades, who became a romantic figure in antiquity. Besides the artistic merit of the portrait, the mosaic is interesting because Alcibiades' name in the upper right corner is misspelled. (Photo: Caroline Buckler)*

fleet in the Aegean and blockaded Athens by land and sea. Finally, in 404 B.C., the Athenians surrendered and watched helplessly while the Spartans and their allies destroyed the walls of Athens to the music of flute girls. The Peloponnesian War lasted twenty-seven years, and it dealt Greek civilization a serious blow.

THE BIRTH OF HISTORICAL AWARENESS

One positive development grew out of the Persian and Peloponnesian wars: the beginnings of historical writing. Herodotus (ca 485–425 B.C.), known as "the Father of History," was born at Halicarnassus in Asia Minor. As a young man he traveled widely, visiting Egypt, Phoenicia, and probably Babylon. Later he migrated to Athens, which became his intellectual home. In the first lines of his book, *The Histories,* Herodotus explained his reasons for writing history:

This is the publication of the researches of Herodotus of Halicarnassus – so that past deeds will not be forgotten by men through lapse of time – which points out the great and admirable achievements, both those of the Greeks and those of the barbarians, lest they be uncelebrated, and which points out why they waged war against each other.[17]

This introduction bears some resemblance to that of the *Iliad,* and indeed *The Histories* has been called a prose epic. The basic difference is that Herodotus dealt with the real and factual, not with legend. He even gave history its name; his word *historia* originally meant "investigation." Only after his book appeared did the word *historia* gain its modern meaning.

Herodotus chronicled the rise of the Persian Empire, sketched the background of Athens and Sparta, and described the land and customs of the Egyptians and the Scythians, who lived in the region of the modern Crimea. The sheer scope of this work is awesome. Lacking newspapers, sophisticated communications, and easy means of travel, Herodotus nevertheless wrote a history that covered the major events of the Near East and Greece.

Perhaps Herodotus' most striking characteristic is his curiosity. He loved to travel, and like most travelers he accumulated a stock of fine stories. He was an excellent storyteller, and the customs of non-Greek peoples fascinated him. But tales and digressions never obscure the central theme of his work. Herodotus diligently questioned everyone who could tell him anything about the Persian wars. The confrontation between East and West unfolds relentlessly in *The Histories,* reaching its climax in the great battles of Salamis and Plataea.

In Herodotus' opinion the victory of the Greeks was due to their ability to live life simply, without luxury or wealth. He emphasized this point in describing a meeting between the Persian king Xerxes and a Greek deserter. Xerxes was about to invade Greece, so he questioned the deserter about the Greeks and their land. The deserter told him that

in Greece poverty is ever-present, but excellence is acquired, attained from wisdom and hard law. By making use of them Greece wards off both poverty and despotism.[18]

Herodotus turned to this thought again when he concluded his history with a moral: "Those accustomed to soft lands are themselves soft."

The outbreak of the Peloponnesian War prompted Thucydides (ca 460–ca 400 B.C.) to write a history of its course in the belief that

it would be great and more noteworthy than previous wars, considering that both states were in the prime of all their preparations and seeing that the other Greeks were taking sides with one or the other, some immediately, others intending to do so. For this was the greatest movement among the Greeks and some of the barbarians, and so to speak among most of mankind.[19]

A politician and a general, Thucydides saw action in the war until he was exiled for a defeat. Exile gave him the time and opportunity to question eyewitnesses about the details of events and to visit battlefields. Since he was an aristocrat and a prominent man, he had access to the inner circles of men who made the decisions.

Thucydides was intensely interested in human nature and how it manifested itself during the war. In 430 B.C., a terrible plague struck Athens. Thucydides described both the symptoms of the plague and the reactions of the Athenians in the same clinical terms. He portrayed the virtual breakdown of a society beset by war, disease, desperation, and despair. Similarly, he chronicled the bloody civil war on the island of Corcyra. Instead of condemning the injustice and inhumanity of the fighting, in which citizen turned on citizen and people ruthlessly betrayed their friends, he coolly observed that such things are normal as long as human nature is what it is.

Thucydides saw the Peloponnesian War as highly destructive to Greek character. He noted – with a visible touch of regret – that the old, the noble, and the simple fell before ambition and lust for power. Thucydides interpreted the war and its effects in purely human terms. He firmly rejected any notion that the gods intervened in human affairs. In his view the fate of men and women was, for good or ill, entirely in their own hands.

ATHENIAN ARTS IN THE AGE OF PERICLES

In the last half of the fifth century B.C., Pericles turned Athens into the showplace of Greece. He appropriated Delian League funds to pay for a huge building program, planning temples and other buildings to honor Athena, the patron goddess of the city, and to display to all Greeks the glory of the Athenian polis. Pericles also pointed out that his program would employ a great many Athenians and bring economic prosperity to the city.

Thus began the undertaking that turned the Acropolis into a monument for all time. Construction of the Parthenon began in 447 B.C., followed by the Propylaea, the temple of Athena Nike (Athena the Victorious), and the Erechtheion. Even today in their ruined state they still evoke awe. Plutarch, a Greek writer who lived in the first century A.D., observed:

In beauty each of them was from the outset antique, and even now in its prime fresh and newly made. Thus each of them is always in bloom, maintaining its appearance as though untouched by time, as though an ever-green breath and undecaying spirit had been mixed in its construction.[20]

Even the pollution of modern Athens, although it is destroying the ancient buildings, cannot rob them of their splendor and charm.

The planning of the architects and the skill of the workmen who erected these buildings were both very sophisticated. Visitors approaching the Acropolis first saw the Propylaea, the ceremonial gateway, a building of complicated layout and grand design whose Doric columns seem to hold up the sky.

On the right was the small temple of Athena Nike, whose dimensions harmonize with those of the Propylaea. The temple was built to commemorate the victory over the Persians, and the Ionic frieze above its columns depicted the battle of the Greeks and the Persians. Here for all the world to see was a tribute to Athenian and Greek valor – and a reminder of Athens' part in the victory.

Ahead of the visitors as they stood in the Propylaea was the huge statue of Athena Promachus (the Front-Line Fighter), so gigantic that the crest of Athena's helmet and the point of her spear could be seen by sailors entering the harbor of Athens. This statue celebrated the Athenian victory at the battle of Marathon, and was paid for by the spoils taken from the Persians. To the left stood the Erechtheion, an Ionic temple that housed several ancient shrines. On its southern side is the famous Portico of the Caryatids, a porch whose roof is supported by statues of Athenian maidens. The graceful Ionic columns of the Erechtheion provide a delicate relief from

THE PARTHENON *Stately and graceful, the Parthenon symbolizes the logic, order, and sense of beauty of Greek architecture. The Parthenon was also the centerpiece of Pericles' plan to make Athens the artistic showcase of the Greek world. (Photo: Caroline Buckler)*

the prevailing Doric order of the massive Propylaea and Parthenon.

As visitors walked on they obtained a full view of the Parthenon, thought by many to be the perfect Doric temple. The Parthenon was the chief monument to Athena and her city. The sculptures that adorned the temple portrayed the greatness of Athens and its goddess. The figures on the eastern pediment depicted Athena's birth, those on the west the victory of Athena over the god Poseidon for the possession of Attica. Inside the Parthenon stood a huge statue of Athena, the masterpiece of Phidias, one of the greatest sculptors of all time.

The Parthenon appears to be all rectangle and triangle, yet it is a structure of curves. Both the pavement that supports the columns and the beam above the columns are curved to avoid the illusion of flatness. The columns themselves are gently curved from bottom to top. The Parthenon also appears rigorously regular, but it is actually a collection of irregularities, all designed to compensate for the effects of optical illusion. For instance, the columns are not regularly spaced, and they incline inward; those at the rear are stockier than those at the front end. In all these refinements the Athenian architect showed his knowledge of mathematics, optics, and design. The impression the Parthenon creates is one of perfection. Well might all Athenians, no matter how humble, feel a great burst of pride in themselves, their goddess, and their polis when they gazed on the Parthenon.

In many ways the Athenian Acropolis is

the epitome of Greek art and its spirit. Although the buildings were dedicated to the gods and most of the sculptures portrayed gods, these works nonetheless express the Greek fascination with the human and rational. Greek deities were anthropomorphic, and Greek artists portrayed them as human beings. While honoring the gods, Greek artists were thus celebrating human beings. In the Parthenon sculptures it is visually impossible to distinguish the men and women from the gods and goddesses. This aspect of Greek art made a powerful impression on the American novelist Mark Twain, who visited the Acropolis at night:

As we wandered thoughtfully down the marble-paved length of this stately temple [the Parthenon] the scene about us was strangely impressive. Here and there in lavish profusion were gleaming white statues of men and women, propped against blocks of marble, some of them armless, some without legs, others headless – but all looking mournful in the moonlight and startlingly human![21]

The Acropolis also exhibits the rational side of Greek art. There is no violent emotion in this art, but instead a quiet intensity. Likewise, there is nothing excessive, for "nothing too much" was the canon of artist and philosopher alike. Greek artists portrayed action in a balanced, restrained, and sometimes even serene fashion, capturing the noblest aspects of human beings: their reason, dignity, and promise.

Other aspects of Athenian cultural life were as rooted in the life of the polis as were the architecture and sculpture of the Acropolis. The development of drama was tied to the religious festivals of the city. The polis sponsored the production of plays and required that wealthy citizens pay the expenses of their production. At the beginning of the year dramatists submitted their plays to the archon. He chose those he considered best and assigned a theatrical troupe to each playwright. Although most Athenian drama has perished, enough has survived to prove that the archons had superb taste. Many plays were highly controversial, but the archons neither suppressed nor censored them.

The Athenian dramatists were the first artists in Western society to examine such basic questions as the rights of the individual, the demands of society on the individual, and the nature of good and evil. Conflict is a constant element in Athenian drama. The dramatists used their art to portray, understand, and resolve life's basic conflicts.

Aeschylus (525–456 B.C.), the first of the great Athenian dramatists, was also the first to express the agony of the individual caught in conflict. In his trilogy of plays, *The Oresteia,* Aeschylus deals with the themes of betrayal, murder, and reconciliation. *The Agamemnon,* the first play of the trilogy, depicts Agamemnon's return from the Trojan War and his murder by his wife Clytemnestra and her lover Aegisthus. In the second play, *The Libation Bearers,* Orestes, the son of Agamemnon and Clytemnestra, avenges his father's death by killing his mother and her lover. His act of vengeance is the work of a dutiful son, but the murder of his mother is a sin against his own blood.

The last play of the trilogy, *The Eumenides,* works out the atonement and absolution of Orestes. The Furies, goddesses who avenged murder and unfilial conduct, demand Orestes' death. Orestes stands trial at Athens, with Athena as judge and Apollo as counsel for the defense. When the jury casts six votes to condemn Orestes and six to acquit him, Athena casts the deciding vote in favor of mercy and compassion. Aeschylus used *The Eumenides* to urge reason and justice to reconcile fundamental conflicts. The play concludes with a prayer that civil dissension never be allowed to destroy the city and that the life of the city be one of harmony and grace.

Sophocles (496–406 B.C.) too dealt with matters personal and political. In *Antigone* he examined the relationship between the individual and the state by exploring a conflict between the ties of kinship and the demands of the polis. In the play Polynices has attacked his own state, Thebes, and has fallen in battle. Creon, the Theban king, refuses to allow Polynices' body to be buried. Polynices' sister Antigone is appalled by Creon's action because custom demands that she bury her brother's corpse. Creon is right in refusing to allow Polynices' body to be buried in the polis, but wrong to refuse any burial at all. He continues in his misguided and willful error. As the play progresses, Antigone comes to stand for the precedence of divine law over human defects. Sophocles touches upon the need for recognition of the law and adherence to it as a prerequisite for a tranquil state.

Sophocles' masterpieces have become classics of Western literature, and his themes have inspired generations of playwrights. Perhaps his most famous plays are *Oedipus the King* and its sequel, *Oedipus at Colonus*. *Oedipus the King* is the ironic story of a man doomed by the gods to kill his father and marry his mother. Try as he might to avoid his fate, Oedipus' every action brings him closer to its fulfillment. When at last he realizes that he has carried out the decree of the gods, Oedipus blinds himself and flees into exile. In *Oedipus at Colonus* Sophocles dramatizes the last days of the broken king, whose patient suffering and uncomplaining piety win him an exalted position. In the end the gods honor him for his virtue. The interpretation of these two plays has been hotly debated, but Sophocles seems to be saying that human beings should do the will of the gods, even without fully understanding it, for the gods stand for justice and order.

Euripides (ca 480–406 B.C.), the last of the three great Greek dramatists, also explored the theme of personal conflict within the polis and sounded the depths of the individual. With Euripides drama entered a new, and in many ways more personal, phase. To him the gods were far less important than human beings. Euripides viewed the human soul as a place where opposing forces struggle with each other, where strong passions such as hatred and jealousy come into conflict with reason. The essence of Euripides' tragedy is the flawed character – the men and women who bring disaster on themselves and their loved ones because their passions overwhelm reason. Although Euripides' plays were less popular in his own lifetime than those of Aeschylus and Sophocles, Euripides was a dramatist of genius, and his work later had a significant impact on Roman drama.

Writers of comedy treated the affairs of the polis bawdily and often coarsely. Even so, their plays too were performed at religious festivals. The comic playwrights dealt primarily with the political affairs of the polis and the conduct of its leading politicians. Best known are the comedies of Aristophanes (ca 445–386 B.C.), an ardent lover of his city and a merciless critic of cranks and quacks. He lampooned eminent generals, at times depicting them as morons. He commented snidely on Pericles, poked fun at Socrates and hooted at Euripides. He saved some of his strongest venom for Cleon, a prominent politician. It is a tribute to the Athenians that such devastating attacks could openly and freely be made on the city's leaders and foreign policy. Even at the height of the Peloponnesian War, Aristophanes proclaimed that peace was preferable to the ravages of war. Like Aeschylus, Sophocles, and Euripides, Aristophanes used his art to dramatize his ideas on the right conduct of the citizen and the value of the polis.

Perhaps never were art and political life so intimately and congenially bound together as at Athens. Athenian art was the product of deep and genuine love of the polis. It aimed at bettering the lives of the citizens and the quality of life in the state.

DAILY LIFE IN PERICLEAN ATHENS

In sharp contrast with the rich intellectual and cultural life of Periclean Athens is the simplicity of its material life. The Athenians – and in this respect they were typical of Greeks in general – lived very happily with comparatively few material possessions. In the first place, there were very few material goods to own. The thousands of machines, tools, and gadgets considered essential for modern life had no counterpart in Athenian life. The inventory of Alcibiades' goods, which the Athenians confiscated after his desertion, is enlightening. His household possessions consisted of chests, beds, couches, tables, screens, stools, baskets, and mats. Other necessities of the Greek home included pottery, metal utensils for cooking, tools, luxury goods such as jewelry, and a few other things. These items they had to buy from craftsmen. Whatever else they needed, such as clothes and blankets, they produced at home.

The Athenian house was rather simple. Whether large or small, the typical house consisted of a series of rooms built around a central courtyard, with doors opening onto the courtyard. Many houses had bedrooms on an upper floor. Artisans and craftsmen often set aside a room to use as a shop or work area. The two principal rooms were the men's dining room and the room where the women worked wool. Other rooms included the kitchen and bathroom. By modern standards there was not much furniture. In the men's dining room were couches, a sideboard, and small tables. Cups and other pottery were often hung on the wall from pegs. Other household furnishings included items such as those confiscated from Alcibiades.

In the courtyard were the well, a small altar, and a washbasin. If the family lived in the country, the stalls of the animals faced the courtyard. The countryman kept oxen for plowing, pigs for slaughtering, sheep for wool, goats for cheese, and mules and donkeys for transportation. Even in the city, chickens and perhaps a goat or two roamed the courtyard together with dogs and cats.

Cooking, done over a hearth in the house, provided welcome warmth in the winter. Baking and roasting were done in ovens. Food consisted of various grains, especially wheat and barley, as well as lentils, olives, figs, and grapes. Garlic and onion were popular garnishes, and wine was always on hand. These foods were stored at home in large jars, and with them the Greek family ate fish, chicken, and vegetables. Women ground wheat into flour at home, baked it into bread, and on special occasions made honey or sesame cakes. The Greeks used olive oil for cooking, as families still do in modern Greece; they also used it as an unguent and as fuel for lamps.

By American standards the Greeks did not eat much meat. On special occasions, such as important religious festivals, the family ate the animal sacrificed to the god and gave the god the exquisite delicacy of the thighbone wrapped in fat. The only Greeks who consistently ate meat were the Spartan warriors. They received a small portion of meat each day, together with the infamous Spartan black broth, a ghastly concoction of pork cooked in blood, vinegar, and salt. One Greek, after tasting the broth, commented that he could easily understand why the Spartans were so willing to die.

In the city a man might support himself as a craftsman – a potter, bronzesmith, sailmaker, or tanner – or he could contract with the polis to work on public buildings, such as the Parthenon and Erechtheion. Men without skills worked as paid laborers but competed with slaves for work. Slaves – usually foreigners, both barbarian and Greek – were paid as much for their labor as were free men.

Slavery was commonplace in Greece, as it was throughout the ancient world. In its essentials Greek slavery resembled Mesopotamian slavery. Slaves received some protection under the law and could buy their freedom. On the other hand, masters could mistreat or neglect their slaves short of killing them, which was illegal. The worst-treated slaves were those of the silver mines at Laurium, who lived, worked, and died in wretchedness. Yet slavery elsewhere was not generally brutal. One crusty aristocrat complained that in Athens one could not tell the slaves from the free. Most slaves in Athens served as domestics and performed light labor around the house. Nurses for children, teachers of reading and writing, and guardians for young men were often slaves. The lives of these slaves were much like those of their owners. Other slaves were skilled workers, who could be found working on public buildings or in small workshops.

The importance of slavery in Athens must not be exaggerated. Apart from the owners of the Laurium mines, Athenians did not own huge gangs of slaves as did Roman owners of large estates. Slave labor competed with free labor and kept wages down, but it never replaced the free labor that was the mainstay of the Athenian economy.

Most Athenians supported themselves by agriculture, but unless the family was fortunate enough to possess holdings in a plain more fertile than most of the land, they found it difficult to reap a good crop from the soil. Wealthy landowners sold their excess produce in the urban marketplace, but many people must have consumed nearly everything they raised. The plow, though wooden, sometimes had an iron share, and was pulled by oxen. Attic farmers were free men. Though hardly prosperous, they were by no means destitute. Greek farmers could usually expect yields of five bushels of wheat and ten of barley per acre for every bushel of grain sown. A bad harvest meant a lean year. In many places farmers grew more barley than wheat because of the nature of the soil. Wherever possible farmers also cultivated vines and olive trees.

For sport both the countryman and the city dweller often hunted for rabbits, deer, or wild boar. A successful hunt supplemented the family's regular diet. Wealthy men hunted on horseback; most others hunted on foot with their dogs. Hunting also allowed a man to display to his fellows his bravery and prowess in the chase. If wild boar were the prey, the sport could be dangerous, as Odysseus discovered when a charging boar slashed open his foot.

The social condition of Athenian women has been the subject of much debate and little agreement. One thing is certain: the status of a free woman of the citizen class was strictly protected by law. Only her children, not those of foreigners or slaves, could be citizens. Only she was in charge of the household and the family's possessions. Yet the law protected her primarily to protect her husband's interests. Raping a free woman was a lesser crime than seducing her because seduction involved the winning of her affections. This law was not concerned with the husband's feelings but with ensuring that he need not doubt the legitimacy of his children.

Ideally, respectable women lived a secluded life in which the only men they saw were relatives. How far this ideal was actually put into practice is impossible to say. At least Athenian women seem to have enjoyed a social circle of other women of their own class. They also attended public festivals, sacrifices, and funerals. Nonetheless, prosperous and respectable women probably spent much of their time in the house. A white complexion – a sign that a woman did not have to work in the fields – was valued highly.

Courtesans lived the freest lives of all Athenian women. Although some courtesans were simply prostitutes, others added intellectual accomplishments to physical beauty. In constant demand, cultured courtesans moved freely in male society. Their artistic talents and intellectual abilities appealed to men who wanted more than sex. The most famous of all courtesans was Aspasia, mistress of Pericles and supposedly friend of Socrates. Under Pericles' roof, she participated in intellectual discussions equally with some of the most stimulating thinkers of the day. Yet her position, like that of most other courtesans, was precarious. After Pericles' death, Aspasia fended for herself, ending her days as the madam of a house of prostitution.

A woman's main functions were to raise the children, oversee the domestic slaves and hired labor, and together with her maids work wool into cloth. The women washed the wool in the courtyard and then brought it into the women's room, where the loom stood. They spun the wool into thread and wove the thread into cloth. They also dyed wool at home and decorated the cloth by weaving in colors and designs. The woman of the household either did the cooking herself or directed her maids. In a sense, poor women lived freer lives than did wealthier women. They performed manual labor in the fields or sold goods in the agora, going about their affairs much as men did.

A distinctive feature of Athenian life, and Greek life in general, was acceptance of homosexuality. The distinguished English scholar K.J. Dover has succinctly described the difference between Greek and modern outlooks on human sexuality:

Greek culture differed from ours in its readiness to recognize the alternation of homosexual and heterosexual preferences in the same individual, its implicit denial that such alternation or coexistence created peculiar problems for the individual or for society, its sympathetic response to the open expression of homosexual desire in words and behavior, and its taste for the uninhibited treatment of homosexual subjects in literature and the visual arts.[22]

No one has satisfactorily explained how the Greek attitude toward homosexual love developed, or determined how common homosexual behavior was. Homosexuality was probably far more common among the aristocracy than among the lower classes. It is impossible to be sure, simply because most of what the modern world knows of ancient Greece and Rome comes from the writings of aristocrats. Since aristocratic boys and girls were often brought up separately, the likelihood of homosexual relationships was very great. This style of life was impossible for the common folk because every member of the family – husband and wife, son and daughter – got out and worked. Among the poorer classes the sexes mingled freely.

Even among the aristocracy attitudes toward homosexuality were complex and sometimes conflicting. Most people saw homosexual love affairs among the young as a stage in the development of a mature heterosexual life. Yet some Athenian aristocrats ridiculed homosexual practices. Comic writers habitually made fun of "boy-crazy men" and "effeminate youths." Others, such as the Spartans and the philosopher Plato, saw in homosexual relationships the opportunity for older men to train their juniors in practical wisdom. For them, the sexual element was supposed to give way to the benefits of education. In Sparta, as in Sappho's Lesbos, noble women loved girls for the same reasons. Warrior-aristocracies generally emphasized the physical side of the relationship in the belief that warriors who were also lovers would fight all the harder to impress each other. They would also be less likely to desert their lovers in battle. Whatever their intellectual and educational content, homosexual love affairs were also overtly sexual.

What effect did homosexual love have on the Greeks? An American psychologist has concluded that the "Greek adolescent . . . ended up as a non-neurotic, completely (or predominantly) heterosexual adult."[23] Most of Sappho's young lovers went on to marry and raise families. They never regretted the homosexual loves of their past or thought them unusual. Their previous relationships did not prevent them from devoting their primary affection to their new mates. For many Greeks, homosexuality was a normal practice, and they treated it as straightforwardly and honestly as they did heterosexual love and other aspects of life.

Despite some modern speculation to the contrary, relations between Athenian husbands and wives were probably close. The presence of female slaves in the home could be a source of trouble; men were always free to resort to prostitutes; and some men and women engaged in homosexual love affairs. But basically husbands and wives depended on each other for mutual love and support. The wife's position and status in the household were guaranteed by her dowry, which came from her father and remained her property throughout her married life. If the wife felt that her marriage was intolerable, she could divorce her husband far more easily than could a Mesopotamian wife.

To judge by the evidence of funerary reliefs, there seems to have been nothing radically odd about the relationships of Athenian wives and husbands. One scholar has noted that funerary reliefs express the sorrow of the entire household – husband, children, and slaves – at the death of a wife. An epitaph of the fourth or third century B.C. reads:

Chaerestrate lies in this tomb. When she was alive her husband loved her. When she died he lamented.[24]

THE FLOWERING OF PHILOSOPHY

The myths and epics of the Mesopotamians are ample testimony that speculation about the origin of the universe and of mankind did not begin with the Greeks. The signal achievement of the Greeks was their willingness to treat these questions in rational rather than mythological terms. Although Greek philosophy did not fully flower until the Classical Period, Ionian thinkers had already begun in the Lyric Age to ask what the universe was made of. These men are called the Pre-Socratics, for their work preceded the philosophical revolution begun by the Athenian Socrates. Though they were born observers, the Pre-Socratics rarely undertook deliberate experimentation. Instead they took individual facts and wove them into general theories. Despite appearances, they believed, the universe was actually simple and subject to natural laws. Drawing upon their observations, they speculated about the basic building blocks of the universe.

The first of the Pre-Socratics, Thales (ca

600 B.C.), learned mathematics and astronomy from the Babylonians and geometry from the Egyptians. Yet there was an immense and fundamental difference between Near Eastern thought and the philosophy of Thales. The Near Eastern peoples considered such events as eclipses as evil omens. Thales viewed them as natural phenomena that could be explained in natural terms. In short, he asked *why* things happened. He believed the basic element of the universe to be water. Although he was wrong, the way in which he had asked the question was momentous: it was the beginning of the scientific method.

Thales' follower Anaximander continued his work. Anaximander was the first of the Pre-Socratics to use general concepts, which are essential to abstract thought. One of the most brilliant of the Pre-Socratics, a man of striking originality, Anaximander theorized that the basic element of the universe is "the boundless" or "endless" — something infinite and indestructible. In his view, the earth floats in a void, held in balance by its distance from everything else in the universe.

Anaximander even concluded that mankind had evolved naturally from lower organisms: "In water the first animal arose covered with spiny skin, and with the lapse of time some crawled onto dry land and breaking off their skins in a short time they survived."[25] This remarkable speculation corresponds crudely to Darwin's theory of evolution of species, which it predated by two-and-a-half millennia.

Another Ionian, Heraclitus (ca 500 B.C.) declared the primal element to be fire. He also declared that the world had neither beginning nor end: "This world, the world of all things, neither any god nor man made, but it always was and it is and it will be: an everlasting fire, measures kindling and measures going out."[26] Although the universe was eternal, according to Heraclitus, it changed constantly. An out-growth of this line of speculation was the theory of Democritus that the universe is made of invisible, indestructible atoms. The culmination of Pre-Socratic thought was the theory that four simple substances make up the universe: fire, air, earth, and water.

With this impressive heritage behind them, the philosophers of the Classical Period ventured into new areas of speculation. This development was partly due to the work of Hippocrates (second half of the fifth century B.C.), the father of medicine.

Like Thales, Hippocrates sought natural explanations for natural phenomena. Basing his opinions on empirical knowledge, not on religion or magic, he taught that natural means could be employed to fight disease. In his treatise On Airs, Waters, and Places, he noted the influence of climate and environment on health. Hippocrates and his followers put forth a theory that was to prevail in medical circles until the eighteenth century. The human body, they declared, contains four humors, or fluids: blood, phlegm, black bile, and yellow bile. In a healthy body the four humors are in perfect balance; too much or too little of any particular humor causes illness. Hippocrates and his pupils shared the Ionian belief that they were dealing with phenomena that could be explained purely in natural terms. But Hippocrates broke away from the mainstream of Ionian speculation by declaring that medicine was a separate craft — just as ironworking was a craft — and that it had its own principles.

The distinction between natural science and philosophy, upon which Hippocrates insisted, was also promoted by the sophists, who traveled the Greek world teaching young men. Despite differences of opinion on philosophical matters, the sophists all agreed that human beings were the proper subject of study. They also believed that excellence could be taught, and used philosophy and rhetoric to prepare young men for life in the polis. The sophists laid great emphasis on logic and the meanings of words. They criticized traditional beliefs, religion, rituals, and myth, and even questioned the laws of the polis. In essence they argued that nothing is absolute, that everything – even the customs and constitution of the state – is relative. Hence, many Greeks of more traditional inclination considered them wanton and harmful, men who were interested in "making the worse seem the better cause."

One of those whose contemporaries thought him a sophist was Socrates (ca 470–399 B.C.), who sprang from the class of small artisans. Socrates spent his life in investigation and definition. Not strictly speaking a sophist, because he never formally taught or collected fees from anyone, Socrates shared the sophists' belief that human beings and their environment are the essential subjects of philosophical inquiry. Like the sophists, Socrates thought that excellence could be learned and passed on to others. His approach when posing ethical questions and defining concepts was to start with a general topic or problem and to narrow the matter to its essentials. He did so by continuous questioning, a running dialogue. Never did he lecture. Socrates thought that by constantly pursuing excellence, an essential part of which was knowledge, human beings could approach the supreme good and thus find true happiness. Yet, in 399 B.C., Socrates was brought to trial, convicted, and executed on charges of corrupting the youth of the city and introducing new gods.

Socrates' student Plato (427–347 B.C.) carried on his master's search for truth. Unlike Socrates, Plato wrote down his thoughts and theories and founded a philosophical school, the Academy. Plato developed the theory that all visible, tangible things are unreal and temporary, copies of "forms" or "ideas" that are constant and indestructible. Only the mind – not the senses – can perceive the eternal forms. In Plato's view the highest form is the idea of good.

In *The Republic* Plato applied his theory of forms to politics in an effort to describe the ideal polis. His perfect polis is utopian; it aims at providing the greatest good and happiness to all its members. Plato thought that the ideal polis could exist only if its rulers were philosophers. He divided society into rulers, guardians of the polis, and workers. The role of people in each category is decided by the education, wisdom, and ability of the individual. In Plato's republic men and women are equal to one another, and women can become rulers. The utopian polis is a balance, with each individual doing what he or she can to support the state and with each receiving from the state his or her just due.

In a later work, *The Laws,* Plato discarded the ideal polis of *The Republic* in favor of a second-best state. The polis of *The Laws* is grimly reminiscent of the modern dictatorship. At its head is a young tyrant, who is just and good. He meets with a council that sits only at night, and together they maintain the spirit of the laws. Nearly everything about this state is coercive; the free will of the citizens counts for little. The laws speak to every aspect of life; their sole purpose is to make people happy.

Aristotle (384–322 B.C.) carried on the philosophical tradition of Socrates and Plato. A student of Plato, Aristotle went far beyond his teacher in his efforts to understand the universe. The very range of Aristotle's thought is staggering. Everything within human experience was fit subject for his inquiry. In his *Politics* Aristotle followed Plato's lead by writing about the ideal polis. Yet

Aristotle approached the question more realistically than Plato had, and he criticized *The Republic* and *The Laws* on many points. In the *Politics* and elsewhere, Aristotle stressed moderation and concluded that the balance of his ideal state depended on people of talent and education who could avoid extremes.

Not content to examine old questions, Aristotle opened up whole new fields of inquiry. He tried to understand the changes of nature – what caused them and where they led. In the *Physics* and *Metaphysics* he evolved a theory of nature in which he developed the notions of matter, form, and motion. He attempted to bridge the gap between abstract truth and concrete perception that Plato had created.

In *On the Heaven,* Aristotle took up the thread of Ionian speculation. His theory of cosmology added ether to air, fire, water, and earth as building-blocks of the universe. He concluded that the universe revolves and that it is spherical and eternal. He wrongly thought that the earth is the center of the universe, with the stars and other planets revolving around it. The Hellenistic scientist Aristarchus of Samos later realized that the earth revolves around the sun, but Aristotle's view was accepted until the time of the fifteenth-century astronomer Nicolaus Copernicus.

Aristotle's scientific interests also included zoology. In several works he describes various animals and makes observations on animal habits, animal anatomy, and how animals move. He also explored the process of reproduction. Intending to examine the entire animal kingdom, he assigned the world of plants to his follower Theophrastus (see Chapter 4).

Aristotle possessed one of the keenest and most curious philosophical minds of Western civilization. While rethinking the old topics

DEPARTING WARRIOR *Scenes like this were all too common from 431 to 338 B.C., as young men donned their armor and left for battle. This warrior and a young woman, probably his sister, pour a libation to the gods before he leaves for the war. (Museum of Fine Arts, Boston)*

explored by the Pre-Socratics, he also created whole new areas of study. In short, he tried to learn everything possible about the universe and everything in it. He did so in the belief that all knowledge could be synthesized to produce a simple explanation of the universe and of humanity.

THE FINAL ACT (403–338 B.C.)

The end of the Peloponnesian War only punctuated a century of nearly constant war-

THE LION OF CHAERONEA   *Alone on his base, this stylized lion marks the mass grave of nearly 300 elite Theban soldiers who valiantly died fighting the Macedonians at the battle of Chaeronea. After the battle, when Philip viewed the bodies of these brave troops, he said to those around him: "May those who suppose that these men did or suffered anything dishonorable perish wretchedly." (Photo: Caroline Buckler)*

fare that lasted from 431 to 338 B.C. The events of the fourth century demonstrated that no single Greek state possessed enough power and resources to dominate the others. There nevertheless ensued an exhausting struggle for hegemony among the great powers, especially Sparta, Athens, and Thebes. Immediately after the Peloponnesian War, with Athens humbled, Sparta began striving for empire over the Greeks. The arrogance and imperialism of the Spartans turned their former allies against them. Even with Persian help Sparta could not maintain its hold on Greece. In 371 B.C. the Spartans met their match on the plain of Leuctra in Boeotia. A Theban army under the command of Epaminondas, one of Greece's most brilliant generals, destroyed the flower of the Spartan army on a single summer day. The victory at Leuctra left Thebes the most powerful state in Greece. Under Epaminondas the Thebans destroyed Sparta as a first-rank power and checked the ambitions of Athens, but they were unable to bring peace to Greece. In 362 B.C. Epaminondas was killed in battle, and a period of stalemate set in. The Greek states were virtually exhausted.

The man who turned the situation to his own advantage was Philip II, king of Macedonia (359–336 B.C.). Throughout most of Greek history Macedonia, which bordered Greece in the north, in modern Greece and Yugoslavia, had been a backward and disunited kingdom, but Philip's genius, courage, and drive turned it into a major power. One of the ablest statesmen of antiquity, Philip united his powerful kingdom behind him, built a redoubtable army, and pursued his ambition with drive and determination. His horizon was not limited to Macedonia, for he realized that he could turn the rivalry and exhaustion of the Greek states to his own purposes. By clever use of his wealth and superb army Philip won control of the northern Aegean and awakened fear in Athens, which had vital interests there. Demosthenes, an Athenian patriot and a fine orator, warned his fellow citizens against Philip:

Most of all there is this to fear. This cunning and terrible man makes use of his accomplishments, yielding on points when he must, threatening (and he certainly appears to mean it) on others. He slanders us and our inactivity. He fosters and takes for himself anything of value.[27]

Others too saw Philip as a threat. A comic playwright depicted one of Philip's ambassadors warning the Athenians:

*Do you know that your battle will be with men
Who dine on sharpened swords,
And gulp burning firebrands for wine?
Then immediately after dinner the slave
Brings us dessert — Cretan arrows
Or pieces of broken spears.
We have shields and breastplates for
Cushions and at our feet slings and arrows,
And we are crowned with catapults.*[28]

Finally the Athenians joined forces with Thebes, which also appreciated the Macedonian threat, to stop Philip. In 338 B.C. the combined Theban-Athenian army met Philip's veterans at the Boeotian city of Chaeronea. Philip's army won a hard-fought victory: he had conquered Greece and put an end to Greek freedom. Because the Greeks could not put aside their quarrels, they fell to an invader.

———

In a comparatively brief span of time the Greeks progressed from a primitive folk, backward and rude compared to their Near Eastern neighbors, to one of the most influential peoples of history. The originators of science and philosophy asked penetrating questions about the nature of life and society, and came up with deathless responses to many of their own questions. Greek achievements range from the development of sophisticated political institutions to the creation of a stunningly rich literature. Brilliant but quarrelsome, they were their own worst enemies. As the Roman historian Pompeius Trogus later said of their fall:

The states of Greece, while each one wished to rule alone, all squandered sovereignty. Indeed, hastening without moderation to destroy one another in mutual ruin, they did not realize, until they were all crushed, that every one of them lost in the end.[29]

Nonetheless, their achievement outlived their political squabbles to become the cornerstone of all later Western development.

NOTES

1. K. J. Beloch, *Griechische Geschichte,* vol. I, pt. I, K. J. Trübner, Strassburg, 1912, p. 49.

2. Aristotle *Politics* 1253a3-4.

3. Herodotus *The Histories* 2.53.

4. Hesiod *Works and Days* 263-266.

5. Ibid., 511-514.

6. F. Lasserre, *Archiloque,* Société d'Edition "Les Belles Lettres," Paris, 1958, frag. 9, p. 4.

7. W. Barnstable, *Sappho,* Doubleday, Garden City, N.Y., 1965, frag. 24, p. 22.

8. Ibid., frag. 132, p. 106.

9. Ibid., frag. 23, p. 20.

10. J. M. Edmonds, *Greek Elegy and Iambus,* Harvard University Press, Cambridge, Mass., 1931, I.70, frag. 10.

11. Ibid., frag. 11, p. 72.

12. Edmonds, *Greek Elegy and Iambus,* frag. 4, p. 118.

13. R. Meiggs and D. Lewis, *A Selection of Greek Historical Inscriptions,* Clarendon Press, Oxford, 1969, no. 52, lines 21-32.

14. Ibid., no. 40, lines 9-11.

15. Thucydides *History of the Peloponnesian War* 1.23.

16. Ibid.

17. Herodotus *The Histories* 1.1.

18. Ibid., 7.102.

19. Thucydides *The Peloponnesian War* 1.1.

20. Plutarch *Life of Pericles* 13.5.

21. Mark Twain, *The Innocents Abroad,* Signet Classics, New York, 1966, p. 249.

22. K. J. Dover, *Greek Homosexuality,* Random House, New York, 1980, p.1.

23. G. Devereux, "Greek Pseudo-Homosexuality and the 'Greek Miracle'," *Symbolae Osloenses* (1968): 70.

24. S. B. Pomeroy, *Goddesses, Whores, Wives and Slaves,* Schocken, New York, 1975, p. 92.

25. E. Diels and W. Krantz, *Fragmente der Vorsokratiker,* 8th ed. Weidmannsche Verlagsbuchhandlung, Berlin, 1960, Anaximander frag. A30.

26. Ibid., Heraclitus frag. B30.

27. Demosthenes *First Olynthiac* 3.

28. J. M. Edmonds, *The Fragments of Attic Comedy,* E. J. Brill, Leiden, 2.366-369, Mnesimachos frag. 7.

29. Justin 8.1.1-2.

SUGGESTED READING

Translations of the most important writings of the Greeks and Romans can be found in the volumes of the Loeb Classical Library, published by Harvard University Press. Paperback editions of the major Greek and Latin authors are available in the Penguin Classics. Recent translations of documents include those by N. Lewis, *Greek Historical Documents: The Fifth Century B.C.* (1971); J. Wickersham and G. Verbrugghe, *Greek Historical Documents: The Fourth Century B.C.* (1973); and C. Fornara, *Translated Documents of Greece and Rome,* vol. 1: *Archaic Times to the End of the Peloponnesian War* (1977).

Among the many general treatments of Greek history, H. D. F. Kitto, *The Greeks* (1951), is a delightful introduction. V. Ehrenberg in two works, *From Solon to Socrates,* 2nd. ed. (1973) and *The Greek State* (1960), covers major areas of Greek history.

For early Greece the most recent treatments include R. J. Hopper, *The Early Greeks* (1976), and L. H. Jeffery, *Archaic Greece* (1976). No finer introduction to the Lyric Age can be found than A. R. Burn's *The Lyric Age* (1960) and its sequel, *Persia and the Greeks* (1962). A good recent survey of work on Sparta is P. Oliva, *Sparta and Her Social Problems* (1971). Sound discussions of Athenian democracy are available in A. H. M. Jones, *Athenian Democracy* (1957), and C. Hignett, *History of the Athenian Constitution* (1952).

A. J. Graham, *Colony and Mother City in Ancient Greece* (1964), gives a good account of Greek colonization. Athens in the fifth century and the outbreak of the Peloponnesian War are covered in G. E. M. de Ste Croix, *The Origins of the Peloponnesian War* (1972), and R. Meiggs, *The Athenian Empire* (1972).

Several books on fourth-century history have recently appeared. D. M. Lewis' *Sparta and Persia* (1977) is rich in information on the administration of the Persian Empire, Spartan diplomacy, and much else. J. Buckler, *The Theban Hegemony, 371-362 B.C.* (1980) treats the period of Theban ascendancy. J. Cargill, *The Second Athenian League* (1981), a significant new study, traces Athenian policy during the century. J. R. Ellis, *Philip II and Macedonian Imperialism* (1976), and G. Cawkwell, *Philip of Macedon* (1978), analyze the career of the great conqueror.

Daily life, the family, women, and homosexuality receive treatment in Pomeroy's book cited in the Notes; T. B. L. Webster, *Life in Classical Greece* (1969); M. and C. H. B. Quennell, *Everyday Things in Ancient Greece* (1954); and a special issue of the Journal *Arethusa* 6 (1973).

For Greek literature, culture, and science, see A. Lesky, *A History of Greek Literature* (English trans., 1963); W. Jaeger, *Paideia,* 3 vols., (English trans., 1944-1945); H. C. Baldry, *The Greek Tragic Theater* (1971); J. Burnet, *Early Greek Philosophy,* 4th ed.

(1930), and *Greek Philosophy, Thales to Plato* (1914); M. Clagett, *Greek Science in Antiquity* (1971); and E. R. Dodds, *The Greeks and the Irrational* (1951).

The classic treatment of Greek architecture is W. B. Dinsmoor, *The Architecture of the Ancient Greeks,* 3rd ed. (1950). More recent (and perhaps more readable) is A. W. Lawrence, *Greek Architecture,* 3rd ed. (1973). J. Boardman, *Greek Art,* rev. ed. (1973), is both perceptive and sound, as is J. J. Pollitt, *Art and Experience in Classical Greece* (1972).

D. Haynes, *Greek Art and the Idea of Freedom* (1981), traces the evolving freedom of the human personality in Greek art.

J. Pinsent, *Greek Mythology* (1969), is a handy introduction. M. P. Nilsson, *Cults, Myths, Oracles and Politics in Ancient Greece* (1951), examines Greek religion and myth in the contemporary context. See also G. S. Kirk, *The Nature of Greek Myths* (1974).

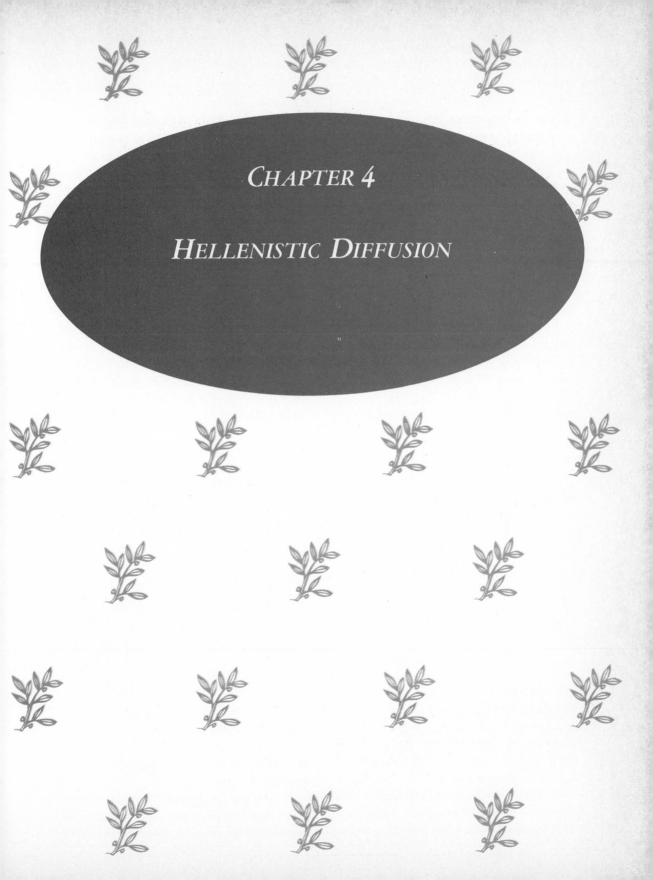

CHAPTER 4

HELLENISTIC DIFFUSION

TWO YEARS AFTER his conquest of Greece, Philip of Macedon fell victim to an assassin's dagger. Philip's twenty-year-old son, known to history as Alexander the Great (336–323 B.C.) assumed the Macedonian throne. This young man, one of the most remarkable personalities of Western civilization, was to have a profound impact on history. "For in twelve years having conquered not a small part of Europe and nearly all of Asia, he was justly famous and his glory was equal to that of the heroes of old and of the demigods."[1]

By overthrowing the Persian Empire and by spreading Hellenism – Greek culture, language, thought and the Greek way of life – as far as India, Alexander was instrumental in creating a new era, traditionally called Hellenistic to distinguish it from the Hellenic. As a result of Alexander's exploits, the individualistic and energetic culture of the Greeks came into intimate contact with the venerable older cultures of the Near East.

What did the spread of Hellenism mean to the Greeks and the peoples of the Near East? What did the meeting of West and East hold for the development of philosophy, religion, science, medicine, and economics? These are the questions this chapter will explore.

ALEXANDER AND THE GREAT CRUSADE

In 336 B.C., Alexander inherited not only Philip's crown but also his policies. After his victory at Chaeronea, Philip had organized the states of Greece into a huge league under his leadership, and announced to the Greeks his plan to lead them and his Macedonians against the Persian Empire. Fully intending to carry out Philip's designs, Alexander proclaimed to the Greek world that the invasion of Persia was to be a great crusade, a mighty

act of revenge for the Persian invasion of Greece in 480 B.C.

Despite his youth, Alexander was well prepared to lead the attack. Philip had groomed his son to become king, and had given him the best education possible. In 343 B.C., Philip invited the philosopher Aristotle to tutor his son. From Aristotle Alexander learned to appreciate Greek culture and literature, and the teachings of the great philosopher left a lasting mark on him. Alexander must also have profited from Aristotle's practical knowledge, but he never accepted Aristotle's political theories. At the age of sixteen Alexander became regent of Macedonia, and two years later at the battle of Chaeronea he helped defeat the Greeks. By 336 B.C., Alexander had acquired both the theoretical and the practical knowledge to rule peoples and lead armies.

In 334 B.C., Alexander led an army of Macedonians and Greeks into Asia Minor. With him went a staff of philosophers and poets, scientists whose job was to map the country and to study strange animals and plants, and the historian Callisthenes, who was to write an account of the campaign. Alexander planned not only to conquer the Persians but to lead an expedition of discovery to open up the East to Greek knowledge.

In the next three years Alexander won three major battles at the Granicus River, Issus, and Gaugamela. As Map 4.1 shows, these battle sites stand almost as road signs marking his march to the East. After his victory at Gaugamela, Alexander captured the principal Persian capital of Persepolis, where he performed a symbolic act of retribution by burning the buildings of Xerxes, the invader of Greece. In 330 B.C., he took Ecbatana, the last Persian capital, and pursued the Persian king to his death.

The Persian Empire had fallen and the war of revenge was over, but Alexander had no intention of stopping. He dismissed his Greek troops, but permitted many of them to serve on as mercenaries. Alexander then began his personal odyssey. With his Macedonian soldiers and Greek mercenaries he set out to conquer the rest of Asia. He plunged deeper into the East, into lands completely unknown to the Greek world. Alexander's way was marked by bitter fighting and bloodshed. It took four more years to conquer Bactria and the easternmost parts of the now-defunct Persian Empire, but still Alexander was determined to march on.

In 326 B.C., Alexander crossed the Indus River and entered India. There too he saw hard fighting, and finally at the Hyphasis River his troops refused to go farther. Alexander was enraged by the mutiny, for he believed that he was near the end of the world. Nonetheless, the army stood firm, and Alexander had to relent. Still eager to explore the limits of the world, Alexander returned south to the Indian Ocean. Even though the tribes in the area did not oppose him, he waged a bloody, ruthless, and unnecessary war against them. After reaching the Indian Ocean and turning west, he led his army through the grim Gedrosian Desert, apparently to punish his troops for their mutiny at the Hyphasis. The army suffered fearfully, and many men died along the way, but in 324 B.C. Alexander reached his camp at Susa. The great crusade was over, and Alexander himself died the next year in Babylon.

ALEXANDER'S LEGACY

Of Alexander the man history knows little: he too quickly became a figure of legend, a figure larger than life. Of Alexander's plans and intentions history likewise knows little. Although some scholars have seen him as a high-minded philosopher, his bloody and sav-

COIN OF ALEXANDER *The head on this coin is that of the demigod Heracles, whom Alexander admired and imitated. Alexander claimed that he was descended from Heracles, and on several occasions he even dressed like Heracles. (Courtesy, World Heritage Museum. Photo: Caroline Buckler)*

age campaigns in the East seem the work of a ruthless and callous conqueror. Yet for the Hellenistic period and for Western civilization in general, what Alexander intended was less important than what he actually did (see Map 4.1).

Alexander was instrumental in changing the face of politics in the eastern Mediterranean. His campaign swept away the Persian Empire, which had ruled the East for over two hundred years. In its place he established a Macedonian monarchy. More important in the long run was his foundation of new cities and military colonies, which scattered Greeks and Macedonians throughout the East. Thus the practical result of Alexander's campaign was to open the East to the tide of Hellenism.

THE POLITICAL LEGACY

In 323 B.C., Alexander the Great died at the age of thirty-two. The main question at his death was whether his vast empire could be

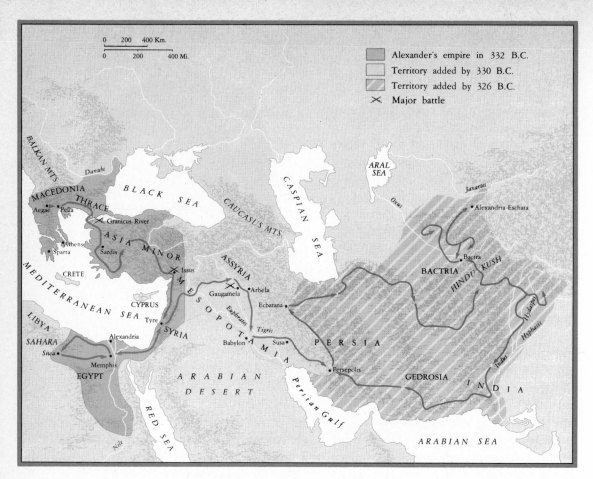

MAP 4.1 ALEXANDER'S CONQUESTS This
map shows the course of Alexander's invasion of the
Persian Empire and the speed of his progress.

held together. The answer became obvious
immediately. Within a week of Alexander's
death began a round of fighting that was to
continue for forty years. No single Macedonian general was able to replace Alexander as
emperor of his entire domain. By 275 B.C., as
Map 4.2 shows, three of Alexander's officers
had divided it into large monarchies. Antig-
onus Gonatas became king of Macedonia and
established the Antigonid dynasty, which
ruled until the Roman conquest in 168 B.C.
Ptolemy Lagus made himself king of Egypt,
and his descendants, the Ptolemies, assumed
the powers and position of pharaohs. Se-

leucus, founder of the Seleucid dynasty, carved
out a kingdom that stretched from the coast
of Asia Minor to India. In 263 B.C., Eumenes,
the Greek ruler of Pergamum, a city in western Asia Minor, won his independence from
the Seleucids and created the Pergamene
monarchy. Though the Seleucid kings soon
lost control of their easternmost provinces,
Greek influence in this area did not wane. In
modern Turkestan and Afghanistan another
line of Greek kings established the kingdom
of Bactria, and even managed to spread their
power and culture into northern India.

The political face of Greece itself changed

ALEXANDER AT THE BATTLE OF ISSOS   At the left, Alexander the Great, bareheaded and wearing a breastplate, charges King Darius, who is standing in a chariot. This moment marks the turning point of the battle, as Darius turns to flee from the attack. (Museo Nazionale, Naples. Alinari/Scala)

during the Hellenistic period. The day of the polis was over, and in its place arose leagues of city-states. The two most powerful and most extensive were the Aetolian League in western and central Greece, and the Achaean League in the Peloponnesus. Once-powerful city-states like Athens and Sparta sank to the level of third-rate powers.

The political history of the Hellenistic period was dominated by the great monarchies and the Greek leagues. The political fragmentation and incessant warfare that marked the Hellenic period continued on an even wider and larger scale during the Hel-lenistic period. Never did the Hellenistic world achieve political stability or lasting peace. Hellenistic kings never forgot the vision of Alexander's empire, spanning Europe and Asia, secure under the rule of one man. Try as they did, they were never able to re-create it. In this respect, Alexander's legacy fell not to his generals but to the Romans of a later era.

THE CULTURAL LEGACY

As Alexander waded ever deeper into the East, distance alone presented him with a serious problem: how was he to retain contact with the Greek world behind him? Communications were vital, for he drew supplies and reinforcements from Greece and Macedonia. Alexander had to be sure that he was never cut off and stranded far from the Mediterranean world. His solution was to plant cities and military colonies in strategic places. In these settlements Alexander left Greek mercenaries and Macedonian veterans no longer up to active campaigning. Besides keeping the road open to the West, these settlements dominated the countryside around them.

Their military significance apart, Alexander's cities and colonies became powerful instruments in the spread of Hellenism throughout the East. Plutarch described Alexander's achievement in glowing terms: "Having founded over 70 cities among barbarian peoples and having planted Greek magistracies in Asia, Alexander overcame its wild and savage way of life."[2] Alexander had indeed opened the East to an enormous wave of immigration, and his successors continued his policy by inviting Greek colonists to settle in their realms. For seventy-five years after Alexander's death, Greek immigrants poured into the East. At least 250 new Hellenistic colonies were established. The Mediterranean world had seen no comparable movement of peoples since the days of Archilochus (see page 82), when wave after wave of Greeks had turned the Mediterranean basin into a Greek-speaking region.

The overall result of Alexander's settlements and those of his successors was the spread of Hellenism as far east as India. Throughout the Hellenistic period Greeks and Easterners became familiar with and adapted themselves to each other's customs, religions, and ways of life. Although Greek culture did not completely conquer the East, it gave the East a vehicle of expression that linked it to the West. Hellenism became a common bond among the East, peninsular Greece, and the western Mediterranean. This pre-existing cultural bond was later to prove supremely valuable to Rome – itself heavily influenced by Hellenism – in its efforts to impose a comparable political unity on the known world.

THE SPREAD OF HELLENISM

When the Greeks and Macedonians entered Asia Minor, Egypt, and the more remote East, they encountered civilizations older than their own. In some ways the Eastern cultures were more advanced than the Greek, in others less so. Thus this third great tide of Greek migration differed from preceding waves, which had spread over land that was uninhabited or inhabited by less-developed peoples.

What did the Hellenistic monarchies offer Greek immigrants, both politically and materially? More broadly, how did Hellenism and the cultures of the East affect one another? What did the meeting of East and West entail for the history of the world?

CITIES AND KINGDOMS

Although Alexander's generals created huge kingdoms, the concept of monarchy never replaced the ideal of the polis. Consequently, the monarchies never won the deep emotional loyalty that Greeks had once felt for the polis. Hellenistic kings needed large numbers of Greeks to run their kingdoms. Otherwise, royal business would grind to a halt, and the conquerors would soon be swallowed up by the far more numerous conquered population. Obviously, then, the kings had to encourage Greeks to immigrate and build new homes.

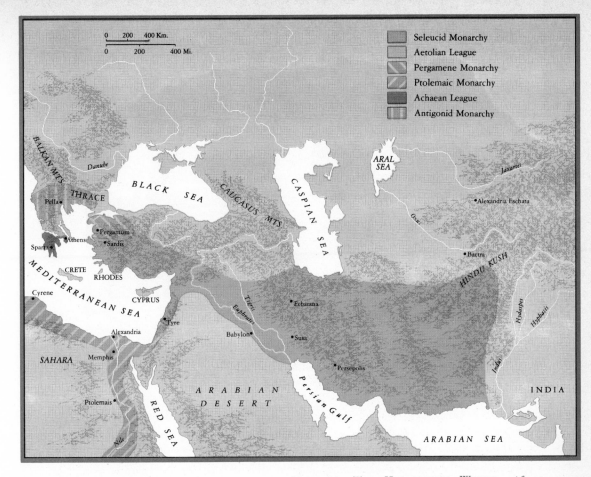

	Seleucid Monarchy
	Aetolian League
	Pergamene Monarchy
	Ptolemaic Monarchy
	Achaean League
	Antigonid Monarchy

MAP 4.2 THE HELLENISTIC WORLD *After Alexander's death, no single commander could hold his vast conquests together, resulting in the empire's break-up into several kingdoms and leagues.*

To these Greeks monarchy was something out of the heroic past, something found in Homer's *Iliad* but not in daily life. The Hellenistic kings thus confronted the problem of making life in the new monarchies resemble the traditional Greek way of life. Since Greek civilization was urban, the kings continued Alexander's policy of establishing cities throughout their kingdoms in order to entice Greeks to immigrate. Yet the creation of these cities posed a serious problem, which the Hellenistic kings failed to solve.

To the Greeks civilized life was unthinkable without the polis, which was far more than a mere city. The Greek polis was by definition sovereign – an independent, autonomous state run by its citizens free from any outside power or restraint. Hellenistic kings, however, refused to grant sovereignty to their cities. In effect, these kings willingly built cities, but refused to build a polis. Instead they attempted a compromise that ultimately failed.

Hellenistic monarchs gave to their cities all the external trappings of a polis. Each had an assembly of citizens, a council to prepare legislation, and a board of magistrates to conduct the political business of the city. Yet however similar to the Greek city-state they appeared,

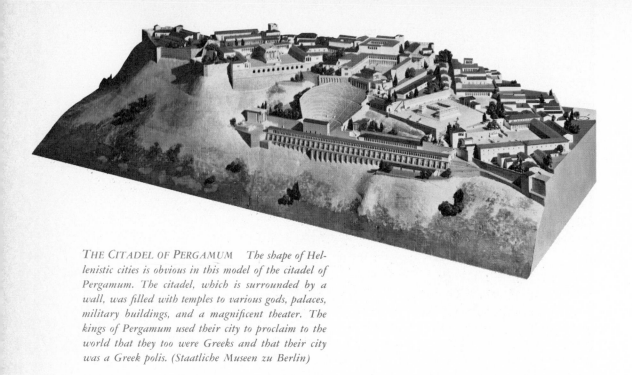

THE CITADEL OF PERGAMUM *The shape of Hellenistic cities is obvious in this model of the citadel of Pergamum. The citadel, which is surrounded by a wall, was filled with temples to various gods, palaces, military buildings, and a magnificent theater. The kings of Pergamum used their city to proclaim to the world that they too were Greeks and that their city was a Greek polis. (Staatliche Museen zu Berlin)*

these cities could not engage in diplomatic dealings, make treaties, pursue their own foreign policy, or wage their own wars. None could govern its own affairs without interference from the king, who, even if he stood in the background, was the real sovereign. In the eyes of the king the cities were important parts of the kingdom, but the welfare of the kingdom as a whole came first. The cities had to follow royal orders, and the king often placed his own officials in the cities to see that his decrees were carried out.

A new Hellenistic city differed from a Greek polis in other ways as well. The Greek polis had enjoyed political and social unity even though it was normally composed of citizens, slaves, and resident aliens. The polis had one body of law and one set of customs. In the Hellenistic city the Greeks represented an elite citizen class. Natives and non-Greek foreigners who lived in Hellenistic cities usually possessed lesser rights than those of the Greeks and often had their own laws. In some instances this disparity spurred natives to assimilate Greek culture in order to rise both politically and socially. Other peoples, such as the Jews, firmly resisted the essence of Hellenism. The Hellenistic city was not homogeneous, and it could not spark the intensity of feeling that marked the polis.

In many respects, the Hellenistic city resembled a modern city. It was a cultural center with theaters, temples, and libraries. It was a seat of learning, the home of poets, writers, scholars, teachers, and artists. It was the place where people could find amusement. The Hellenistic city was also an economic center that provided a ready market for the grain and produce raised in the surrounding countryside. The city was an emporium, the scene of trade and manufacturing. In short, the Hellenistic city offered cultural and economic opportunities, but did not foster a sense of united, integrated enterprise.

There were no constitutional links between the city and the king. The city was simply his possession. It and its citizens had no voice in how the kingdom was run. The city had no rights except for those the king granted, and even those he could summarily take away. Ambassadors from the city could entreat the king for favors and petition him on such matters as taxes, boundary disputes, and legal cases. But the city had no right to advise the king on royal policy, and it enjoyed no political function within the kingdom.

Hellenistic kings tried to make the kingdom the political focus of citizens' allegiance. If the king could secure the frontiers of his kingdom, he could give it a geographical identity. He could then hope that his subjects would direct their primary loyalty to the kingdom rather than a particular city. However, the kings' efforts to fix their borders led only to sustained warfare. Boundaries were determined by military power, and rule by force became the chief political principle of the Hellenistic world.

Border wars were frequent and exhausting. The Seleucids and the Ptolemies, for instance, waged five wars for the possession of southern Syria. Other kings refused to acknowledge any boundaries at all. These men followed the example of Alexander and waged wars to reunify his empire under their own authority. By the third century B.C., a weary balance of power was reached, but only as the result of stalemate. It was not maintained by any political principle.

The Hellenistic kings failed to create in their kingdoms a political unit to replace the polis. Even the Hellenistic city, despite its beauty and Hellenic trappings, failed to win the devotion and love that the Greeks had readily and enthusiastically given the polis.

Nor did the Hellenistic kings ever give the Greeks anything else to which to attach their political loyalty.

THE GREEKS AND THE OPENING OF THE EAST

If the Hellenistic kings failed to satisfy the Greeks' political yearnings, they nonetheless succeeded in giving them unequaled economic and social opportunities. The ruling dynasties of the Hellenistic world were Macedonian, and Greeks filled all important political, military, and diplomatic positions. These people constituted an upper class that sustained Hellenism in the barbarian East. Besides building Greek cities, Hellenistic kings offered Greeks land and money as a lure to further immigration.

The more splendid, prestigious, and famous the kingdom, the easier it was to attract settlers. Each kingdom strove to be more philhellenic — more Greek-like and more appreciative of Greek culture — than the others. Each claimed the ability to provide Greeks with the necessities of Greek life. The burden of these policies fell upon the native population of the various kingdoms. Easterners paid for these enticements through heavy taxation.

The opening of the East offered ambitious Greeks opportunities for well-paying jobs and economic success. The Hellenistic monarchy, unlike the Greek polis, did not depend solely on its citizens to fulfill its political needs. Talented Greeks could expect to rise quickly within the governmental bureaucracy. Appointed by the king, these administrators did not have to stand for election each year, as had many of the officials of a Greek polis. Since they held their jobs year after year, they had ample time to evolve new administrative techniques. Naturally, they became more efficient than the amateur officials common in the Greek city-states of the Hellenic period. The needs of the Hellenistic monarchy and the opportunities it offered thus gave rise to a professional corps of Greek administrators.

Greeks and Macedonians also found ready employment in the armies and navies of the Hellenistic monarchies. Alexander had proved the Greco-Macedonian style of warfare to be far superior to that of the Easterners, and Alexander's successors, themselves experienced officers, realized the importance of trained Greek and Macedonian soldiers. Moreover, Hellenistic kings were extremely reluctant to arm the native population or to allow them to serve in the army, fearing military rebellions among their conquered subjects. The result of this situation was the emergence of professional armies and navies consisting entirely of Greeks and Macedonians.

Greeks were able to dominate other professions as well. In order to be really philhellenic, the kingdoms and their cities needed Greek writers and artists to create Greek literature, art, and culture on Asian soil. Architects, engineers, and skilled craftsmen found their services in great demand because of the building policies of the Hellenistic monarchs. If Hellenistic kingdoms were to have Greek cities, those cities needed Greek buildings — temples, porticoes, gymnasia, theaters, fountains, and houses. Architects and engineers were sometimes commissioned to design and build whole cities, which they laid out in checkerboard fashion and filled with typical Greek buildings. A truly enormous wave of construction took place during the Hellenistic period.

Despite the opportunities they offered, the Hellenistic monarchies were hampered by their artificial origins. Their failure to win the political loyalty of their Greek subjects and their policy of wooing Greeks with lucrative positions encouraged a feeling of uprootedness and self-serving individualism among Greek immigrants. Once a Greek had left home to take service with, for instance, the army or the bureaucracy of the Ptolemies, he had no incentive beyond his pay and the comforts of life in Egypt to keep him there. If the Seleucid king offered him more money or a promotion, he might well accept it and take his talents to Asia Minor. Why not? In the realm of the Seleucids he, a Greek, would find the same sort of life and environment that the kingdom of the Ptolemies had provided him. Thus professional Greek soldiers and administrators were highly mobile and prone to look to their own interests, not those of the kingdom they joined.

As long as Greeks continued to replenish their professional ranks, the kingdoms remained strong. In the process they drew an immense amount of talent from the Greek peninsula, draining the vitality of the Greek homeland. However, the Hellenistic monarchies could not keep recruiting Greeks forever, in spite of their wealth and willingness to spend lavishly to attract and keep the Greeks coming. In time, the huge surge of immigration slowed greatly. Even then the Hellenistic monarchs were reluctant to recruit Easterners to fill posts normally held by Greeks. The result was at first the stagnation of the Hellenistic world and finally, after 202 B.C., collapse in the face of the young and vigorous Roman Republic.

GREEKS AND EASTERNERS

The Greeks in the East were a minority, and Hellenistic cities were islands of Greek culture in an Eastern sea. But Hellenistic monarchies were remarkably successful in at least partially hellenizing Easterners and spreading a uniform culture throughout the East, a culture to which Rome eventually fell heir. The prevailing institutions, laws, and language of the East became Greek. Indeed, the Near East had seen nothing comparable since the days when Mesopotamian culture had spread throughout the area.

Yet the spread of Greek culture was wider than it was deep. At best it was a veneer, thicker in some places than in others. Hellenistic kingdoms were never entirely unified in language, customs, and thought. Greek culture took firmest hold along the shores of the Mediterranean, but in the Far East, in Persia and Bactria, it eventually gave way to Eastern cultures.

The Ptolemies in Egypt made no effort to spread Greek culture, and unlike other Hellenistic kings they were not city builders. Indeed, they founded only the city of Ptolemais near Thebes. At first the native Egyptian population, the descendants of the pharaoh's people, retained their traditional language, outlook, religion, and way of life. Initially untouched by Hellenism, the natives continued to be the foundation of the state: they fed it by their labor in the fields, and they financed its operations by their taxes.

Under the pharaohs, talented Egyptians had been able to rise to high office, but during the third century B.C. the Ptolemies cut off this avenue of advancement. They tied the natives to the land ever more tightly, making it nearly impossible for them to leave their villages. The bureaucracy of the Ptolemies was ruthlessly efficient, and the native population was viciously and cruelly exploited. Even in times of hardship the king's taxes came first, though payment might mean starvation for the natives. The desperation of the native population was summed up by one Egyptian, who scrawled the warning: "We are worn out; we will run away."[3] To many Egyptians revolt or a life of brigandage was certainly preferable to working the land under the harsh Ptolemies.

Throughout the third century B.C., the Greek upper class had little to do with the native population. Many Greek bureaucrats established homes in Alexandria and Ptolemais, where they managed finances, served as magistrates, and administered the law. Other Greeks settled in military colonies and supplied the monarchy with fighting men.

In the second century B.C., Greeks and native Egyptians began to intermarry and mingle their cultures. The language of the native population influenced Greek, and many Greeks adopted Egyptian religion and ways of life. Simultaneously, natives adopted Greek customs and language, and began to play a role in the administration of the kingdom and even to serve in the army. While many Greeks and Egyptians remained aloof from each other, the overall result was the evolution of a widespread Greco-Egyptian culture.

Meanwhile the Seleucid kings established many cities and military colonies in western Asia Minor and along the banks of the Tigris and Euphrates rivers in order to nurture a vigorous and numerous Greek population. Especially important to the Seleucids were the military colonies, for they depended on Greeks to defend the kingdom. The Seleucids had no elaborate plan for hellenizing the native population, but the arrival of so many Greeks was bound to have an impact. Seleucid military colonies were generally founded near native villages, thus exposing Easterners to all aspects of Greek life. Many Easterners found Greek political and cultural forms attractive, and imitated them. In Asia Minor and Syria, for instance, numerous native villages and towns developed along Greek lines, and some of them became hellenized cities. Farther East the Greek kings who replaced the Seleucids in the third century B.C. spread Greek culture to their neighbors and even into the Indian sub-continent.

For Easterners the prime advantage of Greek culture was its very pervasiveness. The Greek language became the common speech of the East. Indeed, a common dialect, called *koine,* even influenced the speech of peninsular Greece itself. Greek became the speech of the royal court, the bureaucracy, and the military. It was also the speech of commerce: any Easterner who wanted to compete in business had to learn Greek. As early as the third century B.C., some Greek cities were giving citizenship to hellenized natives.

The vast majority of hellenized Easterners, however, took only the externals of Greek culture while retaining the essentials of their own way of life. Though Greeks and Easterners adapted themselves to each others' ways, there was never a true fusion of cultures. Nonetheless, each found useful things in the civilization of the other, and the two fertilized each other. This fertilization, this mingling of Greek and Eastern elements, is what makes Hellenistic culture unique and distinctive.

HELLENISM AND THE JEWS A prime illustration of how the East took what it wanted from Hellenism while remaining true to itself is the impact of Greek culture on the Jews. At first Jews in Hellenistic cities were treated as resident aliens. As they grew more numerous, they received permission to form a political corporation, a *politeuma,* which gave them a great deal of autonomy. The *politeuma* allowed Jews to attend to their religious and internal affairs without interference from the Greek municipal government. The Jewish politeuma had its own officials, the leaders of the synagogue. In time the Jewish politeuma gained the special right to be judged by its own law and its own officials, thus becoming in effect a Jewish city within a Hellenistic city.

The Jewish politeuma, like the Hellenistic city, obeyed the commands of the king, but there was virtually no royal interference with the Jewish religion. Indeed, the Greeks were always very reluctant to tamper with anyone's religion. Only the Seleucid king Antiochus Epiphanes (175–ca 164 B.C.) tried to suppress the Jewish religion in Judaea. He did so not because he hated the Jews (who were a small part of his kingdom), but because he was trying to unify his realm culturally to meet the threat of Rome. To the Jews he extended the same policy that he applied to all of his subjects. Apart from this instance, Hellenistic Jews suffered no official religious persecution. Some Jews were given the right to become full citizens of Hellenistic cities, but few exercised that right. Citizenship would have allowed them to vote in the assembly and serve as magistrates, but it would also have obliged them to worship the gods of the city – a practice few Jews chose to follow.

Jews living in Hellenistic cities often embraced a good deal of Hellenism. So many Jews learned Greek, especially in Alexandria, that the Old Testament was translated into Greek, and services in the synagogue came to be conducted in Greek. Jews often took Greek names, used Greek political forms, adopted Greek practice by forming their own trade associations, put inscriptions on graves as the Greeks did, and much else. Yet no matter how much of Greek culture or its externals Jews borrowed, they normally remained true to their religion. Their ideas and those of the Greeks were different. The exceptions were some Jews in Asia Minor and Syria who incorporated Greek or local Eastern cults into their worship. To some degree this development was due not only to the strength and attraction of these cults but also to the growing belief among Greeks and Easterners that all peoples, despite differences in cult and ritual, actually worshiped the same gods.

Thus, in spite of their Hellenistic trappings, hellenized Jews remained Jews at heart. The value of Hellenism both to Jews and to other Easterners was its gift of a common cultural background and means of expression.

THE ECONOMIC SCOPE OF THE HELLENISTIC WORLD

Alexander's conquest of the Persian Empire not only changed the political face of the ancient world, it also brought the East fully into the sphere of Greek economics. Yet the Hellenistic period did not see a revolution in the way people lived and worked. The material demands of Hellenistic society remained as simple as those of Athenian society in the fifth century B.C. Clothes and furniture were essentially unchanged, as were household goods, tools, and jewelry. The real achievement of Alexander and his successors was linking East and West in a broad commercial network. The spread of Greeks throughout the East created new markets and stimulated trade. The economic unity of the Hellenistic world, like its cultural bonds, would later prove valuable to the Romans.

COMMERCE

Alexander's conquest of the Persian Empire had immediate effects on trade. In the Persian capitals Alexander had found vast sums of gold, silver, and other treasure. This wealth financed the creation of new cities, the building of roads, and the development of harbors.

Most of the great monarchies coined their money on the Attic standard, which meant that much of the money used in the Hellenistic kingdoms had the same value. Traders were less in need of moneychangers than in the days when each major power coined money on a different standard. As a result of Alexander's conquests, geographical knowledge of the East increased dramatically, making the East far better known to the Greeks than previously. The Greeks spread their law and methods of transacting business throughout the East. Whole new fields lay open to Greek merchants, and they eagerly took advantage of the new opportunities. Commerce itself was a leading area where Greeks and Easterners met on grounds of common interest. In bazaars, ports, and trading centers Greeks learned of Eastern customs and traditions, while spreading knowledge of their own culture.

The Seleucid and Ptolemaic dynasties traded as far afield as India, Arabia, and Africa. Overland trade with India and Arabia was conducted by caravan and was largely in the hands of Easterners. The caravan trade never dealt in bulk items or essential commodities, for only luxury goods could be transported in this very expensive fashion. Once the goods reached the Hellenistic monarchies, Greek merchants took a hand in the trade.

In the early Hellenistic period the Seleucids and Ptolemies ensured that the caravan trade proceeded efficiently. Later in the period — a time of increased war and confusion — they left the caravans unprotected. Taking advantage of this situation, Palmyra in the Syrian desert and Nabataean Petra in Arabia arose as caravan states. Such states protected the caravans from bandits and marauders, and served as dispersal areas of caravan goods.

The Ptolemies discovered how to use monsoon winds to establish direct contact with India. One hardy merchant has left a firsthand account of sailing this important maritime link:

Hippalos, the pilot, observing the position of the ports and the conditions of the sea, first discovered how to sail across the ocean. Concerning the winds of the ocean in this region, when with us the Etesian winds begin, in India a wind between southwest and south, named for Hippalos, sets in from the open sea. From then until now some mariners set forth from Kanes and some from the Cape of Spices. Those sailing to Dimurikes [in southern India] throw the bow of the ship farther out to sea. Those bound for Barygaza and the realm of the Sakas [in northern India] hold to the land no more than three days; and if the wind remains favorable, they hold the same course through the outer sea, and they sail along past the previously mentioned gulfs.[4]

Although this sea route never replaced overland caravan traffic, it kept alive direct relations with the East, stimulating the exchange of ideas as well as goods.

More economically important than this exotic trade were commercial dealings in essential commodities like raw materials, grain, and industrial products. The Hellenistic monarchies usually raised enough grain for their own needs as well as a surplus for export. For the cities of Greece and the Aegean this trade in grain was essential, because many of them could not grow enough of their own. Fortunately for them, abundant supplies of wheat were available nearby in Egypt and in the Crimea in southern Russia.

The large-scale wars of the Hellenistic period often interrupted both the production and distribution of grain. This was especially true when the successors of Alexander were trying to carve out their kingdoms. In addi-

tion, natural calamities, such as excessive rain or drought, frequently damaged harvests. Throughout the Hellenistic period famine or severe food shortage remained a grim possibility.

Most trade in bulk commodities was seaborne, and the Hellenistic merchant ship was the workhorse of the day. The merchant ship had a broad beam and relied on sails for propulsion. It was far more seaworthy than the contemporary warship, which was long, narrow, and built for speed. A small crew of experienced sailors could handle it easily. Maritime trade gave rise to other industries and trades: sailors and shipbuilders, dock workers, merchants, accountants, teamsters, and pirates. Piracy was always a factor in the Hellenistic world and remained so until Rome extended its power throughout the East.

The Greek cities paid for their grain by exporting olive oil and wine. When agriculture and oil production developed in Syria, Greek products began to encounter competition from the Seleucid monarchy. Later in the Hellenistic period Greek oil and wine found a lucrative market in Italy. Another significant commodity was fish, which for export was either salted, pickled, or dried. This trade was doubly important because fish provided poor people with an essential element of their diet. Salt too was often imported, and there was some very slight trade in salted meat, which was a luxury item. Far more important was the trade in honey, dried fruit, nuts, and vegetables. Among raw materials wood ranked high in demand, but there was little trade in manufactured goods.

Slaves were a staple of Hellenistic trade. The wars provided prisoners for the slave market, and to a lesser extent so did kidnapping and capture by pirates. The number of slaves involved cannot be estimated, but there

HARBOR AND WAREHOUSES AT DELOS During the Hellenistic period Delos became a thriving trading center. Shown here is the row of warehouses at water's edge. From Delos cargoes were shipped to virtually every part of the Mediterranean. (Photo: Caroline Buckler)

is no doubt that slavery flourished. Both the old Greek states and the new Hellenistic kingdoms were ready markets for slaves, as was Rome when it emerged triumphant from the Second Punic War (Chapter 5). The war took a huge toll of Italian manpower, and Rome bought slaves in vast numbers to replace them in the fields.

Throughout the Mediterranean world, slaves were almost always in demand. Only the Ptolemies discouraged both the trade and slavery itself, and they did so only for economic reasons. Their system had no room for slaves, who would only have competed with free labor. Otherwise, slave labor was to be found in the cities and temples of the Hellenistic world, in the factories and fields, and in the homes of wealthier people. In Italy and some parts of the East, slaves performed the manual labor for large estates and worked the mines. They were vitally important to the Hellenistic economy.

SCENE FROM DAILY LIFE *Art in the Hellenistic period often pursued two themes: increased realism and scenes from daily life. This statuette illustrates both themes. Either a peasant or a slave, the man carries a wine jar over his left shoulder and in his right hand a bag, perhaps his lunch. On his back is a basket. He is so heavily loaded that he is walking with difficulty. (Reproduced by Courtesy of the Trustees of the British Museum)*

Although demand for goods increased during the Hellenistic period, no new techniques of production appear to have developed. The discoveries of Hellenistic mathematicians and thinkers failed to produce any significant corresponding technological development. Manual labor, not machinery, continued to turn out the raw materials and few manufactured goods the Hellenistic world used. Human labor was so cheap and so abundant that kings had no incentive to encourage the invention and manufacture of laborsaving machinery.

Perhaps only one noteworthy technological innovation dates to the Hellenistic period — the introduction of the Archimedean screw for pumping water out of mines. At Thoricus in Attica miners dug ore by hand and hauled it from the mines for processing. This was grueling work, and invariably miners were slaves, criminals, or forced laborers. The conditions under which they worked were frightful. At Laurium, which provided silver ore for the processing plant at Thoricus, one can still crawl into the labyrinthine shafts. They are narrow and have very low ceilings. The miners dug out the ore on their hands and knees; never did they have a chance to stand upright. Once a miner passed the entrance of the mine and crawled inside, his only light came from the oil lamp that he carried. Ventilation was poor, and the air must have been foul and stifling.

The Ptolemies ran their gold mines along the same harsh lines. One historian gave a grim picture of the miners' lives:

The kings of Egypt condemn [to the mines] those found guilty of wrong-doing and those taken prisoner in war, those who were victims of false accusations and were put into jail because of royal anger. . . . The condemned — and they are very many — all of them are put in chains, and they work persistently and continually, both by day and throughout the night, getting no rest, and carefully cut off from escape.[5]

The Ptolemies even condemned women and children to work in the mines. The strongest men lived and died swinging iron sledgehammers to break up the gold-bearing quartz rock. Others worked underground following the seams of quartz, men who labored with lamps bound to their foreheads and who were whipped by overseers if they slacked off. Once the diggers had cut out blocks of quartz, young boys gathered up the blocks and carried them outside. All of them — men, women, and boys — worked until they died.

Apart from gold and silver, which were used primarily for coins and jewelry, iron was the most important metal, and saw the most varied use. Even so, the method of its production never became very sophisticated. The Hellenistic Greeks did manage to produce a low-grade steel by adding carbon to iron.

Pottery remained an important commodity, and most of it was made locally. The pottery used in the kitchen, the coarse ware, did not change at all. Indeed, it is impossible to tell whether specimens of this type of pottery are Hellenic or Hellenistic. Fancier pots and bowls, decorated with a shiny black glaze, came into use during the Hellenistic period. This ware originated in Athens, but potters in other places began to imitate its style, heavily cutting into the Athenian market. In the second century B.C., a red-glazed ware, often called Samian, burst upon the market and soon dominated it. Athens still held its own, however, in the production of fine pottery. Despite the change in pottery styles, the method of production of all pottery, whether plain or fine, remained essentially unchanged.

Although new techniques of production and wider use of machinery in industry did not occur, the volume of goods produced increased in the Hellenistic period. Such goods were mostly made locally. Small manufacturing establishments existed in nearly all parts of the Hellenistic world.

AGRICULTURE

Hellenistic kings paid special attention to agriculture. Much of their revenue was derived from it: from the produce of royal lands, rents paid by the tenants of royal land, and taxation of agricultural land. Some Hellenistic kings even sought out and supported agricultural experts. The Ptolemies, for instance, sponsored experiments on seed grain, selecting seeds that seemed hardy and productive and trying to improve their characteristics. Hellenistic authors wrote handbooks that discussed how farms and large estates could be most profitably run. These handbooks described soil types, covered the proper times for planting and reaping, and discussed care of farm animals. Whether these efforts had any impact on the average farmer is difficult to determine.

The Ptolemies made the greatest strides in agriculture, but their success was largely political. Egypt had a strong tradition of central authority dating back to the pharaohs, which the Ptolemies inherited and tightened. They could decree what crops Egyptian farmers would plant and what animals would be raised, and they had the power to carry out their commands. The Ptolemies recognized the need for well-planned and constant irrigation, and much native labor went into the digging and maintenance of canals and ditches. The Ptolemies also reclaimed a great deal of land from the desert, including the Fayum, a dried lake bed.

The centralized authority of the Ptolemies

explains how agricultural advances occurred at the local level in Egypt. But such progress was not possible in any other Hellenistic monarchy. Despite royal interest in agriculture and a more studied approach to it in the Hellenistic period, there is no evidence that agricultural productivity increased. Whether Hellenistic agricultural methods had any influence on Eastern practices is unknown.

RELIGION IN THE HELLENISTIC WORLD

In religion Hellenism gave Easterners far less than the East gave the Greeks. At first the Hellenistic period saw the spread of Greek religious cults throughout the East. When Hellenistic kings founded cities, they also built temples and established new cults and priesthoods for the old Olympian gods. The new cults enjoyed the prestige of being the religion of the conquerors, and they were supported by public money.

The most attractive aspects of the Greek cults were their rituals and festivities. Greek cults sponsored literary, musical, and athletic contests, which were staged in beautiful surroundings among impressive Greek buildings. In short, the cults offered bright and lively entertainment, both intellectual and physical. They fostered Greek culture and traditional sports, and thus were a splendid means of displaying Greek civilization in the East.

Despite various advantages, Greek cults suffered from some severe shortcomings. They were primarily concerned with ritual. Participation in the civic cults did not even involve belief. Greeks and others could observe the rituals without believing in the existence of the deities being worshiped. Nor did civic cults impose an ethical code of conduct. Greeks did not have to follow any particular

rule of life, practice certain virtues, or even live decent lives in order to participate in the cults. On the whole, the civic cults neither appealed to religious emotions nor embraced matters such as sin and redemption. Greek mystery religions helped fill this gap, but the centers of these religions were in old Greece. Although the new civic cults were lavish in pomp and display, they could not satisfy deep religious feelings or spiritual yearnings.

Even though the Greeks participated in the new cults for cultural reasons, they felt little genuine religious attachment to them. In comparison to the emotional and sometimes passionate religions of the East, the Greek cults seemed sterile. Greeks increasingly sought solace from other sources. Educated and thoughtful people turned to philosophy as a guide to life, while others turned to superstition, magic, or astrology. Still others might shrug and speak of *Tyche,* which meant Fate or Chance.

In view of the spiritual decline of Greek religion, it is surprising that Eastern religions did not make more immediate headway among the Greeks, but at first they did not. Although Hellenistic Greeks clung to their own cults as expressions of their Greekness rather than for any ethical principles, they did not rush to embrace native religions. Only in the second century B.C., after a century of exposure to Eastern religions, did Greeks begin to adopt them.

Nor did Hellenistic kings make any effort to spread Greek religion among their Eastern subjects. The Greeks always considered religion a matter best left to the individual. Greek cults were attractive only to those socially aspiring Easterners who adopted Greek culture for personal advancement. Otherwise, Easterners were little affected by Greek religion. Nor did native religions suffer from the arrival of the Greeks. Some Hellenistic kings limited the power of native priesthoods, but

RELIGIOUS SYNCRETISM This relief was found at the Greek outpost of Dura-Europus, located on the Euphrates. In the center sits Zeus Olympius-Baalshamin, a combination of a Greek and a Semitic god. The eastern priest at the left is burning incense on an altar, while the figure on the right in Macedonian dress crowns the god. Both the religious sentiments and the style of art show the meeting of East and West. (Yale University Art Gallery, Dura-Europos Collection)

they also subsidized some Eastern cults with public money. Alexander the Great actually reinstated several Eastern cults that the Persians had suppressed.

The only significant junction of Greek and Eastern religious traditions was the growth and spread of new mystery religions, so called because they featured a body of ritual not to be divulged to anyone not initiated into the cult. The new mystery cults incorporated aspects of both Greek and Eastern religions, and had broad appeal for both Greeks and Easterners who yearned for personal immortality. Since the Greeks were already familiar with old mystery cults, such as the Eleusinian mys-

teries in Attica, the new cults did not strike them as alien or barbarian. Familiar too was the concept of preparation for an initiation. Devotees of the Eleusinian mysteries and other such cults had to prepare themselves mentally and physically before entering the presence of the gods. Thus the new mystery cults fit well with traditional Greek usage.

The new religions enjoyed one tremendous advantage over the old Greek mystery cults. Whereas old Greek mysteries were tied to particular places, such as Eleusis, the new religions spread throughout the Hellenistic world. People did not have to undertake long and expensive pilgrimages just to become members of the religion. In that sense, the new mystery religions came to the people, for temples of the new deities sprang up wherever Greeks lived.

The mystery religions all claimed to save their adherents from the worst that Tyche could do, and they promised life for the soul after death. They all had a single concept in common: the belief that by the rites of initiation the devotees became united with the god, who had himself died and risen from the dead. The sacrifice of the god and his victory over death saved the devotee from eternal death. Similarly, all mystery religions demanded a period of preparation in which the convert strove to become holy — that is, to live by the precepts taught by the religion. Once aspirants had prepared themselves, they went through an initiation in which they learned the secrets of the religion. The initiation was usually a ritual of great emotional intensity, a baptism into a new life.

The Eastern mystery religions that took the Hellenistic world by storm were the Egyptian cults of Serapis and Isis. Serapis, who was invented by King Ptolemy, combined elements of the Egyptian god Osiris with aspects of the Greek gods Zeus, Pluto the prince of the underworld, and Asclepius. Serapis was believed to be the judge of souls, who rewarded virtuous and righteous people with eternal life. Like Asclepius he was a god of healing. Serapis became an international god, and many Hellenistic Greeks thought of him as Zeus. Associated with Isis and Serapis was Anubis, the old Egyptian god who, like Charon in the Greek pantheon, guided the souls of initiates to the realm of eternal life.

The cult of Isis enjoyed even wider appeal than that of Serapis. Isis, the wife of Osiris, claimed to have conquered Tyche, and promised to save any mortal who came to her. She became the most important goddess of the

STATUE OF ISIS *Though originally Egyptian, Isis became a Greek goddess during the Hellenistic period. Her cult spread throughout the Hellenistic world, and she became identified with many purely Greek goddesses. Still popular in the Roman period, her cult profoundly influenced the Christian cult of Mary, the mother of Jesus. (Museo Nazionale, Naples)*

Hellenistic world, and her worship was very popular among women. Her priests claimed that she bestowed upon humanity the gift of civilization and that she founded law and literature. She was the goddess of marriage, conception, and childbirth, and like Serapis a deity who promised to save the souls of her believers.

There was neither conflict between Greek and Eastern religions nor wholesale acceptance of one or the other. Nonetheless, the Hellenistic world was slowly moving toward belief in a single god who ruled over all people. Greeks and Easterners noticed similarities among one another's deities and assumed that they were worshiping the same gods in different garb. These tendencies toward religious universalism and the desire for personal immortality would prove significant when the Hellenistic world came under the sway of Rome, for Hellenistic developments paved the way for the spread of Christianity.

PHILOSOPHY AND THE COMMON MAN

Philosophy during the Hellenic period was the exclusive province of the wealthy, for only they had leisure enough to pursue philosophical studies. During the Hellenistic period, however, philosophy reached out to touch the lives of more men and women than ever before. The reasons for this development were several. Since the ideal of the polis had declined, politics no longer offered people an intellectual outlet. Moreover, much of Hellenistic life, especially in the new cities of the East, seemed unstable and without venerable traditions. Greeks were far more mobile than they had ever been before, but their very mobility left them feeling uprooted. Many people

in search of something permanent, something unchanging in a changing world, turned to philosophy. Another reason for the increased influence of philosophy was the decline of traditional religion and a growing belief in Tyche. Tyche was more than Fate – it was Chance and Doom, capricious and sometimes malevolent. To protect against the worst that Tyche could do, many Greeks looked to philosophy.

Philosophers themselves became much more numerous, and several new schools of philosophical thought emerged. The Cynics preached the joy of a simple life. The Epicureans taught that pleasure is the chief good. The Stoics emphasized the importance of deeds well done. There was a good deal of rivalry as philosophers tried to demonstrate the superiority of their views, but in spite of their differences the major branches of philosophy agreed on the necessity of making people self-sufficient. They all recognized the need to equip men and women to deal successfully with Tyche. The major schools of Hellenistic philosophy all taught that people could be truly happy only when they had turned their backs on the world around them and focused full attention on one enduring thing. They differed chiefly on what that enduring thing was.

CYNICS

Undoubtedly the most unusual of the new philosophers were the Cynics, who urged a return to nature. They advised men and women to discard traditional customs and conventions (which were in decline anyway) and to live simply. The Cynics believed that by rejecting material things people become free, and that nature will provide all necessities.

The founder of the Cynics was Antisthenes

(b. ca 440 B.C.), but it was Diogenes of Sinope (ca 412–323 B.C.), one of the most colorful men of the period, who spread the philosophy. Diogenes came to Athens to study philosophy and soon evolved his own ideas on the ideal life. He hit upon the solution that happiness was possible only by living according to nature and forgoing luxuries. He attacked social conventions because he considered them contrary to nature. Throughout Greece he gained fame for the rigorous way in which he put his beliefs into practice.

Diogenes' disdain for luxury and social pretense also became legendary. Once when he was living at Corinth, he was supposedly visited by Alexander the Great: "While Diogenes was sunning himself . . . Alexander stood over him and said: 'Ask me whatever gift you like.' In answer Diogenes said to him: 'Get out of my sunlight.' "⁶ The story underlines the essence of Diogenes' teachings: even a great, powerful, and wealthy conqueror like Alexander could give people nothing of any real value. Nature had already provided people with everything essential.

Diogenes did not establish a philosophical school in the manner of Plato and Aristotle. Instead, he and his followers took their teaching to the streets and marketplaces. They more than any other philosophical group tried to reach the common man. As part of their return to nature they often did without warm clothing, sufficient food, or adequate housing, which they considered unnecessary. The Cynics also tried to break down political barriers by declaring that people owed no allegiance to any city or monarchy. Rather, they said, all people are cosmopolitan – that is, citizens of the world. The Cynics reached across political boundaries to create a community of people, all sharing their humanity and living as close to nature as humanly possible. The Cynics set a striking example of

how people could turn away from materialism. Although comparatively few men and women could follow such rigorous precepts, the Cynics influenced all the other major schools of philosophy.

EPICUREANS

Epicurus (340–270 B.C.), who founded his own school of philosophy at Athens, based his view of life on scientific theories. Accepting Democritus' theory that the universe is composed of indestructible particles, Epicurus put forth a naturalistic theory of the universe. Although he did not deny the existence of the gods, he taught that they had no effect on human life. The essence of Epicurus' belief was that the principal good of human life is pleasure, which he defined as the absence of pain. He was not advocating drunken revels or sensual dissipation, which he thought actually caused pain. Instead, Epicurus concluded that any violent emotion is undesirable. Drawing on the teachings of the Cynics, he advocated mild self-discipline. Even poverty he considered good, as long as people have enough food, clothing, and shelter. Epicurus also taught that individuals can most easily attain peace and serenity by ignoring the outside world and looking into their personal feelings and reactions. Thus Epicureanism led to quietism.

Epicureanism taught its followers to ignore politics and the issues of the day, for politics led to tumult, which would disturb the soul. Although the Epicureans thought that the state originated through a social contract among individuals, they did not care about the political structure of the state. They were content to live in a democracy, oligarchy, monarchy, or whatever, and they never speculated about the ideal state. Their very ideals stood outside all political forms.

Opposed to the passivity of the Epicureans, Zeno (335–262 B.C.), a Hellenized Phoenician, put forth a different concept of human beings and the universe. When Zeno first came to Athens, he listened avidly to the Cynics. Concluding, however, that the Cynics were extreme, he stayed in Athens to form his own school, the Stoa, named after the building where he preferred to teach.

Stoicism became the most popular philosophy of the Hellenistic world, and the one that later captured the mind of Rome. Zeno and his followers considered nature an expression of divine will, and in their view people could be happy only when they lived in accordance with nature. They stressed the unity of man and the universe, stating that all men were brothers and obliged to help one another. Stoicism's science was derived from Heraclitus, but its broad and warm humanity was the work of Zeno and his followers.

Unlike the Epicureans, the Stoics taught that people should participate in politics and worldly affairs. Yet this idea never led to the belief that individuals ought to try to change the order of things. Time and again the Stoics used the image of an actor in a play: the Stoic plays an assigned part and never tries to change the play. To the Stoics the important question was not whether they achieved anything, but whether they lived virtuous lives. In that way they could triumph over Tyche: for Tyche could destroy achievements but not the goodness and nobility of their lives.

Even though the Stoics evolved the concept of a world order, they thought of it strictly in terms of the individual. Like the Epicureans, they were indifferent to specific political forms. They believed that people should do their duty to the state in which they found themselves. The universal state they preached about was ethical, not political. The most significant practical achievement of the Stoics was the creation of the concept of natural law. The Stoics concluded that since all men were brothers, since all men partook of divine reason, and since all good men were in harmony with the universe, one law – a part of the natural order of life – governed them all.

The Stoic concept of a universal state governed by natural law is one of the finest heirlooms the Hellenistic world passed on to Rome. The Stoic concept of natural law, of one law for all people, became a valuable tool when the Romans began to deal with many different peoples with different laws. The ideal of the universal state gave the Romans a rationale for extending their empire to the farthest reaches of the world. The duty of individuals to their fellows served the citizens of the Roman Empire as the philosophical justification for doing their duty. In this respect, too, the real fruit of Hellenism was to ripen only under the cultivation of Rome.

HELLENISTIC WOMEN

With the growth of monarchy in the Hellenistic period came a major new development: the importance of royal women, many of whom played an active part in political and diplomatic life. In the Hellenic period the polis had replaced kingship, except at Sparta, and queens were virtually unknown, apart from myth and legend. Even in Sparta queens did not participate in politics. Hellenistic queens, however, did exercise political power, either in their own right or by manipulating their husbands. Many Hellenistic queens were depicted as willful or ruthless, especially in power struggles over the throne, and in some cases those charges are accurate. Other Hel-

STATUE OF A PRIESTESS   Women in the Hellenistic period continued to play an important part in society and religion by serving as priestesses. Here the young priestess holds a tray, on which she carries the cult objects used in the god's ritual. (Museo Nazionale Romano)

lenistic royal women, however, set an example of courage and nobility. This is especially true of Cratesiclea, mother of the king Cleomenes.

In 224 B.C., Cleomenes was trying to rebuild Sparta as a major power, but he needed money. King Ptolemy of Egypt promised to help the Spartans because doing so would further his own diplomatic ends. In return for his support Ptolemy demanded that Cleomenes give him his mother, Cratesiclea, as a hostage. Ptolemy's demand was an insult and a grave dishonor to the Spartan lady, yet Cleomenes' plans could not succeed without Ptolemy's money. Reluctant to agree to Ptolemy's terms, Cleomenes was also reluctant to mention the matter to his mother. Plutarch related her reaction:

Finally, when Cleomenes worked up his courage to speak about the matter, Cratesiclea laughed aloud and said: "Is this what you often started to say but flinched from? Rather put me aboard a ship and send me away, wherever you think this body of mine will be most useful to Sparta, before sitting here it is destroyed by old age."[7]

Cratesiclea's selflessness and love of her state became legendary. Other Hellenistic queens and women of royal blood demonstrated the same qualities of self-sacrifice and devotion to duty.

The example of the queens had a profound effect on Hellenistic attitudes toward women in general. In fact, the Hellenistic period saw a great expansion in social and economic opportunities for women. More women than ever before received educations that enabled them to enter the professions and medicine. As the American scholar Sarah Pomeroy has observed: "The serious pursuit of intellectual, artistic, or scientific goals, as an addition, or as a prelude, or even as an alternative to marriage, was a new phenomenon for Greek women."[8] Literacy among women increased dramatically, and their options expanded accordingly. Some won fame as poets, while others studied with philosophers and contributed to the intellectual life of the age. As a rule, however, these developments touched only wealthier women. Poor women, and probably the majority of women, were barely literate, if literate at all.

Women began to participate in politics on at least a limited basis. Often they served as priestesses, as they had in the Hellenic period, but they also began to serve in civil capacities. For their services to the state they received public acknowledgment. Women sometimes received honorary citizenship from foreign cities because of aid given in times of crisis. Few women achieved these honors, however, and those who did were from the upper classes.

This major development was not due to male enlightenment. Although Hellenistic philosophy addressed itself to many new questions, the position of women was not one of them. The Stoics, in spite of their theory of the brotherhood of man, thought of women as men's inferiors. Only the Cynics, who waged war on all accepted customs, treated women as men's equals. The Cynics were interested in women as individuals, not as members of a family or as citizens of the state. Their view did not make much headway. Like other aspects of Cynic philosophy, this attitude was more admired than followed.

The new prominence of women was largely due instead to their increased participation in economic affairs. During the Hellenistic period some women took part in commercial transactions. Nonetheless, they still lived under legal handicaps. In Egypt, for example, a Greek woman needed a male guardian to buy, sell, or lease land, to borrow money, and to represent her in other transactions. Yet often such a guardian was present only to fulfill the letter of the law. The woman was the real agent, and she handled the business being transacted. In Hellenistic Sparta women accumulated large fortunes and vast amounts of land. As early as the beginning of the Hellenistic period women owned two-fifths of the land of Laconia. Spartan women, however, were exceptional. In most other areas, even women who were very wealthy in their own right were at least formally under the protection of a male relative.

These changes do not amount to a social revolution. Women had begun to participate in business, politics, and legal activities. Yet such women were rare, and they labored under handicaps that men did not have. Even so, it was a start.

HELLENISTIC SCIENCE

The area in which Hellenistic culture achieved its greatest triumphs was science. Here too the ancient Near East made contributions to Greek thought. The patient observations of the Babylonians, who for generations had scanned the skies, had provided the raw materials for Thales' speculations, which were the foundation of Hellenistic astronomy. The most notable of the Hellenistic astronomers was Aristarchus of Samos (ca. 310–230 B.C.), who was educated in Aristotle's school. Aristarchus concluded that the sun is far larger than the earth and that the stars are enormously distant from the earth. He argued against Aristotle's view that the earth is the center of the universe. Instead, Aristarchus propounded the heliocentric theory – that is, that the earth and the planets revolve around the sun. His work is all the more impressive because he lacked even a rudimentary telescope. Aristarchus had only the human eye and the human brain, but they were more than enough.

Unfortunately, Aristarchus' theories did not persuade the ancient world. In the second century A.D., Claudius Ptolemy, a mathematician and astronomer in Alexandria, accepted Aristotle's theory of the earth as the center of the universe, and their view prevailed for 1400 years. Aristarchus' heliocentric theory lay dormant until resurrected by the brilliant Polish astronomer Nicolaus Copernicus (1473–1543).

In geometry Hellenistic thinkers discovered little that was new, but Euclid (ca 300 B.C.), a mathematician who lived in Alexandria, compiled a valuable textbook of existing knowledge. His book, *The Elements of Geometry,* has exerted immense influence on Western civilization, for it rapidly became the standard introduction to geometry. Generations of students, from the Hellenistic period to the present day, have learned the essentials of geometry from it.

The greatest thinker of the Hellenistic period was Archimedes (ca 287–212 B.C.), who was a clever inventor as well. He lived in Syracuse in Sicily and watched Rome emerge as a power in the Mediterranean. When the Romans laid siege to Syracuse in the Second Punic War (see Chapter 5), Archimedes invented a number of machines to thwart the Roman army. His catapults threw rocks large enough to sink ships and disrupt battle lines. His grappling devices lifted warships out of the water. The Romans developed a healthy respect for Archimedes, as Plutarch reports: "At last the Romans were so terrified . . . that if a small piece of rope or a small timber was seen protruding from the walls, they bellowed

'There's the thing; Archimedes is unleashing some machine against us,' and turned around and fled."[9]

In the Hellenistic period the practical applications of the principles of mechanics were primarily military, for the building of artillery and siege engines. Archimedes built such machines out of necessity, but they were of little real interest to him. In a more peaceful vein, he invented the Archimedean screw, a device used to pump water into irrigation ditches and out of mines. He also invented the compound pulley. Plutarch described Archimedes' dramatic demonstration of how easily it could move huge weights with little effort:

A three-masted merchant ship of the royal fleet had been hauled on land by hard work and many hands. Archimedes put aboard her many men and the usual freight. He sat far away from her; without haste, but gently working a compound pulley with his hand, he drew her towards him smoothly and without faltering, just as though she were running on the surface of the sea.[10]

Archimedes was far more interested in pure mathematics than in practical inventions. His mathematical research, which covered many fields, was his greatest contribution to Western thought. In his book *On Plane Equilibriums* Archimedes dealt for the first time with the basic principles of mechanics, including the principle of the lever. He once said that if he were given a lever and a suitable place to stand, he could move the world. In his treatise *Sand-Counter* Archimedes devised a system to express large numbers, a difficult matter considering the deficiencies of Greek numerical notation. *Sand-Counter* also discussed the heliocentric theory of Aristarchus. With his treatise *On Floating Bodies* Archimedes founded the science of hydrostatics. He concluded that whenever a solid floats in a liquid, the weight of the solid is equal to the volume of liquid displaced. The way in which he made his discovery has become famous:

When he was devoting his attention to this problem, he happened to go to a public bath. When he climbed down into the bathtub there, he noticed that water in the tub equal to the bulk of his body flowed out. Thus, when he observed this method of solving the problem, he did not wait. Instead, moved with joy, he sprang out of the tub, and rushing home naked he kept indicating in a loud voice that he had indeed discovered what he was seeking. For while running he was shouting repeatedly in Greek, "eureka, eureka" ("I have found it, I have found it").[11]

Archimedes' other works include *On the Measurement of a Circle, On the Sphere and Cylinder, On Conoids and Spheroids,* and *On Spirals.*

Archimedes was willing to share his work, and one of those with whom he communicated was Eratosthenes (285–ca 204 B.C.), a man of almost universal interests. From his native Cyrene in North Africa, Eratosthenes traveled to Athens, where he studied philosophy and learned mathematics. He refused to join any of the philosophical schools, for he was interested in too many things to follow any particular dogma. Hence, his thought was eclectic: he took his doctrines from many schools of thought. For instance, in philosophy Eratosthenes was influenced by Zeno, but Stoicism could not satisfy his mathematical and geographical interests. Besides his scientific work, he devoted time to poetry, in which he showed genuine talent, and he wrote a book on Attic comedy.

Around 245 B.C., King Ptolemy invited Eratosthenes to Alexandria. The Ptolemies had done much to make Alexandria an intellectual, cultural, and scientific center. They had established a lavish library and museum, undoubtedly the greatest seat of learning in the Hellenistic world. At the crown's expense, the Ptolemies maintained a number of distinguished scholars and poets. Eratosthenes came to Alexandria to become the librarian of the royal library, a position of great prestige. While there he continued his mathematical work and by letter struck up a friendship with Archimedes. Eratosthenes solved the problem of how to double a cube, built a machine to illustrate his proof, and in a short poem dedicated his work to King Ptolemy.

Unlike his friend Archimedes, Eratosthenes did not devote his life entirely to mathematics, although he never lost interest in it. He used his mathematics to further the geographical studies for which he is most famous. He calculated the circumference of the earth geometrically, estimating it as about 24,675 miles. He was not wrong by much: the earth is actually 24,860 miles in circumference. Of this achievement Carl Sagan, the noted contemporary astronomer, has said:

Eratosthenes' only tools were sticks, eyes, feet, and brains, plus a taste for experiment. With them he deduced the circumference of the earth with an error of only a few percent, a remarkable achievement for 2,200 years ago. He was the first person accurately to measure the size of a planet.[12]

Eratosthenes also concluded that the earth is a spherical globe, that the landmass is roughly foursided, and that the land is surrounded by ocean. He discussed the shapes and sizes of land and ocean and the irregularities of the earth's surface. He drew a map of the earth and used his own system of explaining the divisions of the earth's landmass.

Using geographical information gained by Alexander the Great's scientists, Eratosthenes tried to fit the East into Greek geographical knowledge. Although for some reason he ignored the western Mediterranean and Europe, he declared that a ship could sail from Spain either around Africa to India or directly westward to India. Not until the great days of Western exploration did sailors such as Vasco da Gama and Magellan actually prove Eratosthenes' theories. Greek geographers like Eratosthenes also turned their attention southward to Africa. During this period the people of the Mediterranean learned of the climate and customs of Ethiopia, and gleaned some scant information about equatorial Africa.

In his life and work Eratosthenes exemplifies the range and vitality of Hellenistic science. His interests were varied and included the cultural and humanistic as well as the purely scientific. Although his chief interest was in the realm of speculative thought, he did not ignore the practical. He was quite willing to deal with old problems and to break new ground.

In the Hellenistic period the scientific study of botany had its origin. Aristotle's pupil Theophrastus (ca 372–288 B.C.), who became head of the Lyceum, the school established by Aristotle, studied the botanical information made available by Alexander's penetration of the East. Aristotle had devoted a good deal of his attention to zoology, and Theophrastus extended his work to plants. He wrote two books on the subject, *History of Plants* and *Causes of Plants*. He carefully observed phenomena and based his conclusions on what he had actually seen. Theophrastus classified plants and accurately described their parts. He detected the process of germination and realized the importance of climate and soil to plants. Some of Theophrastus' work found its way into agricultural handbooks, but for the most part Hellenistic science did not carry the study of botany any further.

HELLENISTIC MEDICINE

The study of medicine flourished during the Hellenistic period, and Hellenistic physicians carried the work of Hippocrates into new areas. Herophilus, who lived in the first half of the third century B.C., worked at Alexandria and studied the writings of Hippocrates. He accepted Hippocrates' theory of the four humors, and approached the study of medicine in a systematic, scientific fashion. He dissected dead bodies and measured what he observed. He discovered the nervous system and concluded that two types of nerves, motor and sensory, exist. Herophilus also studied the brain, which he considered the center of intelligence, and discerned the cerebrum and cerebellum. His other work dealt with the liver, lungs, and uterus. His younger contemporary, Erasistratus, also conducted research on the brain and the nervous system, and he improved on Herophilus' work. He too followed in the tradition of Hippocrates and preferred to let the body heal itself by means of diet and air.

Both Herophilus and Erasistratus were members of the Dogmatic school of medicine at Alexandria. In this school speculation played an important part in research. So too did the study of anatomy. To learn more about human anatomy Herophilus and Erasistratus dissected corpses and even vivisected criminals whom King Ptolemy contributed for the purpose. Vivisection – cutting into the body of a living animal or person – was seen as a necessary cruelty: the Dogmatists argued that the knowledge gained from the suffering of a few evil men benefited many others. Nonetheless, the practice of vivisection seems to have been short-lived, although dissection continued. Better knowledge of anatomy led to improvements in surgery. These advances enabled the Dogmatists to invent new surgical instruments and new techniques.

In about 280 B.C., Philinus and Serapion, two pupils of Herophilus, led a reaction to the Dogmatists. Believing that the Dogmatists had become too speculative, they founded the Empiric school of medicine at Alexandria. Claiming that the Dogmatists' emphasis on anatomy and physiology was misplaced, they concentrated instead on the observation and cure of illnesses. They also laid heavier stress on the use of drugs and medicine to treat illnesses. Heraclides of Tarentum (perhaps first century B.C.) carried on the Empirical tradition and dedicated himself to observation and use of medicines. He discovered the benefits of opium and worked with other drugs that relieved pain. He also steadfastly rejected magic and sorcery as pertinent to the application of drugs and medicines.

Hellenistic medicine had its dark side, for many physicians were moneygrubbers, fools, and quacks. One of the angriest complaints comes from the days of the Roman Empire:

Of all men only a physician can kill a man with total impunity. Oh no, on the contrary, censure goes to him who dies and he is guilty of excess, and furthermore he is blamed. . . . Let me not accuse their [physicians'] avarice, their greedy deals with those whose fate hangs in the balance, their setting a price on pain, and their demands for down payment in case of death, and their secret doctrines.[13]

Abuses such as these existed already in the Hellenistic period. As is true today, many Hellenistic physicians did not take the Hippocratic oath very seriously.

Besides incompetent and greedy physicians, the Hellenistic world was plagued by people who claimed to cure illnesses through incantations and magic. Their potions included such concoctions as blood from the ear of an ass mixed with water to cure fever, or the liver of a cat, killed when the moon was waning, and preserved in salt. Broken bones could be cured by applying the ashes of a pig's jawbone to the break. The dung of a goat mixed with old wine was good for healing broken ribs. One charlatan claimed that he could cure epilepsy by making the patient drink, from the skull of a man who had been killed but not cremated, water drawn from a spring at night. These quacks even claimed that they could cure mental illness with their remedies. The treatment for a person suffering from melancholy was calf dung boiled in wine. No doubt the patient became too sick to be depressed.

Quacks who prescribed such treatments were very popular, but they did untold harm to the sick and injured. They and the greedy physicians also damaged the reputation of dedicated doctors who honestly and intelligently tried to heal and alleviate pain. The medical abuses that arose in the Hellenistic period were so flagrant that the Romans who later entered the Hellenistic world developed an intense dislike and distrust of physicians. The Romans considered the study of Hellenistic medicine beneath the dignity of a Roman, and even as late as the Roman Empire few Romans undertook the study of Greek medicine. Nonetheless, the work of men like Herophilus and Serapion made valuable contributions to the knowledge of medicine, and the fruits of their work were preserved and handed on to the West.

———◆———

The Hellenistic period fostered the spread of Hellenism throughout the East, disseminating the knowledge, customs, and laws of the Greeks and bringing East and West into intimate contact. Though often called degenerate and stagnant, the Hellenistic period could boast of numerous advances, especially in the sciences and medicine. Hellenistic thinkers created a golden age of scientific discovery and speculation, while Hellenistic philosophy reached out to touch the lives of rich and poor, princes and peasants.

The Hellenistic period also prepared the way for Rome. Although the Hellenistic monarchies, like the Greek city-states, fought to a standstill and seriously weakened each other, they made something new of the East. Greek and Easterner alike changed the East, and into this world Rome moved. Rome brought political stability and Roman law, but in doing so it built upon the society and culture created by Hellenistic men and women.

NOTES

1. Diodorus 17.1.4.

2. Plutarch *Moralia* 328E.

3. Quoted in W. W. Tarn and G. T. Griffith, *Hellenistic Civilisation,* Meridian Books, Cleveland and New York, 1961, p. 199.

4. *Periplous of the Erythraian Sea* 57.

5. Diodorus 3.12.2–3.

6. Diogenes Laertius 6.38.

7. Plutarch *Lives of Agis and Cleomenes* 22.5.

8. S. B. Pomeroy, "Technikai kai Mousikai," *American Journal of Ancient History* 2 (1977): 51.

9. Plutarch *Life of Marcellus* 17.4.

10. Ibid., 14.13.

11. Vitruvius *On Architecture* 9 Preface, 10.

12. Carl Sagan, "The Measure of Eratosthenes," *Harvard Magazine* 83 (1980): 10.

13. Pliny the Elder *Natural History* 29.8.18, 21.

SUGGESTED READING

General treatments of Hellenistic political, social, and economic history can be found in S. A. Cook, et al., *The Cambridge Ancient History,* vol. 7 (1928), and in the shorter and handier works of M. Cary, *A History of the Greek World 323–146 B.C.,* 2nd ed. (1951), and W. W. Tarn and G. T. Griffith, *Hellenistic Civilisation,* 3rd ed. (1951, 1961). M. M. Austin, *The Hellenistic World from Alexander to the Roman Conquest* (1981) is an excellent selection of primary sources in an accurate and readable translation. F. W. Walbank, *The Hellenistic World* (1981) is a fresh new appraisal by one of the foremost scholars of the period. The undisputed classic in this field is M. Rostovtzeff, *The Social and Economic History of the Hellenistic World,* 3 vols. (1941).

Each year brings a new crop of biographies of Alexander the Great. Still the best, however, is J. R. Hamilton, *Alexander the Great* (1973). Old but still useful is U. Wilcken, *Alexander the Great* (English translation, 1967), which has had a considerable impact on scholars and students alike. On the topic of Alexander's place in history, see A. R. Burn, *Alexander the Great and the Hellenistic World* (1947), a lively and sane treatment. Newer is C. B. Welles, *Alexander and the Hellenistic World* (1970). Recent political studies of the Hellenistic period include G. J. D. Aalders, *Political Theory in Hellenistic Times* (1975), and E. V. Hansen, *The Attalids of Pergamon,* 2nd ed. (1971).

On the spread of Hellenism throughout the Near East, see F. E. Peters, *The Harvest of Hellenism* (1970), and most recently, A. Momigliano, *Alien Wisdom: The Limits of Hellenization* (1975).

A. H. M. Jones, *The Greek City from Alexander to Justinian* (1940), deals with urban life during the Hellenistic, Roman, and early Byzantine periods. P. M. Fraser, *Ptolemaic Alexandria,* 3 vols. (1972), covers the life, history, and culture of the most flourishing and prominent of the Hellenistic cities. G. Downey, *A History of Antioch in Syria from Seleucus to the Arab Conquest* (1961), gives a good account of a major city in Asia Minor. Hellenistic Athens is described by C. Mossé, *Athens in Decline, 404–86 B.C.* (1973). G. M. Cohen, *The Seleucid Colo-*

nies (1978), treats all aspects of the Seleucid colonizing effort.

Two general studies of religion within the Hellenistic world are F. Grant, *Hellenistic Religion: The Age of Syncretism* (1953), and H. J. Rose, *Religion in Greece and Rome* (1959). For the effects of Hellenistic religious developments on Christianity, see A. D. Nock, *Early Gentile Christianity and Its Hellenistic Background* (1964). V. Tscherikover, *Hellenistic Civilization and the Jews* (1959) treats the impact of Hellenism on Judaism, and R. E. Witt, *Isis in the Graeco-Roman World* (1971), which is illustrated, studies the origins and growth of the Isis cult. The cult of her consort Osiris is the subject of J. G. Griffiths, *The Origins of Osiris and His Cult* (1980).

Hellenistic philosophy and science have attracted the attention of a number of scholars, and the various philosophical schools are especially well covered. A convenient survey of Hellenistic philosophy is A. A. Long, *Hellenistic Philosophy* (1974). F. Sayre, *The Greek Cynics* (1948), focuses on Diogenes' thought and manners, while C. Bailey, *Epicureans* (1926), although dated, is still a useful study of the origins and nature of Epicureanism. Two recent treatments of Stoicism are J. Rist, *Stoic Philosophy* (1969), and F. H. Sandbach, *The Stoics* (1975). A good survey of Hellenistic science is G. E. R. Lloyd, *Greek Science after Aristotle* (1963), and specific studies of major figures can be found in T. L. Heath's solid work, *Aristarchus of Samos* (1920), still unsurpassed, and E. J. Dijksterhuis, *Archimedes* (1956).

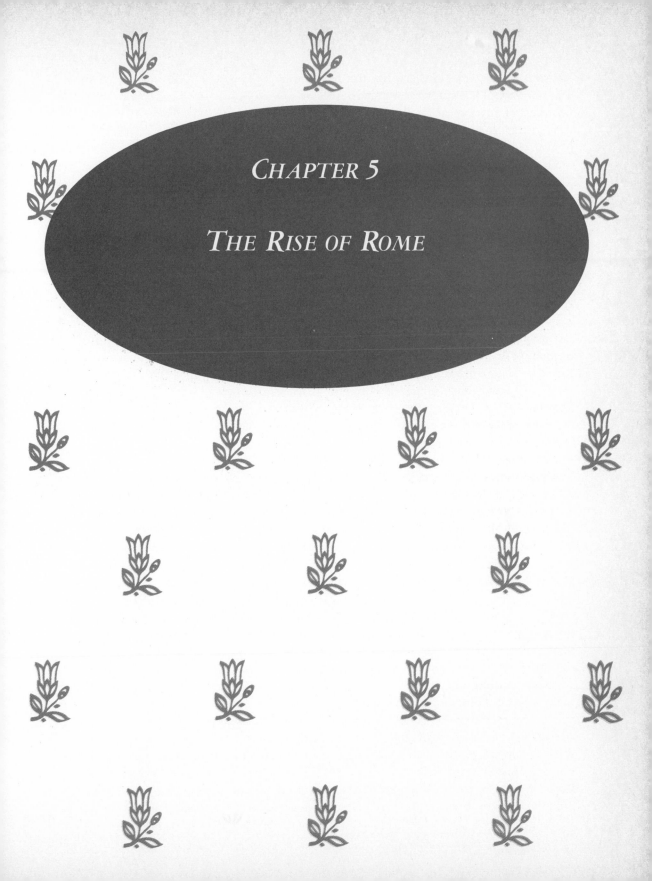

CHAPTER 5

THE RISE OF ROME

"WHO IS SO THOUGHTLESS and lazy that he does not want to know in what way and with what kind of government the Romans in less than 53 years conquered nearly the entire inhabited world and brought it under their rule – an achievement previously unheard of?"[1] This question was first asked by Polybius, a Greek historian who lived in the second century B.C. With keen awareness Polybius realized that the Romans were achieving something unique in world history.

What was that achievement? Was it simply the creation of a huge empire? Hardly. The Persians had done the same thing. For that matter, Alexander the Great had conquered vast territories in a shorter time. Was it the creation of a superior culture? Even the Romans admitted that in matters of art, literature, philosophy, and culture they learned from the Greeks. Rome's achievement lay in the ability of the Romans not only to conquer peoples but to incorporate them into the Roman system. Rome succeeded where the Greek polis had failed. Unlike the Greeks, who refused to share citizenship, the Romans extended their citizenship first to the Italians and later to the peoples of the provinces. With that citizenship went Roman government and Roman law. Rome created a world state that embraced the entire Mediterranean area.

Nor was Rome's achievement limited to the ancient world. Rome's law, language, and administrative practices were a precious heritage to medieval and modern Europe. London, Paris, Vienna, and many other modern European cities began as Roman colonies or military camps. When the Founding Fathers created the American Republic they looked to Rome as a model. On the darker side, Napoleon and Mussolini paid their own tribute to Rome by aping its forms. Whether Founding Father or modern autocrat, they were all ac-

MAP 5.1 ITALY AND THE CITY OF ROME *The geographical configuration of the Italian peninsula shows how Rome stood astride north-south communications and how the state that united Italy stood poised to move into Sicily and northern Africa.*

knowledging their admiration for the Roman achievement.

Roman history is usually divided into two periods: the Republic, the age in which Rome grew from a small city-state to ruler of an empire, and the Empire, the period when the republican constitution gave way to constitutional monarchy. How did Rome rise to greatness? What effects did the conquest of the Mediterranean have on the Romans themselves? Finally, why did the republic collapse? These are the questions this chapter will attempt to answer.

THE LAND AND THE SEA

To the west of Greece the boot-shaped peninsula of Italy, with Sicily at its toe, occupies the center of the Mediterranean basin. As Map 5.1 shows, Italy and Sicily thrust southward toward Africa: the distance between southwestern Sicily and the northern African coast is at one point only about a hundred miles. Italy and Sicily literally divide the Mediterranean into two basins and form the focal point between the halves.

Like Greece and other Mediterranean lands, Italy enjoys a genial, almost subtropical climate. The winters are rainy, but the summer months are dry. Because of the climate the rivers of Italy usually carry little water during the summer, and some go entirely dry. The low water level of the Arno, one of the principal rivers of Italy, once led Mark Twain to describe it as "a great historical creek with four feet in the channel and some scows

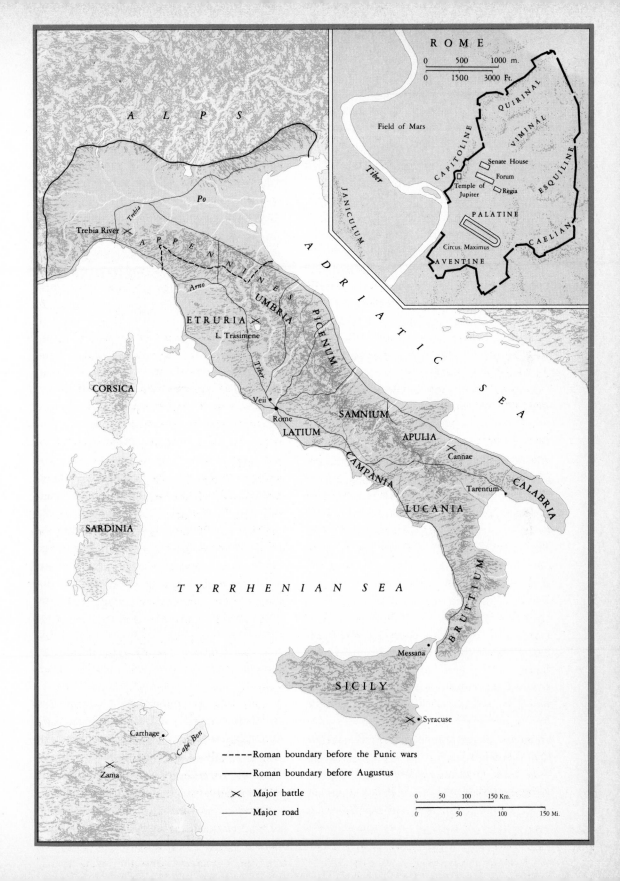

ALPS

Po

Trebia

Trebia River ✕

A
P
P
E
N
N
I
N
E
S

Arno

UMBRIA

ETRURIA

L. Trasimene ✕

Tiber

PICENUM

Veii •

Rome •

LATIUM

SAMNIUM

CAMPANIA

APULIA

Cannae ✕

Tarentum •

LUCANIA

CALABRIA

BRUTTIUM

A D R I A T I C   S E A

CORSICA

SARDINIA

T Y R R H E N I A N   S E A

Messana •

Carthage •

Cape Bon

SICILY

✕ • Syracuse

✕
Zama

ROME

0   500   1000 m.

0   1500   3000 Ft.

Field of Mars

Tiber

JANICULUM

CAPITOLINE

QUIRINAL

VIMINAL

Senate House

Forum

Temple of Jupiter

Regia

ESQUILINE

PALATINE

CAELIAN

Circus Maximus

AVENTINE

- - - - - Roman boundary before the Punic wars

———— Roman boundary before Augustus

✕ Major battle

———— Major road

0   50   100   150 Km.

0   50   100   150 Mi.

floating around. It would be a very plausible river if they would pump some water into it."[2] The Arno at least is navigable. Most of Italy's other rivers are not. Clearly, these small rivers were unsuitable for regular, large-scale shipping. Italian rivers, unlike Twain's beloved Mississippi, never became major thoroughfares for commerce and communications.

Geography discouraged maritime trade as well. Italy lacks the numerous good harbors that are such a prominent feature of the Greek landscape. Only in the south are there good harbors, and Greek colonists had early claimed those ports for themselves. Yet geography gave rise to – and the rivers nourished – a bountiful agriculture that sustained a large population. The strength of Italy lay in the land and its produce.

Geography encouraged Italy to look to the Mediterranean. In the north Italy is protected by the Apennine Mountains, which break off from the Alps and form a natural barrier. The Apennines retarded but did not prevent peoples from penetrating Italy from the north. Throughout history, in modern times as well as ancient, various invaders have entered Italy by this route. From the north the Apennines run southward the entire length of the Italian boot; they virtually cut off access to the Adriatic Sea, which further induced Italy to look west to Spain and Carthage rather than east to Greece. Even though most of the land is mountainous, the hill country is not as inhospitable as are the Greek highlands. In antiquity the general fertility of the soil provided the basis for a large population. Nor did the mountains of Italy so carve up the land as to prevent the development of political unity. Geography proved kinder to Italy than to Greece.

In their southward course the Apennines leave two broad and fertile plains, those of Latium and Campania. These plains attracted settlers and invaders from the time when peoples began to move into Italy. Among these peoples were the Romans, who established their city on the Tiber River in Latium.

This site enjoyed several advantages. The Tiber provided Rome with a constant source of water. Located at an easy crossing-point on the Tiber, Rome thus stood astride the main avenue of communications between northern and southern Italy. The famous seven hills of Rome were defensible and safe from the floods of the Tiber. Rome was in an excellent position to develop the resources of Latium and maintain contact with the rest of Italy.

THE ETRUSCANS AND ROME
(750–509 B.C.)

In recent years archaeologists have found traces of numerous early peoples in Italy. The origins of these cultures and their precise relations with one another are not yet well understood. In fact, no clear account of the prehistory of Italy is yet possible. Of the period before the appearance of the Etruscans (1200–750 B.C.) one fundamental fact is indisputable: peoples speaking Indo-European languages were moving into Italy from the north, probably in small groups. They were part of the awesome but imperfectly understood movement of peoples that spread the Indo-European family of languages from Spain to India.

Only with the coming of the Greeks does Italy enter the light of history. A great wave of Greek immigration swept into southern Italy and Sicily during the eighth century B.C., as was described on pages 81–82. The Greeks brought urban life to these regions, spreading cultural influence far beyond the walls of their city-states.

In the north the Greeks encountered the Etruscans, one of the truly mysterious peoples of antiquity. Who the Etruscans were, where they came from, and what language they spoke are unknown. Nonetheless, this fascinating people was to leave an indelible mark on the Romans. Skillful metal workers, the Etruscans amassed extensive wealth by trading their manufactured goods in Italy and beyond. The strength of their political and military institutions enabled them to form a loosely organized league of cities whose dominion extended as far north as the Po valley and as far south as Latium and Campania (see Map 5.1). In Latium they founded cities and took over control of Rome. Like the Greeks, the Etruscans promoted urban life, and one of the places that benefited from Etruscan influence was Rome.

The Etruscans found the Romans settled on three of Rome's seven hills. The site of the future Forum Romanum, the famous public square and center of political life, was originally the cemetery of the small community. According to Roman legend, Romulus and Remus founded Rome in 753 B.C. Romulus built his settlement on the Palatine Hill, while Remus chose the Aventine (see inset, Map 5.1). Jealous of his brother's work, Remus ridiculed it by jumping over Romulus's unfinished wall. In a rage, Romulus killed his brother and vowed, "So will die whoever else shall leap over my walls." In this instance legend preserves some facts. Archaeological investigation has confirmed that the earliest settlement at Rome was situated on the Palatine and that it dates to the first half of the eighth century B.C. The legend also shows traces of Etruscan influence on Roman customs. The inviolability of Romulus's walls

STATUETTE OF AN ETRUSCAN WARRIOR *The warrior shows the Etruscan military debt to Greece. He wears Greek armor and carries the spear of the Greek heavy infantryman. The artistic rendering of the warrior, however, shows that Italic artists were moving away from Greek models and were creating a style of their own. (Collection of the University Museum, The University of Pennsylvania)*

recalls the Etruscan concept of the *pomerium,* a sacred boundary intended to keep out anything evil or unclean.

During the years 753–509 B.C., the Romans picked up many Etruscan customs. They adopted the Etruscan alphabet, which the Etruscans themselves had adopted from the Greeks. The Romans later handed on this alphabet to medieval Europe and thence to the modern Western world. The Romans also adopted symbols of political authority from the Etruscans. The symbol of the Etruscan king's right to execute or scourge his subjects was a bundle of rods and an ax, called in Latin the *fasces,* which the king's retainer carried before him on official occasions. When the Romans expelled the Etruscan kings, they created special attendants called lictors to carry the fasces before their new magistrates, the consuls. Even the toga, the white woolen robe worn by citizens, came from the Etruscans. In engineering and architecture the Romans adopted from the Etruscans the vault and the arch. Above all, it was thanks to the Etruscans that the Romans truly became urban dwellers.

Etruscan power and influence at Rome were so strong that Roman traditions preserved the memory of Etruscan kings who ruled the city. Under the Etruscans, Rome enjoyed contacts with the larger Mediterranean world, and the city began to grow. In the years 575–550 B.C., temples and public buildings began to grace the city. The Capitoline Hill became the religious center of the city when the temple of Jupiter Optimus Maximus (Jupiter the Best and Greatest) was built there. The forum ceased to be a cemetery and began its history as a public meeting place, much like the agora of a Greek city. Metalwork became common, and the wealthier classes began to import large numbers of fine Greek vases. The Etruscans had found Rome a collection of villages and made of it a city.

THE ROMAN CONQUEST OF ITALY
(509–290 B.C.)

Early Roman history is an uneven mixture of fact and legend. Roman traditions often contain an important kernel of truth, but that does not make them history. In many cases they are significant because they illustrate the ethics, morals, and ideals that Roman society considered valuable. Rome's early history also presents the historian with another problem. Historical writing did not begin among the Romans until the third century B.C., hundreds of years after the founding of Rome. Much later still, around the time of Jesus, the historian Livy (59 B.C.–A.D. 17) gave final form to these legends.

How much genuine information about the early years did Romans like Livy have? Or did they simply take what they knew and try to make of it an intelligible story? Livy gave his own answer to these questions: "Events before Rome was born or thought of have come down to us in old tales with more of the charm of poetry than of sound historical record, and such traditions I propose neither to affirm nor refute."[3] Livy also admitted that these legends and tales depicted men and women not necessarily as they were, but as Romans should be. For him, the story of early Rome was an impressive moral tale. Today, historians would say that Livy took these legends and made of them a sweeping epic. But they would also admit that the epic preserved the broad outlines of the Roman conquest of Italy and the development of Rome's internal

THE ROMAN FORUM   *The forum was the center of Roman political life. From simple beginnings it developed into the very symbol of Rome's imperial majesty. (Italian Government Travel Office)*

affairs. Both parts of the epic – legend and fact – are worth examining for what they say about the Romans.

According to Roman tradition, the Romans expelled the Etruscan king Tarquin the Proud from Rome in 509 B.C. and founded the republic. In the years that followed, the Romans fought numerous wars with their neighbors on the Italian peninsula. They became soldiers, and the grim fighting bred tenacity, a prominent Roman trait. War also involved diplomacy, at which the Romans became masters. At an early date they learned the value of alliances and how to provide leadership for their allies. Alliances with the Latin towns around them provided them with a large reservoir of manpower. Their alliances also involved the Romans in still other wars and took them farther and farther afield in the Italian peninsula.

One of the earliest wars was with two nearby peoples, the Aequi and the Volsci, and from this contest arose the legend of Cincinnatus. At one point, when the Aequi had launched a serious invasion, the Romans called upon Cincinnatus to assume the office of dictator. In this period the Roman dictator, unlike modern dictators, was a legitimate magistrate given ultimate powers for a specified period of time. The Roman officials found Cincinnatus working his three-acre farm. Wiping the sweat from himself, he listened to the appeal of his countrymen and accepted the office. Fifteen days later, after he had defeated the Aequi, he returned to his farm. Cincinnatus personified the ideal of the Roman citizen – a man of simplicity, a man who put his duty to Rome before any consideration of personal interest or wealth.

Roman tradition tells of grand campaigns

and continuous Roman success in these wars. In reality, most campaigns were neither grand nor always victorious. A good idea of what the fighting was like comes from the legend of the Fabii, one of Rome's noblest families. On one occasion 306 members of the Fabii set out toward Etruscan territory on what was nothing more than a cattle raid. What could be more patriotic than to reduce the enemy's wealth while increasing your own? The Etruscans, however, ambushed the Fabii and surrounded them. One boy escaped from the fighting, but the rest of the Fabii died to the last man, as good Romans were supposed to do. The excessive losses belong to the realm of legend, but the Fabii's type of combat was no doubt typical of the hard-fought border skirmishes and raids, in which the Romans at times took a beating. Gradually, Roman tenacity and numbers exhausted the strength of the enemy. The conflicts also taught the Romans to bounce back from defeat and to modify their institutions to deal effectively with changing problems and situations.

The growth of Roman power was slow but steady. Not until roughly a century after the founding of the republic did the Romans try to drive the Etruscans entirely out of Latium. In 405 B.C. they laid siege to Veii, the last neighboring Etruscan city. Ten years later they captured it. The story of the siege of Veii is in some ways the Roman equivalent of the Greek siege of Troy. But once again tradition preserves a kernel of truth, confirmed now by archaeological exploration of Veii. This was an important Roman victory, for the land of Veii went to the Romans and provided additional resources for Rome's growing population. Rome's concentrated landholdings formed a strong, unified core in central Italy. After the destruction of Veii, Rome overshadowed its Latin allies and its enemies alike.

Although the Romans slowly but steadily advanced their power in central Italy, they suffered a major setback about 390 B.C. A new people, the Celts – or Gauls, as the Romans called them – had been spreading their culture throughout the regions of modern France, Belgium, and southern Germany. By about 550 B.C. the Gauls were trading with the Greek colony of Massilia (modern Marseilles) and with Etruscan cities in the Po valley. Lured by the wealth of northern Italy, bands of Gauls began to push into the Po valley. Around 390 B.C. one band struck as far south as Latium. The great German historian Eduard Meyer has vividly recaptured the terror of the event:

With gloomy fear the sons of the Mediterranean looked upon these giants [the Gauls], with their long red hair and huge moustaches. They were a wild warrior folk who trampled down whatever stood in their way. With the severed heads of their enemies they bedecked their horses and their huts with skulls. Half naked they went into battle, their necks and arms adorned with thick gold rings and chains. Their many-colored mantles they threw aside; only shields covered their bodies. Their weapons were spears and mighty, but slender and wickedly-shaped, swords.[4]

The Gauls swept aside a Roman army and sacked Rome. More intent on loot than land, they agreed to abandon Rome in return for a thousand pounds of gold. The decision to buy off the Gauls made a lasting impression on the Romans. According to Roman tradition, when the Gauls produced their own scale, the Romans howled with indignation. The Gallic chieftain then threw his sword on the scale, exclaiming "Vae victis" – "woe to the conquered." These words, though legendary, became a challenge to the Romans. Thereafter they made it their policy never to accept peace, much less to surrender, as long as the enemy were still in the field.

Although the Gauls left Rome in rubble – another fact confirmed by modern archaeology – they also inadvertently helped the Romans: on their way to central Italy they broke forever the power of the Etruscans. When the Gauls took their gold and returned to the Alps, they left the north open to Roman expansion.

During the century from 390 to 290 B.C., Romans rebuilt their city and recouped their losses. They also reorganized their army to create the mobile legion, a flexible unit capable of fighting on either broken or open terrain. The Romans finally brought Latium and their Latin allies fully under their control, and they conquered Etruria. In 343 B.C., they grappled with the Samnites in a series of bitter wars for the possession of Campania and southern Italy. The Samnites were a formidable enemy, and they inflicted some serious losses on the Romans. But the superior organization, institutions, and manpower of the Romans won out in the end. Although Rome had yet to subdue the whole peninsula, for the first time in history the city stood unchallenged in Italy.

Rome's success in diplomacy and politics was as important as its military victories. Unlike the Greeks, the Romans did not simply conquer and then dominate. Instead, they shared with other Italians both political power and degrees of Roman citizenship. The Romans did not start out to build a system. They were always a practical people – that was one of their greatest strengths. When they found a treaty or a political arrangement that worked, they used it wherever possible. When it did not, they turned to something else. Consequently, Rome had a network of alliances and treaties with other peoples and states.

With many of their oldest allies, such as the Italian cities, they shared full Roman citizenship. In other instances they granted citizenship without the franchise (*civitas sine suffragio*). Allies who held this status enjoyed all the rights of Roman citizenship except that they could not vote or hold Roman offices. They were subject to Roman taxes and calls for military service, but they ran their own local affairs. The Latin allies were able to acquire full Roman citizenship by moving to Rome.

By their willingness to extend their citizenship the Romans took Italy into partnership. Here the political genius of Rome triumphed where Greece had failed: Rome proved itself superior to the Greek polis because it both conquered and shared the fruits of conquest with the conquered. Rome could consolidate where Greece could only dominate. The unwillingness of the Greek polis to share its citizenship condemned it to a limited horizon. Not so with Rome. The extension of Roman citizenship strengthened the state, gave it additional manpower and wealth, and laid the foundations of the Roman Empire itself.

THE ROMAN STATE

The Romans summed up their political existence in a single phrase: *senatus populusque Romanus,* the Roman senate and the people. The real genius of the Romans lay in the fields of politics and law. Unlike the Greeks, they did not often speculate on the ideal state or on political forms; instead, they realistically met actual challenges and created institutions, magistracies, and legal concepts to deal with practical problems. Change was consequently a commonplace feature of Roman political life, and the constitution of 509 B.C. was far simpler than that of 27 B.C. Nonetheless, the principal magistracies and political organs of the state can be briefly sketched.

In the early republic, social divisions determined the shape of politics. Political power was in the hands of the aristocracy – the patricians, who were wealthy landowners. Patrician families formed clans, as did aristocrats in early Greece. They dominated the affairs of state, provided military leadership in time of war, and monopolized knowledge of law and legal procedure. The common people of Rome, the plebeians, had few of the advantages of the patricians. Some plebeians formed clans of their own, and rivaled the patricians in wealth. Many plebeian merchants increased their wealth in the course of Roman expansion, but most plebeians were poor. They were the artisans, the small farmers, and the landless urban dwellers. The plebeians, rich and poor alike, were free citizens and had a voice in politics. Nonetheless, they were overshadowed by the patricians.

Perhaps the greatest institution of the republic was the senate, which had originated under the Etruscans as a council of noble elders who advised the king. During the republic the senate advised the consuls and the other magistrates. Because the senate sat year after year, while magistrates changed annually, it provided stability and continuity. It also served as a reservoir of experience and knowledge. Technically, the senate could not pass legislation; it could only offer its advice. But increasingly because of the senate's prestige its advice came to have the force of law.

The Romans created several assemblies through which the people elected magistrates and passed legislation. The earliest was the *comitia curiata,* which had religious, political, and military functions. According to Roman tradition, king Servius Tullius (578–535 B.C.), who reorganized the state into 193 centuries (military and political units) for military purposes, created the *comitia centuriata.* Since the patricians shouldered most of the burden of defense, they dominated the *comitia centuriata,* and could easily outvote the plebeians. In 471 B.C., the plebeians won the right to meet in an assembly of their own, the *concilium plebis,* and to pass ordinances. In 287 B.C., the bills passed in the concilium plebis were recognized as binding on the entire population, patrician and plebeian alike.

The chief magistrates of the republic were the two consuls, elected for one-year terms. At first the consulship was open only to the patricians. The consuls commanded the army in battle, administered state business, convened the comitia centuriata, and supervised financial affairs. In effect, they and the senate ran the state. The consuls appointed quaestors to assist them in their duties, and in 421 B.C. the quaestorship became an elective office open to the plebeians. The quaestors took charge of the public treasury and prosecuted criminals in the popular courts.

In 366 B.C., the Romans created a new office, that of praetor, and in 227 B.C. the number of praetors was increased to four. When the consuls were away from Rome, the praetor could act in their place. The praetor dealt primarily with the administration of justice. When he took office, the praetor issued a proclamation declaring the principles along which he would interpret the law. These proclamations became very important because they usually covered areas where the law was vague. Thus, they helped clarify the law.

The lowest officials were the aediles, four in number, who supervised streets and markets and presided over public festivals.

After the age of overseas conquest (pages 154–157), the Romans divided the Mediterranean area into provinces, which were governed by ex-consuls and ex-praetors. Because of their experience in Roman politics, they were well suited to administer the affairs of the provincials and to fit Roman law and custom into new contexts that they might encounter.

One of the most splendid achievements of the Romans was their development of law. Roman law began as a set of rules that regulated the lives and relations of citizens. This civil law, or *ius civile,* consisted of statutes, customs, and forms of procedure. Roman assemblies added to the body of law, and praetors interpreted it. The spirit of the law aimed at protecting the property, lives, and reputations of citizens, redressing wrongs, and giving satisfaction to the victims of injustice.

As the Romans came into more frequent contact with foreigners, they had to devise laws to deal with disputes between Romans and foreigners and between foreigners under Roman jurisdiction. In these instances, where there was no precedent to guide the Romans, the legal decisions of the praetors proved to be of immense importance. The praetors adopted aspects of other legal systems, and they resorted to the law of equity – what they thought was right and just to all parties. Thus, the praetors were in effect free to determine law, and they enjoyed a great deal of flexibility. This situation illustrates the practicality and the genius of the Romans. By addressing specific, actual circumstances the praetors developed a body of law, the *ius gentium,* that applied to Romans and foreigners and that laid the foundation for a universal conception of law. By the time of the late republic Roman jurists were reaching decisions on the basis of the Stoic concept of *ius naturale,* natural law, a universal law that could be applied to all societies.

SOCIAL CONFLICT IN ROME

War was not the only aspect of Rome's early history. In Rome itself a great social conflict, usually known as the Struggle of the Orders, developed between the patricians and the plebeians. What the plebeians wanted was real political representation and safeguards against patrician domination. The efforts of the plebeians to obtain recognition of their rights is the crux of the Struggle of the Orders.

Rome's early wars gave the plebeians the leverage they needed: Rome's survival depended on the army, and the army needed the plebeians. The first showdown between the plebeians and the patricians came, according to tradition, in 494 B.C. To force the patricians to grant concessions, the plebeians seceded from the state; they literally walked out of Rome and refused to serve in the army. Livy tells how Menenius Agrippa, acting as spokesman for the senate, persuaded them to return by relating the story of the belly and the limbs.

Agrippa said that the limbs of the body once went on strike against the stomach because it did nothing but enjoy all the good things it received from the limbs. Yet the limbs found that by starving the stomach they also starved themselves. (In the same vein Benjamin Franklin once told the Founding Fathers that unless they all hung together they would all hang separately.) Livy's story is legend, but once again the legend preserves truth. The Struggle of the Orders was marked by hard bargaining, but also by compromise and concession. Throughout the conflict plebeian and patrician alike were sincerely concerned for the welfare of Rome. Only this true patriotism prevented the conflict from becoming civil war.

The general strike of the plebeians worked. Because of it the patricians made important concessions. They recognized the right of the plebeians to elect their own officials, the tribunes. The tribunes in turn had the right to protect the plebeians from the arbitrary conduct of patrician magistrates. The tribunes brought plebeian complaints and grievances to the senate for resolution. In 471 B.C., when the plebeians won the right to hold their own assembly, the concilium plebis, and to enact ordinances that concerned only themselves, the plebeians became a state within a state. This situation could have led to chaos, but Rome was not a house divided against itself. The plebeians were not bent on undermining the state. Rather, they used their gains only to win full equality under the law.

The law itself was the next target of the plebeians. Only the patricians knew what the law was, and only they could argue cases in court. All too often they had used the law for their own benefit. The plebeians wanted the law codified and published. The result of their agitation was the Law of the Twelve Tables, so called because the laws, which covered civil and criminal matters, were inscribed on large bronze plaques. Like Draco's law code, the Law of the Twelve Tables seems stiff and even harsh. For instance, Table IV commands, "A seriously deformed child should be quickly killed." Table VIII deals handily with slander: "If anyone has sung or composed a song which caused dishonor or disgrace to another, he should be beaten to death with clubs." But at least all Romans could learn their rights and guard against arbitrary judgments. Later still, the plebeians forced the patricians to publish legal procedures as well. They had broken the patricians' legal monopoly. Henceforth, they enjoyed full protection under the law.

The decisive plebeian victory came with the passage of the Licinian-Sextian rogations (or laws) in 367 B.C. Licinius and Sextus were two plebeian tribunes who led a ten-year fight for further reform. Rich plebeians, like Licinius and Sextus themselves, joined the poor to mount a sweeping assault on patrician privilege. Wealthy plebeians wanted the opportunity to provide political leadership for the state. They demanded that the patricians allow them access to all the magistracies of the state. If they could hold the consulship, they could also sit in the senate and advise the senate on policy. The two tribunes won approval from the senate for a law that stipulated that one of the two annual consuls had to be a plebeian.

Licinius and Sextus also protected the interests of the plebeian poor, those who owned little or no land and whose poverty had driven them into debt. These plebeians wanted access to public land so that they could make a new start. The two tribunes sponsored legislation that limited the amount of public land an individual could hold. This restriction struck hard at the patricians, many of whom had used large tracts of public land for their own profit. The new law allowed magistrates to parcel out land in small lots, which plebeians could claim and work for themselves.

The Struggle of the Orders resulted in a Rome stronger and better united than before. It could have led to anarchy, but again the Roman political genius triumphed. Resistance and confrontation never exploded into class warfare. Instead, both sides resorted to compromises to hammer out a realistic solution. Important too were Roman patience and tenacity – and a healthy sense of the practical. These qualities enabled both sides to keep working until they had resolved the crisis. The Struggle of the Orders ended in 367 B.C. with a new concept of Roman citizenship. All citizens shared equally under the law. Theoretically, all could aspire to the highest

THE ROMAN REPUBLIC

509 B.C.	Expulsion of the Etruscan king and founding of the Roman republic
471 B.C.	Plebians win official recognition of their assembly, the *concilium plebis*
ca 450 B.C.	Law of the Twelve Tables
390 B.C.	The Gauls sack Rome
390–290 B.C.	Rebuilding of Rome; reorganization of the army; Roman expansion in Italy
367 B.C.	Licinian-Sextian rogations
287 B.C.	Legislation of the *concilium plebis* made binding on entire population
282–146 B.C.	The era of overseas conquest
264–241 B.C.	First Punic War: Rome builds a navy, defeats Carthage, acquires Sicily
218–202 B.C.	Second Punic War: Scipio defeats Hannibal; Rome dominates the western Mediterranean
200–148 B.C.	Rome conquers the Hellenistic east
149–146 B.C.	Third Punic War: savage destruction of Carthage
133–121 B.C.	The Gracchi introduce land reform; murder of the Gracchi by some senators.
107 B.C.	Marius becomes consul and begins the professionalization of the army.
91–88 B.C.	War with Rome's Italian allies
88 B.C.	Sulla marches on Rome and seizes dictatorship
79 B.C.	Sulla abdicates
78–27 B.C.	Era of civil war
60–49 B.C.	First Triumvirate: Pompey, Crassus, Julius Caesar
45 B.C.	Julius Caesar defeats Pompey's forces and becomes dictator
44 B.C.	Assassination of Julius Caesar
43–36 B.C.	Second Triumvirate: Marc Antony, Lepidus, Octavian
31 B.C.	Octavian defeats Antony and Cleopatra at Actium

political offices. Patrician or plebeian, rich or poor, Roman citizenship was equal for all.

THE AGE OF OVERSEAS CONQUEST (282–146 B.C.)

In 282 B.C., Rome embarked on a series of wars that left it the ruler of the Mediterranean world. There was nothing ideological about these wars. Unlike Napoleon or Hitler, the Romans did not map out grandiose strategies for world conquest. In 282 B.C., they had no idea of what lay in store for them. If they could have looked into the future, they would have stood amazed. In many instances the Romans did not even initiate action; they simply responded to situations as they arose. Nineteenth-century Englishmen were fond of saying, "We got our empire in a fit of absence of mind." The Romans could not go quite that far. Even though they sometimes declared war reluctantly, they nonetheless felt the need to dominate, to eliminate any state that could threaten them.

Rome was imperialistic, and its imperialism took two forms. In the barbarian West, the home of fierce tribes, Rome resorted to bald aggression to conquer new territory. In areas like Spain, and later in Gaul, the fighting was fierce and savage, and gains came slowly. In the civilized East, the world of Hellenistic states, Rome tried to avoid annexing territory. The East was already heavily populated, and those people would have become Rome's responsibility. New responsibilities meant new problems, and such headaches the Romans shunned. In the East the Romans preferred to be patrons rather than masters. Only when that policy failed did they directly annex land. But in 282 B.C., all this lay in the future.

The Samnite wars had drawn the Romans into the political world of southern Italy. In 282 B.C., alarmed by the powerful newcomer, the Greek city of Tarentum in southern Italy called for help from Pyrrhus, king of Epirus in western Greece. A relative of Alexander the Great and an excellent general, Pyrrhus won two furious battles but suffered heavy casualties – thus the phrase "Pyrrhic victory" for a victory involving severe losses. Roman bravery and tenacity led him to comment: "If we win one more battle with the Romans, we'll be completely washed up." Against Pyrrhus's army the Romans threw new legions, and in the end Roman manpower proved decisive. In 275 B.C., the Romans drove Pyrrhus from Italy and extended their sway over southern Italy. Once they did, the island of Sicily became important to them.

Pyrrhus once described Sicily as a future "wrestling ground for the Carthaginians and Romans." The Phoenician city of Carthage, in North Africa (see Map 5.2), had for centuries dominated the western Mediterranean. Sicily had long been a Carthaginian target. Since Sicily is the steppingstone to Italy, the Romans could not let it fall to an enemy. In 264 B.C., Carthage and Rome came to blows over the city of Messina, which commanded the straits between Sicily and Italy. This conflict, the First Punic War, lasted for twenty-three years. The Romans quickly learned that they could not conquer Sicily unless they controlled the sea. Yet they lacked a fleet and hated the sea as fervently as cats hate water. Nevertheless, with grim resolution the Romans built a navy and challenged the Carthaginians at sea. The Romans fought seven major naval battles with the Carthaginians and won six. Twice their fleet went down in gales. But finally the Romans wore down the Carthaginians. In 241 B.C., the Romans de-

MODEL OF A ROMAN WARSHIP This rare ancient model was found off the southern coast of the Peloponnesus near Sparta. The bow of the warship is capped by a ram, behind which run the seats for the rowers. At the stern is the poop, the station of the officers and steersmen. (Photo: Caroline Buckler)

feated them and took possession of Sicily, which became their first real province. Once again Rome's resources, manpower, and determination proved decisive.

The First Punic War was a beginning, not an end. Carthage was still a formidable enemy. After the First Punic War the Carthaginians expanded their power to Spain and turned the Iberian Peninsula into a rich field of operations. By 219 B.C., Carthage had found its avenger – Hannibal. In Spain, Hannibal learned how to lead armies and to wage war on a large scale. A brilliant general, he realized the advantages of swift mobile forces, and he was an innovator in tactics.

In 219 B.C., Hannibal defied the Romans by laying siege to the small city of Saguntum in Spain. When the Romans declared war the following year, he gathered his forces and led them on one of the most spectacular marches in ancient history. Hannibal carried the Second Punic War to the very gates of Rome. Starting in Spain, he led his troops – infantry,

cavalry, and elephants – over the Alps and into Italy on a march of more than a thousand miles. Once in Italy, he defeated one Roman army at the battle of Trebia and later another at the battle of Lake Trasimene in 217 B.C. At the battle of Cannae in 216 B.C. Hannibal inflicted some forty thousand casualties on the Romans. He spread devastation throughout Italy, but failed to crush Rome's iron circle of Latium, Etruria, and Samnium. The wisdom of Rome's political policy of extending rights and citizenship to its allies showed itself in these dark hours. Italy stood solidly with Rome against the invader. And Rome fought back.

The Roman general Scipio Africanus copied Hannibal's methods of mobile warfare. He streamlined the legions by making their components capable of independent action and by introducing new weapons. Scipio gave his new army combat experience in Spain, which he wrested from the Carthaginians. Meanwhile the Roman fleet dominated the western

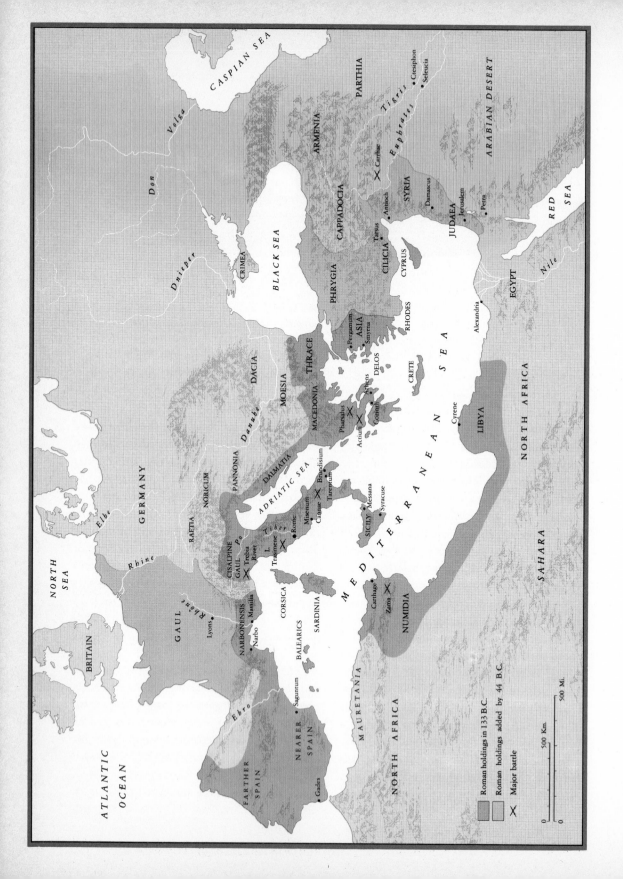

CASPIAN SEA

Volga

Don

PARTHIA

• Ctesiphon
• Seleucia

ARMENIA

Tigris

Euphrates

ARABIAN DESERT

✗ Carrhae

Dnieper

CAPPADOCIA

SYRIA
• Damascus

CRIMEA

BLACK SEA

PHRYGIA

Tarsus •

CILICIA

• Antioch

JUDAEA

• Jerusalem
• Petra

RED SEA

CYPRUS

Nile

EGYPT

Pergamum •

ASIA
• Smyrna

RHODES

• Alexandria

THRACE

DELOS

CRETE

DACIA

MOESIA

MACEDONIA

Athens •

MEDITERRANEAN SEA

Corinth •

Danube

Pharsalus ✗

Actium ✗

Cyrene •

LIBYA

GERMANY

Elbe

NORICUM

PANNONIA

DALMATIA

ADRIATIC SEA

Brundisium
✗
Tarentum

NORTH AFRICA

RAETIA

Rhine

CISALPINE
GAUL
✗
Po

Trebia
River

L.
Trasimene
✗

Tiber

Rome •

Misenum •

Capua •

Messana •
SICILY
Syracuse •

SAHARA

NORTH SEA

GAUL

Rhône

Lyons •

NARBONENSIS
Narbo •

Massilia •

CORSICA

SARDINIA

Carthage •
✗
Zama ✗

NUMIDIA

BRITAIN

BALEARICS

MAURETANIA

NORTH AFRICA

Ebro

• Saguntum

NEARER
SPAIN

ATLANTIC OCEAN

FARTHER
SPAIN

Gades •

Roman holdings in 133 B.C.

Roman holdings added by 44 B.C.

✗ Major battle

500 Km.

500 Mi.

0

0

MAP 5.2 ROMAN EXPANSION DURING THE REPUBLIC *The main spurt of Roman expansion occurred between 264 and 133 B.C., when most of the Mediterranean fell to Rome, followed by the conquest of Gaul and the eastern Mediterranean by 44 B.C.*

Mediterranean and interfered with Carthaginian attempts to reinforce Hannibal. In 204 B.C., the Roman fleet landed Scipio in Africa, which prompted the Carthaginians to recall Hannibal from Italy to defend the homeland.

In 202 B.C., near the town of Zama (see Map 5.2), Scipio Africanus defeated Hannibal in one of the world's truly decisive battles. Scipio's victory meant that the world of the western Mediterranean would henceforth be Roman. Roman language, law, and culture, fertilized by Greek influences, would in time permeate this entire region. The victory at Zama meant that Rome's heritage – not Carthage's – would be passed on to the Western world.

The Second Punic War contained the seeds of still other wars. Unabated fear of Carthage led to the Third Punic War, a needless, unjust, and savage conflict that ended in 146 B.C., when Scipio Aemilianus, grandson of Scipio Africanus, destroyed the old hated rival. As the Roman conqueror watched the death pangs of that great city, he turned to his friend Polybius with the words: "I fear and foresee that someday someone will give the same order about my fatherland." It would, however, be centuries before an invader would stand before the gates of Rome.

During the war with Hannibal the Romans had invaded Spain, a peninsula rich in material resources and the home of fierce warriors. When the Roman legions tried to reduce Spanish tribesmen, they met with bloody and determined resistance. Not until 133 B.C., after years of brutal and ruthless warfare, did Scipio Aemilianus finally conquer Spain.

When the Romans intervened in the Hellenistic East, they went from triumph to triumph. The Romans dealt with the Greeks in a civilized fashion. There were hard-fought battles in the East, but the bloodletting and carnage that marked the battles in the West were not repeated in the cultured East. Even so, the results were essentially the same. The kingdom of Macedonia fell to the Roman legions, as did Greece and the Seleucid monarchy. By 146 B.C., the Romans stood unchallenged in the eastern Mediterranean, and they had turned many states and kingdoms into provinces. In 133 B.C., the king of Pergamum in Asia Minor left his kingdom to the Romans in his will. The Ptolemies of Egypt meekly obeyed Roman wishes. The following years would bring the Romans new victories, and they would establish their system of provincial administration. But by 146 B.C., the work of conquest was largely done. The Romans had turned the entire Mediterranean basin into *mare nostrum* – "our sea."

OLD VALUES AND GREEK CULTURE

Rome had conquered the Mediterranean world, but some Romans considered that victory a misfortune. The historian Sallust (86–34 B.C.), writing from hindsight, complained that the acquisition of an empire was the beginning of Rome's troubles:

But when through labor and justice our Republic grew powerful, great kings defeated in war, fierce nations and mighty peoples subdued by force, when Carthage the rival of the Roman people was wiped out root and branch, all the seas and lands lay open, then fortune began to be harsh and to throw everything into confusion. The Romans had easily

BATTLE BETWEEN THE ROMANS AND THE
GAULS   All the brutality and fury of Rome's wars
with the barbarians of western Europe come to life in
this Roman sarcophagus of 225 B.C. Even the bravery
and strength of the Gauls were no match for the stead-
iness and discipline of the Roman legions. (Alinari/
Scala)

*borne labor, danger, uncertainty, and hardship. To
them leisure, riches – otherwise desirable – proved
to be burdens and torments. So at first money, then
desire for power grew great. These things were a
sort of cause of all evils.*[5]

Sallust was not alone in his feelings. At the
time, some senators had opposed the destruction of Carthage on the grounds that fear of
their old rival would keep the Romans in
check. Did Rome gain the whole world only
to lose its soul? Sallust obviously thought so,
and he could have made a good case. It is true
that the new empire provided many Romans
with golden opportunities to amass fortunes
wrung from the conquered. It is true that numerous generals, provincial governors, and
other magistrates oppressed the vanquished
for their personal gain. But it is also true that
Rome continued to produce patriotic, noble,
and hard-working men and women, just as it
had in the past. Rome did not suddenly become weak and evil, but Roman society was

undergoing a fundamental change. In the
process, Rome's early period became senti-
mentalized as the "good old days," a golden
age of virtue the early Romans themselves
would never have recognized.

In the second century B.C., Romans learned
that they could not return to what they fondly
considered a simple life. They were world
rulers. The responsibilities they faced were
complex and awesome. They had to change
their institutions, their social patterns, and
their way of thinking to meet the new era.
They were in fact building the foundations of
a great imperial system. It was an awesome
challenge, and there were failures along the
way. Roman generals and politicians would
destroy each other. Even the republican constitution would eventually be discarded. But
in the end Rome triumphed here just as it had
on the battlefield, for out of the turmoil
would come the pax Romana – the Roman
peace.

How did the Romans of the day meet these

challenges? How did they lead their lives and cope with these momentous changes? Obviously, there are as many answers to these questions as there were Romans. Yet two men can be taken to represent the major trends of the second century B.C. Cato the Elder shared the mentality of those who longed for the good old days and idealized the traditional agrarian way of life. Scipio Aemilianus led those who embraced the new urban life with its eager acceptance of Greek culture. Forty-nine years older than Scipio, Cato was a product of an earlier generation, one that confronted a rapidly changing world. Cato and Scipio were both aristocrats and neither of them was typical, even of the aristocracy. But they do exemplify opposing sets of attitudes that marked Roman society and politics in the age of conquest.

CATO AND THE TRADITIONAL IDEAL

Marcus Cato was born a plebeian, but his talent and energy carried him to Rome's highest offices. He cherished the old virtues and consistently imitated the old ways. Cato had inherited an estate north of Rome and began his career as a man of moderate means. Near his estate were the fields and cottage of Manius Curius, the general who had driven Pyrrhus from Italy forty years before Cato was born. Curius had been another Cincinnatus; although Curius had held the consulship and commanded armies, he worked his small farm alone. He once refused a large bribe, saying that a man of his simple tastes did not need gold. It was the example of Curius that Cato constantly held before his eyes.

In Roman society ties within the family were very strong. In this sense Cato and his family were typical. Cato was *paterfamilias,* a term that meant far more than merely "father." The paterfamilias was the oldest

dominant male of the family. He held nearly absolute power over the lives of his wife and children so long as he lived. He could legally kill his wife for adultery or divorce her at will. He could kill his children or sell them into slavery. He could force them to marry against their will. Until the paterfamilias died, his sons could not legally own property. At his death, his wife and children inherited his property.

Despite his immense power, the paterfamilias did not necessarily act alone or arbitrarily. To deal with important family matters he usually called a council of the adult males. In this way the leading members of the family aired their views. They had the opportunity to give their support to the paterfamilias or to dissuade him from harsh decisions. In these councils the women of the family had no formal part, but it can safely be assumed that they played an important behind-the-scenes role. Although the possibility of serious conflicts between a paterfamilias and his grown sons is obvious, no one in ancient Rome ever complained about the institution. Perhaps in practice the paterfamilias preferred to be lenient rather than absolute.

Cato's wife (whose name is unknown) was the matron of the family, a position of authority and respect. The virtues expected of a Roman matron were those of Lucretia, a legendary figure from the early republic. According to Livy's account, the son of the last Etruscan king wanted to sleep with Lucretia. One night while her husband was away, the king's son slipped into her room and tried to seduce her. When she refused him, he threatened to kill her and then he raped her. When he had gone, Lucretia sent for her father and husband and told them the whole story. They tried to console her, telling her that she had been helpless and was free from any shame. Her answer was short: "Never shall Lucretia

provide a precedent for unchaste women to escape what they deserve." She demanded vengeance, the death of the king's son. Then, innocent though she was, she drew a knife and killed herself. Clearly, Lucretia was the ideal, but numerous funerary inscriptions testify that the virtues of chastity and modesty were highly valued. The tribute of one husband to his wife is typical of many:

Here is laid a woman dutiful, temperate, pure, chaste, Sempronia Moschis, to whom thanks are returned by her husband for her merits.[6]

Like most Romans, Cato and his family began the day early in the morning. The Romans divided the period of daylight into twelve hours and the darkness into another twelve. The day might begin as early as half past four in summer, as late as half past seven in winter. Because Mediterranean summers are invariably hot, the farmer and his wife liked to take every advantage of the cool mornings. Cato and his family, like modern Italians, ordinarily started the morning with a light breakfast, usually nothing more than some bread and cheese. After breakfast the family went about its work.

Because of his political aspirations Cato often used the mornings to plead law cases. He walked to the marketplace of the nearby town and defended anyone who wished his help. He received no fees for these services, but did put his neighbors in his debt. In matters of law and politics Roman custom was very strong. It demanded that Cato's clients give him their political support or their votes in repayment whenever he asked for them. These clients knew and accepted their obligations to Cato for his help.

Cato's wife shared her husband's love for the old ways. While he was in town, she ran the household. She spent the morning spinning and weaving wool for the clothes they wore. She supervised the domestic slaves, planned the meals, and devoted a good deal of attention to her son. In wealthy homes during this period the matron had begun to employ a slave as a wet nurse. Cato's wife refused to delegate her maternal duties. Like most ordinary Roman women, she nursed her son herself. She also bathed and swaddled him daily. Later, the boy was allowed to play with toys and terra-cotta dolls. Roman children, like children everywhere, kept pets. Dogs were especially popular, and they were valuable as house guards. Children played all sorts of games, and games of chance were very popular. Until the age of seven the child was under the matron's care. During this time the mother began to educate her daughter in the management of the household. After the age of seven, the son – and in many wealthy households the daughter too – began formal education.

In the country, Romans like Cato continued to take their main meal at midday. This meal included either coarse bread made from the entire husk of wheat or porridge made with milk or water; it also included turnips, cabbage, olives, and beans. When Romans ate meat, they preferred pork. Unless they lived by the sea, the average farm family did not eat fish, which was an expensive delicacy. Cato once complained that Rome was a place where a fish could cost more than a cow. With the midday meal the family drank an ordinary wine mixed with water. Afterward any Roman who could took a nap. This was especially true in the summer, when the Mediterranean heat can be fierce. Slaves, artisans, and hired laborers, however, went about their work. In the evening the Romans ate a light meal and went to bed about nightfall.

The agricultural year followed the sun and the stars; they were the farmer's calendar. Like Hesiod in Boeotia, the Roman farmer looked to the sky to determine when to plant, weed, shear sheep, and perform other chores. Varro (116–27 B.C.), one of the most famous writers on agriculture, did everything by the sun and stars. He advised farmers in Italy to harvest their grain crops between the summer solstice and the rising of the Dog Star. He suggested that they sow at the setting of the Pleiades. Varro's book on agriculture owed much to Hellenistic Greek manuals, but it also reflected actual Roman practice. Besides, the farmer could not depend on the civil calendar. The lunar year is 354 days long, and the solar year is 365¼ days long. So the civil calendar had to be adjusted to both lunar and solar years. To make matters worse, politicans often tampered with the calendar. In 46 B.C., when Julius Caesar reformed the civil calendar, it was some 2½ months out of step with the solar year. Obviously, farmers had to depend on something more reliable than this. Their solution was the sun, moon, and stars.

Spring was the season for plowing. Roman farmers plowed their land at least twice and preferably three times. The third plowing was to cover the sown seed in ridges and to use the furrows to drain off excess water. The Romans used a variety of plows. Some had detachable shares. Some were heavy for thick soil, others light for thin, crumbly soil. Farmers used oxen and donkeys to pull the plow. They collected the dung of their animals for fertilizer. Besides spreading manure, some farmers fertilized their fields by planting lupines and beans; when they began to pod, farmers plowed them under. The main money crops, at least for rich soils, were wheat and flax. Forage crops included clover, vetch, and alfalfa. Prosperous farmers like Cato raised olive trees chiefly for the oil. They also raised grapevines for the production of wine. Cato and his neighbors harvested their cereal crops in summer and their grapes in autumn. Harvests varied depending on the soil, but farmers could usually expect yields of 5½ bushels of wheat or 10½ bushels of barley per acre.

MANUMISSION OF SLAVES   During the Republic some Roman masters began to free slaves in public ceremonies. Here two slaves come before their master or a magistrate, who is in the process of freeing the kneeling slave by touching him with a manumission-rod. The other slave shows his gratitude and his good faith with a handshake. (Collection Waroque, Mariemont, Belgium. © A. C. L. Brussels)

Rome as the spoils of war. The Roman attitude toward slaves and slavery had little in common with modern views. To the Romans slavery was a misfortune that befell some people. But slavery did not entail any racial theories. Races were not enslaved because the Romans thought them inferior. The black African slave was treated no worse – and no better – than the Spaniard. Indeed, some slaves were valued because of their physical distinctiveness: black Africans and blond Germans were particular favorites. For the talented slave, the Romans always held out the hope of eventual freedom. Manumission – the freeing of individual slaves by their masters – became so common that it had to be limited by law. Not even Christians questioned the institution of slavery. It was just a fact of life.

Slaves were entirely the property of their master, and they might be treated with great cruelty. Many Romans were practical enough to realize that they got more out of their slaves by kindness than by severity. Yet in Sicily slave owners treated their slaves viciously. They bought slaves in huge numbers, branded them for identification, put them in irons, and often made them go without food and clothing. In 135 B.C., these conditions gave rise to a major slave revolt, during which many of the most brutal masters died at the hands of their slaves. Italy too had trouble with slave unrest, but conditions there were generally better than in Sicily.

Cato urged his countrymen to treat slaves humanely. Varro suggested that masters should control slaves with knowledge and not with whips. Yet even Cato could be hardhearted. Although he worked and ate with his slaves, he never forgot their money value. When they grew too old to work, he sold them to save the expense of feeding them.

In the early republic the master of the household worked the farm himself. By the second century B.C., however, Cato was noticeably old-fashioned because he stripped to the waist in summer and sweated alongside his slaves and day laborers.

An influx of slaves resulted from Rome's wars and conquests. Prisoners from Spain, Africa, and the Hellenistic East, and even some blacks from Hannibal's army, came to

Not all Romans were Catos, though. Between many slaves and masters there developed genuine bonds of affection. On numerous occasions slaves risked or gave their lives to protect kind masters.

Part of the reason for such good relations probably stems from the fact that many slaves came from the Hellenistic East. They were certainly not barbarians. Many of them were more cultured than their owners. Greek male slaves frequently became the tutors of the master's children. These men especially were likely to receive their freedom. Slaves who gained their freedom also became Roman citizens. Freedmen and freedwomen often continued to live with their previous owners. And it was not unusual for Romans to permit their ex-slaves to be buried with them.

For Cato and most other Romans, religion played an important part in life. Originally, the Romans thought of the gods as invisible and shapeless natural forces. Only through Etruscan and Greek influence did Roman deities take on human form. Jupiter, the sky god, and his wife Juno became equivalent to the Greek Zeus and Hera. Mars was the god of war, but he was also the god who guaranteed the fertility of the farm and protected it from danger. Cato habitually sacrificed a pig, a ram, and a bull to Mars to obtain his help and protection. Cato or one of his farmhands led the animals around the boundaries of the farm and then called upon Mars the Father

that you hold back, repel, and turn away disease seen and unseen, blight and devastation; that you allow my crops, grain, vines, and thickets to increase and flourish; that you keep my shepherd and flocks safe; that you watch over and give good health and strength to me, my house, and household.[7]

Cato then sacrificed the animals to Mars and offered the god small cakes. The Romans used a similar ritual, the Robigalia, to protect the grain crops from mildew. The Robigalia later gave rise to the Christian practice of purifying farms on Rogation Days, when the priest and his congregation marched in procession around the farms while calling upon Jesus and the saints for protection. Cato would have approved.

These two religious practices are illustrative of Roman religion in general. The gods of the Romans were not loving and personal. They were stern, powerful, and aloof. But as long as the Romans honored the cults of their gods, they could expect divine favor.

Along with the great gods the Romans believed in spirits who haunted fields, forests, crossroads, and even the home itself. Some of these deities were hostile, and only magic could ward them off. The spirits of the dead, like ghosts in modern horror films, frequented the places where they had lived. They too had to be placated, but they were ordinarily benign. As the poet Ovid (43 B.C.–A.D. 17) put it:

The spirits of the dead ask for little.
They are more grateful for piety than for an expensive gift –
Not greedy are the gods who haunt the Styx below.
A rooftile covered with a sacrificial crown,
Scattered kernels, a few grains of salt,
Bread dipped in wine, and loose violets –
These are enough.
Put them in a potsherd and leave them in the middle of the road.[8]

A good deal of Roman religion consisted of such rituals as those Ovid describes. These practices lived on long after the Romans had lost interest in the great gods. Even Christianity could not entirely wipe them out. Instead, Christianity was to incorporate many of these rituals into its own style of worship.

SCIPIO: GREEK CULTURE AND URBAN LIFE

The old-fashioned ideals that Cato represented came into conflict with a new spirit of wealth and leisure. The conquest of the Mediterranean world and the spoils of war made Rome a great city. Some, like the historian Velleius Paterculus (first century A.D.), viewed these developments with distaste:

Scipio Africanus opened the way for Roman power. Scipio Aemilianus opened the way for luxury. Indeed, when Rome was free of the fear of Carthage, and its rival in empire was removed, Rome fell, not gradually but in headlong course, from virtue towards vice. The old discipline was deserted and the new introduced. The state turned from vigilance to sleep, from military affairs to pleasures, from work to leisure.[9]

Roman life, especially in the cities, *was* changing and becoming less austere. The spoils of war went to the building of baths, theaters, and other places of amusement. Romans and Italian townsmen began to spend more of their time in leisure pursuits. But simultaneously the new responsibilities of governing the world produced in Rome a sophisticated society. Romans developed new tastes and a liking for Greek culture and literature. They began to learn the Greek language. It became common for an educated Roman to speak both Latin and Greek. Hellenism dominated the cultural life of Rome. Even diehards like Cato found a knowledge of Greek essential for political and diplomatic affairs. The poet Horace (64–8 B.C.) summed it up well: "Captive Greece captured her rough conqueror and introduced the arts into rustic Latium."

One of the most avid devotees of Hellenism and the new was Scipio Aemilianus, the destroyer of Carthage. Scipio was also the man whom Velleius had accused of introducing luxury into Rome. Scipio realized that broad and worldly views had to replace the old Roman narrowness. The new situation called for new ways. Rome was no longer a small city on the Tiber; it was the capital of the world, and Romans had to adapt themselves to that fact. Scipio was ready to become an innovator both in politics and culture. He broke with the past in the conduct of his political career. He embraced Hellenism wholeheartedly. Perhaps more than anyone else of his day, Scipio represented the new Roman – imperial, cultured, and independent.

Scipio even dared to be independent in his political career, which differed from that of traditional politicians. He set out on a course of personal politics, determined to carve out a career for himself on the strength of his own merits. In doing so he set an example for future politicians. One of the most successful of Scipio's imitators would be Julius Caesar.

In his education and interests, too, Scipio broke with the past. As a boy, he had received the traditional Roman training, learning to read and write Latin and becoming acquainted with the law. He mastered the fundamentals of rhetoric and learned how to throw the javelin, fight in armor, and ride a horse. But later Scipio also learned Greek and became a fervent Hellenist. As a young man he formed a lasting friendship with the historian Polybius, who actively encouraged him in his study of Greek culture and in his intellectual pursuits. In later life Scipio's love of Greek learning, rhetoric, and philosophy became legendary. Scipio also promoted the spread of Hellenism in Roman society. He became the center of the Scipionic Circle, a small group of Greek and Roman artists, philosophers, historians, and poets. Conservatives like Cato tried to stem the rising tide of Hellenism, but men like Scipio carried the day and helped make the heritage of Greece an abiding factor in Roman life.

The new Hellenism profoundly stimulated the growth and development of Roman art and literature. The Roman conquest of the Hellenistic East resulted in wholesale confiscation of Greek paintings and sculpture to grace Roman temples, public buildings, and private homes. Roman artists copied many aspects of Greek art, but their emphasis on realistic portraiture carried on a native tradition.

Fabius Pictor (second half of the third century B.C.), a senator, wrote the first *History of Rome* in Greek. Other Romans translated Greek classics into Latin. Still others, like the poet Ennius (239–169 B.C.), the father of Latin poetry, studied Greek philosophy, wrote comedies in Latin, and adapted many of Euripides' tragedies for the Roman stage. Ennius also wrote a history of Rome in Latin verse. Plautus (ca 254–184 B.C.) specialized in rough humor. He too decked out Greek plays in Roman dress, but was no mere imitator. Indeed, his play *Amphitruo* was itself copied eighteen hundred years later by the French playwright Molière and the English poet John Dryden. The Roman dramatist Terence (ca 195–159 B.C.), a member of the Scipionic Circle, wrote comedies of refinement and grace that owed their essentials to Greek models. His plays lacked the energy and the slapstick of Plautus's rowdy plays. All of early Roman literature was derived from the Greeks, but it managed in time to speak in its own voice and to flourish because it had something of its own to say.

The conquest of the Mediterranean world brought the Romans leisure, and Hellenism influenced how they spent their free time. During the second century B.C., the Greek custom of bathing became a Roman passion and an important part of the day. In the early republic Romans had bathed infrequently, especially in the winter. Now large buildings containing pools and exercise rooms went up in great numbers, and the baths became an essential part of the Roman city. Architects built intricate systems of aqueducts to supply the bathing establishments with water. Conservatives railed at this Greek custom too, calling it a waste of time and an encouragement to idleness. The conservatives were correct in that bathing establishments were more than just places to take a bath. They included gymnasia, where men exercised and played ball. Women had places of their own to bathe, generally sections of the same baths used by men; for some reason, women's facilities lacked gymnasia. The baths contained hot-air rooms to induce a good sweat and pools of hot and cold water to finish the actual bathing. They also contained snack bars and halls where people chatted and read. The baths were socially important places where men and women went to see and be seen: social climbers tried to talk to "the right people" and wangle invitations to dinner; politicians took advantage of the occasion to discuss the affairs of the day. Despite the protests of conservatives and moralists, the baths at least provided people – rich and poor – with places for clean and healthy relaxation.

This period also saw a change in the eating habits of urban dwellers. The main meal of the day shifted from midday to evening. Dinner became a more elaborate meal and dinner parties became fashionable. Although Scipio Aemilianus detested fat people, more and more Romans began to eat excessively. Rich men and women displayed their wealth by serving exotic dishes and gourmet foods. After a course of vegetables and olives came the main course of meat, fish, or fowl. Pig was a favorite dish, and a whole suckling pig might be stuffed with sausage. A lucky guest might even dine on peacock and ostrich, each

BATHS OF CARACALLA   Once introduced into the Roman world, social bathing became a passion. These baths, which date to the Roman Empire, are the ultimate development of sophistication and size. (Italian Government Travel Office)

served with rich sauces. Dessert, as in Italy today, usually consisted of fruit. With the meal the Romans served wine, and during this period vintage wines became very popular. Household slaves sometimes read poetry or performed music during the meal. People of more vulgar tastes hired jesters. Dwarves were in great demand, and the evening's entertainment consisted of buffoonery and coarse jokes. After dinner the party drank wine and talked, often late into the night.

Although the wealthy gorged themselves whenever they could, poor artisans and workers could rarely afford rich meals. Their dinners resembled Cato's. Yet they too occasionally spent generously on food, especially during the major festivals. The Roman calendar was crowded with religious festivals, occasions not of dreary piety but of cheerful celebration. One such was the festival of Anna Perenna, a festival of fertility, longevity, and prosperity. It was an occasion for fun and exuberant but harmless excess. The poet Ovid caught all the joy and charm of the event in these lines:

The ordinary people come [to the banks of the Tiber];
   And scattering themselves over the green grass,
They drink and lie down, each man with his woman.
Some remain under the open sky, a few put up tents,
   Others build leafy huts of twigs.
Some set up reeds instead of unbending columns,
   Over which they spread their togas.
Yet they grow warm with sun and wine, and pray
   For as many years as cups of wine they take, and they drink that many.

. . . .

*There also they sing the songs they have heard in
the theaters,*
   *And they beat time to the words with lively
   hands.*
*Putting down the bowl, they join in rough ring
dances,*
   *And the trim girlfriend dances with her hair
   flying.*
*As they return home, they stagger and are a spec-
tacle to the vulgar.*
   *When meeting them, the crowd calls them
   blessed.*
*The procession came my way recently (a worthy
sight in my opinion):*
   *A drunk woman dragged along a drunk old
   man.*[10]

Robust religious festivals and a decided love
of good food and drink were characteristics of
the average Roman, whether rich or poor.

Did Hellenism and the new social customs
corrupt the Romans? Perhaps the best answer
is simply this: the Roman state and the empire it ruled continued to exist for six more
centuries. Rome did not collapse; the state
continued to prosper. The golden age of literature was still before it. The high tide of its
prosperity still lay in the future. The Romans
did not like change, but they took it in stride.
That was part of their practical turn of mind
and part of their genius.

THE LATE REPUBLIC (133–27 B.C)

The wars of conquest created serious problems for the Romans, some of the most
pressing of which were political. The republican constitution had suited the needs of a
simple city-state, but it was inadequate to
meet the requirements of Rome's new position in international affairs (see Map 5.2).

Sweeping changes and reforms were necessary
to make it serve the demands of empire. A
whole system of provincial administration
had to be established. Officials had to be
appointed to govern the provinces and to
administer the law. These officials and
administrative organs had to find places
within the constitution. Armies had to be
provided to defend the provinces, and a system of tax collection had to be created.

Other political problems were equally serious. During the wars Roman generals commanded huge numbers of troops for long
periods of time. Men such as Scipio Aemilianus were on the point of becoming too
mighty for the state to control. Although
Rome's Italian allies had borne much of the
burden of the fighting, they received fewer
rewards than did Roman officers and soldiers.
Italians began to agitate for full Roman citizenship and a voice in politics.

There were serious economic problems too.
Hannibal's operations and the warfare in Italy
had left the countryside a shambles. The
movements of numerous armies had disrupted
agriculture. The prolonged fighting had also
drawn untold numbers of Roman and Italian
men away from their farms for long periods.
The families of these soldiers could not keep
the land under full cultivation. The people
who defended Rome and conquered the world
for Rome became impoverished for having
done their duty.

These problems, complex and explosive,
largely account for the turmoil of the closing
years of the republic. The late republic was
one of the most dramatic eras in Roman history. It produced some of Rome's most
famous figures: Marius, Sulla, Cicero, Pompey, and Julius Caesar, among others. In one
way or another each of these men attempted
to solve Rome's problems.

When the legionaries returned to their

farms in Italy, they encountered an appalling situation. All too often their farms looked like the farms of people they had conquered. Two courses of action were open to them. They could rebuild as their forefathers had done. Or they could take advantage of an alternative not open to their ancestors: they could sell their holdings. The wars of conquest had made some men astoundingly rich. These men wanted to invest their wealth in land. They bought up small farms to create huge estates, which the Romans called latifundia.

The purchase offers of the rich landowners appealed to the veterans for a variety of reasons. Many veterans had seen service in the East, where they had tasted the rich city life of the Hellenistic states. They were reluctant to return home and settle down to a dull life on the farm. Often their farms were so badly damaged that rebuilding hardly seemed worth the effort. Besides, it was hard to make big profits from small farms. Nor could the veterans supplement their income by working on the latifundia. Although the owners of the latifundia occasionally hired free men as day laborers, they preferred to use slaves to work their land. Slaves could not strike, and they could not be drafted into the army. Confronted by these conditions, veterans and their families opted to sell their land. They took what they could get for their broken farms and tried their luck elsewhere.

Most veterans migrated to the cities, especially to Rome. Although some found work, most did not. Industry and small manufacturing were generally in the hands of slaves. Even when there was work, slave labor kept the wages of free men low. Instead of a new start, veterans and their families encountered slum conditions that matched those of modern American cities. Sanitation was virtually nonexistent. Housing was frequently shabby and

structurally unsound, but expensive nonetheless. Fire and police protection were unknown. These conditions were especially prevalent in Rome and some larger cities. Within a brief period of time Rome became the home of a large body of urban poor.

This trend held ominous consequences for the strength of Rome's armies. The Romans had always believed that only landowners should serve in the army, for only they had something to fight for. Landless men, even if they were Romans and lived in Rome, could not be conscripted into the army. These landless men may have been veterans of major battles and numerous campaigns; they may have won distinction on the battlefield. But once they sold their land they became ineligible for further military service. A large pool of experienced manpower was going to waste. The landless ex-legionaries wanted a new start, and they were willing to support any leader who would provide it.

One man who recognized the plight of Rome's peasant farmers and urban poor was an aristocrat, Tiberius Gracchus (163–133 B.C.). Appalled by what he saw, Tiberius warned his countrymen that the legionaries were losing their land even while fighting Rome's wars:

The wild beasts that roam over Italy have every one of them a cave or lair to lurk in. But the men who fight and die for Italy enjoy the common air and light, indeed, but nothing else. Houseless and homeless they wander about with their wives and children. And it is with lying lips that their generals exhort the soldiers in their battles to defend sepulchres and shrines from the enemy, for not a man of them has an hereditary altar, not one of all these many Romans an ancestral tomb, but they fight and die to support others in luxury, and though they are styled masters of the world, they have not a single clod of earth that is their own.[11]

Until his death, Tiberius Gracchus sought a solution to the problems of the veterans and the urban poor.

After his election as tribune of the people, Tiberius in 133 B.C. proposed that public land be given to the poor in small lots. His was an easy and sensible plan, but it angered many wealthy and noble people who had usurped large tracts of public land for their own use. They had no desire to give any of it back, and they bitterly resisted Tiberius's efforts. Violence broke out in Rome when a large body of senators killed Tiberius in cold blood. It was a black day in Roman history. The very people who directed the affairs of state and administered the law had taken the law into their own hands. The death of Tiberius was the beginning of an era of political violence. In the end that violence would bring down the republic.

Although Tiberius was dead, his land bill became law. Furthermore, Tiberius's brother Gaius (153–121 B.C.) took up the cause of reform. Gaius was a veteran soldier with an enviable record, but this fiery orator made his mark in the political arena. Gaius also became tribune, and demanded even more extensive reform than had his brother. To help the urban poor Gaius pushed legislation to provide them with cheap grain for bread. He defended his brother's land law and suggested other measures for helping the landless. He proposed that Rome send many of its poor and propertyless people out to form colonies in southern Italy. The poor would have a new start and could lead productive lives. The city of Rome would immediately benefit because excess and nonproductive families would leave for new opportunities abroad. Rome would be less crowded, sordid, and dangerous.

Gaius went a step further and urged that all Italians be granted full rights of Roman citizenship. This measure provoked a storm of opposition, and it was not passed in Gaius's

UNUSUAL ROMAN HELMET Not standard issue, this metal helmet is a craftsman's masterpiece. The helmet itself is decorated with battle scenes and originally probably bore a crest. The molded face is actually a hinged visor. (Reproduced by Courtesy of the Trustees of the British Museum)

lifetime. Yet in the long run he proved wiser than his opponents. In 91 B.C., many Italians revolted against Rome over the issue of full citizenship. After a brief but hard-fought war the senate gave Roman citizenship to all Italians. Had the senate listened to Gaius earlier, it could have prevented a great deal of bloodshed. Instead, reactionary senators rose against Gaius and murdered him and three thousand of his supporters. Once again the cause of reform had met with violence. Once again it was Rome's leading citizens who flouted the law.

More trouble for Rome came from an unexpected source. In 112 B.C., war broke out in North Africa, when a Numidian king named Jugurtha rebelled against Rome. The Roman legions made little headway against him until 107 B.C., when Gaius Marius, an Italian "new man" (a politician not from the traditional Roman aristocracy), became consul. Marius's values were those of the military camp. A man of fierce vigor and courage, Marius saw the army as the tool of his ambition. To prepare for the war with Jugurtha, Marius reformed the Roman army. He was the first Roman officer to recruit an army by permitting landless men to serve in the legions. Marius thus tapped Rome's vast reservoir of idle manpower. His volunteer army was a professional force, not a body of draftees. Marius also reorganized the Roman legion into smaller units, called cohorts, which made the legion more mobile and flexible. He rearmed the legion by making the sword and javelin the standard weapons of the legionaries.

There was, however, a disturbing side to Marius's reforms, one that would henceforth haunt the republic. To encourage enlistments, Marius promised land to his volunteers after the war. Poor and landless veterans flocked to him, and together they handily defeated Jugurtha. When Marius proposed a bill to grant land to his veterans, the senate refused to act, in effect turning its back on the soldiers of Rome. This was a disastrous mistake. Henceforth, the legionaries expected their commanders — not the senate or the state — to protect their interests. Through Marius's reforms the Roman army became a professional force, but it owed little allegiance to the state. By failing to reward the loyalty of Rome's troops, the senate set the stage for military rebellion and political anarchy.

Nor was trouble long in coming. The senate's refusal to honor Marius's promises to his soldiers, and the brief but bitter war between the Romans and their Italian allies (91–88 B.C.), set off serious political disturbances in Rome. In 88 B.C., the Roman general and conqueror Sulla marched on Rome with his army to put an end to the turmoil. Sulla made himself dictator — a far cry from Cincinnatus's dictatorship. He put his enemies to death and confiscated their land. The constitution thus disrupted was never effectively put back together.

In 79 B.C. Sulla voluntarily abdicated as dictator and permitted the republican constitution to function normally once again. Yet his dictatorship cast a long shadow over the late republic. Sulla the political reformer proved far less influential than Sulla the successful general and dictator. Civil war was to be the constant lot of Rome for the next fifty years, until the republican constitution gave way to the empire of Augustus in 27 B.C. The history of the late republic is the story of the power struggles of some of Rome's most famous figures: Julius Caesar and Pompey, Augustus and Marc Antony. One figure who stands apart is Cicero (106–43 B.C.), a practical politician whose greatest legacy to the Roman world and to Western civilization is his mass of political and oratorical writings.

Pompous, vain, and sometimes silly, Cicero was nonetheless one of the few men of the period to urge peace and public order. As consul in 63 B.C. he put down a conspiracy against the republic, but he refused to use force to win political power. Instead, he developed the idea of "concord of the orders," an idealistic and probably unattainable balance among the elements that constituted the Roman state. A truly brilliant master of Latin prose and undoubtedly Rome's finest orator, Cicero used his vast literary ability to promote political and social reforms and to explore the underlying principles of statecraft. Yet Cicero commanded no legions, and only legions commanded respect.

In the late republic the Romans were grappling with the simple and inescapable fact that their old city-state constitution was unequal to the demands of overseas possessions and the problems of governing provinces. Thus even Sulla's efforts to put the constitution back together again proved hollow. Once the senate and the other institutions of the Roman state had failed to come to grips with the needs of empire, once the authorities had lost control of their own generals and soldiers, and once the armies put their faith in their commanders instead of in Rome, the republic was doomed.

Sulla's real political heirs were Pompey and Julius Caesar, who realized that the days of the old republican constitution were numbered. Pompey, a man of boundless ambition, began his career as one of Sulla's lieutenants. After his army put down a rebellion in Spain, he himself threatened to rebel unless the senate allowed him to run for consul. He and another ambitious politician, Crassus, pooled their political resources and both won the consulship. They dominated Roman politics until the rise of Julius Caesar, who became consul in 59 B.C. Together the three concluded a political alliance, the First Triumvirate, in which they agreed to advance each other's interests.

The man who cast the longest shadow over these troubled years was Julius Caesar (100–44 B.C.). More than a mere soldier, Caesar was a cultivated man. Born of a noble family, he received an excellent education, which he furthered by studying in Greece with some of the most eminent teachers of the day. He had serious intellectual interests, and his literary ability was immense. Caesar was a superb orator, though second to Cicero, and his affable personality and wit made him popular. He was also a shrewd politician of unbridled ambition. Since military service was an effective stepping-stone to politics, Caesar launched his military career in Spain, where his courage won the respect and affection of his troops. Personally brave and tireless, Caesar was a military genius who knew how to win battles and how to turn victories into permanent gains.

In 58 B.C., Caesar became governor of Gaul, the region of modern France, a huge area he had conquered in the name of Rome. Caesar's account of his operations, his *Commentaries* on the Gallic wars, became a classic in Western literature and most schoolchildren's introduction to Latin. By 49 B.C., the First Triumvirate had fallen apart. Crassus had died in battle, and Caesar and Pompey, each suspecting the other of treachery, came to blows. The result was a long and bloody civil war, which raged from Spain across northern Africa to Egypt. Although Pompey enjoyed the official support of the government, Caesar finally defeated Pompey's forces in 45 B.C. He had overthrown the republic and made himself dictator.

Julius Caesar was not merely another victorious general. Politically brilliant, he was determined to make basic reforms, even at the expense of the old constitution. He took the first long step to break down the barriers between Italy and the provinces, extending citizenship to many of the provincials who had supported him. Caesar also took measures to cope with Rome's burgeoning population. By Caesar's day perhaps 750,000 people lived in Rome. Caesar drew up plans to send his veterans and some 80,000 of the poor and unemployed to colonies throughout the Mediterranean. He founded at least twenty colonies, most of which were located in Gaul,

Spain, and North Africa. These colonies were important agents in spreading Roman culture in the western Mediterranean. Caesar's work would eventually lead to a Roman empire composed of citizens, not subjects.

In 44 B.C., a group of conspirators assassinated Caesar and set off another round of civil war. Caesar had named his eighteen-year-old grandnephew, Octavian – or Augustus, as he is better known to history – as his heir. Augustus joined forces with two of Caesar's lieutenants, Marc Antony and Lepidus, in a pact known as the Second Triumvirate, and together they hunted down and defeated Caesar's murderers. In the process, however, Augustus and Antony came into conflict. Antony, "boastful, arrogant, and full of empty exultation and capricious ambition," proved to be the major threat to Augustus's designs.[12] In 33 B.C., Augustus branded Antony a traitor and a rebel. Augustus painted lurid pictures of Antony lingering in the eastern Mediterranean, a romantic and foolish captive of the seductive Cleopatra, queen of Egypt and bitter enemy of Rome. In 31 B.C., with the might of Rome at his back, Augustus met and defeated the army and navy of Antony and Cleopatra at the battle of Actium in Greece. Augustus's victory put an end to an age of civil war that had lasted since the days of Sulla.

———◆———

The final days of the republic, even though filled with war and chaos, should not obscure the fact that much of the Roman achievement survived the march of armies. The Romans had conquered the Mediterranean world only to find that conquest required them to change their way of life. Socially, they imbibed Greek culture and adjusted themselves to the superior civilization of the Hellenistic East. Politically, their city-state constitution broke down

and expired in the wars of the late republic. Even so, men like Caesar and later Augustus sought new solutions to the problems confronting Rome. The result, as Chapter 6 will describe, was a system of government capable of administering an empire with justice and fairness. Out of the failure of the republic arose the pax Romana of the empire.

NOTES

1. Polybius *The Histories* 1.1.5.

2. Mark Twain, *The Innocents Abroad,* Signet Classics, New York, 1966, p. 176.

3. Livy *History of Rome* Preface 6.

4. E. Meyer, *Geschichte des Altertums,* 6th ed., vol 5, Wissenschaftliche Buchgesellschaft, Darmstadt, 1975, pp. 144–145.

5. Sallust *War with Catiline* 10.1–3.

6. *Corpus Inscriptionum Latinarum,* vol. 6, G. Reimer, Berlin, 1882, no. 26192.

7. Cato *On Agriculture* 141.2–3.

8. Ovid *Fasti* 2.535–539.

9. Velleius Paterculus *History of Rome* 2.1.1.

10. Ovid *Fasti* 3.525–542.

11. Plutarch *Life of Tiberius Gracchus* 9.5–6.

12. Plutarch *Life of Antony* 2.8.

SUGGESTED READING

H. H. Scullard covers much of Roman history in a series of books: *The Etruscan Cities and Rome* (1967), *A History of the Roman World,* 753–146 B.C., 3rd ed. (1961), and *From the Gracchi to Nero,* 4th ed. (1976). The Etruscans have inspired much new work, most notably L. Banti, *The Etruscan Cities and Their Culture* (English translation, 1973), M. Pallottino, *The Etruscans,* rev. ed. (1975), and R. M. Ogilvie, *Early Rome and the Etruscans* (1976), an excellent account of Rome's early relations with them.

Roman expansion is the subject of J. Heurgon, *The Rise of Rome to 264 B.C.* (English translation, 1973), R. M. Errington, *The Dawn of Empire* (1971), and W. V. Harris, *War and Imperialism in Republican Rome 327–70 B.C.* (1979). J. F. Lazenby, *Hannibal's War: A Military History of the Second Punic War* (1978), is a recent and detailed treatment of one of Rome's greatest struggles. More general and encompassing is E. Gabba, *Republican Rome, the Army, and the Allies* (English translation, 1976). One of the best studies of Rome's political evolution is the classic, A. N. Sherwin-White, *The Roman Citizenship*, 2nd ed. (1973), a work of enduring value.

The great figures and events of the late republic have been the object of much new work. E. S. Gruen, *The Last Generation of the Roman Republic* (1974), treats the period as a whole. Very important are the studies of E. Badian, *Roman Imperialism in the Late Republic* (1968) and *Publicans and Sinners* (1972). R. Syme, *The Roman Revolution,* revised ed. (1952) is a classic. Valuable also are P. A. Brunt, *Social Conflicts in the Roman Republic* (1971); A. J. Toynbee, *Hannibal's Legacy,* 2 vols. (1965); and A. W. Lintott, *Violence in the Roman Republic* (1968).

Many new works deal with individual Romans who left their mark on this period. H. C. Boren, *The Gracchi* (1968), treats the work of the two brothers, and B. Levick, *Tiberius the Politician* (1976), offers closer scrutiny of the elder of the brothers, as does A. Bernstein, *Tiberius Sempronius Gracchus, Tradition and Apostacy* (1978). A. E. Astin has produced two works that are far more extensive than their titles indicate: *Scipio Aemilianus* (1967) and *Cato the Censor* (1978). J. Leach, *Pompey the Great* (1978), surveys the career of this politician, and B. Rawson, *The Politics of Friendship, Pompey and Cicero* (1978), treats both figures in their political environment. M. Gelzer, *Caesar, Politician and Statesman* (English translation, 1968) is easily the best study of one of history's most significant figures. Those interested in learning more about Caesar and the importance of his writings in the late Republic should see the fine article by L. Raditsa, "Julius Caesar and His Writings," in *Aufstieg und Niedergang der römischen Welt,* vol. I, part 3 (1973), pp. 417–456. His one-time colleague Marcus Crassus is treated in B. A. Marshall, *Crassus: A Political Biography* (1976), and A. Ward, *Marcus Crassus and the Late Roman Republic* (1977).

K. D. White, *Roman Farming* (1970), deals with agriculture, and J. P. V. D. Balsdon covers social life in the republic and the empire in two works: *Life and Leisure in Ancient Rome* (1969) and *Roman Women,* revised ed. (1974). Greek cultural influence on Roman life is the subject of A. Wardman, *Rome's Debt to Greece* (1976). F. Schulz, *Classical Roman Law* (1951) is a useful introduction to an important topic. Lastly, H. H. Scullard, *Festivals and Ceremonies of the Roman Republic* (1981), gives a fresh look at religious practices.

CHAPTER 6

THE PAX ROMANA

HAD THE ROMANS conquered the entire Mediterranean world only to turn it into their battlefield? Would they, like the Greeks before them, become their own worst enemies, destroying each other and wasting their strength until they perished? At Julius Caesar's death in 44 B.C. it must have seemed so to many. Yet finally, in 31 B.C., Augustus restored peace to a tortured world, and with peace came prosperity, new hope, and a new vision of Rome and Rome's destiny. The Roman poet Virgil expressed this vision most nobly:

You, Roman, remember — these are your arts:
To rule nations, and to impose the ways of peace,
To spare the humble and to war down the proud.[1]

In place of the republic, Augustus established a constitutional monarchy. He attempted to achieve a lasting cooperation in government and a balance among the people, the magistrates, the senate, and the army. His efforts were not always successful. His settlement of Roman affairs did not permanently end civil war. Yet he carried on Caesar's work. It was Augustus who created the structure that the modern world calls the Roman Empire. He did his work so well, and his successors so capably added to it, that Rome realized Virgil's hope. For the first and second centuries A.D. the lot of the Mediterranean world was peace — the *pax Romana,* a period of security, order, and harmony, of flourishing culture and expanding economy. It was a period that saw the wilds of Gaul, Spain, Germany, and eastern Europe introduced to Greco-Roman culture. By the third century A.D., when the empire gave way to the medieval world, the greatness of Rome and the blessings of Roman culture had left an indelible mark on the yet-unseen ages to come.

How did the Roman emperors govern the empire, and how did they spread Roman influence into northern Europe? What were the fruits of the pax Romana? Why did Christianity, originally a minor and local religion, sweep across the Roman world to change it fundamentally? Finally, how did the empire meet the grim challenge of barbarian invasion and economic decline? These are the main questions this chapter will consider.

AUGUSTUS'S SETTLEMENT (31 B.C.–A.D. 14)

When Augustus put an end to the civil wars that had raged since 83 B.C., he faced monumental problems of reconstruction. Rome and the entire Mediterranean world were in his power, and the legions were obedient to his word. Sole ruler as no Roman had ever been, he had a rare opportunity to shape the future. But how was that to be accomplished?

Augustus could easily have declared himself dictator as Caesar had, but the thought was repugnant to him. Augustus was neither an autocrat nor a revolutionary. His solution was to restore the republic. But was that possible? Some eighteen years of anarchy and civil war had shattered the republican constitution. It could not be rebuilt in a day. Augustus recognized these problems, but did not let them stop him. From 29 to 23 B.C., he toiled to heal Rome's wounds. The first problem facing him was to rebuild the constitution and the organs of government. Next he had to demobilize the army and care for the welfare of the provinces. Then he had to meet the danger of barbarians at Rome's European frontiers. Augustus was highly successful in meeting these challenges; his gift of peace to a war-torn world sowed the seeds of a literary flowering that produced some of the finest fruits of the Roman mind.

The Principate and the Restored Republic

Restoring the republic and creating a place for himself in it proved to be the biggest challenges to Augustus. Typically Roman, he preferred not to create anything new; he intended instead to modify republican forms and offices to meet new circumstances. Augustus planned for the senate to take upon itself a serious burden of duty and responsibility. He expected it to administer some of the provinces, to continue to be the chief deliberative body of the state, and to act as a court of law. Yet he did not give the senate enough power to become his partner in government. As a result, the senate failed to live up to its responsibilities, and increasingly its prerogatives shifted to Augustus by default.

Augustus's own position within the restored republic was something of an anomaly. He could not simply surrender the reins of power, for someone else would only have seized them. But how was he to fit into a republican constitution? Again Augustus had his own answer. He became *princeps civitatis,* "the First Citizen of the State." This prestigious title carried no power; it indicated only that Augustus was the most distinguished of all Roman citizens. In effect, it designated Augustus as the first among equals and a little more equal than anyone else in the state. His real power resided in the magistracies he held, the powers granted him by the senate, and his control of the army. Clearly, much of the principate, as the position of First Citizen is known, was a legal fiction. Yet that need not imply that Augustus, like a modern dictator, tried to clothe himself with constitutional legitimacy. In an inscription known as *Res Gestae (The Deeds of Augustus),* Augustus described his constitutional position in these terms:

COIN OF AUGUSTUS   This portrait shows Augustus as a mature princeps. *Like many of his coins, this one too has a propaganda value. On the reverse is his grandson Gaius. Augustus may have minted this coin to publicize Gaius's participation in Tiberius's campaign against the Germans. (Courtesy, World Heritage Museum. Photo: Caroline Buckler)*

In my sixth and seventh consulships [28–27 B.C.], I had ended the civil war, having obtained through universal consent total control of affairs. I transferred the Republic from my power to the authority of the Roman people and the senate.... After that time I stood before all in rank, but I had power no greater than those who were my colleagues in any magistracy.[2]

Augustus was not being a hypocrite. As consul he had no more constitutional and legal power than his fellow consul. Yet in addition to the consulship Augustus held many other magistracies, which his fellow consul did not. Constitutionally, his ascendancy within the state stemmed from the number of magistracies he held and the power granted him by the senate. At first he held the consulship annually, and then the senate voted him permanent proconsular power. The senate also voted him *tribunicia potestas* – the full power of the tribunes. Tribunician power gave Augustus the right to call the senate into session, present legislation to the people, and defend their rights. He held either high office or the powers of the chief magistrate year in and year out. No other magistrate could do the same. In 12 B.C., he became *pontifex maximus,* chief priest of the state. By assuming this position of great honor, Augustus became the chief religious official within the state.

The main source of Augustus's power was his position as commander of the Roman army. His title *imperator,* with which Rome customarily honored a general after a major victory, came to mean "emperor" in the modern sense of the term. Augustus governed the provinces where troops were needed for defense. The frontiers were his special concern. There Roman legionaries held the German barbarians at arm's length. The frontiers were also the areas where fighting could be expected to break out. Augustus made sure that Rome went to war only at his command. He controlled the deployment of the Roman army and paid its wages. He granted it bonuses and gave veterans retirement benefits. Thus, he avoided the problems with the army that the old senate had created for itself. Augustus never shared control of the army, and no Roman found it easy to defy him militarily.

The very size of the army was a special problem for Augustus. Rome's legions numbered thousands of men, far more than were necessary to maintain peace. What was Augustus to do with so many soldiers? This sort of problem had constantly plagued the late republic, whose leaders never found a solution to it. Augustus gave his own answer in the *Res Gestae:* "I founded colonies of soldiers in Africa, Sicily, Macedonia, Spain, Achaea, Gaul, and Pisidia. Moreover, Italy has 28 colonies under my auspices."[3] At least forty new colonies arose, most of them in the western Mediterranean. Augustus's veterans took abroad with them their Roman language and culture. His colonies, like those of Julius Caesar, were a significant tool in the further spread of Roman culture throughout the West.

Roman colonies were very different from the Greek colonies of Archilochus's time (pages 81–82). Greek colonies were independent. Once founded, they went their own way. Roman colonies were part of a system — the Roman Empire — that linked East with West in a mighty political, social, and economic network. The glory of the Roman Empire was its great success in uniting the Mediterranean world and spreading Greco-Roman culture throughout it. Roman colonies played a crucial part in that process, and deservedly did Augustus boast of his foundations.

What is to be made of Augustus's constitutional settlement? Despite his claims to the contrary, Augustus had not restored the republic. In fact, he would probably have agreed with the words of John Stuart Mill, the nineteenth-century English philosopher: "When society requires to be rebuilt, there is no use in attempting to rebuild it on the old plan." Augustus had created a constitutional monarchy, something completely new in Roman history. The title *princeps,* "First Citizen," came to mean in Rome, as it does today, "prince" in the sense of a sovereign ruler.

Augustus also failed to solve a momentous problem. He never found a way to institutionalize his position with the army. The ties between the princeps and the army were always personal. The army was loyal to the princeps but not necessarily to the state. The

Augustan Principate worked well at first, but by the third century A.D. the army would make and break emperors at will. Nonetheless, it is a measure of Augustus's success that his settlement survived as long and as well as it did.

AUGUSTUS'S ADMINISTRATION OF THE PROVINCES

To gain an accurate idea of the total population of the empire, Augustus ordered a census to be taken in 28 B.C. In Augustus's day the population of the Roman empire was between 70 and 100 million people, fully 75 percent of whom lived in the provinces. In the areas under his immediate jurisdiction Augustus put provincial administration on an ordered basis. He improved its functioning as well. Believing that the cities of the empire should look after their own affairs, he encouraged and fostered local self-government and urbanism. Augustus respected local customs and ordered his governors to do the same. The lengths he was willing to go to can be seen in Judaea.

Augustus wished to avoid antagonizing the Jews. As early as 40 B.C., long before he had put an end to the civil war, he and Antony had prevailed upon the senate to give the Jews their own king, Herod the Great, as a gesture of goodwill. Also, when the Roman legionaries stationed outside of Jerusalem entered the city, they left their standards behind in deference to the Jewish belief that the standards showed graven images. This was a magnanimous gesture, the equivalent of a modern army leaving its national flags behind. Augustus saw no reason to interfere with the customs, institutions, and traditions of cities as long as they functioned peacefully and effectively.

As a spiritual bond between the provinces and Rome, Augustus encouraged the cult of Roma, the goddess and guardian of the state. In the Hellenistic East, where king-worship was an established custom, the cult of Roma et Augustus grew up and spread rapidly. Augustus then introduced it in the West. By the time of his death in A.D. 14, nearly every province in the Empire could boast an altar or shrine to Roma et Augustus. In the West it was not the person of the emperor who was worshiped but his *genius* – his guardian spirit. In praying for the good health and welfare of the emperor Romans and provincials were praying for the empire itself. The cult became a symbol of Roman unity.

ROMAN EXPANSION INTO NORTHERN AND WESTERN EUROPE

For the history of Western civilization one of the most momentous aspects of Augustus's reign was Roman expansion into the wilderness of northern and western Europe (see Map 6.1). In this Augustus was following in Julius Caesar's footsteps. Between 58 and 51 B.C., Caesar had subdued Gaul and unsuccessfully attacked Britain. Carrying on his work, Augustus pushed Rome's frontier into the region of modern Germany. The Germanic tribes were tough opponents, and the Roman legions saw much bitter fighting against them in the north.

For the common soldier this fighting must have been exceptionally grim. Forests were believed to be the haunts of evil spirits, places of dim light and unidentifiable sounds. As early as the third century B.C. Roman armies habitually skirted the forests of Etruria. The vast forests of central Germany, with their thick, impenetrable gloom, must have oppressed even veteran legionaries. The thought of coming suddenly onto a war party of tall bearded Germans was not particularly pleasing either. Even so, the Roman legionary was

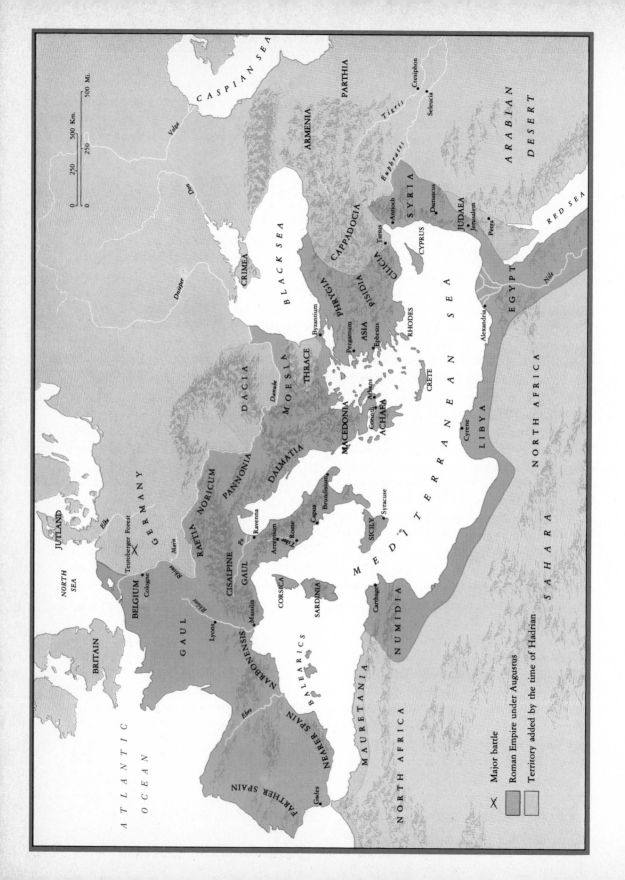

CASPIAN SEA

Volga

PARTHIA

ARMENIA

Tigris

Ctesiphon •
Seleucia •

ARABIAN DESERT

Don

CAPPADOCIA

SYRIA

Antioch • Damascus •

Tarsus •

CILICIA

PISIDIA

JUDAEA

Jerusalem •
Petra •

RED SEA

CRIMEA

BLACK SEA

Byzantium •

PHRYGIA

Pergamum •

ASIA

Ephesus •

CYPRUS

RHODES

EGYPT

Alexandria •

Nile

Euphrates

500 Mi.

500 Km.

250

250

250

0

0

Dnieper

DACIA

Danube

MOESIA

THRACE

MACEDONIA

Corinth • Athens •

ACHAEA

CRETE

MEDITERRANEAN SEA

LIBYA

Cyrene •

NORTH AFRICA

SAHARA

NORTH SEA

JUTLAND

Elbe

GERMANY

Teutoberger Forest ✕

Main

Rhine

BELGIUM

Cologne •

NORICUM

RAETIA

PANNONIA

DALMATIA

CISALPINE

GAUL

Po

Ravenna •

Arretium •

Rome •

Capua •

Brundisium •

SICILY

Syracuse •

Carthage •

NUMIDIA

BRITAIN

ATLANTIC OCEAN

GAUL

Lyons •

NARBONENSIS

Massilia •

CORSICA

SARDINIA

BALEARICS

NEARER SPAIN

Ebro

FARTHER SPAIN

Gades •

MAURETANIA

NORTH AFRICA

✕ Major battle

Roman Empire under Augustus

Territory added by the time of Hadrian

stouthearted, and these obstacles did not stop Roman expansion.

Augustus began his work in the north by completing the conquest of Spain. In Gaul, apart from minor campaigns, most of his work was peaceful. He founded twelve new towns. The Roman road system linked new settlements with one another and with Italy. But the German frontier, along the Rhine River, was the scene of hard fighting. In 12 B.C., Augustus ordered a major invasion of Germany beyond the Rhine. Roman legions advanced to the Elbe River, and a Roman fleet explored the North Sea and Jutland. The area north of the Main River and west of the Elbe was on the point of becoming Roman. But in 9 B.C., Augustus's general Varus lost some twenty thousand troops at the battle of the Teutoburger Forest. Thereafter the Rhine remained the Roman frontier.

Meanwhile, more successful generals extended the Roman standards as far as the Danube. Roman legions penetrated the area of modern Austria and western Hungary. The regions of modern Serbia, Bulgaria, and Rumania fell to Roman troops. Within this area the legionaries built fortified camps. Roads linked these camps with one another, and settlements grew up around the camps. Traders began to frequent the frontier and to traffic with the barbarians. Thus Roman culture — the rough-and-ready kind found in military camps — gradually spread into the northern wilderness.

Augustus's achievements in the north were monumental. For the first time in history, Greco-Roman culture spread beyond the sunny Mediterranean into the heart of Europe.

Amid the vast expanse of forests, Roman towns, trade, language, and law began to exert a civilizing influence on the barbarians. The Roman way of life attracted the barbarians, who soon recognized the benefits of assimilating Roman culture. Military camps often became towns; many modern European cities owe their origins to the forts of the Roman army. For the first time, the barbarian north came into direct, immediate, and continuous contact with Mediterranean culture.

LITERARY FLOWERING

The Augustan settlement's gift of peace inspired a literary flowering unparalleled in Roman history. With good reason this period is known as the golden age of Latin literature. Augustus and many of his friends actively encouraged poets and writers. As Virgil, Rome's greatest poet, summed up Augustus and his era:

Here is the man, here is he whom you often hear promised to you,
Augustus Caesar, offspring of the deified [Julius Caesar], who will establish
Once more a golden age in Latium.[4]

Virgil was not alone in this sentiment. The poet Horace felt the same:

With Caesar [Augustus] the guardian of the state
Not civil rage nor violence shall drive out peace, Nor wrath which forges swords
And turns unhappy cities against each other.[5]

These lines are not empty flattery, despite Augustus's support of many contemporary Latin writers. To a generation that had known only vicious civil war, Augustus's settlement was an unbelievable blessing.

The tone and ideal of Roman literature, like that of the Greeks, was humanistic and

ARA PACIS   This scene from the Ara Pacis, the Altar of Peace, celebrates Augustus's restoration of peace and the fruits of peace. Here Mother Earth is depicted with her children. The cow and the sheep under the goddess represent the prosperity brought by peace, especially the agricultural prosperity so highly cherished by Virgil. (Alinari/Scala)

worldly. Roman poets and prose writers celebrated the dignity of humanity and the range of its accomplishments. They stressed the physical and emotional joys of a comfortable, peaceful life. Their works were highly polished, elegant in style, and intellectual in conception. Roman poets referred to the gods frequently and treated mythological themes, but always the core of their work was human, not divine.

Virgil (70–19 B.C.) celebrated the new age in the *Georgics,* four books of poems on agriculture. Virgil delighted in his own farm, and his poems sing of the pleasures of peaceful farm life. The *Georgics* are also a manual of agriculture written in meter. The poet tells how to keep bees, grow grapes and olives, plow, and manage a farm. Throughout the

Georgics Virgil wrote about things he himself had seen, rather than drawing his theme from the writings of others. For instance, he describes the worker bees returning to the hive at nightfall:

*The weary young bees come back late at night,
Their legs full of thyme. Far and wide they feed
     on arbutus and grey-green willows and red
     crocus
And rich linden and rust-colored hyacinth.*[6]

Virgil could be vivid and graphic as well as pastoral. Even a small event could be a drama for him. The death of a bull while plowing is hardly epic material; yet Virgil captures the sadness of the event in the image of the farmer unyoking the remaining animal:

Look, the bull, shining under the rough plough,
    falls to the ground
    and vomits from his mouth blood mixed with
        foam,
    and releases his dying groan.
Sadly moves the ploughman, unharnessing the
    young steer grieving for the death of his brother
    and leaves in the middle of the job
    the plough stuck fast.[7]

Virgil's poetry is robust yet graceful. A sensitive man who delighted in simple things, Virgil left in his *Georgics* a charming picture of life in the Italian countryside in a period of peace.

Virgil's masterpiece is the *Aeneid,* an epic poem that is the Latin equivalent of the Greek *Iliad* and *Odyssey.* In the *Aeneid* Virgil expressed his admiration for Augustus's work by celebrating the shining ideal of a world blessed by the pax Romana. Virgil's account of the founding of Rome and the early years of the city gave final form to the legend of Aeneas, the Trojan hero who escaped to Italy at the fall of Troy. The principal Roman tradition held that Romulus was the founder of Rome, but the legend of Aeneas was also very old; it was known by the Etruscans as early as the fifth century B.C. Although Rome could not have had two founders, Virgil linked the legends of Aeneas and Romulus and kept them both. In so doing he also connected Rome with Greece's heroic past. Recounting the story of Aeneas and Dido, the queen of Carthage, Virgil made their ill-fated love affair the cause of the Punic wars. But above all, the *Aeneid* is the expression of Virgil's passionate belief in Rome's greatness. It is a vision of Rome as the protector of the good and noble against the forces of darkness and disruption.

In its own way Livy's history of Rome, entitled simply *Ab Urbe Condita (From the Founding of the City),* is the prose counterpart

of the *Aeneid.* Livy (59 B.C.–A.D. 17) received training in Greek and Latin literature, rhetoric, and philosophy. He even urged the future emperor Claudius to write history. Livy loved and admired the heroes and the great deeds of the republic, but he was also a friend of Augustus and a supporter of the principate. He especially approved of Augustus's efforts to restore the old republican virtues and morality.

Livy's history began with the legend of Aeneas and ended with the reign of Augustus. His theme of the greatness of the republic fitted admirably with Augustus's program of restoring the republic. Livy's history was colossal, consisting of 142 books of which only 25 percent still exists. Livy was a sensitive writer, and something of a moralist. Like Thucydides, he felt that history should be applied to the present. His history later became one of Rome's legacies to the modern world. During the Renaissance *Ab Urbe Condita* found a warm admirer in the poet Petrarch and left its mark on Machiavelli, who read it avidly.

The poet Horace (65–8 B.C.) rose from humble beginnings to friendship with Augustus. The son of an ex-slave and tax collector, Horace nonetheless received an excellent education. He loved Greek literature and finished his education in Athens. After Augustus's victory he returned to Rome and became Virgil's friend. Horace acquired a small farm north of Rome, which delighted him. He was as content as Virgil on his farm, and expressed his joy in a few lines:

Strive to add nothing to the myrtle plant!
The myrtle befits both you, the servant,
And me the master, as I drink under the
Thick-leaved vine.[8]

Horace happily turned his pen to celebrating Rome's newly won peace and prosperity. One of his finest odes commemorates Augustus's victory over Cleopatra at Actium in 31 B.C. Cleopatra is depicted as a frenzied queen, drunk with desire to destroy Rome. Horace saw in Augustus's victory the triumph of West over East, of simplicity over oriental excess. One of the truly moving aspects of Horace's poetry, like Virgil's, is his deep and abiding gratitude for the pax Romana.

For Rome, Augustus's age was one of hope and new beginnings. Augustus had put the empire on a new foundation. Constitutional monarchy was firmly established, and government was to all appearances a partnership between the princeps and the senate. The Augustan settlement was a delicate structure, and parts of it would in time be discarded. Nevertheless it worked, and by building on it later emperors would carry on Augustus's work.

The solidity of Augustus's work became obvious at his death in A.D. 14. Since the principate was not technically an office, Augustus could not legally hand it to a successor. Augustus had recognized this problem, and long before his death had found a way to solve it. He shared his consular and tribunician powers with his adopted son Tiberius, thus grooming him for the principate. In his will Augustus left most of his vast fortune to Tiberius, and the senate formally requested Tiberius to assume the burdens of the principate. All the formalities apart, Augustus had succeeded in creating a dynasty.

JUDAISM AND THE RISE OF CHRISTIANITY

During the reign of the emperor Tiberius (A.D. 14–37), perhaps in A.D. 29, Pontius Pilate, prefect of Judaea, condemned Jesus of Nazareth to death. At the time a minor event, this has become one of the best-known moments in history. How did these two men come to their historic meeting? The question is not idle, for Rome was as important as Judaea to Christianity. Jesus was born in a troubled time, when Roman rule aroused hatred and unrest among the Jews. This climate of hostility affected the lives of all who lived in Judaea, Roman and Jew alike. It forms the backdrop of Jesus' life, and it had a fundamental impact on his ministry. Without an understanding of this age of anxiety in Judaea, Jesus and early Christianity cannot properly be appreciated.

The entry of Rome into Jewish affairs was anything but peaceful. The civil wars that destroyed the republic wasted the prosperity of Judaea and the entire eastern Mediterranean world. Jewish leaders took sides in the fighting, and Judaea suffered its share of ravages and military confiscations. Peace brought little satisfaction to the Jews. Although Augustus treated Judaea generously, the Romans won no popularity by making Herod king of Judaea. King Herod gave Judaea prosperity and security, but the Jews hated his acceptance of Greek culture. He was also a bloodthirsty prince, who murdered his own wife and sons. Upon his death, the Jews broke out in revolt. For the next ten years Herod's successor waged almost constant war against the rebels. Added to the horrors of civil war were years of crop failure, which caused famine and plague. Men who called themselves prophets proclaimed the approach of the end of the world and the coming of the Messiah, the savior of Israel.

At length the Romans intervened to restore order. Augustus put Judaea under the charge of a prefect answerable directly to the emperor. Religious matters and local affairs became the responsibility of the Sanhedrin, the highest Jewish judicial body. Although many prefects tried to perform their duties scrupulously and conscientiously, many others were rapacious and indifferent to Jewish culture. Often acting from fear rather than cruelty, some prefects fiercely stamped out any signs of popular discontent. Pontius Pilate, prefect in A.D. 26–36, is typical of such incompetent officials. Although eventually relieved of his duties in disgrace, Pilate brutally put down even innocent demonstrations. Especially hated were the Roman tax collectors, called publicans, many of whom pitilessly gouged the Jews. Publicans and sinners – the words became synonymous. Clashes between Roman troops and Jewish guerrillas inflamed the anger of both sides.

In A.D. 40 the emperor Caligula undid part of Augustus's good work by ordering his statue erected in the temple at Jerusalem. The order, though never carried out, further intensified Jewish resentment. Thus, the Jews became embittered by Roman rule because of taxes, sometimes unduly harsh enforcement of the law, and a misguided interference in their religion.

Among the Jews two movements spread. First was the rise of the Zealots, extremists who worked and fought to rid Judaea of the Romans. Resolute in their worship of Yahweh, they refused to pay any but the tax levied by the Jewish temple. Their battles with the Roman legionaries were marked by savagery on both sides. As usual, the innocent caught in the middle suffered grievously. As Roman policy grew tougher, even moderate Jews began to hate the conquerors. Judaea came more and more to resemble a tinderbox, ready to burst into flames at a single spark.

The second movement was the growth of militant apocalyptic sentiment – the belief that the coming of the Messiah was near. This belief was an old one among the Jews. But by the first century A.D. it had become more widespread and fervent than ever before. Typical was the Apocalypse of Baruch, which foretold the destruction of the Roman Empire. First would come a period of great tribulation, misery, and injustice. At the worst of the suffering, the Messiah would appear. The Messiah would destroy the Roman legions and all the kingdoms that had ruled Israel. Then the Messiah would inaugurate a period of happiness and plenty.

This was no abstract notion among the Jews. As the ravages of war became ever more widespread and conditions worsened, more and more people prophesied the imminent coming of the Messiah. One such was John the Baptist, "the voice of one crying in the wilderness, prepare ye the way of the lord."[9] Many Jews did just that. The sect described in the Dead Sea Scrolls readied itself for the end of the world. Its members were probably Essenes, and their social organization closely resembled that of the early Christians. Members of this group shared their possessions, precisely as John the Baptist urged people to do. Yet this sect, unlike the Christians, also made military preparations for the day of the Messiah.

Into this climate of Roman severity, fanatical Zealotry, and Messianic hope came Jesus of Nazareth (ca 3 B.C.–A.D. 29). He was raised in Galilee, the stronghold of the Zealots. Yet Jesus himself was a man of peace. Jesus urged his listeners to love god as their father and each other as god's children. The kingdom that he proclaimed was no earthly one, but one of eternal happiness in a life after death. Jesus' teachings are strikingly similar to those of Hillel (30 B.C.–A.D. 9), a great rabbi and interpreter of the Scriptures. Hillel taught the Jews to love one another as they loved god. He taught them to treat others as they themselves wished to be treated. Jesus' preaching was in this same serene tradition.

Jesus' teachings were entirely and thoroughly Jewish. He declared that he would change not one jot or tittle of the Jewish law. His orthodoxy enabled him to preach in the synagogue and the temple. His only deviation from orthodoxy was his insistence that he taught in his own name, not in the name of Yahweh. Was he then the Messiah? A small band of followers thought so, and Jesus revealed himself to them as the Messiah. Yet Jesus had his own conception of the Messiah. Unlike the Messiah of the Apocalypse of Baruch, Jesus would not destroy the Roman Empire. He told his disciples flatly that they were to "render unto Caesar the things that are Caesar's." Jesus would establish a spiritual kingdom, not an earthly one. Repeatedly he told his disciples that his kingdom was "not of this world."

Of Jesus' life and teachings the prefect Pontius Pilate knew little and cared even less. All that concerned him was the maintenance of peace and order. The crowds following Jesus at the time of the Passover, a highly emotional time in the Jewish year, alarmed Pilate, who faced a volatile situation. Some Jews believed that Jesus was the long-awaited Messiah. Others were disappointed because he refused to preach rebellion against Rome. Still others who hated and feared Jesus wanted to be rid of him. The last thing that Pilate wanted was a riot on his hands. Christian tradition has made much of Pontius Pilate. In the medieval West he was considered a monster. In the Ethiopian church he is considered a saint. Neither monster nor saint, Pilate was simply a hard-bitten Roman official. He did his duty, at times harshly. In Judaea his duty was to enforce the law and to keep the peace. These were the problems on his mind when Jesus stood before him. Jesus as King of the Jews did not worry him. The popular agitation surrounding Jesus did. To avert a riot

and bloodshed Pilate condemned Jesus to death.

Once Pilate's soldiers had carried out the sentence, the entire matter seemed to be closed. There were rumors that Jesus had risen from the dead or that his disciples had stolen his body, but otherwise the tumult subsided. Jesus' followers lived quietly and peacefully, unmolested by Roman or Jew. Pilate had no quarrel with them, and Judaism already had many minor sects. Peter (d. A.D. 67?), the first of Jesus' followers, became the head of the sect, which continued to observe Jewish law and religious customs. Peter, a man of traditional Jewish beliefs, felt that Jesus' teachings were meant exclusively for the Jews. Only in their practices of baptism and the Lord's Supper did the sect differ from normal Jewish custom. Meanwhile, they awaited the return of Jesus.

Christianity might have remained a purely Jewish sect had it not been for Paul of Tarsus (A.D. 5?–67?). The conversion of Hellenized Jews and of Gentiles (non-Jews) to Christianity caused the sect grave problems. Were the Gentiles subject to the law of Moses? If not, was Christianity to have two sets of laws? The answer to these questions was Paul's momentous contribution to Christianity. Paul was unlike Jesus or Peter. Born in a thriving and busy city filled with Romans, Greeks, Jews, Syrians, and others, he was at home in the world of Greco-Roman culture. After his conversion to Christianity he taught that his native Judaism was the preparation for the Messiah, and that Jesus by his death and resurrection had fulfilled the prophesy of Judaism and initiated a new age. Paul taught that Jesus was the Son of God, the beginning of a new law, and he preached that Jesus' teachings were to be proclaimed to all people, whether Jew or Gentile. Paul thus made a significant break with Judaism, Christianity's parent religion, for Judaism was exclusive and did not seek converts.

Paul's influence was far greater than that of any other early Christian. He traveled the length and breadth of the eastern Roman world, spreading his doctrine and preaching of Jesus. To little assemblies of believers in cities as distant as Rome and Corinth he taught that Jesus had died to save all people. Paul's vision of Christianity won out over Peter's traditionalism. Christianity broke with Judaism and embarked on its own course.

What was Christianity's appeal to the Roman world? What did this obscure sect give people that other religions did not? Christianity possessed many different attractions. One of its appeals was its willingness to embrace both men and women, slaves and nobles. Many of the Eastern mystery religions with which Christianity competed were exclusive in one way or another. Mithraism, a mystery religion descended from Zoroastrianism, spread throughout the entire empire. Mithras the sun god embodied good and warred against evil. Like Christianity, Mithraism offered elaborate and moving rituals including a form of baptism, a code of moral conduct, and the promise of life after death. Unlike Christianity, however, Mithraism permitted only men to become devotees. Much the same was true of the ancient Eleusinian mysteries of Greece, which were open only to Greeks and Romans.

Christianity appealed to common people and to the poor. Its communal celebration of the Lord's Supper gave men and women a sense of belonging. Christianity also offered its adherents the promise of salvation. Christians believed that Jesus on the cross had defeated evil, and that he would reward his followers with eternal life after death. Christianity also offered the possibility of forgiveness. Human nature was weak, and even the best Christians would fall into sin. But Jesus loved sinners and forgave those who repented. In its doctrine of salvation and forgiveness alone Christianity had a powerful ability to give solace and strength to those who believed.

Christianity was attractive to many because it gave the Roman world a cause. Hellenistic philosophy had attempted to make men and women self-sufficient: people who became indifferent to the outside world could no longer be hurt by it. That goal alone ruled out any cause except the attainment of serenity. The Romans, who were never innovators in philosophy, merely elaborated this lonely and austere message. Instead of passivity Christianity stressed the ideal of striving for a goal. Each and every Christian, no matter how poor or humble, worked to realize the triumph of Christianity on earth. This was God's will, a sacred duty for every Christian. By spreading the word of Christ, Christians played their part in God's plan. No matter how small a part each Christian played, that part was important. Since this duty was God's will, Christians believed that sooner or later the goal would be achieved. The Christian was not to be discouraged by temporary setbacks, believing Christianity to be invincible.

Christianity gave its devotees a sense of community. No Christian was alone. All members of the Christian community strived toward the same goal of fulfilling God's plan. Each individual community was in turn a member of a greater community. And that community, the Church General, was indestructible. After all, Jesus himself had promised, "Thou art Peter, and upon this rock I will build my church; and the gates of hell shall not prevail against it."[10]

So Christianity's attractions were many, from forgiveness of sin to an exalted purpose for each individual. Its insistence on the importance of the individual gave solace and encouragement, especially to the poor and meek. Its claim to divine protection fed hope in the eventual success of the Christian community. Christianity made participation in the universal possible for each and every person. The ultimate reward promised by Christianity was eternal bliss after death. Though at first the educated and wealthy scoffed at this message, they too succumbed to its charm. It was unlike anything the average man and woman had ever known.

THE JULIO-CLAUDIANS AND THE FLAVIANS (27 B.C.–A.D. 96)

For fifty years after Augustus's death the dynasty that he established – known as the Julio-Claudians because they were all members of the Julian and Claudian clans – provided the emperors of Rome. Some of the Julio-Claudians, like Tiberius and Claudius, were sound rulers and able administrators. Others, like Caligula and Nero, were weak and frivolous men who exercised their power stupidly and brought misery to the empire. Writers such as the biting and brilliant historian Tacitus (ca A.D. 55–ca 116) and the gossipy Suetonius (ca A.D. 75–150) have left unforgettable – and generally hostile – portraits of these emperors that are literary masterpieces. Yet the venom of Tacitus and Suetonius cannot obscure the fact that Julio-Claudians were responsible for some notable achievements and that during their reigns the empire on the whole prospered.

One of the most momentous achievements of the Julio-Claudians was Claudius's creation of an imperial bureaucracy composed of professional administrators. Even the most energetic emperor could not run the empire alone.

The numerous duties and immense reponsibilities of the emperor prompted Claudius to delegate power. He began by giving the freedmen of his household official duties, especially in the field of finances. It was a simple, workable system. Claudius knew his ex-slaves well and could discipline them at will. The effect of Claudius's innovations was to enable the emperor to rule the empire more easily and efficiently.

One of the worst defects of Augustus's settlement – the army's ability to interfere in politics – became obvious during the Julio-Claudian period. Augustus had created a special standing force, the Praetorian Guard, as an imperial bodyguard. In A.D. 41 one of the praetorians murdered Caligula while others hailed Claudius as the emperor. Under the threat of violence the senate ratified the praetorians' choice. It was a story repeated frequently. During the first three centuries of the empire the Praetorian Guard all too often murdered emperors they were supposed to protect and saluted emperors of their own choosing.

In A.D. 69, Nero's inept rule led to an extensive military uprising that caused widespread disruption. No fewer than four men became emperor that year, known as the Year of the Four Emperors. Roman armies in Gaul, on the Rhine, and in the East marched on Rome to make their commanders emperor. The man who emerged triumphant was Vespasian, commander of the eastern armies, who entered Rome in 70 and restored order. Nonetheless, the Year of the Four Emperors proved that the Augustan settlement had failed to end civil war.

Not a brilliant politician, Vespasian did not institute reforms as had Augustus or tackle the problem of the army in politics. To prevent usurpers from claiming the throne Vespasian designated his sons Titus and Domitian as his successors. By establishing the Flavian (the name of Vespasian's clan) dynasty Vespasian turned the principate into an open and admitted monarchy. He also expanded the power of the emperor by increasing the size of the budding bureaucracy Claudius had created.

One of Vespasian's first tasks was to suppress rebellions that had erupted at the end of Nero's reign. The most famous had taken place in Judaea, which still seethed long after Jesus' crucifixion. Long-standing popular unrest and atrocities committed by Jews and Romans alike sparked a massive revolt in A.D. 66. Four years later a Roman army reconquered Judaea and reduced Jerusalem by siege. The Jewish survivors were enslaved, their state destroyed. The mismanagement of Judaea was one of the few — and worst — failures of Roman imperial administration.

The Flavians carried on Augustus's work on the frontiers. Domitian, the last of the Flavians, won additional territory in Germany and consolidated it in two new provinces. He defeated barbarian tribes on the Danube frontier and strengthened that area as well. Nonetheless, Domitian was one of the most hated of Roman emperors, and he fell victim to an assassin's dagger. Nevertheless, the Flavians had given the Roman world peace and had kept the legions in line. Their work paved the way for the era of the "Five Good Emperors," the golden age of the empire.

THE AGE OF THE FIVE GOOD EMPERORS (A.D. 96–180)

In the second century of the Christian era, the Empire of Rome comprehended the fairest part of the earth, and the most civilised portion of mankind. The frontiers of that extensive monarchy

THE PRAETORIAN GUARD *Instituted by Augustus as the imperial bodyguard, the Praetorian Guard began making and breaking emperors as early as the Julio-Claudian period. For all of their power, they were not crack troops, but their access to the emperor gave them an influence far greater than their numerical strength or fighting ability. (Giraudon)*

were guarded by ancient renown and disciplined valour. The gentle but powerful influence of laws and manners had gradually cemented the union of the provinces. Their peaceful inhabitants enjoyed and abused the advantages of wealth and luxury. The image of a free constitution was preserved with decent reverence: the Roman senate appeared to possess the sovereign authority, and devolved on the emperors all the executive powers of government. During a happy period (A.D. 98–180) of more than fourscore years, the public administration was conducted by the virtue and abilities of Nerva, Trajan, Hadrian, and the two Antonines.[11]

Thus Edward Gibbon (1737–1794) began his monumental *History of the Decline and Fall of the Roman Empire.* Gibbon saw the era of Nerva, Trajan, Hadrian, Antoninus Pius, and Marcus Aurelius – the "five good emperors" – as the happiest period in human history, the last burst of summer before the autumn of failure and barbarism. Gibbon recognized a great truth: the age of the Antonines, as the "five good emperors" are often called, was one of almost unparalleled prosperity. Wars were minor and confined to the frontiers. Even the serenity of Augustus's day seemed to pale in comparison. These emperors were among the noblest, most dedicated, and ablest men in Roman history. Yet fundamental political and military changes had taken place since Augustus's day.

THE ANTONINE MONARCHY

The age of the Antonines was the age of full-blown monarchy. Gibbon wrote:

The obvious definition of a monarchy seems to be that of a state, in which a single person, by whatsoever name he may be distinguished, is entrusted with the execution of the laws, the management of the revenue, and the command of the army.[12]

Augustus clearly fits Gibbon's definition of a monarch in all essentials. But there is a significant difference between Augustus's position and that of an emperor like Hadrian.

Augustus claimed that his influence arose from the collection of offices the senate had bestowed upon him. However, there was in law no such office as emperor. Augustus was merely the First Citizen. Under the Flavians the principate became a full-blown monarchy, and by the time of the Antonines the principate was an office with definite rights, powers, and prerogatives. In the years between Augustus and the Antonines the emperor had become an indispensable part of the imperial machinery. In short, without the emperor the

empire would quickly fall to pieces. Augustus had been monarch in fact but not in theory; the Antonines were monarchs in both.

The Antonines were not power-hungry autocrats. The concentration of power was the result of empire, as the American historian M. Hammond has pointed out:

Monarchy was indeed an inescapable result of the existence of the empire; the more efficient the imperial government became, the more it assumed new functions; and the more that increasing pressure made its task heavier, so much the more it became monarchical.[13]

In short, the easiest and most efficient way to run the Roman Empire was to invest the emperor with vast powers. Furthermore, Roman emperors on the whole proved to be effective rulers and administrators. As capable and efficient emperors took on new tasks and functions, the hand of the emperor was felt in more and more areas of life and government. Increasingly, the emperors became the source of all authority and guidance within the empire. The five good emperors were benevolent and exercised their power intelligently, but they were absolute kings all the same. Lesser men would later throw off the façade of constitutionality and use this same power in a despotic fashion.

Typical of the five good emperors is the career of Hadrian, who became emperor in A.D. 117. He was born in Spain, a fact that illustrates the importance of the provinces in Roman politics. Hadrian received his education at Rome and became an ardent admirer of Greek culture. He caught the attention of his elder cousin Trajan – the future emperor – who started him on a military career. At age nineteen Hadrian served on the Danube frontier, where he learned the details of how the Roman army lived and fought and saw for himself the problems of defending the fron-

ROMAN HISTORY AFTER AUGUSTUS

PERIOD	IMPORTANT EMPERORS	SIGNIFICANT EVENTS
Julio-Claudians 27 B.C.–A.D. 68	Augustus, 27 B.C.–A.D. 14 Tiberius, 14–37 Caligula, 37–41 Claudius, 41–54 Nero, 54–68	Augustan settlement Beginning of the principate Birth and death of Jesus Expansion into northern and western Europe Creation of the imperial bureaucracy
Year of the Four Emperors, 68–69	Nero Galba Otho Vitellius	Civil war Major breakdown of the concept of the principate
Flavians 69–96	Vespasian, 69–79 Titus, 79–81 Domitian, 81–96	Growing trend toward the concept of monarchy Defense and further consolidation of the European frontiers
Antonines 96–192	Nerva, 96–98 Trajan, 98–117 Hadrian, 117–138 Antoninus Pius, 138–161 Marcus Aurelius, 161–180 Commodus, 180–192	The "golden age" – the era of the "five good emperors" Economic prosperity Trade and growth of cities in northern Europe Beginning of barbarian menace on the frontiers
Severi 193–235	Septimius Severus, 193–211 Caracalla, 211–217 Elagabalus, 218–222 Severus Alexander, 222–235	Military monarchy All free men within the empire given Roman citizenship
"Barracks Emperors" 235–284	Twenty-two emperors in forty-nine years	Civil war Breakdown of the Empire Barbarian invasions Severe economic decline
Tetrarchy 284–337	Diocletian, 284–305 Constantine, 306–337	Political recovery Autocracy Legalization of Christianity Transition to the Middle Ages in the West Birth of the Byzantine Empire in the East

tiers. When Trajan became emperor in A.D. 98, he began giving Hadrian high military and administrative positions in which he learned how to defend and run the empire. At Trajan's death in 117, Hadrian assumed the reins of power.

Roman government had changed since Augustus's day. One of the most significant changes was the enormous growth of the imperial bureaucracy created by Claudius. Hadrian reformed this system by putting the bureaucracy on an organized, official basis. He established imperial administrative departments to handle the work formerly done by the imperial freedmen. Hadrian also separated civil service from military service. Men with little talent or taste for the army could instead serve the state as administrators. Hadrian's bureaucracy demanded professionalism from its members. Administrators made a career of the civil service. These innovations made for more efficient running of the empire, and increased the authority of the emperor, who was the ruling power of the bureaucracy.

CHANGES IN THE ARMY

The Roman army had also changed since Augustus's time. The Roman legion had once been a mobile unit, but its duties under the empire no longer called for mobility. The successors of Augustus called a halt to further conquests. The army was expected to defend what had already been won. Under the Flavian emperors (A.D. 69–96) the frontiers became firmly fixed. Forts and watch stations guarded the borders. Behind the forts the Romans built a system of roads, which allowed the forts to be quickly supplied and reinforced in times of trouble. The army had evolved into a garrison force, with legions guarding specific areas for long periods.

The personnel of the legions was changing too. Italy could no longer supply all the recruits needed for the army. Increasingly, only the officers came from Italy and from the more Romanized provinces. The legionaries were mostly drawn from the less civilized provinces, especially the ones closest to the frontiers. A major trend was already obvious in Hadrian's day: fewer and fewer Roman soldiers were really Roman. In the third century A.D., the barbarization of the army would result in an army indifferent to Rome and its traditions. In the age of the Antonines, however, the army was still a source of economic stability and a Romanizing agent. Provincials and even barbarians joined the army to learn a trade and to gain Roman citizenship. Even so, the signs were ominous. Julius Caesar's veterans would hardly have recognized Hadrian's troops as Roman legionaries.

LIFE IN THE GOLDEN AGE

If a man were called to fix the period in the history of the world, during which the condition of the human race was most happy and prosperous, he would without hesitation, name that which elapsed from the death of Domitian to the accession of Commodus.[14]

Thus, according to Gibbon, the age of the five good emperors was a golden age in human history. How does Gibbon's picture correspond to the popular image of Rome as a city of bread, brothels, and gladiatorial games? If the Romans were degenerates who spent their time carousing, who kept Rome and the empire running? Can life in Rome be taken as representative of life in other parts of the empire?

Truth and exaggeration are mixed both in Gibbon's view and in the popular image of Rome. Rome and the provinces must be treated separately. Rome no more resembled a provincial city like Cologne than New York resembles Keokuk, Iowa. Rome was unique and must be seen as such. Only then can one turn to the provinces to obtain a full and reasonable picture of the empire under the Antonines.

IMPERIAL ROME

Rome was truly an extraordinary city, especially by ancient standards. It was also an enormous city, with a population somewhere between 500,000 and 750,000. Although Rome could boast of stately palaces, noble buildings, and beautiful residential areas, most people lived in jerrybuilt apartment houses. Fire and crime were perennial problems, even after Augustus created fire and urban police forces. Streets were narrow and drainage inadequate. During the republic sanitation had been a common problem. Numerous inscriptions record prohibitions against the dumping of human refuse and even cadavers within the grounds of sanctuaries and cemeteries. Under the empire this situation improved. By comparison with medieval and early modern European cities, Rome was a healthy enough place to live.

Rome was such a huge city that the surrounding countryside could not feed it. Because of the danger of starvation, the emperor, following republican practice, provided the citizen population with free grain for bread, and later included oil and wine. By feeding the citizenry the emperor prevented bread riots caused by shortages and high prices. For the rest of the urban population who did not enjoy the rights of citizenship,

COIN OF HADRIAN   *The emperor Hadrian not only energetically ruled the Roman Empire, he also helped to set a new fashion in Rome by sporting a full beard. Since Scipio Aemilianus's day, Romans had ordinarily been clean-shaven. (Courtesy, World Heritage Museum. Photo: Caroline Buckler)*

the emperor provided grain at low prices. This measure was designed to prevent speculators from forcing up the price of grain in times of crisis. By maintaining the grain supply the emperor kept the favor of the people and insured that Rome's poor and idle did not starve.

The emperor also entertained the Roman populace, often at vast expense. The most popular forms of public entertainment were gladiatorial contests and chariot racing. Gladiatorial fighting was originally an Etruscan funerary custom, a blood sacrifice for the dead. Even a humane man like Hadrian staged extravagant contests. In A.D. 126 he sponsored six days of such combats, during which 1,835

pairs of gladiators dueled, usually with swords and shields. Many gladiators were criminals, some of whom were sentenced to be slaughtered in the arena. These convicts were given no defensive weapons and stood little real chance of survival. Other criminals were sentenced to fight in the arena as fully armed gladiators. Some gladiators were the slaves of gladiatorial trainers; others were prisoners of war. Still others were free men who volunteered for the arena. Even women at times engaged in gladiatorial combat. What drove these men and women? Some obviously had no other choice. For a criminal condemned to death, the arena was preferable to the imperial mines, where convicts worked digging ore and died under wretched conditions. At least in the arena the gladiator might fight well enough to win his or her freedom. Others no doubt fought for the love of danger and for fame. Although some Romans protested against gladiatorial fighting, most delighted in it — one of their least attractive sides. Not until the fifth century did Christianity put a stop to it.

The Romans were even more addicted to chariot racing than to gladiatorial shows. Under the empire four permanent teams competed against one another. Each team had its own color — red, white, green, or blue. Some Romans claimed that people cared more about their favorite team than about the race itself. Two-horse and four-horse chariots ran a course of seven laps, about five miles. A successful driver could be the hero of the hour. One charioteer, Gaius Appuleius Diocles, raced for twenty-four years. During that time he drove 4,257 starts and won 1,462 of them. His admirers honored him with an inscription that proclaimed him the champion of all charioteers.

But people like the charioteer Diocles were no more typical of the common Roman than Babe Ruth is of the average American. Ordinary Romans have left their mark in the inscriptions that grace their graves. These inscriptions offer a glimpse of Roman life. Ordinary Romans were proud of their work and accomplishments. They were affectionate toward their families and friends, and eager to be remembered after death. They did not spend their lives in idleness, watching gladiators or chariot races. They had to make a living. They dealt with everyday problems and rejoiced over small pleasures. An impression of them and their cares can be gained from their epitaphs. The funerary inscription of Paprius Vitalis to his wife is particularly engaging:

If there is anything good in the lower regions — I, however, finish a poor life without you — be happy there too, sweetest Thalassia . . . married to me for 40 years.[15]

As moving is the final tribute of a patron to his ex-slave:

To Grania Clara, freedwoman of Aulus, a temperate freedwoman. She lived 23 years. She was never vexatious to me except when she died.[16]

In another epitaph the wife of a merchant honored her husband for his honest dealings. Even the personal philosophies of typical Romans have come down from antiquity. Marcus Antonius Encolpus erected a funerary inscription to his wife that reads in part:

Do not pass by my epitaph, traveler.
But having stopped, listen and learn, then go your way.
There is no boat in Hades, no ferryman Charon,
no caretaker Aiakos, no dog Cerberus.
All we who are dead below
have become bones and ashes, but nothing else.
I have spoken to you honestly, go on, traveler,
lest even while dead I seem loquacious to you.[17]

Others put it more simply: "I was, I am not, I don't care." "To each his own tombstone." These Romans went about their lives much as people have always done. Though fond of brutal spectacles, they also had their loves and their dreams.

THE PROVINCES

In the provinces and even on the frontiers many men and women would have agreed with Gibbon's opinion of the second century. The age of the Antonines was one of extensive prosperity, especially in western Europe. The Roman army had beaten back the barbarians and exposed them to the civilizing effects of Roman traders. The resulting peace and security opened Britain, Gaul, Germany, and the lands of the Danube to immigration. Agriculture flourished as large tracts of land came under cultivation. Most of this land was in the hands of free tenant farmers. From the time of Augustus slavery had declined in the empire, as had the growth of latifundia (see page 168). Augustus and his successors encouraged the rise of free farmers. Under the Antonines this trend continued, and the holders of small parcels of land thrived as never before. The Antonines provided loans on easy terms to farmers. These loans enabled them to rent land previously worked by slaves. It also permitted them to cultivate the

SCENE FROM TRAJAN'S COLUMN From 101 to 107 Trajan fought the barbarian tribes along the Danube. This scene depicts Roman soldiers unloading supplies at a frontier city, which forms the background. Not only did such walled cities serve as Roman strong points, they were also centers of Roman civilization, with their shops, homes, temples, and amphitheaters. (Alinari/Scala)

new lands that were being opened up. Consequently, the small tenant farmer was becoming the backbone of Roman agriculture.

In continental Europe the army was largely responsible for the new burst of expansion. The areas where the legions were stationed readily became Romanized. When legionaries retired from the army, they often settled in the locality where they had served. Since they had usually learned a trade in the army, they brought essential skills to areas that badly needed trained men. These veterans took their retirement pay and used it to set themselves up in business.

Since the time of Augustus towns had gradually grown up around the camps and forts. The roads that linked the frontier with the rearward areas served as commercial lifelines for the new towns and villages. Part Roman, part barbarian, these towns were truly outposts of civilization, much like the raw towns of the American West. In the course of time many of them grew to be Romanized cities. As they did, emperors gave them the status of full Roman municipalities, with charters and constitutions. This development was very pronounced along the Rhine and Danube frontiers. Thus while defending the borders, the army also spread Roman culture. This process would go so far that in A.D. 212 the emperor Caracalla would grant Roman citizenship to every free man within the empire.

The eastern part of the empire also participated in the boom. The Roman navy had swept the sea of pirates, and Eastern merchants traded their wares throughout the Mediterranean. The flow of goods and produce in the East matched that of the West. Venerable cities like Corinth, Antioch, and Ephesus flourished as rarely before. The cities of the East built extensively, bedecking themselves with new amphitheaters, temples, fountains, and public buildings. For the East, the age of the Antonines was the heyday of the city. Urban life there grew ever richer and more comfortable.

Trade among the provinces increased dramatically. Britain and Belgium became prime producers of grain, much of their harvests going to the armies of the Rhine. Britain's famous wool industry probably got its start under the Romans. Italy and southern Gaul produced wine in huge quantities. The wines of Italy went principally to Rome and the Danube, while Gallic wines were shipped to Britain and the Rhineland. Roman colonists had introduced the olive to southern Spain and northern Africa, an experiment so successful that these regions produced most of the oil consumed in the western empire. In the East, Syrian farmers continued to cultivate the olive, and the production of oil reached an all-time high. Egypt was the prime grain producer of the East, and tons of Egyptian wheat went to feed the populace of Rome. The

Roman army in Mesopotamia consumed a high percentage of the raw materials and manufactured products of Syria and Asia Minor. The spread of trade meant the end of isolated and self-contained economies. By the time of the Antonines the empire had become an economic reality as well as a political one.

One of the most striking features of this period was the growth of industry in the provinces. Cities in Gaul and Germany eclipsed the old Mediterranean manufacturing centers. Italian cities were particularly hard-hit by this development. Cities like Arrentium and Capua had dominated the production of glass, pottery, and bronze ware. Yet in the second century A.D. Gaul and Germany took over the pottery market. Lyons in Gaul became the new center of the glassmaking industry. The technique of glass blowing spread to Britain and Germany, and later in the second century Cologne replaced Lyons in glass production. The cities of Gaul were nearly unrivaled in the manufacture of bronze and brass. Gallic craftsmen invented a new technique of tin-plating and decorated their work with Celtic designs. Their wares soon drove Italian products out of the northern European market. For the first time in history northern Europe was able to rival the Mediterranean as a producer of manufactured goods. Europe had entered fully into the economic and cultural life of the Mediterranean world.

The age of the Antonines was generally one of peace, progress, and prosperity. The work of the Romans in northern and western Europe was a permanent contribution to the history of Western society. The cities that grew up in Britain, Belgium, Gaul, Germany, Austria, and elsewhere survived the civil wars that racked the empire in the third century A.D. Likewise, they survived the barbarian invasions that destroyed the western empire, and handed on a precious heritage, both cultural and material, to the medieval world. The period of the Antonine monarchy was also one of consolidation. Roads and secure sea-lanes linked the empire in one vast web. The empire had become a commonwealth of cities, and urban life was the hallmark of this civilization.

CIVIL WARS AND INVASION IN THE THIRD CENTURY

The age of the Antonines gave way to a period of chaos and stress. During the third century A.D., the empire was stunned by civil wars and barbarian invasions. By the time peace was restored, the economy was shattered, cities had shrunk in size, and agriculture was becoming manorial (see pages 203–204). In the disruption of the third century and the reconstruction of the fourth, the medieval world had its origins.

After the death of Marcus Aurelius, the last of the five good emperors, his son Commodus came to the throne, a man who was totally unsuited to govern the empire. His misrule led to his murder and a renewal of civil war. After a brief but intense spasm of fighting, the African general Septimius Severus defeated other rival commanders and established the Severan dynasty (A.D. 193–235). Although Septimius Severus was able to stabilize the empire, his successors proved incapable of disciplining the legions. When the last of the Severi was killed by one of his own soldiers, the empire plunged into still another grim, destructive, and this time prolonged round of civil war.

Over twenty different emperors ascended the throne in the forty-nine years between 235

and 284, and many rebels died in the attempt to seize power. At various times, parts of the empire were lost to rebel generals, one of whom, Postumus, set up his own empire in Gaul for about ten years (A.D. 259–269). Yet other men like the iron-willed Aurelian (A.D. 270–275) dedicated their energies to restoring order. So many military commanders seized rule that the middle of the third century has become known as the age of the "barracks emperors." The Augustan Principate had become a military monarchy, and that monarchy was nakedly autocratic.

The disruption caused by civil war opened the way for widespread barbarian invasions. Throughout the empire, barbarian invasions and civil war devastated towns, villages, and farms and caused a catastrophic economic depression. Indeed, the Roman Empire seemed on the point of collapse.

BARBARIANS ON THE FRONTIERS

The first and most disastrous result of the civil wars was trouble on the frontiers. It was Rome's misfortune that this era of anarchy coincided with immense movements of barbarian peoples. Historians still dispute the precise reason for these migrations, though their immediate cause was pressure from tribes moving westward across Asia. In the sixth century A.D., Jordanes, a Christianized Goth, preserved the memory of innumerable wars among the barbarians in his *History of the Goths*. Goths fought Vandals, Huns fought Goths. Steadily, the defeated and displaced tribes moved toward the Roman frontiers. Finally, like "a swarm of bees" – to use Jordanes's image – the Goths burst into Europe in A.D. 258.

When the barbarians reached the Rhine and Danube frontiers, they often found huge gaps in the Roman defenses. Typical is the case of Decius, a general who guarded the Danube frontier in Dacia (modern Rumania). In A.D. 249, he revolted and invaded Italy in an effort to become emperor. Decius left the frontier deserted, and the Goths easily poured in looking for new homes. Through much of the third century A.D., bands of Goths devastated the Balkans as far south as Greece. They even penetrated Asia Minor. The Alamanni, a German people, swept across the Danube. At one point they entered Italy and reached Milan before they were beaten back. Meanwhile the Franks, still another German folk, hit the Rhine frontier. The Franks then invaded eastern and central Gaul and northeastern Spain. Saxons from Scandinavia entered the English Channel in search of loot. In the East the Sassanids, of Persian stock, overran Mesopotamia. If the army had been guarding the borders instead of creating and destroying emperors, none of these invasions would have been possible. The "barracks emperors" should be credited with one accomplishment, however: they fought barbarians when they were not fighting each other. Only that kept the empire from total ruin.

TURMOIL IN FARM AND VILLAGE LIFE

How did the ordinary people cope with this period of iron and blood? What did it mean to the lives of men and women on farms and in villages? How did local officials continue to serve their emperor and their neighbors? Some people became outlaws. Others lived their lives more prosaically. Some voiced their grievances to the emperor, thereby leaving a record of the problems they faced. In a sur-

prising number of cases the barbarians were less of a problem than the lawlessness of soldiers, imperial officials, and local agents. For many ordinary people official corruption was the tangible and immediate result of the breakdown of central authority. In one instance some tenant farmers in Lydia (modern Turkey) complained to the emperor about arbitrary arrest and the killing of prisoners. They claimed that police agents had threatened them and prevented them from cultivating the land. Tenant farmers in Phrygia (modern Turkey) voiced similar complaints. They suffered extortion at the hands of public officials. Military commanders, soldiers, and imperial agents requisitioned their livestock and compelled the farmers to forced labor. The farmers were becoming impoverished, and many people deserted the land to seek safety elsewhere. The inhabitants of an entire village in Thrace (modern Bulgaria) complained that they were being driven from their homes. From imperial and local officials they suffered insolence and violence. Soldiers demanded to be quartered and given supplies. Many villagers had already abandoned their homes to escape. The remaining villagers warned the emperor that unless order was restored, they too would flee.

Local officials were sometimes unsympathetic or violent toward farmers and villagers because of their own plight. They were responsible for the collection of imperial revenues. If their area could not meet its tax quota, they paid the deficit from their own pockets. For instance, Aurelius Hermophilus complained that he could no longer perform public duties because he had gone bankrupt. When Aemilius Stephanus, a wealthy Roman in Egypt, learned that he had been nominated to the local council of his town, he surrendered all his property to the man who had nominated him. In one Egyptian municipality fistfights broke out among the officials. Finally the emperor had to forbid fighting in the council house. Because the local officials were so hard-pressed, they squeezed whatever they could from the villagers and farmers.

RECONSTRUCTION UNDER DIOCLETIAN AND CONSTANTINE (A.D. 284–337)

At the close of the third century A.D., the emperor Diocletian (284–305) put an end to the period of turmoil. Repairing the damage done in the third century was the major work of the emperor Constantine (306–337) in the fourth. But the price was high.

Under Diocletian, Augustus's polite fiction of the emperor as "first among equals" gave way to the emperor as absolute autocrat. The princeps became *dominus* – lord. The emperor claimed that he was "the elect of god" – that he ruled because of god's favor. Constantine even claimed to be the equal of Jesus' first twelve followers. To underline the emperor's exalted position, Diocletian and Constantine adopted the gaudy court ceremonies and trappings of the Persian Empire. People entering the emperor's presence prostrated themselves before him and kissed the hem of his robes. Constantine went so far as to import Persian eunuchs to run the palace. The Roman emperor had become an oriental monarch.

No mere soldier, Diocletian gave serious thought to the ailments of the empire. He recognized that the empire and its difficulties had become too great for one man to handle. He also realized that during the third century provincial governors had frequently used their positions to foment or participate in rebellions. To solve the first of these problems

MAP 6.2 THE ROMAN WORLD DIVIDED Under Diocletian, the Roman empire was first divided into a western and an eastern half, a development that foreshadowed the medieval division between the Latin West and the Byzantine East.

Diocletian divided the empire into a western half and an eastern half (see Map 6.2). Diocletian assumed direct control of the eastern part; he gave the rule of the western part to a colleague, along with the title *augustus,* which had become synonymous with emperor. Diocletian and his fellow augustus further delegated power by appointing two men to assist them. Each man was given the title of *caesar* to indicate his exalted rank. Although this system is known as the Tetrarchy because four men ruled the empire, Diocletian was clearly the senior partner and the final source of authority.

Each half of the empire was further split into two prefectures, governed by a prefect responsible to an augustus. Diocletian reduced the power of the old provincial governors by dividing provinces into smaller units: he organized the prefectures into smaller administrative units called dioceses, which were in turn subdivided into small provinces. Provincial governors were also deprived of their military power, leaving them only civil and administrative duties.

Diocletian's division of the empire into two parts was a momentous step, for it became permanent. Constantine and later emperors tried hard to keep the empire together, but without success. Throughout the fourth century A.D., the East and the West drifted apart. In later centuries the western part witnessed the fall of Roman government and the rise of barbarian kingdoms, while the eastern empire evolved into the majestic Byzantine Empire.

The most serious immediate matters con-

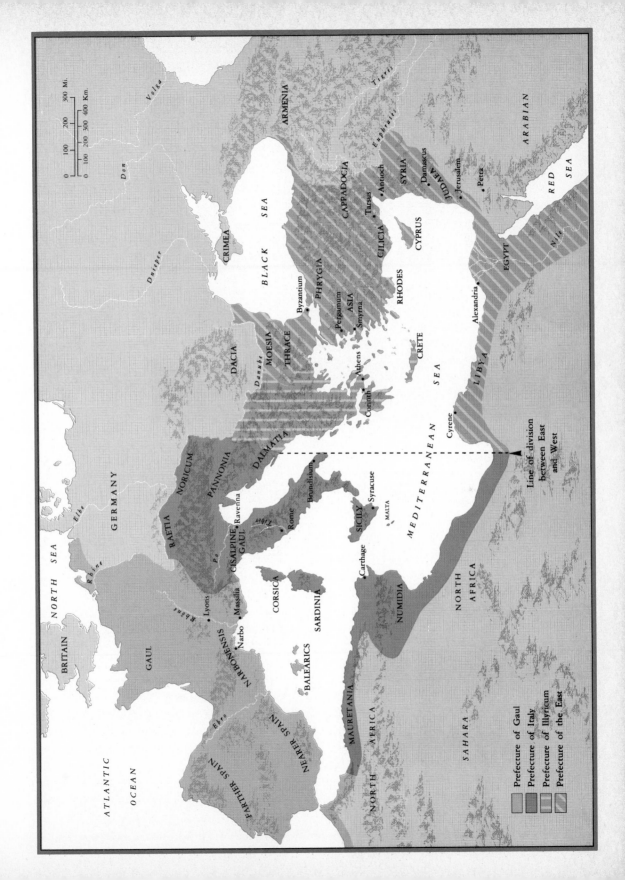

300 Mi.
0   100   200
0 100 200 300 400 Km.

ATLANTIC
OCEAN

NORTH
SEA

BRITAIN

Elbe

GERMANY

Rhine

GAUL

NARBONENSIS

Lyons
Massilia
Narbo

Rhône

Ebro

NEARER SPAIN

FARTHER SPAIN

BALEARICS

CORSICA

SARDINIA

MAURETANIA

NORTH AFRICA

SAHARA

RAETIA

NORICUM

PANNONIA

DALMATIA

CISALPINE GAUL

Ravenna
Po
Rome
Tiber

Brundisium

SICILY
Syracuse
MALTA

Carthage

NUMIDIA

NORTH AFRICA

MEDITERRANEAN SEA

DACIA

MOESIA

THRACE

Danube

Byzantium

PHRYGIA

Pergamum
ASIA
Smyrna

Athens

Corinth

CRETE

CRIMEA

Dnieper

Don

Volga

BLACK SEA

ARMENIA

CAPPADOCIA

Tarsus

CILICIA

Antioch

SYRIA

Damascus

JUDAEA

Jerusalem

Petra

Euphrates

Tigris

CYPRUS

RHODES

LIBYA

Cyrene

EGYPT

Alexandria

Nile

ARABIAN

RED SEA

Line of division
between East
and West

Prefecure of Gaul
Prefecture of Italy
Prefecture of Illyricum
Prefecure of the East

THE ARCH OF CONSTANTINE   *To celebrate the victory which made him emperor, Constantine built this triumphal arch at Rome. Rather than decorate the arch with the inferior work of his own day, Constantine plundered other Roman monuments, including those of Trajan and Marcus Aurelius. (Italian Government Travel Office)*

fronting Diocletian and Constantine were economic, social, and religious. They needed additional revenues to support the army and the imperial court. Yet the wars and the barbarian invasions had caused widespread destruction and poverty. The fighting had struck a serious blow to Roman agriculture, which the emperors tried to revive. Christianity had become too strong either to ignore or to crush. How Diocletian, Constantine, and their successors dealt with those problems helped create the economic and social patterns medieval Europe inherited.

INFLATION AND TAXES

The barracks emperors had dealt with economic hardship by depreciating the currency: they cut the silver content of coins until money was virtually worthless. As a result the entire monetary system fell into ruin. In Egypt governors had to order bankers to accept imperial money. The immediate result was a crippling inflation throughout the empire.

The empire was less capable of recovery than in earlier times. Wars and invasions had disrupted normal commerce and the means of production. Mines were exhausted in the attempt to supply much-needed ores, especially gold and silver. War and invasion had hit the cities especially hard. Markets were disrupted, and travel became dangerous. Craftsmen, artisans, and traders rapidly left devastated regions. The prosperous industry and commerce of Gaul and the Rhineland declined markedly. Those who owed their prosperity to commerce and the needs of urban life likewise suffered. Cities were no longer places where trade and industry thrived. The devastation of the countryside increased the difficulty of feeding and supplying the cities. The destruction was so extensive that many wondered whether the ravages could be repaired at all.

The response of Diocletian and Constantine to these problems was marked by compulsion, rigidity, and loss of individual freedom. Diocletian's attempt to curb inflation illustrates the methods of absolute monarchy: in a move unprecedented in Roman history, he issued an edict that fixed maximum prices and wages throughout the empire. The measure failed because it was unrealistic and unenforceable.

The emperors dealt with the tax system just as strictly and inflexibly. As in the past, local officials bore the responsibility of collecting imperial taxes. Constantine made these officials into a hereditary class; son followed father whether he wanted to or not. In this period of severe depression, many localities could not pay their taxes. In such cases these local officials had to make up the difference from their own funds. This system soon wiped out a whole class of moderately wealthy people.

With the monetary system in ruins, most imperial taxes became payable in kind — that is, in goods or produce instead of money. The major drawback of payment in kind is its demands on transportation. Goods have to be moved from where they are grown or manufactured to where they are needed. Accordingly, the emperors locked into their occupations all those involved in the growing, preparation, and transportation of food and essential commodities. A baker or shipper could not go into any other business, and his son took up the trade upon his death. The late Roman Empire had a place for everyone, and everyone had a place.

THE DECLINE OF SMALL FARMS

The late Roman heritage to the medieval world is most obvious in agriculture. Because of worsening conditions, free tenant farmers were reduced to serfdom. During the third century A.D., many were killed or fled the land to escape the barbarians, or abandoned farms ravaged in the fighting. Consequently, large tracts of land lay deserted. Great landlords with ample resources began at once to reclaim as much of this land as they could. The huge estates that resulted were the forerunners of medieval manors. Like manors, villas were self-sufficient. Since they often produced more than they consumed, they successfully competed with the declining cities by selling their surplus in the countryside. They became islands of stability in an unsettled world.

While the villas were growing, the small farmers who remained on the land barely held their own. They were too poor and powerless to stand against the tide of chaos. They were exposed to the raids of barbarians or brigands and to the tyranny of imperial officials. For relief they turned to the great landlords. After all, the landowners were men of considerable resources, lords in their own right. They were wealthy, and they had many people working

A LARGE ROMAN VILLA   During the third and fourth centuries, as the Roman Empire was breaking up, large villas such as this often became the focus of life. The villa was at once a fortress, as can be seen by the towers at the corner of the building, and the economic and social center of the neighborhood. (Courtesy, German Archeological Institute)

their land. They were independent and capable of defending themselves. If need be, they could — and at times did — field a small force of their own. Already influential, they stood up to imperial officials.

In return for the protection and security that landlords could offer, the small landholders gave over their lands. Free men and their families became clients of the landlords, and lost much of their freedom. To guarantee a steady supply of labor the landlords bound them to the soil. They could no longer decide to move elsewhere. Henceforth, they and their families worked the land of their patrons. Free men and women were in effect becoming serfs.

THE LEGALIZATION OF CHRISTIANITY

In religious affairs Constantine took the decisive step of recognizing Christianity as a legitimate religion. No longer would Christians suffer persecution for their beliefs. Constantine himself died a Christian in 337. Constantine has been depicted both as a devout convert to Christianity and as a realistic opportunist who used the young religion to his own imperial ends. Certainly Constantine was realistic enough to recognize and appreciate Christianity's spread and hold on his subjects. He correctly gauged the strength of the Christian ecclesiastical organization, and realized that the new church could serve as a friend of his empire. Yet there is no solid reason to doubt the sincerity of his conversion to the Christian religion. In short, Constantine was a man personally inclined toward Christianity and an emperor who could bestow on it a legal and legitimate place within the Roman empire.

Why had the pagans – those who believed in the Greco-Roman gods – persecuted Christians in the first place? Polytheism is by nature tolerant of new gods and accommodating in religious matters. Why was Christianity singled out for violence? These questions are still matters of scholarly debate, but some broad answers can be given.

Even an educated and cultured man like the historian Tacitus opposed Christianity. He believed that Christians hated the whole human race. As a rule early Christians, like Jews, kept to themselves. Romans distrusted and feared their exclusiveness, which seemed unsociable and even subversive. Most pagans genuinely misunderstood Christian practices. They thought that the Lord's Supper, at which Christians said they ate and drank the body and blood of Jesus, was an act of cannibalism. Pagans thought that Christians indulged in immoral and indecent rituals. They considered Christianity one of the worst of the oriental mystery cults, for one of the hallmarks of many of those cults was disgusting rituals.

Even these feelings of distrust and revulsion do not entirely account for persecution. The main reason seems to have been sincere

religious conviction on the part of the pagans. Time and again they accused Christians of atheism. Indeed, Christians either denied the existence of pagan gods or called them evil spirits. For this same reason many Romans hated the Jews. Tacitus no doubt expressed the common view when he said that Jews despised the gods. Christians went even further than Jews – they said that no one should worship pagan gods.

At first, some pagans were repelled by the fanaticism of these monotheists. No good could come from scorning the gods. The whole community might end up paying for the wickedness and blasphemy of the Christians. Besides – and this is important – pagans did not demand that Christians *believe* in pagan gods. Greek and Roman religion was never a matter of belief or ethics. It was purely a religion of ritual. One of the clearest statements of pagan theological attitudes comes from the Roman senator Symmachus:

We watch the same stars; heaven is the same for us all; the same universe envelops us: what importance is it in what way anyone looks for truth? It is impossible to arrive by one route at such a great secret.[18]

Yet Roman religion was inseparable from the state. An attack on one was an attack on the other. The Romans were being no more fanatical or intolerant than an eighteenth-century English judge who declared the Christian religion part of the law of the land. All the pagans expected was performance of the ritual act, a small token sacrifice. Any Christian who sacrificed went free, no matter what he or she personally believed. The earliest persecutions of the Christians were minor and limited. Even Nero's famous persecution was temporary and limited to Rome. Subsequent persecutions were sporadic and local. As time went on, pagan hostility decreased.

Pagans gradually realized that Christians were not working to overthrow the state and that Jesus was no rival of Caesar. The emperor Trajan forbade his governors to hunt down Christians. Trajan admitted that he thought Christianity an abomination, but he preferred to leave Christians in peace.

The stress of the third century, however, seemed to some emperors the punishment of the gods. What else could account for such anarchy? With the empire threatened on every side, a few emperors thought that one way to appease the gods was by offering them the proper sacrifices. Such sacrifices would be a sign of loyalty to the empire, a show of Roman solidarity. Consequently, a new wave of persecutions began. Yet even they were never very widespread or long-lived; by the late third century, pagans had become used to Christianity. Although a few emperors, including Diocletian, vigorously persecuted Christians, most pagans left them alone. Nor were they very sympathetic to the new round of persecutions. Pagan and Christian alike must have been relieved when Constantine legalized Christianity.

In time the Christian triumph would be complete. In 380, the emperor Theodosius made Christianity the official religion of the Roman Empire. At that point Christians began to persecute the pagans for their beliefs. History had come full circle.

THE CONSTRUCTION OF CONSTANTINOPLE

The triumph of Christianity was not the only event that made Constantine's reign a turning-point in Roman history. Constantine took the bold step of building a new capital for the empire. Constantinople, the New Rome, was constructed on the site of Byzantium, an old Greek city on the Bosporus. Throughout the third century, emperors had found Rome and the West hard to defend. The eastern part of the empire was more easily defensible, and escaped the worst of the barbarian devastation. It was wealthy and its urban life still vibrant. Moreover, Christianity was more widespread in the East than in the West, and Constantinople was intended to be a Christian city.

THE AWFUL REVOLUTION

On the evening of October 15, 1764, Edward Gibbon, a young Englishman, sat in Rome among the ruins of the Capitol listening to the chanting of some monks. As the voices of the Christian present echoed against the stones of the pagan past, Gibbon wondered how the Roman Empire had given way to the medieval world. His curiosity aroused, he dedicated himself to the study of what he considered the greatest problem in history.

Twelve years later, in 1776, Gibbon published *The History of the Decline and Fall of the Roman Empire,* one of the monuments of English literature, a brilliant work fashioned with wit, learning, humor, and elegance.

Gibbon's thesis is, as the title of his work indicates, that the Roman Empire, after the first two centuries of existence, declined in strength, vitality, and prosperity and then fell into ruin. His concept of Rome's "decline and fall," a process he called "the awful revolution," has dominated historical thought for two hundred years. Even those who disagree with Gibbon over details have usually accepted his concept of "decline and fall." What explanations did Gibbon give for the fate of the Roman Empire, and how have others responded to his views? Is Gibbon's concept valid, and is it the only way of looking at this problem?

GIBBON'S RATIONALISTIC THEORIES

Gibbon was a true son of the Enlightenment, the eighteenth-century mode of thought that honored reason and despised faith. He regarded Christianity with contempt and as nothing more than vile superstition. In Gibbon's view the glory of the ancient world, with its learning, arts, manners, and philosophy, gleamed in comparison with the "Dark Ages" of the medieval period, when the church held Europe in the thrall of ignorance and sorcery. Christianity emphasized the virtues of humility, patience, and piety – qualities hardly masculine or imperial and totally inadequate for the maintenance of a proud and vigorous empire. Christianity praised chastity and the monastic life, which, in Gibbon's view, drained the empire of vitality and creativity. Nor did he admire the Germans who invaded and infiltrated the empire. Uncivilized and uncouth, they were, in Gibbon's eyes, even incapable of using reason. Although he acknowledged their hardiness and manly vigor, he scorned them as savages who ate horsemeat.

Despite the value of Gibbon's work, Christianity cannot reasonably be made the villain of the piece. True, many very able minds and forceful characters devoted their lives and energies to the Christian church and not to the empire. True, monasticism flourished and led to a passive and politically unproductive existence. Yet the numbers involved in these pursuits were small in proportion to the total population. Furthermore, the Byzantine Empire, which evolved from the eastern part of the Roman Empire, demonstrated that Christians could handle the sword and spear as well as the cross.

Gibbon also argued that the empire had grown so large that it fell of its own weight. In his words, "the decline of Rome was the natural and inevitable effect of immoderate greatness.... The story of its ruin is simple and obvious; and instead of inquiring *why* the Roman empire was destroyed, we should rather be surprised that it had subsisted so long."[19] In effect, Gibbon begs his own question, and instead chronicles the later history of the Roman world.

PSEUDOSCIENTIFIC THEORIES: SCIENCE ABUSED

Gibbon is not alone in trying to explain Rome's fate. The question has absorbed the attention of many, some of whom have misused scientific techniques in their search. They have applied bits of scientific fact and method to a vast and imperfectly known historical development, ignoring the simple fact that the end of the Roman Empire, unlike the composition of DNA, cannot be scientifically determined.

A slightly altered form of Gibbon's view of natural decline has recently found supporters who look at historical developments in biological terms. According to them, states and empires develop like living organisms, progressing through periods of birth and growth to maturity and consolidation, followed by decrepitude, decline, and collapse. This argument is simply false analogy, unsupported by any scientific evidence.

Some twentieth-century writers have resorted to pseudoscientific theories blaming the "collapse" of the empire on racial corruption. As the physically strong, morally pure, and creatively intelligent Romans conquered inferior Asian and African peoples, so the explanation goes, they intermingled with them. The physical and intellectual traits of the less fit came to predominate. This "mongrelization" of the empire steadily sapped the physical and moral fiber of the Romans. When faced with a military crisis, Rome was too weak to cope. Even taken on its own terms, this theory is nonsense. The eastern half of the empire, the home of the "inferior" Asiatics, survived a thousand years longer than the "superior" western one.

Not all those who have used science to explain Rome's fate have been cranks. Some writers have tried to use statistical information and demographic arguments to explain Rome's fall. According to this view, a sharp decline in population diminishes a society's ability to defend itself and weakens its economy and ultimately the entire civilization. In 167 A.D., they argue, the bubonic plague swept the empire and apparently killed large numbers of people. Yet it is a serious error to conclude that the ravages of disease in the second century were responsible for later catastrophes. Economic historians have demonstrated that even severe epidemics have only a short-term economic effect, after which conditions quickly normalize themselves. There was ample time for the empire to recover from this plague.

Population did decline in the third and fourth centuries, for which the most likely explanation is losses due to war and devastation. Even so, the population of the Roman Empire outnumbered the invading barbarians, and there were more than enough people to defend the empire.

THE SOCIOECONOMIC THEORIES OF FERDINAND LOT

The twentieth-century French scholar Ferdinand Lot relied on economics to explain "the awful revolution." He acknowledged that the causes of Rome's "decline" were many and interrelated, but maintained that the basic causes were socioeconomic. Lot pointed out that the Roman economy was badly adjusted;

in fact, according to him, it never really developed. Although the Romans had technological skill, Rome never industrialized. An almost limitless supply of slaves provided cheap labor and discouraged the development of labor-saving methods. Roman conquests brought a steady stream of slaves to the West. Slaves worked the land on the latifundia and produced what little was manufactured in the West. The Roman aristocracy lived on the revenues from their estates. The few people involved in trade and commerce served as middlemen, moneylenders, tax collectors, or civil bureaucrats. A commercial and industrial middle class failed to develop.

Western products – primarily, in Lot's view, raw materials – did not begin to equal the value of imports. Increasingly, the balance of trade within the empire worsened: the western part bought much more than it sold and paid for purchases with precious metals. The pressure of the German invasions made social and economic conditions worse. Once the West was cut off from sources of goods and without goods of its own to export, it reverted to an agrarian and isolated economy. The level of learning deteriorated and technical skills were lost. According to Lot, economic collapse accelerated political ruin. Moreover, great cities in the West drastically declined in population, and simultaneously trade and commerce slowed to a trickle. With the tax base gone, cultural movements and intellectual activities could not be maintained.

The force of Lot's argument is weakened by the fact that large-scale emancipation of slaves occurred during the empire. Roman emperors encouraged the growth of a prosperous class of small tenant farmers. Slavery also existed in the East, and did not prevent the West from industrializing. Cities in Gaul and Germany became centers of manufacturing, and even managed to dominate the production of glass, pottery, and bronze ware. Furthermore, these industries were usually manned by free labor, not slaves.

Lot's theories also make too little of political factors. The economic woes of the empire began during the civil wars and invasions of the middle of the third century – wars that left wide tracts of land desolate and manufacturing centers in shambles. Roman failure to create a stable form of government exposed the empire to serious disruption that could not fail to have dire economic effects. Though enlightening in many respects, Lot's theories are incapable of explaining the "decline and fall."

POLITICAL EXPLANATIONS

Over the years political explanations have won the widest acceptance. The Roman imperial government never solved the problem of succession: it never devised a peaceful and regular way to pass on the imperial power when an emperor died. The legions enjoyed too much power, often creating and destroying civil governments at will, and in the process disrupting the state. The assassinations of emperors and frequent changes of government produced chronic instability, weakening the state's ability to solve its problems.

From the late third century onward, successive approaches to Rome's economic difficulties proved disastrous. Emperors depreciated the coinage. The middle classes carried an increasingly heavy burden of taxation, and all the while the imperial bureaucracy grew bigger, though not more efficient. These factors combined to destroy the ordinary citizen's confidence in the state. Consequently, according to the political explanation, with the economy and society undermined, the empire was destroyed by its internal difficulties.

There is no question that the Roman Empire suffered from severe political problems, which were never solved. Energy that could have been spent defending the frontiers or policing the sea-lanes was all too often squandered in bloody and costly civil war. The same fate had overtaken the republic, but at least then there were no land-hungry barbarian tribes ready to turn Roman weakness to their own advantage. Political explanations, too, have their defects, for emperors such as Diocletian showed how the empire could survive even fearful ravages. Nor do political theories adequately explain why the West "fell" while the East survived for another millennium.

CONTINUITY AND CHANGE

Some writers have rejected the whole idea of decline. As early as 1744, before Gibbon had contemplated writing the *Decline and Fall of the Roman Empire,* the Frenchman Abbé Galliani wrote: "The fall of empires? What can that mean? Empires being neither up nor down do not fall. They change their appearance."[20] The concept of change and development, instead of decline, has much to recommend it, inasmuch as many aspects of the Roman world survived to influence the medieval and eventually the modern world. Roman law left its traces on the legal and political systems of most European countries. Roman roads, aqueducts, bridges, and buildings remained in use, standing as constant reminders of the Roman past and its link with the present. The Latin language, with its rich vocabulary and its strict but rational grammatical rules, facilitated communication over a wide area and allowed for precision of expression. For almost two thousand years Latin language and literature remained the core of all education in the West. Those who studied Latin came to some degree under the spell of

Rome, as Roman attitudes and patterns of thought fertilized the intellectual lives of generation after generation of Europeans. Slowly, almost imperceptibly, the Roman Empire gave way to the medieval world.

———◆———

Never before in Western history and not again until modern times did one state govern so many people over so much of the world for so long a span of time. The true heritage of Rome is its long tradition of law and freedom. Under Roman law and government the West enjoyed relative peace and security for extensive periods of time. Under the auspices of Rome northern Europe entered into the civilized world of the Mediterranean. Through Rome the best of ancient thought and culture was preserved to make its contribution to modern life. Perhaps no better epitaph for Rome can be found than the words of Virgil:

While rivers shall run to the sea,
While shadows shall move across the valleys of
mountains,
While the heavens shall nourish the stars,
Always shall your honor and your name and your
fame endure.[21]

NOTES

1. Virgil *Aeneid* 6.851–853.

2. Augustus *Res Gestae* 6.34.

3. Ibid., 5.28.

4. Virgil *Aeneid* 6.791–794.

5. Horace *Odes* 4.15.

6. Virgil *Georgics* 4.180–183.

7. Ibid., 3.515–519.

8. Horace *Odes* 1.38.

9. Matthew 3:3.

10. Matthew 16:18.

11. Edward Gibbon, *The History of the Decline and Fall of the Roman Empire,* Modern Library, New York, n.d., 1.1.

12. Ibid., 1.52.

13. M. Hammond, *The Antonine Monarchy,* American Academy in Rome, Rome, 1959, p. x.

14. Gibbon, 1.70.

15. *Corpus Inscriptionum Latinarum,* vol. 6, G. Reimer, Berlin, 1882, no. 9792.

16. Ibid., vol. 10, no. 8192.

17. Ibid., vol. 6, no. 14672.

18. Symmachus *Relations* 3.10.

19. Gibbon, 2.438.

20. Quoted in F. W. Walbank, *The Awful Revolution,* University of Toronto Press, Toronto, 1969, p. 121.

21. Virgil *Aeneid* 1.607–609.

SUGGESTED READING

Of the works cited in the Notes, that by Hammond is a classic in the field, and Gibbon's *Decline and Fall* is of course one of the masterpieces of English literature. Some good general treatments of the empire include B. Cunliffe, *Rome and Her Empire* (1978), which is profusely illustrated, and P. Petit, *Pax Romana* (English translation, 1976). The role of the emperor is superbly treated by F. Millar, *The Emperor in the Roman World* (1977), and the defense of the empire is brilliantly studied by E. N. Luttwak, *The Grand Strategy of the Roman Empire* (1976). The army that carried out that strategy is the subject of G. Webster, *The Roman Imperial Army* (1969).

Favorable to Augustus is M. Hammond, *The Augustan Principate* (1933), and G. W. Bowersock, *Augustus and the Greek World* (1965), is excellent intellectual history. C. M. Wells, *The German Policy of Augustus* (1972), uses archaeological findings to illustrate Roman expansion into northern Europe.

The commercial life of the empire is the subject of M. P. Charlesworth, *Trade Routes and Commerce of* the Roman Empire, 2nd ed. (1926). Newer, if briefer, is the stimulating article by L. Casson, "Rome's Trade with the East: The Sea Voyage to Africa and India," *Transactions of the American Philological Association* 110 (1980): 21–36. R. Duncan-Jones, *The Economy of the Roman Empire: Quantitative Studies,* 2nd ed. (1982), employs new techniques of historical inquiry. J. Percival, *The Roman Villa* (1976), is a lively study of an important institution. The classic treatment, which ranges across the empire, is M. Rostovtzeff, *The Economic and Social History of the Roman Empire* (1957).

Social aspects of the empire are the subject of R. Auguet, *Cruelty and Civilization: The Roman Games* (English translation, 1972); P. Garnsey, *Social Status and Legal Privilege in the Roman Empire* (1970); and A. N. Sherwin-White, *Racial Prejudice in Imperial Rome* (1967). A general treatment is R. MacMullen, *Roman Social Relations, 50 B.C. to A.D. 284* (1981). N. Kampen, *Image and Status: Roman Working Women in Ostia* (1981) is distinctive for its treatment of ordinary Roman women. An important feature of Roman history is treated by R. P. Saller, *Personal Patronage under the Early Empire* (1982).

Christianity, paganism, and Judaism receive treatment in E. M. Smallwood, *The Jews under Roman Rule* (corrected ed., 1981); R. A. Markus, *Christianity in the Roman World* (1975); and A. D. Momigliano, *The Conflict between Paganism and Christianity in the Fourth Century* (1963). Two important topics in the study of early Christianity are treated in W. H. C. Frend, *Martyrdom and Persecution in the Early Church* (1965); and M. Hengel, *Acts and the History of Earliest Christianity* (1979). The significance of the cult of Roma in the empire is well treated by R. Mellor, "The Goddess Roma", in *Aufstieg und Niedergang der römischen Welt,* vol. II, part 17 (1981), pp. 952–1030.

A convenient survey of Roman literature is J. W. Duff, *Literary History of Rome from the Origins to the Close of the Golden Age* (1953) and *Literary History of Rome in the Silver Age,* 3rd ed. (1964).

The fall of Rome continues to be a fertile field of investigation: A. H. M. Jones, *The Decline of the Ancient World* (1966); F. W. Walbank, *The Awful Revolution* (1969); and R. MacMullen's two books: *Soldier and Civilian in the Later Roman Empire* (1963) and *Enemies of the Roman Order: Treason, Unrest, and Alienation in the Empire* (1966).

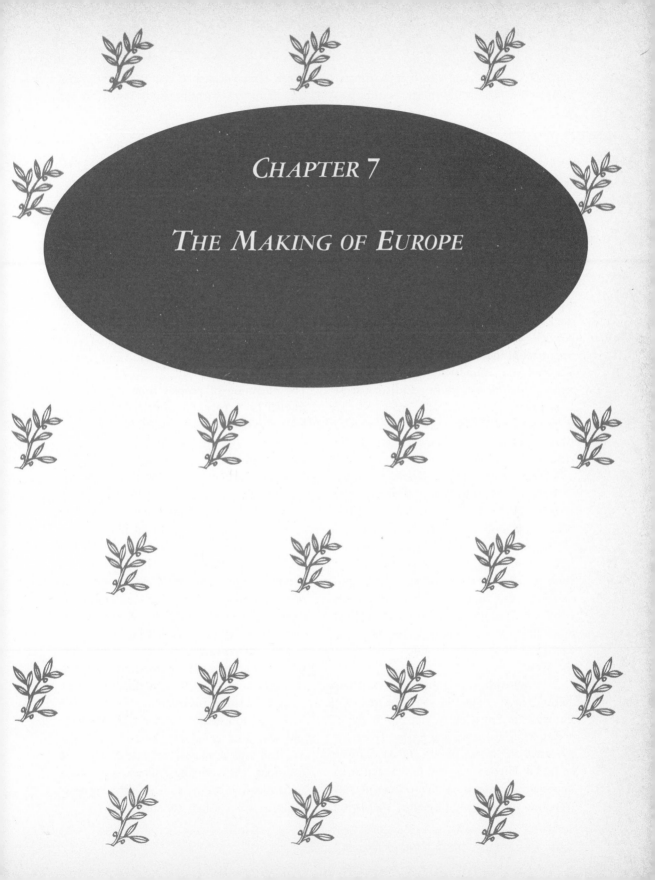

CHAPTER 7

THE MAKING OF EUROPE

THE CENTURIES BETWEEN approximately 400 and 900 present the student with a paradox. These years witnessed the disintegration of the Roman Empire, which had been one of humanity's great political and cultural achievements. On the other hand, these five centuries were a creative and important period, during which Europeans laid the foundations for the development of medieval and modern Europe. It is not too much to say that this period saw the making of Europe.

The basic ingredients that went into the making of a distinctly European civilization were the cultural legacy of Greece and Rome, the customs and traditions of the Germanic peoples, and the Christian faith. The most important of these was Christianity, because it absorbed and assimilated the other two. It reinterpreted the classics in a Christian sense. It instructed the Germanic peoples and gave them new ideals of living and social behavior. Christianity became the cement that held European society together.

During this period the Byzantine Empire centered at Constantinople served as a protective buffer between Europe and savage peoples to the east. The Greeks preserved the philosophical and scientific texts of the ancient world, which later formed the basis for study in science and medicine; and they produced a great synthesis of Roman law, the Justinian Code. In the urbane and sophisticated life led at Constantinople, the Greeks set a standard far above the primitive existence of the West.

In the seventh and eighth centuries, Arabic culture spread around the southern fringes of Europe – to Spain, Sicily, and North Africa, and to Syria, Palestine, and Egypt. The Arabs translated the works of such Greek thinkers as Euclid, Hippocrates, and Galen, and made important contributions in mathematics, astronomy, and physics. In Arabic translation,

Greek texts trickled to the West, and most later European scientific study rested on the Arabic work.

European civilization resulted from the fusion of Germanic traditions, the Greco-Roman heritage, and the Christian faith. How did these components act upon one another? How did they bring about the making of Europe? What influence did the Byzantine and Islamic cultures have on the making of European civilization? These are the questions discussed in this chapter.

THE MIGRATION OF THE GERMANIC PEOPLES

The migration of peoples from one area to another has been a dominant and continuing feature of European history. Mass movements of Europeans occurred in the fourth through sixth centuries, in the ninth and tenth centuries, and in the twelfth and thirteenth centuries. From the sixteenth century to the present such movements have been almost continuous, and have involved not just the European continent but the entire world. The causes of these migrations varied, and they are not thoroughly understood by scholars. But there is no question that they profoundly affected both the regions to which peoples moved and the ones they left behind.

The *völkerwanderungen,* or migrations of the Germanic peoples, was an important factor in the decline of the Roman Empire. Many twentieth-century historians and sociologists have tried to explain who the Germans were and why they emigrated, but scholars have not had much success at answering these questions. The surviving evidence is primarily archaeological, scanty, and not yet adequately explored. Conclusions are still tentative.

VANDAL LANDOWNER *The adoption of Roman dress — short tunic, cloak, and sandals — reflects the way the Germanic tribes accepted Roman lifestyles. Likewise both the mosaic art form and the man's stylized appearance show the Germans' assimilation of Roman influences. (Notice that the rider has a saddle but not stirrups.) (The British Museum)*

What answers do exist rest on archaeological evidence found later inside the borders of the Roman Empire: bone fossils, cooking utensils, jewelry, instruments of war, and other surviving artifacts. Like the Vikings, who first terrorized and then settled in many sections of Europe in the ninth and tenth centuries, the Germans came from eastern Germany and the areas of modern Denmark, Sweden, and Norway. Ethnically they were Scandinavians.

Since about 250, Germanic tribes had pressed along the Rhine-Danube frontier of the Roman Empire. Depending upon their closeness to that border, these tribes differed considerably from one another in level of civilization. Some tribes, such as the Visigoths and Ostrogoths, led a settled existence, engaged in agriculture and trade, and accepted an unorthodox form of Christianity called Arianism. Long acquaintance with Roman ways made them very civilized, and some had been welcomed into the empire and served as mercenaries in the imperial army. Tribes such as the Anglo-Saxons and the Huns, who lived far from the Roman frontiers, were not af-

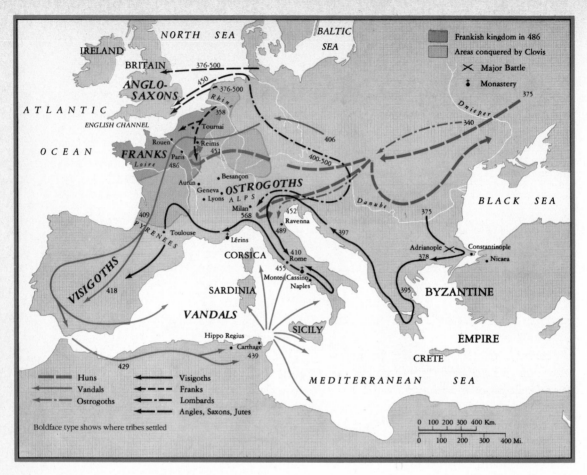

MAP 7.1. THE GERMANIC MIGRATIONS *The Germanic tribes infiltrated and settled in all parts of Western Europe. The Huns, who were not German ethnically, originated in central Asia.*

fected by the civilizing influences of Rome. They remained primitive, nomadic, even barbaric peoples.

Historians do not know exactly when the Mongolian tribe called the Huns began to move westward from China, but about 370 they pressured the Goths living along the Rhine-Danube frontier. The Huns easily defeated the Ostrogoths, and the frightened Visigoths petitioned the emperor to be allowed to settle within the empire. Once inside, however, they revolted. In 378, a Visigothic army decisively defeated the emperor's army. This date marks the beginning of massive Germanic invasions; Germans flooded into the empire (see Map 7.1).

Why did the Germans emigrate? In the absence of literary evidence one can only speculate. Perhaps overpopulation and food shortages resulting from polygamy (the practice of having several wives simultaneously) caused migration. Perhaps victorious tribes forced the vanquished ones to move south. Perhaps tales of the luxurious lifestyle of the cities of the Roman Empire attracted settlers. Perhaps the Germans migrated for a combination of all these reasons.

Some tribes that settled within the borders of the Roman Empire numbered perhaps no more than ten thousand individuals. Others, such as the Ostrogoths and Visigoths, were about twenty or thirty times larger. Because they settled near and quickly intermingled with Romans and Romanized peoples, it is impossible to specify numbers of the original migrators. Dense forests, poor soil, and inadequate equipment probably kept food production low. This meant that the Germans could not increase very rapidly in their new locations.

Except for the Lombards, whose conquests of Italy persisted through the sixth and seventh centuries, the movements of Germanic peoples on the Continent ended about 600. Between 450 and 565, the Germans established a number of kingdoms, but none except the Frankish kingdom lasted very long. Since the German kingdoms were not states with definite geographical boundaries, their locations are approximate. The Visigoths overran much of southwestern Gaul. Establishing their headquarters at Toulouse, they exercised a weak domination over Spain until a great Muslim victory at Guadalete in 711 ended Visigothic rule. The Vandals, whose destructive ways are commemorated in the word *vandal,* settled in North Africa. In northern and western Europe in the sixth century, the Burgundians established rule over lands roughly circumscribed by the old Roman army camps at Lyons, Besançon, Geneva, and Autun.

In northern Italy, the sixth-century Ostrogothic king Theodoric pursued a policy of assimilation between Germans and Romans. He maintained close relations with the Roman emperor at Constantinople and drew Roman scholars and diplomats into the royal civil service. He was a crude German, however, and his reign was disliked by the pagan Roman aristocrats. Moreover, he was an Arian Christian, so Roman Catholics hated him as heretical. His royal administration fell apart during the reconquest of Italy by the Byzantine emperor Justinian in the sixth century. Weakness, war, and plague then made northern Italy ripe for the Lombard conquest in the seventh century.

The most enduring Germanic kingdom was established by the Frankish chieftain Clovis (481-511). Originally only a petty chieftain with headquarters in the region of Tournai in northwestern Gaul (modern Belgium), Clovis began to expand his territories in 486. His defeat of the Gallo-Roman general Syagrius extended his jurisdiction to the Loire. Clovis's conversion to orthodox Christianity in 496 won him the crucial support of the papacy and the bishops of Gaul. As the defender of Roman Catholicism against heretical German tribes, he went on to conquer the Visigoths, extending his domain as far as the Pyrenees and making Paris his headquarters. Because he was descended from the half-legendary chieftain Merovech, the dynasty Clovis founded has been called Merovingian. Clovis's sons subjugated the Burgundians in eastern Gaul and the Ostrogothic tribes living north of the Alps.

GERMANIC SOCIETY

The Germans replaced the Romans as rulers of most of the European continent, and German customs and traditions formed the basis of European society for centuries. What pat-

THE BAPTISM OF CLOVIS In this thirteenth-century representation, Remigius, Bishop of Rheims, blesses Clovis, a noble holds the crown symbolizing royal victory, while the Holy Spirit descends with holy oil. Clovis respected Remigius and supported his work of conversion; Remegius urged obedience to Clovis. (Bibliothèque Nationale, Paris)

terns of social and political life characterized the Germans? What kind of economy did they practice?

Scholars are hampered in answering these questions because the Germans could not write, and so kept no written records before their conversion to Christianity. The earliest information about them comes from moralistic accounts by such Romans as the historian Tacitus, who was acquainted only with the tribes living closest to the borders of the empire. Furthermore, Tacitus wrote his *Germania* at the end of the first century A.D., and by the fifth century German practices differed from those of Tacitus's time. Our knowledge of the Germans depends largely on information in records written in the sixth and seventh centuries and projected backward.

KINSHIP AND CUSTOM

The Germans had no notion of the state as we in the twentieth century use that concept; they thought in social, not political, terms. The basic social unit of the Germans was the tribe, or folk. Members of the folk believed they were all descended from a common ancestor. Blood united them. Kinship protected them. Law was custom – unwritten, preserved in the minds of the elders of the tribe, and handed down by word of mouth from generation to generation. Custom regulated everything. Every tribe had its customs, and every member of the tribe knew what they were. Members were subject to their tribe's customary law wherever they went, and friendly tribes respected one another's laws.

Germanic tribes were led by a king, or tribal chieftain. The chief was that member of the folk recognized as the strongest, the bravest in battle. He was elected from among the male members of the strongest family. He led the tribe in war, settled disputes among tribal members, conducted negotiations with outside powers, and offered sacrifices to the gods. Closely associated with the king was the *gesith,* or war band (known in Latin as the *comitatus*). The members of the war band were usually the bravest young men in the tribe. They swore loyalty to the chief and fought with him in battle. They were not supposed to leave the battlefield without him; to do so implied cowardice and disloyalty and brought terrible disgrace.

LAW

As long as custom determined all behavior, the early Germans had no need for written law. Beginning in the late sixth century, however, German tribal chieftains began to collect, write, and publish lists of their customs. Why then? The Christian missionaries who were slowly converting the Germans to Christianity wanted to know the tribal customs, and they encouraged German rulers to set down their customs in written form. Churchmen wanted to read about German ways in order to assimilate the tribes to Christianity. Moreover, by the sixth century the German kings needed rules and regulations for the Romans living under their jurisdiction as well as for their own people.

Today if a person holds up a bank, American law maintains that the robber attacks both the bank and the state in which it exists. That is a sophisticated notion involving the abstract idea of the state. In early German law, all crimes were regarded as crimes against a person.

According to the code of the Salian Franks, every person had a particular monetary value to the tribe. This value was called the *wergeld,* which literally means man-money or "money to buy off the spear." Men of fighting age had the highest wergeld, then women of childbearing age, then children, and finally the aged. Everyone's value reflected his or her potential military worthiness. If a person accused of a crime agreed to pay the wergeld, and if the victim and his or her family accepted the payment, there was peace (hence the expression "money to buy off the spear"). If the accused refused to pay the wergeld, or if the victim's family refused to accept it, a blood feud ensued. Individuals depended on their kin for protection, and kinship served as a force of social control.

Historians and sociologists have difficulty applying the early law codes, partly because they are patchwork affairs studded with additions made in later centuries. For example, the Salic Law — the law code of the Salian Franks — was issued by Clovis in the late fifth century and amended first in the eighth and again in the ninth century. Thus it cannot be taken as an entirely accurate representation of conditions in the sixth century. Nevertheless, it does offer a general picture of Germanic life and problems in the early Middle Ages, and it is typical of the law codes of other tribes, such as the Visigoths, the Burgundians, the Lombards, and the Anglo-Saxons.

The Salic Law lists the money fines to be paid to the victim or the family for such injuries as theft, rape, assault, arson, and murder:

If any person strike another on the head so that the

brain appears, and the three bones which lie above the brain shall project, he shall be sentenced to 1200 denars, which make 300 shillings.

But if it shall have been between the ribs or in the stomach, so that the wound appears and reaches to the entrails, he shall be sentenced to 1200 denars – which make 300 shillings – besides five shillings for the physician's pay.

If any one have hit a free woman who is pregnant, and she dies, he shall be sentenced to 2800 denars, which make 700 shillings.

If any one have killed a free woman after she has begun bearing children, he shall be sentenced to 2400 denars, which make 600 shillings.

If any one shall have drawn a harrow through another's harvest after it has sprouted, or shall have gone through it with a waggon where there was no road, he shall be sentenced to 120 denars, which make 30 shillings.

If any one shall have killed a free Frank, or a barbarian living under the Salic law, and it have been proved on him, he shall be sentenced to 8000 denars.

But if any one have slain a man who is in the service of the king, he shall be sentenced to 2400 denars, which make 600 shillings.

If any one have slain a Roman who eats in the king's palace, and it have been proved on him, he shall be sentenced to 1200 denars, which make 300 shillings.[1]

This is not really a code of law at all, but a list of tariffs or fines for particular offenses. German law aimed at the prevention or reduction of violence. It was not concerned with justice.

At first Romans had been subject to Roman law, and Germans to Germanic custom. As German kings accepted Christianity, and as Romans and Germans increasingly intermarried, the distinction between the two laws blurred and, in the course of the seventh and eighth centuries, disappeared. The result of the fusion would be the new feudal law, to which all people were subject.

LIFE IN THE FORESTS

How did the Germans live? The dark, dense forests that dotted the continent of Europe were the most important physical and psychological factor in the lives of the Germanic peoples who were not quickly Romanized. Forests separated one tribe from another. The pagan Germans believed that gods and spirits inhabited the forests. Trees were holy, and to cut them down was an act of grave sacrilege. Thus the Germans cut no trees. They also feared building a mill or a bridge on a river, lest the river spirit be offended. This attitude prevented the clearing of land for farming and tended to keep the Germans isolated.

In the course of the sixth through eighth centuries, the Germans slowly adapted to Greco-Roman and Christian attitudes and patterns of behavior. Acceptance of Christianity and the end of animistic beliefs that spiritual forces live in natural objects had profound consequences. In fact, the decline of animistic beliefs marks a turning-point in the economic and intellectual progress of the West. A more settled and less nomadic way of life developed as people no longer feared to make use of natural resources such as rivers and forests. Once animistic beliefs were dispelled, the forests were opened to use, and all members of the community had common rights in them. Trees provided everyone with wood for building and for fuel; the forests served as the perfect place for grazing animals throughout the Middle Ages. The steady reduction of forest land between the sixth and thirteenth centuries was a major step in the agricultural development of Europe.

Within the forests the Germans clustered in small villages of a few families. Individual families lived in huts made of mud, wood, or wattle (poles intertwined with twigs or reeds) and thatched with straw. Recent archaeological excavations at Thetford in East Anglia in England uncovered a sixth-century village. Evidence from places on the Continent suggests that this English village was typical. It contained a number of one-room huts about twelve feet long, most without a fireplace. Uprights in the center of the gable supported the roof. These dwellings were scattered over a small cleared area, without alignment or evidence of town planning.

Each German family owned its plot of land and passed it on to the next generation. All members of the small community worked together to cultivate the clearing. Apparently, the land farmed was adjacent to the dwellings. Farmers helped one another to plow and harvest, and all had to agree on the uniform rotation of crops. It is difficult to generalize about agricultural methods. The German plow dug deeper than the Roman plow, but it was hard to turn around at the end of the furrow. The difficulty of this operation probably brought about the division of arable land into long narrow strips.

Bread was the basic food, and oats and rye the predominant grains in the fifth and sixth centuries. Later these cereals were held in low esteem, and wheat was raised everywhere it would grow. Peas and beans (a source of protein), turnips, onions, and cabbage supplemented the diet. Beside the field under cultivation, another stood fallow. Cattle grazed on it and fertilized it.

ANGLO-SAXON ENGLAND

The island of Britain, conquered by Rome during the reign of Claudius, shared fully in the life of the Roman Empire during the first four centuries of the Christian era. A military

THE TARA BROOCH   Men and women of the Germanic tribes wore brooches to fasten their cloaks at the shoulder. This elaborately decorated brooch (a reproduction) was worn by a person of the warrior aristocracy. Ordinary people used a thorn. (Courtesy, World Heritage Museum. Photo: Caroline Buckler)

aristocracy governed, and the official religion was the cult of the emperor. Towns were planned in the Roman fashion, with temples, public baths, theaters, and amphitheaters. In the countryside large manors controlled the surrounding lands. Roman merchants brought Eastern luxury goods and Eastern religions – including Christianity – into Britain. The native Britons, a gentle Celtic people, had become thoroughly Romanized. Their language was Latin. Their lifestyle was Roman.

But an event in the distant eastern province of Thrace changed all this. In 378, the Visigoths crossed the Danube and inflicted a severe defeat on the Roman emperor Valens at Adrianople. Even Britain felt the consequences. Rome was forced to retrench, and in 407 Roman troops were withdrawn from the island, leaving it unprotected. The savage Picts from Scotland continued to harass the

MAP 7.2. ANGLO-SAXON ENGLAND *Can you identify the seven kingdoms of the Heptarchy? Where is Bede's monastery Jarrow?*

The beginnings of the Germanic kingdoms in Britain are very obscure, but scholars suspect they came into being in the seventh and eighth centuries. Writing in the eighth century, the scholar Bede (pages 266–267) described seven kingdoms: the Jutish kingdom of Kent; the Saxon kingdoms of the East Saxons (Essex), South Saxons (Sussex), and West Saxons (Wessex); and the kingdoms of the Angles, Mercians, and Northumbrians (see Map 7.2). The names imply that these peoples thought of themselves in tribal rather than geographical terms. They referred to the kingdom of the West Saxons, for example, rather than simply Wessex. Because of Bede's categorization, scholars refer to the Heptarchy, or seven kingdoms of Anglo-Saxon Britain. The suggestion of total Anglo-Saxon domination, however, is not entirely accurate. Germanic tribes never subdued Scotland, where the Picts remained strong, or Wales, where the Celts and native Britons continued to put up stubborn resistance.

Thus Anglo-Saxon England was divided along racial and political lines. The Teutonic kingdoms in the south, east, and center were opposed by the Britons in the west, who wanted to get rid of the invaders. The Anglo-Saxon kingdoms also fought among themselves, with the result that boundaries shifted constantly. Finally in the ninth century, under pressure of the Danish, or Viking, invasions, the Britons and the Germanic peoples were molded together under the leadership of King Alfred of Wessex (871–899).

north. Teutonic tribes from Scandinavia and modern-day Belgium – the Angles, Saxons, and Jutes – stepped up their assaults, attacking in a hit-and-run fashion. Their goal was plunder, and at first their invasions led to no permanent settlements. As more Germans arrived, however, they took over the best lands and humbled the Britons. Increasingly, the natives fled to the west and settled in Wales. These sporadic raids continued for over a century and led to Germanic control of most of Britain. Historians have labeled the period 500 to 1066 Anglo-Saxon.

Except for the Jutes, who probably came from Frisia (modern Belgium), the Teutonic tribes came from the least Romanized and least civilized parts of Europe. They destroyed Roman culture in Britain. Tribal custom superseded Roman law.

THE SURVIVAL AND GROWTH OF THE EARLY CHRISTIAN CHURCH

While many elements of the Roman Empire disintegrated, the Christian church survived and grew. Having gained the support of the fourth-century emperors, the church gradually adopted the Roman system of organization. Christianity had a dynamic missionary policy, and the church slowly succeeded in assimilating – that is, adapting – pagan peoples, both Germans and Romans, to Christian teaching. Moreover, the church possessed able administrators and leaders and highly literate and creative thinkers. These factors help to explain the survival and growth of the early Christian church in the face of repeated Germanic invasions.

THE CHURCH AND THE ROMAN EMPERORS

The early church benefited considerably from the support of the emperors. In return, the emperors expected the support of the Christian church in the maintenance of order and unity. Constantine had legalized the practice of Christianity within the empire in 312. Although he himself was not baptized until he was on his deathbed, Constantine encouraged Christianity throughout his reign. He freed the clergy from imperial taxation. At the churchmen's request, he helped to settle theological disputes and thus to preserve doctrinal unity within the church. Constantine generously endowed the building of Christian churches, and one of his gifts – the Lateran Palace in Rome – remained the official residence of the popes until the fourteenth century. Constantine also declared Sunday a public holiday, a day of rest for the service of God. As the result of its favored position within the empire, Christianity slowly became the leading religion.

At the end of the fourth century, the emperor Theodosius went further than Constantine and made Christianity the official religion of the empire. Theodosius stripped Roman pagan temples of their statues, made the prac-

tice of the old Roman state religion a treasonable offense, and persecuted Christians who dissented from orthodox doctrine. Most significant, he allowed the church to establish its own courts. Church courts began to develop their own body of law, called canon law. These courts, not the Roman government, had jurisdiction over the clergy and ecclesiastical disputes. At the death of Theodosius, the Christian church was completely independent of the authority of the Roman state. The foundation for the power of the medieval church had been laid.

What was to be the church's relationship to secular powers? How was the Christian to render unto Caesar the things that were his while returning to God his due? This problem had troubled the earliest disciples of Christ. The toleration of Christianity and the coming to power of Christian emperors in the fourth century did not make it any easier. Striking a balance between responsibility to secular rulers and loyalty to spiritual duties was difficult.

In the fourth century, theological disputes arose within Christianity – primarily disagreements about the nature of Christ. Constantine, to whom religious disagreement meant civil disorder, intervened. In 325, Constantine summoned a council of church leaders to Nicaea in Asia Minor, and presided over it personally.

The council debated whether Christ was of a different substance from God, as Arius, a priest of Alexandria, maintained, or of the same substance, as Bishop Athanasius of Alexandria held. The council decided against the Arians and supported the doctrine that Christ was of the same substance as God. This became the orthodox position. Anxious to preserve the unity of the empire, Constantine insisted on its acceptance by all Christians. The participation of the emperor in a theological dispute within the church paved the way for later rulers to claim they could do the same.

So active was the emperor Theodosius's participation in church matters that he eventually came to loggerheads with Bishop Ambrose of Milan (339–397). Theodosius ordered Ambrose to hand over his cathedral church to the emperor. Ambrose's response had important consequences for the future:

At length came the command, "Deliver up the Basilica"; I reply, "It is not lawful for us to deliver it up, nor for your Majesty to receive it. By no law can you violate the house of a private man, and do you think that the house of God may be taken away? It is asserted that all things are lawful to the Emperor, that all things are his. But do not burden your conscience with the thought that you have any right as Emperor over sacred things. Exalt not yourself, but if you would reign the longer, be subject to God. It is written, God's to God and Caesar's to Caesar. The palace is the Emperor's, the Churches are the Bishop's. To you is committed jurisdiction over public, not over sacred buildings."[2]

Ambrose's statement was to serve as the cornerstone of the ecclesiastical theory of state-church relations throughout the Middle Ages. Ambrose insisted that the church was independent of the state's jurisdiction. The two powers were, he maintained, separate and autonomous. He insisted that in matters relating to the faith or the church, the bishops were to be the judges of emperors, not the other way around. In a Christian society, harmony and peace depended upon agreement between the bishop and the secular ruler. But if disagreement developed, the church was ultimately the superior power because the church was responsible for the salvation of all individuals (including the emperor).

Theodosius accepted Ambrose's argument and bowed to the church. In later centuries

theologians, canonists, and propagandists repeatedly cited Ambrose's position as the basis of relations between the two powers. The precedent set by Theodosius was repeatedly recalled by church leaders in the Middle Ages as proof that secular power had to yield to ecclesiastical authority.

INSPIRED LEADERSHIP

The early Christian church benefited from the brilliant administrative abilities of some church leaders and from identification of the authority and dignity of the bishop of Rome with the grand imperial traditions of the city. Some highly able Roman citizens accepted baptism and applied their intellectual powers and administrative skills to the service of the church rather than the empire. With the empire in decay, educated people joined and worked for the church in the belief that it was the one institution able to provide leadership. Bishop Ambrose, for example, was the son of the Roman prefect of Gaul, a trained lawyer and governor of a province. As bishop of Milan, he exercised considerable responsibility and influence in the temporal as well as ecclesiastical affairs of northern Italy.

During the reign of Diocletian (284–305), the Roman Empire had been divided for administrative purposes into geographical units called dioceses. Gradually the church made use of this organizational structure. Christian bishops – the leaders of early Christian communities, popularly elected by the Christian people – established their headquarters, or sees, in the urban centers of the old Roman dioceses. Their jurisdiction extended throughout all parts of the diocese. The center of the bishop's authority was his cathedral (the word derives from the Latin *cathedra*, meaning "chair"). Thus church leaders capitalized on the Roman imperial method of organization and adapted it to ecclesiastical purposes.

After the removal of the capital and the emperor to Constantinople (page 206), the bishop of Rome exercised vast influence in the West because he had no real competitor there. Bishops of Rome – known as popes from the Latin word *papa*, meaning "father" – began to identify their religious offices with the imperial traditions of the city. They stressed that Rome had been the capital of a worldwide empire, and they emphasized the special importance of Rome within the framework of that empire. Successive bishops of Rome reminded Christians in other parts of the world that Rome was the burial-place of Saint Peter and Saint Paul. Moreover, according to tradition Saint Peter, the chief of Christ's first twelve followers, had lived and been executed in Rome. No other city in the world could make such claims.

In the fifth century, the bishops of Rome began to stress their supremacy over other Christian communities and to urge other churches to appeal to Rome for the resolution of complicated doctrinal issues. Thus Pope Innocent I (401–417) wrote to the bishops of Africa:

[*We approve your action in following the principle*] *that nothing which was done even in the most remote and distant provinces should be taken as finally settled unless it came to the notice of this See, that any just pronouncement might be confirmed by all the authority of this See, and that the other churches might from thence gather what they should teach. . . .*[3]

The prestige of Rome and the church as a whole was also enhanced by the courage and leadership of the Roman bishops. According to tradition, Pope Leo I (440–461) met the advancing army of Attila the Hun in 452 and, through his power of persuasion, saved Rome

from a terrible sacking. Three years later, Leo repeated this performance and secured concessions from the Vandal leader Gaiseric.

By the time Gregory I (590–604) became pope, there was no civic authority left to handle the problems pressing the city. Flood, famine, plague, and invasion by the Lombards made for an almost disastrous situation. Pope Gregory concluded a peace with the Lombards, organized relief services that provided water and food for the citizens, and established hospitals for the sick and dying. The fact that it was Christian leaders, rather than imperial administrators, who responded to the city's dire needs could not help but increase the prestige and influence of the church.

MISSIONARY ACTIVITY

The word *catholic* derives from a Greek word meaning "general," "universal," or "worldwide." Early Christians believed that Christ's teaching was intended for all peoples, and they sought to make their faith catholic – that is, believed everywhere. This could be accomplished only through missionary activity. As Saint Paul had written to the Christian community at Colossae in Asia Minor:

You have stripped off your old behavior with your old self, and you have put on a new self which will progress towards true knowledge the more it is renewed in the image of its creator; and in that image there is no room for distinction between Greek and Jew, between the circumcised or the uncircumcised, or between barbarian or Scythian, slave and free man. There is only Christ; he is everything and he is in everything.[4]

Paul urged Christians to bring the "good news" of Christ to all peoples. The Mediterranean served as the highway over which Christianity spread to the cities of the empire.

During the Roman occupation, there were

also scattered and isolated Christian communities in Gaul, Britain, and Ireland. However, they had no wide impact on the populations of their countries, and the migration of the German tribes in the fourth and fifth centuries virtually destroyed Christianity in remote and isolated Britain. The Christianization of the Germans really began in 597, when Pope Gregory I sent a delegation of monks under the Roman Augustine to Britain to convert the Britons. Augustine's approach, adopted by all subsequent missionaries, was to concentrate on converting the king. When he succeeded in converting Ethelbert, king of Kent, the baptism of Ethelbert's people took place as a matter of course. Augustine established his headquarters, or cathedral seat, at Canterbury, the capital of Kent.

In the course of the seventh century, two Christian forces competed for the conversion of the pagan Anglo-Saxons: Roman-oriented missionaries traveling north from Canterbury, and Celtic monks from Ireland and northwestern Britain. Monasteries were established at Iona, Lindisfarne, Jarrow, Whitby, and York (see Map 7.2).

The Roman and Celtic traditions differed completely in their forms of church organization, types of monastic life, and methods of arriving at the date of the central feast of the Christian calendar, Easter. At the Synod (ecclesiastical council) of Whitby in 664, the Roman tradition was completely victorious. The conversion of the English, and the close attachment of the English church to Rome, had far-reaching consequences, because Britain later served as a base for the Christianization of the Continent.

Between the fifth and tenth centuries, the great majority of peoples living on the European continent and the nearby islands accepted the Christian religion – that is, they received baptism, though baptism in itself did not automatically transform people into Christians.

Religion influenced all aspects of tribal life. All members of the tribe participated in religious observances, because doing so was a social duty. Religion was not a private or individual matter; the religion of the chieftain or king determined the religion of the people. Thus missionaries concentrated their initial efforts not on the people but on kings or tribal chieftains. According to custom, tribal chiefs negotiated with all foreign powers, including the gods. Because the Christian missionaries represented a "foreign" power (the Christian God), the king dealt with them. If the ruler accepted Christian baptism, his people did so too. The result was mass baptism.

Once a ruler had marched his people to the waters of baptism, however, the work of Christianization had only begun. Baptism meant either sprinkling the head or immersing the body in water. Conversion meant mental and heartfelt acceptance of the beliefs of Christianity. What does it mean to be a Christian? This question has troubled sincere people from the time of Saint Paul to the present. The problem rests in part in the basic teaching of Jesus in the Gospel:

Then fixing his eyes on his disciples he said:
"How happy are you who are poor: yours is the kingdom of God. Happy you who are hungry now: you shall be satisfied. Happy you who weep now: you shall laugh.
"Happy are you when people hate you, drive you out, abuse you, denounce your name as criminal, on account of the Son of man. Rejoice when that day comes and dance for joy, then your reward will be great in heaven. This was the way their ancestors treated the prophets."

THE CURSES
"But alas for you who are rich: you are having

your consolation now. Alas for you who have your fill now: you shall go hungry. Alas for you who laugh now: you shall mourn and weep.

"Alas for you when the world speaks well of you: This was the way their ancestors treated the false prophets."

LOVE OF ENEMIES

"But I say this to you who are listening: Love your enemies, do good to those who hate you, bless those who curse you, pray for those who treat you badly. To the man who slaps you on one cheek, present the other cheek too; to the man who takes your cloak from you, do not refuse your tunic. Give to everyone who asks you, and do not ask of your property back from the man who robs you. Treat others as you would like them to treat you."[5]

These ideas are among the most radical and revolutionary the world has heard, and it has proved very difficult to get people to live by them.

The German peoples were warriors who idealized the military virtues of physical strength, ferocity in battle, and loyalty to the leader. Victors in battle enjoyed the spoils of success and plundered the vanquished. The greater the fighter, the more trophies and material goods he collected. Thus the Germans had trouble accepting the Christian precepts of "love your enemies" and "turn the other cheek." How could a person be poor and happy at the same time, as Christians claimed?

The Germanic tribes found the Christian notions of sin and repentance virtually incomprehensible. Sin in Christian thought meant disobedience to the will of God as revealed in the Ten Commandments and the teachings of Christ. Good or "moral" behavior to the barbarians meant the observance of tribal customs and practices. Dishonorable behavior caused social ostracism. The inculcation of Christian ideals took a very long time.

CONVERSION AND ASSIMILATION

In Christian theology, conversion involves a turning toward God – that is, a conscious effort to live according to the gospel message. How did missionaries and priests get masses of pagan and illiterate peoples to understand and live by Christian ideals and teachings? Through preaching, through assimilation, and through the penitential system. Preaching aimed at instruction and edification. Instruction presented the basic teachings of Christianity. Edification was intended to strengthen the newly baptized in their faith through stories about the lives of Christ and the saints. Deeply ingrained pagan customs and practices could not be stamped out by words alone, or even by imperial edicts. Christian missionaries often pursued a policy of assimilation, easing the conversion of pagan men and women by stressing similarities between their customs and beliefs and those of Christianity. A letter that Pope Gregory I wrote to Augustine of Canterbury beautifully illustrates this policy. The letter, carried to Augustine in Britain by one Mellitus in 601, expresses the pope's intention that pagan buildings and practices be given a Christian significance:

To our well beloved son Abbot Mellitus: Gregory servant of the servants of God.... Therefore, when by God's help you reach our most reverent brother, Bishop Augustine, we wish you to inform him that we have been giving careful thought to the affairs of the English, and have come to the conclusion that the temples of the idols among that people should on no account be destroyed. The idols are to be destroyed, but the temples themselves are to be aspersed with holy water, altars set up in them, and relics deposited there. For if these temples are well-built, they must be purified from the worship of demons and dedicated to the service of the true God. In this way, we hope that the people, seeing

THE PANTHEON (INTERIOR) *Originally a temple for the gods, the Pantheon later served as a Christian church. As such, it symbolizes the adaptation of pagan elements to Christian purposes. (Alinari/Scala)*

that their temples are not destroyed, may abandon their error and, flocking more readily to their accustomed resorts, may come to know and adore the true God. And since they have a custom of sacrificing many oxen to demons, let some other solemnity be substituted in its place, such as a day of Dedication or the Festivals of the holy martyrs whose relics are enshrined there. On such occasions they might well construct shelters of boughs for themselves around the churches that were once temples, and celebrate the solemnity with devout feasting. . . . For it is certainly impossible to eradicate all errors from obstinate minds at one stroke, and whoever wishes to climb to a mountain top climbs gradually step by step, and not in one leap.[6]

How assimilation works is perhaps best appreciated through the example of a festival familiar to all Americans, Saint Valentine's Day. There were two Romans named Valentine. Both were Christian priests, and both were martyred for their beliefs around the middle of February in the third century. Since about 150 B.C. the Romans had celebrated the festival of Lupercalia, at which they asked the gods for fertility for themselves, their fields, and their flocks. This celebration occurred in mid-February, shortly before the Roman New Year and the arrival of spring. Thus the early church "converted" the old festival of Lupercalia into Saint Valentine's Day. (Nothing in the lives of the two Christian martyrs connects them with lovers or the exchange of messages and gifts. That practice began in the later Middle Ages.) February 14 was still celebrated as a festival, but it had taken on Christian meaning.

Assimilation is a slow process. Probably more immediate in its impact on the unconverted masses was the penitential system. Penitentials were manuals for the examination of conscience. Irish priests wrote the earliest ones, which English missionaries then carried to the Continent. The illiterate penitent knelt beside the priest, who questioned the penitential about sins he or she might have committed. The recommended penance was then imposed. Penance usually meant fasting for three days each week on bread and water, which served as a "medicine" for the soul. Here is a section of the penitential prepared by Archbishop Theodore of Canterbury (668–690), which circulated widely at the time:

If anyone commits fornication with a virgin he shall do penance for one year. If with a married woman, he shall do penance for four years, two of these entire, and in the other two during the three forty-day periods and three days a week.

A male who commits fornication with a male shall do penance for three years.

If a woman practices vice with a woman, she shall do penance for three years.

Whoever has often committed theft, seven years is his penance, or such a sentence as his priest shall determine, that is, according to what can be arranged with those whom he has wronged. And he who used to steal, when he becomes penitent, ought always to be reconciled to him against whom he has offended and to make restitution according to the wrong he has done to him; and [in such case] he shall greatly shorten his penance.

If a layman slays another with malice aforethought, if he will not lay aside his arms, he shall do penance for seven years; without flesh and wine, three years.

If one slays a monk or a cleric, he shall lay aside his arms and serve God, or he shall do penance for seven years.

He who defiles his neighbor's wife, deprived of his own wife, shall fast for three years two days a week and in the three forty-day periods.

If [the woman] is a virgin, he shall do penance for one year without meat and wine and mead.

If he defiles a vowed virgin, he shall do penance for three years, as we said above, whether a child is born of her or not.

Women who commit abortion before [the fetus] has life, shall do penance for one year or for the three forty-day periods or for forty days, according to the nature of the offense; and if later, that is, more than forty days after conception, they shall do penance as murderesses, that is for three years on Wednesdays and Fridays and in the three forty-day periods. This according to the canons is judged [punishable by] ten years.

If a mother slays her child, if she commits homicide, she shall do penance for fifteen years, and never change except on Sunday.

If a poor woman slays her child, she shall do penance for seven years. In the canon it is said that if it is a case of homicide, she shall do penance for ten years.[7]

As this sample suggests, writers of penitentials were preoccupied with sexual transgressions. Penitentials are much more akin to the Jewish law of the Old Testament than to the spirit of the New Testament. They provide an enormous amount of information about the ascetic ideals of early Christianity and about the crime-ridden realities of Celtic and Germanic societies. Penitentials also reveal the ecclesiastical foundations of some modern attitudes toward sex, birth control, and abortion. Most important, the penitential system led to the growth of a different attitude toward religion: formerly public, corporate, and social, religious observances became private, personal, and individual.[8]

CHRISTIAN ATTITUDES TOWARD CLASSICAL CULTURE

Probably the major dilemma the early Christian church faced concerned Greco-Roman culture. The Roman Empire as a social, political, and economic force gradually disintegrated. Its culture, however, survived. In Greek philosophy, art, and architecture, in Roman law, literature, education, and engineering, the legacy of a great civilization continued. The Christian religion had begun and spread within this intellectual and psychological milieu. What was to be the attitude of Christians to the Greco-Roman world of ideas?

HOSTILITY

Christians in the first and second centuries believed that the end of the world was near. Christ had promised to return, and Christians expected to witness that return. Therefore they considered knowledge useless and learning a waste of time. The important duty of the Christian was to prepare for the Second Coming of the Lord.

Early Christians harbored a strong hatred of pagan Roman culture – in fact, of all Roman civilization. Had not the Romans crucified Christ? Had not the Romans persecuted Christians and subjected them to the most horrible tortures? Did not the Book of Revelation in the New Testament call Rome the great whore of the world, filled with corruption, sin, and every kind of evil? Roman culture was sexual, sensual, and materialistic. The sensual poetry of Ovid, the pornographic descriptions of the satirist Petronius, the political poetry of Virgil, even the rhetorical brilliance of Cicero represented a threat, in the eyes of serious Christians, to the spiritual aims and ideals of Christianity. Good Christians who sought the Kingdom of Heaven through the imitation of Christ believed they had to disassociate themselves from the filth that Roman culture embodied.

As Saint Paul wrote, "The wisdom of the world is foolishness, we preach Christ crucified." Tertullian (ca 160–220), an influential African Christian writer, condemned all secular literature as foolishness in the eyes of God. He called the Greek philosophers, such as Aristotle, "hucksters of eloquence" and compared them to "animals of self-glorification." "What has Athens to do with Jerusalem," he demanded, "the Academy with the Church? We have no need for curiosity since Jesus Christ, nor for inquiry since the gospel." Tertullian insisted that Christians would find in the Bible all the wisdom they needed.

COMPROMISE AND ADJUSTMENT

At the same time, Christianity encouraged adjustment to the ideas and institutions of the Roman world. Some Biblical texts clearly urged Christians to accept the existing social, economic, and political establishment. In a letter specifically addressed to Christians living among non-Christians in the hostile environment of Rome, Saint Peter had written about the obligations of Christians:

TOWARDS PAGANS
Always behave honourably among pagans, so that they can see your good works for themselves and, when the day of reckoning comes, give thanks to God for the things which now make them denounce you as criminals.

TOWARDS CIVIL AUTHORITY
For the sake of the Lord, accept the authority of every social institution: the emperor, as the supreme authority, and the governors as commissioned by

him to punish criminals and praise good citizenship. God wants you to be good citizens. . . . Have respect for everyone and love for your community; fear God and honour the emperor.[9]

Christians really had little choice. Greco-Roman culture was the only culture they knew. Only men received a formal education, and they went through the traditional curriculum of grammar and rhetoric. They learned to be effective speakers in the forum or law courts. No other system of education existed. Many early Christians had grown up as pagans, been educated as pagans, and were converted only as adults. Toward homosexuality, for example, Christians of the first three or four centuries simply imbibed the attitude of the world in which they lived. Many Romans indulged in homosexual activity, and contemporaries did not consider such behavior (or inclinations to it) immoral, bizarre, or harmful. Several emperors were openly homosexual, and homosexuals participated freely in all aspects of Roman life and culture. Early Christians too considered homosexuality a conventional expression of physical desire, and they were no more susceptible to anti-homosexual prejudices than pagans were. Some prominent Christians experienced loving same-gender relationships that probably had a sexual element. What eventually led to a change in public and Christian attitudes toward sexual behavior was the shift from the sophisticated urban culture of the Greco-Roman world to the rural culture of medieval Europe.[10]

Even had early Christians wanted to give up their classical ideas and patterns of thought, they would have had great difficulty doing so. Therefore, they had to adapt or adjust their Roman education to their Christian beliefs. Saint Paul himself believed there was a good deal of truth in pagan thought, as long

THE ANTIOCH CHALICE *This earliest surviving Christian chalice, which dates from the fourth century A.D., combines the typical Roman shape with Christian motifs. The chalice is decorated with figures of Christ and the apostles, leaves, and grapes, which represent the sacrament of the Eucharist. (The Metropolitan Museum of Art; the Cloisters Collection; purchase, 1950)*

as it was correctly interpreted and properly understood.

The result was a compromise. Christians gradually came to terms with Greco-Roman culture. Saint Jerome (340–419), a distinguished theologian and linguist, remains famous for his translation of the Old and New Testaments from the Hebrew and Greek into vernacular Latin. Called the Vulgate, his edition of the Bible served as the official translation until the sixteenth century, and even today scholars rely on it. Saint Jerome was also familiar with the writings of such classical authors as Cicero, Virgil, and Terence. He believed that Christians should study the best of ancient thought, because it would direct their minds to God. Jerome maintained that the best ancient literature should be interpreted in light of the Christian faith.

SYNTHESIS: SAINT AUGUSTINE

The finest representative of the blending of classical and Christian ideas, and indeed one of the most brilliant thinkers in the history of the Western world, was Saint Augustine of Hippo (354–430). Aside from the scriptural writers, no one else has had a greater impact on Christian thought in succeeding centuries. Saint Augustine was born into an urban family in what is now Algeria in North Africa. His father was a pagan, his mother a devout Christian. Because his family was poor — his father was a minor civil servant — the only avenue to success in a highly competitive world was a classical education.

Augustine's mother believed that a good classical education, though pagan, would make her son a better Christian, so Augustine's father scraped together the money to educate him. The child received his basic education in the local school. By modern and even medieval standards, that education was extremely narrow: textual study of the writings of the poet Virgil, the orator-politician Cicero, the historian Sallust, and the playwright Terence. At that time, learning meant memorization. Education in the late Roman world aimed at appreciation of words, par-

ticularly those of renowned and eloquent orators.

At the age of seventeen, Augustine went to nearby Carthage to continue his education. There he took a mistress with whom he lived for fifteen years. At Carthage, Augustine entered a difficult psychological phase and began an intellectual and spiritual pilgrimage that led him through experiments with several philosophies and heretical Christian sects. In 383, he traveled to Rome, where he endured illness and disappointment in his teaching: his students fled when their bills were due.

Finally, in Milan in 387, through his friendship with Ambrose and the insights he gained from reading Saint Paul's Letter to the Romans, Augustine was converted and received Christian baptism. He later became bishop of the seacoast city of Hippo Regius in his native North Africa. He was a renowned preacher to Christians there, a vigorous defender of orthodox Christianity, and the author of over ninety-three books and treatises.

Augustine's autobiography, *The Confessions,* is a literary masterpiece and one of the most influential books in the history of Europe. Written in the form of a prayer to God, its language is often incredibly beautiful:

Great are thou, O Lord, and exceedingly to be praised: great is thy power and of thy wisdom there is no reckoning. And man, indeed, one part of thy creation, has the will to praise thee: yea, man, though he bears his mortality about with him . . . even man, a small portion of thy creation, has the will to praise thee. Thou dost stir him up, that it may delight him to praise thee, for thou hast made us for thyself, and our hearts are restless till they find repose in thee.[11]

Too late have I loved thee, O beauty ever ancient and ever new, too late have I loved thee! And be-

hold! Thou wert within and I without, and it was *without that I sought thee. Thou wert with me, and I was not with thee. Those creatures held me far from thee which, were they not in thee, were not at all. Thou didst call, thou didst cry, thou didst break in upon my deafness; thou didst gleam forth, thou didst shine out, thou didst banish my blindness; thou didst send forth thy fragrance, and I drew breath and yearned for thee; I tasted and still hunger and thirst; thou didst touch me, and I was on flame to find thy peace.*[12]

The Confessions describes Augustine's moral struggle, the conflict between his spiritual and intellectual aspirations and his sensual and material self. It tells the eternally human story of a man constantly tempted by sin but aware also of the providence of God. *The Confessions* reveals the change and development of a human mind and personality steeped in the philosophy and culture of the ancient world.

Greek and Roman philosophers had taught that knowledge and virtue are the same thing: a person who really knows what is right will do what is right. Augustine rejected this idea. He believed that a person may know what is right but fail to act righteously because of the innate weakness of the human will. People do not always act on the basis of rational knowledge. Here Augustine made a profound contribution to the understanding of human nature: he demonstrated that a very learned person can also be corrupt and evil. *The Confessions,* written in the rhetorical style and language of late Roman antiquity, marks the synthesis of Greco-Roman forms and Christian thought.

When the Visigothic chieftain Alaric conquered Rome in 410, horrified pagans blamed the disaster on the Christians. In response, Augustine wrote *City of God.* This profoundly original work contrasts Christianity with the secular society in which it existed. *City of God* presents a moral interpretation of the Roman government, and in fact of all history. Written in Latin and filled with references to ancient history and mythology, it is the best statement of the Christian philosophy of history.

According to Augustine, history is the account of God acting in time. Human history reveals that there are two kinds of people: those who live according to the flesh in the city of Babylon and those who live according to the spirit in the City of God. In other words, humanity is composed of individuals who live entirely according to their selfish inclinations and individuals who live according to the Word of God. The former will endure eternal hellfire, the latter eternal bliss.

Augustine maintained that states came into existence as the result of Adam's fall and people's inclination to sin. The state is a necessary evil, responsible only for providing the peace and order Christians need in order to pursue their pilgrimage to the City of God. The particular form of government – whether monarchy, aristocracy, or democracy – is basically irrelevant. Any civil government that fails to provide order, law, and justice is no more than a band of gangsters.

Since the state results from moral lapse, from sin, it follows that the church, which is concerned with salvation, is responsible for everyone, including Christian rulers. Churchmen in the Middle Ages used Augustine's theory to defend their belief in the ultimate superiority of the spiritual power over the temporal. This remained the dominant political theory until the late thirteenth century.

Augustine had no objection to drawing on pagan knowledge to support Christian thought. Augustine used Roman history as evidence to defend Christian theology. In doing so he assimilated Roman history, and indeed all of classical culture, into Christian teaching.

MONASTICISM AND THE RULE OF SAINT BENEDICT

Christianity began and spread as a city religion. Since the first century, however, some especially pious Christians had felt that the only alternative to the decadence of urban life was complete separation from the world. All-consuming pursuit of material things, gross sexual promiscuity, and general political corruption disgusted them. They believed that the Christian life as set forth in the Gospel could not be lived in the midst of such immorality. They rejected the established values of Roman society and were the first real nonconformists in the church.

At first individuals and small groups left the cities and went to live in caves or rude shelters in the desert or the mountains. These people were called hermits, from the Greek word *eremos*, meaning "desert." There is no way of knowing how many hermits there were in the fourth and fifth centuries, partly because their conscious aim was a secret and hidden life known only to God.

Several factors worked against the eremitical variety of monasticism in western Europe. First was the climate. The cold, snow, ice, and fog that covered much of Europe for many months of the year discouraged isolated living. Dense forests filled with wild animals and wandering barbaric German tribes presented obvious dangers. Furthermore, church leaders did not really approve of the eremitical life. Hermits sometimes claimed to have mystical experiences, direct communications with God. No one could verify these experiences.

But if hermits could communicate directly with the Lord, what need had they for the priest and the institutional church? The church hierarchy, or leaders, encouraged coenobitic monasticism – that is, communal living in monasteries.

In the fifth and sixth centuries, many experiments in communal monasticism were made in Gaul, Italy, Spain, Anglo-Saxon England, and Ireland. John Cassian, after studying both eremitical and coenobitic mysticism in Egypt and Syria, established two monasteries near Marseilles in Gaul around 415. One of Cassian's books, *Conferences,* based on conversations he had had with holy men in the East, discussed the dangers of the isolated hermit's life. The abbey or monastery of Lérins on the Mediterranean Sea near Cannes (ca 410) also had significant contacts with monastic centers in the Middle East and North Africa. Lérins encouraged the severely penitential and extremely ascetic behavior common in the East, such as long hours of prayer, fasting, and self-flagellation. It was this tradition of harsh self-mortification that the Roman-British monk Saint Patrick carried from Lérins to Ireland in the fifth century. Church organization in Ireland became closely associated with the monasteries, and Irish monastic life followed the ascetic Eastern form.

Around 540, the Roman senator Cassiodorus retired from public service and established a monastery, the Vivarium, on his estate in Italy. Cassiodorus wanted the Vivarium to become an educational and cultural center, and enlisted highly educated and sophisticated men for it. He set the monks to copying both sacred and secular manuscripts, intending this to be their sole occupation. Cassiodorus started the association of monasticism with scholarship and learning. This developed into a great tradition in the medieval and modern worlds. But Cassiodorus's experiment did not become the most influential form of monasticism in European society. The fifth and sixth centuries witnessed the appearance of many other monastic lifestyles.

In 529 Benedict of Nursia (480–543), who had experimented with both the eremitical and the communal forms of monastic life, wrote a brief set of regulations, or rules, for the monks who had gathered around him at Monte Cassino between Rome and Naples. This guide for monastic life slowly replaced all others. *The Rule of Saint Benedict* has influenced all forms of organized religious life in the Roman church.

THE RULE OF SAINT BENEDICT

Saint Benedict conceived of his *Rule* as a simple code for ordinary men. It outlined a monastic life of regularity, discipline, and moderation. Each monk had ample food and adequate sleep. Self-destructive acts of mortification were forbidden. In an atmosphere of silence, the monk spent part of the day in formal prayer, which Benedict called the Work of God. This consisted of chanting psalms and other prayers from the Bible in that part of the monastery church called the choir. The rest of the day was passed in study and manual labor. After a year of probation, the monk made three vows.

First, the monk vowed stability: he promised to live his entire life in the monastery of his profession. The vow of stability was Saint Benedict's major contribution to Western monasticism; his object was to prevent the wandering so common in his day. Second, the monk vowed conversion of manners – that is, to strive to improve himself and to come closer to God. Third, he promised obedience, the most difficult vow because it meant the complete surrender of his will to the abbot, or head of the monastery. The first sentence of

ST. BENEDICT from Agnolo Gaddi, Madonna Enthroned with Saints, *ca 1385. The first word of his* Rule, *which Benedict holds in his left hand, is "Listen." Listening was the posture of students, and St. Benedict called his monastery a "School of the Lord's Service," where the monks listened not only to their abbot but through the abbot to Christ himself. In his right hand, Benedict carries the rods of correction. (National Gallery of Art, Washington, Andrew W. Mellon Collection)*

the *Rule* urged the monk, by the labor of obedience, to return to God, from whom he had departed "by the sloth of disobedience."

The Rule of Saint Benedict expresses the assimilation of the Roman spirit into Western monasticism. It reveals the logical mind of its creator and the Roman concern for order, organization, and respect for law. Its spirit of moderation and flexibility is reflected in the patience, wisdom, and understanding with which the abbot is to govern, and, indeed, the entire life is to be led. The *Rule* could be used in vastly different physical and geographical circumstances, in damp and cold Germany as well as in warm and sunny Italy. The *Rule* was quickly adapted for women, and many convents of nuns were established in the early Middle Ages.

Saint Benedict's *Rule* implies that a person who wants to become a monk or nun need have no previous ascetic experience or even a particularly strong bent toward the religious life. Thus, it allowed for the admission of newcomers with different backgrounds and personalities. This flexibility helps to explain the attractiveness of Benedictine monasticism throughout the centuries. *The Rule of Saint Benedict* is a superior example of the way in which the Greco-Roman heritage and Roman patterns of thought were preserved.

At the same time, the *Rule* no more provides a picture of actual life within a Benedictine abbey of the seventh or eighth (or twentieth) century than the American Constitution of 1789 describes living conditions in the United States today. A code of laws cannot do that. Monasteries were composed of individuals, and human beings defy strict classification according to rules, laws, or statistics. *The Rule of Saint Benedict* had one fundamental purpose. The exercises of the monastic life were designed to draw the individual, slowly but steadily, away from attachment to the world and love of self and toward the love of God.

THE SUCCESS OF BENEDICTINE MONASTICISM

Why was the Benedictine form of monasticism so successful? Why did it eventually replace other forms of Western monasticism? The answer lies partly in its spirit of flexibility and moderation and partly in the balanced life it provided. Early Benedictine monks and nuns spent part of the day in prayer, part in study or some other form of intellectual activity, and part in manual labor. The monastic life as conceived by Saint Benedict did not lean too heavily in any one direction; it struck a balance between asceticism and idleness. It thus provided opportunities for persons of entirely different abilities and talents — from mechanics to gardeners to literary scholars. Benedict's *Rule* contrasts sharply with Cassiodorus's narrow concept of the monastery as a place for aristocratic scholars and bibliophiles.

Benedictine monasticism also suited the social circumstances of early medieval society. The German invasions had fragmented European life: the self-sufficient rural estate replaced the city as the basic unit of civilization. A monastery too had to be economically self-sufficient. It was supposed to produce from its lands and properties all that was needed for food, clothing, buildings, and liturgical service of the altar. The monastery fitted in — indeed, represented — the trend toward localism.

Benedictine monasticism also succeeded partly because it was so materially successful. In the seventh and eighth centuries, monasteries pushed back forest and wasteland, drained swamps, and experimented with crop rotation. For example, the abbey of Saint Wandrille, founded in 645 near Rouen in northwestern Gaul, sent squads of monks to clear the forests that surrounded it. Within seventy-five years the abbey was immensely wealthy. The abbey of Jumièges, also in the diocese of Rouen, followed much the same pattern. Such Benedictine houses made a significant contribution to the agricultural development of Europe. The socialistic nature of their organization, whereby property was held in common and profits pooled and reinvested, made this contribution possible.

Finally, monasteries conducted schools for the education of the young people of the neighborhood. Some learned about prescriptions and herbal remedies for disease, and

JUSTINIAN AND HIS COURT   The Emperor Justinian (center) with ecclesiastical and court officials personifies the unity of the Byzantine state and the orthodox church in the person of the emperor. Just as the emperor was both king and priest, so all his Greek subjects belonged to the orthodox church. (Alinari/Scala)

went on to provide medical treatment for their localities. A few copied manuscripts and wrote books. This training did not go unappreciated in a society desperately in need of it. Local and royal governments drew upon the services of the literate men, the able administrators whom the monasteries produced. This was not what Saint Benedict had intended, but the effectiveness of the institution he designed made it perhaps inevitable.

THE BYZANTINE EAST
(CA 400–788)

Constantine (306–337) had tried to maintain the unity of the Roman Empire, but during the fifth and sixth centuries the western and eastern halves drifted apart. Later emperors worked to hold the empire together. Justinian (527–565) waged long and hard-fought wars against the Ostrogoths and temporarily regained Italy and North Africa. But his conquests had disastrous consequences. Justinian's wars exhausted the resources of the Byzantine state, destroyed Italy's economy, and killed a large part of its population. The wars paved the way for the easy conquest of Italy by another Germanic tribe, the Lombards, shortly after Justinian's death. In the late sixth century, the territory of the western Roman Empire came under Germanic sway, while in the East the Byzantine Empire continued the traditions and institutions of the caesars.

Latin Christian culture was only one legacy the Roman Empire bequeathed to the Western world. The Byzantine culture centered at Constantinople – Constantine's New Rome – was another. The Byzantine Empire maintained a high standard of living, and for centuries the Greeks were the most civilized people in the Western world. The Byzantine Empire held at bay, or at least hindered, barbarian peoples who could otherwise have wreaked additional devastation on western Europe, retarding its development. Most important, however, is the role of Byzantium as preserver of the wisdom of the ancient world. Throughout the long years when barbarians in western Europe trampled down the old and then painfully built something new, Byzantium protected and then handed on to the West the intellectual heritage of Greco-Roman civilization.

BYZANTINE EAST AND GERMANIC WEST

As imperial authority disintegrated in the West during the fifth century, civic functions were performed first by church leaders and then by German chieftains. As we have seen, Pope Leo I negotiated with Attila the Hun and persuaded him to withdraw from Rome. There was no other authority in Rome to do so. The death of the Roman emperor Romulus Augustus in 476 signaled the end of the empire in the West. Thereafter, German chieftains held power.

Meanwhile in the East, the Byzantines preserved the forms and traditions of the old Roman Empire, and even called themselves Romans. Byzantine emperors traced their lines back past Constantine to Augustus. The senate that sat in Constantinople carried on the traditions and preserved the glory of the old Roman senate. The army that defended the empire was the direct descendant of the

old Roman legions. Even the chariot factions of the Roman Empire lived on under the Byzantines, who cheered their favorites as enthusiastically as had the Romans of Hadrian's day.

The position of the church differed considerably in the Byzantine East and the Germanic West. The fourth-century emperors Constantine and Theodosius had wanted the church to act as a unifying force within the empire, but the Germanic invasions made that impossible. The bishops of Rome repeatedly called upon the emperors at Constantinople for military support against the invaders, but rarely could the emperors send it. The church in the West steadily grew away from the empire and became involved in the social and political affairs of Italy and the West. Nevertheless, until the eighth century, the popes, who were selected by the clergy of Rome, continued to send announcements of their elections to the emperors at Constantinople – a sign that the Roman popes long thought of themselves as bishops of the Roman Empire.

The popes were preoccupied with conversion of the Germans, the Christian attitude toward classical culture, and relations with the German rulers. The church in the West concentrated on its missionary function. It took time for the clergy to be organized and for the papacy to get in touch with all clerics. Most of the theology of the church in the West came from the East, and the overwhelming majority of popes were themselves of Eastern origin.

Tensions occasionally developed between church officials and secular authorities in the West. The dispute between Bishop Ambrose of Milan and the emperor Theodosius is a good example. A century later, Pope Gelasius I (492–496) insisted that bishops, not civil authorities, were responsible for the administration of the church. Gelasius maintained that two powers governed the world, the sacred authority of the popes and the royal power of kings. Because priests have to answer to God even for kings, the sacred power was the greater.

Such an assertion was virtually unheard of in the East, where the emperor's jurisdiction over the church was fully acknowledged. The emperor in Constantinople nominated the patriarch, as the highest prelate of the church in the East was called. The emperor looked upon religion as a branch of the state. Religion was such a vital aspect of the social life of the people that the emperor devoted considerable attention to it. He considered it his duty to protect the faith, not only against heathen enemies but also against heretics within the empire. In case of doctrinal disputes, the emperor, following Constantine's example at Nicaea, summoned councils of bishops and theologians to settle problems.

In the East, Christianity was the established religion. All citizens of the Byzantine Empire were Christians; to be Byzantine meant to be Christian. The Greek church was an imperial state church subject to and guided by the emperor. The clergy were well organized. The level of theological debate was high. Fine points of Christian theology held the attention of the leaders of the Greek church.

The expansion of the Arabs in the Mediterranean in the seventh and eighth centuries furthered the separation of the churches by dividing the two parts of Christendom. Separation bred isolation. Isolation, combined with prejudice on both sides, bred hostility. Finally, in 1054, a theological disagreement led the bishop of Rome and the patriarch of Constantinople to excommunicate each other. The outcome was a permanent schism, or split, between the Roman Catholic and the Greek Orthodox churches.

In spite of religious differences, the Byzantine Empire served as a bulwark for the West, protecting it against invasions from the east. The Greeks stopped the Persians in the seventh century. They blunted — though they could not stop — Arab attacks in the seventh and eighth centuries, and they fought courageously against Turkish invaders until the fifteenth century, when they were finally overwhelmed. Byzantine Greeks slowed the impetus of the Slavic incursions in the Balkans and held the Russians at arm's length.

Turning from war to the arts of peace, the Byzantines set about civilizing the Slavs, both in the Balkans and in Russia. Byzantine missionaries spread the word of Christ, and one of their triumphs was the conversion of the Russians. The Byzantine missionary Cyril adapted the Greek alphabet to the Russian language, and this script (called the Cyrillic alphabet) is still in use today. Cyrillic script made possible the birth of Russian literature. Similarly, Byzantine art and architecture became the basis and inspiration of Russian forms. The Byzantines were so successful that the Russians claimed to be the successors of the Byzantine Empire. For a time Moscow was even known as "the Third Rome" (the second Rome being Constantinople).

THE LAW CODE OF JUSTINIAN

One of the most splendid achievements of the Byzantine emperors was the preservation of Roman law for the medieval and modern worlds. Roman law had developed from many sources — decisions by judges, edicts of the emperors, legislation passed by the senate, and the opinions of jurists expert in the theory and practice of law. By the fourth century, Roman law had become a huge bewildering mass. Its sheer bulk made it almost unusable. Some laws had become outdated, some repeated others, and some contradicted others. Faced with this vast, complex, and confusing hodgepodge, the emperor Theodosius decided to clarify and codify the law. He explained the need to do so:

When we consider the enormous multitude of books, the diverse modes of process and the difficulty of legal cases, and further the huge mass of imperial constitutions, which hidden as it were under a rampart of gross mist and darkness precludes men's intellects from gaining a knowledge of them, we feel that we have met a real need of our age, and dispelling the darkness have given light to the laws by a short compendium. . . . Thus having swept away the clouds of volumes, on which many wasted their lives and explained nothing in the end, we established a compendious knowledge of the Imperial constitutions since the time of the divine Constantine.[13]

Theodosius's work was only a beginning. He left centuries of Roman law untouched.

A far more sweeping and systematic codification took place under the emperor Justinian. Justinian intended to simplify the law and to make it known to everyone. He appointed a committee of eminent jurists to sort through and organize the laws. In 529, Justinian published the *Code,* which distilled the legal genius of the Romans into a coherent whole, eliminated outmoded laws, eliminated contradictions, and clarified the law itself. Not content with the *Code,* Justinian set about bringing order to the equally huge body of Roman jurisprudence, the science or philosophy of law.

During the second and third centuries the foremost Roman jurists, at the request of the emperors, had expressed learned opinions on complex legal problems, but often these opinions differed from one another. To harmonize this body of knowledge, Justinian directed his jurists to clear up disputed points and to issue definitive rulings. Accordingly, in 533 his lawyers published the *Digest,* which codified Roman legal thought. Finally, Justinian's lawyers compiled a handbook of civil law, the *Institutes.*

These three works – the *Code, Digest,* and *Institutes* – are the backbone of the *corpus juris civilis,* the body of civil law, which is the foundation of law for nearly every modern European nation. Even England, which developed its own common law, has been influenced by it. The work of Justinian and his dedicated band of jurists still affects the life of the modern world nearly fifteen hundred years later.

BYZANTINE INTELLECTUAL LIFE

Among the Byzantines education was highly prized, and because of them many masterpieces of ancient Greek literature survived to fertilize the intellectual life of the modern world. The literature of the Byzantine Empire was predominantly Greek, although Latin was long spoken among top politicians, scholars, and lawyers. Indeed, Justinian's *Code* was first written in Latin. Among the reading public, which was quite large, history was a favorite subject. Generations of Byzantines read the historical works of Herodotus, Thucydides, and others. Some Byzantine historians abbreviated long histories, such as those of Polybius, while others wrote detailed narratives of their own days.

The most remarkable Byzantine historian was Procopius (ca 500–ca 562), who left a rousing account of Justinian's reconquest of North Africa and Italy. Proof that the wit and venom of ancient writers like Archilochus and Aristophanes lived on in the Byzantine era can be found in Procopius's *Secret History,* a vicious and uproarious attack on Justinian and his wife, the empress Theodora. Although the

Byzantines are often depicted as dull and lifeless, such opinions are hard to defend in the face of Procopius's descriptions of Justinian's character:

For he was at once villainous and amenable; as people say colloquially, a moron. He was never truthful with anyone, but always guileful in what he said and did, yet easily hoodwinked by any who wanted to deceive him. His nature was an unnatural mixture of folly and wickedness.[14]

Procopius even accused Justinian of being a demon who possessed strange powers:

And some of those who have been with Justinian at the palace late at night, men who were pure of spirit, have thought they saw a strange demonaic form taking his throne and walked about, and indeed he was never wont to remain sitting for long, and immediately Justinian's head vanished, while the rest of his body seemed to ebb and flow; whereat the beholder stood aghast and fearful, wondering if his eyes were deceiving him. But presently he perceived the vanished head filling out and joining the body again as strangely as it had left it.[15]

The *Secret History* may not be great history, but it is robust literature.

Later Byzantine historians chronicled the victories of their emperors and the progress of their barbarian foes. Like Herodotus before them, they were curious about foreigners. They have left striking descriptions of the Turks, who eventually overwhelmed Byzantium. They painted unflattering pictures of the uncouth and grasping princes of France and England, who saw in the Crusades the perfect combination of faith and piety, bloodshed and profit.

In mathematics and geometry the Byzantines discovered nothing new. Yet they were exceptionally important as catalysts, for they passed Greco-Roman learning on to the

LID–BYZANTINE BOX *Probably made in Alexandria, Egypt in the fifth century, this medicine box (15.2 cm. high and 8.9 cm. wide) was divided into six compartments intended to hold various medicines. The female figure on the lid carries a rudder in one hand, symbolizing Alexandria's maritime activities, and a cornucopia suggesting material prosperity or good health in the other. Alexandria was a great medical center until about 700 A.D., after which leadership in medical practice passed to Constantinople. (Dumbarton Oaks Center for Byzantine Studies, Trustees of Harvard University)*

Arabs, who assimilated it and made remarkable advances upon it. The Byzantines were equally uncreative in astronomy and natural science, but they at least faithfully learned what the ancients had to teach.

Only when science could be put to military use did the Byzantines make advances. The best-known Byzantine scientific discovery was chemical – "Greek fire," a combustible liquid that was the medieval equivalent of the flame thrower. In mechanics the Byzantines continued the work of Hellenistic and Roman inventors of artillery and seige machinery. Just as Archimedes had devised machines to stop the Romans, so Byzantine scientists improved and modified devices for defending their empire.

The Byzantines devoted a great deal of attention to medicine, and the general level of medical competence was far higher in the Byzantine Empire than it was in the medieval West. The Byzantines assimilated the discoveries of Hellenic and Hellenistic medicine but added very few of their own. The basis of their medical theory was Hippocrates' concept of the four humors of the body (page 101). Byzantine physicians emphasized the importance of diet and rest, and relied heavily on drugs made from herbs. Perhaps their chief weakness was their excessive use of bleeding and burning, which often succeeded only in further weakening an already feeble patient. Hospitals were a prominent feature of Byzantine life, and the army too had a medical corps.

THE ARABS AND ISLAM

Around 610, in the obscure town of Mecca in what is now Saudi Arabia, a moderately successful merchant called Mohammed began to

ISLAMIC RELIGIOUS HERITAGE In these two miniature paintings a Muslim artist acknowledges the Islamic debt to Judaism and to Christianity. Above, Samson destroys the temple of the Philistines (Judges 16: 28–30). Below, Christ at a window watches Mohammed's flight from Mecca. (Edinburgh University Library)

have religious visions. By the time he died in 632, all Arabia had accepted his creed. A century later his followers controlled Syria, Palestine, Egypt, all of North Africa, Spain, and part of France. This Arabic expansion profoundly affected the development of European culture. Through centers at Salerno in southern Italy and Toledo in central Spain, Arabic and Greek learning reached the West. Arabic mathematicians not only preserved ancient learning but also made original contributions. Western knowledge, especially in medicine, mathematics, and engineering, rests heavily on Arabic achievements.

THE ARABS

In Mohammed's time, Arabia was inhabited by Semitic tribes, most of whom were Bedouins. These primitive and warlike peoples grazed their goats and sheep on the sparse patches of grass that dotted the vast semi-arid peninsula. Other Arabs, called Hejaz, lived in the southern valleys and coastal towns along the Red Sea – in Yemen, Mecca, and Medina. The Hejaz led a more sophisticated life and supported themselves by agriculture and trade. Their caravan routes crisscrossed Arabia and carried goods to Byzantium, Persia, and Syria. The Hejaz had wide commercial dealings, but avoided cultural contacts with their Jewish, Christian, and Persian neighbors. The wealth produced by their business transactions led to luxurious and extravagant living in the towns.

لهفاستجب لهفاستندالی الاسطوانات الیمنی وقبض علی اسطوانیرکیورین علی جذبهما بکل قوته حتی هدجام کان بهماووقت الحیة وهلک کل رکان فی امرالکا والملوک

وبقی تسعون عشرین سنة امامافا لبنی اسرائیل وردینا فیم قبل هذه الواقعة وبقی بنواسرائیل بعد عشرسنین بلاامام ولاریس حتی جاربنی اسرائیل ویکن

ملک المعبد رفعوقصد ماقعد ماوسائلته وفی زمان تولته ظفراها فلسطین بالتابوت وتعرف بصندوق الشهادة فاخذوه وهذمن بنی اسرائیل ویهکن ملک

Although the nomadic Bedouins condemned the urbanized lifestyle of the Hejaz as immoral and corrupt, Arabs of both types deeply respected each other's local tribal customs. They had no political unity beyond their tribal bonds. Tribal custom regulated their lives. Custom demanded the rigid observance of family obligations and the performance of religious rituals. Custom insisted that an Arab be proud, generous, and swift to take revenge. Custom required manly courage in public and avoidance of shameful behavior that could bring social disgrace.

Although the various tribes differed markedly, they did have certain religious rules in common. For example, all Arabs kept three months of the year as sacred, and during that time fighting stopped so that everyone could attend the holy ceremonies in peace. The city of Mecca was the religious center of the Arab world, and fighting was never tolerated there. All Arabs prayed at the Kaaba, the sanctuary in Mecca. Within the Kaaba was a sacred black stone that Arabs revered because they believed it had fallen from heaven.

What eventually molded the diverse Arab tribes into a powerful political and social unity was the religion founded by Mohammed.

MOHAMMED AND THE FAITH OF ISLAM

Except for a few vague autobiographical remarks in the Koran, the sacred book of Islam, Mohammed (ca 571–632) left no account of his life. Arab tradition accepts as historically true some of the sacred legends that developed about him, but those legends were not written down until about a century after his death. Orphaned at the age of six, Mohammed was brought up by his grandfather. As a young man he became a merchant in the caravan trade. Later he entered the service of a

wealthy widow, and their subsequent marriage brought him financial independence. The Koran reveals him as an extremely devout man, ascetic, self-disciplined, literate but not educated.

Since childhood Mohammed had had strange seizures, or fits, during which he completely lost consciousness and had visions. After 610, these attacks and the accompanying visions apparently became more frequent. Unsure for a time what he should do, Mohammed discovered his mission after a vision in which the angel Gabriel instructed him to preach. Mohammed described his visions in verse form and used these verses as his Qur'an (Koran) or prayer recitation. During his lifetime Mohammed's secretary, Zaid ibn Thabit, jotted down these revelations haphazardly. After Mohammed's death, scribes organized the revelations into chapters, and in 651 Mohammed's second successor as religious leader, Othman, published an official version of them known as the Koran.

The religion Mohammed founded is called Islam; a believer in that faith is called a Muslim. Mohammed's religion eventually attracted great numbers of people, partly because of the simplicity of its doctrines. The subtle and complex reasoning Christianity had acquired by the seventh century was absent from Islam. Nor did Islam emphasize study and learning, as did Judaism.

The strictly monotheistic theology outlined in the Koran has only a few tenets. Allah, the Muslim god, is all-powerful and all-knowing. Mohammed, Allah's prophet, preached his word and carried his message. Mohammed described himself as the successor both of the Jewish patriarch Abraham and of Christ, and claimed that his teachings replaced theirs. Mohammed invited and won converts from Judaism and Christianity.

Because Allah is all-powerful, believers

must submit themselves to him. ("Islam" literally means "submission to the word of God.") This Islamic belief is closely related to the central feature of Muslim doctrine, the coming Day of Judgment. Muslims need not be concerned about *when* judgment will occur, but they must believe with absolute and total conviction that the Day of Judgment *will* come. Consequently, all of a Muslim's thoughts and actions at every hour of every day should be oriented toward the Last Judgment.

The Islamic Day of Judgment will be very similar to the Christian one: on that day God will separate the saved and the damned. Mohammed described in lengthy detail the frightful tortures with which Allah will punish the damned: scourgings, beatings with iron clubs, burnings, and forced drinking of boiling water. The prophet's depiction of the heavenly rewards of the saved and the blessed are just as graphic but different in kind from those of Christian theology. The Muslim vision of heaven features lush green gardens surrounded by refreshing streams. There the saved, clothed in rich silks, lounge about on soft cushions and couches, nibbling ripe fruits, sipping delicious beverages served by handsome youths, and enjoying the companionship of plump black-eyed maidens. It is not difficult to understand how these particular sensual delights would appeal to a people living in or near the hot, dry desert.

In order to merit the rewards of heaven, Mohammed prescribed a strict code of morality and behavior. The Muslim must recite a profession of faith in Allah and in Mohammed as God's prophet: "There is no god but Allah and Mohammed is his prophet." The believer must pray five times a day, fast and pray during the sacred month of Ramadan, make a pilgrimage to the holy city of Mecca once during his or her lifetime, and give alms to the poor. The Koran forbids alcoholic beverages and gambling. It condemns usury in business – that is, lending money at high interest rates or taking advantage of market demands for products by charging high prices for them. Some foods, such as pork, are forbidden, a dietary regulation adopted directly from the Mosaic law of the Jews.

By earlier Arab standards, the Koran sets forth an austere sexual morality. Muslim jurisprudence condemned licentious behavior on the part of men as well as women, and the status of women in Muslim society gradually improved. About marriage, illicit intercourse, and inheritance, the Koran states:

(Of) . . . women who seem good in your eyes, marry but two, three, or four; and if ye still fear that ye shall not act equitably, then only one; or the slaves whom ye have acquired: this will make justice on your part easier.
The whore and the fornicator: whip each of them a hundred times. . . .
The fornicator shall not marry other than a whore; and the whore shall not marry other than a fornicator. . . .
They who defame virtuous women, and fail to bring four witnesses (to swear that they did not), are to be whipped eighty times. . . .
Men who die and leave wives behind shall bequeath to them a year's maintenance. . . .
And your wives shall have a fourth part of what you leave, if you have no issue; but if you have issue, then they shall have an eighth part. . . .
With regard to your children, God commands you to give the male the portion of two females; and if there be more than two females, then they shall have two-thirds of what their father leaves; but if there be one daughter only, she shall have the half. (The man who is shamed at the birth of a daughter) hides himself from the people because of the ill tidings: shall he keep it with disgrace or

bury it in the dust? Are not his judgments wrong? . . . Kill not your children for fear of want: for them and for you will we provide. Verily, the killing of them is a great wickedness.

By contrast, Western law has tended to punish prostitutes but not their clients. Westerners tend to think polygamy degrading to women, but in a military society where there are apt to be many widows, polygamy provided women a measure of security. The prohibition against killing unwanted female infants by burial obviously represents a more humane attitude. With respect to matters of property, Muslim women were more emancipated than Western women. For example, a Muslim woman retained complete jurisdiction over one-third of her property when she married, and she could dispose of it in any way she wished. A Western woman had no such power.[16]

The Muslim who faithfully observed the laws of the Koran could hope for salvation. The believer who suffered and died for his faith in battle was assured the sensual rewards of the Muslim heaven immediately. According to the Koran, salvation is by Allah's grace and choice alone. A Muslim will not "win" salvation as a reward for good behavior. Because Allah is all-knowing and all-powerful, he knows from the moment of a person's conception whether or not that person will be saved. Nevertheless, Mohammed maintained, predestination gave the believer the will and the courage to try to achieve the impossible. Devout Muslims came to believe that mechanical performance of the basic rules of the faith would automatically gain them salvation.

Historians and ecumenically minded theologians have pointed out many similarities among Islam, Christianity, and Judaism. All three religions are monotheistic. Like Jews, Muslims are forbidden to eat pork. Like Christians, Muslims are urged to practice charity and to be generous to the poor and the weak. And like Christians, Muslims believe in the Last Judgment. Mohammed probably had a general familiarity with the Old and New Testaments, and he must have learned something about Jewish and Christian cultures on his commercial travels.

In the Koran, Mohammed gave his believers a holy book of revelation, moral principles, and history on a par with the Old and New Testaments. Like Jews and Christians, Muslims became people with a sacred book. But the Koran was not only a sacred book. It was written with great eloquence and poetic charm, qualities the Arabs of Mohammed's day especially valued.

MUSLIM EXPANSION IN THE WEST

Mohammed's preaching at first did not appeal to many people. Legend has it that for the first three years he attracted only fourteen believers. One explanation for the slow acceptance of Islam is that Mohammed urged the destruction of the idols in the sanctuary at Mecca. This site drew thousands of devout Arabs annually and thus brought important revenue to the city. The townspeople turned against Mohammed, and he and his followers were forced to flee to Medina. This Hegira, or flight, occurred in 622, and Muslims subsequently dated the beginning of their era from that event. At Medina, Mohammed attracted increasing numbers of believers, and his teachings began to have an impact.

The social and political effects of Islam were massive. Mohammed destroyed the communal and tribal quality of Arab life. Individuals could perform the religious rituals, such as the five daily prayers, alone. Although

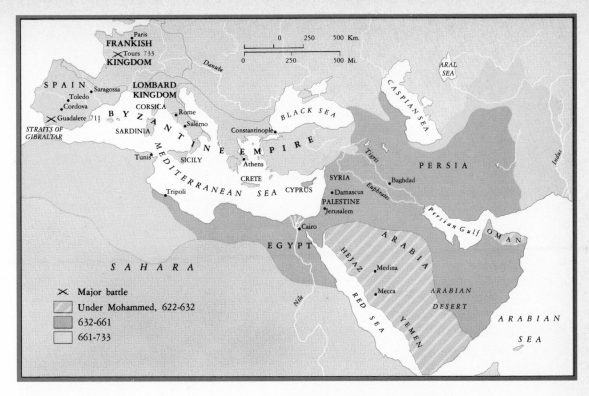

MAP 7.3. THE EXPANSION OF ISLAM TO
733 *Political weaknesses in the territories they conquered, as well as superior fighting skills, help explain
the speed with which the Muslims expanded.*

Muslims customarily worshiped together at
sundown on Fridays, no assembly or organized church was essential. Islam lacked the
public and corporate aspects of tribal religion.
Every Muslim hoped that by following the
simple requirements of Islam he or she could
achieve salvation. For the believer, the significance of the petty disputes and conflicts of
tribal society paled before the simple teachings of Allah. On this basis Mohammed
united the nomads of the desert and the merchants of the cities. The doctrines of Islam,
instead of the ties of local custom, bound all
Arabs.

The faith of Allah, having united the
Arabs, redirected their warlike energies. Hostilities were launched outward. By the time

Mohammed died in 632, he had welded together all the Bedouin tribes. The crescent of
Islam, the Muslim symbol, controlled the entire Arabian peninsula. In the following century, between 632 and 733, one rich province
of the old Roman Empire after another came
under Muslim domination – first Syria, then
Egypt and Persia, and then all of North Africa
(see Map 7.3). The governmental headquarters of this vast new empire was established at Damascus in Syria by the ruling
Omayyad family. A contemporary proverb
speaks of the Mediterranean as a Muslim lake.

In 711, a Muslim force crossed the Straits
of Gibraltar and at Gaudalete easily defeated
the weak Visigothic kingdom in Spain. The
Muslims swept across Spain in seven years

DOME OF THE ROCK   Built in 691 by Mohammed's second successor, the Caliph Omar, this domed mosque was the first Islamic religious building in Jerusalem after the Arab conquest of Palestine. Because the Koran *forbade representations of the human figure, geometrical designs decorate the walls. (Israel Government Tourist Administration)*

and, as one scholar has written, "What was lost in seven years, it took seven hundred to regain."[17] A few Christian princes supported by the Frankish rulers held out in northern mountain fortresses, but the Muslims controlled most of Spain until the twelfth century. The political history of Spain in the Middle Ages is the history of the *reconquista,* or Christian reconquest of that country.

In 719, the Arabs pushed beyond the Pyrenees into the kingdom of the Franks. At the battle of Tours in 733, the Frankish ruler Charles Martel defeated the Arabs and halted their further expansion. Ultimately Charlemagne expelled them from France.

Nor was Muslim expansion confined to northern Africa and southern Europe. From the Arabian peninsula, Muslims also carried their faith deep into Africa and across Asia all the way to India. In the West, however, Arab political influence was felt almost exclusively in Spain. A member of the Omayyad dynasty, Abdurrahman (756–788), established the Moorish kingdom of Spain with its capital at

Cordova. (The Spanish kingdom and Spanish culture were called Moorish after the dark-skinned Moors of North Africa, also known as Berber-Arabs, who had conquered the Iberian Peninsula.) Jewish people were generally well treated in Moorish Spain, and Christians were tolerated as long as they paid a small tax.

Toledo became an important center of learning through which Arab intellectual achievements entered and influenced western Europe. Arabic knowledge of science and mathematics, derived from the Chinese, Greeks, and Hindus, was highly sophisticated. The Muslim mathematician Al-Khwarizmi (d.830) wrote the important treatise *Algebra,* the first work in which the word *algebra* is used mathematically, to mean the transposing of negative terms in an equation to the opposite side. Al-Khwarizmi used Arabic numerals in *Algebra,* and applied mathematics to problems of physics and astronomy. Muslims also instructed Westerners in the use of the zero, which permitted the execution of complicated problems of multiplication and long division. Use of the zero represented an enormous advance over the clumsy Roman numerals.

Muslim medical knowledge was also far superior to that of Westerners. By the ninth century, Arab physicians had translated most of the treatises of Hippocrates and Galen. Unfortunately, these Greek treatises came to the West as translations from Greek to Arabic to Latin, and inevitably lost a great deal in translation. Nevertheless, in the ninth and tenth centuries, Arabic knowledge and experience in anatomy and pharmaceutical prescriptions much enriched Western knowledge. Later, Greek philosophical thought passed to the West by way of Arabic translation.

There is no question that Islam was a significant ingredient in the making of Europe.

Muslim expansion meant that Mediterranean civilization would be divided into three spheres of influence, the Byzantine, the Arabic, and the Western. Beginning in the ninth century, Arabic mathematics, medicine, philosophy, and science played a decisive role in the formation of European culture. A few of the words that came into English from Arabic suggest the extent of Arabic influence: alcohol, admiral, algebra, almanac, candy, cipher, coffee, damask, lemon, orange, sherbet, zero.[18]

＊

Saint Augustine died in 430 as the Vandals approached the coastal city of Hippo. Scholars have sometimes described Augustine as standing with one foot in the ancient world and one in the Middle Ages. Indeed, Augustine does represent the end of ancient culture and the birth of what has been called the Middle Ages. A new and different kind of society was gestating in the mid-fifth century.

The world of the Middle Ages combined Germanic practices and institutions, classical ideas and patterns of thought, Christianity, and a significant dash of Islam. Christianity, because it creatively and energetically fashioned the Germanic and the classical legacies, was the most powerful agent in the making of Europe. Saint Augustine of Hippo, dogmatic thinker and Christian bishop, embodies the coming world-view.

NOTES

1. E. F. Henderson, ed., *Select Historical Documents of the Middle Ages,* G. Bell & Sons, London, 1912, pp. 176–189.

2. R. C. Petry, ed., *A History of Christianity: Read-*

ings in the History of Early and Medieval Christianity, Prentice-Hall, Englewood Cliffs, N.J., 1962, p. 70.

3. H. Bettenson, ed., *Documents of the Christian Church,* Oxford University Press, Oxford, 1947, p. 113.

4. Colossians 3:9-11 (*Jerusalem Bible*).

5. Luke 6:20-32 (*Jerusalem Bible*).

6. L. Sherley-Price, trans., *Bede: A History of the English Church and People,* Penguin Books, Baltimore, 1962, pp. 86-87.

7. J. T. McNeill and H. Gamer, trans., *Medieval Handbooks of Penance,* Octagon Books, New York, 1965, pp. 184-197.

8. L. White, "The Life of the Silent Majority," in *Life and Thought in the Early Middle Ages,* ed. R. S. Hoyt, University of Minnesota Press, Minneapolis, 1967, p. 100.

9. I Peter 2:11-20 (*Jerusalem Bible*).

10. See John Boswell, *Christianity, Social Tolerance, and Homosexuality: Gay People in Western Europe from the Beginning of the Christian Era to the Fourteenth Century,* University of Chicago Press, Chicago, 1980, chs. 3 and 5, esp. pp. 87, 127-131.

11. F. J. Sheed, trans., *The Confessions of St. Augustine,* Sheed & Ward, New York, 1953, book I, pt. 3.

12. Ibid., book 10, pt. 27, p. 236.

13. Quoted by J. B. Bury, *History of the Later Roman Empire,* vol. I, Dover Publications, New York, 1958, pp. 233-234.

14. R. Atwater, trans., *Procopius: The Secret History,* University of Michigan Press, Ann Arbor, 1963, book 8.

15. Ibid., book 12.

16. Julia O'Faolain and Lauro Martines, eds., *Not in God's Image: Women in History from the Greeks to the Victorians,* Harper & Row, New York, 1973, pp. 108-115.

17. J. H. Elliott, *Imperial Spain, 1496-1716,* St. Martin's Press, London, 1966, p. 26.

18. F. B. Artz, *The Mind of the Middle Ages,* Alfred A. Knopf, New York, 1967, p. 178.

SUGGESTED READING

In addition to the studies listed in the Notes, this chapter leans on the following works, which students may consult for a broader treatment of the characteristics of the early Middle Ages.

P. Brown, *The World of Late Antiquity, A.D. 150-750* (1971), is a well-illustrated and lucidly written introduction to the entire period, with an emphasis on social and cultural change. B. Lyon, *The Origins of the Middle Ages: Pirenne's Challenge to Gibbon* (1972), is an excellent bibliographical essay with extensive references. For the Germans, see J. M. Wallace-Hadrill, *The Barbarian West, The Early Middle Ages A.D. 400-1000* (1962), and A. Lewis, *Emerging Europe, A.D. 400-1000* (1967), both of which describe German customs and society and the Germanic impact on the Roman Empire. F. Lot, *The End of the Ancient World* (1965), emphasizes the economic and social causes of Rome's decline.

There is a rich literature on the Christian church and its role in the transition between ancient and medieval civilizations. F. Oakley, *The Medieval Experience: Foundations of Western Cultural Singularity* (1974), stresses the Christian roots of Western cultural uniqueness. J. Danielou and H. Marrou, *The Christian Centuries,* vol. 1: *The First Six Hundred Years* (1964), is a clearly written and comprehensive history. G. Le Bras, "The Sociology of the Church in the Early Middle Ages," in S. L. Thrupp, ed., *Early Medieval Society* (1967), discusses the Christianization of the barbarians. Students interested in the synthesis of classical and Christian cultures should see C. N. Cochrane, *Christianity and Classical Culture* (1957), a deeply learned monograph. T. E. Mommsen, "Saint Augustine and the Christian Idea of Progress: The Background of the City of God," *Journal of the History of Ideas* 12 (1951):346-374, and G. B. Ladner, *The Idea of Reform* (1959), examine ideas of history and progress among the early fathers of the Christian church. The best biography of St. Augustine is

P. Brown, *Augustine of Hippo* (1967), which treats him as a symbol of change.

Monasticism has attracted the interest of Westerners from sixth-century Germans to twentieth-century hippies. L. Doyle, trans., *St. Benedict's Rule for Monasteries* (1957), presents the monastic guide in an accessible pocket-size form; a more scholarly edition is J. McCann, ed. and trans., *The Rule of Saint Benedict* (1952). Two beautifully illustrated syntheses by distinguished authorities are D. Knowles, *Christian Monasticism* (1969), which sketches monastic history through the middle of the twentieth century, and G. Zarnecki, *The Monastic Achievement* (1972), which focuses on the medieval centuries. L. J. Daly, *Benedictine Monasticism* (1965), stresses the day-to-day living of the monks, and H. B. Workman, *The Evolution of the Monastic Ideal* (1962), concentrates on monasticism as a spiritual and intellectual ideal.

For Byzantium and the Arabs, see J. Hussey, *The Byzantine World* (1961); A. A. Vasiliev, *History of the Byzantine Empire* (1968); S. Runciman, *Byzantine Civilization* (1956); B. Lewis, *The Arabs in History* (1966); T. Andrae, *Mohammed: The Man and His Faith* (1970); M. Rodinson, *Mohammed* (1974); and G. E. von Grunebaum, *Medieval Islam* (1961), which are all excellent treatments of the subject.

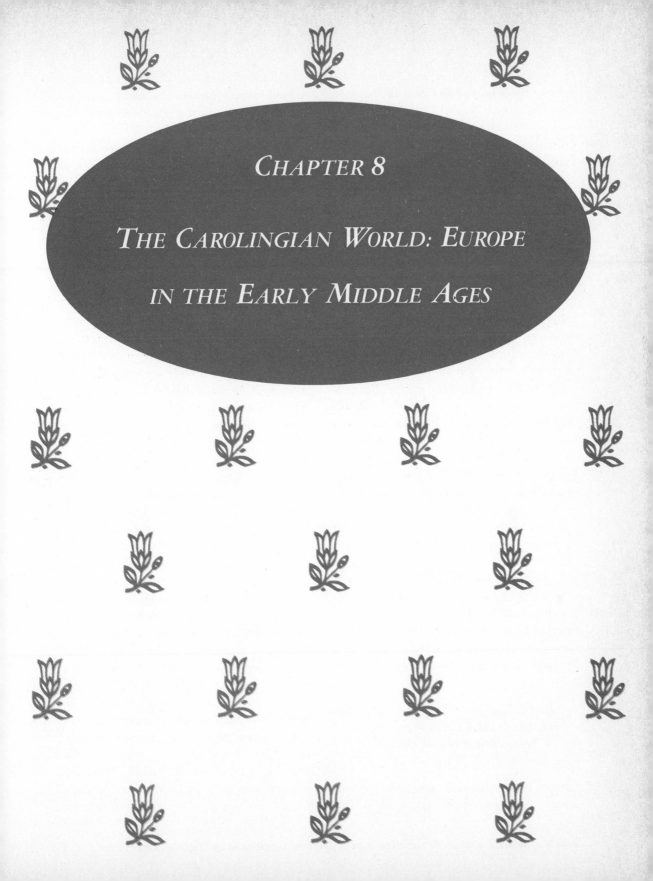

CHAPTER 8

THE CAROLINGIAN WORLD: EUROPE IN THE EARLY MIDDLE AGES

IN 733, the Frankish chieftain Charles Martel defeated the Muslim invaders at the battle of Tours in central France. At the time it was only another skirmish in the struggle between Christians and Muslims, but in retrospect it looms as one of the great battles of history: this Frankish victory halted Arab expansion in Europe. A century later, in 843, Charles Martel's three great-great-grandsons, after a bitter war, concluded the Treaty of Verdun, which divided the European continent among themselves.

Between 733 and 843, a society emerged that was distinctly European. A new kind of social and political organization, later called feudalism, appeared. And for the first time since the collapse of the Roman Empire, most of western Europe was united under one government. That government reached the peak of its development under Charles Martel's grandson, Charlemagne. Christian missionary activity among the Germanic peoples continued, and strong ties were forged with the Roman papacy. A revival of study and learning, sometimes styled the Carolingian Renaissance, occurred under Charlemagne.

This chapter will explore the following questions. What was feudalism? How did it come about? How did Charlemagne acquire and govern his vast empire? What was the significance of the relations between Carolingian rulers and the church? What was the Carolingian Renaissance? The culture of the Carolingian Empire has been described as "the first European civilization." What does this mean?

THE EIGHTH CENTURY: END OF THE ANCIENT WORLD?

Scholars have traditionally designated the fifth century as the end of the ancient world. But an influential twentieth-century historian, the Belgian Henri Pirenne, has argued that the eighth century was the real turning-point in Western civilization.

Pirenne's thesis focuses on the Mediterranean Sea. The Roman Empire had controlled the Mediterranean from the Bosporus in the east to the Straits of Gibraltar in the west. Roman trade, Roman armies, and Greco-Roman ideas had travelled on the Mediterranean; it was the highway that united the empire. Although the German tribes had conquered the western provinces in the fifth and sixth centuries, they had perpetuated many Roman ways. The Germans gradually converted to Christianity, and with Christianization came Romanization. German rulers in the West continued trade and economic relations with the East, and the Germans shared in the economic and cultural unity the Mediterranean provided.

But the Muslim conquests of the seventh and eighth centuries ended all this. The Mediterranean, long the thoroughfare of the Greco-Roman world, became a Muslim lake. By the time of Charlemagne in the late eighth century, the Muslims controlled the Mediterranean and the land bordering three sides of it. According to Pirenne, their control meant the real end of the ancient world, which had centered on the Mediterranean. In the eighth century, western Europe, which had been relying on Eastern imports, was cut off from its sources of supply. An isolated and agrarian economy developed as a result. Charlemagne's capital at Aix-la-Chapelle was a sign of the shift of political and military power to the north, away from the Mediterranean. For the next five hundred years, northern Europe, rather than Rome and Italy, was to be the center of culture and civilization. Thus the imperial coronation of Charlemagne by Pope Leo III on Christmas Day in the year 800 can be seen as the symbolic end of the ancient world and the start of the medieval.

Pirenne's argument rests heavily on Mohammed; indeed, as Pirenne put it, "It is therefore strictly correct to say that without Mohammed, Charlemagne would have been inconceivable."[1] By this he meant that the entire empire of Charlemagne was centered in northern Europe and oriented to the West as the direct consequence of Muslim expansion. Pirenne's interpretation has provoked vigorous debate. Historians have questioned his facts and disputed his conclusions. For one thing, considerable evidence suggests that trade between the East and the West continued through the eighth and ninth centuries and was not shut off by Muslim control of the Mediterranean. As this debate vividly illustrates, the division of time spans into distinct periods is always subject to interpretation. Whatever the merits of Pirenne's thesis, the eighth century deserves attention as a great turning point.

EQUESTRIAN STATUE OF CHARLEMAGNE A *medieval king was expected to be fierce (and successful) in battle, to defend the church and the poor, and to give justice to all. This majestic and idealized figure of Charlemagne conveys these qualities. The horse is both the symbol and the means of his constant travels. (French Embassy Press and Information Division)*

TOWARD A FEUDAL SOCIETY

In the period of the Germanic invasions the Roman imperial government had been compelled to retrench. Roman troops and Roman administrators were withdrawn from the provinces. Gallo-Romans in Gaul and Romanized natives in Britain were forced to cope as best they could. No authority was strong enough to provide peace over a wide area.

Men who could fight, or who owned horses, or who were wealthy and had the time to learn how to fight and ride could join a local band of warriors. But the vast defenseless majority, compelled to work the land for their livelihood, had little choice but to seek out some local strongman and ask that "lord"

for protection. Local lords replaced Roman administrators. Western Europe was governed by the simple law that he should take who has the power, and he should keep who can.

FEUDALISM

Between the sixth and eighth centuries, European society evolved toward a condition that scholars later termed feudalism. Feudalism may be defined as a kind of social organization in which public political power resided in the private hands of a small military elite. The fundamental strength of the feudal elite rested on its military might. The ethos, the values — indeed, the entire culture of feudal society —

was military. Almost everything was determined by war or the preparation for war. Thus, loyalty was the highest virtue. It was the cement that held a warring society together.

In order to ensure the support of his fighters, a lord gave them land in exchange for their loyalty. Charles Martel got land to distribute to his men by confiscating church property. Lesser lords, as they defeated weaker neighbors and seized their property, divided it among their followers. Early feudalism resulted from a fusion of the Germanic custom of swearing allegiance to a warrior leader with the Roman practice of granting an estate or the booty of war to fighters or important servants. The mounted warrior became a vassal (from the Celtic word for "a well-born young man") of the lord. Though he was obliged to perform services in return for holding the land – his feud, or fief – the vassal lost nothing in social status.

The political power of the ruling class rested upon the ability to raise a contingent of fighting men, to hold courts, to coin money, and to conduct relations and make agreements with outside powers. These powers were held by many lords, both lay and ecclesiastical, and not just by monarchs. Many men became the vassals of several lords in order to acquire more land or money and thus improve their economic position. Feudal lords everywhere were out for themselves, and everywhere they tended to resist the centralizing ambitions of kings.

The ceremony by which a man became the vassal of another involved the use of religious objects, such as the Bible or relics of the saints, and the presence of a priest. The vassal knelt, placed his folded hands between those of the lord, and declared his intention to become the lord's man. By this he meant that he would fight for the lord or perform some

other kind of military service, such as castle-guard. The vassal then rose and swore his faith (or fidelity) on the Bible or the relics. Lord and vassal exchanged a kiss on the mouth, symbolizing peace between two social equals. The conclusion of the ceremony was marked by the lord's investing his new vassal with a symbol of his fief, such as a clump of earth.

Because feudal society was a military society, men held the dominant positions in it. A high premium was put on physical strength, fighting skill, and bravery. The legal and social position of women was not as insignificant as might be expected, however. Charters recording gifts to the church indicate that women held land in many areas. Women frequently endowed monasteries, churches, and other religious establishments. The possession of land obviously meant economic power. Moreover, women inherited fiefs. In southern France and Catalonia in Spain, women inherited feudal property as early as the tenth century. Other kinds of evidence attest to the status of women. In parts of northern France, children sometimes identified themselves in legal documents by their mother's name rather than their father's name, indicating that the mother's social position in the community was higher than the father's.

In a treatise he wrote in 822 on the organization of the royal household, Archbishop Hincmar of Reims placed the queen directly above the treasurer. She was responsible for giving the knights their annual salaries. She supervised the manorial accounts. Thus, in the management of large households, with many knights to oversee and complicated manorial records to supervise, the lady of the manor had highly important responsibilities. With such responsibility went power and influence.[2]

MANORIALISM

Feudalism concerned the rights, powers, and lifestyle of the military elite; manorialism involved the services and obligations of the peasant classes. The *economic* power of the warring class rested upon landed estates, which were worked by peasants. Hence feudalism and manorialism were inextricably linked. Peasants needed protection, and lords demanded something in return for that protection. Free peasants surrendered themselves and their lands to the lord's jurisdiction. The land was given back, but the peasants became tied to the land by various kinds of payments and services. In France, England, Germany, and Italy, local custom determined precisely what those services were, but certain practices became common everywhere. The serf was obliged to turn over to the lord a percentage of the annual harvest, usually in produce, sometimes in cash. The peasant paid a fee to marry someone from outside the lord's estate. He paid a fine, often his best beast, to inherit property. Above all, the peasant became part of the lord's permanent labor force. With vast stretches of uncultivated virgin land and a tiny labor population, lords encouraged population growth and immigration. The most profitable form of capital was not land but laborers. The small feudal class led lives devoted to war and leisure; toil was the usual fate of those who were not warriors or clerics.

In entering into a relationship with a feudal lord, the free farmer lost status. His position became servile, and he became a serf. That is, he was bound to the land and could not leave it without the lord's permission. He was also subject to the jurisdiction of the lord's court in any dispute over property or suspicion of criminal behavior.

The transition from freedom to serfdom was slow; its speed was closely related to the degree of political order in a given geographical region. Even in the late eighth century there were still many free men. And within the legal category of serfdom there were many economic levels, ranging from the highly prosperous to the desperately poor. Nevertheless, a social and legal revolution was taking place. Around the year 800, perhaps 60 percent of the population of Western Europe – completely free a century before – had been reduced to serfdom. The ninth-century Viking assaults on Europe created extremely unstable conditions and individual insecurity, leading to additional loss of personal freedom. Chapter 10 will look in detail at the lives of the peasants. As we shall see, although the later Middle Ages witnessed considerable upward social mobility, serfdom remained the condition of most Europeans, in fact if not in law, for almost a thousand years.

THE RISE OF THE CAROLINGIAN DYNASTY

In the seventh century, the kingdom of the Franks steadily deteriorated. Weak and incompetent rulers lost power to local strongmen. Central authority collapsed in the face of brute force. The administrative agencies of the Merovingian kings slipped into the hands of local powers.

The rise of the Carolingian family – whose name derives from the Latin *Carolus*, for "Charles" – began with the efforts of Pippin I in the mid-seventh century. Pippin made himself mayor of the palace of Austrasia, which meant that he was head of the Frankish administration. His grandson Pippin II (d. 714) also gained the title of mayor of the palace, and from that position worked to reduce the power of the Frankish aristocracy.

It was Pippin's son Charles Martel (714–741) who defeated the Muslims at Tours and thus checked Arab expansion into Europe. Charles's wars against the Saxons, the Burgundians, and the Frisians broke those weakening forces. His victory over the infidels and his successful campaigns within the Frankish kingdom added to the prestige of his family the reputation of great military strength. Charles Martel held the real power in the Frankish kingdom; the Merovingians were king in name only.

The rise of the Carolingian dynasty rested partly on papal support. In the early eighth century, while Charles Martel and his son Pippin III were attempting to bring the various Germanic tribes under their jurisdiction, they gained the support of two Anglo-Saxon missionaries, Willibrord and Wynfrith. The Northumbrian monk Willibrord crossed the English Channel and preached to the pagans on the Frisian Islands and in the area of the modern Netherlands, Belgium, and Luxembourg. With enormous zeal Willibrord organized the church of Friesland, established the see of Utrecht, and acted as the first archbishop. He also founded the abbey of Echternach (in what is now Luxembourg), which subsequently became an important missionary center.

Even more spectacular were the achievements of Wynfrith, or Boniface (680–754), as he was later called. A native of Devonshire in England, Boniface preached in Bavaria and Hesse in southern Germany. There, assisted by other monks from Britain, his many conversions attracted the attention of both Charles Martel and Pope Gregory II. Boniface traveled to Rome several times and was made a bishop. He became an enthusiastic champion of ecclesiastical principles and of papal authority in the Frankish kingdom.

Given the semibarbarous peoples with whom he was dealing, Boniface's achievements were remarkable. He founded the see of Mainz, the chief see of Germany, and the abbey of Fulda, which became one of the great centers of Christian culture in the ninth century. He built churches. He established the *Rule of Saint Benedict* in all the monasteries he founded or reformed. With the full support of Pippin III, Boniface held several councils that reformed the Frankish church. He even succeeded in cutting down the famous Oak of Thor, the center of a pagan cult.

Saint Boniface preached throughout Germany against divorce, polygamous unions, and incest. On these matters German custom and ecclesiastical law completely disagreed. The Germans allowed divorce simply by the mutual consent of both parties. The Germanic peoples also practiced polygamy and incest – sexual relations between brothers and sisters or between parents and children – on a wide scale. (Incest, in fact, is a major theme of a seventh-century German legend about the twins Sigmund and Siglinda, whose tragic love and the life of their son Siegfried were immortalized in three operas by the nineteenth-century composer Richard Wagner.) Church councils in the sixth and seventh centuries repeatedly condemned incest, indicating that it was common. And theologians since Saint Augustine had stressed that marriage, validly entered into, could not be ended.

Boniface's preaching was not without impact, for in 802 Charlemagne prohibited incest, and decreed that a husband might separate from an adulterous wife. The woman could be punished, and the man could not remarry in her lifetime. Charlemagne also encouraged severe punishment for adulterous men. In so doing, he contributed to the dignity of marriage, the family, and women.

Saint Boniface, known as the Apostle of Germany, is one of the most important fig-

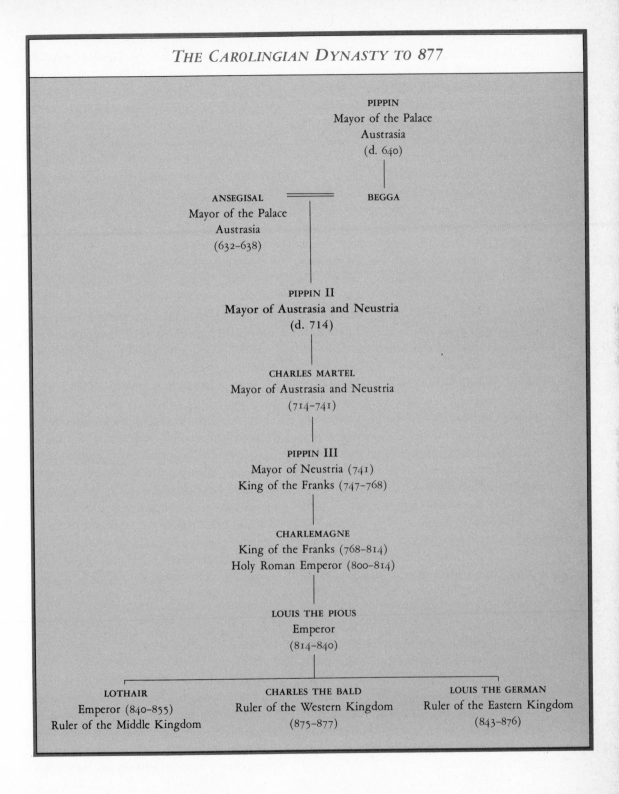

PIPPIN
Mayor of the Palace
Austrasia
(d. 640)

ANSEGISAL ══════ **BEGGA**
Mayor of the Palace
Austrasia
(632–638)

PIPPIN II
Mayor of Austrasia and Neustria
(d. 714)

CHARLES MARTEL
Mayor of Austrasia and Neustria
(714–741)

PIPPIN III
Mayor of Neustria (741)
King of the Franks (747–768)

CHARLEMAGNE
King of the Franks (768–814)
Holy Roman Emperor (800–814)

LOUIS THE PIOUS
Emperor
(814–840)

LOTHAIR
Emperor (840–855)
Ruler of the Middle Kingdom

CHARLES THE BALD
Ruler of the Western Kingdom
(875–877)

LOUIS THE GERMAN
Ruler of the Eastern Kingdom
(843–876)

ures in early European history. In all of his missionary activity he promoted peace and respect for legally established civil authorities. Charles Martel and Pippin III protected Boniface, and he preached Christian obedience to rulers. Because of his staunch adherence to Roman ideas, Roman traditions, and the Roman pope, the Romanization of Europe accompanied Christianization.

Charles Martel had been king of the Franks in fact but not in title. His son Pippin III (747–768) made himself king in title as well as in fact. In Germanic custom – and custom was law – the kingship had to pass to someone with royal blood. Pippin did not want to do away with the ineffectual Merovingian king, but he did want the kingship. Because the missionary activity of Boniface had spread Christian ideals and enhanced papal influence in the Frankish kingdom, Pippin decided to consult the pope about the kingship. Accordingly, Pippin sent Boniface to Rome to ask the pope whether the man who has the power is entitled to be king. Pope Zacharias, guided by the Augustinian principle that the real test of kingship is whether it provides for order and justice, responded in 751 that he who has the power should also have the title. This answer constituted recognition of the Carolingians.

Just as the emperors Constantine and Theodosius in the fourth century had taken actions that would later be cited as precedents in the relations between church and state (pages 223 and 224), so Pippin III in the eighth century took papal confirmation as official approval of his title. In 752, Pippin III was formally elected king of the Franks by the great lords, or magnates, of the Frankish territory. Two years later the pope – who needed Pippin's protection from the Lombards – came to Gaul and personally anointed Pippin king at Paris.

Thus an important alliance was struck between the papacy and the Frankish ruler. In 754, Pope Stephen gave Pippin the title of protector of the Roman church. Pippin in turn agreed to restore to the papacy territories in northern Italy recently seized by the Lombards; he promptly marched into Italy and defeated the Lombards. The Carolingian family had received official recognition and anointment from the leading spiritual power in Europe. The papacy had gained a military protector.

On a second successful campaign in Italy in 756, Pippin made a large donation to the papacy. The gift was estates in central Italy that technically belonged to the Byzantine emperor at Constantinople. Known as the Papal States, they existed over a thousand years, until the newly formed kingdom of Italy abolished them in 1870.

Because of his anointment, Pippin's kingship took on a special spiritual and moral character. Before Pippin, only priests and bishops had received anointment: Pippin became the first lay person to be anointed with the sacred oils. His person was considered sacred. He was acknowledged as *rex et sacerdos* (king and priest). Pippin also cleverly eliminated possible threats to the Frankish throne, and the pope promised him support in the future. When Pippin died, his son Charlemagne succeeded him.

THE EMPIRE OF CHARLEMAGNE

Charles the Great (768–814) built on the military and diplomatic foundations of his ancestors. Charles's secretary and biographer, the Saxon Einhard, wrote a lengthy description of this warrior-ruler. It has serious flaws, partly because it is modeled directly on the Roman author Suetonius's *Life of the Emperor Augustus*. Still, it is the earliest medieval biography of a layman, and historians consider it generally accurate:

Charles was large and strong, and of lofty stature, though not disproportionately tall . . . the upper part of his head was round, his eyes very large and animated, nose a little long, hair fair, and face laughing and merry. Thus his appearance was always stately and dignified . . . although his neck was thick and somewhat short, and his belly rather prominent; but the symmetry of the rest of his body concealed these defects. His gait was firm, his whole carriage manly, and his voice clear, but not so strong as his size led one to expect. His health was excellent, except during the four years preceding his death. . . . Even in those years he consulted rather his own inclinations than the advice of physicians, who were almost hateful to him, because they wanted him to give up roasts, to which he was accustomed, and to eat boiled meat instead. In accordance with the national custom, he took frequent exercise on horseback and in the chase, accomplishments in which scarcely any people in the world can equal the Franks. He enjoyed the exhalations from natural warm springs, and often practiced swimming, in which he was such an adept that none could surpass him; and hence it was that he built his palace at Aix-la-Chapelle, and lived there constantly during his latter years until his death. He used not only to invite his sons to his bath, but his nobles and friends, and now and then a troop of his retinue or bodyguard. . . .

He used to wear the national, that is to say, the Frank, dress – next his skin a linen shirt and linen breeches, and above these a tunic fringed with silk; while hose fastened by bands covered his lower limbs, and shoes his feet, and he protected his shoulder and chest in winter by a close-fitting coat of otter or marten skins. Over all he flung a blue cloak, and he always had a sword girt about him, usually one with a gold or silver hilt and belt; he sometimes carried a jeweled sword, but only on great feastdays or at the reception of ambassadors from foreign nations.[3]

Though crude and brutal, Charlemagne was a man of enormous intelligence. He appreciated good literature, such as Saint Augustine's *City of God,* and Einhard considered him an unusually effective speaker. On the other hand, he could not even write his own name.

For all Charles's concern for moderation in food and wine, he had three wives, one after the other, and after they died, three concubines simultaneously. The austere code of sexual morality he published for the empire reflects the attitude of the clerics who wrote it far more than the behavior of the warrior-king. The most striking feature of Charlemagne's character was his phenomenal energy, which helps to account for his great military achievements.

TERRITORIAL EXPANSION

Continuing the expansionist policies of his ancestors, Charlemagne fought more than fifty campaigns and became the greatest warrior of the early Middle Ages. In what is now France, he subdued all of the north. In the south, the lords of the mountainous ranges of Aquitaine – what is now called Basque country – fought off his efforts at total conquest. The Muslims in northeastern Spain were checked by the establishment of strongly fortified areas known as marches.

Charlemagne's greatest successes were in what is today called Germany. There, his concerns were basically defensive. In the course of a thirty-year war against the semibarbaric Saxons, he added most of the northwestern German tribes to the Frankish kingdom. The story goes that because of their repeated rebellions, Charlemagne ordered more than four thousand Saxons slaughtered on one day.

To the south, he achieved spectacular results. In 773–774, the Lombards in northern Italy once again threatened the papacy. Charlemagne marched south, overran fortresses at Pavia and Spoleto, and incorporated Lombardy – including Venetia, Istria, and Dalmatia – into the Frankish kingdom. To his title as king of the Franks, he added king of the Lombards. This victory ended all serious attempts at the unification of Italy until the nineteenth century.

By around 805, the Frankish kingdom included all of continental Europe except Spain, Scandinavia, southern Italy, and the Slavic fringes of the east (see Map 8.1). Not since the third century A.D. had any ruler controlled so much of the Western world. Not until Napoleon Bonaparte in the early nineteenth century was the feat to be repeated.

THE GOVERNMENT OF THE CAROLINGIAN EMPIRE

Charlemagne ruled a vast rural world dotted with isolated estates and characterized by constant petty violence. His empire was definitely not a state as people today understand that term; it was a collection of primitive peoples and semibarbarian tribes. Apart from a small class of warrior-aristocrats and clergy, almost everyone engaged in agriculture. Trade and commerce played only a small part in the economy. Cities served as the headquarters of bishops and as ecclesiastical centers.

By constant travel, personal appearances, and the sheer force of his personality, Charlemagne sought to awe his conquered peoples with his fierce presence and his terrible justice. By confiscating the estates of the great territorial magnates, he acquired land with which to gain the support of lesser lords.

Charles divided his kingdom into counties, which served as administrative units. Two or three hundred counts were appointed as the king's representatives. They had full military and judicial powers to maintain law and order and to dispense justice at the local level. They held their offices for life. As a link between local authorities and the central government of the emperor, Charles appointed officials called *missi dominici,* agents of the lord king. The empire was divided into visitorial districts. Each year, beginning in 802, two missi, usually a count and a bishop or abbot, visited assigned districts. They held courts and investigated the judicial, financial, and clerical activities of the district. They held commissions to regulate crime, moral conduct, the clergy, education, the poor, and many other matters. The missi checked up on the counts and worked to prevent the counts' positions from becoming hereditary: strong counts with hereditary estates would have weakened the power of the emperor.

In especially barbarous areas, such as the Spanish and Danish borders, Charles set up areas called marks. There, royal officials called margraves had extensive powers to govern their dangerous localities.

A modern state has institutions of government, such as a civil service, courts of law, financial agencies for the collection and apportionment of taxes, and police and military powers with which to maintain order internally and defend against foreign attack. These simply did not exist in Charlemagne's empire. What held society together were relationships of dependence cemented by oaths promising faith and loyalty.

Although the empire lacked viable institutions, some of the Carolingians involved in governing did have vigorous political ideas. The abbots and bishops who served as Charlemagne's advisers worked out what was for

IRELAND

NORTHUMBRIA

+ Jarrow

• York

MERCIA

NORTH WALES

EAST
ANGLIA

ESSEX

WEST WALES

WESSEX

KENT

SUSSEX

DANISH
MARCH

SAXONY
804

+ Fulda

Aix-la-Chapelle ◉

AUSTRASIA

• Mainz

+ Echternach

TRIBUTARY SLAVIC PEOPLES

■ Rouen

BRITTANY
811

• Paris

NEUSTRIA

• Tours

ALEMANNIA

BAVARIA
788

BURGUNDY

• Lyons

AQUITAINE

• Bordeaux

VENETIA

ISTRIA

DALMATIA

Milan
•

• Pavia

Roncevalles
■

Marseilles
•

SPANISH MARCH
811

• Barcelona

CORSICA

PAPAL
STATES

• Spoleto

• Rome

DUCHY
OF
BENEVENTO

OMMAYAD   KINGDOM   OF   SPAIN

• Toledo

Monte Cassino
+

• Salerno

• Cordova

SARDINIA

BYZANTINE   EMPIRE

SICILY

Monasteries

☐ Frankish Kingdom, 768

☐ Areas conquered by Charlemagne

▨ Tributary peoples

▨ Byzantine Empire

| 0 | 100 | 200 Km. |
| 0 | 100 | 200 Mi. |

MAP 8.1.   THE CAROLINGIAN WORLD   *The
extent of Charlemagne's nominal jurisdiction was extraordinary; it was not equalled until the nineteenth
century.*

their time a sophisticated political ideology.
In letters and treatises they set before the emperor high ideals of behavior and of government. They wrote that a ruler may hold
power from God, but he is responsible to the
law. Just as all subjects of the empire were
required to obey him, so he too was obliged
to respect the law. They envisioned a unified
Christian society presided over by a king who
was responsible for the maintenance of peace,
which would enable Christians to pursue their
pilgrimage to the City of God. They encouraged the emperor to maintain law and
order and to do justice, without which neither
the ruler nor the "state" has any justification.
These views derived largely from Saint Augustine's theories of kingship. Inevitably, they
could not be realized in an illiterate, half-
Christianized, and preindustrial society. But
they were the seeds from which medieval and
even modern ideas of government were to
develop.

THE IMPERIAL CORONATION OF
CHARLEMAGNE (800)

In the autumn of the year 800, Charlemagne
paid a momentous visit to Rome. Here are
two accounts of what happened.

According to the Frankish *Royal Annals*, a
year-by-year description of events:

*On the very day of the most holy nativity of the
Lord [Christmas], when the king at Mass had
risen from prayer before the tomb of Blessed Peter
the Apostle, Pope Leo placed the crown on his
head, and by all the people of Rome he was ac-*

claimed: *Long Life and Victory to the* August *Charles, the Great and Peace-Giving Emperor, crowned by God. And after the ovations, the pope did obeisance to him according to the custom observed before the ancient emperors, and the title of* Patricius [Protector] *being dropped, he was called Emperor and* Augustus.[4]

Charlemagne's secretary Einhard wrote:

His last journey there [to Rome] was due to another factor, namely that the Romans, having inflicted many injuries on Pope Leo — plucking out his eyes and tearing out his tongue, he had been compelled to beg the assistance of the king. Accordingly, coming to Rome in order that he might set in order those things which had exceedingly disturbed the condition of the Church, he remained there the whole winter. It was at the time that he accepted the name of Emperor and Augustus. At first he was so much opposed to this that he insisted that although that day was a great [Christian] feast, he would not have entered the Church if he had known beforehand the pope's intention. But he bore very patiently the jealousy of the Roman Emperors [that is, the Byzantine rulers] who were indignant when he received these titles. He overcame their arrogant haughtiness with magnanimity, a virtue in which he was considerably superior to them, by sending frequent ambassadors to them and in his letters addressing them as brothers.[5]

Charlemagne became *Holy* Roman emperor, adding the sacred authority of the Christian church to the universal authority of the Roman emperor. Einhard says that Charlemagne seldom used the imperial title. But the fact that he sometimes used it illustrates a significant point. Charlemagne governed most of continental Europe. He considered himself a Christian king ruling a Christian people. The title expressed his connection with the Rome of the caesars and the Rome of the popes. By using it, Charlemagne was consciously perpetuating the old Roman imperial

notions, while at the same time identifying with the new Rome of the Christian church. Charlemagne and his government represent a combination of German feudal practices and Christian ideals. These two elements were basic constituents of Europe in the early Middle Ages.

For centuries scholars have debated the significance of the imperial coronation of Charlemagne. Did Charles plan the coronation in St. Peter's on Christmas Day? What did he have to gain from the imperial title? Did Pope Leo III arrange the coronation in order to identify the Frankish monarchy with the papacy and papal policy? Did a coronation actually happen, or are accounts of it later inventions?

Although final answers will probably never be found, two things are certain. First, later German rulers were anxious to gain the imperial title and to associate themselves with the legend of Charlemagne and with ancient Rome. They wanted to use the ideology of imperial Rome to strengthen their own positions. Second, ecclesiastical authorities continually cited the event as proof that the dignity of the imperial crown could be granted only by the pope. The imperial coronation of Charlemagne, whether event or nonevent, was to have a profound effect on the course of German history and on the later history of Europe.

THE CAROLINGIAN INTELLECTUAL REVIVAL

It is ironic that Charlemagne's most enduring legacy was the stimulus he gave to scholarship and learning. Barely literate himself, preoccupied with the control of vast territories, much more of a warrior than a thinker, he nevertheless set in motion a cultural revival that had "international" and long-lasting consequences. The revival of learning associated with Charlemagne and his court at Aix-la-Chapelle drew its greatest inspiration from seventh- and eighth-century intellectual developments in the Anglo-Saxon kingdom of Northumbria, situated on the northernmost tip of the old Roman world.

NORTHUMBRIAN CULTURE

The victory of the Roman forms of Christian liturgy and monastic life at the Synod of Whitby in 664 marked the official end of the Celtic church in Britain (page 226). But Whitby did not end the Celtic influence on Christianity in Northumbria. Irish-Celtic culture – through such monasteries as Lindisfarne and York – permeated the Roman church in Britain and resulted in a flowering of artistic and scholarly activity.

Northumbrian creativity owes a great deal to the intellectual curiosity and collecting zeal of Saint Benet Biscop (ca 628–689). Descended from a noble Northumbrian family, Benet Biscop became a monk at Lérins, an island monastery in the Mediterranean that enjoyed valuable contacts with the Eastern monastic tradition of Syria and Egypt. He returned to Britain in the company of the Syrian archbishop of Canterbury, Theodore of Tarsus. Between 674 and 682, Benet Biscop founded the monasteries of Wearmouth and Jarrow. A strong supporter of Benedictine monasticism, he introduced the Roman form of ceremonial into the new religious houses and encouraged it in older ones. Benet Biscop made five dangerous trips to Italy, raided the libraries, and brought back to Northumbria manuscripts, relics, paintings, and other treasures. These books and manuscripts formed the libraries on which much later study was based.

Northumbrian monasteries produced scores of books: missals (used for the celebration of the mass), psalters (which contained the 150 psalms and other prayers used by the monks in their devotions), commentaries on the Scriptures, illuminated manuscripts, law codes, and collections of letters and sermons. The finest product of Northumbrian art is probably the Gospel book produced at Lindisfarne around 700. The incredible expense involved in the publication of such a book – for vellum, coloring, gold leaf – represents in part an aristocratic display of wealth. The script, called uncial, is a Celtic version of contemporary Greek and Roman handwriting. The illustrations have a strong Eastern quality. They combine the abstract style of the Christian Middle East and the narrative approach of classical Roman art. Likewise, the use of geometrical decorative designs shows the influence of Syrian art. Many scribes, artists, and illuminators must have participated in its preparation.

The finest representative of Northumbrian and indeed all Anglo-Saxon scholarship is the Venerable Bede (ca 673–735). The simplicity of Bede's life illustrates his greatness. Given by his parents when he was seven years old as an oblate or "offering" to Benet Biscop's monastery at Wearmouth, he was later sent to the new monastery at Jarrow five miles away. There, surrounded by the books Benet Biscop had brought from Italy, Bede spent the rest of his life.

Bede's scrupulous observance of the *Rule of Saint Benedict* expressed his deep piety. His days were punctuated only by the bells for choir and other religious duties. As a scholar, his patience and diligence reflected his deep love for learning. Contemporaries revered Bede for his learned commentaries on the Scriptures and for the special holiness of his life, which earned him the title "Venerable." He was the most widely read author in the entire Middle Ages.

Modern scholars praise Bede for his *Ecclesiastical History of the English Nation.* Broader in scope than the title suggests, it is the chief source of information about early Britain. Bede searched far and wide for his information, discussed the validity of his evidence, compared various sources, and exercised a rare critical judgment. For these reasons, he has been called "the first scientific intellect among the Germanic peoples of Europe."[6]

Bede was probably the greatest master of chronology of the Middle Ages. He began the system of dating events from the birth of Christ, rather than from the foundation of the city of Rome, as the Romans had done, or from the regnal years of kings, as the Germans did. Bede introduced the term *anno Domini,* "in the year of the Lord," abbreviated A.D. He fit the entire history of the world into this new dating method. (The reverse, or diminishing, dating system of B.C., before Christ, does not seem to have been widely used before 1700.) The Anglo-Saxon missionary Saint Boniface introduced this system of reckoning time throughout the Frankish empire of Charlemagne.

At the very time that monks at Lindisfarne were producing their Gospel book, and Bede at Jarrow was writing his *History,* another Northumbrian monk was at work on a nonreligious epic poem that provides considerable information about the society that produced it. The poem *Beowulf* is perhaps the finest expression of the secular literature of the eighth century. Though the tale is almost childish in its simplicity, scholars have hailed it as a masterpiece of Western heroic literature.

The great hall of the Danish king Hrothgar has been ravaged for twelve years by a half-human monster called Grendel. Hrothgar and his men cannot stop Grendel's attacks. Finally Beowulf, a relative of the Swedish royal house, hears of Grendel's murderous destruc-

THE SCRIBE EZRA   *Monks at Bede's monastery at Jarrow made this copy of an early Christian manuscript showing the Jewish scribe Ezra writing his chronicle. The backless bench on which he works appears very uncomfortable. Books were stored against theft and climate in heavy chests or cabinets. (Scala/Editorial Photocolor Archives)*

tion. With a bodyguard of fourteen trusted warriors, Beowulf sails to Denmark and in a brutal battle destroys Grendel. Hrothgar and his queen, Wealhtheow, give a great banquet for Beowulf and his followers. Afterward, Grendel's mother enters the hall and carries off one of Hrothgar's closest advisers to revenge her son's death. Beowulf ultimately catches and destroys her. This victory is followed by more feasting, and Beowulf returns home to Sweden laden with rich gifts.

Beowulf later becomes king of a Swedish tribe and rules them for fifty years. When his country is ravaged by a terrible dragon, the aged Beowulf challenges him. In the ensuing battle, Beowulf is overwhelmed by the dragon's fiery breath, and all but one of his followers flee. Beowulf defeats the dragon, but is mortally wounded and dies.[7]

The story resembles ordinary Norse legends, but it is actually permeated with classical, Germanic, and Christian elements. Though the poem was written in England, all the action takes place in Scandinavia. This reflects the "international" quality of the culture of the age, or at least the close ties between England and the Continent in the eighth century. (Britain exported wool to the settlements in Frisia that later became the flourishing commercial centers at Ypres and Bruges, which produced cloth.)

Beowulf's entire life was devoted to fighting and war. His values are military and aristocratic: the central institution in the poem is the *gesith,* or Germanic band of warriors united to fight with Beowulf. The highest virtue is loyalty to him, and loyalty is maintained by the giving of gifts. Yet the author was a Christian monk, and the basic theme of the poem is the conflict between good and evil. Beowulf, however, does not exhibit any Christian humility. Never one to hide his light under a bushel, he boasts of his exploits unashamedly. In this, he embodies the classical idea of fame, the notion that fame is the greatest achievement because it is all that a person leaves behind.

Pagan and Germanic symbols and practices suffuse Beowulf. Fighting, feasting, and drinking preoccupy its warrior heroes. There is no glimpse of those who raised and prepared the food they consume. The author did not think peasants deserved mention. In a famous scene Hrothgar's beautiful queen Wealhtheow enters the great hall, dispensing grace and gifts. The scene suggests that women of the upper class served a decorative function in aristocratic society. But Wealhtheow may have been handing out presents to the warriors because she had custody of and responsibility for her husband's treasure.

In another scene the body of a dead king, along with considerable treasure, is put on a ship and floated out to sea. That this was a typical method of burial for Scandinavian kings is known from the ship burial uncovered at Sutton Hoo in England in 1939. Such customs are a far cry from traditional Christian burial. A monk may have composed *Beowulf,* but the persistence of this practice indicates that conversion was still imperfect in much of Europe.

Reading *Beowulf,* one enters a world of darkness, cold, gloom, and pessimism, pierced by a weak ray of Christian hope. It is the foremost expression of the psychological complexities and spiritual contradictions of what has been called the heroic age of Scandinavia – the eighth and ninth centuries.

A less serious literary genre than the epic poem, highly popular in Anglo-Saxon England and Carolingian Europe, was the riddle. Riddles were more than a guessing game for children; in the riddle a poet took on the characteristics or personality of someone or something. Riddles were intended to instruct and to entertain:

Swings by his thigh a thing most magical!
Below the belt, beneath the folds
of his clothes it hangs, a hole in its front end,
stiff-set & stout, but swivels about.

Levelling the head of this hanging instrument,
its wielder hoists his hem above the knee:
it is his will to fill a well-known hole
that it fits fully when at full length.

He has often filled it before. Now he fills it again.[8]

The answer is a key. Riddling was a popular

game in monasteries, and the subjects were not always pious.

The physical circumstances of life in the seventh and eighth centuries make Northumbrian cultural achievements all the more remarkable. Learning was pursued under terribly primitive conditions. Monasteries such as Jarrow and Lindisfarne stood on the very fringes of the European world. The barbarian Picts, just an afternoon's walk from Jarrow, were likely to attack at any time.

Food was not the greatest problem. The North Sea and the nearby rivers, the Tweed and the Tyne, yielded abundant salmon and other fish, which could be salted or smoked for winter, a nutritious if monotonous diet. Climate was another matter. Winter could be extremely harsh. In 664, for example, deep snow was hardened by frost from early winter until mid-spring. When it melted away, many animals, trees, and plants were found dead. To make matters worse, disease and sickness could take terrible tolls. Bede described events in the year 664:

In the same year of our Lord 664 there was an eclipse of the sun on the third day of May at about four o'clock in the afternoon. Also in that year a sudden pestilence first depopulated the southern parts of Britain and then attacked the kingdom of the Northumbrians as well. Raging far and wide for a long time with cruel devastation it struck down a great multitude of men.... This same plague oppressed the island of Ireland with equal destruction.[9]

Damp cold with bitter winds blowing across the North Sea must have pierced everyone and everything, even the stone monasteries. Inside, only one room, the calefactory or warming room, had a fire. Scribes in the scriptorium, or writing room, had to stop frequently to rub the circulation back into their numb hands. These monk-artists and

BINDING OF THE LINDAU GOSPELS *This splendid example of the Carolingian revival combines the geometric forms of Anglo-Irish art with the Roman portrait tradition. The strong face of Christ shows no suffering. The semiprecious stones around the border are raised to catch the light. (The Pierpont Morgan Library)*

monk-writers paid a very high physical price for what they gave to posterity.

Had they remained entirely insular, Northumbrian cultural achievements would have been of slight significance. As it happened, an Englishman from Northumbria played a decisive role in the transmission of English learning to the Carolingian Empire and continental Europe.

THE CAROLINGIAN RENAISSANCE

Charlemagne's empire disintegrated shortly after his death in 814. But the support he gave to education and learning preserved the writings of the ancients and laid the foundations for all subsequent medieval culture. Charlemagne promoted a revival that scholars have named the Carolingian Renaissance.

At his court at Aix-la-Chapelle, Charlemagne assembled learned men from all over Europe. From Visigothic Spain came Theodulf, the best writer of Latin verse of the day. From Pavia in Lombardy came the monk-historian Paul the Deacon, who later wrote the invaluable *History of the Lombards,* still the chief source for the history of the sixth and seventh centuries. From the abbey of Fulda came Einhard, who served as a royal administrator and Charlemagne's closest adviser and biographer.

The most important scholar and the leader of the palace school was the Northumbrian Alcuin. He was born about a year after Bede's death (ca 735) and educated at the cathedral school at York. On a visit to Italy in 781, Alcuin met Charlemagne, who invited him to his court. From then until his death in 804, Alcuin remained the emperor's major adviser on religious and educational matters.

Alcuin was an unusually prolific scholar. He prepared some of the emperor's official documents, and wrote many moral *exempla,* or models, which set high standards for royal behavior and constitute a treatise on kingship. Alcuin's letters to Charlemagne set forth political theories on the authority, power, and responsibilities of a Christian ruler.

What did the scholars at Charlemagne's court do? They copied books and manuscripts and built up libraries. They devised the beautifully clear handwriting known as Carolingian minuscule, from which modern Roman type is derived. (This script is called minuscule because it has lower-case letters; the Romans had only capitals.) They established schools all across Europe, attaching them to

monasteries and cathedrals. They placed great emphasis on the education of priests, trying to make all of them at least able to read, write, and do simple arithmetical calculations. The greatest contribution of the scholars at Aix-la-Chapelle was not so much the originality of their ideas as their hard work of salvaging and preserving the thought and writings of the ancients. Thus the Carolingian Renaissance was a rebirth of interest in, and the study and preservation of, the ideas and achievements of classical Greece and Rome.

Language has been called "the nourishing mother of history." It is the core, the center, of all culture and civilization. Without the ability to communicate ideas, grammatically and effectively, orally and in writing, an individual or a society is barbaric. The revival of learning inspired by Charlemagne and directed by the Northumbrian Alcuin halted the dangers of barbaric illiteracy on the European continent. Although hardly widespread by later standards, basic literacy was established among the clergy and even among some of the nobility. The small group of scholars at Aix-la-Chapelle preserved Greek and Latin culture from total extinction in the West.

Meanwhile, the common people spoke their local or vernacular languages. The Bretons, for example, retained their local dialect, and the Saxons and Bavarians could not understand each other (see Map 8.1). Communication among the diverse peoples of the Carolingian Empire was possible only through the medium of Latin.

Once basic literacy was established, monastic and other scholars went on to more difficult work. By the middle years of the ninth century there was a great outpouring of more sophisticated books. Collections of canon law, illustrated manuscripts, codes of Frankish law, commentaries on the Bible and on the church

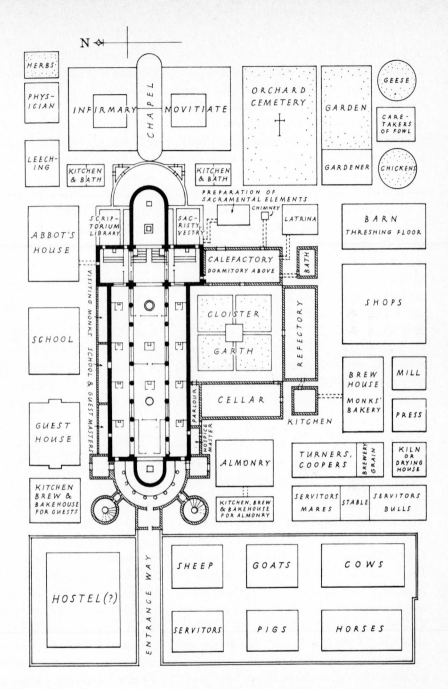

PLAN FOR AN IDEAL MONASTERY *This is a ninth-century architectural design for a self-supporting monastic community of 270 members. The monks' lives centered around the church and the cloister (center). Note the herb garden close to the physician's quarters. The western entrance for visitors was sur-rounded by the hostel for poor guests and pens for farm animals — with all the inevitable smells. (Kenneth John Conant,* Carolingian and Romanesque Architecture, 800–1200. Pelican History of Art, *2nd rev. ed. New York. 1978. p. 57)*

fathers flowed from monastic and cathedral scriptoria. Ecclesiastical writers, imbued with the legal ideas of ancient Rome and the theocratic ideals of Saint Augustine, instructed the semibarbarian rulers of the West. And it is no accident that medical study in the West began, at Salerno in southern Italy, in the late ninth century, *after* the Carolingian Renaissance.

Alcuin completed the work of his countryman Boniface – the Christianization of northern Europe. Latin Christian attitudes penetrated deeply into the consciousness of European peoples. By the tenth century, the patterns of thought and lifestyles of educated western Europeans were those of Rome and Latin Christianity. Even the violence and destruction of the great invasions of the late ninth and tenth centuries could not destroy the strong foundations laid by the Northumbrian Alcuin and his colleagues.

HEALTH AND MEDICAL CARE IN THE EARLY MIDDLE AGES

Scholars' careful examination of medical treatises, prescription (or herbal) books, manuscript illustrations, and archaeological evidence has recently revealed a surprising amount of information about medical treatment in the early Middle Ages. In a society devoted to fighting, warriors and civilians alike stood a strong chance of wounds from sword, spear, battle-axe, or some blunt instrument. Trying to eke a living from poor soil with poor tools, perpetually involved in pushing back forest and wasteland, the farmer and his family daily ran the risk of accidents. Poor diet weakened everyone's resistance to disease. People bathed rarely. Low standards of personal hygiene increased the danger of

infection. This being the case, what medical or surgical attention was available to medieval people?

The Germanic peoples had no rational understanding of the causes of and cures for disease. They believed that sickness was due to one of three factors: elf-shot, in which elves hurled darts that produced disease and pain; wormlike creatures in the body; and the number 9. Treatment involved the use of charms, amulets, priestly incantations, and potions. Drinks prepared from mistletoe, for example, were thought to serve as an antidote to poison and to make women fertile.

Medical practice consisted primarily of drug and prescription therapy. Through the monks' efforts and through the recovery of Greek and Arabic manuscripts, a large body of the ancients' prescriptions was preserved and passed on. For almost any ailment, several recipes were likely to exist in the prescription lists. Balsam was recommended for coughs. For asthma an ointment combining chicken, wormwood, laurel berries, and oil of roses was to be rubbed on the chest. The scores of prescriptions to rid the body of lice, fleas, and other filth reflect the frightful standards of personal hygiene. The large number of prescriptions for eye troubles suggests that they too must have been very common. This is understandable, given the widespread practice of locating the fireplace in the center of the room. A lot of smoke and soot filtered into the room, rather than going up the chimney. One remedy calls for bathing the eyes in a solution of herbs mixed with honey, balsam, rainwater, saltwater, or wine.

Poor diet caused frequent stomach disorders and related ailments such as dysentery, constipation, and diarrhea. The value of dieting and avoiding greasy foods was recognized. For poor circulation, a potion of meadow wort, oak rind, and lustmock was recommended. Pregnant women were advised to abstain from eating the flesh of almost all male animals, because their meat might deform the child. Men with unusually strong sexual appetites were advised to fast and to drink at night the juice from agrimony (an herb of the rose family) boiled in ale. If a man suffered from a lack of drive, the same plant boiled in milk gave him "courage."

Physicians were not concerned with the treatment of specific diseases or illnesses. They did not examine patients. The physician, or leech, as he was known in Anglo-Saxon England, treated only what he could see or deduce from the patient's obvious symptoms. Treatment consisted of the application of herbal, animal, or superstitious remedies to these symptoms. The physician knew little about the pathology of disease or physiological functions. He knew little of internal medicine. He had no accurate standards of weights and measures. Prescriptions called for "a pinch of" or "a handful" or "an eggshell full."

Warfare and the dangers inherent in working the land made broken bones, wounds, and burns common. All wounds and open injuries invited infection, and infection invited gangrene. Several remedies were known for wounds. Physicians appreciated the antiseptic properties of honey, and prescriptions recommended that wounds be cleaned with it. When an area or limb had become gangrenous, a good technique of amputation existed. The physician was instructed to cut above the diseased flesh, that is, to cut away some healthy tissue and bone, in order to hasten cure. The juice of white poppy plants – the source of heroin – could be added to wine and drunk as an anesthetic. White poppies, however, grew only in southern Europe and North Africa. If a heavy slug of wine was not enough to dull the patient, he or she had to be held down forcibly while the physician

MEDICAL INSTRUMENTS   *Medieval physicians invented hundreds of instruments for surgical operations. This page shows a number of knives and saws. The accompanying text explains which instrument to use for various operations. (Yale Medical Library)*

cut. Butter and egg whites, which have a soothing effect, were prescribed for burns.

Teeth survive long periods of burial and give reasonably good information about disease. Evidence from early medieval England shows that the incidence of tooth decay was very low. In the adult population, the rate of cavities was only one-sixth that of the present day. Cavities below the gum line, however, were very common, due to the prevalence of carbohydrates and starch in the diet. The result was abscesses of the gums. These and other forms of periodontal disease were widespread after the age of thirty.[10]

The spread of Christianity in the Carolingian era had a beneficial effect on medical knowledge and treatment. Several of the church fathers expressed serious interest in medicine. Some of them even knew something about it. The church was deeply concerned about human suffering, whether physical or mental. Christian teaching vigorously supported concern for the poor, sick, downtrodden, and miserable. Churchmen taught that while all knowledge came from God, he had supplied it so that people could use it for their own benefit.

In the period of the bloodiest violence, the sixth and seventh centuries, medical treatment was provided by the monasteries. No other places offered the calm and quiet atmosphere necessary for treatment and recuperation. Monks took care of the sick. They collected and translated the ancient medical treatises. They cultivated herb gardens from which medicines were prepared. Monks practiced medicine throughout the Middle Ages, as did lay people.

The foundation of a school at Salerno in southern Italy sometime in the ninth century gave a tremendous impetus to medical study by lay people. Its location attracted Arabic, Greek, and Jewish physicians from all over the Mediterranean region. Students flocked there from northern Europe. The Jewish physician Shabbathai Ben Abraham (931–982) left behind pharmacological notes that were widely studied in later centuries.

By the eleventh century, the medical school at Salerno enjoyed international fame. Its most distinguished professor then was Constantine the African. A native of Carthage, he had studied medicine throughout the Middle East and, because of his thorough knowledge of oriental languages, served as an important transmitter of Arabic culture to the West. Constantine taught and practiced medicine at Salerno for some years before becoming a monk at Monte Cassino.

Several women physicians also contributed to the celebrity of the school. Trotula, an authority on gynecological problems, wrote a book called *On Female Disorders*. Though not connected with the Salerno medical school, the abbess Hildegard (1098–1179) of Rupertsberg in Hesse, Germany, reputedly treated the emperor Frederick Barbarossa. Hildegard's treatise *On the Physical Elements* shows a remarkable degree of careful scientific observation.

How available was medical treatment? Most people lived on isolated rural estates, and had to take such advice and help as was available locally. Physicians were very few. They charged a fee, which only the rich could afford. Most illnesses, apparently, simply took their course. People had to develop a stoical attitude. Death came early. A person of forty was considered old. People's vulnerability to ailments for which there was no probable cure contributed to a fatalistic acceptance of death at an early age. Early medical literature shows that attempts to relieve pain and suffering were primitive and crude. Still, it is significant that serious attempts *were* made.

DIVISION AND DISINTEGRATION OF THE CAROLINGIAN EMPIRE (814–887)

Charlemagne left his vast empire to his only surviving son, Louis the Pious (814–840), who had actually been crowned emperor in his father's lifetime. Deeply religious he was, and well educated, but Louis was no soldier. Thus he could not retain the respect and loyalty of the warrior-aristocracy on whom he depended for troops and for administration of his territories. Disintegration began almost at once.

The basic reason for the collapse of the Carolingian Empire is simply that it was too big. In Charlemagne's lifetime it was held together by the sheer force of his personality and driving energy. After his death, it began to fall apart. The empire lacked a bureaucracy like that of the Roman Empire — the administrative machinery necessary for strong and enduring government. It was a collection of tribes held together at the pleasure of warrior-aristocrats, men most interested in strengthening their own local positions and insuring that they could pass on to their sons the offices and estates they had amassed. Counts, abbots, bishops — both lay and ecclesiastical magnates needed estates to support themselves and reward their followers. In their localities, they simply assumed judicial, military, and financial functions. Why should they obey an unimpressive distant ruler who represented a centralizing power, a power that threatened their localistic interests? What counted was strength in one's own region and the preservation of family holdings.

Bad roads filled with thugs and rivers swarming with pirates made communication within the empire very difficult. Add to this the Frankish custom of dividing estates among all male heirs. Between 817 and his death in 840, Louis the Pious made several divisions of the empire. Dissatisfied with their portions and anxious to gain the imperial title, Louis's sons, Lothair, Louis the German, and Charles the Bald fought bitterly among themselves. Finally, in the Treaty of Verdun of 843, the brothers agreed to partition the empire (see Map 8.2).

MAP 8.2. THE DIVISION OF THE CAROLINGIAN EMPIRES, 843   *The treaty of Verdun (843), which divided the empire among Charlemagne's grandsons, is frequently taken as the start of the separate development of Germany, France, and Italy. The "Middle Kingdom" of Lothair, however, lacking defensive borders and any political or linguistic unity, soon broke up into several territories.*

Lothair, the eldest, received the now-empty title of emperor and the "middle kingdom," which included Italy and the territories bordered by the Meuse, Saône, and Rhône rivers in the west and the Rhine in the east. Almost immediately this kingdom broke up into many petty principalities extending diagonally across Europe from Flanders to Lombardy. When the French and German monarchs were trying to build strong central governments in the twelfth and thirteenth centuries, this area was constantly contested between them. Even in modern times, the "middle kingdom" of Lothair has been blood-soaked.

The eastern and most Germanic part of the Carolingian Empire passed to Louis the German. The western kingdom went to Charles the Bald; it included the provinces of Aquitaine and Gascony and formed the basis of medieval and modern France. The descendants of Charles the Bald held on in the west until 987, when the leading magnates elected Hugh Capet as king. The heirs of Louis the German ruled the eastern kingdom until 911, but real power was in the hands of local chieftains. Everywhere in the tenth century, fratricidal warfare among the descendants of Charlemagne accelerated the spread of feudalism.

GREAT INVASIONS OF THE NINTH CENTURY

After the Treaty of Verdun and the division of Charlemagne's empire among his grandsons, continental Europe presented an easy target for foreign invaders. All three kingdoms were torn by domestic dissension and disorder. No European political power was strong enough to put up effective resistance to external attacks. The frontier and coastal defenses erected by Charlemagne and maintained by Louis the Pious were completely neglected.

From the moors of Scotland to the mountains of Sicily there arose in the ninth century the Christian prayer "Save us, O God, from the violence of the Northmen." The Northmen, also known as Normans or Vikings, were Germanic peoples from Norway, Sweden, and Denmark who had remained beyond the sway of the Christianizing and civilizing influences of the Carolingian Empire. Some scholars believe that the name "Viking" derives from the Old Norse word *vik*, meaning creek. A Viking, then, was a pirate who waited in a creek or bay to attack passing vessels.

Charlemagne had established marches, fortresses, and watchtowers along his northern coasts to defend his territory against Viking raids. Their assaults began around 787, and by the mid-tenth century they had brought large chunks of continental Europe and Britain under their sway. In the east they pierced the rivers of Russia as far as the Black Sea. In the west they sailed as far as Greenland and even to the coast of North America, perhaps as far south as Boston.

The Vikings were superb seamen. Their advanced methods of boatbuilding gave them great speed and maneuverability. Propelled either by oars or sails, deckless, about sixty-five feet long, a Viking ship could carry between forty and sixty men — quite enough to harass an isolated monastery or village effectively. These boats, navigated by thoroughly experienced and utterly fearless sailors, moved through the most complicated rivers, estuaries, and waterways in Europe. They could move swiftly, attack, and get away before help could arrive.

Scholars disagree about the reasons for these migrations. Some maintain that because the Vikings practiced polygamy, their countries were vastly overpopulated. Since the property of a family passed to the oldest son, other sons had to emigrate. Others argue that climatic conditions and crop failures forced migration. Still others insist that the Northmen were looking for trade and new commercial contacts. What better targets of plunder, for example, than the mercantile centers of northern France and Frisia?

Plunder they did. Viking attacks were bitterly savage. At first they attacked and sailed off laden with booty. Later, they returned, settled down, and colonized the areas they had conquered. For example, the Vikings overran a large part of northwestern France and called

VIKING SHIP MODEL *The Norwegian original was built entirely of oak, weighed over twenty tons, and could carry a sizable contingent of men and horses. With fleets of these ships, the Vikings conducted* *piratical raids, territorial conquests, and colonizing ventures. (Courtesy, World Heritage Museum. Photo: Caroline Buckler)*

the territory Norsemanland, from which the word "Normandy" is derived.

Scarcely had the savagery of the Viking assaults begun to subside when Europe was hit from the east and south (see Map 8.3). Beginning around 862, Magyar, or Hungarian, tribes crossed the Danube and pushed steadily westward. They subdued northern Italy, compelled Bavaria and Saxony to pay tribute, and penetrated even into the Rhineland and Burgundy. These roving bandits attacked isolated villages and monasteries, taking prisoners and selling them in the Eastern slave markets. The Magyars were not colonizers; their sole object was booty and plunder.

The Magyars and Vikings depended upon fear. In their initial attacks on isolated settlements, every man, woman, and child was put to the sword. A few attractive women might be spared to satisfy the lusts of the conquerors or to be sold into slavery. The Hungarians and Scandinavians struck such terror in rural and defenseless peoples that they often gave up without a struggle. Many communities bought peace by paying tribute.

From the south the Muslims began new encroachments, concentrating on the two southern peninsulas, Italy and Spain. Their goal too was plunder. In Italy the monks of Monte Cassino were forced to flee. The Muslims drove northward and sacked Rome in 846. Most of Spain had remained under their

TO GREENLAND AND
NORTH AMERICA

ICELAND

874

FAEROES
800

SHETLANDS
700

VIKINGS

Novgorod 820

Volga

866-878

IRELAND
839

841-884

BRITAIN

Vistula

Elbe

Oder

882

Dnieper

Rouen

Aix-la-Chapelle

NORMANDY

Seine

Rhine

895

Loire
896-911

900

MAGYARS

883

843-882

Bordeaux

917

Rhine

899

Santiago

Garonne

Marseilles

CORSICA

895

Lisbon
844

Tagus

Barcelona

859-861

SARDINIA

BALEARICS

Rome

846

Monte
Cassino

Danube

Constantinople

866 907 941

844

842

SICILY

827

840-896

MUSLIMS

Monastery

Vikings

Magyars

Muslims

0   200   400 Km.

0   200   400 Mi.

MAP 8.3. THE GREAT INVASIONS OF THE
NINTH CENTURY   Note the Viking penetration of
eastern Europe and their probable expeditions to
North America. What impact did their various invasions have on European society?

domination since the sixth century (page 247). Expert seamen, they sailed around the Iberian peninsula, braved the notoriously dangerous shoals and winds of the Atlantic coast, and attacked the settlements along the coast of Provence. Muslim attacks on the European continent in the ninth and tenth centuries were less destructive, primarily because in comparison to the rich and sophisticated culture of the Arab capitals, northern Europe was primitive, backward, and offered little.

What was the effect of these invasions on the structure of European society? Viking, Magyar, and Muslim attacks accelerated the development of feudalism. Lords capable of rallying fighting men, supporting them, and putting up resistance to the invaders did so. They also assumed political power in their territories. Weak and defenseless people sought the protection of local strongmen. Free men sank to the level of serfs. Consequently, European society became further fragmented. Public power became increasingly decentralized.

FEUDALISM AND HISTORY

The adjective *feudal* is often used disparagingly to describe something antiquated and barbaric. It is similarly commonplace to think of medieval feudalism as a system that let a small group of lazy military leaders exploit the producing class, the tillers of the soil. This is not a very useful approach. Preindustrial societies from ancient Greece to the American South before the Civil War to some twentieth-century Latin American countries have been characterized by sharp divisions between the "exploiters" and the "exploited." To call all such societies feudal strips the term

of significant meaning and distorts our understanding of medieval feudalism. As many twentieth-century scholars have demonstrated, when feudalism developed it served the needs of medieval society.

The term *feudalism* was first coined in the late seventeenth century. The men who used it meant a type of government in which political power was treated as a private possession and divided among a large number of lords. Later, abolition of feudalism was among the main rallying-cries of the French Revolution and other eighteenth-century democratic revolutions. (What the revolutionaries really meant was manorialism and aristocratic privilege; by that time, feudalism had not existed in France for several hundred years.)

Scholars agree that feudalism was a persistent feature of medieval European culture. It was, however, far from uniform. The feudalism developing in Charlemagne's ninth-century Frankish kingdom was vastly different from the feudalism of thirteenth-century France under Louis IX. The feudalism of eleventh-century Normandy was considerably different from that of eleventh-century Anglo-Saxon England just twenty-six miles away. The word itself inaccurately implies the constancy of the feud, the land a lord gave to a vassal in return for his promise to fight or perform some other service. In fact, the giving of land was largely a tenth-century development. Eighth-century lords maintained their vassals in their own households, and even in the tenth century most vassals in France held no land. Some lords gave their vassals cash instead of land.

Feudalism is often characterized as a pyramid with weak men at the bottom, ever more important lords in the middle, and the king at the top. But lords and kings never arranged themselves so neatly. Many men became vassals of several lords in order to acquire more land or money. Medieval European feudalism frequently lacked organization, regularity, and rational connections. Feudal lords everywhere were out for themselves, and everywhere they tended to oppose the centralizing ambitions of kings.

The central point about medieval society is that economic and political power were in the hands of military leaders. Successful lords provided protection for the peasants who worked the land. They also exercised political and judicial authority over the dependent serfs. When the lord was a bishop or abbot, he had ecclesiastical as well as civil jurisdiction over his peasants. Because almost all communities were rural, isolated, and vulnerable to attack, the basic need of society was physical security. Consequently, the military virtues and values of the feudal nobility infused all aspects of the culture.

———◆———

The culture that emerged in Europe between 733 and 843 has justifiably been called the first European civilization. That civilization had definite characteristics: it was feudal, Christian, and infused with Latin ideas and models. A military elite controlled most forms of economic and political power. Almost all peoples were baptized Christians. Latin was the common language of educated people everywhere; what was written was written in Latin. In spite of the disasters of the ninth and tenth centuries, these features remained basic aspects of European culture for centuries to come.

The century and a half after the death of Charlemagne in 814 witnessed a degree of disintegration, destruction, and disorder un-

paralleled in Europe until the twentieth century. The Viking, Magyar, and Muslim invasions made a frightful situation absolutely disastrous. The Carolingian Empire was split into several parts, each tending to go its own way. No civil or religious authority could maintain stable government over a very wide area. Local strongmen provided what little security existed. Commerce and long-distance trade were drastically reduced. Leadership of the church became the political football of Roman aristocratic families. The rich became warriors; the poor sought protection. The result was that society underwent feudalization.

NOTES

1. H. Pirenne, *Mohammed and Charlemagne,* Barnes & Noble, New York, 1955, pp. 234–235.

2. See D. Herlihy, "Land, Family, and Women in Continental Europe, 701–1200," in *Women in Medieval Society,* ed. S. M. Stuart, University of Pennsylvania Press, Philadelphia, 1976, pp. 13–45.

3. Einhard, *The Life of Charlemagne,* with a foreword by S. Painter, University of Michigan Press, Ann Arbor, 1960, pp. 50–51.

4. B. D. Hill, ed., *Church and State in the Middle Ages,* John Wiley & Sons, New York, 1970, p. 45.

5. Ibid., pp. 46–47.

6. R. W. Southern, *Medieval Humanism and Other Studies,* Basil Blackwell, Oxford, 1970, p. 3.

7. D. Wright, trans., *Beowulf,* Penguin Books, Baltimore, 1957, pp. 9–19.

8. M. Alexander, trans., *The Earliest English Poems,* Penguin Books, Baltimore, 1972, p. 99.

9. L. Sherley-Price, trans., *Bede: A History of the English Church and Peoples,* Penguin Books, Baltimore, 1962, book 3, chap. 27, p. 191.

10. See S. Rubin, *English Medieval Medicine,* Barnes & Noble, New York, 1974.

SUGGESTED READING

In spite of centuries of war, violence, and destruction, a sizable literature survives from the period once inaccurately described as the Dark Ages. Scholars have devoted considerable attention to that literature because it was produced in such a crucial period, and the enterprising student who seeks further information about it may find the following works useful.

Chapters 4, 5, and 6 of J. B. Russell, *A History of Medieval Christianity: Prophecy and Order* (1968), describe the mind of the Christian church and show how it gradually made an impact on pagan Germanic peoples. C. Dawson, *Religion and the Rise of Western Culture* (1958), emphasizes the religious origins of Western culture. C. H. Talbot, ed., *The Anglo-Saxon Missionaries in Germany* (1954), gives a good picture, through biographies and correspondence, of eighth-century religious life.

Einhard's *Life of Charlemagne* is probably the best starting point for study of the great chieftain. There is no easily accessible and thorough treatment of the man and his government, but the advanced student with a knowledge of French should see L. Halphen, *Charlemagne et L'Empire Carolingien* (1949), the standard scholarly treatment. Recent research has been incorporated in E. Perroy, "Carolingian Administration," in S. Thrupp, ed., *Early Medieval Society* (1967). J. Brondsted, *The Vikings* (1960), is an excellently illustrated study of many facets of the culture of the Northmen.

In addition to the references to Bede, Beowulf, and Anglo-Saxon poetry in the Notes, D. L. Sayers, trans., *The Song of Roland* (1957), provides an excellent key, in epic form, to the values and lifestyles of the feudal classes. For the eighth-century revival of learning, see W. Levison, *England and the Continent in the Eighth Century* (1946); M. L. W. Laistner, *Thought and Letters in Western Europe, 500–900* (1931); and the beautifully written evocation by P. H. Blair, *Northumbria in the Days of Bede* (1976). E. S. Duckett, *Alcuin, Friend of Charlemagne* (1951),

makes light and enjoyable reading. L. Wallach, *Alcuin and Charlemagne,* rev. ed. (1968), is a technical study of Alcuin's treatises for the advanced student. The best treatment of the theological and political ideas of the period is probably K. F. Morrison, *The Two Kingdoms: Ecclesiology in Carolingian Political Thought* (1964), a difficult book.

Those interested in the role of women and children in early medieval society should see two articles: D. Herlihy, "Land, Family, and Women in Continental Europe, 701–1200," and E. Coleman, "Infanticide in the Early Middle Ages," both in S. M. Stuart, ed., *Women in Medieval Society* (1976).

For health and medical treatment, the curious student should consult S. Rubin, *Medieval English Medicine, A.D. 500–1300* (1974), especially pp. 97–149; W. H. McNeill, *Plagues and Peoples* (1976); A. Castiglioni, *A History of Medicine,* trans. E. B. Krumbhaar (1941); and the important article by J. M. Riddle, "Theory and Practice in Medieval Medicine," *Viator* 5 (1974): 157–184.

The literature on feudalism and manorialism is very rich. F. L. Ganshof, *Feudalism* (1961), and J. R. Strayer, "Feudalism in Western Europe," in *Feudalism in History,* ed. R. Coulborn (1956), are probably the best introductions. M. Bloch, *Feudal Society,* trans. L. A. Manyon (1961) remains the standard scholarly study. The more recent treatments of Perry Anderson, *Passages from Antiquity to Feudalism* (1978), and Georges Duby, *The Early Growth of the European Economy: Warriors and Peasants from the Seventh to the Twelfth Century* (1978), stress the evolution of social structures and mental attitudes. For the significance of the ceremony of vassalage, see Jacques Le Goff, "The Symbolic Ritual of Vassalage," in his *Time, Work, & Culture in the Middle Ages,* trans. Arthur Goldhammer (1982), a collection of provocative but difficult essays that includes his "The Peasants and the Rural World in the Literature of the Early Middle Ages." The best broad treatment of peasant life and conditions is Georges Duby, *Rural Economy and Country Life in the Medieval West,* trans. C. Postan (1968).

CHAPTER 9

REVIVAL, RECOVERY, AND REFORM

BY THE LAST QUARTER of the tenth century, after a long and bitter winter of discontent, the first signs of European spring were appearing. The European springtime lasted from the early eleventh century to the end of the thirteenth century. This period from about 1050 to 1300 has often been called the High Middle Ages. The term designates a time of crucial growth and remarkable cultural achievement between two eras of economic, political, and social crisis.

What were the ingredients of revival? How did they come about? What was the social and economic impact of the recovery of Europe? How did reform of the Christian church affect relations between the church and civil authorities? These are the questions discussed in this chapter.

POLITICAL REVIVAL

The eleventh century witnessed the beginnings of political stability in western Europe. Foreign invasions gradually declined, and domestic disorder subsided. This development gave people security in their persons and property. Security and political stability, supported by the peace movements of the church, contributed to a slow increase in population. Political order and stability paved the way for economic recovery.

THE DECLINE OF INVASION AND CIVIL DISORDER

The most important factor in the revival of Europe after the disasters of the ninth century was the gradual decline in foreign invasions and the reduction of domestic violence. In 911 the Norwegian leader Rollo subdued large parts of what was later called Normandy. The West Frankish ruler Charles the Simple, unable to oust the Northmen, went along with that territorial conquest. He recognized Rollo as duke of Normandy on the condition that Rollo swear allegiance to him and hold the territory as a sort of barrier against future Viking assaults. This agreement, embodied in the treaty of Saint-Clair-sur-Epte, marks the beginning of the rise of Normandy.

Rollo kept his word. He exerted strong authority over Normandy and in troubled times supported the weak Frankish king. Rollo and his men were baptized as Christians. Although additional Viking settlers arrived, they were easily pacified. The tenth and eleventh centuries saw the steady assimilation of Normans and French. Major attacks on France had ended.

Rollo's descendant, Duke William I (1035–1087), made feudalism work as a system of government in Normandy. William attached specific quotas of military or knight service to the lands he distributed. Vassals who defaulted on their military obligations or refused attendance at the duke's court were ruthlessly executed. William forbade the construction of private castles, always the symbol of feudal independence. He limited private warfare and vigorously supported a peace movement sponsored by the church. He kept strict control over the coinage and maintained strong supervision over the church, actively participating in church councils and in the selection of abbots and bishops. By 1066 – the year William and the Normans invaded England – the duchy of Normandy was the strongest and the most peaceful territory in Western Europe.

Recovery followed a somewhat different pattern in England. Between 960 and 1040,

England was part of a vast Scandinavian empire that stretched from Normandy to Iceland and even to the eastern coast of North America. The Danish ruler Canute, king of England (1016-1035) and after 1030 king of Norway as well, made England the center of his empire. Canute promoted a policy of assimilation and reconciliation between Anglo-Saxons and Vikings.

Canute governed with the help of a *witan* — literally, a council of wise men — composed of Anglo-Saxons and Danes. He republished the laws of tenth-century Anglo-Saxon kings to show the continuity of his government with theirs. Canute and his followers accepted Christianity and Christian ideas about the responsibilities of a good and just king. Slowly the two peoples were molded together. The assimilation of Viking and Anglo-Saxon was personified by King Edward the Confessor (1042-1066), the son of an Anglo-Saxon father and a Norman mother who had taken Canute as her second husband.

In the East the German king Otto I (936-973) inflicted a crushing defeat on the Hungarians on the banks of the Lech River in 955. This battle halted the Magyars' westward expansion and threat to Germany, and made Otto a great hero to the Germans. It also signified the revival of the German monarchy and demonstrated that Otto was a worthy successor to Charlemagne.

When he was chosen king, Otto had selected Aix-la-Chapelle as the site of his coronation to symbolize his intention to continue the work and tradition of Charlemagne. The basis of his power was to be an alliance with, and control of, the church. Otto asserted the right to invest bishops and abbots with the symbols of their office — the ring, which symbolized the bishop's union with his dioceses, and the staff, which was the symbol of his pastoral authority. This assertion gave Otto effective control over ecclesiastical appointments. Before receiving religious consecration, bishops and abbots had to perform feudal homage for the lands that accompanied the church office. (This practice, later known as lay investiture, was to create a grave crisis in the eleventh century.)

Otto realized that he had to use the financial and military resources of the church to halt feudal anarchy. He used the higher clergy extensively in his administration, and the bulk of his army came from monastic and other church lands. Between 936 and 955, Otto succeeded in breaking the territorial power of the great German dukes.

In 962 Otto was crowned Holy Roman emperor by the pope. The imperial coronation had important results. It revived the Holy Roman Empire and its traditions, and it showed that Otto had the full support of the church in Germany and Italy. The uniting of the kingship with the imperial crown advanced German interests. Otto filled a power vacuum in northern Italy and brought about peace among the great aristocratic families. He established stable government there for the first time in over a century. Peace and political stability in turn promoted the revival of northern Italian cities, such as Venice.

By the start of the eleventh century, the Italian maritime cities were seeking a place in the rich Mediterranean trade. Pisa and Genoa fought to break Muslim control of the trade and shipping with the Byzantine Empire and the Orient. Once the Muslim fleets had been destroyed, the Italian cities of Venice, Genoa, and Pisa embarked on the road to prosperity. The eleventh century witnessed their steadily rising strength and wealth. Freedom from invasion and domestic security made economic growth possible all over western Europe.

Meanwhile the church was working to end arson, rape, homicide, and wanton destruction. The knights were developing a consciousness of themselves as a class, and the social gap between knight and serf was widening. Local lords ignored all laws and restraints, and attacks on churches were common. Physical assaults on the peasants and the devastation of their fields caused terrible suffering.

In the last quarter of the tenth century, councils of bishops met in Burgundy. The place is significant, for Burgundy was the part of the Carolingian Empire where anarchy was worst and where the clergy and the poor had no defenders whatsoever. The bishops accordingly proclaimed the Peace of God. It placed certain persons – monks who lived in monasteries, clergy who lived in villages and cathedral cities, and the poor – and certain places – church buildings and peasant fields – under ecclesiastical protection. Those who attacked such persons and places were anathematized, which meant that they were to be totally excluded from contact with all Christians. The bishops convinced their relatives among the aristocracy to participate in trying to enforce the peace.

In 1027, a council published the Truce of God, which attempted to regulate the times of fighting. An agreement was sworn that "in order to enable every man to show respect for the Lord's Day," no one was to attack an enemy between Saturday evening and Monday morning. Before 1050, the number of restricted days was increased. Thursday, Friday, and Saturday were added as reminders of the Last Supper, the Crucifixion, and the Entombment. Gradually, some saints' days were added and then the seasons of Advent (the four weeks before Christmas) and Lent (the six weeks before Easter). Lords and knights were urged to form groups to preserve the peace. How effective they were is not known, but without strong and determined lay support they would not have been very successful.

The chief importance of the peace movements lies in their influence on secular rulers. Around 1050, Duke William of Normandy compelled his vassals to join the movement. His backing, and eventually that of other leaders, was an important element in the promotion of peace.

INCREASING POPULATION AND MILD CLIMATE

A steady growth of population also contributed to the general recovery of Europe. The decline of foreign invasions and of internal civil disorder reduced the number of people killed and maimed. Feudal armies in the eleventh through thirteenth centuries continued their destruction, but they were very small by modern standards and fought few pitched battles. Most medieval warfare consisted of the besieging of castles or fortifications. As few as twelve men could defend a castle. With sufficient food and an adequate water supply, they could hold out for a long time. Monastic chroniclers, frequently bored and almost always writing from hearsay evidence, tended to romanticize medieval warfare (as long as it was not in their own neighborhoods). Most conflicts were petty skirmishes with slight loss of life. The survival of more young people, those most often involved in warring activities, and those usually the most sexually active meant a population rise.

Nor was there any "natural," or biological, hindrance to population expansion. Between the tenth and fourteenth centuries, Europe was not hit by any major plague or other medical scourge, though leprosy and malaria did strike down some people. Leprosy had entered Europe in the early Middle Ages. Although caused by a virus, the disease was not very contagious and, if contracted, worked slowly. Lepers presented a frightful appearance: the victim's arms and legs rotted away, and gangrenous sores emitted a horrible smell. Physicians had no cure. For these reasons, and because of the command in the thirteenth chapter of Leviticus that lepers be isolated, medieval lepers were segregated in hospitals called leprosaria.

Malaria, spread by protozoa-carrying mosquitoes that infested swampy areas, also caused problems. Malaria is characterized by alternate chills and fevers, and leaves the afflicted person extremely weak. Peter the Venerable, the ninth abbot of the monastery of Cluny (1122–1156), suffered for many of his later years from recurring bouts of malaria contracted on a youthful trip to Rome. Still, relatively few people caught malaria or leprosy. Crop failure and the ever-present danger of starvation were much more pressing threats.

The weather cooperated with the revival. Meteorologists believe that a slow but steady retreat of polar ice occurred between the ninth and the eleventh centuries. A significant warming trend occurred and continued until about 1200. The century between 1080 and 1180 witnessed exceptionally clement weather in England, France, and Germany, with mild winters and dry summers.

Good weather helps to explain advances in population growth, land reclamation, and agricultural yield. Increased agricultural output had a profound impact on society: it affected Europeans' health, commerce, trade, industry, and general lifestyle.

The greatest manifestation of the recovery of Europe was the rise of towns and the development of a new business and commercial class. This development was to lay the foundations for Europe's transformation, centuries later, from a rural and agricultural society into an industrial and urban society. This change, which had global implications, had its beginnings in the Middle Ages.

Why did these developments occur when they did? What sorts of people first populated the towns and where did they come from? What is known of town life in the High Middle Ages? What relevance did towns have for medieval culture? Part of the answer to at least one of these questions has already been given. Without increased agricultural output, there would not have been an adequate food supply for new town dwellers. Without a rise in population, there would have been no one to people the towns. Without a minimum of peace and political stability, merchants could not have transported and sold goods. (Merchants dislike nothing more than domestic disorder.)

THE RISE OF TOWNS

Medieval society was traditional, agricultural, and rural. The emergence of a new class that was none of these constituted a social revolution. The new class — artisans and merchants — came from the peasantry. They were landless younger sons of large families, driven away by land shortage. Or they were forced by war and famine to seek new possibilities. Or they were unusually enterprising and adventurous, curious and willing to take a chance.

One of the most exciting aspects of the

THE CITY WALLS OF MANTUA *Town walls
protected citizens from theft and physical attack. Up-
keep of the walls was usually the town's heaviest expense.* (The Granger Collection)

study of history is that facts and evidence may
be explained in a variety of ways. There is no
final or definitive interpretation. Serious investigation of the origin of European towns
began only in the twentieth century. Historians have proposed three basic theories. Some
scholars believe towns began as boroughs —
that is, as forts or fortifications erected during
the ninth-century Viking invasions. According to this view, towns were at first places of

defense or security into which farmers from
the surrounding countryside moved when
their area was attacked. Later, merchants were
attracted to the fortifications because they had
something to sell and wanted to be where the
potential customers were. But most residents
of the early towns made their livings by
farming outside the town.

The Belgian historian Henri Pirenne maintained that towns sprang up when merchants

who engaged in long-distance trade gravitated toward attractive or favorable spots, such as near a fort. Usually traders settled just outside the walls, in the *faubourgs* or *suburbs* – both of which mean "outside," or "in the shelter of the walls." As their markets prospered and as their number outside the walls grew, the merchants built a new wall around themselves. Such construction might be necessary every century or so. According to Pirenne, a medieval town consisted architecturally of a number of concentric walls, and the chief economic pursuit of its residents was trade and commerce.

A third explanation focuses on the great cathedrals and monasteries. The large numbers of clergy attached to a cathedral or monastery represented a demand for goods and services. Cathedrals such as Notre Dame in Paris conducted schools, which drew students from far and wide. Consequently, traders and merchants settled near the religious establishments to cater to the residents' economic needs. Concentrations of people accumulated, and towns came into being.

All three theories have validity, though none of them explains the origins of *all* medieval towns. Few towns of the tenth and eleventh centuries were "new" in the sense that American towns and cities were new in the seventeenth and eighteenth centuries. They were not carved out of forest and wilderness. Some medieval towns that had become flourishing centers of trade by the mid-twelfth century had originally been Roman army camps: York in northern England, Bordeaux in west central France, and Cologne in west central Germany are good examples of ancient towns that underwent revitalization in the eleventh century. Some Italian seaport cities, such as Pisa and Genoa, had been centers of shipping and commerce in earlier times. Muslim attacks and domestic squabbles had cut their populations and drastically reduced the volume of their trade in the early Middle Ages, but trade with Constantinople and the Orient had never stopped entirely. The restoration of order and political stability promoted rebirth and new development. Pirenne's interpretation accurately describes the Flemish towns of Bruges and Ypres. It does not fit the course of development in the Italian cities or in such centers as London.

Whether evolving from a newly fortified place or an old Roman army camp, from a cathedral site or a river junction or a place where several overland routes met, all medieval towns had a few common characteristics. Walls enclosed the town. (The terms "burgher" and "bourgeois" derive from the Old English and Old German words *burg, burgh, borg,* and *borough* for a walled or fortified place. Thus, a burgher or bourgeois was originally a person who lived or worked inside the walls.) The town had a marketplace. It often had a mint for the coining of money and a court to settle disputes.

In each town many people inhabited a small, cramped area. Census records do not exist for most of Europe before the early eighteenth century, but tax returns reveal the populations of many English towns in 1377. The largest city, London, had 23,314 people. The second largest city, Bristol, had only 6,345 citizens. Some continental cities, such as Paris, were probably much bigger. Size was not important; the real strength of the medieval towns rested in their people (see Map 9.1).

By the late eleventh century many towns in Western Europe had small Jewish populations. Jews had emigrated in post-Roman times from the large cities of the Mediterranean region to France, the Rhineland, and Britain. During the Carolingian period Jews had the reputation of being richer and more

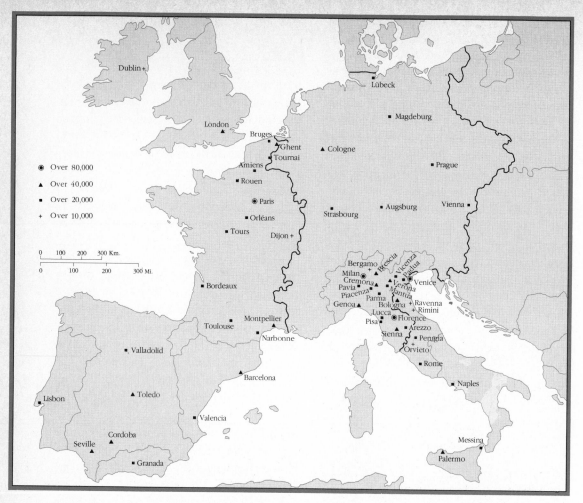

MAP 9.1 POPULATION OF EUROPEAN URBAN
AREAS, CA LATE THIRTEENTH CENTURY
Although there were scores of urban centers in the

*thirteenth century, the Italian and Flemish towns had
the largest concentrations of people. By modern standards, Paris was Europe's only real city.*

learned than the semibarbarian peoples among
whom they lived. They typically earned their
livelihoods in the lesser trades or by lending
money at interest, and Jews engaged in trade
had to be literate to keep records. The laws of
most countries forbade Jews to own land,
though they could hold land pledged to them
for debts. As townspeople they often possessed cultural eminence over their neighbors.
By the twelfth century many Jews were
usurers: they lent to consumers but primarily

to new or growing business enterprises. New
towns and underdeveloped areas where cash
was scarce welcomed Jewish settlers. Like
other businesspeople, the Jews preferred to
live near their work; they also settled close to
their synagogue or school. Thus originated
the Jews' street or quarter or ghetto. Such
neighborhoods gradually became legally defined sections where Jews were required to
live.

In their backgrounds and abilities, townspeople represented diversity and change. They constituted an entirely new element in medieval society. They fit into none of the traditional categories. Their occupations, their preoccupations, their very lives were different from those of the feudal nobility and the laboring peasantry. They were the "middle" class.

The aristocratic nobility glanced down with contempt and derision at the money-grubbing townspeople, but were not above borrowing from them. The rural peasantry peered up with suspicion and fear at the town dwellers. What was the point, the farmers wondered, of making money? Only land had real permanence.

Nor did the new commercial classes make much sense initially to churchmen. The immediate goal of the middle class was obviously not salvation. It was to be a good while before churchmen developed a theological justification for the new classes.

TOWN LIBERTIES

In the words of the Greek poet Alcaeus, "Not houses finely roofed or well built walls, nor canals or dockyards make a city, but men able to use their opportunity."[1] Men and opportunity. That is fundamentally what medieval towns meant — concentrations of people and varieties of chances. No matter where groups of traders congregated, they settled on someone's land and had to secure from king or count, abbot or bishop, permission to live and trade. Aristocratic nobles and churchmen were suspicious of and hostile to the middle class. They soon realized, however, that profits and benefits flowed to them and their territories from the markets set up on their land.

The history of towns in the eleventh through thirteenth centuries consists largely of the efforts of merchants to acquire "liberties." In the Middle Ages, liberties meant special privileges. For the town dweller, liberties included the privilege of living and trading on the lord's land. The most important privilege a medieval townsperson could gain was freedom. It gradually developed that an individual who lived in a town for a year and a day was free of servile obligations and status. More than anything else, perhaps, the liberty of personal freedom that came with residence in a town contributed to the emancipation of the serfs in the High Middle Ages. Liberty meant citizenship, and citizenship in a town implied the right to buy and sell goods there. Unlike foreigners and outsiders of any kind, the full citizen did not have to pay taxes and tolls in the market. Obviously, this increased profits.

In the twelfth and thirteenth centuries towns fought for, and slowly gained, legal and political rights. Since the tenth century, some English boroughs had held courts with jurisdiction over members of the town in civil and criminal matters. In the twelfth century, such English towns as London and Norwich developed courts that applied a special kind of law, called law merchant. It dealt with commercial transactions, debt, bankruptcy, proof of sales, and contracts. Law merchant was especially suitable to the needs of the new bourgeoisie. Around 1116, the count of Flanders granted to the burgesses of Ypres the right to hold a municipal court that alone could judge members of the town. Gradually, other towns across Europe acquired the same right. In effect it gave them judicial independence.[2]

In the acquisition of full rights of self-government, the merchant guilds played a large role. Medieval men were long accustomed to communal enterprises. In the late tenth and early eleventh centuries, men who were engaged in foreign trade joined together in merchant guilds; united enterprise provided them greater security and less risk of losses than did individual action. At about the same time, the artisans and craftsmen of particular trades formed guilds of their own. These were the butchers, the bakers, and the candlestick makers. Members of the craft guilds determined the quality, quantity, and price of the goods produced and the number of apprentices and journeymen affiliated with the guild. Terrible conflicts were to arise between the craft guilds and the merchant guilds in the thirteenth and fourteenth centuries, but that is a later story.

Women engaged in every kind of urban commercial activity, both as helpmates to their husbands and independently. In many manufacturing trades women predominated, and in some places women were a large percentage of the labor force. In fourteenth-century Frankfurt, for example, about 33 percent of the crafts and trades were entirely female, about 40 percent wholly male, and the remaining crafts roughly divided between the sexes. Craft guilds provided greater opportunity for women than did merchant guilds. In late twelfth-century Cologne, women and men had equal rights in the turners' guild (those who made wooden objects on a lathe). Most members of the Paris silk and woolen trades were women, and some achieved the mastership. Widows frequently followed their late husbands' professions, but if they remarried outside the craft they lost the mastership. Between 1254 and 1271 the chief magistrate of Paris drew up the following regulations for the silk industry:

Any woman who wishes to be a silk spinster (woman who spins) on large spindles in the city of Paris — i.e. reeling, spinning, doubling and re-twisting — may freely do so, provided she observe the following customs and usages of the craft:

No spinster on large spindles may have more than three apprentices, unless they be her own or her husband's children born in true wedlock; nor may she contract with them for an apprenticeship of less than seven years or for a fee of less than 20 Parisian sols to be paid to her, their mistress. . . . If a working woman comes from outside Paris and wishes to practice the said craft in the city, she must swear before the guardians of the craft that she will practice it well and loyally and conform to its customs and usages. . . . No man of this craft who is without a wife may have more than one apprentice; . . if, however, both husband and wife practice the craft, they may have two apprentices and as many journeymen as they wish.[3]

Guild records show that women received lower wages than men for the same work, on the grounds that they needed less income.

By the late eleventh century, especially in the towns of the Low Countries (present-day Belgium and Holland) and northern Italy, the leading men in the merchant guilds were quite rich and powerful. They constituted an oligarchy in their towns, controlling economic life and bargaining with kings and lords for political independence. Full rights of self-government included the right to hold a town court, the right to select the mayor and other municipal officials, and the right to tax and collect taxes. Kings often levied on their serfs and unfree townspeople arbitrary taxes called tallage, or the taille. Such taxes (also known as customs) called attention to the fact that men were not free. Citizens of a town much preferred to levy and collect their own taxes.

A charter that King Henry II of England granted to the merchants of Lincoln around

1157 nicely illustrates the town's rights. The emphasized passages clearly suggest that the merchant guild had been the governing body in the city for almost a century and that anyone who lived in Lincoln for a year and a day was considered free:

Henry, by the grace of God, etc., to the bishop of Lincoln, and to the justices, sheriffs, barons, servants and all his liegemen, both French and English, of Lincoln, greeting. Know that I have granted to my citizens of Lincoln all their liberties and customs and laws which they had in the time of Edward [King Edward the Confessor] *and William and Henry, kings of England.* And I have granted them their gild-merchant, comprising men of the city and other merchants of the shire, as well and freely as they had it in the time of our aforesaid predecessors, kings of England. *And all the men who live within the four divisions of the city and attend the market, shall stand in relation to gelds* [taxes] *and customs and the assizes* [ordinances or laws] *of the city as well as ever they stood in the time of Edward, William and Henry, kings of England. I also confirm to them that if anyone has lived in Lincoln for a year and a day without dispute from any claimant, and has paid the customs, and if the citizens can show by the laws and customs of the city that the claimant has remained in England during that period and has made no claim,* then let the defendant remain in peace in my city of Lincoln as my citizen, *without* [having to defend his] *right.*[4]

Kings and lords were reluctant to grant towns self-government, fearing loss of authority and revenue if they gave the merchant guilds full independence. But the lords discovered that towns attracted increasing numbers of people to an area — people whom the lords could tax. Moreover, when burghers

bargained for a town's political independence, they offered sizable amounts of ready cash. Consequently, feudal lords ultimately agreed to self-government.

TOWN LIFE

Protective walls surrounded almost all medieval towns and cities. The valuable goods inside a town were too much of a temptation to marauding bands for the town to be without the security of bricks and mortar. The walls were pierced by gates, and visitors waited at the gates to gain entrance to the town. When the gates were opened early in the morning, guards inspected the quantity and quality of the goods brought in and collected the customary taxes. Part of the taxes went to the king or lord on whose land the town stood, part to the town council for civic purposes. Constant repair of the walls was usually the town's greatest expense.

Peasants coming from the countryside and merchants traveling from afar set up their carts as stalls just inside the gates. The result was that the road nearest the gate was the widest thoroughfare. It was the ideal place for a market, because everyone coming in or going out used it. Most streets in a medieval town were marketplaces as much as passages for transit. They were narrow, just wide enough to transport goods through.

Medieval cities served, above all else, as markets. In some respects the entire city was a marketplace. The place where a product was made and sold was also typically the merchant's residence. Usually the ground floor was the scene of production. A window or door opened from the main workroom directly onto the street. The window displayed the finished product, and passersby could look in and see the goods being produced. The

MEDIEVAL STREET SCENE *Merchants displayed their goods from shop windows on the ground floor: tailors, furriers, a barber, and a grocer. Merchants with shops on the street that linked the two main town* *gates naturally profited more than did those on side streets which were blocked by the town wall. (Bibliothèque Nationale, Paris)*

merchant and his family lived above the business on the second or third floor. As his business and his family expanded, he built additional stories on top of his house.

Because space within the walls of the town was limited, expansion occurred upward. Second and third stories were built jutting out over the ground floor and thus over the street. Neighbors on the opposite side of the road did the same. Since the streets were narrow to begin with, houses thus lacked fresh air and light. Initially, houses were made of wood and thatched with straw. Fire represented a con-

stant danger, and because houses were built so close together, fires spread rapidly. Municipal governments consequently urged construction in stone or brick.

Most medieval cities developed haphazardly. There was little town planning. As the population increased, space became more and more limited. Air and water pollution presented serious problems. Many families raised pigs for household consumption in sties next to the house. Horses and oxen, the chief means of transportation and power, dropped tons of dung on the streets every year. It was universal practice in the early towns to dump household waste, both animal and human, into the road in front of one's house. The stench must have been abominable. In 1298, the burgesses of the town of Boutham in Yorkshire, England, received the following order (one long, vivid sentence):

To the bailiffs of the abbot of St. Mary's York, at Boutham. Whereas it is sufficiently evident that the pavement of the said town of Boutham is so very greatly broken up and that all the singular passing and going through that town sustain immoderate damages and grievances, and in addition the air is so corrupted and infected by the pigsties situated in the king's highways and in the lanes of that town and by the swine feeding and frequently wandering about in the streets and lanes and by dung and dunghills and many other foul things placed in the streets and lanes, that great repugnance overtakes the king's ministers staying in that town and also others there dwelling and passing through, the advantage of more wholesome air is impeded, the state of men is grievously injured, and other unbearable inconveniences and many other injuries are known to proceed from such corruption, to the nuisance of the king's ministers aforesaid and of others there dwelling and passing through, and to the peril of their lives, and to the manifest shame and reproach of the bailiffs and other the inhabitants of that town: the king, being unwilling longer to tolerate such great and unbearable defects there, orders the bailiffs to cause the pavement to be suitably repaired within their liberty before All Saints next, and to cause the pigsties, aforesaid streets and lanes to be cleansed from all dung and dunghills, and to cause them to be kept thus cleansed hereafter, and to cause proclamation to be made throughout their bailiwick forbidding any one, under pain of grievous forfeiture, to cause or permit their swine to feed or wander outside his house in the king's streets or the lanes aforesaid.[5]

A great deal of traffic passed through Boutham in 1298 because of the movement of the English troops to battlefronts in Scotland. Conditions there were probably not typical. Still, this document suggests that problems of space, air pollution, and sanitation bedeviled urban people in medieval times just as they do today.

The church took a great interest in townspeople as Christians. Parish clergy catered to their spiritual needs. As the bourgeoisie gained in wealth, they expressed their continuing Christian faith by refurbishing old churches, constructing new ones, and giving stained-glass windows, statues, and carvings. The twelfth-century chronicler William of Newburgh, writing about 1170, could proudly boast that the city of London had 126 parish churches, in addition to 13 monastic churches and the great cathedral of St. Paul's.

Some literary descriptions of medieval cities survive, but they do not tell all that we would like to know. Most illustrations of walls, streets, and houses date only from the fifteenth century. Medieval cities, like modern ones, changed a great deal in the course of decades and, of course, centuries. A fifteenth-century picture is not a very accurate representation of twelfth-century conditions. William of Newburgh, however, left a detailed description of the city of London around 1175:

Among the noble and celebrated cities of the world that of London, the capital of the kingdom of the English, is one which extends its glory farther than all the others and sends its wealth and merchandise more widely into distant lands. Higher than all the rest does it lift its head. . . .

It has on the east the Palatine castle [the Tower of London], very great and strong: the keep and walls rise from very deep foundations and are fixed with a mortar tempered by the blood of an-

A FIFTEENTH-CENTURY HOUSE *Medieval merchants conducted their business on the ground floor and lived with their families on the floors above. As additional stories were added on, they jutted out one over the other. Since this form of building was done on both sides of the street, streets received little light during the day and were dangerously dark at night. (Royal Commission on Historical Monuments, England)*

south, but the mighty Thames, so full of fish, has with the sea's ebb and flow washed against, loosened, and thrown down those walls in the course of time. Upstream to the west there is the royal palace [the Palace of Westminster]. . . .

Everywhere outside the houses of those living in the suburbs, and adjacent to them, are the spacious and beautiful gardens of the citizens, and these are planted with trees. Also there are on the north side pastures and pleasant meadow lands through which flow streams wherein the turning of millwheels makes a cheerful sound. Very near lies a great forest with woodland pastures in which there are the lairs of wild animals: stags, fallow deer, wild boars and bulls. . . .

Those engaged in business of various kinds, sellers of merchandise, hirers of labour, are distributed every morning into their several localities according to their trade. Besides, there is in London on the river bank among the wines for sale in ships and in the cellars of the vintners a public cook-shop. There daily you may find food according to the season, dishes of meat, roast, fried and boiled, large and small fish, coarser meats for the poor and more delicate for the rich, such as venison and big and small birds. If any of the citizens should unexpectedly receive visitors, weary from their journey, who would fain not wait until fresh food is bought and cooked, or until the servants have brought bread or water for washing, they hasten to the river bank and there find all they need. . . .

Immediately outside one of the gates there is a field [Smithfield] which is smooth both in fact and in name. On every sixth day of the week, unless it be a major feast-day, there takes place there a famous exhibition of fine horses for sale. Earls, barons and knights, who are in the town, and many citizens come out to see or to buy. It is pleasant to see the high-stepping palfreys with their gleaming coats, as they go through their paces, putting down their feet alternately on one side together. . . .

imals. On the west there are two castles very strongly fortified, and from these there runs a high and massive wall with seven double gates and with towers along the north at regular intervals. London was once also walled and turreted on the

By themselves in another part of the field stand the goods of the countryfolk: implements of husbandry, swine with long flanks, cows with full udders, oxen of immense size, and woolly sheep. There also stand the mares fit for plough, some big with foal, and others with brisk young colts closely following them.

To this city from every nation under heaven merchants delight to bring their trade by sea. The Arabian sends gold; the Sabaean spice and incense. The Scythian brings arms, and from the rich, fat lands of Babylon comes oil of palms. The Nile sends precious stones; the men of Norway and Russia, furs and sables; nor is China absent with purple silk. The Gauls come with their wines....

We now come to speak of the sports of the city, for it is not fitting that a city should be merely useful and serious-minded, unless it be also pleasant and cheerful....

Furthermore, every year on the day called Carnival – to begin with the sports of boys (for we were all boys once) – scholars from the different schools bring fighting-cocks to their masters, and the whole morning is set apart to watch their cocks do battle in the schools, for the boys are given a holiday that day. After dinner all the young men of the town go out into the fields in the suburbs to play ball. The scholars of the various schools have their own ball, and almost all the followers of each occupation have theirs also. The seniors and the fathers and the wealthy magnates of the city come on horseback to watch the contests of the younger generation, and in their turn recover their lost youth: the motions of their natural heat seem to be stirred in them at the mere sight of such strenuous activity and by their participation in the joys of unbridled youth.

Every Sunday in Lent after dinner a fresh swarm of young men goes forth into the fields on war-horses, steeds foremost in the contest, each of which is skilled and schooled to run in circles. From the gates there sallies forth a host of laymen, sons of the citizens, equipped with lances and shields, the younger ones with spears forked at the top, but with the steel point removed. They make a pretence at war, carry out field-exercises and indulge in mimic combats. Thither too come many courtiers, when the king is in town, and from the households of bishops, earls and barons come youths and adolescents, not yet girt with the belt of knighthood, for the pleasure of engaging in combat with one another. Each is inflamed with the hope of victory....

On feast-days throughout the summer the young men indulge in the sports of archery, running, jumping, wrestling, slinging the stone, hurling the javelin beyond a mark and fighting with sword and buckler....

Others, more skilled at winter sports, put on their feet the shin-bones of animals, binding them firmly around their ankles, and, holding poles shod with iron in their hands, which they strike from time to time against the ice, they are propelled swift as a bird in flight or a bolt shot from an engine of war....[6]

People wanted to get into medieval cities because they represented a means of economic advancement, social mobility, and improvement in legal status. For the adventurous, the ambitious, and the shrewd, cities offered tremendous opportunities.

THE REVIVAL OF LONG-DISTANCE TRADE

The eleventh century witnessed a remarkable revival of trade as artisans and craftsmen manufactured goods for local and foreign consumption (see Map 9.2). Most trade centered in towns and was controlled by professional traders. Because long-distance trade was risky and required large investments of capital, it could be practiced only by professionals. The transportation of goods involved serious risks. Shipwrecks were common. Pirates infested the sea-lanes, and robbers and thieves roamed virtually all of the land routes. Since the risks were so great, merchants preferred to share them. A group of men would thus pool some of their capital to finance an expedition to a distant place. When the ship or caravan returned and the goods brought back were sold, the investors would share the profits. If disaster struck the caravan, an investor's loss was limited to the amount of his investment.

What goods were exchanged? What towns took the lead in medieval "international" trade? In the late eleventh century, the Italian cities, especially Venice, led the West in trade in general and completely dominated the oriental market. Ships carried salt from the Venetian lagoon, pepper and other spices from North Africa, and silks and purple textiles from the Orient to northern and western Europe. Venetian caravans brought slaves from the Crimea and Chinese silks from Mongolia to the town markets and regional fairs of France, Flanders, and England. (Fairs were periodic gatherings that attracted buyers, sellers, and goods from all over Europe.) Flanders controlled the cloth industry. The towns of Bruges, Ghent, and Ypres built up a vast industry in the manufacture of cloth. Italian merchants exchanged their products for Flemish tapestries, fine broadcloths, and various other textiles.

Two circumstances help to explain the lead Venice and the Flemish towns gained in long-distance trade. Both enjoyed a high degree of peace and political stability. Geographical factors were equally if not more important. Venice was ideally located at the northwestern end of the Adriatic Sea, with easy access to both the transalpine land routes and the Adriatic and Mediterranean sea-lanes. The markets of North Africa, Byzantium, and Russia and the great fairs of Ghent in Flanders and Champagne in France provided commercial opportunities that Venice quickly seized. The

geographical situation of Flanders also offered unusual possibilities. Just across the Channel from England, Flanders had easy access to English wool. Indeed, Flanders and England developed a very close economic relationship.

Sheep had been raised for their wool in England since Roman times. The rocky soil and damp climate of Yorkshire and Lincolnshire, though poorly suited for agriculture, were excellent for sheep farming. Beginning in the early twelfth century, but especially after the arrival of Cistercian monks around 1130, the size of the English flocks doubled and then tripled. Scholars have estimated that by the end of the twelfth century roughly 6 million sheep grazed on the English moors and downs. They produced fifty thousand sacks of wool a year.[7] Originally, a "sack" of wool was the burden one packhorse could carry, an amount eventually fixed at 364 pounds; fifty thousand sacks, then, represented huge production.

Wool was the cornerstone of the English medieval economy. Population growth in the twelfth century and the success of the Flemish and Italian textile industries created foreign demand for English wool. The production of English wool stimulated Flemish manufacturing, and the expansion of the Flemish cloth industry in turn spurred the production of English wool. The availability of raw wool also encouraged the development of domestic cloth manufacture within England. The towns of Lincoln and York in the north, Leicester and Northampton in the central counties, Winchester in the south, and Exeter in the west became important cloth-producing

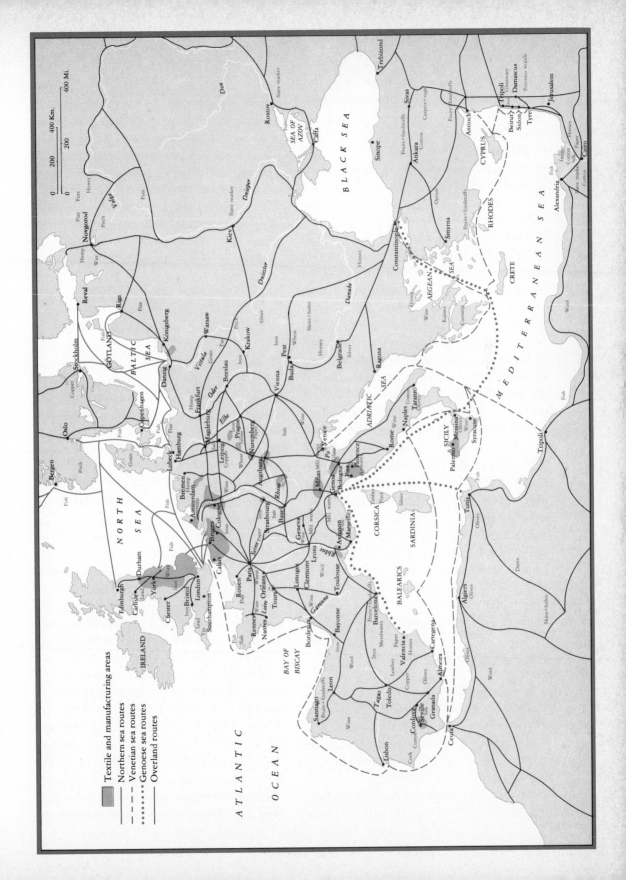

towns. The port cities of London, Hull, Boston, and Bristol thrived on the wool trade. In the thirteenth century commercial families in these towns grew fabulously rich.

The wool and cloth trades serve as a good barometer of the economic growth and decline of English towns. The supply of wool depended upon such natural factors as the amount of land devoted to grazing, the weather, and the prevalence of sheep disease or scab. The price of wool, unlike that of wheat or other foodstuffs, was determined not by supply but by demand. Changes in demand – often the result of political developments over which merchants had no control – could severely damage the wool trade. In the 1320s, for example, violent disorder exploded in the Flemish towns, causing a sharp drop in demand for English wool. When wool exports fell, the economies of London, Hull, and Southampton slumped. Then, during the Hundred Years War (pages 402–403), the English Crown laid increasingly high export taxes on raw wool, and again the wool trade hurt. On the other hand, the decline of wool exports encouraged the growth of cloth manufacturing in older centers such as Lincoln and in new ones such as Tiverton and Lavenham. In the fourteenth century these towns experienced some population growth and considerable prosperity – a prosperity directly linked to the cloth industry.

THE COMMERCIAL REVOLUTION

A steadily expanding volume of international trade from the late eleventh through the thirteenth centuries was a sign of the great economic surge, but it was not the only one. In cities all across Europe trading and transportation firms opened branch offices. Credit was widely extended, considerably facilitating exchange. Merchants devised the letter of credit, which made unnecessary the slow and dangerous shipment of coin for payment.

A new capitalistic spirit developed. Professional merchants were always on the lookout for new markets and new opportunities. They invested their surplus capital in new enterprises to make more money. They diversified their interests and got involved in a wide variety of operations. The typical prosperous merchant in the later thirteenth century might well be involved in buying and selling, in shipping, in lending some capital at interest, and in other types of banking. Medieval merchants were fiercely competitive.

Some scholars consider capitalism a modern phenomenon, beginning in the fifteenth or sixteenth century. But in their use of capital to make more money, in their speculative pursuits and willingness to gamble, in their competitive spirit, and in the variety of their interests and operations, medieval businessmen displayed the essential traits of capitalists.

The ventures of the English cloth industry in the fourteenth century illustrate these impulses. Profits had steadily accumulated in the cloth-producing towns, where manufacturers often had close ties with wool dealers. With the Flemish cloth industry in trouble, English merchant-manufacturers invaded Flemish markets on the continent and invested their capital in a variety of enterprises. Cloth merchants began to deal in French wines, Flemish tapestries, Baltic fish, furs, and naval stores, and Italian silks. English businessmen established trading centers called factories with long-term residents at Antwerp, Bergen in Norway, Danzig on the Baltic, and Cologne on the Rhine; a single English company might have factories in all of these cities. The foreign commodities exchanged for finished cloth or raw wool were imported into England for domestic sale. These activities re-

A FLEMISH DOCK SCENE Flemish towns early developed commercial ties with neighboring countries. The Flemish purchased wool from England and manufactured excellent textiles, which they sold to merchants from all over Europe. This print shows bales of cloth being loaded at dockside for transport abroad. (Bodleian Library)

quired capital, willingness to take risks, and the aggressive pursuit of opportunities — the essential ingredients of capitalism. They also yielded fat profits.

These developments added up to what one modern scholar who knows the period well has called "a commercial revolution, .. probably the greatest turning point in the history of our civilization."[8] This is not a wildly extravagant statement. In the long run the commercial revolution of the High Middle Ages brought about radical change in European society and culture. One remarkable aspect of this change is that the commercial classes did not constitute a large part of the total population – never more than 10 percent. They exercised an influence far in excess of their actual numbers.

The commercial revolution created a great deal of new wealth. Wealth meant a higher standard of living. The new availability of something as simple as spices, for example, allowed for variety in food. Dietary habits gradually changed. Taste became more sophisticated. Contact with Eastern civilizations introduced Europeans to eating utensils such as forks. Table manners improved. People learned to eat with forks and knives, instead of tearing the meat from the roast with their hands. They began to use napkins, instead of wiping their greasy fingers on the dogs lying under the table.

The existence of wealth did not escape the attention of kings and other rulers. Wealth could be taxed, and through taxation kings could create strong and centralized states. In the years to come, alliances with the middle classes were to enable kings to defeat feudal powers and aristocratic interests and to build the states that came to be called modern.

The commercial revolution also provided the opportunity for thousands of serfs to improve their social position. The slow but steady transformation of European society from almost completely rural and isolated to relatively more sophisticated constituted the greatest effect of the commercial revolution that began in the eleventh century.

Even so, merchants and businesspeople did not run medieval communities, except in central and northern Italy and in the county of Flanders. Towns remained small: as late as the 1320s a town of 5000 people was considered sizable, and Paris with about 80,000 souls was Europe's greatest city. The castle, the manorial village, and the monastery dominated the landscape. The feudal nobility and churchmen determined the preponderant social attitudes, values, and patterns of thought and behavior. The commercial changes of the eleventh and

twelfth centuries did, however, lay the economic foundations for the development of urban life and culture that occurred during the Renaissance.

REVIVAL AND REFORM IN THE CHRISTIAN CHURCH

The eleventh century also witnessed the beginnings of a remarkable religious revival. Monasteries, always the leaders in ecclesiastical reform, remodeled themselves under the leadership of the Burgundian abbey of Cluny. Subsequently, new religious orders, such as the Cistercians, were founded and became a broad spiritual movement.

The papacy itself, after a century of corruption and decadence, was cleaned up. The popes worked to clarify church doctrine and to codify church law. They and their officials sought to communicate with all the clergy and peoples of Europe through a clearly defined and obedient hierarchy of bishops. The popes wanted the basic loyalty of all members of the clergy. Pope Gregory VII (1073–1085) tried to enforce an entirely new theory of Christian kingship, and his assertion of papal power caused profound changes and serious conflicts with secular authorities. The revival of the Christian church was manifested in the twelfth and thirteenth centuries by a flowering of popular piety, reflected in the building of magnificent cathedrals.

MONASTIC REVIVAL

In the early Middle Ages the best Benedictine monasteries had been citadels of good Christian living and centers of education and learning. Between the seventh and ninth centuries,

MONT ST.-MICHEL At the summit of a 250-foot cone of rock rising out of the sea and accessible only at low tide, Mont St.-Michel combined fortified castle and monastery. Thirteenth century monarchs considered it crucial to their power in northwestern France, *and it played a decisive role in French defenses against the English during the Hundred Years War. The abbots so planned the architecture that monastic life went on undisturbed by military activity. (Mark Sheridan OSB)*

religious houses like Bobbio in northern Italy, Luxeuil in France, and Jarrow in England copied and preserved manuscripts, maintained schools, and set high standards of monastic observance. Charlemagne had encouraged and supported these monastic activities, and the collapse of the Carolingian Empire had disastrous effects.

The Viking and Muslim invaders attacked and ransacked many monasteries across Europe. Some communities fled and dispersed. In the period of political disorder that followed the disintegration of the Carolingian Empire, many religious houses fell under the control and domination of local feudal lords. Powerful laymen appointed themselves or their relatives as abbots, while keeping their wives or mistresses. They took for themselves the lands and goods of monasteries. They spent monastic revenues and sold monastic offices. Temporal powers all over Europe dominated the monasteries. The level of spiritual observance and intellectual activity declined.

In 909 William the Pious, duke of Aquitaine, established the abbey of Cluny near Mâcon in Burgundy. This was to be a very important event. In his charter of endowment Duke William declared that Cluny was to enjoy complete independence from all feudal or secular lordship. The new monastery was to be subordinate only to the authority of Saints Peter and Paul as represented by the pope. The duke then renounced his own possession of and influence over Cluny.

This monastery and its foundation charter came to exert vast religious influence. The first two abbots of Cluny, Berno (910–927) and Odo (927–942), set very high standards of religious behavior. They stressed strict observance of the *Rule of Saint Benedict,* the development of a personal spiritual life by the individual monk, and the importance of the liturgy. In the church as a whole, Cluny gradually came to stand for clerical celibacy and the suppression of simony (the sale of church offices). Within a generation neighboring monasteries sought Cluny's help and were reformed along Cluniac lines.

In the course of the eleventh century, Cluny was fortunate in having a series of extremely able abbots, who all ruled for a long time. They paid careful attention to sound economic management and to the principle of independence from lay influence. In the Holy Roman Empire, Cluniac reform had the strong and significant support of the emperor Henry III (1039–1056). He aided the religious houses in their struggle for independence from the lay aristocracy. Hundreds of monasteries across Europe, in France, Germany, Italy, Spain, and England, placed themselves under Cluny's jurisdiction. By the time of the sixty-year reign of Abbot Hugh (1049–1109), the Cluniac reforming spirit was felt everywhere.

Success for an institution, as for an individual, is measured by the degree to which it lives up to the goals it sets for itself. In religion nothing leads to failure like material success. By the last quarter of the eleventh century, some monasteries enjoyed wide reputations for the beauty and richness of their chant and the piety of the monks' lives. Deeply impressed laymen showered gifts upon them. Jewelry, rich vestments and elaborately carved sacred vessels, lands and properties poured into some houses. With this wealth came the influence of laymen. As the monasteries became richer, the lifestyle of the monks became luxurious. Monastic observance and spiritual fervor declined.

Once again the ideals of the pristine Benedictine life were threatened. Fresh demands for reform were heard, and the result was the founding of new religious orders in the late eleventh and early twelfth centuries. The best representatives of the new reforming spirit and monastic piety of the twelfth century were the Cistercians.

In 1098 a group of monks left the rich abbey of Molesmes in Burgundy and founded a new house in the swampy forest of Cîteaux. They had specific goals and high ideals. They planned to avoid all involvement with secular feudal society. They decided to accept only uncultivated lands far from regular habitation. They intended to refuse all gifts of mills, serfs, tithes, ovens – the traditional manorial sources of income. The early Cistercians determined to avoid elaborate liturgy and ceremony and to keep their chant simple. Finally, they refused to allow the presence of high and powerful laymen in their monasteries, because they knew that such influence was usually harmful to careful observance.

To the Cistercian reformers the older Benedictine monasteries represented power, wealth, and luxurious living, which violated the spirit of the *Rule of Saint Benedict*. The Cistercian life was to be a new kind of commune. It was to be simple, isolated, austere, and purified of all the economic and religious complexities found in the Benedictine houses.

These Cistercian goals coincided perfectly with the needs of twelfth-century society. The late eleventh and early twelfth centuries witnessed energetic agricultural expansion and land reclamation all across Europe. The early Cistercians wanted to farm only land that had previously been uncultivated, or swampland, or fenland, and that was exactly what needed to be done. They thus became the great pioneers of the twelfth century. Their churches had to be plain, and they wanted their daily lives to be simple. A pioneer existence in a commune where all had to work hard and all resources were pooled obviously had enormous economic and social possibilities. Unavoidably the success of the Cistercians' efforts brought wealth, and wealth brought power and influence.

The first monks at Citeaux experienced sickness, a dearth of recruits, and terrible privations. Their obvious sincerity and high idealism eventually attracted attention. In 1112, a twenty-three-year-old nobleman called Bernard joined the community at Citeaux, together with thirty of his aristocratic friends and companions. Thereafter, this reforming movement gained wide impetus. Citeaux founded hundreds of new monasteries in the course of the twelfth century, and its influence on European society was profound.

REFORM OF THE PAPACY

Some scholars believe that the monastic revival spreading from Cluny influenced reform of the Roman papacy and eventually of the entire Christian church. Certainly, Abbot Odilo of Cluny (994-1048) was a close friend of the German emperor Henry III, who promoted reform throughout the empire. Pope Gregory VII, who carried the ideals of reform to extreme lengths, had spent some time at Cluny. And the man who consolidated the reform movement and strengthened the medieval papal monarchy, Pope Urban II (1088-1099), had been a monk and prior at Cluny. The precise degree of Cluny's impact on the reform movement cannot be measured. But the broad goals of the Cluniac movement and those of the Roman papacy were the same.

The papacy provided little leadership to the Christian peoples of western Europe in the tenth century. Factions in Rome sought to control the papacy for their own material gain. Popes were appointed to advance the political ambitions of their families – the great aristocratic families of the city – and not because of special spiritual qualifications. The office of pope, including its spiritual powers and influence, was frequently bought and sold, though this grave crime, called simony, had been condemned by Saint Peter. The licentiousness and debauchery of the papal court scandalized people. According to a contemporary chronicler, for example, Pope John XII (955-963), who had secured the papal office at the age of eighteen, wore himself out from sexual excesses before he was twenty-eight. Such conditions weakened the religious prestige and moral authority of the pope.

At the local parish level there were many married priests. Taking Christ as the model for the priestly life, the Roman church had always encouraged clerical celibacy, and it had been an obligation for ordination since the fourth century. But in the tenth and eleventh

POPE LEO IX *Called the "founder of the medieval papal monarchy," Leo IX stood for the ideal of the papacy as a moral force throughout Europe. A strong supporter of the Cluniac reform movement, Leo is portrayed here blessing an abbey church. (Burgerbibliothek, Bern. Cod. 292, fol. 73)*

centuries, probably a majority of the priests of Europe were married or living with a woman. Such priests were called Nicolaites from a reference in the Book of Revelation to early Christians who advocated a return to pagan sexual practices.

Several factors may account for the uncelibate state of the clergy. The explanation may lie in the basic need for warmth and human companionship. Perhaps village priests could not survive economically on their small sala-

ries and needed the help of a mate. Perhaps the tradition of a married clergy was so deeprooted by the tenth century that each generation simply followed the example of its predecessor. In any case, the disparity between the law and the reality shocked people in the lay community and bred disrespect for the clergy.

Serious efforts at reform began under Pope Leo IX (1049-1054). Not only was Leo related to Emperor Henry III but, as bishop of Toul and a German, he was also an outsider who owed nothing to any Roman faction. Leo traveled widely and held councils at Pavia, Reims, and Mainz that issued decrees against simony, Nicolaism, and violence. Leo's representatives held church councils across Europe, pressing for moral reform. They urged individuals who could not secure justice at home to appeal to the pope, the ultimate source of justice.

Leo himself was a man of deep humility and great pastoral zeal. By his character and his actions, he set high moral standards for the West. The reform of the papacy had legal as well as moral aspects. During Leo's pontificate a new collection of ecclesiastical law was prepared – the Collection of 74 Titles. Based on letters of popes and the decrees of councils, the Collection of 74 Titles laid great emphasis on papal authority. The substance of the Collection was to stress the rights, the legal position, and the supreme spiritual prerogatives of the bishop of Rome as the successor of Saint Peter.

Papal reform continued after Leo IX. In the short reign of Nicholas II (1058-1061), a council held in the ancient church of St. John Lateran in 1059 reached a momentous decision. A new method was devised for electing the pope. Since the eighth century the priests of the major churches in and around Rome had constituted a special group, called a college, that advised the pope when he summoned them to meetings. These chief priests were called cardinals from the Latin word *cardo,* meaning "hinge." The cardinals were the hinges on which the church turned. The Lateran Synod of 1059 decreed that the authority and power to elect the pope rested solely in this college of cardinals. The college retains that power today.

The object of the decree was to remove this crucial decision from the secular squabbling of Roman aristocratic factions. When the office of pope was vacant, the cardinals were responsible for the government of the church. (In the Middle Ages the college of cardinals numbered around twenty-five or thirty, most of them from Italy. In 1586, the figure was set at seventy. In the 1960s, Pope Paul VI virtually doubled that number, appointing men from the remotest parts of the globe to reflect the international character of the church.) By 1073, the progress of reform in the Christian church was well advanced. The election of Cardinal Hildebrand as Pope Gregory VII changed the direction of reform from a moral to a political one.

THE GREGORIAN REVOLUTION

The papal reform movement of the eleventh century is frequently called the Gregorian reform movement, after Pope Gregory VII. The label is not accurate, in that reform began long before Gregory's pontificate and continued after it. Gregory's reign did, however, inaugurate a radical or revolutionary phase that had important political and social consequences.

In contrast to his predecessors and successors in the eleventh century, Cardinal Hildebrand – who took the name Gregory when he was elected pope – was not of aristocratic descent but the son of poor Tuscan peasants. Some historians have argued that his bitter clash with the German emperor Henry IV was the result of a lowborn upstart's desire to humble the chief secular power in Europe. This idea is intriguing, if not thoroughly convincing. Gregory's education probably had more influence on his mature attitudes than his social origins did. He received a good education at Rome and spent some time at Cluny, where his strict views of clerical life were strengthened. Hildebrand had served in the papal secretariat under Leo IX, and after 1065 was probably the chief influence there.

Hildebrand was dogmatic, inflexible, and unalterably convinced of the truth of his own views. He believed that the pope, as the successor of Saint Peter, was the Vicar of God on earth and that papal orders were the orders of God. His ideas of kingship were even more notorious – and threatening – to his contemporaries. In a Christian society, he believed, the king was responsible for providing peace and order so that Christians could pursue their pilgrimage to the City of God.

The king was obliged to act righteously. If he did not, he was a tyrant, to whom *no one* owed allegiance. Who was to decide if a ruler was a tyrant? The pope, as the Vicar of God, would make that decision and, Hildebrand maintained, could release subjects from their duty of obedience. This had been the Christian view of kingship since the time of Saint Augustine. But Hildebrand wanted to put the theory into practice, and in that respect he was very much a radical.

Once Hildebrand became pope, the reform of the papacy took on a new dimension. Its goal was not just the moral regeneration of the clergy and centralization of the church under papal authority. Gregory and his assistants began to insist upon "the freedom of the church." By this they meant the freedom of all churchmen to obey the newly codified canon law, and freedom from control and interference by laymen.

"Freedom of the church" pointed to the end of lay investiture – the selection and appointment of church officials by secular authority. Ecclesiastical opposition to lay investiture was not new in the eleventh century. It too had been part of church theory for centuries. But Gregory's attempt to put theory into practice was a radical departure from tradition. Since feudal monarchs depended upon churchmen for the operation of their governments, Gregory's program seemed to spell disaster for stable royal administration. It provoked a terrible crisis.

THE CONTROVERSY OVER LAY INVESTITURE

In February 1075, Pope Gregory held a council at Rome. It published decrees not only against Nicolaism and simony but also, for the first time, against lay investiture:

If anyone henceforth shall receive a bishopric or abbey from the hands of a lay person, he shall not be considered as among the number of bishops and abbots.... Likewise if any emperor, king ... or any one at all of the secular powers, shall presume to perform investiture with bishoprics or with any other ecclesiastical dignity ... he shall feel the divine displeasure as well with regard to his body as to his other belongings.[9]

In short, clerics who accepted investiture

from laymen were to be deposed, and laymen who invested clerics were to be excommunicated (cut off from contact with other Christians).

The church's penalty of excommunication relied for its effectiveness on public opinion. Since most Europeans favored Gregory's moral reforms, he believed that excommunication would compel rulers to abide by his changes. Immediately, however, Henry IV in the German Empire, William the Conqueror in England, and Philip I in France protested.

The strongest reaction came from Germany. Henry IV had strongly supported the moral aspects of church reform within the empire. In fact, they would not have achieved much success without his support. But of all the countries of Europe, the Holy Roman Empire most depended upon the services of churchmen. Governing a vast territory of half Christianized and half pagan peoples, the emperor relied heavily upon the assistance of churchmen. His fledgling bureaucracy could not survive without the literacy and administrative knowhow of bishops and abbots. Naturally, then, he had selected and invested most of them.

Over and beyond the subject of lay investiture, however, a more fundamental issue was at stake. Gregory's decree raised the question of the proper role of the monarch in a Christian society. Did a king have ultimate jurisdiction over all his subjects, including the clergy? For centuries tradition had answered this question in favor of the ruler; so it is no wonder that Henry vigorously protested the papal assertions about lay investiture. By implication they undermined imperial power and sought to make papal authority supreme.

An increasingly bitter exchange of letters ensued. Gregory accused Henry of lack of respect for the papacy and insisted that disobedience to the pope was disobedience to God. Henry protested in a now-famous letter beginning, "Henry King not by usurpation, but by the pious ordination of God, to Hildebrand, now not Pope, but false monk."

Within the empire, those who had most to gain from the dispute quickly took advantage of it. In January 1076, in the southwestern German city of Worms on the Rhine, the German bishops who had been invested by Henry withdrew their allegiance from the pope. Gregory replied by excommunicating them and the emperor. The lay nobility delighted in the bind the emperor had been placed in: with Henry IV excommunicated and cast outside the fold of the Christian faithful, they did not have to obey him and could advance their own interests. Gregory hastened to support them. The Christmas season of 1075 witnessed an ironic situation within Germany: the greater clergy supported the emperor, while the great nobility favored the pope.

Henry outwitted Gregory. Crossing the Alps in January, he approached the pope's residence at Canossa in northern Italy. According to legend, Henry stood for three days in the snow seeking forgiveness. As a priest, Pope Gregory was obliged to grant absolution and to readmit the emperor to the Christian community. Henry's going to Canossa is often described as the most dramatic incident in the High Middle Ages. Some historians claim that it marked the peak of papal power because the most powerful ruler in Europe, the Holy Roman emperor, had bowed before the pope. Actually, Henry scored a temporary victory. When the sentence of excommunication was lifted, Henry regained the kingship and his authority over his rebellious subjects. But in the long run, in Germany and elsewhere, secular rulers were reluctant to pose a

TWELFTH-CENTURY ROMANESQUE CROZIER
This ivory crozier or staff (a reproduction) shows Saint John baptizing Christ in the Jordan River, while the Holy Spirit in the form of a dove descends and God the Father blesses the event. Old Testament prophets with scrolls surround the head of the crozier. (Courtesy, World Heritage Museum. Photo: Caroline Buckler)

serious challenge to the papacy for the next two hundred years.

For the German empire the incident at Canossa settled nothing. The controversy over lay investiture and the position of the king in Christian society continued. In 1080 Gregory VII again excommunicated and deposed the emperor, but this time it appeared to public opinion that Henry was being persecuted. The papal edicts had little effect. Moreover, Henry invaded Italy, captured Rome, and controlled the city when Gregory died in exile in 1085. But Henry won no lasting victory. Gregory's successors encouraged Henry's sons to revolt against their father. With lay investiture the ostensible issue, the conflict between the papacy and the successors of Henry IV continued into the twelfth century.

The kings of England and France were just as guilty of lay investiture as the German emperor. William the Conqueror (1066-1087) ignored papal decrees against the practice. He selected bishops and counted them among his most important tenants-in-chief. He presided over church councils and refused to allow papal letters or legates into England without his permission. He did, though, work to achieve in England the moral goals of reform. Under the Conqueror's sons William Rufus and Henry I, however, disagreement with the popes over lay investiture was long and violent.

Philip I (1060-1108) of France also quarreled with Gregory, but the subject of their dispute was more Philip's adulterous marriage than lay investiture. Philip enjoyed the profits he received from the sale of church offices. And he probably thought that a church independent of royal control would be a real threat to the French monarchy. Rome's conflict with the western rulers never reached the proportions of the dispute with the German emperor. Gregory VII and his successors had the diplomatic sense to avoid creating three enemies at once.

A long and exhausting propaganda campaign followed the confrontation at Canossa. Finally, in 1122, at a conference held at Worms, the issue was settled by compromise. The terms, as it happened, were the same as those agreed on by the papacy and the English king Henry I in 1107. Bishops were to be chosen according to canon law — that is, by the clergy — in the presence of the emperor or his delegate. The emperor surrendered the

right of investing bishops with the ring and staff. But, since lay rulers were permitted to be present at ecclesiastical elections and to accept or refuse feudal homage from the new prelates, they still possessed an effective veto over ecclesiastical appointments. At the same time, the papacy achieved technical success, because rulers could no longer invest. Papal power was enhanced. Thus neither side won a clear victory. The real winners in Germany were the great princes and the lay aristocracy.

The long controversy had tremendous social and political consequences in Germany. For half a century, between 1075 and 1125, civil war was chronic within the empire. Preoccupied with Italy and the quarrel with the papacy, emperors could do little about it. To control their lands, great lords built castles, symbolizing their increased power and growing independence. (In no European country do more castles survive today.) The castles were both military strongholds and centers of administration for the surrounding territories. The German aristocracy subordinated the knights and reinforced their dependency with strong feudal ties. They reduced freemen and serfs to an extremely humble and servile position. Henry IV and Henry V were compelled to surrender rights and privileges to the nobility. Particularism, localism, and feudal independence characterized the Holy Roman Empire in the High Middle Ages. The investiture controversy had a catastrophic effect there, severely retarding the development of a strong centralized monarchy.

THE PAPACY IN THE HIGH MIDDLE AGES

In the late eleventh century and throughout the twelfth, the papacy pressed Gregory's campaign for reform of the church. Pope

Urban II laid the real foundations for the papal monarchy by reorganizing the central government of the Roman church, the papal writing office (the chancery) and papal finances. He recognized the college of cardinals as a definite consultative body. These agencies, together with the papal chapel, constituted the papal court, or curia – the papacy's administrative bureaucracy and its court of law. The papal curia, although not fully developed until the mid-twelfth century, was the first well-organized institution of monarchial authority in medieval Europe.

The Roman curia had its greatest impact as a court of law. As the highest ecclesiastical tribunal, it formulated canon law for all of Christendom. It was the instrument with which the popes pressed the goals of reform and centralized the church. The curia sent legates to hold councils in various parts of Europe. Councils published decrees and sought to enforce the law. When individuals in any part of Christian Europe felt they were being denied justice in their local church courts, they could appeal to Rome. Slowly but surely, in the High Middle Ages the papal curia developed into the court of final appeal for all of Christian Europe.

In the course of the twelfth century, appeals to the curia steadily increased. The majority of cases related to disputes over church property or ecclesiastical elections and above all to questions of marriage and annulment. Significantly, most of the popes in the twelfth and thirteenth centuries were themselves canon lawyers. The most famous of them, the man whose pontificate represented the height of medieval papal power, was Innocent III (1198–1216).

Innocent judged a vast number of cases. He compelled King Philip Augustus of France to take back his wife, Ingeborg of Denmark. He arbitrated the rival claims of two disputants to the imperial crown of Germany. He forced King John of England to accept as archbishop of Canterbury a man whom John did not really want. Innocent exerted papal authority in the Iberian Peninsula, in Norway and Sweden, in the Balkans, and even in distant Cyprus and Armenia.

By the early thirteenth century, papal efforts at reform begun more than a century before had attained phenomenal success. The popes themselves were men of high principles and strict moral behavior. The frequency of clerical marriage had declined considerably. The level of violence had dropped sharply. Simony was much more the exception than the rule. The church enjoyed a huge success in most places and provided leadership for Christian Europe.

Yet the seeds of future difficulties were being planted. As the volume of appeals to Rome multiplied, so did the size of papal bureaucracy. As the number of lawyers increased, so did concern for legal niceties and technicalities, fees, and church offices. As early as the mid-twelfth century, John of Salisbury, an Englishman working in the papal curia, had written a blistering critique of the expanding curial bureaucracy. The people, he wrote, condemned the curia for its greed and indifference to human suffering. Nevertheless, the trend continued.

Thirteenth-century popes, a long series of canon lawyers, devoted their attention to the bureaucracy and to their conflicts with the German emperor Frederick II. Some, like Gregory IX (1227–1241), abused their prerogatives to such an extent that their moral impact was seriously weakened. Even worse, Innocent IV (1243–1254) used secular weapons, including military force, to maintain his leadership. These popes badly damaged papal prestige and influence. By the early fourteenth century, the seeds of disorder would grow into a vast and sprawling tree, and once again cries for reform would be heard.

———◆———

The end of the great invasions signaled the beginning of profound changes in European society – economic, social, political, and ecclesiastical. In the year 1000, having enough to eat was the rare privilege of a few noblemen, priests, and monks. In the course of the eleventh century, however, manorial communities slowly improved their agricultural equipment; this advance, aided by warmer weather, meant more food and increasing population. Surplus population on the land led to the growth of old towns and the foundation of new ones. Towns and cities represented an entirely new social class, new opportunities, and a more sophisticated way of life.

In the eleventh century, also, rulers and local authorities gradually imposed some degree of order within their territories. Peace and domestic security, vigorously pushed by the church, meant larger crops for the peasants and improved trading conditions for the townspeople. The church overthrew the domination of lay influences, and the spread of the Cluniac and the Cistercian orders marked the ascendancy of monasticism. Having put its own house in order, the Roman papacy in the twelfth and thirteenth centuries built the first strong governmental bureaucracy. In the High Middle Ages the church exercised general leadership of European society.

NOTES

1. Quoted by R. S. Lopez, "Of Towns and Trade," in *Life and Thought in the Early Middle Ages,* ed. R.

S. Hoyt, University of Minnesota Press, Minneapolis, 1967, p. 33.

2. H. Pirenne, *Economic and Social History of Medieval Europe,* Harcourt Brace, New York, 1956, p. 53.

3. Quoted by Julia O'Faolain and Lauro Martines, eds., *Not In God's Image: Women in History from the Greeks to the Victorians,* Harper & Row, New York, 1973, pp. 155-156.

4. D. Douglas and G. W. Greenaway, eds., *English Historical Documents,* Eyre & Spottiswoode, London, 1961, 2.969.

5. H. Rothwell, ed., *English Historical Documents,* Eyre & Spottiswoode, London, 1975, 3.854.

6. Douglas and Greenaway, 2.956-961.

7. M. M. Postan, *The Medieval Economy and Society: An Economic History of Britain in the Middle Ages,* Penguin Books, Baltimore, 1975, pp. 213-214.

8. R. S. Lopez, "The Trade of Medieval Europe: The South," in *The Cambridge Economic History of Europe,* ed. M. M. Postan and E. E. Rich, Cambridge University Press, Cambridge, 1952, 2.289.

9. B. D. Hill, ed., *Church and State in the Middle Ages,* John Wiley & Sons, New York, 1970, p. 68.

SUGGESTED READING

In addition to the references in the Notes, the curious student will find a fuller treatment of many of the topics raised in this chapter in the following works.

Both C. D. Burns, *The First Europe* (1948), and G. Barraclough, *The Crucible of Europe: The Ninth and Tenth Centuries in European History* (1976), survey the entire period and emphasize the transformation from a time of anarchy to one of great creativity; Barraclough also stresses the importance of stable government. His *The Origins of Modern Germany* (1963) is essential for central and eastern Europe. For the social significance of the peace movements, see H. E. J. Cowdray, "The Peace and the Truce of God in the Eleventh Century," *Past and Present* 46 (1970): 42-67.

For economic and social history, see Gerald A. J.

Hodgett, *A Social and Economic History of Medieval Europe* (1974), a broad survey, and Carlo M. Cipolla, *Before the Industrial Revolution: European Society and Economy, 1000–1700* (1980), which draws on a wealth of recent research to treat demographic shifts, technological change, and business practices. The effect of climate on population and economic growth is discussed in the remarkable work of E. L. Ladurie, *Times of Feast, Times of Famine: A History of Climate since the Year 1000,* trans. B. Bray (1971). A masterful account of agricultural changes and their sociological implications is to be found in G. Duby, *The Early Growth of the European Economy: Warriors and Peasants from the Seventh to the Twelfth Centuries* (1978).

Students interested in the origins of medieval towns and cities will learn how historians use the evidence of coins, archeology, tax records, geography, and laws in J. F. Benton, ed., *Town Origins: The Evidence of Medieval England* (1968). H. Pirenne, *Medieval Cities* (1956), is an important and standard work, which concentrates on the Low Countries. H. Saalman, *Medieval Cities* (1968), gives a fresh description of the layouts of medieval cities, with an emphasis on Germany, and shows how they were places of production and exchange. Colin Platt's well-illustrated *The English Medieval Town* (1979) makes excellent use of archeological evidence and contains detailed information on the wool and cloth trades. Richard Muir, *The English Village* (1980), offers a broad survey of many aspects of the daily lives of ordinary people. For readability, few works surpass J. and F. Gies, *Life in a Medieval City* (1973).

For the Christian church, the papacy, and ecclesiastical developments, G. Barraclough's richly illustrated *The Medieval Papacy* (1968) is a good general survey that emphasizes the development of administrative bureaucracy. The advanced student may tackle W. Ullmann, *A Short History of the Papacy in the Middle Ages* (1972). S. Williams, ed., *The Gregorian Epoch: Reformation, Revolution, Reaction?* (1964), contains significant interpretations of the eleventh-century reform movements. Ullmann's *The Growth of Papal Government in the Middle Ages,* rev. ed. (1970) traces the evolution of papal law and government. G. Tellenbach, *Church, State, and Christian Society at the Time of the Investiture Contest* (1959), emphasizes the revolutionary aspects of the Gregorian reform program. The relationship of the monks to the ecclesiastical crisis of the late eleventh century is discussed by N. F. Cantor, "The Crisis of Western Monasticism," *American Historical Review* 66 (1960), and by H. E. J. Cowdray, *The Cluniacs and the Gregorian Reform* (1970), an impressive but difficult study. J. B. Russell, *A History of Medieval Christianity: Prophecy and Order* (1968), is an important and sensitively written work.

CHAPTER 10

LIFE IN CHRISTIAN EUROPE IN THE HIGH MIDDLE AGES

THE REVIVAL OF TRADE and commerce in the eleventh century brought into being a new class of merchants and businessmen. However, traders and other city dwellers were not typical of medieval society. They may have represented the wave of the future, but in the twelfth century that future was far in the distance. Some historians, trying to show the links between medieval and modern urban society, have concentrated their attention on the medieval commercial classes. In doing so, they have presented a distorted and anachronistic picture of medieval society. Other scholars have painted medieval society as static and unchanging. This picture also is inaccurate, because there was a good deal of movement, change, and migration.

In his biography of the Anglo-Saxon king Alfred, the tenth-century monk Asser described Christian society as composed of those who pray (the monks), those who fight (the nobles), and those who work (the peasants). This description, which was widely accepted and frequently repeated by other writers in the High Middle Ages, set forth the basic social composition of the medieval world. It does not take into consideration the emerging commercial classes. But medieval people were usually contemptuous (at least officially) of profit-making activities, and long after the appearance of commercial and urban groups, the general medieval view of Christian society remained the one formulated by Asser in the tenth century.

The most representative figures of Christian society in the High Middle Ages were peasants, monks, and nobles. How did these people actually live? What were their preoccupations and lifestyles? To what extent was social mobility possible for them? These are some of the questions this chapter seeks to answer.

THOSE WHO WORK

The largest and economically most productive group in medieval European society was the peasants. The men and women who worked the land in the twelfth and thirteenth centuries made up the overwhelming majority of the population, probably more than 90 percent. Yet it is difficult to form a coherent picture of them. The records that serve as historical sources were written by and for the aristocratic classes. Since farmers did not perform what were considered "noble" deeds, the aristocratic monks and clerics did not waste time or precious paper and ink on them. When peasants were mentioned, it was usually with contempt or in terms of the services and obligations they owed.

Usually – but not always. In the early twelfth century, Honorius, a monk and teacher at Autun who composed a popular handbook of sermons, wrote: "What do you say about the agricultural classes? Most of them will be saved because they live simply and feed God's people by means of their sweat."[1] This sentiment circulated widely. Honorius's comment suggests that peasant workers may have been appreciated and in a sense respected more than is generally believed.

In the last twenty-five years, historians have made remarkable advances in their knowledge of the medieval European peasantry. They have been able to do so by bringing fresh and different questions to old documents, by paying greater attention to such natural factors as geography and climate, and by studying demographic changes. Nevertheless, this new information raises additional questions, and a good deal remains unknown.

In 1932, a distinguished economic historian

wrote, "The student of medieval social and economic history who commits himself to a generalization is digging a pit into which he will later assuredly fall and nowhere does the pit yawn deeper than in the realm of rural history."[2] This remark is virtually as true today as when it was written. It is, therefore, important to remember that peasants' conditions varied widely across Europe, that geographical and climatic features as much as human initiative and local custom determined the peculiar quality of rural life. The problems that faced the farmer in Yorkshire, England, where the soil was rocky and the climate rainy, were very different from those of the Italian peasant in the sun-drenched Po valley.

Another difficulty has been historians' tendency to group all peasants into one social class. That is a serious mistake. It is true that medieval theologians simply lumped everyone who worked the land into the category of "those who work." In actual fact, however, there were many gradations, classes, and levels of peasants, ranging all the way from complete slaves to free and very rich farmers. The period from 1050 to 1250 was one of considerable fluidity with no little social mobility. The status of the peasantry varied widely all across Europe.

SLAVERY, SERFDOM, AND UPWARD MOBILITY

Slaves were found in western Europe in the High Middle Ages, but in steadily declining numbers. That the word *slave* derives from "Slav" attests to the widespread trade in men and women from the Slavic areas in the early Middle Ages. Around the year 1200, there were in aristocratic and upper-middle-class households in Provence, Catalonia, Italy, and Germany a few slaves – blond Slavs from the Baltic, olive-skinned Syrians, and blacks from Africa.

Since ancient times, it had been a universally accepted practice to reduce conquered peoples to slavery. The church had long taught that all baptized Christians were brothers in Christ and that all Christians belonged to one "international" community. Although the church never issued a blanket condemnation of slavery, it did vigorously oppose the enslaving of Christians. In attacking the enslavement of Christians and in criticizing the reduction of pagans and infidels to slavery, the church made a contribution to the development of human liberty.

In western Europe during the Middle Ages legal language differed considerably from place to place, and the distinction between slave and serf was not always clear. Both lacked freedom – the power to do as one wished – and were subject to the arbitrary will of one man, the lord. A serf, however, could not be bought and sold like an animal or an inanimate object, as the slave could.

The serf was required to perform labor services on the lord's land. The number of workdays varied but it was usually three days a week, except in the planting or harvest seasons, when it would be more. Serfs frequently had to pay arbitrary taxes. When a man married, he had to pay his lord a fee. When he died, his son or heir had to pay an inheritance tax to inherit his parcels of land. The precise amounts of tax paid to the lord on these important occasions depended upon local custom and tradition. Every manor had its particular obligations. A free person had to do none of these things. For his or her landholding, rent had to be paid to the lord, and that was often the sole obligation. A free person could move and live as he or she wished.

Serfs were tied to the land, and serfdom was a hereditary condition. A person born a serf was likely to die a serf, though many did secure their freedom. About 1187, Glanvill, an official of King Henry II and an expert on English law, described how villeins (literally, inhabitants of small villages) – as English serfs were called – could be made free:

A person of villein status can be made free in several ways. For example, his lord, wishing him to achieve freedom from the villeinage by which he is subject to him, may quit-claim him from himself and his heirs; or he may give or sell him to another with intent to free him. It should be noted, however, that no person of villein status can seek his freedom with his own money, for in such a case he could, according to the law and custom of the realm, be recalled to villeinage by his lord, because all the chattels of a villein are deemed to such an extent the property of his lord that he cannot redeem himself from villeinage with his own money, as against his lord. If, however, a third party pro-

vides the money and buys the villein in order to free him, then he can maintain himself for ever in a state of freedom as against his lord who sold him. . . . If any villein stays peaceably for a year and a day in a privileged town and is admitted as a citizen into their commune, that is to say, their gild, he is thereby freed from villeinage.[3]

Many energetic and hardworking serfs acquired their freedom in the High Middle Ages. More than anything else, the economic revival that began in the eleventh century advanced the cause of individual liberty. The revival saw the rise of towns, increased land productivity, the growth of long-distance trade, and the development of a money economy. With the advent of a money economy, serfs could save money and buy their freedom.

Another opportunity for increased personal freedom, or at least for a reduction in traditional manorial obligations and dues, was provided by the reclamation of waste and forest land in the eleventh and twelfth centuries. Resettlement on newly cleared land offered unusual possibilities for younger sons and for those living in areas of acute land shortage or on overworked, exhausted soil. Historians still do not know very much about this movement: how the new frontier territory was advertised, how men were recruited, how they and their households were transported, and how the new lands were distributed. It is certain, however, that there was significant migration and that only a lord with considerable authority over a wide territory could sponsor such a movement. Great lords supported the fight against the marshes of northern and eastern Germany and against the sea in the Low Countries.

As land long considered poor was brought under cultivation, there was a steady nibbling away at the wasteland on the edges of old vil-lages. Clearings were made in forests. Marshes and fens were drained and slowly made arable. This type of agricultural advancement frequently improved the peasants' social and legal condition. A serf could clear a patch of fen or forest land, make it productive, and, through prudent saving, buy more land and eventually purchase his freedom. There were in the thirteenth century many free tenants on the lands of the bishop of Ely in eastern England, tenants who had moved into the area in the twelfth century and drained the fens. Likewise, settlers on the low lands of the abbey of Bourbourg in Flanders, who had erected dikes and extended the arable lands, possessed hereditary tenures by 1159. They secured personal liberty and owed their overlord only small payments.

Peasants who remained in the villages of their birth often benefited because landlords, threatened with the loss of serfs, relaxed ancient obligations and duties. While it would be unwise to exaggerate the social impact of the settling of new territories, frontier lands in the Middle Ages did provide opportunities for upward mobility.

THE MANOR

In the High Middle Ages, most European peasants, free and unfree, lived on estates called manors. The word *manor* derives from a Latin term meaning "dwelling," "residence," or "homestead." In the twelfth century it meant the estate of a lord and his dependent tenants.

The manor was the basic unit of medieval rural organization and the center of rural life. All other generalizations about manors and manorial life have to be limited by variations in the quality of the soil, local climatic conditions, and methods of cultivation. Some

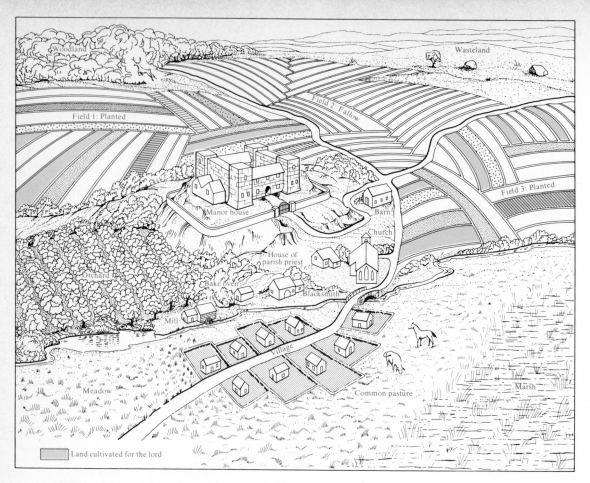

FIGURE 10.1 A MEDIEVAL MANOR *The basic unit of rural organization and the center of life for most people, the manor constituted the medieval peasants' world. Since manors had to be economically self-sufficient, life meant endless toil.*

manors were vast, covering several thousand acres of farmland; others were no larger than 120 acres. A manor might include several villages or none at all, but usually it contained a single village and was subject to one lord (see Figure 10.1).

The arable land of the manor was divided into two sections. The demesne, or home farm, was cultivated for the lord. The other part was held by the peasantry. Usually, the peasants' portion was larger, held on condition that they cultivate the lord's demesne. All the arable, both the lord's and the peasants',

was divided into strips, and the strips belonging to any given individual were scattered throughout the manor. All peasants cooperated in the cultivation of the land, working it as a group. This meant that all shared in any disaster as well as any large harvest.

A manor usually held pasture or meadowland for the grazing of cattle, sheep, and sometimes goats. Often the manor had some forest land as well. Forests had enormous economic importance: they were the source of wood for building and resin for lighting; ash for candles, and ash and lime for fertilizers and all sorts of sterilizing products; wood for fuel and bark for the manufacture of rope. From the forests came wood for the construction of barrels, vats, and all sorts of storage containers. Last but hardly least, the forests were used for the feeding of pigs, cattle, and domestic animals on nuts, roots, and wild berries. If the manor was intersected by a river, it had a welcome source of fish and eels.

Agricultural Methods

The fundamental objective of all medieval agriculture was the production of an adequate food supply. According to the method historians have called the open-field system, at any one time half the manorial land was under cultivation and the other half lay fallow; the length of the fallow period was usually one year. Every peasant farmer had strips scattered in both halves. One part of the land under cultivation was sown with winter cereals, such as wheat and rye, the other with spring crops, such as peas, beans, and barley. What was planted in a particular field varied each year when the crops were rotated.

Local needs, the fertility of the soil, and dietary customs determined what was planted and the method of crop rotation. Where one or several manors belonged to a great aristocratic establishment, such as the abbey of Cluny, which needed large quantities of oats for horses, more of the arable land would be planted in oats than in other cereals. Where the land was extremely fertile, such as the Alsace region of France, a biennial cycle was used: one crop of wheat was sown and harvested every other year, and in alternate years all the land lay fallow. The author of an English agricultural treatise advised his readers to stick to a two-field method of cultivation and insisted that a rich harvest every second year was preferable to two mediocre ones every three years. Farmers everywhere obviously sought to use the land in the most productive way and to get the greatest output.

Nor were they ignorant of the value of animal fertilizers. Chicken manure, because of its high nitrogen content, was the richest but limited in quantity. Sheep manure was also valuable. Gifts to English Cistercian monasteries were frequently given on condition that the monks' sheep be allowed to graze at certain periods on the benefactor's demesne. Because cattle were fed on the common pasture and were rarely stabled, gathering their manure was laborious and time-consuming. Nevertheless, whenever possible, animal manure was gathered and thinly spread. So also was house garbage — eggshells, fruit cores, onion skins — that had disintegrated on a compost heap.

Tools and farm implements are often shown in medieval manuscripts. But accepting such representations at face value is misleading. Rather than going out into a field to look at a tool, medieval artists simply copied drawings from classical and other treatises. Thus a plow or harrow pictured in a book written in the Ile-de-France may actually have been used in England or Italy a half century before.

In the early twelfth century the production of iron increased greatly. There is considerable evidence for the manufacture of iron plowshares (the part of the plow that cuts the furrow into and grinds up the earth). In the thirteenth century the wooden plow continued to be the basic instrument of agricultural production, but its edge was strengthened with iron. Only after the start of the fourteenth century, when lists of manorial equipment began to be kept, is there evidence for pitchforks, spades, axes, and harrows. Harrows were used to smooth out the soil after it had been broken up. A crude harrow appears

LATE MEDIEVAL WHEELLESS PLOW   This plow has a sharp-pointed colter, which cut the earth while the attached mold-board lifted, turned, and pulverized the soil. As the man steers the plow, his wife prods the oxen. The caption reads, "God speed the plow, and send us corn (wheat) now." (Trinity College Library, Cambridge)

in the illustration for the month of October in the *Très riches heures du duc de Berry,* completed in the mid-fifteenth century. The harrow is made of wood and weighted down with a large stone to force it to cut more deeply into the earth.

The harrow was drawn by horses. The use of horses rather than oxen in the agricultural economy increased in the later thirteenth century. Horses were a large investment, perhaps comparable to a modern tractor. They had to be shod (another indication of increased iron production) and the oats they ate were costly. But horses represented an important element in the improvement of the medieval agricultural economy. Because of their greater strength, horses brought far greater efficiency to farming than oxen. Indeed, some scholars believe that the use of the horse in agriculture is one of the decisive ways in which western Europe advanced over the rest of the world. But horses were not universally adopted. The Mediterranean countries, for example, did not use horsepower. And, at the same time, tools remained pitifully primitive.

Agricultural yields varied widely from place to place and from year to year. Even with good iron tools, horsepower, and careful use of seed and fertilizer, medieval peasants were at the mercy of the weather. Even today, lack of rain or too much rain can cause terrible financial loss and extreme hardship. How much more vulnerable was the medieval peasant with his primitive tools! By twentieth-century standards medieval agricultural yields were very low. The inadequate preparation of the soil, the poor selection of seed, the lack of sufficient manure – all made this virtually inevitable.

Yet there was striking improvement over time. Between the ninth and early thirteenth centuries, it appears that yields of cereals approximately doubled, and that on the best-managed estates, for every bushel of seed planted, the farmer harvested five bushels of grain. This is a very tentative conclusion. Because of the great scarcity of manorial inventories before the thirteenth century, the student of medieval agriculture has great difficulty determining how much the land produced. The author of a treatise on land husbandry, Walter of Henley, who lived in the mid-thirteenth century, wrote that the land should yield three times its seed; that amount was necessary for sheer survival. The surplus would be sold to grain merchants in the nearest town. Townspeople were wholly dependent on the surrounding countryside for food, which could not be shipped a long distance. A poor harvest meant that both town and rural people suffered.

Grain yields were probably greatest on the large manorial estates, where there was more professional management. For example, the estates of Battle Abbey in Sussex, England, enjoyed a very high yield of wheat, rye, and oats in the century and a half between 1350 and 1499. This was due to heavy seeding, good crop rotation, and the use of manure from the monastery's sheep flocks. Battle Abbey's yields seem to have been double those of smaller, less efficiently run farms. A modern Illinois farmer expects to get 40 bushels of soybeans, 150 bushels of corn, and 50 bushels of wheat for every bushel of seeds planted. Of course, modern costs of production in labor, seed, and fertilizer are quite high, but this yield is at least ten times that of the farmer's medieval ancestor. The average manor probably got a yield of 5:1 in the thirteenth century.[4] As low as that may seem by current standards, it marked a rise in the level of productivity equal to that of the years just before the great agricultural revolution of the eighteenth century.

LIFE ON THE MANOR

Life for most people in medieval Europe meant country life. A person's horizons were largely restricted to the manor on which he or she was born. People rarely traveled more than twenty-five miles beyond their villages. Everyone's world was small, narrow, and provincial in the original sense of the word: limited by the boundaries of the province. This way of life did not have entirely unfortunate results. A farmer had a strong sense of family and the certainty of its support and help in time of trouble. People knew what their life's work would be – the same as their mother's or father's. They had a sense of place, and pride in that place was reflected in adornment of the village church. Religion and the village gave people a sure sense of identity and with it psychological peace. Modern people – urban, isolated, industrialized, rootless, and thoroughly secular – have lost many of these reinforcements.

On the other hand, even aside from the unending physical labor, life on the manor was dull. Medieval men and women must have had a crushing sense of frustration. They lived lives of quiet desperation. Often they sought escape in heavy drinking. English judicial records of the thirteenth century reveal

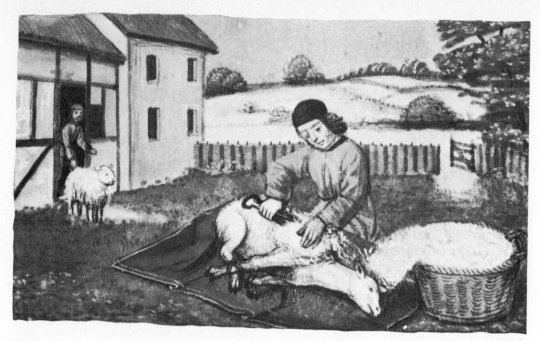

SHEEPSHEARING   *After the sheep was tied up, the farmer clipped the wool and bagged it. English wool was internationally famous for its fine quality, and the English and the Flemish economies depended upon the wool trade. (The British Museum)*

a surprisingly large number of "accidental" deaths. Strong, robust, and commonsensical farmers do not ordinarily fall down on their knives and stab themselves, or slip out of a boat and drown, or get lost in the woods on a winter's night, or fall from their horses and get trampled. They were probably drunk. Many of these accidents occurred, as the court records say, "coming from an ale." Brawls and violent fights were frequent at taverns. They reflect in part the drudgery of life and simple human frustration.

Women played a significant role in the agricultural life of medieval Europe. This obvious fact is often overlooked by historians. Women shared with their fathers and husbands the backbreaking labor in the fields, work that was probably all the more difficult for them because of weaker muscular development and frequent pregnancies. The adage from the Book of Proverbs – "Houses and riches are the inheritances of fathers: but a prudent wife is from the Lord" – was seldom more true than in an age when the wife's prudent management was often all that separated a household from starvation in a year of crisis. And starvation was a very real danger to the peasantry until the eighteenth century.

Women managed the house. The size and quality of peasants' houses varied according to their relative prosperity, and that prosperity usually depended upon the amount of land held. Poorer peasants lived in windowless cottages built of wood and clay or wattle and thatched with straw. These cottages consisted of one large room that served as the kitchen and living quarters for all. Everyone slept there. The house had an earthen floor and a fireplace. The lack of windows meant that the room was very sooty. A trestle table, several stools, one or two beds, and a chest for storing clothes constituted the furniture. A shed attached to the house provided storage for tools and shelter for animals. Prosperous peasants added rooms and furniture as they could be afforded, and some wealthy peasants in the early fourteenth century had two-story houses with separate bedrooms for parents and children.

Every house had a small garden and an outbuilding. Onions, garlic, turnips, and carrots were grown and stored through the winter in the main room of the dwelling or in the shed attached to it. Cabbage was raised almost everywhere and, after being shredded, salted, and packed in vats in hot water, was turned into kraut. Peasants ate vegetables not because they appreciated their importance for good health but because there was usually little else. Some manors had fruit trees – apple, cherry, and pear in northern Europe; lemon, lime, and olive in the south. But because of the high price of sugar, when it was available, fruit could not be preserved. Preserving and storing other foods were the basic responsibility of the women and children.

Women also had to know the correct proportions of barley, water, yeast, and hops to make beer – the universal drink of the common people in northern Europe. By modern American standards the rate of beer consumption was heroic. Each monk of Abingdon Abbey in England in the twelfth century was allotted three gallons a day, and a man working in the fields for ten or twelve hours a day probably drank much more.

The mainstay of the diet for peasants everywhere – and for all other classes – was bread. It was a hard, black substance made of barley, millet, and oats, rarely of expensive wheat flour. The housewife usually baked the supply for the household once a week. Where sheep, cows, or goats were raised, she also made cheese. In places like the Bavarian Alps region of southern Germany, where hundreds of sheep grazed on the mountainsides, or at Cheddar in southwestern England, cheese was a staple of the diet.

The diet of those living in an area with access to a river, lake, or stream would be supplemented with fish, which could be preserved by salting. In many places there were severe laws against hunting and trapping in the forests. Deer, wild boars, and other game were strictly reserved for the king and nobility. These laws were flagrantly violated, however, and stolen rabbits and wild game often found their way to the peasants' tables. Woods and forests also provided nuts, which housewives and small children would gather in the fall.

Lists of peasant obligations and services to the lord, such as the following from a manor in Battle Abbey in England, commonly included the payment of chickens and eggs:

John of Coyworth holds a house and thirty acres of land, and owes yearly 2 p at Easter and Michaelmas; and he owes a cock and two hens at Christmas, of the value of 4 d.[5]

Chickens and eggs must have been highly valued in the prudently managed household. Except for the rare chicken or the illegally caught wild game, meat appeared on the table only on the great feast days of the Christian year: Christmas, Easter, and Pentecost. Then, the meat was likely to be pork from the pig that had been slaughtered in the fall and salted for the rest of the year. Some scholars believe that by the mid-thirteenth century there was a great increase in the consumption of meat generally. If so, this improvement in

WORKING IN THE FIELDS *Women shared with men all the difficult agricultural work. These farm scenes show women hoeing, sowing seed, cutting and tying the grain, and carrying it to the mill. Although the sickles and the spade appear to have an iron tip, the hoe is entirely wooden. (Rheinisches Landesmuseum, Bonn)*

the diet is further evidence of a better standard of living.

Breakfast, eaten at dawn before the farmer departed for his work, might well consist of bread, an onion (easily stored through the winter months), and a piece of cheese, washed down with milk or beer. Farmers then as now ate their main meal around noon. This was often soup – a thick *potage* of boiled cabbage, onions, turnips, and peas, seasoned with a bone or perhaps a sliver of meat. The evening meal, taken at sunset, consisted of leftovers from the noon meal, perhaps with bread, cheese, milk, or beer.

Once children were able to walk, they helped their parents in the hundreds of chores that had to be done. Small children were set to collecting eggs, if the family possessed chickens, or gathering twigs and sticks for firewood. As they grew older, children had more responsible tasks, such as weeding the family vegetable garden, milking the cows, shearing the sheep, cutting wood for fires, helping with the planting or harvesting, and assisting their mothers in the endless tasks of baking, cooking, and preserving. Because of poor diet, terrible sanitation, and lack of medical care, the death rate among children was phenomenally high.

POPULAR RELIGION

Apart from the land and the weather and the peculiar conditions that existed on each manor, the Christian religion had the greatest impact on the daily lives of ordinary people in the High Middle Ages. Religious practices varied widely from country to country and even from province to province. But nowhere was religion a one-hour-on-Sunday or High Holy Days affair. Christian practices and attitudes shaded and permeated virtually all aspects of everyday life.

In the ancient world participation in religious rituals was a public and social duty. As the Germanic and Celtic peoples were Christianized, their new religion became a fusion of Jewish, pagan, Roman, and Christian practices. By the High Middle Ages, religious rituals and practices represented a synthesis of many elements, and all people shared as a natural and public duty in the religious life of the community.

The village church was the center of manorial life — social, political, and economic as well as religious. Most of the important events in a person's life took place in or around the church. A person was baptized there, within hours of birth. Men and women confessed their sins to the village priest there and received, usually at Easter and Christmas, the sacrament of the Eucharist. In front of the church, the bishop reached down from his horse and confirmed a person as a Christian by placing his hands over the candidate's head and making the sign of the cross on the forehead. (Bishops Thomas Becket of Canterbury and Hugh of Lincoln were considered especially holy men because they got down from their horses to confirm.) Young people courted in the churchyard and, so the sermons of the priests complained, made love in the church cemetery. They were married before the altar in the church.

The stone in the church altar contained relics of the saints, often a local saint to whom the church itself had been dedicated. In the church women and men could pray to the Virgin and the local saints. The saints had once lived on earth and thus could well understand human problems. They could be helpful intercessors with Christ or God the Father. According to official church doctrine, the center of the Christian religious life was the mass, the re-enactment of Christ's sacrifice on the cross. Every Sunday and on holy days, the villager stood at mass or squatted on the floor (there were no chairs), breaking the painful routine of work. Finally, people wanted to be buried in the church cemetery, close to the holy place and the saints believed to reside there.

The church was the center of village social life. The feasts that accompanied baptisms, weddings, funerals, and other celebrations were commonly held in the churchyard. Medieval drama originated within the church. Mystery plays, based on biblical episodes, were performed first in the sanctuary, then on the church porch, and finally in the village square, which was often in front of the west door.

From the church porch the priest read to his parishioners orders and messages from royal and ecclesiastical authorities. Royal judges traveling on circuit opened their courts on the church porch. The west front of the

Thirteenth-Century Crucifix Christian teaching in the High Middle Ages stressed the humanity, compassion, and understanding of Christ, as the face of Christ on this richly enamelled crucifix suggests. (Courtesy, World Heritage Museum. Photo: Caroline Buckler)

church, with its scenes of the Last Judgment, was the background against which the justices disposed of civil and criminal cases. Farmers from outlying districts pushed their carts to the marketplace in the village square near the west front. In busy mercantile centers such as London, business agreements and commercial exchanges were made in the aisles of the church itself, as at St. Paul's.

Popular religion consisted largely of rituals heavy with symbolism. Before slicing a loaf of bread, the good wife tapped the sign of the cross on it with her knife. Before the planting, the village priest customarily went out and sprinkled the fields with water, symbolizing refreshment and life. Shortly after a woman had successfully delivered a child, she was "churched." This was a ceremony of thanksgiving, based on the Jewish rite of purification. When a child was baptized, a few grains of salt were dropped on its tongue. Salt had been the symbol of purity, strength, and incorruptibility for the ancient Hebrews, and the Romans had used it in their sacrifices. It was used in Christian baptism both to drive away demons and to strengthen the infant in its new faith.

The entire calendar was designed with reference to the great festivals of the Christian year — Easter, Christmas, and Pentecost. Saints' days were legion. Everyone participated in village processions. The colored vestments the priests wore at mass gave the villagers a sense of the changing seasons of the church's liturgical year. The signs and symbols of Christianity were visible everywhere.

Was popular religion entirely a matter of ritualistic formulas and ceremonies? What did the peasants actually *believe?* They accepted what family, customs, and the clergy ingrained in them. They learned the fundamental teachings of the church from the homilies of the village priests. The mass was in Latin, but the priest delivered homilies on the gospel in the vernacular. People grasped the meaning of biblical stories and church doctrines from the paintings on the village church wall. If their parish was wealthy, the scenes depicted in the church's stained-glass windows instructed them. Illiterate and uneducated, they certainly could not reason out the increasingly sophisticated propositions of clever theologians. Still, scriptural references and proverbs dotted everyone's language. Christianity was a basic element in the common people's culture; indeed, it was their culture.

Christians had long had special reverence and affection for the Virgin Mary, as the Mother of Christ. In the eleventh century theologians began to emphasize the depiction of Mary at the crucifixion in the Gospel of John:

But standing by the cross of Jesus were his mother, and his mother's sister, Mary the wife of Clopas, and Mary Magdalene. When Jesus saw his mother and the disciple whom he loved standing near, he said to his mother, "Woman, behold, your son!" Then he said to the disciple, "Behold, your mother!"[6]

Medieval scholars interpreted this passage as expressing Christ's compassionate concern for all humanity and Mary's spiritual motherhood of all Christians. The huge outpouring of popular devotions to Mary concentrated on her role as Queen of Heaven and, because of her special relationship to Christ, as all-powerful intercessor with Him. Masses on Saturdays specially commemorated her, sermons focused on her unique influence with Christ, and hymns and prayers to her multiplied. The most famous prayer, *Salve Regina*, perfectly expresses medieval people's attitude toward Mary:

Hail, holy Queen, Mother of Mercy! Our life, our sweetness, and our hope. To thee we cry, poor banished children of Eve; to thee we send up our sighs, mourning and weeping in this valley of tears. Turn, then, most gracious advocate, thy merciful eyes upon us; and after this our exile show us the blessed fruit of thy womb, Jesus. O merciful, O loving, O sweet Virgin Mary!

The prayer vividly and lovingly declares medieval people's confidence in Mary, to whom they recommend themselves as the exiled sons

BURIAL OF THE VIRGIN *Carved in a piece of ivory 5" × 2½", this detailed scene of Mary's burial reflects both the profound faith of the age and the incredible skill of medieval artists. (Courtesy, World Heritage Museum. Photo: Caroline Buckler)*

of Eve in this world, and in her power as advocate with Christ.

Peasants had a strong sense of the universal presence of God. They believed that God intervened directly in human affairs and could reward the virtuous and bring peace, health, and material prosperity. They believed, too, that God punished men and women for their sins with disease, poor harvests, and the destructions of war. Sin was caused by the Devil, who lurked everywhere. The Devil constantly incited people to evil deeds and sin, especially sins of the flesh. Sin frequently took place in the dark. Thus, evil and the Devil were connected in the peasant's mind with darkness or blackness. In medieval literature the Devil is often portrayed as a Negro, an identification that has had a profound and sorry impact on Western racial attitudes.

For peasants, life was not only hard but short. Few lived much beyond the age of forty. They had a great fear of nature: storms, thunder, and lightning terrified them. They had a terror of hell, whose geography and awful tortures they knew from sermons. And they certainly saw that the virtuous were not always rewarded but sometimes suffered considerably on earth. These things, which they could not explain, bred in them a deep pessimism.

No wonder, then, that pilgrimages to shrines of the saints were so popular. They offered hope in a world of gloom. They satisfied a strong emotional need. They meant change, adventure, excitement. The church granted indulgences to those who visited the shrines of great saints. Though indulgences only reduced the priest-imposed penalties for sin, people equated them with salvation. They generally believed that the indulgence received from a pilgrimage cut down the amount of time one would spend in hell. Thus pilgrimages "promised" salvation. Vast numbers embarked on pilgrimages to the shrines of St. James at Santiago de Compostella in Spain, Thomas Becket at Canterbury, St.-Gilles de Provence, and Saints Peter and Paul at Rome.

THOSE WHO FIGHT

In the High Middle Ages members of the nobility were those who fought. Also from the nobility came the great majority of monks and clerics, as well as the opinions, attitudes, and behavior that, to a considerable extent, shaped the lives of other classes. How did the lifestyle and social status of the nobility in the twelfth and thirteenth centuries differ from what they had been in the tenth century? What political and economic role did the nobility play?

Nobility was a legal status that a person acquired automatically at birth or received from a king or ruler as a reward for outstanding fighting skill or unusual services. Nobles considered themselves aristocrats – the word *aristocrat* derives from a Greek term meaning "the best" – but only toward the end of the twelfth century did the European nobility begin to develop a definite class consciousness. Nobles had a way of life based on a chivalric code and the observance – at least among those they considered social equals – of ideals of courtesy, generosity, graciousness, and hospitality. Most monks came from noble families, and the opinions they expressed were aristocratic.

The aristocratic nobility, though a small fraction of the total population, strongly influenced all aspects of culture – political, economic, religious, educational, and artistic. For that reason European society in the twelfth and thirteenth centuries may be termed aristocratic. In spite of scientific, industrial, and political revolutions, the nobility continued to hold the real political and social power in Europe down to the nineteenth century. In order to account for this continuing influence in later centuries, it is important to understand its development in the High Middle Ages.

The noble was almost always a military man, and he frequently used the Latin title *miles,* or knight, to indicate his nobility. He possessed a horse and a sword. These, and the leisure time in which to learn how to use them in combat, were the visible signs of his nobility.

Members of the nobility enjoyed a special legal status. The noble was free personally and in his possessions. He had immunity from almost all outside authorities. He was limited only by his military obligation to king, duke, or prince. As the result of his liberty, he had certain rights and responsibilities. He raised troops and commanded them in the field. He held courts that dispensed a sort of justice. Sometimes he coined money for use within his territories. He conducted relations with outside powers. He was the political, military, and judicial lord of the people who settled on his lands. He made political decisions affecting them, he resolved disputes among them, and he protected them in time of attack. The liberty of the noble and the privileges that went with his liberty were inheritable; they were perpetuated by blood and not by wealth alone.

Women whose fathers or husbands were noble were considered noble too, but not in their own right. Noble ladies often performed the political and military obligations of the men of their class, but there is no evidence of a woman being raised to the nobility. The values of a society are largely determined by its needs, and in the High Middle Ages those needs were military. Fighting was usually done by men, and so men were given noble status.

In the course of the twelfth century, the aristocratic knights slowly evolved into a distinct and closely knit class with feelings of superiority and an attitude of exclusivity. They had a common culture based on consciousness of family, the veneration of ancestors, and a sense of their own worth. Those who were or aspired to be aristocrats wanted

CHAIN MAIL   *This long shirt of interlinked metal rings, though heavy and uncomfortable, was flexible and allowed movement. Knights wore it because before the manufacture of plate armor, chain mail provided a fair degree of protection. (Courtesy, World Heritage Museum. Photo: Caroline Buckler)*

to possess a castle, the symbol of feudal independence and of a military lifestyle. Nobles almost always married within their class.

INFANCY AND CHILDHOOD

Some very exciting research has been done on childbirth in the Middle Ages. Most information comes from manuscript illuminations, which depict the birth process from the moment of coitus through pregnancy to delivery. An interesting thirteenth-century German miniature from Vienna shows a woman in labor. She is sitting on a chair or stool surrounded by four other women, who are pres-

Ti. cura euis adlumbricos.
Et coriandrum coque ad triasin oleo in capite mitte:
mulier ut cito pariat:
Accipe coriandri sem grana xi ali xiii et involucolo mundo filo
de tela alligab a puer aut puella ligo ad fem sinistri ppe inguine tene
at et mox ut omnis partus fuit gactus remedia cito tollat ne intestine
equantur.

*MIDWIVES HASTENING DELIVERY   Relatives or
midwives assist the woman in childbirth by shaking
her up and down. Significantly, no physician is present. With such treatment, the death-rate for both
mothers and infants was high. (Bildarchiv der Öster-
reichischen Nationalbibliothek)*

ent to help her in the delivery. They could be
relatives or neighbors. If they are midwives,
the woman in labor is probably noble or rich,
since midwives charged a fee. Two midwives
seem to be shaking the mother up and down
to hasten delivery. One of the women is
holding a coriander seed near the mother's
vagina. Coriander is an herb of the carrot
family, and its seeds were used for cleaning
purposes. They were thought to be helpful for
expelling gas from the alimentary canal —
hence their value for speeding up delivery.

The rate of infant mortality in the High Middle Ages must have been staggering. Such practices as jolting the pregnant woman up and down and inserting a seed into her surely contributed to the death rate of both the newborn and the mother. Natural causes – disease and poor or insufficient food – also resulted in many deaths. Infanticide, however, which was common in the ancient world, seems to have declined in the High Middle Ages. Ecclesiastical pressure worked steadily against it. High mortality due to foreign invasions and the generally violent and unstable conditions of the ninth and tenth centuries also made unnecessary the deliberate killing of one's own children. On the other hand, English court records from the counties of Warwickshire, Staffordshire, and Gloucestershire for 1221 reveal a suspiciously large number of children dying from "accidental deaths" – drowning, falling from carts, disappearing into the woods, falling into the fire. Still, accidental deaths in rural conditions are more common than is usually thought. Until more research is done, we cannot be certain about the prevalence of infanticide in the High Middle Ages.

Noble women did not nurse their own children. They sent newborns out to wet nurses – women who had recently given birth and therefore had milk. When Richard Plantagenet was born to Henry II and Eleanor on September 8, 1157, his mother immediately gave him to a woman of St. Alban's to nurse. The wet nurse had also had a son on September 8. How long the infant Richard and other medieval children were nursed is not known.

Swaddling appears to have been common in the Middle Ages. Strips of cloth were wrapped tightly around the child's arms, legs, and entire body until it was immobile. The infant was often strapped to a board, which could be set down in a corner or hung up in an out-of-the-way spot. Swaddling depressed the bodily functions: the heartbeat slowed, the child slept more and cried less. Theoretically, this practice arose from adult fears that the child would harm itself if its limbs were free. Probably, too, swaddling was a convenience to the nurse or parent. A swaddled child could be ignored for hours.[7] Any number of unfortunate things could happen to the inert infant, not the least of which was lying for a long time in its own filth. Swaddling surely led to body rashes, disease, and death.

For children of aristocratic birth, the years from infancy to around the age of seven or eight were primarily years of play. Infants had their rattles, as the twelfth-century monk Guibert of Nogent reports, and young children their special toys. Of course, then as now, children would play with anything handy – balls, rings, pretty stones, horns, any small household object. Gerald of Wales, who later became a courtier of King Henry II, describes how as a child he built monasteries and churches in the sand while his brothers were making castles and palaces. Vincent of Beauvais, who composed a great encyclopedia around 1250, recommended that children be bathed twice a day, fed well, and given ample playtime.

Guibert of Nogent speaks in several places in his autobiography of "the tender years of childhood" – the years from six to twelve. Describing the severity of the tutor whom his mother assigned to him, Guibert wrote:

Placed under him, I was taught with such purity and checked with such honesty from the vices which commonly spring up in youth that I was kept from ordinary games and never allowed to leave my master's company, or to eat anywhere else than at home, or to accept gifts from anyone without his leave; in everything I had to show self-control in word, look, and deed, so that he seemed to require of me the conduct of a monk rather than a clerk. While others of my age wandered everywhere at will and were unchecked in the indulgence of such inclinations as were natural at their age, I, hedged in with constant restraints and dressed in my clerical garb, would sit and look at the troops of players like a beast awaiting sacrifice. Even on Sundays and saints' days I had to submit to the severity of school exercises. At hardly any time, and never for a whole day, was I allowed to take a holiday; in fact, in every way and at all times I was driven to study. Moreover, he devoted himself exclusively to my education, since he was allowed to have no other pupil.[8]

Guibert's mother had intended him for the church. Other boys and girls had more playtime and more freedom.

Aristocrats deliberately had large families in order to insure the continuation of the family. Although many women died in childbirth and many children died before the age of seven, the survival of four or five children was not uncommon. Parents decided upon the futures of their children as soon as they were born or when they were still toddlers. Sons were prepared for one of the two positions considered suitable to their birth and position. Careers for the youngest sons might well be found in the church; for the rest, a suitable position meant a military career. Likewise, parents determined early which daughters would be married – and to whom – and which would become nuns.

At about the age of seven a boy of the noble class who was not intended for the church was placed in the household of one of his father's friends or relatives. There he became a servant to the lord and received his formal training in arms. He was expected to serve the lord at the table, to assist him as a private valet when called upon to do so, and, as he gained experience, to care for the lord's

horses and equipment. The boy might have a great deal of work to do, depending upon the size of the household and the personality of the lord. The work children did, medieval people believed, gave them experience and preparation for later life.

Training was in the arts of war. The boy learned to ride and to manage a horse. He had to acquire skill in wielding a sword, which sometimes weighed as much as twenty-five pounds. He had to be able to hurl a lance, shoot with a bow and arrow, and care for armor and other equipment. In the eleventh and twelfth centuries, noble youths were rarely taught to read and write. On thousands of charters from that period nobles signed with a cross ($+$) or some other mark. Literacy for the nobility became a little more common in the thirteenth century. Formal training was concluded around the age of eighteen with the ceremony of knighthood.

By the twelfth century, all men who were legally and socially noble had been formally knighted and could use the titles *dominus* and *messire,* which mean "lord." The ceremony of knighthood was one of the most important in a man's life. Once knighted, a young man was supposed to be courteous, generous, and if possible handsome and rich. Above all, he was to be loyal to his lord and brave in battle. Loyalty was the greatest and most important virtue. In a society lacking strong institutions of government, loyalty was the cement that held aristocratic society together. That is why the greatest crime was called a felony, which meant treachery to one's lord.

YOUTH

Knighthood, however, did not mean adulthood, power, and responsibility. Sons were completely dependent upon their fathers for support. Unless a young man's father was dead, he was still considered a youth. He remained a youth until he was in a financial position to marry – that is, until his father died. That might not happen until he was in his late thirties, and marriage at forty was not uncommon. A famous English soldier of fortune, William Marshal, had to wait until he was forty-five to take a wife. One factor – the inheritance of land and the division of properties – determined the lifestyle of the aristocratic nobility. The result was tension, frustration, and sometimes violence.

Once he had been knighted, the young man traveled. His father selected a group of friends to accompany, guide, and protect him. The band's chief pursuit was fighting. They meddled in local conflicts. Sometimes they departed on crusades. They did the tournament circuit. The tournament, in which a number of men competed from horseback (in contrast to the joust, which involved only two competitors), gave the bachelor knight experience in pitched battle. Since the horses and equipment of the vanquished were forfeited to the victors, the knight could also gain a reputation and a profit. The group hunted. They took great delight in spending money on horses, armor, gambling, drinking, and women. Everywhere these bands of youths went they stirred up trouble. It is no wonder that kings supported the Crusades. Those foreign excursions rid their countries of considerable violence caused by bands of footloose young knights.

The period of traveling lasted two or three years. Although some young men met violent death and others were maimed or injured, many returned home, still totally dependent upon their fathers for support. Serious trouble frequently developed at this stage, for the father was determined to preserve intact the properties of the lordship and to maintain his power and position within the family. Young men could not marry and set up a household on their own without the father's approval.

When fathers survived until advanced years, marriage and independence had to be long postponed.

Parents often wanted to settle their daughters' futures as soon as possible. Men, even older men, tended to prefer young brides. A woman in her late twenties or thirties would have fewer years of married fertility, limiting the number of children she could produce and thus threatening the survival of the family. Therefore, aristocratic girls in the High Middle Ages were married at around the age of sixteen.

The future of many young women was not enviable. For a girl of sixteen, marriage to a man in his thirties was not the most attractive prospect, and marriage to a widower in his forties and fifties would be even less so. If there were a large number of marriageable young girls in a particular locality, their market value was reduced. In the early Middle Ages it had been the custom for the groom to present a dowry to the bride and her family, but by the late twelfth century the process was reversed. Thereafter, the size of the marriage portions offered by brides and their families rose higher and higher.

Many girls of aristocratic families did not marry at all, although there were few professions a well-born lady could honorably enter. She certainly could not be apprenticed to a trader or artisan. Even less did her blood and dignity allow her to perform any manual labor. The sole alternative was the religious life. Benedictine abbeys for women provided "career opportunities" for some unmarriageable girls. Parents commonly decided upon this option, especially if there were several daughters in the family, when the child was under ten. If a girl felt no particular inclination toward becoming a nun, her mother changed her mind quickly enough. The girl of eleven or twelve years was taken to the childbed of a relative or neighbor to observe the pain and blood that was the lot of married women. It was an event she would not quickly forget. This traumatic experience made her willing to go along with her parent's wishes.

In England in the later Middle Ages there were 138 nunneries, whose residents were overwhelmingly women from the nobility and the upper middle classes. Most convents were small, however, and did not have places for everyone desiring entrance. The new religious orders of the thirteenth century, the Franciscan and the Dominican, provided some relief by establishing many convents for girls and women of the upper class.

Within noble families and within medieval society as a whole, paternal control of the family property and wealth led to serious difficulties. Because marriage was long delayed for men, a considerable age difference existed between husbands and wives and between fathers and their sons. Because of this generation gap, as one scholar has written, "the father became an older, distant, but still powerful figure. He could do favors for his sons, but his very presence, once his sons had reached maturity, blocked them in the attainment and enjoyment of property and in the possession of a wife."[9] Consequently, disputes between the generations were common in the twelfth and thirteenth centuries. Older men held on to property and power. Younger sons wanted a "piece of the action." This helps explain the conflicts and rebellions that occurred in the years 1173–1189 between Henry II of England and his sons Henry, Geoffrey, and John. Their case was quite typical.

The relationship between the mother and her sons was also affected. Closer in years to her children than her husband, she was perhaps better able to understand their needs and frustrations. She often served as a mediator between conflicting male generations. One

authority, discussing the role of the mother in French epic poetry, has written, "In extreme need, the heroes betake themselves to their mother, with whom they always find love, counsel and help. She takes them under her protection, even against their father."[10]

When society included so many married young women and unmarried young men, sexual tensions also arose. The young male noble, unable to marry for a long time, could satisfy his lust with peasant girls or prostitutes. But what was a young woman unhappily married to a much older man to do? The literature of courtly love is filled with stories of young bachelors in love with young married women. How hopeless their love was is not known. The cuckolded husband is a stock figure in such masterpieces as *The Romance of Tristan and Isolde,* Chaucer's *The Merchant's Tale,* and Boccaccio's *Fiammetta's Tale.*

In the High Middle Ages, for economic reasons, a man might remain a bachelor knight – a "youth" – for a very long time. The identification of bachelorhood with youth has survived into modern times, and the social attitude persists that marriage makes a man mature – an adult. Marriage, however, is no guarantee of that.

POWER AND RESPONSIBILITY

A member of the nobility became an adult when he came into the possession of his property. He then acquired vast authority over lands and people. With it went responsibility. The first obligation of the noble was to fight. He was supposed to be the protector and the defender of Christian society against its enemies. In the words of Honorius of Autun:

Soldiers: You are the arm of the Church, because you should defend it against its enemies. Your duty

is to aid the oppressed, to restrain yourself from rapine and fornication, to repress those who impugn the Church with evil acts, and to resist those who are rebels against priests. Performing such a service, you will obtain the most splendid of benefices from the greatest of Kings.[11]

Nobles rarely lived up to this ideal, and there are countless examples of nobles attacking the church. In the early thirteenth century, Peter of Dreux, count of Brittany, spent so much of his time attacking the church that he was known as "the Scourge of the Clergy."

The nobles' conception of rewards and gratification did not involve the kind of postponement envisioned by the clergy. They wanted rewards immediately. Since by definition a military class is devoted to war, those rewards came through the pursuit of arms. When nobles were not involved in local squabbles with neighbors — usually disputes over property or over real or imagined slights — they participated in tournaments.

Complete jurisdiction over his properties allowed the noble, at long last, to gratify his desire for display and lavish living. Since his status in medieval society depended upon the size of his household, he would be anxious to increase the number of his household retainers. The elegance of his clothes, the variety and richness of his table, the number of his horses and followers, the freedom with which he spent money – all these things were public indications of his social standing. The aristocratic lifestyle was luxurious and extravagant. To maintain it, nobles often had to borrow from Jewish financiers or wealthy monasteries.

At the same time nobles had a great deal of work to do. The responsibilities of a noble in the High Middle Ages depended upon the size and extent of his estates, the number of his dependents, and his position in his territory relative to others of his class and to the king. As a vassal he was required to fight for his lord or for the king when called upon to do so. By the mid-twelfth century this service was limited in most parts of western Europe to forty days a year. He might have to perform guard duty at his lord's castle for a certain number of days a year. He was obliged to attend his lord's court on important occasions when the lord wanted to put on great displays, such as at Easter, Pentecost, and Christmas. When the lord knighted his eldest son or married off his eldest daughter, he called his vassals to his court. They were expected to attend and to present a contribution known as a gracious aid.

Throughout the year a noble had to look after his own estates. He had to appoint prudent and honest overseers and to make sure that they paid him the customary revenues and services. Since the estates of a great lord were usually widely scattered, he had to travel frequently.

Until the late thirteenth century, when royal authority intervened, a noble in France or England had great power over the knights and peasants on his estates. He maintained order among them and dispensed justice to them. Holding the manorial court, which

punished criminal acts and settled disputes, was one of his gravest obligations. The quality of justice varied widely: some lords were vicious tyrants who exploited and persecuted their peasants; others were reasonable and evenhanded. In any case, the quality of life on the manor and its productivity were related in no small way to the temperament and decency of the lord – and his lady.

Women played a large and important role in the functioning of the estate. They were responsible for the practical management of the household's "inner economy" – cooking, brewing, spinning, weaving, overseeing servants, caring for yard animals. The lifestyle of the medieval warrior nobles required constant travel, both for purposes of war and for the supervision of distant properties. When the lord was away for long periods, the women frequently managed the herds, barns, granaries, and outlying fields as well.

Frequent pregnancies and the reluctance to expose women to hostile conditions kept the lady at home and therefore able to assume supervision over the family's fixed properties. When a husband went away on crusade – and his absence could last anywhere from two to five years, if he returned at all – his wife was often the sole manager of the family properties. When her husband went to the Holy Land between 1060 and 1080, the lady Hersendis was the sole manager of the family properties in the Vendomois region in northern France.

Nor were the activities of women confined to managing family households and estates in the absence of their husbands. Medieval warfare was largely a matter of brief skirmishes, and few men were killed in any single encounter. But altogether the number slain ran high, and there were many widows. Aristocratic widows frequently controlled family properties and fortunes and exercised great authority. Although the evidence is scattered and sketchy, there are indications that women performed many of the functions of men. In Spain, France and Germany they bought, sold, and otherwise transferred property. Gertrude, labeled "Saxony's almighty widow" by the chronicler Ekkehard of Aaura, took a leading role in the conspiracies against the emperor Henry V. Sophia, wife of Berthold of Zohringer, assisted her brother Henry the Proud with eight hundred knights at the siege of Falkenstein in 1129. And Eilika Billung, the widow of Count Otto of Ballenstedt, built a castle at Burgwerben on the Saale River and, as advocate of the monastery of Goseck, removed one abbot and selected his successor. From her castle at Bernburg, the countess Eilika was also reputed to ravage the countryside.

Throughout the High Middle Ages fighting remained the dominant feature of the noble lifestyle. The church's preachings and condemnations reduced but did not stop violence. Lateness of inheritance, depriving the nobility of constructive outlets for their energy, together with the military ethos of their culture, encouraged petty warfare and disorder. The nobility thus represented a constant source of trouble for monarchy. In the thirteenth century kings drew on the financial support of the middle classes to build the administrative machinery that gradually laid the foundations for strong royal government. The Crusades relieved the rulers of France, England, and the German Empire of some of their most dangerous elements. Complete royal control of the nobility, however, came only in modern times.

THOSE WHO PRAY

According to Asser, monks performed the most important service to society. In the

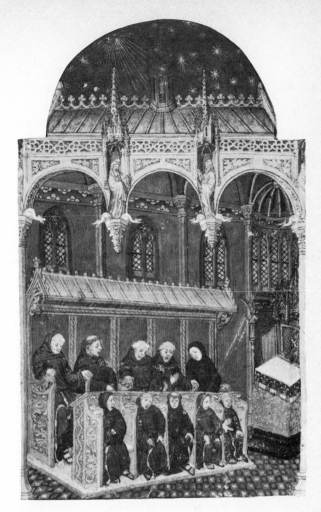

MONKS IN CHOIR   *Seven times during the day and once during the night monks went to the church to chant the psalms and other prayers, performing what everyone believed to be a valuable service for the rest of society. (The British Museum)*

Middle Ages prayer was looked upon as a vital social service, one that was just as crucial as the agricultural labor of the farmers and the military might of the nobles. Just as the knights protected and defended society with the sword, and the peasants provided food and sustenance through their toil, so the monks with their prayers and chants worked to secure God's blessing for society.

Monasticism represented some of the finest aspirations of medieval civilization. The monasteries were devoted to prayer, and their standards of Christian behavior influenced the entire church. The monasteries produced the educated elite that was continually drawn into the administrative services of kings and great lords. Monks kept alive the remains of classical culture and experimented with new styles of architecture and art. They introduced new techniques of estate management and land reclamation. Although relatively few in number in the High Middle Ages, the monks played a significant role in medieval society.

RECRUITMENT

Toward the end of his *Ecclesiastical History of England and Normandy*, when he was a man well into his sixties, Orderic Vitalis, a monk of the Norman abbey of St. Evroul, interrupted his narrative to explain movingly how he happened to become a monk:

It was not thy will, O God, that I should serve thee longer in that place, for fear that I might be less attentive to thee among kinsfolk, who are often a burden and an impediment to thy servants, or might in any way be distracted from obeying the law through human affection for my family. And so, O glorious God, you didst inspire my father Odeleric to renounce me utterly and submit me in all things to thy goverance. So, weeping, he gave me, a weeping child, into the care of the monk Reginald, and sent me away into exile for love of thee, and never saw me again. And I, a mere boy, did not presume to oppose my father's wishes, but obeyed him in all things, for he promised me for his part that if I became a monk I should taste of the joys of Heaven with the Innocents after my death. . . . And so, a boy of ten, I crossed the English channel and came into Normandy as an exile, unknown to all, knowing no one. Like Joseph in Egypt I heard a language which I could not understand. But thou didst suffer me through thy grace to find nothing but kindness among strangers. I was received as an oblate in the abbey of St.

Evroul by the venerable abbot Mainier in the eleventh year of my life. . . . The name of Vitalis was given me in place of my English name, which sounded harsh to the Normans.[12]

Orderic Vitalis (ca 1075– ca 1140) was one of the leading scholars of his times. As such, he is not a representative figure or even a typical monk. Intellectuals, those who earn their living or spend most of their time working with ideas, are never typical figures of their times. In one respect, however, Orderic was quite representative of the monks of the High Middle Ages: although he had no doubt that God wanted him to be a monk, the decision was actually made by his parents who gave him to a monastery as a child-oblate. Orderic was the third son of Odeleric, a knight who fought for William the Conqueror at the battle of Hastings (1066). For his participation in the Norman conquest of England, Odeleric was rewarded with lands in western England. Concern for the provision of his two older sons probably led him to give his youngest to the monastery.

Medieval monasteries were religious institutions whose organization and structure fulfilled the social needs of the feudal nobility. Between the tenth and thirteenth centuries, economic necessities compelled great families, or aspiring ones, to seek a life in the church for some members. There simply were not sufficient resources or career opportunities to provide suitable, honorable positions in life for all the children in aristocratic families. The monasteries provided these children an honorable and aristocratic life and opportunities for ecclesiastical careers.[13]

Until well into modern times, and certainly in the Middle Ages, almost everyone believed in and accepted the thorough subjection of children to their parents. This belief was the logical consequence of the fact that young noblemen were not expected to work and were therefore totally dependent on their fathers. Some men did become monks as adults, and apparently for a wide variety of reasons: belief in a direct call from God, disgust with the materialism and violence of the secular world, the encouragement and inspiration of others, economic failure or lack of opportunity, poverty, sickness, the fear of hell. However, most men who became monks, until about the early thirteenth century, seem to have been given as child-oblates by their parents.

In the thirteenth century, the older Benedictine and Cistercian orders had to compete with the new orders of friars — the Franciscans and the Dominicans. More and more monks had to be recruited from the middle class, that is, from small landholders or traders in the district near the abbey. As medieval society changed economically, and as European society ever so slowly developed middle-class traits, the monasteries almost inevitably drew their manpower, when they were able, from the middle classes. Until that time, they were preserves of the aristocratic nobility.

MONK HARVESTING GRAIN *Saint Benedict wrote, "they are truly monks when they live by the labor of their hands" (Rule, chapter 48). The isolated and localized nature of life in the early Middle Ages required that monasteries be entirely self-supporting. (Bibliothèque Publique de Dijon)*

PRAYER AND OTHER WORK

The pattern of life within individual monasteries varied widely from house to house and from region to region. Each monastic community was shaped by the circumstances of its foundation and endowment, by tradition, by the interests of its abbots and members, and by local conditions. It would therefore be a mistake to think that Christian monasticism in the High Middle Ages was everywhere the same. One central activity, however — the work of God — was performed everywhere. Daily life centered around the liturgy.

Seven times a day and once during the night, the monks went to choir to chant the psalms and other prayers prescribed by Saint

Benedict. Prayers were offered for peace, rain, good harvests, the civil authorities, the monks' families, and their benefactors. Monastic patrons in turn lavished gifts upon the monasteries, which often became very wealthy. Through their prayers the monks performed a valuable service for the rest of society.

Prayer justified the monks spending a large percentage of their income on splendid objects to enhance the liturgy; monks praised God, they believed, not only in prayer but in everything connected with prayer. They sought to accumulate priestly vestments of the finest silks, velvets, and embroideries; and sacred vessels — chalices, patens, and thuribles — of embossed silver and gold. Thuribles

MONK INSTRUCTING ILLUMINATOR *All monks had to learn to read in order to perform the religious services. A few of the intellectually and artistically gifted were often taught to copy and to illuminate manuscripts. (The Pierpont Morgan Library)*

containing sweet-smelling incense brought at great expense from the Orient were used for the incensation of the altars, following ancient Jewish ritual. The pages of gospel books were richly decorated with gold leaf and the books' bindings were ornamented and bejewelled. Every monastery tried to acquire the relics of its patron saint, which necessitated the production of a beautiful reliquary to house the relics. The liturgy, then, inspired a great deal of art, and the monasteries became the crucibles of art in Western Christendom.

The monks fulfilled their social responsibility by praying. It was generally agreed that they could best carry out this duty if they were not distracted by worldly matters. Thus, great and lesser lords gave the monasteries lands that would supply the community with

necessities. Each manorial unit was responsible for provisioning the abbey for a definite period of time, and the expenses of each manor were supposed to equal its income.

The administration of the abbey's estates and properties consumed considerable time. The operation of a large establishment, such as Cluny in Burgundy or Bury St. Edmunds in England, which by 1150 had several hundred monks, involved planning, prudence and wise management. Although the abbot or prior had absolute authority in making assignments, common sense advised that tasks be allotted according to the ability and talents of individual monks.

The usual method of economic organization was the manor. Many monastic manors were small enough and close enough to the abbey to be supervised directly by the abbot. But if a monastery held and farmed vast estates, the properties were divided into administrative units under the supervision of one of the monks of the house. The lands of the German abbey of St. Emmeran at Regensburg, for example, were divided into thirty-three manorial centers.

Because the choir monks were aristocrats, they did not till the land themselves. In each house one monk, the cellarer or general financial manager, was responsible for supervising the peasants or lay brothers who did the actual agricultural labor. Lay brothers were vowed religious drawn from the servile classes, with simpler religious and intellectual obligations than those of the choir monks. The cellarer had to see to it that the estates of the monastery produced enough income to cover its expenses. Another monk, the almoner, was responsible for feeding and caring for the poor of the neighborhood. At the French abbey of St.-Requier in the eleventh century, 110 persons were fed every day. At Corbie, fifty loaves of bread were distributed daily to the poor.

The precentor, or cantor, was responsible for the library and the careful preservation of books. The sacristan of the abbey had in his charge all the materials and objects connected with the liturgy — vestments, candles, incense, sacred vessels, altar cloths, and hangings. The novice master was responsible for the training of recruits, instructing them in the *Rule,* the chant, the Scriptures, and the history and traditions of the house. For a few of the monks, work was some form of intellectual activity, such as the copying of books and manuscripts, the preparation of manuals, and the writing of letters.

Although the church forbade monks to study law and medicine, that rule was often ignored. In the twelfth and thirteenth cen-

turies, many monks gained considerable reputations for their knowledge and experience in the practice of both the canon law of the church and the civil law of their countries. For example, the Norman monk Lanfranc, because of his legal knowledge and administrative ability, became the chief adviser of William the Conqueror.

Although knowledge of medicine was primitive by twentieth-century standards, monastic practitioners were less ignorant than one would suspect. Long before 1066, a rich medical literature had been produced in England. The most important of these treatises was *The Leech Book of Bald* ("leech" means medical). This work exhibits a wide knowledge of herbal prescriptions, familiarity with ancient authorities, and evidence based on empirical practice. Bald discusses diseases of the lungs and stomach together with their remedies and demonstrates his acquaintance with surgery. *The Leech Book of Bald* was copied and circulated widely in the eleventh through thirteenth centuries, and many monastic libraries in England and on the Continent had a copy of it. Medical knowledge was sometimes rewarded. King Henry II of England made his medical adviser, the monk Robert de Veneys, abbot of Malmesbury.

The religious houses of medieval Europe usually took full advantage of whatever resources and opportunities their location offered. For example, the raising of horses could produce income in a world that depended on horses for travel and for warfare. Some monasteries, such as the Cistercian abbey of Jervaulx in Yorkshire, became famous for and quite wealthy from their production of prime breeds. In the eleventh and twelfth centuries, a period of considerable monastic expansion, large tracts of swamp, fen, forest, and wasteland were brought under cultivation — principally by the Cistercians.

The Cistercians, whose constitution insisted that they accept lands far from human habitation and forbade them to be involved in the traditional feudal-manorial structure, were ideally suited to the agricultural needs and trends of their times. In the Low Countries they built dikes to hold back the sea, and the reclaimed land was put to the production of cereals. In the eastern parts of the Holy Roman Empire – in Silesia, Mecklenburg, and Pomerania – they took the lead in draining swamps and cultivating wasteland. Because of a labor shortage, they advertised widely all across Europe for monks and brothers. Because of their efforts, the rich, rolling land of French Burgundy was turned into lush vineyards. In northern and central England, the rocky soil and damp downs of Lincolnshire, poorly suited to agriculture, were turned into sheep runs; by the third quarter of the twelfth century, the Cistercians were raising sheep and playing a very large role in the production of England's staple crop, wool.

Some monasteries got involved in iron and lead mining. In 1291, the Cistercian abbey of Furness operated at least forty forges. The German abbeys of Königsbronn, Waldsassen, and Saarbegen also mined iron in the thirteenth century. The monks entered this industry first to fill their own needs, but in an expanding economy they soon discovered a large market. Iron had hundreds of uses. Nails, hammers, plows, armor, spears, axes, stirrups, horseshoes, and many weapons of war were all made from this basic metal. When King Richard of England was preparing to depart on crusade in 1189, he wanted to take fifty thousand horseshoes with him. Lead also had a great variety of uses. It could be used for the roofing of buildings, and as alloy for strengthening the silver coinage, for framing pane-glass windows in parish, mon-astery, and cathedral churches, and even for lavatory drainpipes.

Whatever work particular monks did and whatever economic activities individual monasteries were involved in, monks also performed social services and exerted an influence for the good. Monasteries often ran schools that gave primary education to young boys. Abbeys like St. Albans, situated north of London on a busy thoroughfare, served as hotels and resting-places for travelers. Monasteries frequently operated "hospitals" and leprosaria, which provided care and attention to the sick, the aged, and the afflicted – primitive care, it is true, but often all that was available. In short, they performed a variety of social services in an age when there was no "state" and no conception of social welfare as a public responsibility.

ECONOMIC DIFFICULTIES

In the twelfth century, expenses in the older Benedictine monastic houses increased more rapidly than did income, leading to a steadily worsening economic situation. Cluny is a good example. Life at Cluny was lavish and extravagant. There were large quantities of rich food. The monks' habits were made of the best cloth available. Cluny's abbots and priors traveled with sizable retinues, as great lords were required to do. The abbots worked to make the liturgy ever more magnificent, and large sums were spent on elaborate vestments and jeweled vessels. Abbot Hugh embarked on an extraordinarily expensive building program. He entirely rebuilt the abbey church, and when Pope Urban II consecrated it in 1095 it was the largest church in Christendom. The monks lived like lords, which in a sense they were.

Revenue came from the hundreds of monasteries scattered across France, Italy, Spain,

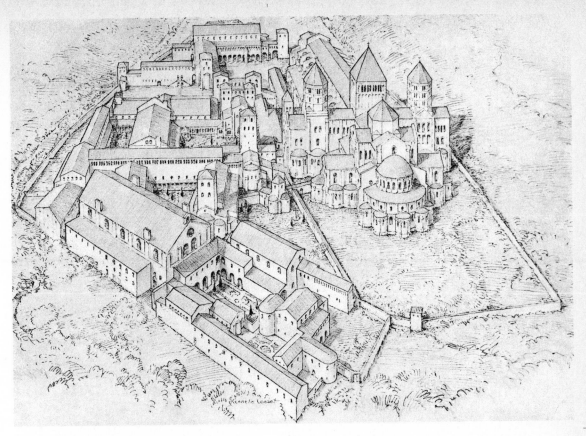

CLUNY, CA 1157 *Begun in 1085 and supported by the generosity of kings and peasants, the church (right center) and monastery of Cluny was the administrative center of a vast monastic and feudal empire. Note* *the apse around the east end of the church and the large foreground complex, which served as monastic infirmary and guest hostel. (The Mediaeval Academy of America)*

and England that Cluny had reformed in the eleventh century; each year they paid Cluny a cash sum. Novices were expected to make a gift of land or cash when they entered. For reasons of security, knights departing on crusade often placed their estates under Cluny's authority. Still, this income was not enough. The management of Cluny's manors all across Europe was entrusted to bailiffs or wardens who were not monks and who were given lifetime contracts. Frequently these bailiffs were poor managers and produced no profits. But they could not be removed and replaced. In order to meet expenses, Cluny had to rely on cash reserves. For example, Cluny's estates produced only a small percentage of needed

food supplies; the rest had to be bought and paid for from cash reserves.

Cluny had two basic alternatives – improve management to cut costs or borrow money. The abbey could have placed the monastic manors under the jurisdiction of monks, rather than hiring bailiffs who would grow rich as middlemen. It could have awarded annual rather than lifetime contracts, supervised all revenues, and tried to cut costs within the monastery. Cluny chose the second alternative – borrowing. Consequently, the abbey spent hoarded reserves of cash and fell into debt.

In contrast to the abbot of Cluny, Suger (1122–1151), the superior of the royal abbey of St.-Denis near Paris, was a shrewd manager. Although he too spared no expense to enhance the beauty of his monastery and church, Suger kept an eye on costs and made sure that his properties were soundly managed. But the management of St.-Denis was unusual. Far more typical was the economic mismanagement at Cluny. By the later twelfth century, small and great monasteries were facing comparable financial difficulties.

———◆———

During the eleventh century the term *chevaliers,* meaning "horsemen" or "knights," gained widespread currency in France. Non-French peoples gradually adopted it to refer to the nobility, "who sat up high on their warhorses, looking down on the poor masses and terrorizing the monks."[14] By 1100 the knightly class was united in its ability to fight on horseback, its insistence that each member was descended from a valorous ancestor, its privileges, and its position at the top of the social hierarchy. The interests and activities of the nobility centered around warfare, but its economic power rested upon its ability to extract labor services and rents from the peasants. Generalizations about peasant life in the High Middle Ages must always be qualified by manorial customs, by the weather in a given year, and by the personalities of local lords. Everywhere, however, the performance of agricultural services and the payment of rents preoccupied peasants. Although they led hard lives, social mobility was possible through exceedingly hard work, luck, or flight to a town.

The monks exercised a profound influence on matters of the spirit. In their prayers the monks battled for the Lord, just as the chivalrous knights did on the battlefield. In their chant and rich ceremonial, in the Romanesque architecture of their buildings, and in the ex-

ample of many monks' lives, the monasteries inspired Christian peoples to an incalculable degree. As the crucibles of sacred art, the monasteries became the cultural centers of Christian Europe.

NOTES

1. Honorius of Autun, "Elucidarium sive Dialogus de Summa Totius Christianae Theologiae," in *Patrologia Latina,* ed. J. P. Migne, Garnier Bros., Paris, 1854, vol. 172, col. 1149.

2. E. Power, "Peasant Life and Rural Conditions," in J. R. Tanner et al., *The Cambridge Medieval History,* Cambridge University Press, Cambridge, 1958, 7.716.

3. Glanvill, "De Legibus Angliae," book 5, chap. 5, in *Social Life in Britain from the Conquest to the Reformation,* ed. G. G. Coulton, Cambridge University Press, London, 1956, pp. 338–339.

4. G. Duby, *Early Growth of the European Economy,* Cornell University Press, Ithaca, N.Y., 1977, pp. 213–219.

5. S. R. Scargill-Bird, ed., *Custumals of Battle Abbey in the Reign of Edward I and Edward II,* Camden Society, London, 1887, p. 19.

6. John 19: 25–27.

7. L. Demause, "The Evolution of Childhood," in *The History of Childhood,* ed. L. Demause, Psychohistory Press, New York, 1974, pp. 32–37.

8. J. F. Benton, ed. and trans., *Self and Society in Medieval France: The Memoirs of Abbot Guibert of Nogent,* Harper & Row, New York, 1970, p. 46.

9. D. Herlihy, "The Generation Gap in Medieval History," *Viator* 5 (1974): 360.

10. Cited in ibid., p. 361.

11. Honorius of Autun in *Patrologia Latina,* vol. 172, col. 1148.

12. M. Chibnall, ed. and trans., *The Ecclesiastical History of Orderic Vitalis,* Oxford University Press, Oxford, 1972, 2.xiii.

13. R. W. Southern, *Western Society and the Church in the Middle Ages,* Penguin Books, Baltimore, 1970, pp. 224–230, esp. p. 228.

14. G. Duby, *The Age of the Cathedrals: Art and Society, 980–1420,* trans. Eleanor Levieux and Barbara Thompson, University of Chicago Press, Chicago, 1981, p. 38.

SUGGESTED READING

The best short introduction to the material of this chapter is C. Brooke, *The Structure of Medieval Society* (1971), a beautifully illustrated book. The student interested in aspects of medieval slavery, serfdom, or the peasantry should begin with M. Bloch, "How Ancient Slavery Came to an End" and "Personal Liberty and Servitude in the Middle Ages, Particularly in France," in *Slavery and Serfdom in the Middle Ages: Selected Essays,* trans. W. R. Beer (1975). There is an excellent discussion of these problems in the magisterial work of G. Duby, *Rural Economy and Country Life in the Medieval West,* trans. C. Postan (1968). G. C. Homans, *English Villagers of the Thirteenth Century* (1975), is a fine combination of sociological and historical scholarship, while the older study of H. S. Bennett, *Life on the English Manor: A Study of Peasant Conditions* (1960), contains much useful information presented in a highly readable fashion. Emmanuel LeRoy Ladurie, *Montaillou: Cathars and Catholics in a French Village, 1294–1324,* trans. Barbara Bray (1978), is a fascinating glimpse of village life. G. Duby, *The Early Growth of the European Economy: Warriors and Peasants from the Seventh to the Twelfth Century* (1977), is a superb synthesis by a leading authority. Advanced students should see the same author's *The Three Orders: Feudal Society Imagined* (1980), a brilliant but difficult book.

For the nobility, see L. Genicot, "The Nobility in Medieval Francia: Continuity, Break, or Evolution?"; A. Borst, "Knighthood in the High Middle Ages: Ideal and Reality"; and two studies by G. Duby, "The Nobility in Eleventh and Twelfth Century Maconnais" and "Northwestern France: The 'Youth' in Twelfth Century Aristocratic Society": all these articles appear in F. L. Cheyette, ed., *Lordship and Community in Medieval Europe: Selected Readings* (1968). Social mobility among both aristocracy and peasantry are discussed in T. Evergates, *Feudal Society in the Bailliage of Troyes under the Counts of Champagne, 1152–1284* (1976). M. Bloch, *Feudal Society* (1966), remains the standard.

E. Power, *Medieval Women* (1976), is a nicely illustrated sketch of the several classes of women. For women, marriage, and the family in the High Middle Ages, J. McNamara and S. F. Wemple, "Sanctity and Power: The Dual Pursuit of Medieval Women," in *Becoming Visible: Women in European History* (1977), ed. R. Bridenthal and C. Koonz; and E. R. Coleman, "Medieval Marriage Characteristics: A Neglected Factor in the History of Medieval Serfdom," in *The Family in History: Interdisciplinary Essays* (1973), ed. T. K. Rabb and R. I. Rotberg, make interesting reading.

There is no dearth of good material on the monks in medieval society. The titles listed in the Suggested Reading for Chapter 7 represent a useful starting point for study. Anne Boyd, *The Monks of Durham* (1975), is an excellently illustrated sketch of many facets of monastic culture in the High Middle Ages. L. J. Lekai, *The Cistercians: Ideals and Reality* (1977), is a broad scholarly survey of the White Monks. Georges Duby, *The Age of the Cathedrals,* cited in the Notes to this chapter, is especially strong on the monastic origins of medieval art. Both W. Braunfels, *Monasteries of Western Europe: the Architecture of the Orders* (1972), and C. Brooke, *The Monastic World* (1974), have splendidly illustrated texts and good bibliographies.

CHAPTER 11

THE CREATIVITY AND VITALITY OF
THE HIGH MIDDLE AGES

THE HIGH MIDDLE AGES witnessed some of the most remarkable achievements in the entire history of Western society. Europeans displayed tremendous creativity and vitality in many realms of culture. Rulers tried to establish contact with all of their peoples, developed new legal and financial institutions, and slowly consolidated power in the hands of the monarchy. The kings of England and France succeeded in laying the foundations of the modern national state. The university, a uniquely Western contribution to civilization and a superb expression of medieval creativity, came into being at the same time. The Gothic cathedral manifested medieval peoples' deep Christian faith and their appreciation for the worlds of nature, man, and God. The Crusades, a series of holy wars to recover the Holy Land from the Muslims, also expressed European Christians' strong, even fanatical, religious faith.

This chapter will discuss the following questions. How did medieval rulers in England, France, and the Holy Roman Empire work to solve their problems of government? How did universities develop, and what needs of medieval society did they serve? What does the Gothic cathedral reveal about the ideals, attitudes, and interests of medieval people? What functions did the cathedral serve? Finally, what combination of motives inspired the Crusades, and what results did they have?

MEDIEVAL ORIGINS OF THE MODERN STATE

Rome's great legacy to Western civilization had been the concepts of the state and the law, but for almost five hundred years after the disintegration of the Roman Empire in the West the state as a reality did not exist. Political authority was completely decentralized. Power was spread among many feudal lords, who gave their localities such protection and security as their strength allowed. The fiefdoms, kingdoms, and territories that covered the continent of Europe did not have the qualities or provide the services of a modern state. They did not have jurisdiction over many people, and their laws affected a relative few. In the mid-eleventh century, there existed many layers of authority — earls, counts, barons, knights — between a king and the ordinary people.

In these circumstances, medieval kings had common goals. The rulers of England, France, and the Holy Roman Empire wanted to strengthen and extend royal authority within their territories. They wanted to establish an effective means of communication with all peoples in order to increase public order. They wanted more revenue and efficient state bureaucracies. The solutions they found to these problems laid the foundations for modern national states.

The modern state is an organized territory with definite geographical boundaries that are recognized by other states. It has a body of law and institutions of government. If the state claims to govern according to law, it is guided in its actions by the law. The modern national state counts on the loyalty of its citizens, or at least a majority of them. It provides order so that citizens can go about their daily work and other activities. It protects its citizens in their persons and property. The state tries to prevent violence and to apprehend and punish those who commit it. It supplies a currency or medium of exchange that permits financial and commercial transactions. The state conducts relations with foreign governments. In order to accomplish even these minimal functions, the state must have officials, bureaucracies, laws and courts

THE BAYEUX TAPESTRY *Measuring 231' by 19½", the Bayeux Tapestry gives a narrative description of the events surrounding the Norman Conquest of England. The tapestry provides an important historical source for the clothing, armor, and lifestyles of the Norman and Anglo-Saxon warrior class. (Tapisserie de la Reine Mathilde, Ville de Bayeux)*

of law, soldiers, information, and money. States with these attributes are relatively recent developments.

UNIFICATION AND COMMUNICATION

ENGLAND   Under the pressure of the Danish (or Viking) invasions of the ninth and tenth centuries, the seven kingdoms of Anglo-Saxon England united under one king. At the same period, for reasons historians still cannot fully explain, England was divided into local units called shires, or counties, each under the jurisdiction of a sheriff appointed by the king. The Danish king Canute (1016–1035) and his successor Edward the Confessor (1042–1066) exercised broader authority than any contemporary ruler on the Continent. All the English thegns, or local chieftains, recognized the central authority of the kingship.

The kingdom of England, therefore, had a political head start on the rest of Europe.

When Edward the Confessor died, his cousin Duke William of Normandy claimed the English throne and in 1066 defeated the Anglo-Saxon claimant on the battlefield of Hastings. As William subdued the rest of the country, he distributed lands to his Norman followers and assigned specific military quotas to each estate. He also required all feudal lords to swear an oath of allegiance to him as king.

William the Conqueror (1066–1087) preserved the Anglo-Saxon institution of sheriffs representing the king at the local level, but replaced Anglo-Saxon sheriffs with Normans. A sheriff, who always lived in the county where he worked, had heavy duties. He maintained order in the shire. He caught criminals and punished them in the shire court, over which he presided. He collected taxes and, when the king ordered him to do so, raised an army of foot soldiers. The sheriff also organized adult males in groups of ten, with each member liable for the good behavior of the others. The Conqueror thus made local people responsible for order in their communities. For all his efforts, the sheriff received no pay. This system, whereby unpaid officials governed the county, served as the basic pattern of English local government for many centuries. It cost the Crown nothing, but restricted opportunities for public service to the well-to-do.

William also retained another Anglo-Saxon device, the writ. This brief administrative order written in the vernacular (Anglo-Saxon) by a government clerk was the means by which the central government communicated with people at the local level. Sheriffs were empowered to issue writs relating to matters in their counties.

In 1086 the Conqueror introduced into England a major innovation, the Norman inquest. At his Christmas court in 1085, William discussed the state of the kingdom with his vassals and decided to conduct a systematic investigation of the entire country. The survey was to be made by means of inquests, or general inquiries, held throughout England. William wanted to determine how much wealth there was in his new kingdom, who held what land, and what lands had been disputed among his vassals since the conquest of 1066. In 1086 groups of royal officials or judges were sent to every part of the country. In every village and farm, the priest and six ordinary people were put under oath to answer the questions asked of them by the king's commissioners. Everybody and everything was counted and listed. In the words of a contemporary chronicler:

He sent his men over all England into every shire and had them find out how many hundred hides

there were in the shire, or what land and cattle the king himself had, or what dues he ought to have in twelve months from the shire. Also . . . what or how much everybody had who was occupying land in England, in land or cattle, and how much money it was worth. So very narrowly did he have it investigated, that there was no single hide nor yard of land, nor indeed . . . one ox nor one cow nor one pig was there left out, and not put down in his record: and all these records were brought to him afterwards.[1]

The resulting record, called *Domesday Book* from the Anglo-Saxon word *doom* meaning "judgment," still survives. It is an invaluable source of social and economic information about medieval England.

The Conqueror's scribes compiled *Domesday Book* in less than a year, using the evidence given by local people. *Domesday Book* provided William and his descendants with information vital for the exploitation and government of the country. Knowing the amount of wealth every area possessed, the king could tax accordingly. Knowing the amount of land his vassals had, he could allot knight service fairly. *Domesday Book* was a unique document. Its inclusion of material about all of England helped enable English kings to think of their country as a single unit and to work to bind it together. Across the English Channel, state building took a different course.

FRANCE In the early twelfth century, France consisted of a number of virtually independent provinces. Each was governed by its local ruler; each had its own laws and customs; each had its own coinage; each had its own dialect. Unlike the king of England, the king of France had jurisdiction over a very small area. Chroniclers called King Louis VI (1108–1137) *roi de St.-Denis,* king of St.-Denis, because the territory he controlled was limited to Paris and the St.-Denis area surrounding the city. This region, called the Ile-de-France or royal domain, became the nucleus of the French state. The clear goal of the medieval French monarchy was to increase the royal domain and extend the power and authority of the king (see Map 11.1).

The work of unifying France began under Louis VI's grandson Philip II (1180-1223). Rigord, Philip's biographer, gave him the title "Augustus" (from a Latin word meaning "to increase") because he vastly enlarged the territory of the kingdom of France. By defeating a baronial plot against the Crown, Philip Augustus acquired the northern counties of Artois and Vermandois. When King John of England, who was Philip's vassal for the rich province of Normandy, defaulted on his feudal obligation to come to the French court, Philip declared Normandy forfeit to the French crown. He enforced this declaration militarily, and in 1204 Normandy fell to the French. Within two years Philip also gained the prosperous farmlands of Maine, Touraine, and Anjou. By the end of his reign Philip was effectively master of northern France.

In the thirteenth century Philip Augustus's descendants made important acquisitions in the south. Louis VIII (1223-1226) added the county of Poitou to the kingdom of France by war. Louis IX (1226-1270) gained Toulouse and a vital interest in the Mediterranean province of Provence through his marriage to Margaret of Provence. Louis' son Philip III (1270-1285) secured Languedoc through inheritance. By the end of the thirteenth century, most of the provinces of modern France had been added to the royal domain through diplomacy, marriage, war, and inheritance. The king of France was stronger than any group of antagonistic French nobles who might try to challenge his authority.

Philip Augustus devised a method of governing the provinces and providing for communication between the central government in Paris and local communities. Philip decided that each province would retain its own institutions and laws. But royal agents, called baillis in the north and seneschals in the south, were sent from Paris into the provinces as the king's official representatives with authority to act for him. Often middle-class lawyers, these men possessed full judicial, financial, and military jurisdiction in their districts. The baillis and seneschals were appointed by, paid by, and responsible to the king. Unlike the English sheriffs, they were never natives of the provinces to which they were assigned, and they could not own land there. This policy reflected the fundamental principle of French administration that royal interests superseded local interests.

While English governmental administration was based on the services of unpaid local officials, France was administered by a professional royal bureaucracy. Bureaucracy was the cornerstone of French royal government. As new territories came under royal control, the bureaucracy expanded. So great was the variety of customs, laws, and provincial institutions that any attempt to impose uniformity would have touched off a rebellion. The French system was characterized by diversity at the local level and centralization at the top. Although it sometimes fell into disrepair, the basic system that Philip Augustus created worked so well that it survived until the Revolution of 1789.

THE HOLY ROMAN EMPIRE The political problems of the Holy Roman Empire differed considerably from those of France and England. The eleventh-century investiture controversy between the German emperor and the Roman papacy had left the empire shattered and divided (pages 308-310). In the twelfth and thirteenth centuries, the Holy Roman Empire was split into hundreds of indepen-

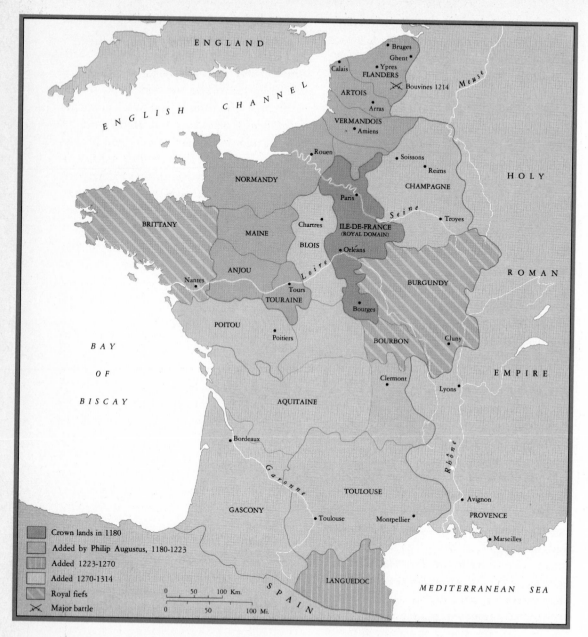

ENGLAND

BRUGES •
GHENT •
Calais • YPRES •
FLANDERS
⚔ Bouvines 1214
ARTOIS
Arras •
VERMANDOIS
Amiens •

ENGLISH CHANNEL

Rouen •

NORMANDY

Soissons •
Reims •
CHAMPAGNE

Paris •

HOLY

ILE-DE-FRANCE
(ROYAL DOMAIN)

Seine

Troyes •

BRITTANY

Chartres •
MAINE
BLOIS

Nantes •

ANJOU

Loire

Tours •
TOURAINE

Orléans •
BOURGES •

ROMAN

BURGUNDY

BAY

POITOU

Poitiers •

BOURBON

Cluny •

OF

Clermont •

EMPIRE

BISCAY

AQUITAINE

Lyons •

Bordeaux •

Garonne

Rhône

GASCONY

TOULOUSE

Toulouse •
Montpellier •

Avignon •
PROVENCE

SPAIN

LANGUEDOC

Marseilles •

MEDITERRANEAN   SEA

Crown lands in 1180
Added by Philip Augustus, 1180–1223
Added 1223–1270
Added 1270–1314
Royal fiefs
Major battle

0   50   100 Km.
0   50   100 Mi.

MAP 11.1   THE GROWTH OF THE KINGDOM OF
FRANCE   *Some scholars believe that Philip II received the title "Augustus" (from a Latin word
meaning "to increase"), because he vastly expanded
the territories of the kingdom of France. In spite of
differences, what similarities among peoples made expansion from Paris likely?*

dent provinces, principalities, bishoprics, duchies, and free cities. Princes, dukes, and local rulers held power over small areas.

There were several barriers to the development of a strong central government. The German rulers lacked a strong royal domain, like that of the French kings, to use as a source of revenue and a base from which to expand royal power. No accepted principle of succession to the throne existed, and as a result the death of the emperor was often followed by disputes, civil war, and anarchy. Moreover, German rulers were continually attracted south by the wealth of the northern Italian cities or by dreams of restoring the imperial glory of Charlemagne. Time after time the German emperors got involved in Italian affairs, and in turn the papacy, fearful of a strong German power in northern Italy, interfered in German affairs. German princes took bribes from whichever authority — the emperor or the pope — best supported their own particular ambitions. Consequently, the centralization of authority in Germany, in contrast to that in France and England, occurred very slowly. In medieval Germany, power remained in the hands of numerous princes instead of the emperor.

Through most of the first half of the twelfth century, civil war wracked the Holy Roman Empire as the emperors tried to strengthen their position by playing off baronial factions against one another. When the emperor Conrad III died in 1152, the resulting anarchy was so terrible that the electors — the seven princes responsible for choosing the emperor — decided that the only alternative to continued chaos was the selection of a strong ruler. They chose Frederick Barbarossa of the house of Hohenstaufen.

Frederick Barbarossa (1152–1190) tried valiantly to unify the empire. Just as the French rulers branched out from their compact domain in the Ile-de-France, Frederick tried to use his family duchy of Swabia in southwestern Germany as a power base (see Map 11.2). Just as William the Conqueror had done, Frederick required all vassals in Swabia to take an oath of allegiance to him as emperor, no matter who their immediate lord might be. He appointed officials called ministeriales, men of low social origin, to exercise the full imperial authority over administrative districts of Swabia. Ministeriales linked the emperor and local communities.

Outside of Swabia, Frederick tried to make feudalism work as a system of government. The princes throughout the empire exercised tremendous power, and Frederick tried to subordinate them to the authority of the royal government. He made alliances with the great lay princes in which they acknowledged that their lands were fiefs of the emperor, and he in turn recognized their military and political jurisdiction over their territories. Frederick also compelled the great churchmen to become his vassals, so that when they died he could control their estates. Frederick solved the problem of chronic violence by making the princes responsible for the establishment of peace within their territories. At a great assembly held at Roncaglia in 1158, private warfare was forbidden and severe penalties were laid down for violations of the peace.

Unfortunately Frederick Barbarossa did not concentrate his efforts and resources in one area. He too became embroiled in the affairs of Italy. He too wanted to restore the Holy Roman Empire, joining Germany and Italy. In the eleventh and twelfth centuries, the northern Italian cities had grown rich on trade, and Frederick believed that if he could gain the imperial crown, he could cash in on Italian wealth. Frederick saw that although the Italian cities were populous and militarily strong, they lacked stable governments and

HOLSTEIN

Lübeck

POMERANIA

Bremen

FRISIA

SAXONY

BRANDENBURG

Brandenburg

LUSATIA

Goslar

POLAND

Cologne

THURINGIA

MEISSEN

Aix-la-Chapelle

LOWER
LORRAINE

FRANCONIA

Mainz

Prague

BOHEMIA

Trier

Worms

MORAVIA

UPPER
LORRAINE

Verdun

FRANCE

Toul

BAVARIA

AUSTRIA

Augsburg

SWABIA

Salzburg

STYRIA

Besançon

CARINTHIA

HUNGARY

BURGUNDY–ARLES

LOMBARDY

Legnano 1176

VERONA

CARNIOLA

Milan

Venice

Pavia

Roncaglia

REPUBLIC OF VENICE

Avignon

PROVENCE

Florence

Arles

Marseilles

TUSCANY

PAPAL
STATES

Rome

APULIA

KINGDOM OF SICILY

Naples

Salerno

Messina

Palermo

SICILY

✕ Major battle

　 Holy Roman Empire, ca 1200

　 Kingdom of Sicily

　 Republic of Venice

0   100   200 Km.

0   100   200 Mi.

were often involved in struggles with one another. The German emperor mistakenly believed that moneygrubbing infantrymen could not stand up against his tough aristocratic knights. He did not realize that the merchant oligarchs who ran the city governments of Milan, Venice, and Florence considered themselves just as noble as he; they prized their independence and were determined to fight for it. Frederick's desire to control the papacy and to end papal claims to suzerainty over the empire also attracted him southward. He did not know that the popes feared a strong German state in northern Italy even more than they feared the rich and (the popes suspected) slightly heretical Italian cities.

Between 1154 and 1188, Frederick made six expeditions into Italy. His scorched-earth policy was successful at first, making for significant conquests in the north. The brutality of his methods, however, provoked revolts, and the Italian cities formed an alliance with the papacy. In 1176, Frederick suffered a catastrophic defeat at Legnano (see Map 11.2). This battle marked the first time a feudal cavalry of armed knights was decisively defeated by bourgeois infantrymen. Frederick was forced to recognize the independence of the northern Italian cities. Germany and Italy remained separate countries and followed separate courses of development.

Frederick Barbarossa's Italian ventures contributed nothing to the unification of the German states. Because the empire lacked a stable bureaucratic system of government, his presence was essential for the maintenance of peace. In Frederick's absences, the fires of independence and disorder spread. The princes

and magnates consolidated their power, and the unsupervised royal ministeriales gained considerable independence. By 1187, Frederick had to accept again the reality of private warfare. The power of the princes grew at the expense of a centralized monarchy.

FINANCE

As medieval rulers expanded their territories and extended their authority, they required more officials, larger armies, and more and more money. Officials and armies had to be paid, and kings had to find ways to raise revenue.

In England, William the Conqueror's son Henry I (1100–1135) established a bureau of finance called the Exchequer (for the checkered cloth at which his officials collected and audited royal accounts). Henry's income came from a variety of sources: from taxes paid by peasants living on the king's estates; from the Danegeld, an old tax originally levied to pay tribute to the Danes; from the *dona,* an annual gift from the church; from money paid to the Crown for settling disputes; and from fines paid by people found guilty of crimes. Henry also received income because of his position as feudal lord. If, for example, one of his vassals died and the son wished to inherit the father's properties, the heir had to pay Henry a relief tax. The sheriff in each county was responsible for collecting all these sums and for paying them twice a year to the king's Exchequer. Henry, like other medieval kings, made no distinction between his private income and state revenues.

An accurate record of expenditures and income is needed to insure a state's solvency. Henry assigned a few of the barons and bishops at his court to keep careful records of the monies paid into and out of the royal treasury. These financial officials, called barons of the Exchequer, gradually developed into a professional organization with its own rules, procedures, and esprit de corps. The Exchequer, which always sat in London, became the first institution of the governmental bureaucracy of England. Because of its work, an almost complete series of financial records for England dating back to 1130 survives; after 1154 the series is complete.

The development of royal financial agencies in most continental countries lagged behind the English Exchequer. Twelfth-century French rulers derived their income from their royal estates in the Ile-de-France. As Philip Augustus and his successors added provinces to the royal domain, the need for money became increasingly acute. Philip made the baillis and seneschals responsible for collecting taxes in their districts. This income came primarily from fines and confiscations imposed by the courts. Three times a year the baillis and seneschals reported to the king's court with the monies they had collected.

In the thirteenth century, French rulers found additional sources of revenue. They acquired some income from the church and some from people living in the towns. Townspeople paid tallage – a tax arbitrarily laid by the king. In all parts of the country feudal vassals owed military service to the king when he called for it. Louis IX converted this military obligation into a cash payment, called host tallage, and thus increased his revenues. Philip Augustus, Louis VIII, and Louis IX all taxed the Jews mercilessly.

Medieval people believed that a good king lived on the income of his own land and taxed only in time of a grave emergency – that is, a just war. Because the church, and not the state, performed what twentieth-century people call social services, such as education and care of the sick, the aged, and orphaned children, there was no ordinary need for the government to tax. Taxation meant war

financing. The French monarchy could not continually justify taxing the people on the grounds of the needs of war. Thus the French kings were slow to develop an efficient bureau of finance. French localism – in contrast to England's early unification – also retarded the growth of a central financial agency. Not until the fourteenth century, as a result of the demands of the Hundred Years' War, did a state financial bureau emerge – the Chamber of Accounts.

The one European government other than England that developed an efficient financial bureaucracy in the High Middle Ages was the kingdom of Sicily. Sicily is a good example of how strong government could be built on a feudal base by determined rulers.

Like England, Sicily had come under Norman domination. Between 1061 and 1091, a bold Norman knight, Roger de Hauteville, with a small band of mercenaries had defeated the Muslims and Greeks who controlled the island. Like William the Conqueror in England, Robert introduced Norman feudalism in Sicily and made it work as a system of government. Roger distributed scattered fiefs to his followers, so that no vassal had a centralized power base. He took an inquest of royal properties and rights, and he forbade private warfare. Roger adapted his Norman experience to Arabic and Greek governmental practices. Thus he retained the Muslims' main financial agency, the *diwan,* a sophisticated bureau for recordkeeping.

His son and heir, Count Roger II (1130–1154), continued the process of state building. He subdued the province of Apulia in southern Italy, united it with his Sicilian lands, and had himself crowned king of Sicily (1130–1154). Roger II organized the economy in the interests of the state; for example, the Crown secured a monopoly on the sale of salt and lumber. With the revenues thus acquired, Roger hired mercenary troops. His judiciary welcomed appeals from local communities. The army, the judiciary, and the *diwan* were staffed by Greeks and Muslims as well as Normans.

Under Frederick II Hohenstaufen (1212-1250), grandson of Roger II, Sicily underwent remarkable development. Frederick, also the grandson and heir of Frederick Barbarossa, was a brilliant legislator and administrator, and he constructed the most advanced bureaucratic state in medieval Europe. The institutions of the kingdom of Sicily were harnessed in the service of the state as represented by the king.

Frederick banned private warfare, and he placed all castles and towers under royal administration. Frederick also replaced town officials with royal governors. In 1231, he published the Constitutions of Melfi, a collection of laws that vastly enhanced royal authority. Both feudal and ecclesiastical courts were subordinated to the king's courts. Each year royal judges visited all parts of the kingdom, and the supreme court at Capua heard appeals from all lesser courts. Thus churchmen accused of crimes were tried in the royal courts. Royal control of the nobility, of the towns, and of the judicial system added up to great centralization, which required a professional bureaucracy and sound state financing.

In 1224, Frederick founded the University of Naples to train clerks and officials for his bureaucracy. University-educated administrators and lawyers emphasized the stiff principles of Roman law, such as the Justinian maxim that "what pleases the prince has the force of law." Frederick's financial experts regulated agriculture, public works, and even business. His customs service carefully supervised all imports and exports, collecting taxes for the Crown on all products. Royal revenues increased tremendously. Moreover, Frederick strictly regulated the currency and forbade the export of gold and silver bullion.

GERMAN BRONZE BIRD   Dating from the twelfth or thirteenth century, this may possibly be the eagle that surmounted the staff of the Emperor Frederick II, or possibly a falcon representing Frederick's interest in falconry, on which he was a great authority. The eagle symbolizes the royal virtues of justice and generosity, whereas the falcon was the favorite aristocratic hunting bird. (Metropolitan Museum of Art, The Cloisters Collection, 1947)

Finally, Frederick secured the tacit consent of his people to regular taxation. This was an incredible achievement in the Middle Ages, when most people believed that taxes should be levied only in time of grave emergency, the just war. Frederick defined emergency broadly. For much of his reign he was involved in a bitter dispute with the papacy. Churchmen hardly considered the emperor's wars with the popes as just, but Frederick's position was so strong that he could ignore criticism and levy taxes.

Frederick's contemporaries called him "The Transformer of the World." He certainly transformed the kingdom of Sicily, creating a state that was in many ways modern. But Frederick was highly ambitious: he wanted to control the entire peninsula of Italy. The popes, fearful of being encircled, waged a long conflict to prevent that. The kingdom of Sicily required constant attention, and Frederick's absences took their toll. Shortly after he died, the unsupervised bureaucracy he had built fell to pieces. The pope, claiming feudal suzerainty over Sicily, called in a French prince to rule.

Frederick showed little interest in Germany. He concentrated his attention on Sicily rather than the historic Hohenstaufen stronghold in Swabia, and the focus of imperial concerns shifted southward. When he visited the empire, in the expectation of securing German support for his Italian policy, he made sweeping concessions to the princes, bishops, duchies, and free cities. In 1220, for example, he exempted German churchmen from taxation and from the jurisdiction of imperial authorities. In 1231, he gave lay princes the same exemptions and even threw in the right to coin money. Frederick gave away so much that imperial authority was seriously weakened. In the later Middle Ages, lay and ecclesiastical princes held sway in the Holy Roman Empire. The centralizing efforts of Frederick Barbarossa were destroyed by his grandson Frederick II.

LAW AND JUSTICE

Throughout Europe, the form and application of laws depended upon local and provincial custom and practice. In the twelfth and thirteenth centuries the law was a hodgepodge of Germanic customs, feudal rights, and provincial practices. Kings wanted to blend these elements into a uniform system of rules acceptable and applicable to all their peoples. In France and England kings successfully contributed to the development of national states through the administration of their laws. Legal developments in continental countries like France were strongly influenced by Roman law, while England slowly built up a unique unwritten common law.

The French king Louis IX was famous in his time for his concern for justice. Each French province, even after being made part of the kingdom of France, retained its unique laws and procedures, but Louis IX created a royal judicial system. He established the Parlement of Paris, a kind of supreme court that welcomed appeals from local administrators and from the courts of feudal lords throughout France. By the very act of appealing the decisions of feudal courts to the Parlement of Paris, French people in far-flung provinces were recognizing the superiority of royal justice. By reviewing the decisions of baronial courts, the Parlement of Paris dispensed the king's justice to all French people.

Louis sent royal judges to all parts of the country to check up on the work of the baillis and seneschals and to hear complaints of injustice. He was the first French monarch to publish laws for the entire kingdom. The Parlement of Paris registered (or announced) these laws, which forbade private warfare, judicial duels, gambling, blaspheming, and prostitution. Louis sought to identify justice with the kingship, and gradually royal justice touched all parts of the kingdom.

Under Henry II (1154–1189), England developed and extended a common law, a law common to and accepted by the entire country. No other country in medieval Europe did so. Henry I had occasionally sent out circuit judges (royal officials who traveled a given circuit or district) to hear civil and criminal cases. Henry II made this way of extending royal justice an annual practice. Every year royal judges left London and set up court in the counties. Wherever the king's judges sat, there sat the king's court. Slowly, the king's court gained jurisdiction over all property disputes and criminal actions.

Henry made an important innovation in civil or property law. Disputes over land and movable property had caused a great deal of violence. Henry established a procedure whereby a person who felt unjustly deprived of possessions could seek a remedy in the royal court. The aggrieved person applied to the sheriff for help. The sheriff summoned a jury of local people before the king's judges, and there in the royal court the jury answered questions about rightful possession. On the basis of the jury's verdict, the disputed property was awarded. Thus, rather than attempting to get property back by force, English people had recourse to the king's court.

Henry also improved procedure in criminal justice. In 1166, he instructed the sheriffs to summon local juries to conduct inquests and draw up lists of known or suspected criminals. These lists, sworn to by the juries, were to be presented to the royal judges when they arrived in the community. This accusing jury is the ancestor of the modern grand jury.

An accused person formally charged with a crime did *not* undergo trial by jury. He or she was tried by ordeal. The accused was tied hand and foot and dropped in a lake or river. People believed that water was a pure substance and would reject anything foul or unclean. Thus a person who sank was considered innocent, and a person who floated was considered guilty. Trial by ordeal was a ritual that appealed to the supernatural for judgment. God determined innocence or guilt, and thus a priest had to be present to bless the water. Henry II and others considered this ancient

Germanic method irrational and a poor way of determining results, but they knew no alternative. In 1215, the Fourth Lateran Council of the church forbade the presence of priests at trials by ordeal and thus effectively abolished them. Gradually, in the course of the thirteenth century, the king's judges adopted the practice of calling upon twelve people (other than the accusing jury) to consider the question of innocence or guilt. This became the jury of trial, but it was very slowly accepted because medieval people had more confidence in the judgment of God than in that of twelve ordinary people.

Henry's innovations in civil procedure, the use of the accusing jury, and regular visits by circuit judges marked a decisive step forward. As the judges advanced the notion that any serious crime belonged under the king's jurisdiction, crime was no longer considered a violent act against an individual to be avenged by the victim and his or her family. Criminal acts became deeds against the state, or against the king as the embodiment of the state.

One aspect of Henry's judicial reforms encountered stiff resistance from an unexpected source: a friend and former chief adviser whom Henry had made archbishop of Canterbury – Thomas Becket. Henry selected Becket as archbishop in 1162 because he believed he could depend on Becket's support. But when Henry wanted to bring all persons in the kingdom under the jurisdiction of the royal courts, Thomas Becket's opposition led to another dramatic conflict between temporal and spiritual powers.

In the 1160s, many literate people accused of crimes claimed "benefit of clergy," even though they were not clerics and often had no intention of being ordained. "Benefit of clergy" gave the accused the right to be tried in church courts, which meted out mild punishments. A person found guilty in the king's court might suffer mutilation – loss of a hand

THE MARTYRDOM OF THOMAS BECKET
Becket's murder evoked many illustrations in the thirteenth century. This illumination faithfully follows the manuscript sources: while one knight held off the archbishop's defenders, the other three attacked. With a powerful stroke, the crown of his head was slashed off and his brains scattered on the cathedral floor. (Walters Art Gallery)

posed to have any contact with an excommunicated person, it appeared that the church could arbitrarily deprive the king of necessary military forces. The disagreement between Henry II and Becket dragged on for years. Becket maintained that as archbishop he had to defend the rights of the church. Henry insisted that the Crown should have full jurisdiction over all its subjects. The king grew increasingly bitter that his appointment of Becket had proved to be such a mistake. Late in December 1170, in a fit of rage, Henry expressed the wish that Becket be destroyed. Four knights took the king at his word, went to Canterbury, and killed the archbishop in his cathedral as he was leaving evening services.

What Thomas Becket could not achieve in life, he gained in death. The assassination of an archbishop in his own church during the Christmas season turned public opinion in England and throughout western Europe against the king. Within months miracles were recorded at Becket's tomb, and in a short time Canterbury Cathedral became a major pilgrimage and tourist site. Henry had to back down. He did public penance for the murder and gave up his attempts to bring clerics under the authority of the royal court.

Henry II's sons Richard I ("the Lion-Hearted") (1189–1199) and John (1199–1216) lacked their father's interest in the work of government. Handsome, athletic, and with an international reputation for military prowess, Richard looked upon England as a source of revenue for his military enterprises. Soon after his accession, he departed on crusade to the Holy Land. During his reign he spent only six months in England, and the government was run by ministers trained under Henry II.

Unlike Richard, King John was incompetent as a soldier and unnecessarily suspicious

or foot, or castration – or even death. Ecclesiastical punishments tended to be an obligation to say certain prayers or to make a pilgrimage. In 1164 Henry II insisted that everyone, including clerics, be subject to the royal courts.

Becket vigorously protested that church law required clerics to be subject to church courts. When he proceeded to excommunicate one of the king's vassals, the issue became more complicated. Because no one was sup-

that the barons were plotting against him. His basic problems, however, were financial. King John inherited a heavy debt from his father and brother. The country had paid dearly for Richard's crusading zeal. Returning from the Holy Land, Richard had been captured, and England had paid an enormous ransom to secure his release. In 1204, John lost the rich province of Normandy to Philip Augustus of France and then spent the rest of his reign trying to get it back. To finance that war, he got in deeper and deeper trouble with his barons. John squeezed as much money as possible from his position as feudal lord. He took scutage, a tax paid by his vassals in lieu of performing knight service. Each time John collected it, he increased the amount due. He forced widows to pay exorbitant fines to avoid unwanted marriages. He sold young girls who were his feudal wards to the highest bidder. These actions antagonized the nobility.

John also alienated the church and the English townspeople. He rejected Pope Innocent III's nominee to the see of Canterbury. And he infuriated the burghers of the towns by extorting money from them and threatening to revoke their charters of self-government.

All the money John raised did not bring him success. In July 1214, John's coalition of Flemish, German, and English cavalry suffered a severe defeat at the hands of Philip Augustus of France at Bouvines in Flanders. This battle ended English hopes for the recovery of territories from France. The battle of Bouvines also strengthened the barons' opposition to John. On top of his heavy taxation, his ineptitude as a soldier in a society that idealized military glory was the final straw. Rebellion begun by a few hotheaded northern barons eventually grew to involve a large number of the English nobility, including the archbishop of Canterbury and the earl of Pembroke, the leading ecclesiastical and lay

peers. After lengthy negotiations in the spring of 1215, John met the barons at Runnymede, a meadow along the Thames River. There he was forced to sign the treaty called Magna Carta, which became the cornerstone of English justice and law.

Magna Carta signifies the principle that the king and the government shall be under the law, that everyone including the king must obey the law. It contains clauses to protect the rights and property of all English people. It defends the interests of widows, orphans, townspeople, and freemen. Some clauses contain the germ of the idea of due process of law and of the right to a fair and speedy trial. Every English king in the Middle Ages reissued Magna Carta as evidence of his promise to observe the law. Because it was reissued frequently, and because later generations appealed to Magna Carta as a written statement of English liberties, it acquired an almost sacred importance as a guarantee of law and justice.

In the thirteenth century, the judicial precedents set under Henry II slowly evolved into permanent institutions. The king's judges asserted the royal authority and applied the same principles everywhere in the country. English people found the king's justice more rational and more evenhanded than the justice meted out in the baronial courts. The royal courts gained popularity, and the baronial courts lost rights and business. Respect for the king's law and the king's courts promoted loyalty to the Crown. By the time of Henry's great-grandson, Edward I (1272–1307), one law, the common law, operated all over England.

In the later Middle Ages, the English common law developed features that differed strikingly from the system of Roman law operative in continental Europe. The common law relied on precedents: a decision in an important case served as an authority for deciding similar cases. By contrast, continental judges, trained in Roman law, used the fixed legal maxims of the Justinian Code (pages 239–240) to decide their cases. Thus the common-law system evolved according to the changing experience of the people, while the Roman-law tradition tended toward an absolutist approach. In countries influenced by the common law, such as Canada and the United States, the court is open to the public; in countries with Roman-law traditions, such as France and the Latin American nations, courts need not be public. Under the common law, the accused in criminal cases has a right to access to the evidence against him; under the other system, he need not. The common law requires that judges be strictly impartial; in the Roman-law system judges interfere freely in many activities in their court rooms. Finally, whereas torture is foreign to the common-law tradition, it was once widely used in the Roman legal system.

The extension of royal law and justice led to a phenomenal amount of legal codification all over Europe. Governments wanted the law written down in an orderly and systematic fashion. The English judge Henry of Bracton (d. 1268) wrote a *Treatise on the Laws and Customs of England,* the French jurist Philippe de Beaumanoir (1250–1296) produced the *Customs of Beauvais,* and an anonymous German scholar compiled the *Sachsenspiegel* (1253). Legal texts and encyclopedias exalted royal authority, consolidated royal power, and emphasized political and social uniformity. The pressure for social conformity in turn contributed to a rising hostility toward minorities, Jews, and homosexuals.

Early Christians, as we have seen (page 231), displayed no special prejudice against homosexuals. While some of the Church Fathers, such as St. John Chrysostom (347–407), preached against them, a general indifference to homosexual activity prevailed throughout the early Middle Ages. In the early twelfth century a large homosexual literature circulated. Publicly known homosexuals such as Ralph, archbishop of Tours (1087–1118), and King Richard the Lion-Hearted of England held high ecclesiastical and political positions.

Beginning in the late twelfth century, however, a profound change occurred in public attitudes toward homosexual behavior. Why, if prejudice against homosexuals cannot be traced to early Christianity? Scholars have only begun to investigate this question, and the root cause of intolerance rarely yields to easy analysis. In the thirteenth century a fear of foreigners, especially Muslims, became associated with the crusading movement. Heretics were the most despised minority in an age that stressed religious and social uniformity. The notion spread that both Muslims and heretics, the great foreign and domestic menaces to the security of Christian Europe, were inclined to homosexual relations. Finally, the systematization of law and the rising strength of the state made any religious or sexual distinctiveness increasingly unacceptable. Whatever the precise cause, "between 1250 and 1300 homosexual activity passed from being completely legal in most of Europe to incurring the death penalty in all but a few legal compilations."[2] Spain, France, England, Norway, and several Italian city-states adopted laws condemning homosexual acts. Most of these laws remained on statute books until the twentieth century.

MEDIEVAL UNIVERSITIES

Just as the first strong secular states emerged in the thirteenth century, so did the first universities. This was no coincidence. The new bureaucratic states needed educated administrators, and universities were a response to this need. The word *university* derives from the Latin *universitas,* meaning "corporation" or "guild." Medieval universities were educational guilds that produced educated and trained individuals. They were also an expression of the tremendous vitality and creativity of the High Middle Ages. Their organization, methods of instruction, and goals continue to influence institutionalized learning in the Western world.

In the early Middle Ages, anyone who received any education got it from a priest. Priests instructed the clever boys on the manor in the Latin words of the mass, and taught them the rudiments of reading and writing. Few boys acquired elementary literacy, however, and girls did not even obtain that. The peasant who wished to send his son to school had to secure the permission of his lord, because the result of formal schooling tended to be a career in the church or some trade. If a young man were to pursue either profession, he had to leave the manor and gain free status. Because the lord stood to lose the services of educated peasants, he carefully limited the number of serfs who were sent to school.

Few schools were available anyway. Society was organized for war and defense and gave slight support to education. By the late eleventh century, however, social conditions had markedly improved. There was greater political stability, and favorable economic conditions had advanced many people beyond the level of bare subsistence. The curious and able felt the lack of schools and teachers.

Since the time of the Carolingian Empire, monasteries and cathedral schools had offered the only formal instruction available. The monasteries were geared to religious concerns, and the monastic curriculum consisted of studying the Scriptures and the writings of the church fathers. Monasteries wished to maintain an atmosphere of seclusion and silence and were unwilling to accept large numbers of noisy lay students. In contrast, schools attached to cathedrals and run by the bishop and his clergy were frequently situated in bustling cities, and in Italian cities like Bologna wealthy businessmen had established municipal schools. Cities inhabited by peoples of many backgrounds and "nationalities" stimulated the growth and exchange of ideas. In the course of the twelfth century, cathedral schools in France and municipal schools in Italy developed into universities (see Map 11.3).

The school at Chartres Cathedral in France became famous for its studies of the Latin classics and for the broad literary interests it fostered in its students. The most famous graduate of Chartres was the Englishman John of Salisbury (d. 1180), who wrote *The Statesman's Book,* an important treatise on the corrupting effects of political power. But Chartres, situated in the center of rich farmland remote from the currents of commercial traffic and intellectual ideas, did not develop into a university. The first European universities appeared in Italy, at Bologna in the north and Salerno in the south.

The growth of the University of Bologna coincided with a revival of interest in Roman law. The study of Roman law as embodied in the Justinian Code had never completely died out in the West, but this sudden burst of interest seems to have been inspired by Irnerius (d. 1125), a great teacher at Bologna. His fame attracted students from all over Europe. Irnerius not only explained the Roman law of the Justinian Code, he applied it to difficult practical situations. An important school of civil law was founded at Montpellier in

BALTIC SEA

NORTH SEA

DENMARK

SCOTLAND

St. Andrews

Glasgow

Copenhagen

Jarrow

Durham

Rivaulx

York

ENGLAND

Peterborough

Cambridge

Bury St. Edmunds

Oxford

Salisbury

Winchester

Canterbury

IRELAND

ATLANTIC OCEAN

Mont St. Michel

Jumièges

Bec

Notre Dame

Savigny

Laon

Reims

St.-Denis

Paris

Chartres

Clairvaux

Orléans

Fleury

Tours

Citeaux

Bourges

Poitiers

Cluny

FRANCE

Bordeaux

Cahors

Montpellier

Avignon

Toulouse

Louvain

Cologne

HOLY

Fulda

Mainz

Heidelberg

Hirsau

Magdeburg

Leipzig

Bamberg

Prague

Lorch

Regensburg

ROMAN

St.-Gall

Basel

Grenoble

EMPIRE

Pavia

Piacenza

Bologna

Florence

Vallombrosa

Perugia

Padua

Vienna

Valladolid

Salamanca

Coimbra

SPAIN

Toledo

Seville

CORSICA

SARDINIA

Rome

Monte Cassino

Naples

Salerno

Palermo

SICILY

MEDITERRANEAN SEA

■ University

† Monastery school

⚜ Cathedral school

0   100   200   300 Km.

0   100   200   300 Mi.

southern France, but Bologna remained the greatest law school throughout the Middle Ages.

At Salerno, interest in medicine had persisted for centuries. Greek and Muslim physicians there had studied the use of herbs as cures for disease, and they had experimented with surgery. The twelfth century ushered in a new interest in Greek medical texts and in the work of Arab and Greek doctors. Students of medicine poured into Salerno, and their study soon attracted royal attention. In 1140, when King Roger II of Sicily took the practice of medicine under royal control, his ordinance stated:

Who, from now on, wishes to practice medicine, has to present himself before our officials and examiners, in order to pass their judgment. Should he be bold enough to disregard this, he will be punished by imprisonment and confiscation of his entire property. In this way we are taking care that our subjects are not endangered by the inexperience of the physicians.

Nobody dare practice medicine unless he has been found fit by the convention of the Salernitan masters.[3]

King Roger sought to protect the people of the kingdom of Sicily from incompetent doctors.

In the first decades of the twelfth century, students converged upon Paris. They crowded into the cathedral school of Notre Dame and spilled over into the area later called the Latin Quarter — whose name probably reflects the Italian origin of many of the students attracted to Paris by the surge of interest in the classics, logic, and theology. The cathedral school's international reputation had already drawn to Paris scholars from all over Europe, one of the most famous of whom was Peter Abélard.

The son of a minor Breton knight, Peter Abélard (1079–1142) studied in Paris, quickly absorbed a large amount of material, and set himself up as a teacher. Abélard was fascinated by logic, which he believed could be used to solve most problems. He had a brilliant mind and, although orthodox in his philosophical teaching, appeared to challenge ecclesiastical authorities. His book *Sic et Non (Yes and No)* was a list of apparently contradictory propositions drawn from the Bible and the writings of the church fathers. One such proposition, for example, stated that sin is pleasing to God and is not pleasing to God. Abélard used a method of systematic doubting in his writing and teaching. As he put it in the preface to *Sic et Non,* "By doubting we come to questioning, and by questioning we perceive the truth." While other scholars merely asserted theological principles, Abélard discussed and analyzed them. Through reasoning he even tried to describe the attributes of the three persons of the Trinity, the central mystery of the Christian faith. Abélard was severely censured by a church council, but his cleverness, boldness, and imagination made him highly popular with students.

The influx of students eager for learning, together with dedicated and imaginative teachers, created the atmosphere in which universities grew. In northern Europe — at Paris and later at Oxford and Cambridge in England — associations or guilds of professors organized universities. They established the curriculum, set the length of time for study, and determined the form and content of examinations. In 1200, King Philip Augustus officially recognized the University of Paris, and in 1208 Pope Innocent III, who had studied there, designated the community of students and scholars a *universitas*.

INSTRUCTION AND CURRICULUM

University faculties grouped themselves according to academic disciplines, called schools – law, medicine, philosophy, and theology. The professors, known as schoolmen or scholastics, developed a method of thinking, reasoning, and writing in which questions were raised and authorities cited on both sides of the question. The goal of the scholastic method was to arrive at definitive answers and to provide a rational explanation for what was believed on faith. Schoolmen held that reason and faith constitute two harmonious realms in which the truths of faith and reason complement each other. The scholastic approach rested upon the recovery of classical philosophical texts.

Ancient Greek and Arabic texts had entered Europe in the early twelfth century, primarily through Toledo in Muslim Spain. Thirteenth-century philosophers relied on Latin translations of these texts, especially those of Aristotle. Aristotle had stressed direct observation of nature, as well as the principles that theory must follow fact and that knowledge of a thing requires an explanation of its causes. The schoolmen reinterpreted Aristotelian texts in a Christian sense.

In exploration of the natural world, Aristotle's axioms were not precisely followed. Medieval scientists argued from authority, such as the Bible, the Justinian Code, or an ancient scientific treatise, rather than from direct observation and experimentation, as modern scientists do. Thus, the conclusions of medieval scientists were often wrong. Nevertheless, natural science gradually emerged as a discipline distinct from philosophy. Scholastics made important contributions to the advancement of knowledge. They preserved the Greek and Arabic texts that contained the body of ancient scientific knowledge, which would otherwise have been lost. And, in asking questions about nature and the universe, scholastics laid the foundations for later scientific work.

Many of the problems that scholastic philosophers raised dealt with theological issues. They addressed, for example, the question that interested all Christians, educated and uneducated: how is a person saved? St. Augustine's thesis – that, as the result of Adam's fall, human beings have a propensity to sin – had become a central feature of medieval church doctrine. The church taught that it possessed the means to forgive the sinful: through grace conveyed through the sacraments. However, although grace provided a predisposition to salvation, the scholastics held that one must also *decide* to use the grace received. In other words, a person must use his or her reason to advance to God.

Thirteenth-century scholastics devoted an enormous amount of time to collecting and organizing knowledge on all topics. These collections were published as *summa,* or reference books. There were summa on law, philosophy, vegetation, animal life, theology. Saint Thomas Aquinas (1225–1274), a professor of theology at Paris, produced the most famous collection, the *Summa Theologica,* which deals with a vast number of theological questions.

Aquinas drew an important distinction between faith and reason. He maintained that, although reason can demonstrate many basic Christian principles such as the existence of God, other fundamental teachings such as the Trinity and original sin cannot be proven by logic. That reason cannot establish them does not, however, mean they are contrary to reason. People can gain an understanding of such

ART: A MIRROR OF SOCIETY

Art reveals the interests and values of society and frequently gives intimate and unique glimpses of how people actually lived. In portraits and statues, whether of saints, generals, philosophers, popes, poets, or merchants, it preserves the memory and fame of men and women who shaped society. In paintings, drawings, and carvings, it also shows how people worked, played, relaxed, suffered, and triumphed. Art, therefore, is extremely useful to the historian, especially for periods such as the ancient and medieval, when written records are scarce. Every work of art and every part of it has meaning and has something of its own to say.

Ancient and medieval art, apart from splendid public buildings, temples, cathedrals, and monasteries, was created by and for an aristocratic elite. It reflected the tastes and the interests of the aristocracy. Only a wealthy Greek could afford to buy a richly painted vase

or wine cup. Only a wealthy Roman family could decorate the floors of their house with dazzling mosaics. The Royal Standard of Ur, below, shows aspects of Sumerian society in peacetime. The upper band of the standard, a triangular box on a pole used on ceremonial occasions, depicts a royal banquet, with the king and his nobles drinking and listening to music. In the lower band herdsmen lead animals. (By courtesy of the British Museum.) Art was also created primarily for the aristocracy in the Middle Ages, when upper-class people commissioned mosaics, illuminated manuscripts, carved and jewelled objects, and miniatures and paintings. Furthermore, in the Middle Ages the primary function of art was to teach. Most medieval artists were clerics or monks, their subject matter was religious, and consequently religious themes pervade their art.

Art also manifests the changes and continuity of European life. Scenes of agricultural work and commerce were popular both in antiquity and in the Middle Ages. As values changed in Europe, so did major artistic themes. The religious art of the early Middle Ages replaced the sensuous pagan art of antiquity. In turn, the art of the later Middle Ages, a time which saw the emergence of a rich urban middle class, increasingly displayed secular interests. Europeans of the sixteenth and seventeenth centuries remained deeply religious but showed a new interest in the world around them: their middle-class attitudes and concerns were harbingers of developments to come.

ATHENIAN WOMEN AT A FOUNTAIN HOUSE (left) The Greeks often decorated their vases with scenes from daily life. Here five well-dressed Athenian women are seen filling their water jugs at a fountain house. They used the occasion to chat and exchange information. Scenes such as this one suggest that Athenian women were not so sheltered as they are often portrayed. (Courtesy, Museum of Fine Arts, Boston.)

BLACKSMITH'S SHOP (right) One blacksmith holds the heated metal in tongs while his husky companion wields a hammer. Hanging from the wall is one man's cloak, a water jug, and knives and axes that the smiths have made or repaired. In the winter the blacksmith's shop, kept warm by a constant fire, was a favorite place for the men to chat and to come in from the cold. (Courtesy, Museum of Fine Arts, Boston.)

PALESTRINA MOSAIC (below) Fish and birds abound as boatsmen steer among rocks and try their hand at spearing fish. The Nile was legendary for its fertility and the exotic animals that could be encountered along its course. Mosaics such as this were common in the ancient world and could be found in temples and the homes of the wealthy. (Scala/EPA.)

THE BURY ST. EDMUNDS' CROSS (above, left) Probably made for the English abbot Samson of Bury St. Edmunds' (1181–1211) and used in ceremonial processions, this walrus ivory cross, 2 ft. high and 14 in. across, contains 8 scenes, 108 figures, and 60 inscriptions from the Old and New Testaments. A superb example of late twelfth-century craftsmanship, piety, and, some inscriptions imply, anti-Semitic attitudes. (The Metropolitan Museum of Art; The Cloisters Collection, 1963.)

LES TRÈS RICHES HEURES DU JEAN, DUC DE BERRY (above, right) This illustrates March in a book of calendar miniatures produced for the duke of Berry, brother of the king of France. With exquisite detail the artists capture four scenes of agricultural life in the early fifteenth century. A shepherd with a dog guards a flock of sheep. Three peasants prune vines while another works in a different field. And an aged farmer guides a wheeled plow and oxen. Symbolically, the vast castle of Lusignan dominates the landscape. (Chantilly, Musée Condé/Giraudon.)

THE CAMPIN ALTARPIECE (ca 1425–1428), by Robert Campin (d. 1444). This 4-by 2-ft. painting in oil on wood was intended to hang behind the altar, facing the people. The Annunciation scene in the center panel occurs in the house of a Flemish burgher. Every detail has significance. For example, the serious, modestly dressed middle-class donors in the left panel are memorialized observing the mystery, the lilies on the table in the center panel represent the Virgin's chastity, and Joseph in front of a delicately painted view of a fifteenth-century city in the right panel carves a mousetrap, symbolizing Christ, the bait set to catch the devil. (The Metropolitan Museum of Art, The Cloisters Collection.)

FEAST OF THE GODS (above) Giovanni Bellini (1430?–1516). In this pastoral scene based on a story of the Roman poet Ovid, Olympian gods picnic in a wooded grove as satyrs and nymphs serve them. The peacock in the tree symbolizes the gods' immortality. The pagan theme, the appreciation for perspective and nature, and the sensual atmosphere make this painting a fine example of Italian Renaissance classicism. (National Gallery of Art, Washington, D.C.)

A WOMAN PEELING APPLES (below left) Pieter de Hooch (1629–1677). Stability, seriousness, and thrift are idealized in this Dutch domestic scene. The light filtering through the window represents a technical achievement and the secular appreciation for the world of nature and of man. (Reproduced by permission of the Trustees of the Wallace Collection.)

GEORG GISZE (below, right) Hans Holbein (1497–1543). Born in Danzig, Gisze became a rich London merchant. Here he is portrayed with quill and ink, seal, scales, and business letters hung on racks behind him. The Caucasian rug covering the desk was probably woven in Asia Minor in the fifteenth century. (Gemäldegalerie, Berlin.)

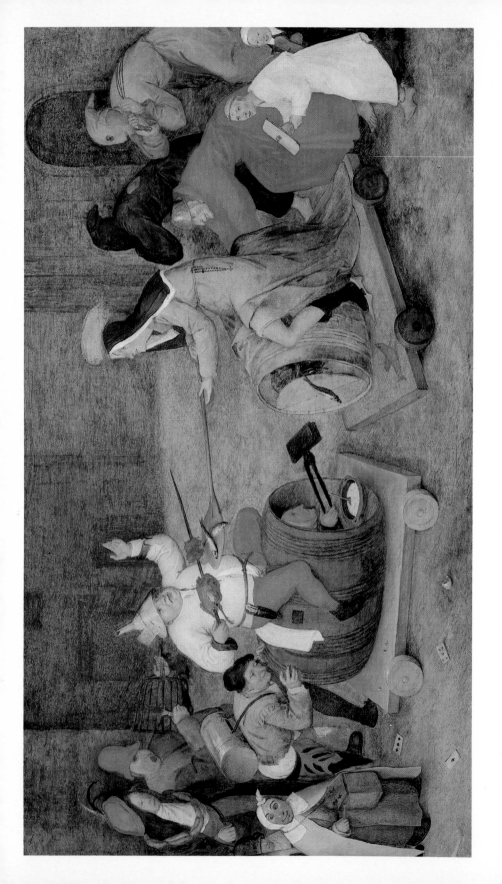

COMBAT BETWEEN CARNIVAL AND LENT (above) Pieter Bruegel the Elder (ca 1525–1559). One of the most original Flemish painters of the sixteenth century, Bruegel concentrated on scenes of peasant life. He treated many subjects satirically. In this conflict between gluttony and asceticism, a common Reformation theme, Bruegel suggests that neither side is a perfect model of Christian living. (Courtesy, Museum of Fine Arts, Boston.)

doctrines through revelation embodied in Scripture. Scripture cannot contradict reason, nor reason Scripture:

The light of faith that is freely infused into us does not destroy the light of natural knowledge [reason] implanted in us naturally. For although the natural light of the human mind is insufficient to show us these things made manifest by faith, it is nevertheless impossible that these things which the divine principle gives us by faith are contrary to those implanted in us by nature [reason]. Indeed, were that the case, one or the other would have to be false, and, since both are given to us by God, God would have to be the author of untruth, which is impossible. . . . it is impossible that those things which are of philosophy can be contrary to those things which are of faith.[4]

Aquinas also investigated the branch of philosophy called epistemology, which is concerned with how a person knows something. Aquinas stated that one knows, first, through sensory perception of the physical world – seeing, hearing, touching, and so on. He maintained that there can be nothing in the mind that is not first in the senses. Secondly, knowledge comes through reason, the mind exercising its natural abilities. Aquinas stressed the power of human reason to know, even to know God. Proofs of the existence of God exemplify the scholastic method of knowing.

Aquinas begins with the things of the natural world – earth, air, trees, water, birds. From these things, he inquires back to their original source or cause, the mover, creator, planner who started it all. Everything, Aquinas maintained, has an ultimate and essential explanation, a reason for existing. Here he was following Aristotle. Aquinas went further and identified the reason for existing, or first mover, with God. Thomas Aquinas and all medieval intellectuals held that the end of both faith and reason was the knowledge of, and union with, God. His work later became the fundamental text of Roman Catholic doctrine.

At all universities, the standard method of teaching was the lecture – that is, a reading. The professor read a passage from the Bible, the Justinian Code, or one of Aristotle's treatises. He then explained and interpreted the passage; his interpretation was called a gloss. Students wrote down everything. Texts and glosses were sometimes collected and reproduced as textbooks. For example, the Italian Peter Lombard (d. 1160), a professor at Paris, wrote what became the standard textbook in theology, *Sententiae (The Sentences),* which was a compilation of basic theological principles.

Because books had to be copied by hand, they were extremely expensive and few students could afford them. Students therefore depended for study on their own or friends' notes accumulated over a period of years. The choice of subjects was narrow. The syllabus at all universities consisted of a core of ancient texts that everyone studied and, if they wanted to get ahead, mastered.

There were no examinations at the end of a series of lectures. Examinations were given after three, four, or five years of study, when the student applied for a degree. The professors determined the amount of material students had to know for each degree, and students frequently insisted that the professors specify precisely what that material was. When the candidate for a degree believed himself prepared, he presented himself to a committee of professors for examination.

Examinations were oral and very difficult. (Not only did paper and ink cost a great deal, the examination was designed to test the student's ability to think quickly on his feet and to express his thoughts effectively.) If the candidate passed, he was awarded the first, or

A UNIVERSITY LECTURE Some students doze, some chat, and some are attentive to the lecturer. All students appear much older than undergraduates today. (Bildarchiv Preussischer Kulturbesitz)

bachelor's, degree. Further study, about as long, arduous, and expensive as it is today, enabled the graduate to try for the master's and doctor's degrees. All degrees certified competence in a given subject, and degrees were technically licenses to teach. Most students, however, did not become teachers.

STUDENT LIFE

The students and faculties of medieval universities were from the middling rungs of society, very much like many of the students and teachers at American state universities today. Most students (all of whom were male) came from families of lesser knights, burgesses of the towns, merchants, and artisans — the group that today would be called middle-class. Undergraduates were usually in their twenties and thirties, poor, ambitious, and aggressively upwardly mobile. They wanted and received an education that was practical, utilitarian, and vocational.

Students wanted to acquire as quickly as

possible the knowledge necessary for a secure, well-paying job in the service of the church or secular government. Consequently, once the first degree had been attained, law was the subject most often pursued for an advanced degree. Students studied law because governments needed the expertise of lawyers. Philip Augustus of France employed law graduates as baillis and seneschals. Frederick II, when he established the University of Naples, had clearly stated in the university's charter that the school's purpose was to train men who would dispense the law throughout his kingdom.

Medieval students exercised more power in their universities than do students today. In the Middle Ages students often traveled long distances to work with great scholars. They arrived as foreigners in the countries where they studied, and, fearful of the natives, formed associations for mutual security. Some guilds were set up for sheer physical protection; others sought to defend students from the high rates charged by local boarding-houses and innkeepers. Student guilds, especially in southern Italy, hired the professors, paid their fees, and demanded that teachers cover the syllabus within an agreed-upon time. If they became dissatisfied with incompetent professors or the financial gouging of townspeople, students did not hesitate to boycott lectures or to leave the town entirely. Cambridge University, for example, began when students at Oxford got fed up with conditions there.

Municipal court records of towns like Paris, Oxford, and Cambridge reveal that in the thirteenth and fourteenth centuries student riots and rebellions were common. Townspeople resented what they considered the wasteful lives of students. Students protested the high costs of living in university towns or what they felt were the unfair decisions of professors or university officials. Friction between students and townspeople or between students and university authorities was common. But the aim of medieval student movements was never to reform society as a whole. Medieval students had no interest in changing the basic social system. They wanted, instead, to get into the system; they wanted a piece of the action.

Medieval universities did not have luxurious dormitories, semiprofessional athletic teams, vast administrations, or even classrooms. The first professors lectured in rented halls. In the later thirteenth century, first at Paris and then at Oxford, noblemen and wealthy businessmen established colleges, or residence halls, and endowed scholarships for poor students. Most students lived in abject poverty, and before the sixteenth century they led a cold, uncomfortable, and hand-to-mouth existence. Nevertheless, in establishing the system of lectures, textbooks, faculties, examinations, and degrees, medieval universities laid the foundations for modern institutional learning.

GOTHIC ART

Medieval churches stand as the most spectacular manifestations of the vitality and creativity of the High Middle Ages. It is difficult for twentieth-century people to appreciate the extraordinary amounts of energy, imagination, and money involved in building them. Between 1180 and 1270 in France alone, eighty cathedrals, about five hundred abbey churches, and tens of thousands of parish churches were constructed. This construction represents a remarkable investment for a country of scarcely 18 million people. More stone was quarried for churches in medieval France than

ROMANESQUE AND GOTHIC ARCHES The
*round barrel vault characterizes the Romanesque
style. Cross vaults built on arches and supported by
buttresses typify the Gothic.*

had been mined in ancient Egypt, where the
Great Pyramid alone consumed 40.5 million
cubic feet of stone. All these churches displayed a new architectural style. Fourteenth-
century critics called the new style "Gothic"
because they mistakenly believed the Goths of
the fifth century had invented it. The Gothic
style actually developed partly in reaction to
an earlier style named Romanesque, which
supposedly resembled ancient Roman architecture.

Gothic cathedrals were built in towns, and
they reflect both bourgeois wealth and enormous civic pride. The manner in which a society spends its wealth expresses its values.
Cathedrals, abbeys, and village churches testify to the deep religious faith and piety of
medieval people. If the dominant aspect of
medieval culture had not been the Christian

faith, the builder's imagination and the merchant's money would have been used in other
ways.

FROM ROMANESQUE GLOOM TO "UNINTERRUPTED LIGHT"

The relative political stability and increase of
ecclesiastical wealth in the eleventh century
encouraged the arts of peace. In the ninth and
tenth centuries, the Vikings and Magyars had
burned hundreds of wooden churches. In the
eleventh century, abbots wanted to rebuild in
a more permanent fashion, and after the year
1000 church building increased on a wide
scale. Because fireproofing was essential, the
ceiling had to be made of stone. Therefore,
builders replaced wooden roofs with arched
stone ceilings called vaults. The stone ceilings
were heavy; only thick walls would support
them. Because the walls were so thick, the
windows were small, allowing little light into
the interior of the church. The basic features
of Romanesque architecture, as this style is
called, are stone vaults in the ceiling, a
rounded arch over the nave (the central part
of the church), and thick, heavy walls. In
northern Europe, twin bell towers often
crowned the Romanesque churches, giving
them a powerful, fortresslike appearance.
Built primarily by the monasteries, Romanesque churches reflect the quasi-military, aristocratic, and pre-urban society that built
them.

The inspiration for the Gothic style originated in the brain of one monk, Suger, abbot
of St.-Denis (1122–1151), whose life is a remarkable medieval success story. Born of very
poor parents, he was given as a child-oblate to
the abbey of St.-Denis. St.-Denis was a royal
abbey, closely associated with the French
monarchy, the custodian of the royal insignia,
and the burial place of the French kings.
Suger became chief adviser to Louis VI and

Louis VII; and when Louis VII was away on crusade, he served as the regent of France. When Suger became abbot, he decided to reconstruct the old Carolingian abbey church at St.-Denis. Work began in 1137. On June 11, 1144, King Louis VII and a large crowd of bishops, dignitaries, and common people witnessed the solemn consecration of the first Gothic church in France.

The basic features of Gothic architecture — the pointed arch, the ribbed vault, and the flying buttress — were not unknown before 1137. What was without precedent was the interior lightness they made possible. Since the ceiling of a Gothic church weighed less, the walls could be thinner. Windows were cut into the stone, allowing the church to be flooded with light. Stained-glass windows crowned the Gothic style. The bright interior was astounding. Suger, describing his achievement, exulted:

Moreover, it was cunningly provided that . . . the central nave of the old nave should be equalized, by means of geometrical and arithmetical instruments, with the central nave of the new addition; and, likewise, that the dimensions of the old side-aisles should be equalized with the dimensions of the new side-aisles, except for that elegant and praiseworthy extension, in [the form of] a circular string of chapels, by virtue of which the whole [church] would shine with the wonderful and uninterrupted light of most sacred windows, pervading the interior beauty.[5]

Thirteenth-century people referred to Gothic architecture as "the new style," or "the Frankish work." Begun in the Ile-de-France, Gothic architecture spread throughout France with the expansion of royal power. French architects were soon invited to design and supervise the construction of churches in other parts of Europe. For example, William of Sens, an experienced architect, was commis-

FOURTEENTH-CENTURY FRENCH STAINED GLASS *Stained glass illuminated both the church and, in the stories told, the minds of the viewers. In the left lancet the prophet Isaiah holds a scroll predicting that a Virgin will bear a son; in the right Mary Magdalene weeps because she cannot find Christ. (Metropolitan Museum of Art, The Cloisters, New York)*

WEST FRONT OF NOTRE DAME CATHEDRAL
In this powerful vision of the Last Judgment, Christ sits
in judgment surrounded by angels, the Virgin, and
Saint John. Scenes of paradise fill the arches on
Christ's right, scenes of hell on the left. In the lower

lintel, the dead arise incorruptible, and in the upper
lintel (below Christ's feet), the saved move off to
heaven, while devils push the damned to hell. Below,
the twelve apostles line the doorway. (Alinari/Scala)

sioned to rebuild Canterbury Cathedral after a disastrous fire in 1174. The distinguished scholar John of Salisbury was then in Canterbury and observed William's work. After John became bishop of Chartres, he wanted William of Sens to assist in the renovation of Chartres Cathedral. Through such contacts "the new style" traveled rapidly over Europe.

THE CREATIVE OUTBURST

The construction of a Gothic cathedral represented a gigantic investment of time, money, and corporate effort. It was the bishop and the clergy of the cathedral who made the decision to build, but they depended on the support of all the social classes. Bishops raised revenue from contributions by people in their dioceses, and the clergy appealed to the king and the nobility. The French rulers were generous benefactors of many cathedrals. Louis IX endowed so many churches in the Ile-de-France – most notably Sainte Chapelle, a small chapel he built to house the crown of thorns – that scholars speak of a "court style" of Gothic. Noble families often gave in order to have their crests in the stained-glass windows. Above all, the church relied on the financial help of those with the greatest amount of ready cash, the commercial classes.

Money was not the only need. A great number of craftsmen had to be assembled: quarrymen, sculptors, stonecutters, masons, mortar makers, carpenters, blacksmiths, glassmakers, roofers. Each master craftsman had his own apprentices, and unskilled laborers had to be recruited for the heavy work. The construction of a large cathedral was rarely completed in one lifetime; many were never finished at all. Because generation after generation of craftsmen added to the building,

many Gothic churches show the architectural influences of two or even three centuries.

The surge of church building in the twelfth and thirteenth centuries is intimately associated with the growth of towns and the increase of commercial wealth. The medieval cathedrals are monuments to the interest and support of the business classes. Townspeople had secured their independence from feudal authorities, and they celebrated that freedom by building splendid cathedrals. A large and magnificent church also reflected the wealth and prosperity of the townspeople – and the cleverness and industry needed to acquire that wealth. What better way to display that wealth than in the house of God?

Since cathedrals were symbols of bourgeois civic pride, towns competed to build the largest and most splendid church. In northern France in the late twelfth and early thirteenth centuries, cathedrals grew progressively taller. In 1163, the citizens of Paris began Notre Dame cathedral, intending it to reach a height of 114 feet. Reconstruction on Chartres Cathedral was begun in 1194: it was to be 119 feet. The people of Beauvais exceeded everyone: their church, started in 1247, reached 157 feet; unfortunately, the weight imposed on the vaults was too great, and the building collapsed in 1284. Medieval people built cathedrals to glorify God – and if mortals were impressed, so much the better.[6]

Cathedrals served secular as well as religious purposes. The sanctuary containing the altar and the bishop's chair belonged to the clergy, but the rest of the church belonged to the people. In addition to marriages, baptisms, and funerals, there were scores of feast days on which the entire town gathered in the cathedral for festivities. Amiens Cathedral could hold the entire town of ten thousand people. Local guilds, which fulfilled the economic, fraternal, and charitable functions of

CROUCHING BLACK MAN *From the north transept of Chartres Cathedral, ca 1230. The thousands of representations of blacks in medieval art show that Europeans were familiar with them — from commercial contacts with Muslim parts of Spain and Italy, the crusades, and the slave trade. Europeans' attitudes reflected a curious fascination with the social feeling, as here implied, that black people should occupy menial positions. The black man supports the Queen of Sheba, who symbolizes the pagan world in need of conversion. (Mark Sheridan OSB)*

modern labor unions, met in the cathedrals to arrange business deals and plan recreational events and the support of disabled members. Magistrates and municipal officials held political meetings there. Some towns never built town halls, because all civic functions took

place in the cathedral. Pilgrims slept there, lovers courted there, traveling actors staged plays there. The cathedral belonged to all.

The structure of the Gothic cathedral mirrored the interests of all classes of medieval society. The clergy planned the design of the building along orderly theological principles, putting into practice the axiom of the fifth-century mystical writer Dennis the Areopagite, "Through the senses man may rise to the contemplation of the divine." The cathedral was intended to teach the people the doctrines of the Christian faith through visual images.

Architecture became the servant of theology. The main altar was at the east end, pointing toward Jerusalem, the city of peace. The west front of the cathedral faced the setting sun, and its wall was usually devoted to scenes of the Last Judgment. The north side, which received the least sunlight, displayed events from the Old Testament. The south side, washed in warm sunshine for much of the day, depicted scenes from the New Testament. This symbolism implied that the Jewish people of the Old Testament lived in darkness and that the gospel brought by Christ illuminated the world. Every piece of sculpture, furniture, and stained glass had some religious or social significance.

Stained glass beautifully reflects the creative energy of the High Middle Ages. It is both an integral part of Gothic architecture and a distinct form of painting. The glassmaker "painted" his picture with small fragments of glass held together with strips of lead. As Gothic churches became more skeletal and had more windows, stained glass replaced manuscript illumination as the leading kind of painting.

Contributors to the cathedral and the workmen left their imprint upon it. The stonecutter cut his mark on every block of stone, partly so that he would be paid, partly

FIFTEENTH-CENTURY FLEMISH TAPESTRY
The weavers of Tournai (in present-day Belgium)
spent twenty-five years (1450–1475) producing this
magnificent tapestry, which is based on the Old Testa-
ment story of Jehu, Jezebel, and the sons of Ahab (2
Kings, 9–10). The elegant costumes show fifteenth-
century upper-class dress styles. (Isabella Stewart
Gardner Museum)

too so that his work would be remembered. At Chartres Cathedral the craft and merchant guilds – drapers, furriers, haberdashers, tanners, butchers, bakers, fishmongers, and wine merchants – donated money and are memorialized in the stained-glass windows. The incredibly beautiful window of the wine merchants depicts their business in three central medallions: a wine merchant and his cart; a man pouring wine from a cask; and the wine being used at the mass. Thousands of scenes in the cathedral celebrate nature,

country life, and the activities of ordinary people. All members of medieval society had a place in the City of God, which the Gothic cathedral represented. No one, from kings to milkmaids, was excluded.

Tapestry making also came into its own in the fourteenth century. Heavy woolen tapestries were first made in monasteries and convents as wall hangings for churches. Because they could be moved and lent an atmosphere of warmth, they subsequently replaced mural paintings. Early tapestries depicted religious scenes, but later hangings produced for the knightly class bore secular designs, especially romantic forests and hunting spectacles.

The drama, derived from the church's liturgy, emerged as a distinct art form during the same period. For centuries skits based on Christ's Resurrection and Nativity had been performed in monasteries and cathedrals. Beginning in the thirteenth century, plays based on these and other biblical themes and on the lives of the saints were performed in the towns. Guilds financed these "mystery plays," so called because they were based on the mysteries of the Christian faith; in a long production, each of a town's guilds was responsible for a different scene. Actors used very simple costumes and props, and comical or vulgar farces from the lives of ordinary people were interspersed with serious religious scenes. Performed first at the cathedral altar, then in the church square, and later in the town marketplace, mystery plays enjoyed great popularity. They allowed the common people to understand and identify with religious figures and the mysteries of their faith. While provoking the individual conscience to reform, mystery plays were also an artistic manifestation of local civic pride.

THE CRUSADES

Crusades in the late eleventh and early twelfth centuries were holy wars sponsored by the papacy for the recovery of the Holy Land from the Muslim Arabs or the Turks. In the later twelfth and through the thirteenth century, crusades were also directed against Europe's domestic enemies, heretics. Between 1096 and 1270 there were at least eight campaigns to wrest the Holy Land from the in-

fidels. Throughout this period Christians alone and in groups left Europe in a steady trickle for the Middle East. Although people of all ages and classes participated in the Crusades, so many knights did so that crusading became a distinctive feature of the upper-class lifestyle. In an aristocratic military society men coveted a reputation as a Crusader; the Christian knight who had been to the Holy Land enjoyed great prestige. The Crusades manifested the religious and chivalric ideals – as well as the tremendous vitality – of medieval society.

The Crusades of the High Middle Ages grew out of earlier conflict between Christians and Muslims in Spain. The concept of a holy war originated in the Spanish peninsula and gradually influenced all parts of western Europe. In the eighth century, the Arabs had overrun the peninsula, and Christian lords had fled into the mountains in the north. In the tenth century, Christians started the *reconquista,* or holy war of reconquest. Christian warriors made slow progress – not until 1492 did Isabella and Ferdinand finally succeed in expelling the Arabs – but by about 1100 Christian kings had regained about a fourth of the peninsula. The *reconquista* dominates the history of medieval Spain.

The Roman papacy supported the holy war in Spain, and by the late eleventh century had strong reasons for wanting to launch an expedition against Muslim infidels in the Middle East as well. The papacy had been involved in a bitter struggle over investiture with the German emperors. If the pope could muster a large army against the enemies of Christianity, his claim to be the leader of Christian society in the West would be strengthened.

Moreover, in 1054 a serious theological disagreement had split the Greek church of Byzantium and the Roman church of the

West. The pope believed that a crusade would lead to strong Roman influence in Greek territories and eventually the reunion of the two churches. Then, in 1071 at Manzikert in eastern Anatolia, Turkish soldiers in the pay of the Arabs defeated a Greek army and occupied much of Asia Minor. The emperor at Constantinople appealed to the West for support. Shortly afterward, the holy city of Jerusalem, the scene of Christ's preaching and burial, fell to the Turks. Pilgrimages to holy places in the Middle East became very dangerous, and the papacy was outraged that the holy city was in the hands of infidels.

In 1095, Pope Urban II journeyed to Clermont in France and called for a great Christian holy war against the infidels. He stressed the sufferings and persecution of Christians in Jerusalem. He urged Christian knights who had been fighting one another to direct their energies against the true enemies of God, the Muslims. Urban proclaimed an indulgence, or remission of sin, to those who would fight for and regain the holy city of Jerusalem. Few speeches in history have had such a dramatic effect as Urban's call at Clermont for the First Crusade.

The response was fantastic. Godfrey of Bouillon, Geoffrey of Lorraine, and many other great lords from northern France immediately had the cross of the Crusader sewn on their tunics. Encouraged by popular preachers like Peter the Hermit, and by papal legates in Germany, Italy, and England, thousands of people of all classes joined the crusade. Although most of the Crusaders were French, pilgrims from all countries streamed southward from the Rhineland, through Germany and the Balkans. No development in the High Middle Ages better reveals Europeans' religious zeal and emotional fervor, and the influence of the reformed papacy, than the incredible outpouring of support for the First Crusade.

Religious convictions inspired many, but mundane motives were also involved. Except for wives, who had to remain at home to manage estates, many people expected to benefit from the crusade. For the curious and the adventurous, it offered foreign travel and excitement; it promised escape from the dullness of everyday life. The crusade provided kings, who were trying to establish order and to build states, the perfect opportunity to get rid of troublemaking knights. It gave land-hungry younger sons a chance to acquire fiefs in the Middle East. Even some members of the middle class who stayed at home profited from the crusade. Nobles often had to borrow money from the middle class to pay for their expeditions, and they put up part of their land as security. If a noble did not return home or could not pay the interest on the loan, the middle-class creditor took over the land.

The First Crusade was successful mostly because of the dynamic enthusiasm of the participants. The Crusaders had little more than religious zeal. They knew nothing about the geography or climate of the Middle East. Although among the host there were several counts with military experience, the Crusaders could never agree on a leader, and the entire expedition was marked by disputes among the great lords. Lines of supply were never set up. Starvation and disease wracked the army, and the Turks slaughtered hundreds of noncombatants. Nevertheless, convinced that "God wills it" — the war cry of the Crusaders — the army pressed on and in 1099 captured Jerusalem. Although the Crusaders fought bravely, Arab disunity was a chief reason for their victory. At Jerusalem, Edessa, Tripoli, and Antioch, Crusader kingdoms were founded on the Western feudal model (see Map 11.4).

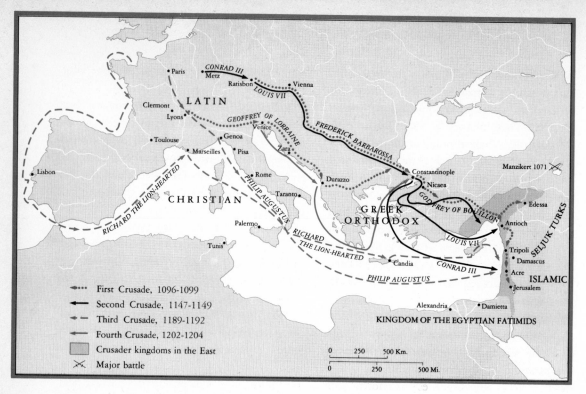

*MAP 11.4   THE ROUTES OF THE CRUSADES
The crusades led to a major cultural encounter between Muslim and Christian values. What significant
intellectual and economic effects resulted?*

Between 1096 and 1270, the crusading ideal
was expressed in eight papally approved expeditions to the East. In addition to those eight,
the papacy in 1208 proclaimed a crusade
against heretics in southern France. In the
same year, two expeditions of children set out
on a crusade to the Holy Land. One contingent turned back; the other was captured and
sold into slavery. And, in 1227 and 1239, the
pope launched a crusade against the emperor
Frederick II. None of the crusades against the
Muslims achieved very much. The third one
(1189–1192) was precipitated by the recapture
of Jerusalem by the sultan Saladin in 1187.
Frederick Barbarossa of the Holy Roman Empire, Richard the Lion-Hearted of England,
and Philip Augustus of France participated,
and the Third Crusade was better financed

than previous ones. But disputes among the
leaders and strategic problems prevented any
lasting results.

During the Fourth Crusade (1198–1204),
careless preparation and inadequate financing
had disastrous consequences for Byzantine-
Latin relations. Hoping to receive material
support from the Greeks, the leaders of the
crusade took the expedition to Constantinople
before advancing to Jerusalem. But once
there, they sacked the city and established the
Latin Empire of Constantinople. This assault
by one Christian people on another, when one
of the goals of the crusade was the reunion of
the Greek and Latin churches, helped to dis-
credit the entire crusading movement. Two
later crusades undertaken by King Louis IX
of France added to his prestige as a pious

ruler. Apart from that, the last of the official crusades accomplished nothing at all.

Crusades were also mounted against groups perceived as Christian Europe's social enemies. In 1208 Pope Innocent III proclaimed a crusade against the Albigensians, a heretical sect. The Albigensians, whose name derived from the southern French town of Albi where they were concentrated, rejected orthodox doctrine on the relationship of God and man, the sacraments, and the hierarchy. Believing the Albigensians a political threat, the French monarchy joined the crusade. Under Count Simon de Montfort the French inflicted a savage defeat on the Albigensians at Muret in 1213; the county of Toulouse passed to the authority of the French Crown. The popes in the mid-thirteenth century, fearful of encirclement by imperial territories, promoted crusades against Emperor Frederick II. This use of force against a Christian ruler backfired, damaging papal credibility as the sponsor of peace.

The Crusades brought few cultural changes to western Europe. By the late eleventh century, strong economic and intellectual ties with the East had already been made. The Crusades testify to the religious enthusiasm of the High Middle Ages. But, as Steven Runciman, a distinguished scholar of the Crusades, concluded in his three-volume history:

The triumphs of the Crusade were the triumphs of faith. But faith without wisdom is a dangerous thing. . . . In the long sequence of interaction and fusion between Orient and Occident out of which our civilization has grown, the Crusades were a tragic and destructive episode. . . . There was so much courage and so little honour, so much devotion and so little understanding. High ideals were besmirched by cruelty and greed, enterprise and endurance by a blind and narrow self-righteousness; and the Holy War itself was nothing more than a long act of intolerance in the name of God, which is the sin against the Holy Ghost.[7]

———————◆———————

Societies, like individuals, cannot maintain a high level of energy indefinitely. In the later years of the thirteenth century, Europeans seemed to run out of steam. The crusading movement gradually fizzled out. No new cathedrals were constructed, and if a cathedral had not been completed by 1300, the chances were that it never would be. The strong rulers of France and England, building on the foundations of their predecessors, increased their authority and gained the loyalty of all their subjects. The vigor of those kings, however, did not pass to their immediate descendants. The church, which for two centuries had guided Christian society, began to face grave difficulties. A violent dispute between the papacy and the kings of France and England badly damaged papal prestige.

In 1296, Kind Edward I of England and Philip the Fair of France declared war upon each other. To finance this war both kings laid taxes on the clergy. Kings had been taxing the church for decades. Pope Boniface VIII (1294–1303), a staunch defender of papal supremacy, forbade churchmen to pay the taxes. But Edward and Philip refused to accept this decree, partly because it hurt royal finances, and partly because the papal order threatened royal authority within their countries. Edward immediately denied the clergy the protection of the law, which meant that they could be attacked with impunity. Philip halted the shipment of all ecclesiastical revenue to Rome. Boniface had to back down.

Philip the Fair and his ministers continued their attack on all powers in France outside royal authority. Philip arrested a French bishop who was also the papal legate. When

THE CAPTURE OF JERUSALEM IN 1099 *As engines hurl stones to breach the walls, crusaders enter on scaling ladders. Scenes from Christ's passion (above) identify the city as Jerusalem. (Bibliothèque Nationale, Paris)*

Boniface defended the ecclesiastical status and diplomatic immunity of the bishop, Philip replied with the trumped-up charge that the pope was a heretic. The papacy and the French monarchy waged a bitter war of propaganda. Finally in 1302, in a letter entitled *Unam Sanctam* (because its opening sentence spoke of one holy Catholic church), Boniface insisted that Philip, like everyone else, submit to papal authority. Philip's university-trained advisers responded with an argument drawn from Roman law: they maintained that the king of France was completely sovereign in his kingdom and responsible to God alone. French mercenary troops went to Italy and arrested the aged pope at Anagni. Although Boniface was soon freed, he died shortly afterward. The incident at Anagni marked a decisive turning point.

The French attack on the leadership of the church signaled the weakening of religious authority. The Christian church had been the strongest influence in medieval society, but now a new power, the national secular state, was emerging in western Europe. Boniface's successors not only retracted *Unam Sanctam* but apologized for it. The centralized power of the French monarchy, which had been growing for over a century, scored a victory over the papacy. The presence of King Philip the Fair at the coronation of Pope Clement V at Lyons in 1305 was symbolic: Clement was French, and he established the papal court at Avignon, within the borders of the Holy Roman Empire but very much a French city. For the next sixty years, the Roman papacy was strongly influenced by France. Anagni foreshadowed serious difficulties within the Christian church, but additional difficulties awaited Western society in the fourteenth century.

NOTES

1. D. C. Douglas and G. E. Greenaway, eds., *English Historical Documents,* II, Eyre & Spottiswoode, London, 1961, p. 853.

2. This section leans heavily on John Boswell, *Christianity, Social Tolerance, and Homosexuality: Gay People in Western Europe from the Beginning of the Christian Era to the Fourteenth Century,* University of Chicago Press, Chicago, 1980, pp. 270–293; the quotation is from p. 293.

3. Quoted by H. E. Sigerist, *Civilization and Disease,* University of Chicago Press, Chicago, 1943, p. 102.

4. Quoted by John H. Mundy, *Europe in the High Middle Ages, 1150–1309,* Basic Books, New York, 1973, pp. 474–475.

5. E. Panofsky, trans., *Abbot Suger on the Abbey Church of St.-Denis and Its Art Treasures,* Princeton University Press, Princeton, 1946, p. 101.

6. See J. Gimpel, *The Cathedral Builders,* Grove Press, New York, 1961, pp. 42–49.

7. S. Runciman, *A History of the Crusades,* vol. 3, *The Kingdom of Acre,* Cambridge University Press, Cambridge, 1955, p. 480.

SUGGESTED READING

The achievements of the High Middle Ages have attracted considerable scholarly attention, and the curious student will have no difficulty finding exciting material on the points raised in this chapter. Three general surveys of the period 1050–1300 are especially recommended: J. R. Strayer, *Western Europe in the Middle Ages* (1955), a masterful synthesis; J. W. Baldwin, *The Scholastic Culture of the Middle Ages* (1971), which stresses the intellectual features of medieval civilization; and F. Heer, *The Medieval World* (1963).

G. O. Sayles, *The Medieval Foundations of England* (1961), traces English conditions to the end of the thirteenth century, while R. Fawtier, *The Capetian Kings of France* (1962), shows how the French monarchy built a nation. G. Barraclough, *Origins of Modern Germany* (1963), provides the best explanation of the problems and peculiarities of the Holy Roman Empire; this is a fine example of a Marxist interpretation of medieval history. Tom Corfe, *Archbishop Thomas Becket and King Henry II* (1980), treats many aspects of the political and religious life of twelfth century England, as well as the conflict between those two persons, in a cleverly illustrated little study: this book is in the Cambridge History of Mankind series. J. R. Strayer, *On the Medieval Origins of the Modern State* (1972), is an excellent treatment of the political and bureaucratic development of European states, also with emphasis on France and England. The advanced student of French medieval administrative history should consult Joseph R. Strayer, *The Reign of Philip the Fair* (1980). Students interested in approaching the High Middle Ages through biographies of leading political figures will find D. C. Douglas, *William the Conqueror* (1964); W. L. Warren, *Henry II* (1974); and E. Kantorowicz, *Frederick II* (1931), interesting and thorough.

For the new currents of thought in the High Middle Ages, see C. Brooke, *The Twelfth Century Renaissance* (1970), a splendidly illustrated book with copious quotations from the sources; E. Gilson, *Héloise and Abélard* (1960) which treats the medieval origins of modern humanism against the background of Abélard the teacher; D. W. Robertson, Jr., *Abélard and Héloise* (1972), which is highly readable, commonsensical, and probably the best recent study of Abélard and the love affair he supposedly had; and C. W. Hollister, ed., *The Twelfth Century Renaissance* (1969), a well-constructed anthology with source materials on many aspects of twelfth-century culture. N. Orme, *English Schools in the Middle Ages* (1973), focuses on the significance of schools and literacy in English Medieval society, while J. Leclercq, *The Love of Learning and the Desire of God* (1974), discusses monastic literary culture.

On the medieval universities, C. H. Haskins, *The Rise of the Universities* (1959), is a good introduction, while H. Rashdall, *The Universities of Europe in the Middle Ages* (1936), is the standard scholarly work. G. Leff, *Paris and Oxford Universities in the Thirteenth and Fourteenth Centuries* (1968), gives a fascinating sketch and includes a useful bibliography.

Students will find a good general introduction to Romanesque and Gothic architecture in N. Pevsner, *An Outline of European Architecture* (1963), a standard work. D. Grivot and G. Zarnecki, *Gislebertus, Sculptor of Autun* (1961), is the finest appreciation of Romanesque architecture written in English. For the actual work of building, see D. Macaulay, *Cathedral: The Story of Its Construction* (1973), a prizewinning, simply written, and cleverly illustrated re-creation of the problems and duration of cathedral building. J. Gimpel, *The Cathedral Builders* (1961), explores the engineering problems involved in cathedral building and places the subject within its social context. Advanced students will enjoy E. Mâle, *The Gothic Image: Religious Art in France in the Thirteenth Century* (1958), which contains a wealth of fascinating and useful detail. For the most important cathedrals in France, architecturally and politically, see A. Temko, *Notre Dame of Paris, the Biography of a Cathedral* (1968); G. Henderson, *Chartres* (1968); and A. Katzenellenbogen, *The Sculptural Programs of Chartres Cathedral* (1959), by a distinguished art historian. E. Panofsky, *Abbot Suger on the Abbey Church of St.-Denis and Its Art Treasures* (1946), provides a contemporary background account of the first Gothic building. E. G. Holt, ed., *A Documentary History of Art* (1957), contains source materials useful for writing papers. J. Gimpel, *The Medieval Machine: The Industrial Revolution of the Middle Ages* (1977), discusses the mechanical and scientific problems involved in the earlier industrial revolution and shows how construction affected the medieval environment; this is an extremely useful book.

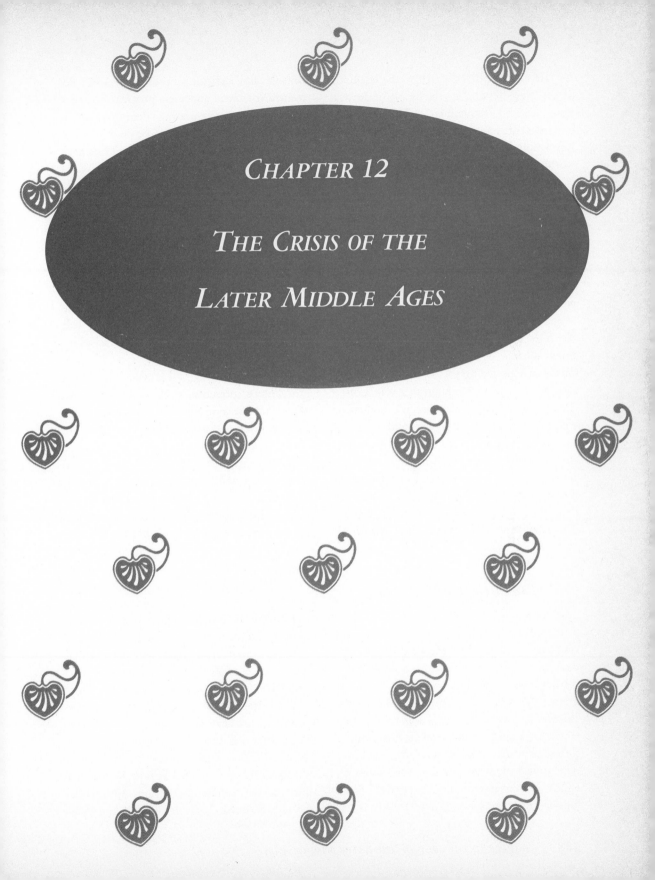

CHAPTER 12

THE CRISIS OF THE

LATER MIDDLE AGES

IN THE LATER MIDDLE AGES, the last book of the New Testament, the Book of Revelation, inspired thousands of sermons and hundreds of religious tracts. The Book of Revelation deals with visions of the end of the world, with disease, war, famine, and death. It is no wonder this part of the Bible was so popular. Between 1300 and 1450, Europeans experienced a frightful series of shocks: economic dislocation, plague, war, social upheaval, and increased crime and violence. Death and preoccupation with death make the fourteenth century one of the gloomiest periods in Western civilization.

The miseries and disasters of the later Middle Ages bring to mind a number of questions. What were the social and psychological effects of repeated attacks of plague and disease? Some scholars maintain that war is often the catalyst for political, economic, and social change. Does this theory have validity for the fourteenth century? Finally, what provoked the division of the church in the fourteenth century? What other ecclesiastical difficulties was the schism a sign of, and what impact did it have on the faith of the common people? This chapter seeks to answer these questions.

PRELUDE TO DISASTER

The fourteenth century began with serious economic problems. In the first decade, the countries of northern Europe experienced a considerable price inflation. The costs of grain, livestock, and dairy products rose sharply. Bad weather made a serious situation worse. An unusual number of storms brought torrential rains. Almost everywhere, heavy rains ruined the wheat, oats, and hay crops on which people and animals depended. Since long-distance transportation of food was ex-

pensive and difficult, most urban areas depended for bread and meat on areas no more than a day's journey away. Poor harvests — and one in four was likely to be poor — led to scarcity and starvation. Almost all of northern Europe suffered a terrible famine in the years 1315–1317.

Hardly had western Europe begun to recover from this disaster when another struck. An epidemic of typhoid fever carried away thousands. In 1316, 10 percent of the population of the city of Ypres in Belgium may have died between May and October alone. Then in 1318 disease hit cattle and sheep, drastically reducing the herds and flocks. Another bad harvest in 1321 brought famine, starvation, and death.

The large province of Languedoc in southern France presents a classic example of agrarian crisis. For over 150 years, Languedoc had enjoyed continual land reclamation, steady agricultural expansion, and enormous population growth. Then the fourteenth century opened with four years of bad harvests, 1302 through 1305. Torrential rains in 1310 ruined the harvest and brought on terrible famine. Harvests failed again in 1322 and 1329. In 1332, desperate peasants survived the winter on raw herbs. In the half-century from 1302 to 1348, poor harvests occurred twenty times. The undernourished population was ripe for the Grim Reaper, who appeared in 1348 in the form of the Black Death.

These catastrophes had inevitable social consequences. Poor harvests meant that marriages had to be postponed. Later marriages and the deaths caused by famine and disease meant a further reduction in population. Thus, after the steady population growth of the twelfth and thirteenth centuries, western Europe suffered a gradual decline in the first third of the fourteenth century. Meanwhile, the international character of trade and commerce meant that a disaster in one country had serious implications elsewhere. For example, the infection that attacked English sheep in 1318 caused a sharp decline in wool exports in the following years. Without wool, Flemish weavers could not work, and thousands were laid off. Without woolen cloth, the businesses of Flemish, French, and English merchants suffered. Unemployment encouraged many men to turn to crime.

To none of these problems did governments have any solutions. In fact, they even lacked policies. After the death of Edward I in 1307, England was governed by the incompetent and weak Edward II (1307–1327), whose reign was dominated by a series of baronial conflicts. In France the three sons of Philip the Fair who followed their father to the French throne between 1314 and 1328 took no interest in the increasing economic difficulties. In the Holy Roman Empire power drifted into the hands of local rulers. The only actions the governments took tended to be in response to the demands of the upper classes. Economic and social problems were aggravated by the appearance in western Europe of a frightful disease.

THE BLACK DEATH

Around 1331, the bubonic plague broke out in China. In the course of the next fifteen years, merchants, traders, and soldiers carried the disease across the Asian caravan routes until, in 1346, it reached the Crimea in southern Russia. From there the plague had easy access to the Mediterranean lands and western Europe.

In 1291, Genoese sailors had opened the Straits of Gibraltar to Italian shipping by defeating the Moroccans. Then, shortly after 1300, important advances were made in the design of Italian merchant ships. A square rig was added to the mainmast, and ships began to carry three masts instead of just one. Additional sails better utilized wind power to propel the ship. The improved design permitted year-round shipping for the first time, and Venetian and Genoese merchant ships could sail the dangerous Atlantic coast even in the winter months. With ships continually at sea, the rats that bore the disease spread rapidly beyond the Mediterranean to Atlantic and North Sea ports.

In October 1347, Genoese ships brought the plague to Messina, from which it spread to Sicily. Venice and Genoa were hit in January 1348, and from the port of Pisa the disease spread south to Rome and north to Florence and all Tuscany. By late spring southern Germany was attacked. Frightened French authorities chased a galley bearing the disease from the port of Marseilles, but not before plague had infected the city, from which it spread to Languedoc and Spain. In June 1348, two ships entered the Bristol Channel and introduced it into England. All Europe felt the scourge of this horrible disease (See Map 12.1).

PATHOLOGY

Modern understanding of the bubonic plague rests on the research of two bacteriologists, one French and one Japanese, who in 1894 independently identified *Pasteurella pestis,* the bacillus that causes the plague (so labeled after the French scientist's teacher, Louis Pasteur). The bacillus liked to live in the bloodstream of an animal or, ideally, in the stomach of a flea. The flea in turn resided in the hair of a rodent, sometimes a squirrel but preferably the hardy, nimble, and vagabond black rat. Why the host black rat moved so much, sci-

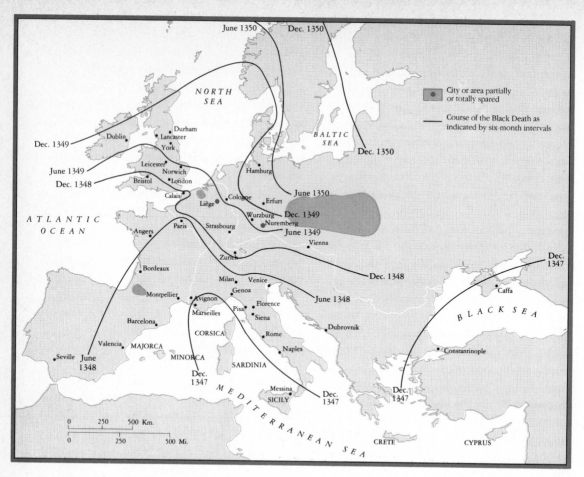

MAP 12.1 *THE COURSE OF THE BLACK DEATH IN FOURTEENTH-CENTURY EUROPE Note the routes that the bubonic plague took across Europe. How do you account for the fact that several regions were spared the "dreadful death"?*

entists still do not know, but it often traveled by ship. There the black rat could feast for months on a cargo of grain or live snugly among bales of cloth. Fleas bearing the bacillus also had no trouble nesting in saddlebags.[1] Comfortable, well fed, and often having greatly multiplied, the black rats ended their ocean voyage and descended upon the great cities of Europe.

Although by the fourteenth century urban authorities from London to Paris to Rome had begun to try to achieve a primitive level of sanitation, urban conditions remained ideal for the spread of disease. Narrow streets filled with mud, refuse, and human excrement were as much cesspools as thoroughfares. Dead animals and sore-covered beggars greeted the traveler. Houses whose upper stories projected over the lower ones eliminated light and air. And extreme overcrowding was commonplace. When all members of an aristocratic family lived and slept in one room, it should not be surprising that six or eight persons in a middle-class or poor household slept in one bed — if they had one. Closeness, after all, provided warmth. Houses were beginning to be constructed of brick, but many remained of wood, clay, and mud. A determined rat had little trouble entering such a house.

Standards of personal hygiene remained frightfully low. Since water was considered dangerous, partly for good reasons, people rarely bathed. Skin infections, consequently, were common. Lack of personal cleanliness, combined with any number of temporary ailments such as diarrhea and the common cold, naturally weakened the body's resistance to serious disease. Fleas and body lice were universal afflictions: everyone from peasants to archbishops had them. One more bite did not cause much alarm. But if that nibble came from a bacillus-bearing flea, an entire household or area was doomed.

The symptoms of the bubonic plague started with a growth the size of a nut or an apple in the armpit, the groin, or on the neck. This was the boil, or *buba,* that gave the disease its name and caused agonizing pain. If the *buba* was lanced and the pus thoroughly drained, the victim had a chance of recovery. The secondary stage was the appearance of black spots or blotches caused by bleeding under the skin. (This syndrome did not give the disease its common name; contemporaries did not call the plague the Black Death. Sometime in the fifteenth century the Latin phrase *atra mors,* meaning "dreadful death" was translated "black death," and the phrase stuck.) Finally, the victim began to cough violently and spit blood. This stage, indicating the presence of thousands of bacilli in the bloodstream, signaled the end, and death followed in two or three days. Rather than evoking compassion for the victim, a French scientist has written, everything about the bubonic plague provoked horror and disgust: "All the matter which exuded from their bodies let off an unbearable stench; sweat, excrement, spittle, breath, so fetid as to be overpowering; urine turbid, thick, black or red."[2]

THE PLAGUE-STRICKEN *Even as the dead were wrapped in shrouds and collected in carts for mass burial, the disease struck others. The man collapsing has the symptomatic buba on his neck. As Saint Sebastian pleads for mercy (above), a winged devil, bearer of the plague, attacks an angel. (Walters Art Gallery)*

Medieval people had no rational explanation for the disease nor any effective medical treatment for it. Fourteenth-century medical literature indicates that physicians could sometimes ease the pain, but they had no cure. Most people — lay, scholarly, and medical — believed that the Black Death was caused by some "vicious property in the air" that carried the disease from place to place. All authorities assumed that some corruption of the atmosphere caused the disease.

PROCESSION OF FLAGELLANTS *The horrors of the Black Death provoked terrible excesses. People believed that the disease was God's punishment for humanity's sins, which could be atoned for only through* *severe penances. In this procession of robed and hooded flagellants, two of the men flog those ahead of them. (Bibliothèque Royale Albert I, Brussels)*

The Italian writer Giovanni Boccaccio (1313–1375), describing the course of the disease in Florence in the preface to his book of tales, *The Decameron,* pinpointed the cause of the spread:

Moreover, the virulence of the pest was the greater by reason that intercourse was apt to convey it from the sick to the whole, just as fire devours things dry or greasy when they are brought close to it. Nay, the evil went yet further, for not merely by speech or association with the sick was the malady communicated to the healthy with consequent peril of common death, but any that touched the clothes of the sick or aught else that had been touched or used by them, seemed thereby to contract the disease.[3]

The highly infectious nature of the plague was recognized by a few sophisticated Arabs.

When the disease struck the town of Salé in Morocco, Ibu Abu Madyan shut in his household with sufficient food and water and allowed no one to enter or leave until the plague had passed. Madyan was entirely successful. In European cities, those who could afford it fled to the countryside, which generally suffered less. Few were so wise or lucky, however, and the plague took a staggering toll.

The mortality rate cannot be specified, because population figures for the period before the arrival of the plague do not exist for most countries and cities. The largest amount of material survives for England, but it is difficult to use and, after enormous scholarly controversy, only educated guesses can be made. Of a total population of perhaps 4.2 million, probably 1.4 million died of the Black Death in its several visits.[4] Densely populated Italian cities endured incredible losses. Florence lost between half and two-thirds of its 1347 population of 85,000 when the plague visited in 1348. In general, rural areas suffered much less than urban ones. The disease recurred intermittently in the 1360s and 1370s and reappeared several times down to 1700. There have been twentieth-century outbreaks in such places as Hong Kong, Bombay, and Uganda.

SOCIAL AND PSYCHOLOGICAL CONSEQUENCES

Predictably, the poor died more rapidly than the rich, because the rich enjoyed better health to begin with; but the powerful were not unaffected. In England two archbishops of Canterbury fell victim to the plague in 1349, King Edward III's daughter Joan died, and many leading members of the London guilds followed her to the grave.

It is noteworthy that in an age of mounting criticism of clerical wealth and luxury, the behavior of the clergy during the plague was often exemplary. Priests, monks, and nuns cared for the sick and buried the dead. In places like Venice, where even physicians ran away, priests remained to give what ministrations they could. Consequently, their mortality rate was phenomenally high. The German clergy, especially, suffered a severe decline in personnel in the years after 1350. With the ablest killed off, the wealth of the German church fell into the hands of the incompetent and weak. The situation was already ripe for reform.

The plague accelerated the economic decline that had begun in the early part of the fourteenth century. In many parts of Europe there had not been enough work for the people to do. The Black Death was a grim remedy to this problem. Population decline, however, led to an increased demand for labor and to considerable mobility among the peasant and working classes. Wages rose sharply. The shortage of labor and steady requests for higher wages put landlords on the defensive. They retaliated with such measures as the English Statute of Laborers (1351), which attempted to freeze salaries and wages at pre-1347 levels. The statute could not be enforced and therefore the move was largely unsuccessful.

Even more frightening than the social effects were the psychological consequences. The knowledge that the disease meant almost certain death provoked the most profound pessimism. Imagine an entire society in the grip of the belief that it was at the mercy of a frightful affliction about which nothing could be done, a disgusting disease from which family and friends would flee, leaving one to die alone and in agony. It is not surprising that some sought release in orgies and gross sensuality while others turned to the severest forms of asceticism and frenzied religious fervor. Some extremists joined groups of flagellants, who collectively whipped and scourged themselves as penance for their and society's sins in the belief that the Black Death was God's punishment for humanity's wickedness.

The literature and art of the fourteenth century reveal a terribly morbid concern with death. One highly popular artistic motif, the Dance of Death, depicted a dancing skeleton leading away a living person. No wonder survivors experienced a sort of shell shock and a terrible crisis of faith. Lack of confidence in the leaders of society, lack of hope for the future, defeatism, and malaise wreaked enormous anguish and contributed to the decline of the Middle Ages. A long international war added further misery to the frightful disasters of the plague.

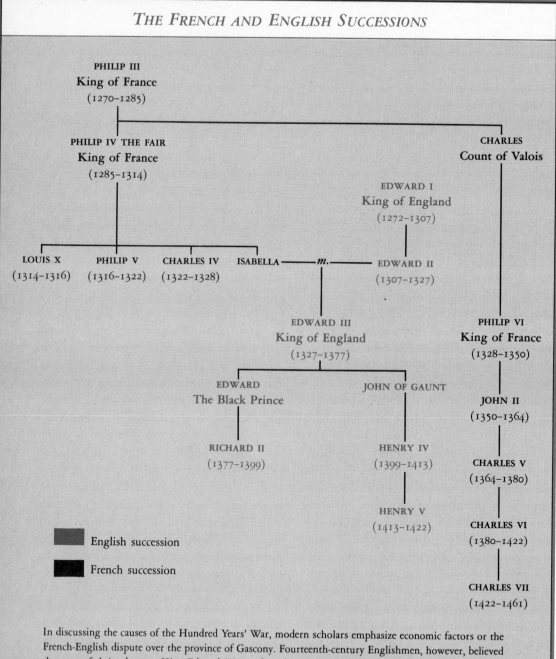

THE FRENCH AND ENGLISH SUCCESSIONS

PHILIP III
King of France
(1270–1285)

PHILIP IV THE FAIR
King of France
(1285–1314)

CHARLES
Count of Valois

EDWARD I
King of England
(1272–1307)

LOUIS X
(1314–1316)

PHILIP V
(1316–1322)

CHARLES IV
(1322–1328)

ISABELLA ——— *m.* ——— **EDWARD II**
(1307–1327)

EDWARD III
King of England
(1327–1377)

PHILIP VI
King of France
(1328–1350)

EDWARD
The Black Prince

JOHN OF GAUNT

JOHN II
(1350–1364)

RICHARD II
(1377–1399)

HENRY IV
(1399–1413)

CHARLES V
(1364–1380)

HENRY V
(1413–1422)

CHARLES VI
(1380–1422)

English succession

French succession

CHARLES VII
(1422–1461)

In discussing the causes of the Hundred Years' War, modern scholars emphasize economic factors or the French-English dispute over the province of Gascony. Fourteenth-century Englishmen, however, believed they were fighting because King Edward III was denied his legal right to the French crown. He was the eldest surviving male descendant of Philip the Fair.

THE HUNDRED YEARS' WAR
(CA 1337-1453)

In January 1327, Queen Isabella of England, her lover Mortimer, and a group of barons, having deposed and murdered Isabella's incompetent husband King Edward II, proclaimed his fifteen-year-old son king as Edward III. A year later Charles IV of France, the last surviving son of the French king Philip the Fair, died childless. With him ended the Capetian dynasty. An assembly of French barons, intending to exclude Isabella – who was Charles's sister and daughter of Philip the Fair – and her son Edward III from the French throne, proclaimed that "no woman nor her son could succeed to the [French] monarchy." The barons passed the crown to Philip VI of Valois (1328–1350), a nephew of Philip the Fair. In these actions lie the origins of another phase of the centuries-old struggle between the English and the French monarchies, one that was fought intermittently from 1337 to 1453.

CAUSES

Edward III of England, as the eldest surviving direct male descendant of Philip the Fair of France, believed he was entitled to the French throne. God had given him the French kingdom, he maintained, and it was his special duty to claim it. Edward was also duke of Aquitaine, in France (see Map 12.2), and in 1329 he did homage to Philip VI for the duchy. Thus Edward was a vassal of the French ruler, though their interests were diametrically opposed. Moreover, the dynastic argument had feudal implications: in order to increase their independent power, French vassals of Philip VI used the excuse that they had to transfer their loyalty to a more legitimate overlord, Edward III. This position resulted in widespread conflicts.

Economic factors involving the wool trade, the ancient dispute over Aquitaine, control of the Flemish towns – for centuries these had served as justifications for war between France and England. The causes of the conflicts known as the Hundred Years' War were dynastic, feudal, political, and economic. Recent historians have stressed the economic factors. The wool trade between England and Flanders served as the cornerstone of the economies of both countries; they were closely interdependent. Flanders was a fief of the French crown, and the Flemish aristocracy was highly sympathetic to the monarchy in Paris. But the wealth of the Flemish merchants and cloth manufacturers depended on English wool, and the Flemish burghers strongly supported the claims of Edward III. The disruption of their commerce with England threatened their prosperity.

It is impossible to measure the precise influence of the Flemings on the cause and course of the war. Certainly, Edward could not ignore their influence, because it represented money he needed to carry on the war. Although the war's impact on commerce fluctuated, over the long run it badly hurt the wool trade and the cloth industry.

Why did the struggle last so long? One historian has written in jest that if Edward III had been locked away in a castle with a pile of toy knights and archers to play with, he would have done far less damage.[5] The same might be said of Philip VI. Both rulers glorified war and saw it as the perfect arena for the realization of their chivalric ideals. Neither king possessed any sort of policy for dealing with his kingdom's social, economic, or political ills. Both sought military adventure as a means of diverting attention from domestic problems.

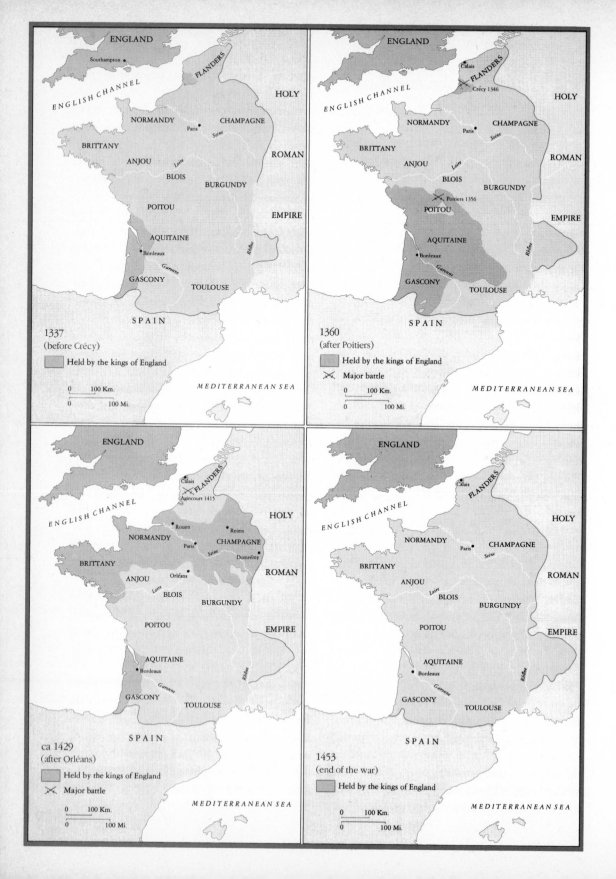

ENGLAND

Southampton

ENGLISH CHANNEL

FLANDERS

HOLY

NORMANDY

CHAMPAGNE

Paris

Seine

BRITTANY

ANJOU

ROMAN

BLOIS

Loire

POITOU

BURGUNDY

EMPIRE

AQUITAINE

Bordeaux

Rhône

Garonne

GASCONY

TOULOUSE

SPAIN

1337
(before Crécy)

Held by the kings of England

MEDITERRANEAN SEA

0   100 Km.

0   100 Mi.

ENGLAND

Calais

FLANDERS

Crécy 1346

HOLY

NORMANDY

CHAMPAGNE

Paris

Seine

BRITTANY

ANJOU

ROMAN

BLOIS

Loire

Poitiers 1356

POITOU

BURGUNDY

EMPIRE

AQUITAINE

Bordeaux

Rhône

Garonne

GASCONY

TOULOUSE

ENGLISH CHANNEL

SPAIN

1360
(after Poitiers)

Held by the kings of England

Major battle

MEDITERRANEAN SEA

0   100 Km.

0   100 Mi.

ENGLAND

Calais

FLANDERS

Agincourt 1415

HOLY

ENGLISH CHANNEL

Rouen

Reims

NORMANDY

CHAMPAGNE

Paris

Seine

Domrémy

BRITTANY

Orléans

ROMAN

ANJOU

Loire

BLOIS

BURGUNDY

POITOU

EMPIRE

AQUITAINE

Bordeaux

Rhône

Garonne

GASCONY

TOULOUSE

SPAIN

ca 1429
(after Orléans)

Held by the kings of England

Major battle

MEDITERRANEAN SEA

0   100 Km.

0   100 Mi.

ENGLAND

Calais

FLANDERS

HOLY

ENGLISH CHANNEL

NORMANDY

CHAMPAGNE

Paris

Seine

BRITTANY

ANJOU

ROMAN

BLOIS

Loire

BURGUNDY

POITOU

EMPIRE

AQUITAINE

Bordeaux

Rhône

Garonne

GASCONY

TOULOUSE

SPAIN

1453
(end of the war)

Held by the kings of England

MEDITERRANEAN SEA

0   100 Km.

0   100 Mi.

MAP 12.2 ENGLISH HOLDINGS IN FRANCE DURING THE HUNDRED YEARS WAR *The year 1429 marked the greatest extent of English holdings in France. Why was it unlikely that England could have held these territories permanently?*

THE POPULAR RESPONSE

The governments of both England and France manipulated public opinion to support the war. Whatever significance modern students ascribe to the economic factor, public opinion in fourteenth-century England held that the war was waged for one reason: to secure for King Edward the French crown he had been denied.[6] Edward III issued letters to the sheriffs describing in graphic terms the evil deeds of the French and listing the royal needs. Royal letters instructed the clergy to deliver sermons filled with patriotic sentiment. Frequent assemblies of Parliament — which theoretically represented the entire nation — spread royal propaganda for the war. The royal courts sensationalized the wickedness of the other side and stressed the great fortunes to be made from the war. Philip VI sent agents to warn communities about the dangers of invasion and to stress the French Crown's revenue needs to meet the attack.

The royal campaign to rally public opinion was highly successful, at least in the early stage of the war. Edward III gained widespread support in the 1340s and 1350s. The English developed a deep hatred of the French and feared that King Philip intended "to have seized and slaughtered the entire realm of England." As England was successful in the field, pride in the country's military proficiency increased.

Most important of all, the war was popular because it presented unusual opportunities for wealth and advancement. Poor and unemployed knights were promised regular wages.

Criminals who enlisted were granted pardons. The great nobles expected to be rewarded with estates. Royal exhortations to the troops before battles repeatedly stressed that, if victorious, the men might keep whatever they seized. The French chronicler Jean Froissart wrote that at the time of Edward III's expedition of 1359, men of all ranks flocked to the king's banner. Some came to acquire honor, but many came in order "to loot and pillage the fair and plenteous land of France."[7]

THE INDIAN SUMMER OF MEDIEVAL CHIVALRY

The period of the Hundred Years' War witnessed the final flowering of the aristocratic code of medieval chivalry. Indeed, the enthusiastic participation of the nobility in both France and England was in response primarily to the opportunity the war provided to display chivalric behavior. Chivalry was a code of conduct originally devised by the clergy to improve the crude and brutal behavior of the knightly class. A knight was supposed to be brave, anxious to win praise, courteous, loyal to his commander, gracious, and generous. What better place to display these qualities than on the field of battle?

War was considered an ennobling experience; there was something elevating, manly, fine, and beautiful about it. When Shakespeare in the sixteenth century wrote of "the pomp and circumstance of glorious war," he was echoing the fourteenth- and fifteenth-century chroniclers who had glorified the trappings of war. Describing the French army before the battle of Poitiers (1356), a contemporary said, "Then you might see banners and pennons unfurled to the wind, whereon fine gold and azure shone, purple, gules and ermine. Trumpets, horns and clarions — you might hear sounding through the camp; the Dauphin's great battle made the earth ring."[8]

The chronicler Froissart repeatedly speaks of the beauty of an army assembled for battle. Writing of the French army before the battle of Bergues in 1383, Froissart reflected the attitudes of the aristocratic classes: it was "a great beauty to see the banners, pennons, and basinets glittering against the sun, and such a great multitude of men-at-arms that the eye of man could not take them in, and it seemed that they bore a veritable forest of lances." At Poitiers, it was marvelous and terrifying to hear the thundering of the horses' hooves, the cries of the wounded, the sound of the trumpets and clarions, and the shouting of war cries. The tumult was heard at a distance of more than three leagues. And it was a great grief to see and behold the flower of all the nobility and chivalry of the world go thus to destruction, to death, and to martyrdom on both sides.

This romantic and "marvelous" view of war holds little appeal for modern men and women, who are more conscious of the slaughter, brutality, dirt, and blood that war inevitably involves. Also, modern thinkers are usually conscious of the broad mass of people, while the chivalric code applied only to the aristocratic military elite. Chivalry had no reference to those outside the knightly class.

The knight was supposed to show courtesy, graciousness, and generosity to his social equals, but certainly not to his social inferiors. When English knights fought French ones, they were social equals fighting according to a mutually accepted code of behavior. The infantry troops were looked upon as inferior beings. When a peasant force at Longueil destroyed a contingent of English knights, their comrades mourned them because "it was too much that so many good fighters had been killed by mere peasants."[9]

Armies in the field were commanded by rulers themselves, by princes of the blood such as Edward III's son Edward, the Black Prince — so-called because of the color of his armor — or by great aristocrats. Knights formed the cavalry; the despised peasantry served as infantrymen, pikemen, and archers. Edward III set up recruiting boards in the counties to enlist the strongest peasants. Perhaps 10 percent of the adult population of England was involved in the actual fighting or in supplying and supporting the troops. The French contingents were even larger. By medieval standards, the force was astronomically large, especially considering the difficulty of transporting men, weapons, and horses across the English Channel. The costs of these armies stretched French and English resources to the breaking point.

The war was fought almost entirely in France and the Low Countries. It consisted mainly of a series of random sieges and cavalry raids. In 1335 the French began supporting Scottish incursions into northern England, ravaging the countryside in Aquitaine, and sacking and burning English coastal towns, such as Southampton. Naturally, such tactics lent weight to Edward III's propaganda campaign. In fact, royal propaganda on both sides fostered a kind of early nationalism.

In the early stages of the war, England was highly successful. At Crécy in northern France in 1346, English longbowmen scored a great victory over French knights and crossbowmen. Although the fire of the longbow was not very accurate, it allowed for rapid reloading, and the English archers could send off three arrows to the French crossbowmen's one. The result was a blinding shower of arrows that unhorsed the French knights and caused mass confusion. The firing of cannon —

THE BATTLE OF CRÉCY, 1346 Pitched battles were unusual in the Hundred Years' War. At Crécy, however, the English (on the right with lions on their royal standard) scored a spectacular victory. The *longbow proved a more effective weapon than the French crossbow, and the low-born English archers withstood a charge of the aristocratic French knights. (Photo: Larousse)*

probably the first use of artillery in the West – created further panic. Thereupon the English horsemen charged and butchered the French.

This was not war according to the chivalric rules that Edward III would have preferred. The English victory at Crécy rests on the skill and swiftness of the despised peasant archers, who had nothing at all to do with the chi-

valric ideals for which the war was being fought. Ten years later Edward the Black Prince, using the same tactics as at Crécy, smashed the French at Poitiers, captured the French king, and held him for ransom. Again at Agincourt near Arras in 1415, the chivalric English soldier-king Henry V (1413–1422) gained the field over vastly superior numbers. Henry followed up his triumph at Agincourt

FIFTEENTH-CENTURY ARMOR This kind of expensive plate armor was worn by the aristocratic nobility in the fifteenth and sixteenth centuries. The use of gunpowder gradually made armor outmoded. (Courtesy, World Heritage Museum. Photo: Caroline Buckler)

with the reconquest of Normandy. By 1419, the English had advanced to the walls of Paris (see Map 12.2).

But the French cause was not lost. Though England had won the initial victories, France won the war.

JOAN OF ARC AND FRANCE'S VICTORY

The ultimate French success rests heavily on the actions of an obscure French peasant girl, Joan of Arc, whose vision and work revived French fortunes and led to victory. A great deal of pious and popular legend surrounds Joan the Maid, because of her peculiar appearance on the scene, her astonishing success, her martyrdom, and her canonization by the Catholic church. The historical fact is that she saved the French monarchy, which was the embodiment of France.

Born in 1412 in the village of Domrémy in Champagne to well-to-do peasants, Joan of Arc grew up in a religious household. During adolescence she began to hear voices, which she later said belonged to Saint Michael, Saint Catherine, and Saint Margaret. In 1428, these voices spoke to her with great urgency, telling her that the dauphin (the uncrowned King Charles VII) had to be crowned and the English expelled from France. Joan went to the French court, persuaded the king to reject the rumor that he was illegitimate, and secured his support for her relief of the besieged city of Orléans.

The astonishing thing is not that Joan the Maid overcame serious obstacles to see the dauphin, not even that Charles and his advisers listened to her. What is amazing is the swiftness with which they were convinced. French fortunes had been so low for so long that the court believed only a miracle could save the country. Because Joan cut her hair short and dressed like a man, she scandalized the court. But hoping she would provide the necessary miracle, Charles allowed her to accompany the army that was preparing to raise the English siege of Orléans.

In the meantime Joan, herself illiterate, dictated the following letter calling upon the English to withdraw:

JHESUS MARIA

King of England, and you Duke of Bedford, calling yourself regent of France, you William Pole, Count of Suffolk John Talbot, and you Thomas Lord Scales, calling yourselves Lieutenants of the said Duke of Bedford, do right in the King of Heaven's sight. Surrender to The Maid *sent hither by God the King of Heaven, the keys of all the good towns you have taken and laid waste in France. She comes in God's name to establish the Blood Royal, ready to make peace if you agree to abandon France and repay what you have taken. And you, archers, comrades in arms, gentles and others, who are before the town of Orléans, retire in God's name to your own country. If you do not, expect to hear tidings from* The Maid *who will shortly come upon you to your very great hurt. And to you, King of England, if you do not thus, I am a chieftain of war, and whenever I meet your followers in France, I will drive them out; if they will not obey, I will put them all to death. I am sent here in God's name, the King of Heaven, to drive you body for body out of all France.*[10]

Joan apparently thought of herself as an agent of God.

Joan arrived before Orléans on April 28, 1429. Seventeen years old, she knew little of warfare and believed that if she could keep the French troops from swearing and frequenting whorehouses, victory would be theirs. On May 8, the English, weakened by disease and lack of supplies, withdrew from Orléans. Ten days later, Charles VII was crowned king at Reims. These two events marked the turning point in the war.

JOAN OF ARC *Later considered the symbol of the French state in its struggle against the English, Joan of Arc here carries a sword in one hand and a banner with the royal symbol of fleur-de-lis in the other. Her face, which scholars believe to be a good resemblance, shows inner strength and calm determination. (Archives Nationales, Paris/Giraudon)*

In 1430 England's allies, the Burgundians, captured Joan and sold her to the English. When the English handed her over to the ecclesiastical authorities for trial, the French court did not intervene. While the English wanted Joan eliminated for obvious political reasons, sorcery (witchcraft) was the ostensible charge at her trial. Witch persecution was increasing in the fifteenth century and Joan's wearing of men's clothes appeared not only aberrant but indicative of contact with the devil. Asked why she did so, Joan replied, "It is a little thing and of small importance. I did not don it by the advice of men of this world. I donned it only by the command of God and the angels."[11]

Joan of Arc's political impact on the course of the Hundred Years' War and on the development of the kingdom of France has led scholars to examine her character and behavior very closely. Besides being an excellent athlete and a superb rider, she usually dressed like a rich and elegant young nobleman. Some students maintain that Joan's manner of dress suggests uncertainty about her own sexual identity. She did not menstruate – very rare in a healthy girl of eighteen – though she was female in every external respect: many men, including several dukes, admired her beautiful breasts. Perhaps, as Joan said, wearing men's clothes meant nothing at all. On the other hand, as some writers believe, she may have wanted to assume a completely new identity. Joan always insisted that God had specially chosen her for her mission. The richness and masculinity of her clothes, therefore, emphasized her uniqueness and made her highly conspicuous.[12] In 1431 the court condemned her as a heretic – her claim of direct inspiration from God, thereby denying the authority of church officials, constituted heresy – and burned her at the stake in the marketplace in Rouen. A fresh trial in 1456 rehabilitated her name. In 1902 she was canonized and declared a holy maiden, and today she is revered as the second patron saint of France. The nineteenth-century French historian Jules Michelet extolled Joan of Arc as a symbol of the vitality and strength of the French peasant classes.

The relief of Orléans stimulated French pride and rallied French resources. In England, as the war dragged on, loss of life mounted, and money appeared to be flowing into a bottomless pit, demands for an end increased. The clergy and the intellectuals pressed for peace. Parliamentary opposition to additional war grants stiffened. Slowly the

French reconquered Normandy and, finally, ejected the English from Aquitaine. At the end of the war, in 1453, only the town of Calais remained in English hands.

COSTS AND CONSEQUENCES

For both France and England, the war proved a disaster. In France, the English had slaughtered thousands of soldiers and civilians. In the years after the sweep of the Black Death, this additional killing meant a grave loss of population. The English had laid waste to hundreds of thousands of acres of rich farmland, leaving the rural economy of many parts of France in a shambles. The war had disrupted trade and the great fairs, resulting in the drastic reduction of French participation in international commerce. Defeat in battle and heavy taxation contributed to widespread dissatisfaction and aggravated peasant grievances.

In England, only the southern coastal ports experienced much destruction; yet England fared little better than France. The costs of war were tremendous: England spent over £5 million in the war effort, a huge sum in the fourteenth and fifteenth centuries. The worst loss was in manpower. Between 10 and 15 percent of the adult male population between the ages of fifteen and forty-five fought in the army or navy. In the decades after the plague, when the country was already suffering a severe manpower shortage, war losses made a bad situation frightful. Peasants serving in France as archers and pikemen were desperately needed to till the fields. The knights who ordinarily handled the work of local government as sheriffs, coroners, jurymen, and justices of the peace were abroad, and their absence contributed to the breakdown of order at the local level. The English government attempted to finance the war effort by raising taxes on the wool crop. Because of steadily increasing costs, the Flemish and Italian buyers could not afford English wool. Consequently, wool exports slumped drastically between 1350 and 1450.

Many men of all social classes had volunteered for service in France in the hope of acquiring booty and becoming rich. The chronicler Walsingham, describing the period of Crécy, tells of the tremendous prosperity and abundance resulting from the spoils of war: "For the woman was of no account who did not possess something from the spoils of . . . cities overseas in clothing, furs, quilts, and utensils . . . tablecloths and jewels, bowls of murra [semiprecious stone] and silver, linen and linen cloths."[13] Walsingham is referring to 1348, in the first generation of war. As time went on, most fortunes seem to have been squandered as fast as they were made.

If English troops returned with cash, they did not invest it in land. In the fifteenth century, returning soldiers were commonly described as beggars and vagabonds, roaming about making mischief. Even the large sums of money received from the ransom of the great – such as the £250,000 paid to Edward III for the freedom of King John of France – and the monies paid as indemnities by captured towns and castles did not begin to equal the £5 million-plus spent. England suffered a serious net loss.[14]

The long war also had a profound impact on the political and cultural lives of the two countries. Most notably, it stimulated the development of the English Parliament. Edward III's constant need for money to pay for the war compelled him to summon not only the great barons and bishops but knights of the shires and burgesses from the towns as well. Between the outbreak of the war in 1337 and the king's death in 1377, parliamentary assemblies met twenty-seven times. Parliament met in thirty-seven of the fifty years of Edward's reign.

The frequency of the meetings is significant. Representative assemblies were becoming a habit, a tradition. Knights and burgesses – or the Commons, as they came to be called – recognized their mutual interests and began to meet apart from the great lords. The Commons gradually realized that they held the country's purse strings, and a parliamentary statute of 1341 required that all nonfeudal levies have parliamentary approval. When Edward III signed the law, he acknowledged that the king of England could not tax without Parliament's consent. Increasingly, during the course of the war, money grants were tied to royal redress of grievances: if the government was to raise money, it had to correct the wrongs its subjects protested.

As the Commons met in a separate chamber – the House of Commons – it also developed its own organization. The speaker came to preside over debates in the House of Commons and to represent the Commons before the House of Lords and the king. Clerks kept a record of what transpired during discussions in the Commons.

In England theoretical consent to taxation and legislation was given in one assembly for the entire country. France had no such single assembly; instead, there were many regional or provincial assemblies. Why did a national representative assembly fail to develop in France? The initiative for convening assemblies rested with the king, who needed revenue almost as much as the English ruler. But the French monarchy found the idea of representative assemblies thoroughly distasteful. The advice of a counselor to King Charles VI (1380–1422), "above all things be sure that no great assemblies of nobles or of *communes* take place in your kingdom,"[15] was accepted. Charles VII (1422–1461) even threatened to punish those proposing a national assembly.

The English Parliament was above all else a court of law, a place where justice was done and grievances remedied. No French assembly (except that of Brittany) had such competence. The national assembly in England met frequently. In France general assemblies were so rare that they never got the opportunity to develop precise procedures or to exercise judicial functions.

No one in France wanted a national assembly. Linguistic, geographic, economic, legal, and political differences were very strong. People tended to think of themselves as Breton, Norman, Burgundian, or whatever, rather than as French. Through much of the fourteenth and early fifteenth centuries, weak monarchs lacked the power to call a national assembly. Provincial assemblies, highly jealous of their independence, did not want a national assembly. The costs of sending delegates to it would be high, and the result was likely to be increased taxation. Finally, the Hundred Year's War itself hindered the growth of a representative body. Violence on dangerous roads discouraged travel. As the fifteenth-century English jurist Sir John Fortescue wrote, "Englishmen made such war in France that the three Estates dared not come together."[16]

In both countries, however, the war did promote the growth of nationalism – the feeling of unity and identity that binds together a people who speak the same language, have a common ancestry and customs, and live in the same area. In the fourteenth century, nationalism largely took the form of hostility to foreigners. Both Philip VI and Edward III drummed up support for the war by portraying the enemy as an alien, evil people. Edward III linked his personal dynastic quarrel with England's national interests. As the Parliament Roll of 1348 states:

The Knights of the shires and the others of the Commons were told that they should withdraw together and take good counsel as to how, for with-standing the malice of the said enemy and for the salvation of our said lord the King and his Kingdom of England . . . the King could be aided.[17]

After victories, each country experienced a surge of pride in its military strength. Just as English patriotism ran strong after Crécy and Poitiers, so French national confidence rose after Orléans. French national feeling demanded the expulsion of the enemy not merely from Normandy and Aquitaine but from French soil. Perhaps no one expressed this national consciousness better than Joan of Arc, when she exulted that the enemy had been "driven out of *France.*"

VERNACULAR LITERATURE

Few developments expressed the emergence of national consciousness more vividly than the emergence of national literatures. Across Europe people spoke the language and dialect of their particular locality and class. In England, for example, the common people spoke regional English dialects, while the upper classes conversed in French. Official documents and works of literature were written in Latin or French. Beginning in the fourteenth century, however, national languages – the vernacular – came into use not only in verbal communication but in literature as well. Three masterpieces of European culture, Dante's *Divine Comedy* (1321), Chaucer's *Canterbury Tales* (1387–1400), and Villon's *Grand Testament* (1461) brilliantly manifest this new national pride.

Dante Aligheri (1265–1321) descended from an aristocratic family in Florence, where he held several positions in the city government. Dante called his work a comedy because

DANTE   In this sixteenth-century allegorical tribute to the most famous of all Florentines, the crowned poet laureate broods over the eternal conflict between the spiritual and the temporal. His right hand protects his beloved Florence, while his left hand holds the Divine Comedy open to paradise, which is seen in the distance surrounded by light. (National Gallery of Art, Washington, D.C. Samual H. Kress Collection 1961)

he wrote it in Italian and in a different style from the "tragic" Latin; a later generation added the adjective "divine," referring both to its sacred subject and to Dante's artistry. The *Divine Comedy* is an allegorical trilogy of one hundred cantos (verses) whose three equal parts ($1+33+33+33$) each describe one of the realms of the next world, Hell, Purgatory, and Paradise. Dante recounts his imaginary journey through these regions toward God. The Roman poet Virgil, representing reason, leads Dante through Hell where he observes the torments of the damned and denounces the disorders of his own time, especially ec-

clesiastical ambition and corruption. Passing up into Purgatory, Virgil shows the poet how souls are purified of their disordered inclinations. In Paradise, home of the angels and saints, St. Bernard – representing mystic contemplation – leads Dante to the Virgin Mary. Through her intercession he at last attains a vision of God.

The *Divine Comedy* portrays contemporary and historical figures, comments on secular and ecclesiastical affairs, and draws on scholastic philosophy. Within the framework of a symbolic pilgrimage to the City of God, the *Divine Comedy* embodies the psychological tensions of the age. A profoundly Christian poem, it also contains bitter criticism of some church authorities. In its symmetrical structure and use of figures from the ancient world, such as Virgil, the poem perpetuates the classical tradition, but as the first major work of literature in the Italian vernacular it is distinctly modern.

Geoffrey Chaucer (1340–1400), the son of a London wine merchant, was an official in the administrations of the English kings Edward III and Richard II who wrote poetry as an avocation. Chaucer's *Canterbury Tales* is a collection of stories in a lengthy rhymed narrative. On a pilgrimage to the shrine of St. Thomas Becket at Canterbury (see page 362), thirty people of various social backgrounds each tell a tale. The Prologue sets the scene and describes the pilgrims, whose characters are further revealed in the story each person tells. For example, the gentle Christian Knight relates a chivalric romance; the gross Miller tells a vulgar story about a deceived husband; the earthy Wife of Bath, who earns her living as a weaver and has buried five husbands, sketches a fable about the selection of a spouse; and the elegant Prioress, who violates her vows by wearing jewelry, delivers a homily on the Virgin. In depicting the interests and behavior of all types of people, Chaucer presents a rich panorama of English social life in the fourteenth century. Like the *Divine Comedy,* the *Canterbury Tales* reflects the cultural tensions of the times. Ostensibly Christian, many of the pilgrims are also materialistic, sensual, and worldly, suggesting the ambivalence of the broader society's concern for the next world and frank enjoyment of this one.

Our knowledge of François Villon (1413–1463), probably the greatest poet of late medieval France, derives from Paris police records and his own poetry. Born to desperately poor parents in the year of Joan of Arc's execution, Villon was sent by his guardian to the University of Paris where he earned the Master of Arts degree. A rowdy and free-spirited student, he disliked the stuffiness of academic life. In 1455 Villon killed a man in a street brawl; banished from Paris, he joined one of the bands of wandering thieves that harassed the countryside after the Hundred Years' War. For his fellow bandits he composed ballads in thieves' jargon.

Villon's *Lais* (1456), a pun on the word *legs* (meaning "legacy"), is a series of farcical bequests to his friends and enemies. *Ballade des Pendus* (Ballad of the Hanged) was written while contemplating that fate in prison. (His execution was commuted.) Villon's greatest and most self-revealing work, the *Grand Testament,* contains another string of bequests, including a legacy to a prostitute, and describes his unshakeable faith in the beauty of life here on earth. The *Grand Testament* possesses elements of social rebellion, bawdy humor, and rare emotional depth. While the themes of Dante's and Chaucer's poetry are distinctly medieval, Villon's celebration of the human condition here on earth brands him as definitely modern. While he used medieval forms of versification, Villon's language was the despised vernacular of the poor and the criminal.

THE DECLINE OF THE CHURCH'S PRESTIGE

In times of crisis or disaster, people of all faiths have sought the consolation of religion. In the fourteenth century, however, the official Christian church offered very little solace. In fact, the leaders of the church added to the sorrow and misery of the times.

From 1309 to 1372, the popes lived in the city of Avignon in southeastern France. In order to control the church and its policies, Philip the Fair of France pressured Pope Clement V to settle in Avignon (page 383). Clement, critically ill with cancer, lacked the will to resist Philip. This period in church history is often called the Babylonian Captivity (referring to the seventy years the ancient Hebrews were held captive in Mesopotamian Babylon).

The Babylonian Captivity badly damaged papal prestige. The Avignon papacy reformed its financial administration and centralized its government. But the seven popes at Avignon concentrated on bureaucratic matters to the exclusion of spiritual objectives. Although some of the popes led austere lives at Avignon, the general atmosphere was one of luxury, splendor, and extravagance. The leadership of the church was cut off from its historic roots and the source of its ancient authority, the city of Rome. In the absence of the papacy, the Papal States in Italy lacked stability and good government. The economy of Rome had long been based on the presence of the papal court and the rich tourist trade the papacy attracted. The Babylonian Captivity left Rome poverty-stricken. As long as the French crown dominated papal policy, papal influence in England (with whom France was intermittently at war) and in Germany declined.

Many devout Christians urged the popes to return to Rome. The Dominican mystic Catherine of Siena, for example, made a special trip to Avignon to plead with the pope to return. In 1377, Pope Gregory XI brought the papal court back to Rome. Unfortunately, he died shortly after the return. At Gregory's death, Roman citizens demanded an Italian pope who would remain in Rome. Determined to influence the papal conclave (the assembly of cardinals who choose the new pope) to elect an Italian, a Roman mob surrounded St. Peter's Basilica, blocked the roads leading out of the city, and seized all boats on the Tiber River. Between the time of Gregory's death and the opening of the conclave, great pressure was put on the cardinals to elect an Italian. At the time, none of them protested this pressure.

Sixteen cardinals — eleven Frenchmen, four Italians, and one Spaniard — entered the conclave on April 7, 1378. After two ballots they unanimously chose a distinguished administrator, the archbishop of Bari, Bartolomeo Prignano, who took the name Urban VI. Each of the cardinals swore that Urban had been elected "sincerely, freely, genuinely, and canonically."

Urban VI (1378–1389) had excellent intentions for church reform: he wanted to abolish simony, pluralism (holding several church offices at the same time), absenteeism, clerical extravagance, and ostentation. These were the very abuses being increasingly criticized by Christian peoples across Europe. Unfortunately, Pope Urban went about the work of reform in a tactless, arrogant, and bullheaded manner. The day after his coronation he delivered a blistering attack on cardinals who lived in Rome while drawing their income from benefices elsewhere. His criticism was well-founded but ill-timed, and provoked opposition among the hierarchy before Urban had consolidated his authority.

In the weeks that followed Urban stepped up attacks on clerical luxury, denouncing individual cardinals by name. He threatened to strike the cardinal archbishop of Amiens. Urban even threatened to excommunicate certain cardinals, and when he was advised that such excommunications would not be lawful unless the guilty had been warned three times, he shouted, "I can do anything, if it be my will and judgment."[18] Urban's quick temper and irrational behavior have led scholars to question his sanity. Whether he was medically insane or just drunk with power is a moot point. In any case, Urban's actions brought on disaster.

In groups of two and three, the cardinals slipped away from Rome and met at Anagni. They declared Urban's election invalid because it had come about under threats from the Roman mob, and they asserted that Urban himself was excommunicated. The cardinals then proceeded to the city of Fondi between Rome and Naples and elected Cardinal Robert of Geneva, the brother of King Charles V of France, as pope. Cardinal Robert took the name Clement VII. There were thus two popes – Urban at Rome and the anti-pope Clement VII (1378–1394), who set himself up at Avignon in opposition to the legally elected Urban. So began the Great Schism, which divided Western Christendom until 1417.

THE GREAT SCHISM

The powers of Europe aligned themselves with Urban or Clement along strictly political lines. France naturally recognized the French anti-pope, Clement. England, France's historic enemy, recognized Pope Urban. Scotland, whose attacks on England were subsidized by France, followed the French and supported Clement. Aragon, Castile, and Portugal hesitated before deciding for Clement at Avignon. The German emperor, who enjoyed the title of king of the Romans and bore ancient hostility to France, recognized Urban VI. At first the Italian city-states recognized Urban; when he alienated them, they opted for Clement.

John of Spoleto, a professor at the law school at Bologna, eloquently summed up intellectual opinion of the schism:

The longer this schism lasts, the more it appears to be costing, and the more harm it does: scandal, massacres, ruination, agitations, troubles and disturbances . . . this dissention is the root of everything: divers tumults, quarrels between kings, seditions, extortions, assassinations, acts of violence, wars, rising tyranny, decreasing freedom, the impunity of villains, grudges, error, disgrace, the madness of steel and of fire given license.[19]

The scandal of competing popes "rent the seamless garment of Christ," as the church was called, and provoked horror and vigorous cries for reform. The common people, wracked by inflation, wars, and plague, were thoroughly confused about which pope was legitimate. The schism weakened the religious faith of many Christians and gave rise to instability and religious excesses. It brought the leadership of the church into serious disrepute. At a time when ordinary Christians needed the consolation of religion and confidence in their religious leaders, church officials were fighting among themselves for power.

THE CONCILIAR MOVEMENT

Calls for reform of the church were not new. A half-century before the Great Schism, in 1324, Marsiglio of Padua, then rector of the University of Paris, had published *Defensor Pacis* (*The Defender of the Peace*). Dealing as it did with the authority of the state and the church, *Defensor Pacis* proved to be one of the most controversial works written in the Middle Ages.

Marsiglio argued that the state was the great unifying power in society and that the church was subordinate to the state. He put forth the revolutionary ideas that the church had no inherent jurisdiction and should own no property. Authority in the Christian church, according to Marsiglio, should rest in a general council, made up of laymen as well as priests and superior to the pope. These ideas directly contradicted the medieval notion of a society governed by the church and the state, with the church ultimately supreme.

Defensor Pacis was condemned by the pope and Marsiglio was excommunicated. But the idea that a general council representing all of the church had a higher authority than the pope was repeated by John Gerson (1363-1429), a later chancellor of the University of Paris and influential theologian.

Even more earthshaking than the theories of Marsiglio of Padua were the ideas of the English scholar and theologian John Wyclif (1329-1384). Wyclif wrote that papal claims of temporal power had no foundation in the Scriptures, and that the Scriptures alone should be the standard of Christian belief and practice. He urged the abolition of such practices as the veneration of saints, pilgrimages, pluralism, and absenteeism. Every sincere Christian, according to Wyclif, should read the Bible for himself. Wyclif's views had broad social and economic significance. He urged that the church be stripped of its property. His idea that every Christian free of mortal sin possessed lordship was seized upon by peasants in England during a revolt in 1381 and used to justify their goals.

In advancing these views, Wyclif struck at the roots of medieval church structure and religious practices. Consequently, he has been hailed as the precursor of the Reformation of the sixteenth century. Although Wyclif's ideas were vigorously condemned by ecclesiastical authorities, they were widely disseminated by humble clerics and enjoyed great popularity in the early fifteenth century. Wyclif's followers were called Lollards. The term, meaning mumblers of prayers and psalms, refers to what they criticized. After the Czech king Wenceslaus's sister Anne married Richard II of England, members of Queen Anne's household carried Lollard principles back to Bohemia, where they were spread by John Hus, rector of the University of Prague.

While John Wyclif's ideas were being spread, two German scholars at the University of Paris, Henry of Langenstein and Conrad of Gelnhausen, produced treatises urging the summoning of a general council. Conrad wrote that the church, as the congregation of all the faithful, was superior to the pope. Although canon law held that only a pope might call a council, a higher law existed, the common good. The common good of Christendom required the convocation of a council.

In response to continued Europe-wide calls for a council, the two colleges of cardinals — one at Rome, the other at Avignon — summoned a council at Pisa in Italy in 1409. A distinguished gathering of prelates and theologians deposed both popes and selected another. Neither the Avignon pope nor the Roman pope would resign, however, and the appalling result was a threefold schism.

Finally, due to the pressure of the German emperor Sigismund, a great council met at Constance in Switzerland (1414-1418). It had three objectives: to end the schism, to reform the church "in head and members" (from top to bottom), and to wipe out heresy. The council condemned the Lollard ideas of John Hus, and he was burned at the stake. The council eventually deposed both the Roman pope and the successor of the pope chosen at Pisa, and it isolated the Avignonese anti-pope. A conclave elected a new leader, the Roman Cardinal Colonna, who took the name Martin V (1417-1431).

Martin proceeded to dissolve the council. Nothing was done about reform. The schism was over, and the conciliar movement in effect ended. For a time thereafter, the papacy concentrated on Italian problems to the exclusion of universal Christian interests. But the schism and the conciliar movement had exposed the crying need for ecclesiastical reform, thus laying the foundations for the great reform efforts of the sixteenth century.

THE LIFE OF THE PEOPLE

In the fourteenth century, economic and political difficulties, disease, and war profoundly affected the lives of European peoples. Decades of slaughter and destruction, punctuated by the decimating visits of the Black Death, made a grave economic situation virtually disastrous. In many parts of France and the Low Countries fields lay in ruin or untilled for lack of manpower. In England, as taxes increased, criticism of government policy and mismanagement multiplied. Crime, always a factor in social history, aggravated economic troubles, and throughout Europe the frustrations of the common people erupted into widespread revolts. For most people, marriage and the local parish church continued to be the center of their lives.

FUR-COLLAR CRIME

The Hundred Years' War had provided employment and opportunity for thousands of idle and fortune-seeking knights. But during periods of truce and after the war finally ended, many nobles once again had little to do. Inflation also hurt them. Although many were living on fixed incomes, their chivalric code demanded lavish generosity and an aristocratic lifestyle. Many nobles turned to crime as a way of raising money. The fourteenth and fifteenth centuries witnessed a great deal of "fur-collar crime," so-called for the miniver fur the nobility alone were allowed to wear on their collars. England provides a good case study of upper-class crime.

Fur-collar crime rarely involved such felonies as homicide, robbery, rape, and arson. Instead, nobles used their superior social status to rob and extort from the weak and then to corrupt the judicial process. Groups of noble brigands roamed the English countryside stealing from both rich and poor. Sir John de Colseby and Sir William Bussy led a gang of thirty-eight knights who stole goods worth £3,000 in various robberies. Operating exactly like modern urban racketeers, knightly gangs demanded that peasants pay "protection money" or else have their hovels burned and their fields destroyed. Members of the household of a certain Lord Robert of Payn beat up a victim and then demanded money for protection from future attack.

Attacks on the rich often took the form of kidnaping and extortion. Individuals were grabbed in their homes, and wealthy travelers were seized on the highways and held for ransom. In northern England a gang of gentry led by Sir Gilbert de Middleton abducted Sir Henry Beaumont and his brother, the bishop-elect of Durham, and two Roman cardinals in England on a peacemaking visit. Only after a ransom was paid were the victims released.[20]

Fur-collar criminals were terrorists, but like some twentieth-century white-collar criminals who commit nonviolent crimes, medieval aristocratic criminals got away with their outrages. When accused of wrongdoing, fur-collar criminals intimidated witnesses. They threatened jurors. They used "pull" or influence or cash to bribe judges. As a fourteenth-century English judge wrote to a young nobleman, "For the love of your father I have hindered charges being brought against you and have prevented execution of indictment actually made."[21]

The ballads of Robin Hood, a collection of folk legends from late medieval England, describe the adventures of the outlaw hero and his band of followers, who lived in Sherwood Forest and attacked and punished those who violated the social system and the law. Most of the villains in these simple tales are fur-collar criminals — grasping landlords, wicked sheriffs such as the famous sheriff of Nottingham, and mercenary churchmen. Robin and his merry men performed a sort of retributive justice. Robin Hood was a popular figure, because he symbolized the deep resentment of aristocratic corruption and abuse; he represented the struggle against tyranny and oppression.

Criminal activity by nobles continued decade after decade because governments were not strong enough to stop it. Then, too, much of the crime was directed against a lord's own serfs, and the line between a noble's legal jurisdiction over his peasants and criminal behavior was a very fine one indeed. Persecution by lords, coming on top of war, disease, and natural disasters, eventually drove long-suffering peasants all across Europe to revolt.

PEASANT REVOLTS

Peasant revolts occurred often in the Middle Ages. Early in the thirteenth century, the French preacher Jacques de Vitry asked rhetorically, "How many serfs have killed their lords or burnt their castles?"[22] Social and economic conditions in the fourteenth and fifteenth centuries caused a great increase in peasant uprisings.

In 1358, when French taxation for the Hundred Years' War fell heavily on the poor, the frustrations of the French peasantry exploded in a massive uprising called the *Jacquerie,* after the nickname of a supposedly happy agricultural laborer, Jacques Bonhomme (Good Fellow). Peasants in Picardy and Champagne went on the rampage.

Crowds swept through the countryside slashing the throats of nobles, burning their castles, raping their wives and daughters, killing or maiming their horses and cattle. Peasants blamed the nobility for oppressive taxes, for the criminal brigandage of the countryside, for defeat in war, and for the general misery. Artisans, small merchants, and parish priests joined the peasants. Urban and rural groups committed terrible destruction, and for several weeks the nobles were on the defensive. Then the upper class united to repress the revolt with savage and merciless ferocity. Thousands of the "Jacques," innocent as well as guilty, were cut down.

This forcible suppppression of social rebellion, without some effort to alleviate its underlying causes, could only serve as a stopgap measure and drive protest underground. Between 1363 and 1484, serious peasant revolts swept the Auvergne; in 1380, uprisings occurred in the Midi; and in 1420, they erupted in the Lyonnais region of France.

The Peasants' Revolt in England in 1381, involving perhaps a hundred thousand people, was probably the largest single uprising of the entire Middle Ages. The causes were complex and varied from place to place. In general, though, the thirteenth century had witnessed the steady commutation of labor services for cash rents, and the Black Death had drastically cut the labor supply. As a result, peasants demanded higher wages and fewer manorial obligations. The parliamentary Statute of Laborers of 1351 (see page 393) declared:

Whereas to curb the malice of servants who after the pestilence were idle and unwilling to serve without securing excessive wages, it was recently ordained . . . that such servants, both men and women, shall be bound to serve in return for salaries and wages that were customary . . . five or six years earlier.[23]

THE JACQUERIE *Because social revolt on the part of war-weary, frustrated poor seemed to threaten the natural order of Christian society, the upper classes everywhere exacted terrible vengeance on peasants and* artisans. In this scene some *jacques* are cut down, some beheaded, and others drowned. (Bibliothèque Nationale, Paris)

This statute was an attempt by landlords to freeze wages and social mobility.

The statute could not be enforced. As a matter of fact, the condition of the English peasantry steadily improved in the course of the fourteenth century. Some scholars believe that the peasantry in most places was better off in the period 1350–1450 than it had been for centuries before or was to be for four centuries after.

Why then was the outburst in 1381 so serious? It was provoked by a crisis of rising expectations. The relative prosperity of the la-boring classes led to demands that the upper classes were unwilling to grant. Unable to climb higher, the peasants' frustration found release in revolt. Economic grievances combined with other factors. Decades of aristocratic violence, much of it perpetrated against the weak peasantry, had bred hostility and bitterness. In France frustration over the lack of permanent victory increased. In England the social and religious agitation of the popular preacher John Ball fanned the embers of discontent. Such sayings as Ball's famous couplet

When Adam delved and Eve span
Who was then the gentleman?

reflect real revolutionary sentiment. But the lords of England believed that God had permanently fixed the hierarchical order of society and that nothing man could do would change that order. Moreover, the south of England, where the revolt broke out, had been subjected to frequent and destructive French raids. The English government did little to protect the south, and villages grew increasingly scared and insecure. Fear erupted into violence.

The straw that broke the camel's back in England was a head tax on all adult males. Although it met widespread opposition in 1380, the royal council ordered the sheriffs to collect it again in 1381 on penalty of a huge fine. Beginning with assaults on the tax collectors, the uprising in England followed much the same course as had the Jacquerie in France. Castles and manors were sacked; manorial records were destroyed. Many nobles, including the archbishop of Canterbury, who had ordered the collection of the tax, were murdered.

Although the center of the revolt was the highly populated and economically advanced south and east, sections of the north and the Midlands also witnessed rebellions. Violence took different forms in different places. The townspeople of Cambridge expressed their hostility to the university by sacking one of the colleges and building a bonfire of academic property. In towns containing skilled Flemish craftsmen, fear of competition led to their attack and murder. Urban discontent merged with rural violence. Apprentices and journeymen, frustrated because the highest positions in the guilds were closed to them, rioted.

The boy-king Richard II (1377–1399) met the leaders of the revolt, agreed to charters insuring peasants' freedom, tricked them with false promises, and then proceeded to crush the uprising with terrible ferocity. Although the nobility tried to restore ancient duties of serfdom, virtually a century of freedom had elapsed, and the commutation of manorial services continued. Rural serfdom had disappeared in England by 1550.

Conditions in England and France were not unique. In Florence in 1378, the *ciompi,* the poorest workmen, revolted. Serious social trouble occurred in Lübeck, Brunswick, and other cities of the Holy Roman Empire. In Spain in 1391, aristocratic attempts to impose new forms of serfdom combined with demands for tax relief led to massive working-class and peasant uprisings in Seville and Barcelona. These took the form of vicious attacks on Jewish communities. Rebellions and uprisings everywhere reveal deep peasant and working-class frustration and the general socioeconomic crisis of the times.

MARRIAGE

Marriage and the family provided such peace and satisfaction as most people attained. In fact, life for those who were not clerics or nuns meant marriage. Apart from sexual and emotional urgency, the community expected people to marry. For a girl, childhood was a preparation for marriage. In addition to the thousands of chores involved in running a household, girls learned obedience, or at least subordination. Adulthood meant living as a wife or widow. However, sweeping statements about marriage in the Middle Ages have limited validity. Most peasants were illiterate and left slight record of their feelings toward their spouses or about marriage as an institution. The gentry, however, often could write, and the letters exchanged between

Margaret and John Paston, upper-middle-class people who lived in Norfolk, England, in the fifteenth century, provide important evidence of the experience of one couple.

John and Margaret Paston were married about 1439, after an arrangement concluded entirely by their parents. John spent most of his time in London fighting through the law courts to increase his family properties and business interests; Margaret remained in Norfolk to supervise the family lands. Her enormous responsibilities involved managing the Paston estates, hiring workers, collecting rents, ordering supplies for the large household, hearing complaints and settling disputes among tenants, and marketing her crops. In these duties she proved herself a remarkably shrewd businessperson. Moreover, when an army of over a thousand men led by the aristocratic thug Lord Moleyns attacked her house, she successfully withstood the siege. When the Black Death entered her area, Margaret moved her family to safety.

Margaret Paston did all this on top of raising eight children (there were probably other children who did not survive childhood). Her husband died before she was forty-three, and she later conducted the negotiations for the children's marriages. Her children's futures, like her estate management, were planned with an eye toward economic and social advancement. When one daughter secretly married the estate bailiff, an alliance considered beneath her, the girl was cut off from the family as if she were dead.[24]

The many letters surviving between Margaret and John reveal slight tenderness toward their children. They seem to have reserved their love for each other, and during many of his frequent absences they wrote to express mutual affection and devotion. How typical the Paston relationship was, modern historians cannot say, but the marriage of John and Margaret, although completely arranged by their parents, was based on respect, responsibility, and love.[25]

In the later Middle Ages, as earlier – indeed, until the late nineteenth century – economic factors, rather than romantic love or physical attraction, determined whom and when a person married. The young agricultural laborer on the manor had to wait until he had sufficient land. Thus most men had to wait until their fathers died or yielded the holding. The age of marriage was late, which in turn affected the number of children a couple had. The journeyman craftsman in the urban guild faced the same material difficulties. Prudent young men selected (or their parents selected for them) girls who would bring the most land or money to the union. Once a couple married, the union ended only with the death of one partner.

Divorce – the complete dissolution of the contract between a woman and man lawfully married – did not exist in the Middle Ages. The church held that a marriage validly entered into could not be dissolved. A valid marriage consisted of the oral consent or promise of the two parties made to each other. Church theologians of the day urged that the marriage be publicized by banns, or announcements made in the parish church, and that the couple's union be celebrated and witnessed in a church ceremony and blessed by a priest.

A great number of couples did not observe the church's regulations. Some treated marriage as a private act – they made the promise and spoke the words of marriage to each other without witnesses and then proceeded to enjoy the sexual pleasures of marriage. This practice led to a great number of disputes, because one or the other of the two parties could later deny having made a marriage agreement. The records of the ecclesiastical courts reveal many cases arising from privately made contracts. Here is a typical case heard by the ecclesiastical court at York in England in 1372:

[The witness says that] one year ago on the feast day of the apostles Philip and James just past, he was present in the house of William Burton, tanner of York. . . . when and where John Beke, saddler . . . called the said Marjory to him and said to her, "Sit with me." Acquiescing in this, she sat down. John said to her, "Marjory, do you wish to be my wife?" And she replied, "I will if you wish." And taking at once the said Marjory's right hand, John said, "Marjory, here I take you as my wife, for better or worse, to have and to hold until the end of my life; and of this I give you my faith." The said Marjory replied to him, "Here I take you John as my husband, to have and to hold until the end of my life, and of this I give you my faith." And then the said John kissed the said Marjory. . . .[26]

This was a private arrangement, made in secret and without the presence of the clergy. Evidence survives of marriages contracted in a garden, in a blacksmith's shop, at a tavern, and, predictably, in a bed. Church courts heard a great number of similar cases. The records of those courts that relate to marriage reveal that rather than suits for divorce, the great majority of petitions asked the court to enforce the marriage contract that one of the parties believed she or he had validly made. Annulments were granted in extraordinary circumstances, such as male impotence, on the grounds that a lawful marriage had never existed.

LIFE IN THE PARISH

In the later Middle Ages, the land and the parish remained the focus of life for the European peasantry. Work on the land continued to be performed collectively. All men, for example, cooperated in the annual tasks of planting and harvesting. The close association

of the cycle of agriculture and the liturgy of the Christian calendar endured. The parish priest blessed the fields before the annual planting, offering prayers on behalf of the people for a good crop. If the harvest was a rich one, the priest led the processions and celebrations of thanksgiving.

How did the common people feel about their work? Since the vast majority were illiterate and inarticulate, it is difficult to say. It is known that the peasants hated the ancient services and obligations on the lords' lands and tried to get them commuted for money rents. When lords attempted to reimpose service duties, the peasants revolted.

In the thirteenth century, the craft guilds provided the small minority of men living in towns and cities with the psychological satisfaction of involvement in the manufacture of a superior product. The guild member also had economic security. The craft guilds set high standards for their merchandise. The guilds looked after the sick, the poor, the widowed, and the orphaned. Masters and journeymen worked side by side.

In the fourteenth century, those ideal conditions began to change. The fundamental objective of the craft guild was to maintain a monopoly on its product, and to do so recruitment and promotion were carefully restricted. Some guilds required a high entrance fee for apprentices; others admitted only the sons or relatives of members. Apprenticeship increasingly lasted a long time, seven years. Even after a young man had satisfied all the tests for full membership in the guild and had attained the rank of master, other hurdles had to be crossed, such as finding the funds to open his own business or special connections just to get in a guild. Restrictions limited the number of apprentices and journeymen to the anticipated openings for masters. The larger a particular business was, the greater was the likelihood that the master did not know his

MASKED MUMMERS *People of all ages and classes enjoyed mummers' shows, which were performed by groups of masked actors who burlesqued some well-known event or person. Sometimes mummers accom-* *panied their shows with primitive musical instruments, such as drums or tambourines. (Bibliothèque Nationale, Paris)*

employees. The separation of master and journeyman and the decreasing number of openings for master craftsmen created serious frustrations. Strikes and riots occurred in the Flemish towns, in France, and in England.

The recreation of all classes reflected the fact that late medieval society was organized for war and that violence was common. The aristocracy engaged in tournaments or jousts; archery and wrestling had great popularity among ordinary people. Everyone enjoyed the cruel sports of bullbaiting and bearbaiting. As the great French scholar Marc Bloch wrote, "Violence was an element in manners. Medieval men had little control over their immediate impulses; they were emotionally insensitive to the spectacle of pain, and they had small regard for human life . . ."[27] Thus, the

hangings and mutilations of criminals were exciting and well-attended events, with all the festivity of a university town before a Saturday football game. Chronicles exulted in describing executions, murders, and massacres. Here a monk gleefully describes the gory execution of William Wallace in 1305:

Wilielmus Waleis, a robber given to sacrilege, arson and homicide . . . was condemned to most cruel but justly deserved death. He was drawn through the streets of London at the tails of horses, until he reached a gallows of unusual height, there he was suspended by a halter; but taken down while yet alive, he was mutilated, his bowels torn out and burned in a fire, his head then cut off, his body divided into four, and his quarters transmitted to four principal parts of Scotland.

Behold the end of the merciless man, who himself perished without mercy.[28]

Violence was as English as roast beef and plum pudding, as French as bread, cheese, and *potage.*

Alcohol, primarily beer or ale, provided solace to the poor, and the frequency of drunkenness reflects their terrible frustrations.

In the fourteenth and fifteenth centuries, the laity began to exercise increasing influence and control over the affairs of the parish. Churchmen were criticized. The constant quarrels of the mendicant orders (the Franciscans and Dominicans), the mercenary and grasping attitude of the parish clergy, the scandal of the Great Schism and a divided Christendom – all these did much to weaken the spiritual mystique of the clergy in the popular mind. The laity steadily took responsibility for the management of parish lands. Laymen and laywomen organized associations to vote on and purchase furnishings for the church. And ordinary lay people secured jurisdiction over the structure of the church building, its vestments, books, and furnishings. These new responsibilities of the laity reflect the increased dignity of the parishioners in the late Middle Ages.[29]

———◆———

Late medieval preachers likened the crises of their times to the Four Horsemen of the Apocalypse in the Book of Revelation, who brought famine, war, disease, and death. The crises of the fourteenth and fifteenth centuries were acids that burned deeply into the fabric of traditional medieval European society. Bad weather brought poor harvests, which contributed to the international economic depression. Disease, over which people also had little control, fostered widespread psychological depression and dissatisfaction. Population losses caused by the Black Death and the

Hundred Years' War encouraged the working classes to try to profit from the labor shortage by selling their services higher: they wanted to move up the economic ladder. The socialistic ideas of thinkers like John Wyclif, John Hus, and John Ball fanned the flames of social discontent. When peasant frustrations exploded in uprisings, the frightened nobility and upper middle class crushed the revolts and condemned heretical preachers as agitators of social rebellion. But the war had heightened social consciousness among the poor.

The Hundred Years' War served as a catalyst for the development of representative government in England. The royal policy of financing the war through Parliament-approved taxation gave the middle classes an increased sense of their economic power. They would pay taxes in return for some influence in shaping royal policies.

In France, on the other hand, the war stiffened opposition to national assemblies. The disasters that wracked France decade after decade led the French people to believe that the best solutions to complicated problems lay not in an assembly but in the hands of a strong monarch. France became the model for continental countries in the evolution toward royal absolutism.

The war also stimulated technological experimentation, especially with artillery. After about 1350, the cannon, although highly inaccurate, was commonly used all over Europe.

Religion remained the cement that held society together. European culture was a Christian culture. But the Great Schism weakened the prestige of the church and people's faith in papal authority. The conciliar movement, by denying the church's universal sovereignty, strengthened the claims of secular governments to jurisdiction over all their peoples. The later Middle Ages witnessed a steady shift of basic loyalty from the Christian church to the emerging national states.

ALBRECHT DÜRER: THE FOUR HORSEMEN OF THE APOCALYPSE From right to left, representatives of war, strife, famine, and death gallop across Christian society leaving thousands dead or in misery. The horrors of the age made this subject extremely popular in art, literature, and sermons. (Courtesy, Museum of Fine Arts, Boston)

NOTES

1. W. H. McNeill, *Plagues and Peoples,* Doubleday, New York, 1976, pp. 151–168.

2. Quoted by P. Ziegler, *The Black Death,* Pelican Books, Harmondsworth, England, 1969, p. 20.

3. J. M. Rigg, trans., *The Decameron of Giovanni Boccaccio,* J. M. Dent & Sons, London, 1903, p. 6.

4. Ziegler, pp. 232–239.

5. N. F. Cantor, *The English: A History of Politics and Society to 1760,* Simon & Schuster, New York, 1967, p. 260.

6. J. Barnie, *War in Medieval English Society: Social Values and the Hundred Years' War,* Cornell University Press, Ithaca, N.Y., 1974, p. 6.

7. Quoted by Barnie, p. 34.

8. Ibid., p. 73.

9. Ibid., pp. 72–73.

10. W. P. Barrett, trans., *The Trial of Jeanne d'Arc,* George Routledge, London, 1931, pp. 165–166.

11. Quoted by Edward A. Lucie-Smith, *Joan of Arc,* W. W. Norton, New York, 1977, p. 32.

12. Ibid., pp. 32–35.

13. Quoted by Barnie, pp. 36–37.

14. M. M. Postan, "The Costs of the Hundred Years' War," *Past and Present* 27 (April 1964):34–53.

15. Quoted by P. S. Lewis, "The Failure of the Medieval French Estates," *Past and Present* 23 (November 1962):6.

16. Ibid., p. 10.

17. C. Stephenson and G. F. Marcham, eds., *Sources of English Constitutional History,* rev. ed., Harper & Row, New York, 1972, p. 217.

18. Quoted by J. H. Smith, *The Great Schism 1378: The Disintegration of the Papacy,* Weybright & Talley, New York, 1970, p. 141.

19. Ibid., p. 15.

20. B. A. Hanawalt, "Fur Collar Crime: The Pattern of Crime Among the Fourteenth-Century English Nobility," *Journal of Social History* 8 (Spring 1975):1–14.

21. Ibid., p. 7.

22. Quoted by M. Bloch, *French Rural History,* trans. Janet Sondheimer, University of California Press, Berkeley, 1966, p. 169.

23. Stephenson and Marcham, p. 225.

24. A. S. Haskell, "The Paston Women on Marriage in Fifteenth Century England," *Viator* 4 (1973):459–469.

25. Ibid., p. 471.

26. Quoted by R. H. Helmholz, *Marriage Litigation in Medieval England,* Cambridge University Press, Cambridge, 1974, pp. 28–29.

27. M. Bloch, *Feudal Society,* trans. L. A. Manyon, Routledge & Kegan Paul, London, 1961, p. 411.

28. A. F. Scott, ed., *Everyone a Witness: The Plantagenet Age,* Thomas Y. Crowell, New York, 1976, p. 263.

29. See E. Mason, "The Role of the English Parishioner, 1000–1500," *Journal of Ecclesiastical History* 27:1 (January 1976):17–29.

SUGGESTED READING

Students who wish further elaboration of the topics covered in this chapter should consult the following studies, on which the chapter leans extensively. For the Black Death and health generally, see W. H. McNeill, *Plagues and Peoples* (1976), a fresh, challenging, and comprehensive study; F. F. Cartwright, *Disease and History* (1972), which contains an interesting section on the Black Death; P. Ziegler, *The Black Death* (1969), a fascinating and highly readable book; and H. E. Sigerist, *Civilization and Disease* (1970), which presents a worthwhile treatment of the many social implications of disease.

The standard study of the long military conflicts of the fourteenth and fifteenth centuries remains that of E. Perroy, *The Hundred Years' War* (1959). J. Henneman, *Royal Taxation in Fourteenth Century France: The Development of War Financing, 1322–1356* (1971), is an important technical work by a distinguished historian. J. Barnie's *War in Medieval English Society: Social Values and the Hundred Years' War* (1974), treats the attitude of patriots, intellectuals, and the general public. Desmond Seward, *The Hundred Years' War: The English in France, 1337–1453* (1981), tells an exciting story, and John Keegan, *The Face of Battle* (1977), Chapter 2, "Agincourt," describes what war meant to the ordinary soldier. Barbara Tuchman, *A Distant Mirror: The Calamitous 14th Century* (1980), gives a vivid picture of many facets of fourteenth-century life, while concentrating on the war. The best treatment of the financial costs of the war is probably M. M. Postan, "The Costs of the Hundred Years' War," *Past and Present* 27 (April 1964):34–53. E. Searle and R. Burghart, "The Defense of England and the Peasants' Revolt," *Viator* 3 (1972), is a fascinating study of the peasants' changing social attitudes.

For political and social conditions in the fourteenth and fifteenth centuries, the following studies are all useful: P. S. Lewis, *Later Medieval France: The Polity* (1968), and "The Failure of the French Medieval Estates," *Past and Present* 23 (November 1962); L. Romier, *A History of France* (1962); G. O. Sayles, *The King's Parliament of England* (1974); M. Bloch, *French Rural History* (1966); I. Kershaw, "The Great Famine and Agrarian Crisis in England, 1315–1322," *Past and Present* 59 (May 1973); B. A. Hanawalt, "Fur Collar Crime: The Pattern of Crime Among the Fourteenth-Century English Nobility," *Journal of Social History* 8 (Spring 1975): 1–17, a fascinating discussion; K. Thomas, "Work and Leisure in Pre-Industrial Society," *Past and Present* 29 (December 1964); M. Keen, *The Outlaws of Medieval Legend* (1961) and "Robin Hood – Peasant or Gentleman?," *Past and Present* 19 (April 1961):7–18; P. Wolff, "The 1391 Pogrom in Spain, Social Crisis or Not?," *Past and Present* 50 (February 1971):4–18; and R. H. Helmholz, *Marriage Litigation in Medieval England* (1974). Students are especially encouraged to consult the brilliant achievement of E. L. Ladurie, *The Peasants of Languedoc,* trans. John Day (1976).

The poetry of Dante, Chaucer, and Villon may be read in the following editions: Dorothy Sayers, trans., *Dante: The Divine Comedy,* 3 vols. (1963); Nevil Coghill, trans., *Chaucer's Canterbury Tales* (1977); Peter Dale, trans., *The Poems of Villon* (1973). The social setting of Chaucer's *Canterbury Tales* is brilliantly evoked in D. W. Robertson, Jr., *Chaucer's London* (1968).

Many of the preceding titles treat the religious history of the period. In addition, the following contain interesting and valuable information: G. Barraclough, *The Medieval Papacy* (1968), which is splendidly illustrated; W. Ullmann, *A Short History of the Papacy in the Middle Ages* (1972); E. Mason, "The Role of the English Parishioner, 1000–1500," *Journal of Ecclesiastical History* 27 (January 1976):17–29; and J. H. Smith, *The Great Schism 1378: The Disintegration of the Medieval Papacy* (1970).

CHAPTER 13

EUROPEAN SOCIETY IN THE AGE OF THE RENAISSANCE

WHILE THE FOUR HORSEMEN of the Apocalypse carried war, plague, famine, and death across the Continent, a new culture was emerging in southern Europe. The fourteenth century witnessed the beginnings of remarkable changes in many aspects of Italian society. In the fifteenth century, these phenomena spread beyond Italy and gradually influenced society in northern Europe. These cultural changes have been collectively labeled the Renaissance. What does the term *Renaissance* mean? How did the Renaissance manifest itself in politics, government, and social organization? What developments occurred in the evolution of the nation state? Did the Renaissance involve shifts in religious attitudes? This chapter explores these questions.

THE IDEA OF THE RENAISSANCE

The Renaissance was an intellectual movement that began in Italy in the fourteenth century. It was characterized by hostility to the culture of the Middle Ages and fascination with the ancient world. Writers and artists of the Renaissance displayed great concern for individualism, a serious interest in human nature based on the study of the Greek and Latin classics, and a new excitement about life in this world. The cultural movement scholars have called the Renaissance was limited to a small, self-conscious, educated elite; it never directly involved the masses of people.

The realization that something new and unique was happening first came to men of letters of the fourteenth century, especially to the poet and humanist Francesco Petrarch (1304-1374). Petrarch thought that he was living at the start of a new age, a period of light following a long night of Gothic gloom. He believed that the first and second centuries of the Roman Empire represented the peak in the development of human civilization. The Germanic invasions had caused a sharp cultural break with the glories of Rome and inaugurated what Petrarch called "the Dark Ages." Medieval people had believed that they were continuing the glories that had been ancient Rome, and had recognized no cultural division between the world of the emperors and their own times. But for Petrarch and many of his contemporaries, the thousand-year period between the fourth and the fourteenth centuries constituted a barbarian, or Gothic, or middle age. The sculptors, painters, and writers of the Renaissance spoke contemptuously of their medieval predecessors and identified themselves with the thinkers and artists of Greco-Roman civilization. Petrarch believed he was witnessing a new golden age of intellectual achievement – a rebirth or, to use the French word that came into English, a renaissance. The division of historical time into periods is often arbitrary and done for the convenience of historians. In terms of the way most people lived and thought, no sharp division exists between the Middle Ages and the Renaissance. Nevertheless, Petrarch's categorization of time periods has had great influence. Most scholars use the word *Renaissance* to mean the artistic and cultural developments in western Europe that began in the fourteenth century and lasted into the seventeenth.

ITALIAN ORIGINS OF THE RENAISSANCE

The Renaissance began in Italy. Why did a brilliant flowering of artistic and intellectual creativity occur in Italy in the fourteenth through sixteenth centuries? This question has troubled scholars for a long time, and they still have not arrived at a definite answer. Some have offered economic explanations for Italy's cultural flowering, emphasizing the material prosperity without which the arts cannot flourish.

By the middle of the fourteenth century, the commercial classes of Florence and other Italian cities had acquired enough money that they could finance non-moneymaking activities. The cornerstone of northern Italian economic activity was international trade, commerce, and banking. The northern Italian cities had led the way in the commercial revival of the eleventh century. By the middle of the twelfth century, Venice, Genoa, Florence, and Milan were enjoying a great volume of trade with the Middle East and with northern Europe. These Italian cities fully exploited their geographical position as natural crossroads for exchange between the East and the West. Venice had profited tremendously from the Fourth Crusade. In the early fourteenth century, furthermore, Genoa and Venice made important strides in shipbuilding, allowing their ships for the first time to sail all year long. Improvements in the construction of cargo ships enabled the Venetians and Genoese to carry more bulk and to navigate the dangerous Atlantic Ocean. Most goods were purchased directly from the producers and sold a good distance away. For example, Italian merchants bought fine English wool directly from the Cistercian abbeys of Yorkshire in northern England. The wool was transported to the bazaars of North Africa either overland or by ship through the Straits of Gibraltar. The risks in such an operation were great, but the profits were enormous. These profits were continually reinvested to earn more.

It is generally agreed that the first manifestations of the Italian Renaissance – in art, ar-

BUSINESS ACTIVITIES IN A FLORENTINE BANK The Florentines early developed new banking devices. One man (left) presents a letter of credit or a bill of exchange, forerunners of the modern check, which allowed credit in distant places. A foreign merchant (right) exchanges one kind of currency for another. The bank profited from the fees it charged for these services. (Prints Division; New York Public Library; Astor, Lenox and Tilden Foundation)

chitecture, and literary creativity – appeared in Florence, and Florence possessed enormous wealth. Geography had not helped Florence; it was an inland city without easy access to water transportation. But toward the end of the thirteenth century, Florentine merchants and bankers acquired control of papal banking. From their position as tax collectors for the papacy, Florentine mercantile families began to dominate European banking on both sides of the Alps. These families had offices in Paris and London, Barcelona and Marseilles, Tunis and the North African ports, and, of course, Naples and Rome. The profits from loans, investments, and money exchanges that poured back to Florence were pumped into urban industries. Such profits contributed to the city's economic vitality.

The Florentine wool industry, however, was the major factor in the city's financial expansion and population increase. Florence purchased the best-quality wool from England and Spain, developed remarkable techniques for its manufacture, and employed thousands of workers to turn it into cloth. Florentine weavers produced immense quantities of superb woolen cloth, which brought the highest prices in the fairs, markets, and bazaars of Europe, Asia, and Africa.

By the first quarter of the fourteenth century, the economic foundations of Florence were so strong that even two severe crises could not destroy the city. In 1344, King Edward III of England repudiated his huge debts to Florentine bankers and forced some of them into bankruptcy. Florence also suffered frightfully from the Black Death, losing perhaps half its population. Still, the basic Florentine economic structure remained stable. Driving enterprise, technical know-how, and competitive spirit saw Florence through the difficult economic period of the late fourteenth century.[1]

One inconsistency in this economic explanation of the origins of the Renaissance lies in the fact that in the middle of the fourteenth century the Florentine wool and banking industries experienced a serious depression. Trade declined, affected by the Black Death and the international business slump. Moreover, such cities as Genoa, which had at one time enjoyed considerable prosperity, made no profound contribution to the Renaissance. It may be, however, that Florentine businessmen who found foreign markets closed invested instead in art, expecting a financial return from art works that increased in value.

A leading interpretation of the Italian Renaissance traces its origins to the development of civic humanism, or public pride, in Florence. In the 1380s, Florence was severely threatened by the conquests of Gian Galeazzo Visconti, duke of Milan. The Florentines put up a heroic and successful resistance, and in so doing came to appreciate the special virtues of their republican form of government – in contrast to the tyranny represented by Visconti. Awareness of their unique political heritage, which they traced back to the time of the Roman Empire, led the Florentines to take great pride in their city. Civic humanism took the form of public respect for Florence's achievements, whether in trade or architecture, education or the arts. They embarked upon a policy of beautification. This civic self-consciousness eventually spread to the other city-states of Italy.

Unlike the countries of northern Europe, Italy had never been heavily feudalized. Italian feudal lords rarely exercised the vast independent powers held by the barons of France, England, and the Holy Roman Empire. Although the volume of urban trade and the size of urban populations severely declined in the early Middle Ages, cities survived as commercial centers. In the twelfth and thirteenth centuries, northern Italian cities like Venice and Milan gained control of their surrounding territories. The wealth they steadily gained was used to acquire and solidify their independence; the Holy Roman emperors never fully exploited the wealth of the cities.

Italian society in the fourteenth century meant urban society, and this fundamental fact helps to account for the Italian origin of the Renaissance. The cities of Milan, Venice, Florence, Genoa, and Pisa were visited by traders and businessmen from all parts of the Western world. Foreigners brought with them their own customs, traditions, and values, and considerable social interchange inevitably took place. The merchant Francesco Datini, for example, was involved in commercial transactions with two hundred cities,

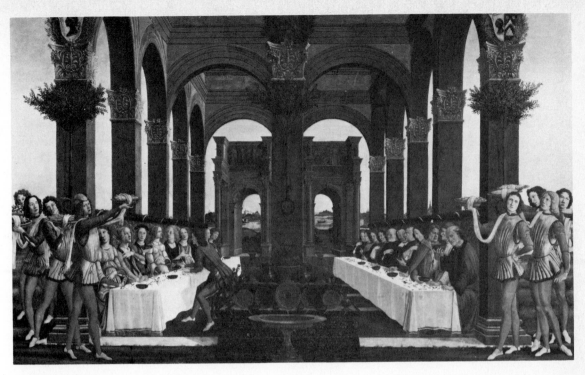

THE WEDDING FEAST   *This picture was one of a series Botticelli produced illustrating a story in Boccaccio's* Decameron. *The classical architecture with its vision of nature beyond, the pomp with which the* meal is served, and the philosophical discussion at the tables — all represent the tastes and ideals of the Florentine aristocracy under the Medici. (Courtesy of Christie's)

from Alexandria and Beirut in the south to Stockholm in the north. Italians gained an awareness of different parts of the world. They grew more refined, more sophisticated in their tastes and lifestyles, more worldly and urbane. Although Italians remained devoted sons and daughters of the church, they grew more secular in their outlook and behavior. Class distinctions remained strong in Renaissance Italy, but those distinctions were based on wealth rather than birth. And enterprise, imagination, and hard work could lead to wealth in the urban environment.

Moreover, the wealthy burghers of the cities began to strike military and marital contracts with the rural nobility of northern Italy. These alliances enabled the nobles to maintain a high standard of living in a rising money economy and gave the cities military support and protection. When the rich merchants united with the rural nobility, two significant developments occurred: the possession of land gradually came into the hands of bankers and merchants, and as a result the cities obtained political as well as economic jurisdiction over the surrounding countryside. In no other part of Europe did cities acquire such political power, primarily because the aristocratic ethos forbade feudal barons to unite with the moneygrubbing bourgeoisie. Nor did cities elsewhere have the commercial and financial strength of the Italian towns.

A foreign element also played a significant role. Beginning in the late fourteenth century, a steady stream of educated Greek refugees came from Byzantium to Italy to escape Turkish domination. Greek scholars like Manuel

Chrysoloras, John Bessarion, and Jonus Lascaris taught the Greek language and translated important Greek literary classics into Latin. Venice became the center of Greek scholarship, but Florence and Rome also gained an international reputation for Greek learning. Greek emigration to Italy broadened the intellectual horizon and enriched Italian Renaissance culture.

Finally, the Renaissance started in Italy because Italian poets, sculptors, painters, and philosophers of the fifteenth and sixteenth centuries considered themselves the natural heirs of the ancient Romans. Italy still possessed the literary manuscripts, the architectural monuments, the roads that constituted the heritage of Roman civilization. The national past of Italy was visible everywhere. Above all, Italians retained the historical memory of Roman power and imperial grandeur, and looked back on Roman antiquity as the golden age, as an ideal to be restored and reborn.

Increased wealth afforded more leisure time. Wealth in itself is usually not sufficient to satisfy the human psyche. When the physical and material needs of life are fulfilled and there is a surplus, then the spirit can be enriched by esthetic and intellectual interests. The Renaissance, then, was an artistic and intellectual movement that began in the Italian cities and was supported and sustained by urban wealth.

HALLMARKS OF THE RENAISSANCE

The Renaissance was characterized, as we have seen, by the self-conscious awareness among fourteenth- and fifteenth-century Italians that they were living in a new era. The Renaissance also manifested itself in a new attitude toward men and women and the world – an attitude that may be described as individualism. A humanism characterized by a deep interest in the Latin classics and the deliberate attempt to revive antique lifestyles emerged, as did a bold new secular spirit.

INDIVIDUALISM

In the Middle Ages individuals thought of themselves as part of a group – as a member of a guild, as a resident of a particular area. The very few people who considered themselves so unusual that they indulged in autobiography – Saint Augustine in the fifth century and Guibert of Nogent in the twelfth, for example – were unique for that very reason. Christian humility and the concept of Western society as an organic entity encouraged people to define themselves in terms of a larger religious, economic, or social group.

This organic view of society eroded during the fourteenth and fifteenth centuries in Italy. The Renaissance witnessed the emergence of many distinctive personalities who gloried in their uniqueness. Italians of unusual abilities were self-consciously aware of their singularity, and unafraid to be unlike their neighbors; they had enormous confidence in their ability to achieve great things. Leon Battista Alberti (1404-1474), a writer, architect, and mathematician, remarked, "Men can do all things if they will."[2] Completely lacking in modesty, real or false, talented people of the Renaissance were proud of their abilities and eager for everyone to know about them. The Florentine goldsmith and sculptor Benvenuto Cellini (1500-1574) prefaced his *Autobiography* with a sonnet that declares:

My cruel fate hath warr'd with me in vain:
Life, glory, worth, and all unmeasur'd skill,
Beauty and grace, themselves in me fulfill
That many I surpass, and to the best attain.[3]

Cellini, certain of his genius, wrote so that the whole world might appreciate it.

Individualism stressed personality, genius, uniqueness, and the fullest development of capabilities and talents. Artist, athlete, painter, scholar, sculptor, whatever – a person's potential should be stretched until fully realized. Thirst for fame, a driving ambition, a burning desire for success drove such people to the complete achievement of their potential. The quest for glory was central to Renaissance individualism.

THE REVIVAL OF ANTIQUITY

In the cities of Italy, and especially in Rome, civic leaders and the wealthy populace showed phenomenal archaeological zeal for the recovery of manuscripts, statues, and monuments. Pope Nicholas V (1447-1455), a distinguished scholar, planned the Vatican Library for the nine thousand manuscripts he had collected. Pope Sixtus IV (1471-1484) built that library, which remains one of the richest repositories of ancient and medieval documents.

Patrician Italians consciously copied the lifestyle of the ancients and even searched out pedigrees dating back to ancient Rome. Aeneas Silvius Piccolomini, a native of Siena who became Pope Pius II (1458-1464), once pretentiously declared, "Rome is as much my home as Siena, for my House, the Piccolomini, came in early times from the capital to Siena, as is proved by the constant use of the names Aeneas and Silvius in my family."[4]

The revival of antiquity also took the form of profound interest in and study of the Latin classics. This feature of the Renaissance became known as the "new learning," or simply "humanism," the term of the Florentine rhetorician and historian Leonardo Bruni (1370-1444). The words *humanism* and *humanist* derive ultimately from the Latin *humanitas,* which Cicero used to mean the literary culture needed by anyone who would be considered educated and civilized. Humanists studied the Latin classics to learn what they reveal about human nature. Humanism emphasized human beings, their achievements, interests, and capabilities. Although churchmen supported the new learning, Italian humanism was a preponderantly lay phenomenon.

Appreciation for the literary culture of the Romans had never died completely in the West. Bede, Alcuin, and Einhard in the eighth century, and Ailred of Rievaulx, Bernard of Clairvaux, and John of Salisbury in the twelfth century had all studied and imitated the writings of the ancients. Medieval writers, however, had studied the ancients in order to come to know God. Medieval thinkers held that human beings are the noblest of god's creatures, and that though they have fallen, they are still capable of regeneration and thus deserving of respect. Medieval scholars interpreted the classics in a Christian sense and invested the ancients' poems and histories with Christian meaning.

Renaissance philosophers and poets also emphasized human dignity, but usually not in a Christian context. In a remarkable essay, "On the Dignity of Man," the Florentine writer Pico della Mirandola maintained that man's place in the universe may be somewhere between the beasts and the angels but that there are no limits to what he can accomplish.

Humanists tried to approach the classical texts with an open mind, to learn what the ancients had thought. They rejected the religious interpretations and systematic and formal scholastic works of the Middle Ages. They hated scholasticism because they believed it denied humanity and destroyed style.

The fourteenth- and fifteenth-century humanists loved the language of the classics and considered it superior to the corrupt Latin of the medieval schoolmen. Renaissance writers were very excited by the purity of ancient Latin. They eventually became concerned more about form than content, more about the way an idea was expressed than about the significance and validity of the idea. Literary humanists of the fourteenth century wrote each other highly stylized letters imitating ancient authors, and they held witty philosophical dialogues in conscious imitation of the Platonic Academy of the fifth century B.C. Wherever they could, Renaissance humanists heaped scorn on the "barbaric" Latin style of the medievalists. The leading humanists of the early Renaissance were rhetoricians, seeking effective and eloquent communication, both oral and written.

SECULAR SPIRIT

Secularism involves a basic concern with the material world instead of eternal and spiritual interests. A secular way of thinking tends to find the ultimate explanation of everything and the final end of human beings within the limits of what the senses can discover. In a religious society, such as the medieval, the focus is on the other-worldly, on life after death. In a secular society, attention is concentrated on the here and now, often on the acquisition of material things. The fourteenth and fifteenth centuries witnessed the slow but steady growth of secularism in Italy.

The economic changes and rising prosperity of the Italian cities in the thirteenth century worked a fundamental change in social and intellectual attitudes and values. In the Middle Ages the feudal nobility and the higher clergy had determined the dominant patterns of culture. The medieval aristocracy expressed disdain for moneymaking. Christian ideas and values infused literature, art, politics, and all other aspects of culture. In the Renaissance, by contrast, the business concerns of the urban bourgeoisie required constant and rational attention.

Worries about shifting rates of interest, shipping routes, personnel costs, and employee relations did not leave much time for thoughts about penance and purgatory. The busy bankers and merchants of the Italian cities calculated ways of making and increasing their money. Money allowed greater material pleasures, a more comfortable life, the leisure time to appreciate and patronize the arts. Money could buy many sensual gratifications, and the rich, social-climbing patricians of Venice, Florence, Genoa, and Rome came to see life more as an opportunity to be enjoyed than as a painful pilgrimage to the City of God.

In *On Pleasure,* the humanist Lorenzo Valla (1406–1457) defended the pleasures of the senses as the highest good. Scholars praise Valla as the father of modern historical criticism. His study *On the False Donation of Constantine* (1444) demonstrated by careful textual examination that an anonymous eighth-century document supposedly giving the papacy jurisdiction over vast territories in western Europe was a forgery. Medieval people had accepted the Donation of Constantine as a reality, and the proof that it was an invention seriously weakened the foundations of papal claims to temporal authority. Lorenzo Valla's work exemplifies the application of critical scholarship to old and almost sacred writings, as well as the new secular spirit of the Renaissance. The tales in the *Decameron* by the Florentine Boccaccio (1313-1375), which describe ambitious merchants, lecherous friars, and cuckolded husbands, portray a frankly acquisitive, sensual, and secular society. The "contempt of the world" theme, so pervasive in medieval literature, had disappeared. Renaissance writers justified the accumulation and enjoyment of wealth with references to ancient authors.

Nor did church leaders do much to combat the new secular spirit or set high moral standards. In the fifteenth and early sixteenth centuries, the papal court and the households of the cardinals were just as worldly as those of great urban patricians. Of course, most of the popes and higher church officials had come from the bourgeois aristocracy. The Medici pope Leo X (1513-1521), for example, supported artists and men of letters because patronage was an activity he had learned in the household of his father, Lorenzo the Magnificent. Renaissance popes beautified the city of Rome and patronized the arts. They expended enormous enthusiasm and huge sums of money on the re-embellishment of the city. A new papal chancellery, begun in 1483 and finished in 1511, stands as one of the architectural masterpieces of the High Renaissance (roughly the period 1500-1530). Pope Julius II (1503-1513) tore down the old St. Peter's Basilica and began work on the present structure in 1506. Michelangelo's dome for St. Peter's is still considered his greatest work. Papal interests, far removed from spiritual concerns, fostered rather than discouraged the new worldly attitude.

But the broad mass of the people and even the intellectuals and leaders of society remained faithful to the Christian church. Few people questioned the basic tenets of the Christian religion. Italian humanists and their aristocratic patrons were antiascetic, antischolastic, and anticlerical, but they were not agnostics or skeptics. The thousands of pious paintings, sculptures, processions, and pilgrimages of the Renaissance period prove that strong religious feeling persisted.

ART AND THE ARTIST

No feature of the Renaissance evokes greater admiration than its artistic masterpieces. The 1400s (quattrocento) and 1500s (cinquecento) witnessed a dazzling creativity in painting, architecture, and sculpture. In all the arts, the city of Florence consistently led the way. According to the Renaissance art historian Giorgio Vasari (1511-1574), the painter Perugino once asked why it was in Florence and not elsewhere that men achieved perfection in the arts. The first answer he received was, "There were so many good critics there, for the air of the city makes men quick and perceptive and impatient of mediocrity."[5]

Some historians and art critics have maintained that the Renaissance "rediscovered" the world of nature and of human beings. This is nonsense, as a quick glance at a Gothic cathedral reveals. The enormous detail applied to the depiction of animals' bodies, the careful carving of leaves, flowers, and all kinds of vegetation, the fine sensitivity frequently shown in human faces — these clearly show medieval and ancient people's appreciation for nature in all its manifestations. Saint Francis of Assisi (1181-1226) encouraged throughout his entire life an awareness of nature. No historical period has a monopoly on the appreciation of nature or beauty.

ART AND SOCIETY

Significant changes in the realm of art did occur in the fourteenth century. Art served

BOTTICELLI: ADORATION OF THE MAGI *The Florentine artist, biographer, and Medici courtier Giorgio Vasari (1511–1574) says that this painting contains the most faithful likenesses of Cosimo (kneel-* *ing before the Christ child) and Lorenzo (far left). Although the subject is Christian, the painting has a secular spirit, introduces individual portraits, and serves to glorify the Medici family. (Alinari/Scala)*

the newly rich middle class as well as the institutional church. The patrons of Renaissance art were more frequently laypeople than ecclesiastics. Patrician merchants and bankers supported the arts as a means of self-glorification and self-perpetuation. Art may also have been a form of financial investment. Great families, such as the Medicis in Florence, used works of art as a means of gaining and maintaining public support for their rule. A magnificent style of living, enriched by works of art, seemed to prove the greatness of the rulers.

As the fifteenth century advanced, the subject matter of art became steadily more secular. The study of classical texts and manuscripts brought deeper understanding of ancient ideas. Classical themes and motifs, such as the lives and loves of pagan gods and goddesses, figured increasingly in painting and sculpture. Religious topics, such as the Annunciation of the Virgin and the Nativity, remained popular among both patrons and artists, but frequently the patron had himself and his family portrayed in the picture. In Botticelli's *Adoration of the Magi,* for example,

Cosimo de' Medici appears as one of the Magi kneeling before the Christ child. People were conscious of their physical uniqueness, and they wanted their individuality immortalized. Paintings cost money and thus were also means of displaying wealth. Although many Renaissance paintings have classical or Christian themes, the appearance of the patron reflects the new spirit of individualism and secularism.

The style of Renaissance art was decidedly different from that of the Middle Ages. The individual portrait emerged as a distinct artistic genre. In the fifteenth century members of the newly-rich middle class often had themselves painted in a scene of romantic chivalry or in courtly society. Rather than reflecting a spiritual ideal, as medieval painting and sculpture tended to do, Renaissance portraits mirrored reality. The Florentine painter Giotto (1276-1337) led the way in the depiction of realism; his treatment of the human body and face replaced the formal stiffness and artificiality that had for so long characterized the representation of the human body. The sculptor Donatello (1386-1466) probably exerted the greatest influence of any Florentine artist before Michelangelo. His many statues express an appreciation of the incredible variety of human nature. While medieval artists had depicted the nude human body only in a spiritualized and moralizing context, Donatello revived the classical figure with its balance and self-awareness. The short-lived Florentine Masaccio (1401-1428), sometimes called the father of modern painting, inspired a new style characterized by great realism, narrative power, and remarkably effective use of light and dark.

Narrative artists depicted the body in a more scientific and natural manner. The female figure is voluptuous and sensual. The male body, as in Michelangelo's *David* and *The Last Judgment,* is strong and heroic. Renaissance glorification of the human body reveals the secular spirit of the age. Filippo Brunelleschi (1377-1446), together with Piero della Francesca (1420-1492), seems to have pioneered perspective in painting, the linear representation of distance and space on a flat surface. *The Last Supper* of Leonardo da Vinci (1452-1519), with its stress on the tension between Christ and the disciples, is an incredibly subtle psychological interpretation.

THE STATUS OF THE ARTIST

In the Renaissance the social status of the artist improved. The lower-middle-class medieval master mason had been viewed in the same light as a mechanic. The artist in the Renaissance was considered an independent intellectual worker. Some artists and architects achieved not only economic security but very great wealth. All aspiring artists received a practical (not theoretical) education in a recognized master's workshop. For example, Michelangelo (1475-1564) was apprenticed at age thirteen to the artist Ghirlandaio (1449-1494), although he later denied the fact to make it appear he never had any formal training. The more famous the artist, the more he attracted assistants or apprentices. Lorenzo Ghiberti (1378-1455) had twenty assistants during the period he was working on the bronze doors of the Baptistery in Florence, his most famous achievement.

Ghiberti's salary of two hundred florins a year compared very favorably with that of the head of the city government, who earned five hundred florins. Moreover, at a time when a man could live in a princely fashion on three hundred ducats a year, Leonardo da Vinci was making two thousand annually. Michelangelo was paid three thousand ducats for painting

HANS MEMLING: MARIA AND TOMMASO POR-
TINARI   A Florentine citizen, Tommaso Portinari
earned a fortune as representative of the Medici banking interests in Bruges, Flanders. Husband and wife
are dressed in a rich but durable black broadcloth;

Maria's necklace displays their wealth. Although both
faces show a sharp intelligence, there is a melancholy
sadness about them, suggestive of the pessimism of
northern religious piety. (The Metropolitan Museum
of Art: Bequest of Benjamin Altman, 1913)

the ceiling of the Sistine Chapel. When he
agreed to work on St. Peter's Basilica, he refused a salary; he was already a wealthy man.[6]

Renaissance society respected and rewarded
the distinguished artist. In 1537, the prolific
letter writer, humanist, and satirizer of
princes Pietro Aretino (1492–1556), wrote to
Michelangelo while he was painting the Sistine Chapel:

TO THE DIVINE MICHELANGELO:
Sir, just as it is disgraceful and sinful to be un-
mindful of God so it is reprehensible and dishon-
ourable for any man of discerning judgement not
to honour you as a brilliant and venerable artist
whom the very stars use as a target at which to
shoot the rival arrows of their favour. You are so
accomplished, therefore, that hidden in your hands

lives the idea of a new king of creation, whereby
the most challenging and subtle problem of all in
the art of painting, namely that of outlines, has
been so mastered by you that in the contours of the
human body you express and contain the purpose of
art.... And it is surely my duty to honour you
with this salutation, since the world has many
kings but only one Michelangelo.[7]

When the Holy Roman emperor Charles V
(1519–1556) visited the workshop of the
great Titian (1477–1576) and stooped to pick
up the artist's dropped paintbrush, the emperor was demonstrating that the patron
himself was honored in the act of honoring
the artist. The social status of the artist of
genius was immortally secured.

Renaissance artists were not only aware of

their creative power; they boasted about it. The architect Brunelleschi had his life written, and Ghiberti and Cellini wrote their autobiographies. Many medieval sculptors and painters had signed their own works; Renaissance artists almost universally did so, and many of them incorporated self-portraits, usually as bystanders, in their paintings. These actions reflect an acute consciousness of creative genius.

The Renaissance, in fact, witnessed the birth of the concept of the artist as genius. In the Middle Ages people believed that only God created, albeit through individuals; the medieval conception recognized no particular value in artistic originality. Renaissance artists and humanists came to think that a work of art was the deliberate creation of a unique personality, of an individual who goes beyond traditions, rules, and theories. A genius has a peculiar gift, which ordinary laws should not inhibit. Cosimo de'Medici described a painter, because of his genius, as "divine," implying that the artist shared in the powers of God. The word *divine* was widely applied to Michelangelo. The Renaissance thus bequeathed the idea of genius to the modern world.

The student must guard against interpreting Italian Renaissance culture in twentieth-century democratic terms. The culture of the Renaissance was that of a small mercantile elite, a business patriciate with aristocratic pretensions. Renaissance culture did not directly affect the broad middle classes, let alone the vast urban proletariat. The typical small tradesman or craftsman could not read the sophisticated Latin essays of the humanists, even if he had the time to do so. He could not afford to buy the art works of the great masters. A small, highly educated minority of literary humanists and artists created the culture of and for an exclusive elite. They cared little

for ordinary people. Castiglione, Machiavelli, and Vergerio, for example, thoroughly despised the masses. Renaissance humanists were a smaller and narrower group than the medieval clergy had ever been. High churchmen had commissioned the construction of the Gothic cathedrals, but, once finished, the buildings were for all to enjoy. The modern visitor can still see the deep ruts in the stone floors of Chartres and Canterbury where the poor pilgrims slept at night. Nothing comparable was built in the Renaissance. Insecure, social-climbing merchant princes were hardly egalitarian.[8] The Renaissance ushered in a gulf between the learned minority and the uneducated multitude that has survived for many centuries.

SOCIAL CHANGE

The Renaissance changed many aspects of Italian, and subsequently European, society. The new developments brought about real breaks with the medieval past. What impact did the Renaissance have on educational theory and practice, on political thought? How did printing, the era's most stunning technological discovery, affect fifteenth- and sixteenth-century society? Did women have a Renaissance?

EDUCATION AND POLITICAL THOUGHT

One of the central preoccupations of the humanists was education and moral behavior. Humanists poured out treatises, often in the form of letters, on the structure and goals of education and the training of rulers. In one of the earliest systematic programs for the young, Peter Paul Vergerio (1370–1444) wrote Ubertinus, the ruler of Carrara:

School of Luca della Robbia: Virgin and Child *In the late fifteenth century, della Robbia's invention of the process of making polychrome-glazed terracottas led contemporaries to consider him a great artistic innovator. The warm humanity of this roundel (circular panel) is characteristic of della Robbia's art. (Marion Gray. By permission of St. Anselm's Abbey, Washington, D.C.)*

The lives of men of position are passed, as it were, in public view; and are fairly expected to serve as witness to personal merit and capacity on the part of those who occupy such exceptional place amongst their fellow men. You therefore, Ubertinus, . . . the representative of a house for many generations sovereign in our ancient and most learned city of Padua, are peculiarly concerned in attaining this excellence in learning of which we speak. . . . Progress in learning . . . as in character, depends largely on ourselves.

For the education of children is a matter of more than private interest; it concerns the State, which indeed regards the right training of the young as, in certain aspects, within its proper sphere. . . . In order to maintain a high standard of purity all enticements of dancing, or suggestive spectacles, should be kept at a distance: and the society of women as a rule carefully avoided. A bad companion may wreck the character. Idleness, of mind and body, is a common source of temptation to indulgence, and unsociable, solitary temper must be disciplined, and on no account encouraged. Tutors and comrades alike should be chosen from amongst those likely to bring out the best qualities, to attract by good example, and to repress the first signs of evil. . . . Above all, respect for Divine ordinances is of the deepest importance; it should be inculcated from the earliest years. Reverence towards elders and parents is an obligation closely akin. In this, antiquity offers us a beautiful illustration. For the youth of Rome used to escort the Senators, the Fathers of the City, to the Senate House: and awaiting them at the entrance, accompany them at the close of their deliberations on their return to their homes. In this the Romans saw an admirable training in endurance and in patience. This same quality of reverence will imply courtesy towards guests, suitable greeting to elders, to friends and to inferiors. . . .

We call those studies liberal *which are worthy of a free man; those studies by which we attain and practise virtue and wisdom; that education*

which calls forth, trains and develops those highest gifts of body and of mind which ennoble men, and which are rightly judged to rank next in dignity to virtue only. . . .[9]

Part of Vergerio's treatise specifies subjects for the instruction of young men in public life: history teaches virtue by examples from the past; ethics focuses on virtue itself; and rhetoric or public speaking trains for eloquence.

No book on education achieved wider fame or broader influence than Baldassare Castiglione's *The Courtier* (1528). This treatise sought to train, discipline, and fashion the young man into the courtly ideal, the gentleman. According to Castiglione, the educated man of the upper class should have a broad background in many academic subjects, and his spiritual and physical, as well as intellectual, capabilities should be trained. The courtier should have easy familiarity with dance, music, and the arts. Castiglione envisioned a man who could compose a sonnet, wrestle, sing a song and accompany himself on an instrument, ride expertly, solve difficult mathematical problems, and, above all, speak and write eloquently. With these accomplishments, he would be the perfect Renaissance man. Whereas the medieval chivalric ideal stressed the military virtues of bravery and loyalty, the Renaissance man had to develop his artistic and intellectual potential as well as his fighting skills.

In contrast to the pattern of medieval education, the Renaissance courtier had the aristocrat's hostility to specialization and professionalism. Medieval higher education, as offered by the universities, had aimed at providing a practical grounding in preparation for a career. After exposure to the rudiments of grammar and rhetoric, which the medieval student learned mainly through memorization, he was trained for a profession

– usually law – in the government of the state or the church. Education was very functional and, by later standards, middle class.

In manner and behavior, the Renaissance courtier had traits his medieval predecessor probably had not had time to acquire. The gentleman was supposed to be relaxed, controlled, always composed and cool, elegant but not ostentatious, doing everything with a casual and seemingly effortless grace. In the sixteenth and seventeenth centuries, *The Courtier* was widely read. It influenced the social mores and patterns of conduct of elite groups in Renaissance and early modern Europe. The courtier became the model of the European gentleman.

No Renaissance book on any topic, however, has been more widely read and studied in all the centuries since its publication than the short political treatise *The Prince,* by Niccolò Machiavelli (1469–1527). Some political scientists maintain that Machiavelli was describing the actual competitive framework of the Italian states with which he was familiar. Other thinkers praise *The Prince* because it revolutionized political theory and destroyed medieval views of the nature of the state. Still other scholars consider this work a classic because it deals with eternal problems of government and society.

Born to a modestly wealthy Tuscan family, Machiavelli received a good education in the Latin classics. He entered the civil service of the Florentine government and served on thirty diplomatic missions. When the exiled Medicis returned to power in the city in 1512, they expelled Machiavelli from his position as officer of the city government. In exile he wrote *The Prince.*

The subject of *The Prince* is political power: how the ruler should gain, maintain, and increase his power. In this, Machiavelli implicitly addresses the question of the citizen's relationship to the state. As a good humanist, he explores the problems of human nature and concludes that human beings are selfish, corrupt, and out to advance their own interests. This pessimistic view leads him to maintain that the prince should manipulate the people in any way he finds necessary:

The manner in which men live is so different from the way in which they ought to live, that he who leaves the common course for that which he ought to follow will find that it leads him to ruin rather than to safety. For a man who, in all respects, will carry out only his professions of good, will be apt to be ruined amongst so many who are evil. A prince therefore who desires to maintain himself must learn to be not always good, but to be so or not as necessity may require.[10]

The prince should combine the cunning of a fox with the ferocity of a lion to achieve his goals. Asking rhetorically whether it is better for a ruler to be loved or feared, Machiavelli wrote:

A prince, therefore, should not mind the ill repute of cruelty, when he can thereby keep his subjects united and loyal; for a few displays of severity will really be more merciful than to allow, by an excess of clemency, disorders to occur, which are apt to result in rapine and murder; for these injure a whole community, whilst the executions ordered by the prince fall only upon a few individuals. And, above all others, the new prince will find it almost impossible to avoid the reputation of cruelty, because new states are generally exposed to many dangers. . . .

. . . This, then, gives rise to the question "whether it be better to be loved than feared, or to be feared than be loved." It will naturally be answered that it would be desirable to be both the one and the other; but as it is difficult to be both at the same time, it is much more safe to be feared than to be loved, when you have to choose between the

two. For it may be said of men in general that they are ungrateful and fickle, dissemblers, avoiders of danger, and greedy of gain. So long as you shower benefits upon them, they are all yours. . . . And the prince who relies upon their words, without having otherwise provided for his security, is ruined; for friendships that are won by rewards, and not by greatness and nobility of soul, although deserved, yet are not real, and cannot be depended upon in time of adversity.[11]

Medieval political theory derived ultimately from Saint Augustine's view that the state arose as a consequence of Adam's fall and people's propensity to sin. The test of good government was whether it provided justice, law and order. Political theorists and theologians from Alcuin to Marsiglio of Padua had stressed the way government ought to be; they set high moral and Christian standards for the ruler's conduct.

Machiavelli divorced government from moral and ethical considerations. He was concerned not with the way things ought to be but with the way they actually are. Consequently, the sole test of a "good" government was whether it was effective, whether the ruler increased his power. The state Machiavelli envisioned was a dynamic, amoral force.

Scholars have debated whether Machiavelli was writing a satire, trying to ingratiate himself with the Medicis, objectively describing contemporary Italian events, or advocating a fierce Italian nationalism that would achieve the unification of the peninsula. In any case, the word *Machiavellian* entered English as a synonym for devious, crafty, and corrupt politics in which the end justifies any means.

THE PRINTED WORD

Sometime in the thirteenth century, paper money and playing cards from China reached the West. They were block printed – that is, Chinese characters or pictures were carved into a wooden block, inked, and the words or illustrations put on paper. Since each word, phrase, or picture was on a separate block, this method of reproduction was extraordinarily expensive and time-consuming.

Around 1455, probably through the combined efforts of three men – Johan Gutenberg, Johan Fust, and Peter Schoffer, all experimenting at Mainz – movable type came into being. The mirror image of each letter (rather than entire words or phrases) was carved in relief on a small block. Individual letters, easily movable, were put together to form words; words separated by blank spaces formed lines of type; and lines of type were brought together to make up a page. Once the printer had placed wooden pegs around the type for a border, and locked the whole in a frame, the page was ready for printing. Since letters could be arranged into any format, an infinite variety of texts could be printed by reusing and rearranging pieces of type.

By the middle of the fifteenth century, paper was no problem. The technologically advanced but extremely isolated Chinese knew how to manufacture paper as early as the first century A.D. This knowledge reached the West in the twelfth century, when the Arabs introduced the process into Spain. Europeans quickly learned that old rags could be shredded, mixed with water, placed in a mold, squeezed, and dried to make a durable paper, far less expensive than the vellum (calfskin) and parchment (sheepskin) on which medieval scribes had relied for centuries.

The effects of the invention of movable-type printing were not felt overnight. Nevertheless, within a half-century of the publication of Gutenberg's Bible in 1456, movable type brought about radical changes. The costs of reproducing books were drasti-

THE PRINT SHOP *Sixteenth-century printing in-volved a division of labor. Two persons (left) at sepa-rate benches set the pieces of type. Another (center, rear) inks the chase (or locked plate containing the set type). Another (right) operates the press which prints the sheets. The boy removes the printed pages and sets them to dry. Meanwhile, a man carries in fresh paper on his head. (BBC Hulton Picture Library)*

cally reduced. It took less time and money to print a book by machine than to make copies by hand. The press also reduced the chances of error. If the type had been accurately set, all the copies would be correct no matter how many were reproduced. The greater the number of pages a scribe copied, the greater the chances for human error.

Printing stimulated the literacy of the laity. Although most of the earliest books dealt with religious subjects, students, business-men, and upper- and middle-class people sought books on all kinds of subjects. Thus, intellectual interests were considerably broad-ened. International communication was enor-mously facilitated. The invention of printing permitted writers and scholars of different countries to learn about one another's ideas and discoveries quickly. Intellectuals working in related fields got in touch with each other and cooperated in the advancement of knowl-edge.

Within the past twenty-five years, two in-ventions have revolutionized life for most Americans, television and the computer. By the late 1960s, the tired business executive or mechanic could return home in the evening, flip on "the tube," and while eating dinner watch battles in Vietnam or Israel that had occurred only a few hours before. The Ameri-can tourist in Copenhagen or Florence or Tokyo who suddenly needs to draw on a bank account in New Orleans or Portland can have the account checked by computer in a matter of minutes. The impact of these relatively recent developments has been absolutely phenomenal. The invention of movable type likewise transformed European society in the fifteenth century.

The process of learning was made much easier by printing. In the past, students had had to memorize everything because only the cathedral, monastery, or professor possessed the book. The greater availability of books meant that students could begin to buy their own. If information was not at the tip of the tongue, it was at the tip of the fingers. The number of students all across Europe multiplied. It is not entirely accidental that between 1450 and 1517 seven new universities were established in Spain, three in France, nine in Germany, and six new colleges were set up at Oxford in England.

Printing also meant that ideas critical of the established order in state or church could be more rapidly disseminated. In the early sixteenth century, for example, the publication of Erasmus's *The Praise of Folly* helped pave the way for the Reformation. After 1517, the printing press played no small role in the spread of Martin Luther's political and social views. Cartoons and satirical engravings of all kinds proliferated. They also provoked state censorship, which had been very rare in the Middle Ages. The printed word eventually influenced every aspect of European culture: educational, economic, religious, political, and social.

WOMEN

The status of upper-class women declined during the Renaissance. If women in the High Middle Ages are compared with those of fifteenth- and sixteenth-century Italy with respect to the education they received, the kind of work they performed, their access to property and political power, and the role they played in shaping the outlook of their society, it is clear that ladies in the Renaissance ruling classes generally had less power than comparable ladies of the feudal age.

In the cities of Renaissance Italy, girls received the same education as boys. Young ladies learned their letters and studied the classics. Many read Greek as well as Latin, knew the poetry of Ovid and Virgil, and could speak one or two "modern" languages, such as French or Spanish. In this respect, Renaissance humanism represented a real educational advance for women. Girls also received some training in painting, music, and dance. What were they to do with this training? They were to be gracious, affable, charming – in short, decorative. Renaissance women were better educated than their medieval counterparts. But whereas education trained a young man to rule and to participate in the public affairs of the city, it prepared a woman for the social functions of the home. An educated lady was supposed to know how to attract artists and literati to her husband's court; she was to grace her husband's household.

A striking difference also exists between the medieval literature of courtly love, the etiquette books and romances, and the widely studied Renaissance manual on courtesy and good behavior, Castiglione's *The Courtier*. In the medieval books manners shaped the man to please the lady; in *The Courtier* the lady was to make herself pleasing to the man. With respect to love and sex, the Renaissance witnessed a downward shift in women's status. In contrast to the medieval tradition of relative sexual equality, Renaissance humanists laid the foundations for the bourgeois double standard. Men, and men alone, operated in the public sphere; women belonged in the home. Castiglione, the foremost spokesman of Renaissance love and manners, completely separated love from sexuality. For women, sex was restricted entirely to marriage. Ladies were bound to chastity, to the roles of wife and mother in a politically arranged marriage. Men, however, could pursue sensual indulgence outside marriage. The Italian Renaissance courts accepted a dual sexual standard, as the medieval courts had not. Although some noble ladies were highly educated and some exercised considerable political power, Renaissance culture did little to advance the dignity of women. They usually served as decorative objects in a male society.[12]

Popular attitudes toward rape provide another index of the status of women in the Renaissance. A careful study of the legal evidence from Venice in the years 1338–1358 is informative. The Venetian shipping and merchant elite held economic and political power and made the laws. Those laws reveal that rape was not considered a particularly serious crime against either the victim or society. Noble youths committed a higher percentage of rapes than their small numbers in Venetian society would imply, despite government-regulated prostitution. The rape of a young girl of marriageable age or a child under twelve was considered a graver crime than the rape of a married woman. Still, the punishment for rape of a noble marriageable girl was only a fine or about six months' imprisonment. In an age when theft and robbery were punished by mutilation, and forgery and sodomy by burning, this penalty was very mild indeed. When a youth of the upper class was convicted of the rape of a nonnoble girl, his punishment was even lighter.

By contrast, the sexual assault on a noblewoman by a man of working-class origin, which was extraordinarily rare, resulted in severe penalization because the crime had social and political overtones.

In the eleventh century, William the Conqueror had decreed that rapists should be castrated, thus implicitly according women protection and a modicum of respect. But in the early Renaissance, rape was treated as a minor offense. Venetian laws and their enforcement show that the populace believed that rape damaged, but only slightly, men's property – women.[13]

Evidence from Florence in the fifteenth century also sheds light on infanticide, which historians are only now beginning to study in the Middle Ages and the Renaissance. Early medieval penitentials and church councils had legislated against abortion and infanticide, though it is known that Pope Innocent III (1198–1216) was moved to establish an orphanage "because so many women were throwing their children into the Tiber."[14] In the fourteenth and early fifteenth centuries, a considerable number of children died in Florence under suspicious circumstances. Some were simply abandoned outdoors. Some were said to have been crushed to death while sleeping in the same bed with their parents. Some died from "crib death" or suffocation. These deaths occurred too frequently to have all been accidental. And far more girls than boys died thus, reflecting societal discrimination against girl children as inferior and less useful than boys. The dire poverty of parents led them to do away with unwanted children.

The gravity of the problem of infanticide, which violated both the canon law of the church and the civil law of the state, forced the Florentine government to build the Foundling Hospital. Supporters of the institution maintained that without public responsibility, "many children would soon be found dead in the rivers, sewers, and ditches, unbaptized."[15] The city fathers commissioned

TITIAN: THE RAPE OF EUROPA *According to Greek myth, the Phoenician princess Europa was carried off to Crete by the god Zeus disguised as a white bull. The story was highly popular in the Renaissance* *with its interests in the classics. In this masterpiece, the erotic and voluptuous female figure reveals the new interest in the human form and the secular element in Renaissance art. (Isabella Stewart Gardner Museum)*

Filippo Brunelleschi, who had recently completed the dome over the Cathedral of Florence, to design the building. (Interestingly enough, the Foundling Hospital — completed in 1445 — is the very first building to use the revitalized Roman classic design that characterizes Renaissance architecture.) The unusually large size of the hospital suggests that great numbers of children were abandoned.

BLACKS IN RENAISSANCE SOCIETY

Ever since the time of the Roman republic, a few black people had lived in Western Europe. They had come, along with white slaves, as the spoils of war. Even after the collapse of the Roman Empire, Muslim and Christian merchants continued to import them. The evidence of medieval art attests to the presence of Africans in the West and Eu-

BALDUNG: ADORATION OF THE MAGI *Early
sixteenth-century German artists produced thousands
of adoration scenes depicting a black man as one of the
three kings: these paintings were based on direct observation, reflecting the increased presence of blacks in
Europe. The elaborate costumes, jewelry, and landscape expressed royal dignity, Christian devotion, and
oriental luxury. (Gemälde galerie. Staatliche Museen
Preussischer Kulturbesitz, Berlin [West])*

ropeans' awareness of them. In the twelfth and thirteenth centuries a large cult surrounded St. Maurice, martyred in the fourth century for refusing to renounce his Christian faith, who was portrayed as a black knight. St. Maurice received the special veneration of the nobility. The numbers of blacks, though, had always been small.

Beginning in the fifteenth century, however, hordes of black slaves entered Europe. Portuguese explorers imported perhaps a thousand a year and sold them at the markets of Seville, Barcelona, Marseilles, and Genoa. The Venetians specialized in the import of white slaves, but blacks were so greatly in demand at the Renaissance courts of northern Italy that the Venetians defied papal threats of excommunication to secure them. What roles did blacks play in Renaissance society? What image did Europeans have of Africans?

The medieval interest in curiosities, the exotic, and the marvelous continued into the Renaissance. Because of their rarity, black servants were highly prized and much sought after. In the late fifteenth century Isabella, the wife of Gian Galeazzo Sforza, took pride in the fact that she had ten blacks, seven of them females; a black lady's maid was both a curiosity and a symbol of wealth. In 1491 Isabella of Este, Duchess of Mantua, instructed her agent to secure a black girl between four and eight years old, "shapely and as black as possible." The duchess saw the child as a source of entertainment: "we shall make her very happy and shall have great fun with her." She hoped that the little girl would become "the best buffoon in the world."[16] The cruel ancient tradition of a noble household retaining a professional "fool" for the family's amusement persisted through the Renaissance — and even down to the twentieth century.

Adult black slaves filled a variety of positions. Many served as maids, valets, domestic servants; Italian aristocrats such as the Marchesa Elena Grimaldi had their portraits painted with their black page boys to indicate their wealth. The Venetians employed blacks – slave and free – as gondoliers and stevedores on the docks. Tradition, stretching back at least as far as the thirteenth century, connected blacks with music and dance. In Renaissance Spain and Italy blacks performed as dancers, as actors and actresses in courtly dramas, and as musicians, sometimes composing full orchestras.[17]

Before the sixteenth-century "discoveries" of the non-European world, Europeans had little interest in Africans and African culture. Consequently, Europeans knew little about them beyond biblical accounts. The European attitude toward Africans was ambivalent. On the one hand, Europeans perceived Africa as a remote place, the home of strange people isolated by heresy and Islam from superior European civilization. Africans' contact even as slaves with Christian Europeans could only "improve" the blacks. Most Europeans' knowledge of the black as a racial type was based entirely on theological speculation. Theologians taught that God is light. Blackness, the opposite of light, therefore represented the hostile forces of the underworld: evil, sin, and the devil. Thus the devil was commonly represented as a black man in medieval and early Renaissance art. Blackness, however, also possessed certain positive qualities. It symbolized the emptiness of worldly goods, the humility of the monastic way of life. Black clothes permitted a conservative and discreet display of wealth. Black vestments and funeral trappings indicated grief, and Christ had said that those who mourn are blessed. Until the exploration and observation of the sixteenth, seventeenth, and nineteenth centuries allowed, ever so slowly, for the development of more scientific knowledge, the Western conception of Africa and black people remained bound up with religious notions.[18]

THE ENVIRONMENT

Historians and natural scientists are only today beginning to study the attitude of peoples in earlier centuries toward their natural environment. An enormous amount of exciting research, which could improve ecological knowledge and aid in the solution of present-day problems, waits to be done. The measures the city of Florence took against water pollution in the fifteenth century provide some interesting information.

In 1450, the Florentine governing body expressed concern that fishermen and others several miles southeast of the city were using toxic substances to harvest more fish from the Arno River, which flowed through the city and was the source of much of Florence's fish. Fewer fresh fish reached the city markets. Ecclesiastical law required Christians to abstain from meat during the Fridays of the year and during the seasons of Advent and Lent. Fish was an obvious substitute, and the fishing industry was large and influential. The law of 1450 states:

Whereas it often happens, especially in parts of the Casentino and areas near there, that poisons and toxic substances are put and inserted into the neighboring rivers and waters to capture and angle fish more easily and in greater number . . .

This is done where those fish are procreated and made which are called Trout, and truly noble and impressive fish they are. The result is that the said fish are destroyed and wasted.

And certainly if this were not so, our city and also other neighboring areas would continually and far more abound in the said fish. So that, therefore, the said genus of fish is preserved, and

our city and the other said areas have a copious and abundant supply of such fish, the magnificent . . . lords priors . . . ordain . . .[19]

The citizens of Florence apparently did not understand the ecological problem and were not concerned about conservation. While they appreciated the beauty of the "noble trout," their concern was only that if upstream waters were polluted and the fish there killed, there would be fewer fish caught and brought to market in Florence. Government officials did not object to the damage to the river as a source of beauty, pleasure, and drinking water. Variations of the law of 1450 were put on the statute books in 1455, 1460, 1471, and 1477,[20] suggesting that these early conservation measures could not be enforced.

THE RENAISSANCE IN THE NORTH

In the last quarter of the fifteenth century, Renaissance thought and ideals penetrated northern Europe. Students from the Low Countries, France, Germany, and England flocked to Italy, imbibed the "new learning," and carried it back to their countries. Northern humanists interpreted Italian ideas about and attitudes toward classical antiquity, individualism, and humanism in terms of their own traditions. The cultural traditions of northern Europe tended to remain more distinctly Christian, or at least pietistic, than those of Italy. Thus while the Renaissance in Italy was characterized by a secular and pagan spirit and focused on Greco-Roman motifs and scholarship, north of the Alps the Renaissance had a religious character and emphasized biblical and early Christian themes. Scholars have termed the northern Renaissance "Christian humanism."

Christian humanists were interested in the development of an ethical way of life. To achieve it they believed that the best elements of classical and Christian cultures should be combined. For example, the classical ideals of calmness, stoical patience, and broad-mindedness should be joined in human conduct with the Christian virtues of love, faith, and hope. Northern humanists also stressed the use of reason, rather than acceptance of dogma, as the foundation for an ethical way of life. Like the Italians, they were extremely impatient with scholastic philosophy. Christian humanists had a profound faith in the power of the human intellect to bring about moral and institutional reform. They believed that although human nature had been corrupted by sin it was fundamentally good and capable of improvement through education, which would lead to piety and an ethical way of life.

This optimistic viewpoint found expression in scores of lectures, treatises, and collections of precepts. Treatises such as Erasmus's *The Education of a Christian Prince* express the naive notion that peace, harmony among nations, and a truly ethical society will result from a new system of education. This hope has been advanced repeatedly in Western history – by the ancient Greeks, by the sixteenth-century Christian humanists, by the eighteenth-century philosophers of the Enlightenment, and by nineteenth-century advocates of progress. The proposition remains highly debatable, but each time the theory has reappeared education has been further democratized.

The work of the French priest Jacques Lefèvre d'Etaples (ca 1455-1536) is one of the early attempts to apply humanistic learning to religious problems. A brilliant thinker and able scholar, he believed that more accurate texts of the Bible would lead people to live better lives. According to Lefèvre, a solid ed-ucation in the Scriptures would increase piety and raise the level of behavior in Christian society. Lefèvre produced an edition of the Psalms and a commentary on Saint Paul's Epistles. In 1516, when Martin Luther lectured to his students at Wittenberg on Paul's Letter to the Romans, he relied on Lefèvre's texts.

Lefèvre's English contemporary John Colet (1466-1519) also published lectures on Saint Paul's Epistles, approaching them in the new critical spirit. Unlike the medieval theologians, who studied the Bible for allegorical meanings, Colet, who was a priest, interpreted the Pauline letters historically – that is, within the social and political context of the times when they were written. Both Colet and Lefèvre d'Etaples were later suspected of heresy, as humanistic scholarship got entangled with the issues of the Reformation.

Colet's friend and countryman Thomas More (1472-1535) towers above other figures in sixteenth-century English social and intellectual history. More's political stance at the time of the Reformation (page 492), a position that in part flowed from his humanist beliefs, got him into serious trouble with King Henry VIII and has tended to obscure his contribution to Christian humanism.

The early career of Thomas More presents a number of paradoxes that reveal the marvelous complexity of the man. Trained as a lawyer, More lived as a student in the London Charterhouse, a Carthusian monastery. He subsequently married and practiced law, but became deeply interested in the classics, and his household served as a model of warm Christian family life and a mecca for foreign and English humanists. Following the career pattern of such Italian humanists as Petrarch, he entered government service under Henry VIII and was sent as ambassador to Flanders. There More found the time to write *Utopia*

THE LATER MIDDLE AGES, RENAISSANCE, AND
PROTESTANT AND CATHOLIC REFORMATIONS, 1300–1600

As is evident in this chronology, early manifestations of the Renaissance and Protestant Reformation coincided in time with major events of the Later Middle Ages.

1300–1321	Dante, *The Divine Comedy*
1304–1374	Petrarch
1309–1372	Babylonian Captivity of the papacy
1337–1453	Hundred Years' War
1347–1351	The Black Death
ca 1350	Boccaccio, *The Decameron*
1356	Golden Bull: transforms the Holy Roman Empire into an aristocratic federation
1358	The Jacquerie
ca 1376	John Wyclif publishes *Civil Dominion* attacking the church's temporal power and asserting the supremacy of Scripture
1377–1417	The Great Schism
1378	Laborers' revolt in Florence
1381	Peasants' Revolt
1385–1400	Chaucer, *Canterbury Tales*
1414–1418	Council of Constance: ends the schism, postpones reform, executes John Hus
1431	Joan of Arc is burned at the stake
1434	Medici domination of Florence begins
1438	Pragmatic Sanction of Bourges: declares autonomy of the French church from papal jurisdiction
1453	Capture of Constantinople by the Ottoman Turks, ending the Byzantine Empire
1453–1471	Wars of the Roses in England
1456	Gutenberg Bible
1492	Columbus reaches the Americas
	Unification of Spain under Ferdinand and Isabella; expulsion of Jews from Spain
1494	France invades Italy, inaugurating sixty years of war on Italian soil
	Florence expels the Medici and restores republican government

1509	Erasmus, *The Praise of Folly*
1512	Restoration of the Medici in Florence
1512–1517	Lateran Council undertakes reform of clerical abuses
1513	Balboa discovers the Pacific
	Macchiavelli, *The Prince*
1516	Concordat of Bologna between France and the papacy: rescinds the Pragmatic Sanction of 1438, strengthens French monarchy, establishes Catholicism as the national religion
	Thomas More, *Utopia*
1517	Martin Luther proclaims the 95 Theses
1519–1522	Magellan's crew circumnavigates the earth
1523	Luther's translation of the New Testament into German
1524	Peasants' Revolt in Germany
1527	Sack of Rome by mercenaries of Holy Roman Emperor Charles
1528	Castiglione, *The Courtier*
1530	Confession of Augsburg, official formulation of Lutheran theology
1534	Act of Supremacy inaugurates the English Reformation
1534–1541	Michelangelo, *The Last Judgment*
1535	Execution of Thomas More for treason
1536	John Calvin, *Institutes of the Christian Religion*
1540	Loyola founds the Society of Jesus (Jesuits)
1541	Calvin establishes a theocracy in Geneva
1543	Copernicus, *On the Revolutions of the Heavenly Spheres*
1545–1563	Council of Trent
1555	Peace of Augsburg: German princes determine the religion of their territories; no privileges for Calvinism
1572	St. Bartholemew's Day Massacre
1588	Spanish Armada
1598	Edict of Nantes grants French Protestants freedom of worship in certain towns
1603	Shakespeare, *Hamlet*
1605	Sir Francis Bacon, *The Advancement of Learning*

(1516), which presented a revolutionary view of society.

Utopia, which literally means "nowhere," describes an ideal socialistic community on a South Sea island. All its children receive a good education, primarily in the Greco-Roman classics, and learning does not cease with maturity, for the goal of all education is to develop rational faculties. Adults divide their days equally between manual labor or business pursuits (the Utopians were thoroughly familiar with advanced Flemish business practices) and various intellectual activities.

Because the profits from business and property are held strictly in common, there is absolute social equality. The Utopians use gold and silver to make chamber pots or to prevent wars by buying off their enemies. By this casual use of precious metals, More meant to suggest that the basic problems in society were caused by greed. Utopian law exalts mercy above justice. Citizens of Utopia lead an ideal and nearly perfect existence because they live by reason; their institutions are perfect.

More's ideas were profoundly original in the sixteenth century. Contrary to the long-prevailing view that vice and violence exist because women and men are basically corrupt, More maintained that *society's* flawed institutions are responsible for corruption and war. Today most people take this view so much for granted that it is difficult to appreciate how radical it was in the sixteenth century. According to More, the key to improvement and reform of the individual was reform of the social institutions that mold the individual.

Better known by his contemporaries than Thomas More was the Dutch humanist Desiderius Erasmus of Rotterdam (1469?–1536). Orphaned as a small boy, Erasmus was forced to enter a monastery. Although he intensely disliked the religious life, he developed there an excellent knowledge of the Latin language and a deep appreciation for the Latin classics. During a visit to England in 1499, Erasmus met John Colet, who decisively influenced his life's work: the application of the best humanistic learning to the study and explanation of the Bible. As a mature scholar with an international reputation stretching from Krakow to London, Erasmus could boast with truth, "I brought it about that humanism, which among the Italians . . . savored of nothing but pure paganism, began nobly to celebrate Christ."[21]

Erasmus's long list of publications includes *The Adages* (1500), a list of Greek and Latin precepts on ethical behavior; *The Education of a Christian Prince* (1504), which combines idealistic and practical suggestions for the formation of a ruler's character through the careful study of Plutarch, Aristotle, Cicero, and Plato; *The Praise of Folly* (1509), a satire on monasticism and a plea for the simple and spontaneous Christian faith of children; and, most important of all, a critical edition of the Greek New Testament (1516). In the preface to the New Testament Erasmus explained the purpose of his great work:

Only bring a pious and open heart, imbued above all things with a pure and simple faith. . . . For I utterly dissent from those who are unwilling that the sacred Scriptures should be read by the unlearned translated into their vulgar tongue, as though Christ had taught such subtleties that they can scarcely be understood even by a few theologians. . . . Christ wished his mysteries to be published as openly as possible. I wish that even the weakest woman should read the Gospel — should read the epistles of Paul. And I wish these were translated into all languages, so that they might be read and understood, not only by Scots and Irishmen, but also by Turks and Saracens. To make them understood is surely the first step. It may be that they might be ridiculed by many, but some would take them to heart. I long that the husbandman should sing portions of them to himself as he follows the plough, that the weaver should hum them to the tune of his shuttle, that the traveller should beguile with their stories the tedium of his journey. . . .

Why do we prefer to study the wisdom of Christ in men's writings rather than in the writing of Christ himself?[22]

Two fundamental themes run through all of Erasmus's scholarly work. First, education was the means to reform, the key to moral and intellectual improvement. The core of education ought to be study of the Bible and the classics. Second, the essence of Erasmus's thought is, in his own phrase, "the philosophy of Christ." By this Erasmus meant that Christianity is an inner attitude of the heart or spirit. Christianity is not formalism, special ceremonies, law; Christianity is Christ — his life and what he said and did, not what theologians and commentators have written about him. The Sermon on the Mount, for Erasmus, expressed the heart of the Christian message.

While the writings of Colet, Erasmus, and More have strong Christian themes and have drawn the attention primarily of scholars, the stories of the French humanist François Rabelais (1490?-1553) possess a distinctly secular flavor and have attracted broad readership among the literate public. Rabelais' *Gargantua* and *Pantagruel* (serialized between 1532 and 1552) belong among the great comic masterpieces of world literature. These stories' gross and robust humor introduced the adjective *Rabelasian* into the language.

Gargantua and *Pantagruel* can be read on several levels: as comic romances about the adventures of the giant Gargantua and his son Pantagruel; as a spoof on contemporary French society; as a program for educational reform; or as illustrations of Rabelais' prodigious learning. The reader enters a world of Renaissance vitality, ribald joviality, and intellectual curiosity. On his travels Gargantua meets various absurd characters, and within their hilarious exchanges there occur serious discussions on religion, politics, philosophy, and education. Rabelais had received an excellent humanistic education in a monastery, and Gargantua discusses the disorders of contemporary religious and secular life. Like More and Erasmus, Rabelais did not denounce institutions directly. Like Erasmus, Rabelais satirized hypocritical monks, pedantic academics, and pompous lawyers. But where Erasmus employed intellectual cleverness and sophisticated wit, Rabelais applied wild and gross humor. Like Thomas More, Rabelais believed that institutions molded individuals and that education was the key to a moral and healthy life. While the middle-class inhabitants of More's *Utopia* lived lives of restrained moderation, the aristocratic residents of Rabelais' Thélème lived for the full gratification of their physical instincts and rational curiosity.

Thélème, the abbey Gargantua establishes, parodies traditional religion and other social institutions. Thélème, whose motto is "Do as Thou Wilt," admits women *and* men, allows all to eat, drink, sleep, and work when they choose, provides excellent facilities for swimming, tennis, and football, and encourages sexual experimentation and marriage. Rabelais believed profoundly in the basic goodness of human beings and the rightness of instinct.

The most roguishly entertaining Renaissance writer, Rabelais was convinced that "laughter is the essence of manhood." A convinced believer in the Roman Catholic faith, he included in Gargantua's education an appreciation for simple and reasonable prayer.

JEROME BOSCH: DEATH AND THE MISER *Netherlandish painters frequently used symbolism, and Bosch (ca 1450–1516) is considered the master-artist of symbolism and fantasy. Here, rats, which because of their destructiveness symbolize evil, control the miser's gold. Bosch's imagery appealed strongly to twentieth-century surrealist painters. (National Gallery of Art, Washington, D.C., Samual H. Kress Collection)*

Rabelais combined the Renaissance zest for life and enjoyment of pleasure with a classical insistence on the cultivation of the body and the mind.

The distinctly religious orientation of the literary works of the Renaissance in the north also characterized northern art and architecture. Some Flemish painters, notably Jan van Eyck (1366–1441), were the equals of Italian painters. One of the earliest artists successfully to use oil on wood panels, van Eyck, in paintings such as the *Ghent Altarpiece* and the portrait of *Giovanni Arnolfini and His Bride,* shows the Flemish love for detail; the effect is great realism. Van Eyck's paintings also demonstrate remarkable attention to human personality, as do those of Hans Memling (d. 1494) in his studies of *Tommaso Portinari and His Wife.* Typical of northern piety, the Portinari are depicted in an attitude of prayer (see p. 432).

Another Flemish painter, Jerome Bosch (c. 1450–1516) frequently used religious themes, but in combination with grotesque fantasies, colorful imagery, and peasant folk legends. Many of Bosch's paintings reflect the confusion and anguish often associated with the end of the Middle Ages. In *Death and the Miser,* Bosch's dramatic treatment of the Dance of Death theme, the miser's gold, increased by usury, is ultimately controlled by diabolical rats and toads, while his guardian angel urges him to choose the crucifix.

A quasi-spiritual aura likewise infuses architectural monuments in the north. The city halls of wealthy Flemish towns like Bruges, Brussels, Louvain, and Ghent strike the viewer more as shrines to house the bones of saints than as settings for the mundane decisions of politicians and businessmen. Northern architecture was little influenced by the classical revival so obvious in Renaissance Rome and Florence.

POLITICS AND THE STATE IN THE RENAISSANCE (CA 1450–1521)

The High Middle Ages had witnessed the origins of many of the basic institutions of the modern national state. Sheriffs, inquests, juries, circuit judges, bureaucracies, and representative assemblies all trace their origins to the twelfth and thirteenth centuries (pages (351–364). The linchpin for the development of states, however, was strong monarchy, and during the period of the Hundred Years' War no ruler in western Europe was able to provide effective leadership. The resurgent power of feudal nobilities weakened the centralizing work begun earlier.

Beginning in the fifteenth century, rulers utilized the aggressive methods implied by Renaissance political ideas to rebuild their governments. First in Italy, then in France, England, and Spain, rulers began the work of reducing violence, curbing unruly nobles and troublesome elements, and establishing domestic order. Within the Holy Roman Empire of Germany, the lack of centralization helps to account for the later German distrust of the Roman papacy. Divided into scores of independent principalities, Germany could not deal with the Roman church as an equal.

The dictators and oligarchs of the Italian city-states, however, together with Louis XI of France, Henry VII of England, and Ferdinand of Spain, were tough, cynical, and calculating rulers. In their ruthless push for power and strong governments, they subordinated morality and considerations of right and wrong to the achievement of hard results. They preferred to be secure, if feared, rather than loved. Whether or not they actually read Machiavelli's *The Prince,* they acted as if they had.

Some historians have called Louis XI (1461–1483), Henry VII (1485–1509), and Ferdinand and Isabella of Spain (1474–1516) "new monarchs." The term is only partly appropriate. These monarchs were new in that they invested kingship with a strong sense of royal authority and national purpose. They stressed that monarchy was the one institution that linked all classes and peoples within definite territorial boundaries. Rulers emphasized the "royal majesty" and royal sovereignty and insisted that all must respect and be loyal to them. They ruthlessly suppressed opposition and rebellion, especially from the nobility. They loved the business of kingship and worked hard at it.

In other respects, however, the methods of these rulers, which varied from country to country, were not so new. They reasserted long-standing ideas and practices of strong monarchs in the Middle Ages. The Holy Roman emperor Frederick Barbarossa, the English Edward I, and the French King Philip the Fair had all applied ideas drawn from Roman law in the High Middle Ages. Renaissance princes also did so. They seized upon the maxim of the Justinian Code, "What pleases the prince has the force of law," to advance their authority. Some medieval rulers, such as Henry I of England, had depended heavily upon middle-class officials. Renaissance rulers too tended to rely on civil servants of middle-class background. With tax revenues, medieval rulers had built armies to crush feudal anarchy. Renaissance townspeople with commercial and business interests naturally wanted a reduction of violence and usually were willing to be taxed in order to achieve domestic order.

Scholars have often described the fifteenth-century "new monarchs" as crafty, devious, and thoroughly Machiavellian in their methods. Yet contemporaries of the Capetian Philip the Fair considered him every bit as devious and crafty as his Valois descendants, Louis XI and Francis I, were considered in the fifteenth and sixteenth centuries. Machiavellian politics were not new in the age of the Renaissance. What was new was a marked acceleration of politics, whose sole rationalization was the acquisition and expansion of power. Renaissance rulers spent precious little time seeking a religious justification for their actions. With these qualifications of the term "new monarchs" in mind, let us consider the development of national states in Italy, France, England, and Spain in the period 1450 to 1521.

THE ITALIAN CITY-STATES

In the fourteenth century, the Holy Roman emperors had made several efforts to impose imperial authority in Italy and continue the tradition begun by Charlemagne. But the German emperors, economically and militarily weak, could not defeat the powerful, though separate, city-states. The Italian city-states were thus entirely independent of the Holy Roman Empire.

In the fifteenth century, five powers dominated the Italian peninsula – Venice, Milan, Florence, the Papal States, and the kingdom of Naples (see Map 13.1). The rulers of the city-states – whether despots in Milan, patrician elitists in Florence, or oligarchs in Venice – governed as monarchs. They crushed proletarian revolts, levied taxes, killed their enemies, and used massive building programs to employ, and the arts to overawe, the masses.

Venice, with enormous trade and a vast colonial empire, ranked as an international power. Although Venice had a sophisticated constitution and was a republic in name, an oligarchy of merchant-aristocrats actually ran

the city. Milan was also called a republic, but despots of the Sforza family ruled harshly and dominated the smaller cities of the north. Likewise in Florence the form of government was republican, with authority vested in several councils of state. In reality, between 1434 and 1494, power in Florence was held by the great Medici banking family. Although they did not hold public office, Cosimo (1434–1464) and Lorenzo (1469–1492) ruled from behind the scenes.

A republic is a state in which political power resides in the people and is exercised by them or their chosen representatives. The Renaissance nostalgia for the Roman form of republican government, combined with a calculating shrewdness, prompted leaders of Venice, Milan, and Florence to preserve the old forms: the people could be deceived into thinking they still possessed the decisive voice.

Central Italy consisted mainly of the Papal States, which during the Babylonian Captivity had come under the sway of important Roman families. Pope Alexander VI (1492–1503), aided militarily and politically by his son Cesare Borgia, reasserted papal authority in the papal lands. Cesare Borgia became the hero of Machiavelli's *The Prince* because he began the work of uniting the peninsula by ruthlessly conquering and exacting total obedience from the principalities making up the Papal States.

South of the Papal States was the kingdom of Naples, consisting of virtually all of southern Italy and, at times, Sicily. The kingdom of Naples had long been disputed by the Aragonese and by the French. In 1435, it passed to Aragon.

The major Italian city-states controlled the smaller ones, such as Siena, Mantua, Ferrara, and Modena, and competed furiously among themselves for territory. The large cities used

HOLY ROMAN EMPIRE

DUCHY OF SAVOY

Turin

SALUZZO

DUCHY OF MILAN

Milan
Lodi
Pavia
Po

REP. OF GENOA

Genoa

M. OF MANTUA

Padua

D. OF FERRARA

D. OF MODENA

Bologna

Ravenna

REP. OF LUCCA

Arno
Florence

Pisa

REP. OF FLORENCE

Siena

REP. OF SIENA

Urbino

PAPAL STATES

Assisi

Tiber

Rome

REPUBLIC OF VENICE

Venice

ADRIATIC SEA

DALMATIA

OTTOMAN EMPIRE

CORSICA
(to Genoa)

SARDINIA

Naples
Salerno

KINGDOM OF NAPLES

Bari

MEDITERRANEAN SEA

Palermo

KINGDOM OF SICILY

0   50   100 Km.

0   50   100 Mi.

MAP 13.1 THE ITALIAN CITY-STATES, CA 1494   In the fifteenth century the Italian city-states represented great wealth and cultural sophistication. The political divisions of the peninsula invited foreign intervention.

UCELLO: BATTLE OF SAN ROMANO *The Medici commissioned this painting ca 1460 to commemorate a lucky Florentine victory over the Sienese in 1432, a victory which contributed to the rise of the Medici dynasty. Although mainly interested in perspective,* Ucello *in this unrealistic and decorative painting seems most concerned with the pageantry of war. (The National Gallery, London. Reproduced by courtesy of the Trustees.)*

diplomacy, spies, paid informers, and any other means to get information that could be used to advance their ambitions. While the states of northern Europe were moving toward centralization and consolidation, the world of Italian politics resembled a jungle where the powerful dominated the weak.

In one significant respect, however, the Italian city-states anticipated future relations among competing European states after 1500. Whenever one Italian state appeared to gain a predominant position within the peninsula, other states combined to establish a balance of power against the major threat. In 1450, for example, Venice went to war against Milan in protest against Francesco Sforza's acquisition of the title of duke of Milan. Cosimo de' Medici of Florence, a long-time supporter of a Florentine-Venetian alliance, switched his po-

sition and aided Milan. Florence and Naples combined with Milan against powerful Venice and the papacy. In the peace treaty signed at Lodi in 1454, Venice received territories in return for recognizing Sforza's right to the duchy. This pattern of shifting alliances continued until 1494.

At the end of the fifteenth century, Venice, Florence, Milan, and the papacy possessed great wealth and represented high cultural achievement. Their imperialistic ambitions at each other's expense, however, and their inability to form a common alliance against potential foreign enemies, made Italy an inviting target for invasion. When Florence and Naples entered into an agreement to acquire Milanese territories, Milan called upon France for support.

At Florence the French invasion had been

predicted by the Dominican friar Girolamo Savonarola (1452-1498). In a number of fiery sermons between 1481 and 1494, Savonarola attacked what he considered the paganism and moral vice of the city, the undemocratic government of Lorenzo de' Medici, and the corruption of Pope Alexander VI. For a time Savonarola enjoyed wide popular support among the ordinary people; he became the religious leader of Florence and as such contributed to the fall of the Medici. Eventually, however, people wearied of his moral denunciations, and he was excommunicated and executed. As an enemy of secularism, Savonarola stands as proof that the common people did not share the worldly outlook of the commercial and intellectual elite. His career also illustrates the internal instability of Italian cities such as Florence, an instability that invited foreign invasion.

The invasion of Italy in 1494 by the French king Charles VIII (1483-1498) inaugurated a new period in Italian and European power politics. Italy became the focus of international ambitions and the battleground of foreign armies. Charles swept down the peninsula with little opposition, and Florence, Rome, and Naples soon bowed before him. When Piero de' Medici, Lorenzo's son, went to the French camp seeking peace, the Florentines exiled the Medicis and restored republican government.

Charles's success simply whetted French appetites. In 1508, his son Louis XII formed the League of Cambrai with the pope and the German emperor Maximilian for the purpose of stripping rich Venice of its mainland possessions. Pope Leo X soon found the French a dangerous friend, and in a new alliance called upon the Spanish and Germans to expel the French from Italy. This anti-French combination was temporarily successful. But the French returned in 1522, and after Charles V

succeeded his grandfather Maximilian as Holy Roman emperor, there began the series of conflicts called the Habsburg-Valois wars (named for the German and French dynasties), whose battlefield was Italy.

In the sixteenth century, the political and social life of Italy was upset by the relentless competition for dominance between France and the empire. The Italian cities suffered severely from the continual warfare, especially in the frightful sack of Rome in 1527 by imperial forces under Charles V. Thus the failure of the city-states to form some federal system, or to consolidate, or at least to establish a common foreign policy, led to the continuation of the centuries-old subjection of the peninsula by outside invaders. Italy was not to achieve unification until 1870.

FRANCE

The Hundred Years' War left France badly divided, drastically depopulated, commercially ruined, and agriculturally weak. Nonetheless, the ruler whom Joan of Arc had seen crowned at Reims, Charles VII (1422-1461), revived the monarchy and France. He seemed an unlikely person to do so. Frail, ugly, feeble, hypochondriacal, mistrustful, called "the son of a madman and a loose woman," Charles VII began France's long recovery.

Charles reconciled the Burgundians and Armagnacs, who had been waging civil war for thirty years. By 1453, French armies had expelled the English from French soil except in Calais. Charles reorganized the royal council, giving increased influence to the middle-class men, and he strengthened royal finances through such taxes as the gabelle (on salt) and the taille (a land tax). These taxes remained the Crown's chief sources of state income until the Revolution of 1789.

Charles also reformed the justice system

FRENCH TRADESMEN *A bootmaker, a cloth merchant (with bolts of material on shelves), and a dealer in gold plate and silver share a stall. Through sales taxes, the French crown received a share of the profits. (Bibliothèque Municipale, Rouen/ Giraudon)*

and remodeled the army. By establishing regular companies of cavalry and archers — recruited, paid, and inspected by the state — Charles created the first permanent royal army. In 1438, Charles published the Pragmatic Sanction of Bourges, asserting the superiority of a general council over the papacy, giving the French crown control over the appointment of bishops, and depriving the pope of French ecclesiastical revenues. The Pragmatic Sanction established the Gallican (or French) liberties, because it affirmed the autonomy of the French church from the Roman papacy. Greater control over the church, the army, and justice helped to consolidate the authority of the French crown.

Charles's son Louis XI, called "the Spider King" by his subjects because of his treacherous and cruel character, was very much a Renaissance prince. Facing the perpetual French problems of unification of the realm and reduction of feudal disorder, he saw money as the answer. Louis promoted new industries, such as silk weaving at Lyons and Tours. He welcomed tradesmen and foreign craftsmen, and he entered into commercial treaties with England, Portugal, and the towns of the Hanseatic League, a group of cities that played an important role in the development of towns and commercial life in northern Germany. The revenues raised through these economic activities and severe taxation were used to improve the army. With the army Louis stopped aristocratic brigandage and slowly cut into urban independence.

Luck favored his goal of expanding royal authority and unifying the kingdom. On the timely death of Charles the Bold, duke of Burgundy, in 1477 Louis invaded Burgundy and gained some territories. Three years later, the extinction of the house of Anjou brought Louis the counties of Anjou, Bar, Maine, and Provence.

Some scholars have credited Louis XI with laying the foundations for later French royal absolutism. Louis summoned only one meeting of the Estates General, and the delegates requested that they not be summoned in the future. Thereafter the king would decide. Building on the system begun by his father, Louis XI worked tirelessly to remodel the government following the debacle of the fourteenth and fifteenth centuries. In his reliance on finances supplied by the middle classes to fight the feudal nobility, Louis is typical of the new monarchs.

Two further developments strengthened the French monarchy. The marriage of Louis XII and Anne of Brittany added the large western duchy of Brittany to the state. Then, the French king Francis I and Pope Leo X reached a mutually satisfactory agreement in 1516. The new treaty, the Concordat of Bologna, rescinded the Pragmatic Sanction's assertion of the superiority of a general council over the papacy and approved the pope's right to receive the first year's income of new bishops and abbots. In return, Leo X recognized the French ruler's right to select French bishops and abbots. French kings thereafter effectively controlled the appointment and thus the policies of church officials within the kingdom.

ENGLAND

English society suffered severely from the disorders of the fifteenth century. The aristocracy dominated the government of Henry IV (1399–1413) and indulged in mischievous violence at the local level. Population, decimated by the Black Death, continued to decline. While Henry V (1413–1422) gained chivalric prestige for his military exploits in France, he was totally dependent upon the feudal magnates who controlled the royal council and Parliament. Henry V's death, leaving a nine-month-old son, the future Henry VI (1422–1461), gave the barons a perfect opportunity to entrench their power. Between 1455 and 1471, adherents of the ducal houses of York and Lancaster waged civil war, commonly called the Wars of the Roses because the symbol of the Yorkists was a white rose and that of the Lancastrians a red one. Although only a small minority of the nobility participated, the chronic disorder hurt trade, agriculture, and domestic industry. Under the pious but spineless Henry VI, the authority of the monarchy sank lower than it had been in centuries.

Edward IV (1461–1483) began establishing domestic tranquility. He succeeded in defeating the Lancastrian forces and after 1471 began to reconstruct the monarchy and consolidate royal power. Edward, his brother Richard III (1483–1485), and Henry VII of the Welsh house of Tudor worked to restore royal prestige, to crush the power of the nobility, and to establish order and law at the local level. All three rulers used methods Machiavelli would have praised – ruthlessness, efficiency, and secrecy.

The Hundred Years' War had cost the nation dearly, and the money to finance it had been raised by Parliament. Dominated by various baronial factions, Parliament had been the arena where the nobility exerted its power. As long as the monarchy was dependent on the lords and the commons for revenue, the king had to call Parliament. Thus Edward IV revived the medieval ideal that he would "live of his own," meaning on his own financial resources. He reluctantly established a policy the monarchy was to follow with rare exceptions down to 1603. Edward, and subsequently the Tudors, conducted foreign policy on the basis of diplomacy, avoiding expensive wars. Thus the English monarchy did not depend on Parliament for money, and the Crown undercut that source of aristocratic influence.

Henry VII did, however, summon several meetings of Parliament in the early years of his reign. He used these assemblies primarily to confirm laws. Parliament remained the highest court in the land, and a statute registered (approved) there by the lords, bishops, and commons gave the appearance of broad national support plus thorough judicial authority.

The center of royal authority was the royal council, which governed at the national level. There too Henry VII revealed his distrust of the nobility: although they were not completely excluded, very few great lords were among the king's closest advisers. Regular representatives on the council numbered between twelve and fifteen men, and while many gained high ecclesiastical rank (the means, as it happened, by which the Crown paid them), their origins were the lesser landowning class and their education was in law. They were in a sense middle class.

The royal council handled any business the king put before it – executive, legislative, judicial. For example, the council conducted negotiations with foreign governments and secured international recognition of the Tudor dynasty through the marriage in 1501 of Henry VII's eldest son Arthur to Catherine of Aragon, the daughter of Ferdinand and Isabella of Spain. The council prepared laws for parliamentary ratification. The council dealt with real or potential aristocratic threats through a judicial offshoot, the court of Star Chamber, so-called because of the stars painted on the ceiling of the room.

The court of Star Chamber applied principles of Roman law, and its methods were terrifying: the accused was not entitled to see evidence against him; sessions were secret; torture could be applied to extract confessions; and juries were not called. These procedures ran directly counter to English common-law precedents, but they effectively reduced aristocratic troublemaking.

Unlike the continental countries of Spain and France, England had no standing army or professional civil-service bureaucracy. The Tudors relied upon the support of unpaid local officials, the justices of the peace. These influential landowners in the shires handled all the work of local government. They apprehended and punished criminals, enforced parliamentary statutes, supervised conditions of service, fixed wages and prices, maintained proper standards of weights and measures, and even checked up on moral behavior. Justices of the peace were appointed and supervised by the council. From the royal point of view, they were an inexpensive method of government.

The Tudors won the support of the influential upper middle class because the Crown linked government policy with their interests. A commercial or agricultural upper class fears and dislikes few things more than disorder and violence. If the Wars of the Roses served any useful purpose, it was killing off dangerous nobles and thus making the Tudors' work easier. The Tudors promoted peace and social order, and the gentry did not object to arbitrary methods like the court of Star Chamber, because the government had halted the long period of anarchy.

Grave, secretive, cautious, and always thrifty, Henry VII rebuilt the monarchy. He encouraged the cloth industry and built up the English merchant marine. Both English exports of wool and the royal export tax on that wool steadily increased. Henry crushed an invasion from Ireland and secured peace with Scotland through the marriage of his daughter Margaret to the Scottish king. When Henry VII died in 1509, he left a country at peace both domestically and internationally, a fat treasury, and the dignity of the royal majesty much enhanced.

SPAIN

Political development in Spain followed a pattern different from that of France and England. The central theme in the history of medieval Spain – or, more accurately, of the separate kingdoms Spain comprised – was disunity and plurality. The various peoples who lived in the Iberian Peninsula lacked a common cultural tradition. Different languages, different laws, and different religious communities made for a rich diversity. Complementing the legacy of Hispanic, Roman, and Visigothic peoples, Muslims and Jews had made significant contributions to Spanish society.

The centuries-long *reconquista* – the attempts of the northern Christian kingdoms to control the entire peninsula – had both military and religious objectives: expulsion or conversion of the Arabs and Jews and political control of the south. By the middle of the fifteenth century, the kingdoms of Castile and Aragon dominated the weaker Navarre, Granada, and Portugal, and, with the exception of Granada, the Iberian Peninsula had been won for Christianity. The wedding in 1469 of the dynamic and aggressive Isabella, heiress of Castile, and the crafty and persistent Ferdinand, heir of Aragon, was the final major step in the unification and Christianization of Spain. This marriage, however, constituted a dynastic union of two royal houses, not the political union of two peoples. Although Ferdinand and Isabella pursued a common foreign policy, Spain under their rule remained a loose confederation of separate states. Each kingdom continued to maintain its own cortes (parliament), laws, courts, bureaucracies, and systems of coinage and taxation.

Isabella and Ferdinand determined to strengthen royal authority. In order to curb the rebellious and warring aristocracy, they revived an old medieval institution. Popular groups in the towns called *hermandades,* or brotherhoods, were given the authority to act both as local police forces and as judicial tribunals. Local communities were made responsible for raising troops and apprehending and punishing criminals. The *hermandades* repressed violence with such savage punishments that by 1498 they could be disbanded. The second step Ferdinand and Isabella took to curb aristocratic power was the restructuring of the royal council. Aristocrats and great territorial magnates were rigorously excluded; thus the influence of the nobility on state policy was greatly reduced. Ferdinand and Isabella intended the council to be the cornerstone of their governmental system, with full executive, judicial, and legislative power under the monarchy. The council was also to be responsible for the supervision of local authorities. The king and queen, therefore, appointed to the council only people of middle-class background. The council and various government boards recruited men trained in Roman law, a system that exalted the power of the Crown as the embodiment of the state.

In the extension of royal authority and the consolidation of the territories of Spain, the church was the linchpin. The church possessed vast power and wealth, and churchmen enjoyed exemption from taxation. Most of the higher clergy were descended from great aristocratic families, controlled armies and strategic fortresses, and fully shared the military ethos of their families.

The major issue confronting Isabella and Ferdinand was the appointment of bishops. If the Spanish crown could select the higher clergy, then the monarchy could influence ecclesiastical policy, wealth, and military resources. Through a diplomatic alliance with the papacy, especially with the Spanish pope Alexander VI, the Spanish monarchs secured the right to appoint bishops in Spain and in the Hispanic territories in America. This power enabled the "Catholic Kings of Spain," a title granted Ferdinand and Isabella by the papacy, to establish, in effect, a national church.[23]

The Spanish rulers used their power to reform the church, and they used some of its wealth for national purposes. For example, they appointed a learned and zealous churchman, Cardinal Jiménez (1436-1517), to reform the monastic and secular clergy. Jiménez proved effective in this task, and established the University of Alcalá in 1499 for the education of the clergy, although instruction did not actually begin until 1508. A highly astute statesman, Jiménez twice served as regent of Castile.

Revenues from ecclesiastical estates provided the means to raise an army to continue the *reconquista*. The victorious entry of Ferdinand and Isabella into Granada on January 6, 1492, signaled the culmination of eight centuries of Spanish struggle against the Arabs in southern Spain and the conclusion of the *reconquista* (see Map 13.2). Granada in the south was incorporated into the Spanish kingdom, and in 1512 Ferdinand conquered Navarre in the north.

Although the Arabs had been defeated, there still remained a sizable and, in the view of the Catholic sovereigns, potentially dangerous minority, the Jews. Since ancient times, governments had never tolerated religious pluralism; religious faiths that differed from the official state religion were considered politically dangerous. Medieval writers quoted the fourth-century Byzantine theologian Saint John Chrysostom, who had asked rhetorically, "Why are the Jews degenerate? Because of their odious assassination of Christ." John Chrysostom and his admirers in the Middle Ages chose to ignore two facts: that it was the Romans who had killed Christ (because they considered him a *political* troublemaker), and that Christ had forgiven his executioners from the cross. France and England had expelled their Jewish populations in the Middle Ages, but in Spain Jews had been tolerated. In fact, Jews had played a decisive role in the economic and intellectual life of the several Spanish kingdoms.

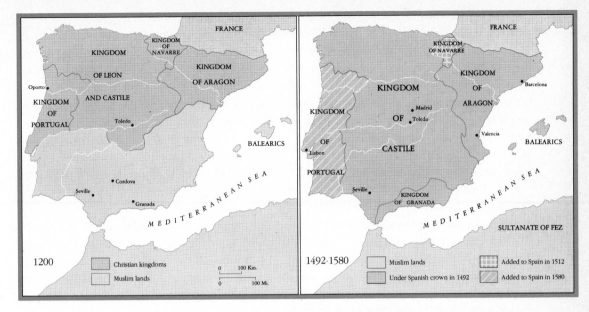

MAP 13.2 THE CHRISTIANIZATION AND UNI-FICATION OF SPAIN *The political unification of Spain was inextricably tied up with conversion or expulsion of the Muslims and the Jews. Why?*

Anti-Semitic riots and pogroms in the late fourteenth century had led many Jews to convert; they were called *conversos.* By the middle of the fifteenth century, many conversos held high positions in Spanish society as financiers, physicians, merchants, tax collectors, and even officials of the church hierarchy. Numbering perhaps 200,000 in a total population of about 7.5 million, Jews exercised an influence quite disproportionate to their numbers. Aristocratic grandees who borrowed heavily from Jews resented their financial dependence, and churchmen questioned the sincerity of Jewish conversions. At first, Isabella and Ferdinand continued the policy of royal toleration — Ferdinand himself had inherited Jewish blood from his mother. But many conversos apparently reverted to the faith of their ancestors, prompting Ferdinand and Isabella to secure Rome's permission to revive the In-

quisition, a medieval judicial procedure for the punishment of heretics.

Although the Inquisition was a religious institution established to insure the Catholic faith, it was controlled only by the Crown and served primarily as a politically unifying force in Spain. Because the Spanish Inquisition commonly applied torture to extract confessions, first from lapsed conversos, then from Muslims, and later from Protestants, it gained a notorious reputation. Thus, the word *inquisition,* meaning "any judicial inquiry conducted with ruthless severity," came into the English language. The methods of the Spanish Inquisition were cruel, though not as cruel as the investigative methods of some twentieth-century governments. In 1478 the deeply pious Ferdinand and Isabella introduced the Inquisition into their kingdoms to handle the problem of backsliding conversos. They solved the problem in a dire and drastic manner. Shortly after the reduction of the Moorish stronghold at Granada in 1492, Isabella and Ferdinand issued an edict expelling all practicing Jews from Spain. Of the community of perhaps 200,000 Jews, 150,000 fled. (Efforts were made through last-minute conversions to retain good Jewish physicians.) Absolute religious orthodoxy served as the foundation of the Spanish national state.

The diplomacy of the Catholic rulers of Spain achieved a success they never anticipated. Partly out of hatred for the French and partly to gain international recognition for their new dynasty, Ferdinand and Isabella in 1496 married their second daughter, Joanna, heiress to Castile, to the archduke Philip, heir through his mother to the Burgundian Netherlands and through his father to the Holy Roman Empire. Philip and Joanna's son, Charles V (1519–1556), thus succeeded to a vast patrimony on two continents. When Charles's son Philip II united Portugal to the Spanish crown in 1580, the Iberian Peninsula was at last politically united.

———————◆———————

Fourteenth-century Italy witnessed the rebirth of a strong interest in the ancient world, a Renaissance whose classicizing influences affected law and literature, government, education, religion, and art. Expanding outside Italy, this movement affected the entire culture of Europe. The chief features of the Renaissance were a secular attitude toward life, a belief in individual potential, and a serious interest in the Latin classics. The printing press revolutionized communication. Meanwhile the status of women in society declined, and black people entered Europe in sizable numbers for the first time since the collapse of the Roman Empire.

These changes rested upon important eco-nomic developments. The growth of Venetian and Genoese shipping and long-distance trade, Florentine banking and manufactures, Milanese and Pisan manufactures – these activities brought into being wealthy urban classes. As commercial oligarchies, they governed their city-states. In northern Europe city merchants and rural gentry allied with rising monarchies. With taxes provided by businesspeople, kings provided a greater degree of domestic peace and order, conditions essential for trade. In Spain, France, and England, rulers also emphasized royal dignity and authority, and they utilized Machiavellian ideas to insure the preservation and continuation of their governments. Feudal monarchies gradually evolved in the direction of nation states.

NOTES

1. A. Brucker, *Renaissance Florence,* John Wiley & Sons, New York, 1969, chap. 2.

2. Quoted by J. Burckhardt, *The Civilization of the Renaissance in Italy,* Phaidon Books, London, 1951, p. 89.

3. *Memoirs of Benvenuto Cellini; A Florentine Artist; Written by Himself,* Everyman's Library, J. M. Dent & Sons, London, 1927, p. 2.

4. Quoted by Burckhardt, p. 111.

5. B. Burroughs, ed., *Vasari's Lives of the Artists,* Simon & Schuster, New York, 1946, pp. 164–165.

6. See chap. 3, "The Social Status of the Artist," in A. Hauser, *The Social History of Art,* vol. 2, Vintage Books, New York, 1959, esp. pp. 60, 68.

7. G. Bull, trans., *Aretino: Selected Letters,* Penguin Books, New York, 1976, p. 109.

8. Hauser, pp. 48–49.

9. Quoted by W. H. Woodward, *Vittorino da Feltre and Other Humanist Educators,* Cambridge University Press, Cambridge, 1897, pp. 96–97.

10. C. E. Detmold, trans., *The Historical, Political*

and *Diplomatic Writings of Niccolò Machiavelli,* J. R. Osgood & Co., Boston, 1882, pp. 51–52.

11. Ibid., pp. 54–55.

12. This account rests on the excellent study of J. Kelly-Gadol, "Did Women Have a Renaissance?" in R. Bridenthal and C. Koonz, eds., *Becoming Visible: Women in European History,* Houghton Mifflin, Boston, 1977, pp. 137–161, esp. p. 161.

13. G. Ruggiero, "Sexual Criminality in the Early Renaissance: Venice 1338-1358," *Journal of Social History* 8 (Spring 1975):18–31.

14. Quoted by R. C. Trexler, "Infanticide in Florence: New Sources and First Results," *History of Childhood Quarterly* 1:1 (Summer 1973): 99.

15. Ibid., p. 100.

16. See Jean Devisse and Michel Mollat, *The Image of the Black in Western Art,* vol. II, part 2, trans. William Granger Ryan, William Morrow and Company, New York, 1979, pp. 187–188.

17. Ibid., pp. 190–194.

18. Ibid., pp. 255–258.

19. Quoted by R. C. Trexler, "Measures against Water Pollution in Fifteenth-Century Florence," *Viator* 5 (1974):463.

20. Ibid., pp. 464–467.

21. Quoted by E. H. Harbison, *The Christian Scholar and His Calling in the Age of the Reformation,* Charles Scribner's Sons, New York, 1956, p. 109.

22. Quoted by F. Seebohm, *The Oxford Reformers,* Everyman's Library, J. M. Dent & Sons, London, 1867, p. 256.

23. See J. H. Elliott, *Imperial Spain 1469–1716,* Mentor Books, New York, 1963, esp. pp. 97–108 and p. 75.

SUGGESTED READING

There are scores of exciting studies available on virtually all aspects of the Renaissance. In addition to the titles given in the Notes, the curious student interested in a broad synthesis should see J. H. Plumb, *The Italian Renaissance* (1965), a superbly written book based on deep knowledge and understanding; this book is probably the best starting point. J. R. Hale, *Renaissance Europe: The Individual and Society, 1480–1520* (1978), is an excellent treatment of individualism by a distinguished authority. F. H. New, *The Renaissance and Reformation: A Short History* (1977), gives a concise, balanced, and up-to-date account. M. P. Gilmore, *The World of Humanism* (1962), is an older but sound study that recent scholarship has not superseded on many subjects. Students interested in the problems the Renaissance has raised for historians should see K. H. Dannenfeld, ed., *The Renaissance: Medieval or Modern* (1959), an anthology with a variety of interpretations, and W. K. Ferguson, *The Renaissance in Historical Thought* (1948), a valuable but difficult book. For the city where much of it originated, G. A. Brucker, *Renaissance Florence* (1969), gives a good description of Florentine economic, political, social, and cultural history.

J. R. Hale, *Machiavelli and Renaissance Italy* (1966), is the best short biography of Machiavelli and broader in scope than the title would imply. G. Bull, trans., *Machiavelli: The Prince* (1959), is a readable and easily accessible edition of the political thinker's major work. C. Singleton, trans., *The Courtier* (1959), presents an excellent picture of Renaissance court life.

The best introduction to the Renaissance in northern Europe and a book that has greatly influenced twentieth-century scholarship is J. Huizinga, *The Waning of the Middle Ages: A Study of the Forms of Life, Thought, and Art in France and the Netherlands in the Dawn of the Renaissance* (1954). The leading northern humanist is sensitively treated in M. M. Philips, *Erasmus and the Northern Renaissance* (1965), and in J. Huizinga, *Erasmus of Rotterdam* (1952), probably the best biography. The standard biography of *Thomas More* remains that of R. W. Chambers (1935), but see also E. E. Reynolds, *Thomas More* (1962). Jacques LeClercq, trans., *The Complete Works of Rabelais* (1963), is easily available.

Renaissance art has understandably inspired vast researches. In addition to Vasari's volume of biographical sketches on the great masters referred to in the Notes, A. Martindale, *The Rise of the Artist in the Middle Ages and Early Renaissance* (1972), is a splendidly illustrated introduction. B. Berenson, *Italian Painters of the Renaissance* (1957), the work of an American expatriate who was an internationally famous art historian, has become a classic. W. Sypher, *Four Stages of Renaissance Style* (1956), relates drama and poetry to the visual arts of painting and sculpture. One of the finest appreciations of Renaissance art, written by one of the greatest art historians of this century, is E. Panofsky, *Meaning in the Visual Arts* (1955). Both Italian and northern painting are treated in the brilliant study of M. Meiss, *The Painter's Choice: Problems in the Interpretation of Renaissance Art* (1976), a collection of essays dealing with Renaissance style, form, and meaning. The splendidly illustrated work of Mary McCarthy, *The Stones of Florence* (1959), celebrates the energy and creativity of the greatest Renaissance city.

The student who wishes to study blacks in medieval and early modern European society should see the rich and original achievement of Jean Devisse and Michel Mollat, *The Image of the Black in Western Art,* vol. II: Part 1, *From the Demonic Threat to the Incarnation of Sainthood,* and Part 2, *Africans in the Christian Ordinance of the World: Fourteenth to Sixteenth Century,* trans. William Granger Ryan, William Morrow & Co., New York, 1979.

The following works are not only useful for the political and economic history of the age of the Renaissance but also contain valuable bibliographical information: A. J. Slavin, ed., *The "New Monarchies" and Representative Assemblies* (1965), a collection of interpretations; R. Lockyer, *Henry VII* (1972), a biography with documents illustrative of the king's reign; J. H. Elliott, *Imperial Spain: 1469–1716* (1966), with a balanced treatment of Isabella and Ferdinand; and I. Origo, *The Merchant of Prato* (1957), a perceptive and detailed account of one busy Florentine businessman.

CHAPTER 14

REFORM AND RENEWAL IN THE

CHRISTIAN CHURCH

THE IDEA OF REFORM is as old as Christianity itself. In his letter to the Christians of Rome, Saint Paul exhorted: "Do not model yourselves on the behavior of the world around you, but let your behavior change, reformed by your new mind. That is the only way to discover the will of God and know what is good, what it is that God wants, what is the perfect thing to do."[1] In the early fifth century, Saint Augustine of Hippo, describing the final stage of world history, wrote, "In the sixth age of the world our reformation becomes manifest, in newness of mind, according to the image of Him who created us." In the middle of the twelfth century, Saint Bernard of Clairvaux complained about the church of his day: "There is as much difference between us and the men of the primitive Church as there is between muck and gold."

The need for reform of the individual Christian and of the institutional church is central to the Christian faith. The Christian humanists of the late fifteenth and early sixteenth centuries – More, Erasmus, Lefèvre d'Etaples, and Jiménez – urged reform of the church on the pattern of the early church primarily through educational and social change. Men and women of every period believed the early Christian church represented a golden age, and critics in every period called for reform.

Sixteenth-century cries, therefore, were hardly new. Why then did sixteenth-century demands for reform lead to revolution in the Christian church and to lasting divisions in Christian society? What role did social and political factors play in the several reformations? What were the consequences of religious division? To resolve these questions, the related issue of the condition of the church within European society must first be explored.

THE CONDITION OF THE CHURCH (CA 1400–1517)

The papal conflict with the German emperor Frederick II in the thirteenth century, followed by the Babylonian Captivity and then by the Great Schism, badly damaged the prestige of church leaders. In the fourteenth and fifteenth centuries, conciliarists reflected educated public opinion when they called for the reform of the church "in head and members." The secular humanists of Italy and the Christian humanists of the north denounced corruption in the church. As Machiavelli put it, "We Italians are irreligious and corrupt above others, because the Church and her representatives set us the worst example."[2] In *The Praise of Folly,* Erasmus condemned the absurd superstitions of the parish clergy and the excessive rituals of the monks. The records of episcopal visitations of parishes, civil court records, and even such literary masterpieces as Chaucer's *Canterbury Tales* and Boccaccio's *Decameron* tend to confirm the sarcasms of the humanists.

Concrete evidence of disorder is spotty and scattered. Since a great deal of corruption may have gone unreported, the moral situation may have been worse than the evidence suggests. On the other hand, bishops' registers and public court records mention the exceptional, not the typical. The thousands of priests who quietly and conscientiously went about their duties and did not warrant correction received no mention in the documents.

The religious life of most people in early sixteenth-century Europe took place at the village or local level. Any assessment of the moral condition of the parish clergy must take into account one fundamental fact: parish priests were peasants, and they were poor. All too frequently the spiritual quality of their lives was not much better than that of the people to whom they ministered. The clergy identified religion with life; that is, they injected religious symbols and practices into everyday living. Some historians, therefore, have accused the clergy of vulgarizing religion. But if the level of belief and practice was vulgarized, still the lives of rural, isolated, and semipagan people were spiritualized.

SIGNS OF DISORDER

In the early sixteenth century, critics of the church concentrated their attacks on three disorders: clerical immorality, clerical ignorance, and clerical pluralism with the related problem of absenteeism. There was little pressure for doctrinal change; the emphasis was on moral and administrative reform.

Since the fourth century, church law had required that candidates for the priesthood accept absolute celibacy. It had always been difficult to enforce. Many priests, especially those ministering to country people, had concubines, and reports of neglect of the rule of celibacy were common. Immorality, of course, included more than sexual transgressions. Clerical drunkenness, gambling, and indulgence in fancy dress were frequent charges. There is no way of knowing how many priests were guilty of such behavior. But because such conduct was so much at odds with the church's rules and moral standards, it scandalized the educated faithful.

The bishops enforced regulations regarding the education of priests very casually. As a result, standards for ordination were shockingly low. Many priests could barely read and write, and critics laughed at the illiterate priest mumbling the Latin words of the mass, which he could not understand. Predictably, this was

the disorder the Christian humanists, with their concern for learning, particularly condemned.

Absenteeism and pluralism constituted the third major abuse. Many clerics, especially higher ecclesiastics, held several benefices (or offices) simultaneously but seldom visited their benefices, let alone performed the spiritual responsibilities those offices entailed. Instead, they collected revenues from all of them and paid a poor priest a fraction of the income to fulfill the spiritual duties of a particular local church.

Many Italian officials in the papal curia held benefices in England, Spain, and Germany. Revenues from those countries paid the Italian priests' salaries, provoking not only charges of absenteeism but nationalistic resentment. King Henry VIII's chancellor Thomas Wolsey was archbishop of York for fifteen years before he set foot in his diocese. The French king Louis XII's famous diplomat Antoine du Prat is perhaps the most notorious example of absenteeism: as archbishop of Sens, the first time he entered his cathedral was in his own funeral procession. Critics condemned pluralism, absenteeism, and the way money seemed to change hands when a bishop entered into his office.

Although royal governments strengthened their positions and consolidated their territories in the fifteenth and sixteenth centuries, rulers lacked sufficient revenues to pay and reward able civil servants. The Christian church, with its dioceses and abbeys, possessed a large proportion of the wealth of the countries of Europe. What better way to reward government officials than with high church offices? After all, the practice was sanctioned by centuries of tradition. Thus in Spain, France, England, and the Holy Roman Empire – in fact, all over Europe – because

THE CHURCH CONTRASTED *Satirical woodcuts as well as the printed word attacked conditions in the church. Here the mercenary spirit of the sixteenth-century papacy is contrasted with the attitude of Christ toward money changers: Christ drove them from the temple, but the pope kept careful records of revenues owed to the church. (Photos: Caroline Buckler)*

church officials served their monarchs, those officials were allowed to govern the church.

The broad mass of the people, in supporting the church, supported everything that churchmen did. Bishops and abbots did a lot of work for secular governments. Churchmen served as royal councilors, diplomats, treasury officials, chancellors, viceroys, and judges. These positions had nothing whatsoever to do with spiritual matters. Bishops worked for their respective states as well as for the church, and they were paid by the church for their services to the state. It is astonishing that so many conscientiously tried to carry out their religious duties on top of their public burdens.

The prodigious wealth of the church inevitably stimulated criticism. For centuries devout laymen and laywomen had bequeathed land, money, rights, and privileges to religious institutions. By the sixteenth century, these gifts and shrewd investments had resulted in vast treasure. Some was spent in the service of civil governments. Much of it was used to alleviate the wretched condition of the poor. But some also provided a luxurious lifestyle for the church hierarchy.

In most countries except England, members of nobility occupied the highest positions in the church. The sixteenth century was definitely not a democratic age. The spectacle of proud, aristocratic prelates living in magnificent splendor contrasted very unfavorably with the simple fishermen who were Christ's first disciples. Nor did the popes of the period 1450–1550 set much of an example. They lived like secular Renaissance princes. Pius II (1458–1464), although deeply learned and a tireless worker, enjoyed a reputation as a clever writer of love stories and witty Latin poetry. Sixtus IV (1471–1484) beautified the city of Rome, built the famous Sistine Chapel, and generously supported several artists. Innocent VIII (1484–1492) made the papal court a model of luxury and scandal. All three popes used papal power and papal wealth to advance the material interests of their own families.

The court of the Spanish pope Rodrigo Borgia, Alexander VI (1492–1503), who publicly acknowledged his mistress and children, reached new heights of impropriety. Because of the prevalence of intrigue, sexual promiscuity, and supposed poisonings, the name Borgia became a synonym for moral corruption. Julius II (1503–1513), the nephew of Sixtus IV, donned military armor and personally led papal troops against the French invaders of Italy in 1506. After him, Giovanni de' Medici, the son of Lorenzo the Magnificent, carried on as Pope Leo X (1513–1521) the Medicean tradition of being a great patron of the arts.

Through the centuries, papal prestige and influence had rested heavily on the moral quality of the popes' lives – that is, on their strong fidelity to Christian teaching as revealed in the Gospel. The lives of Renaissance popes revealed little of this Gospel message.

SIGNS OF VITALITY

Calls for reform testify to the spiritual vitality of the church as well as to its problems. Before a patient can be cured of sickness, he or she must acknowledge that a problem exists. In the late fifteenth and early sixteenth centuries, both individuals and groups within the church were working actively for reform. In Spain, Cardinal Francisco Jiménez visited religious houses, encouraged the monks and friars to keep their rules and constitutions, and set high standards for the training of the diocesan clergy. Jiménez founded the University of Alcalá (1499) partly for the education of priests.

Lefèvre d'Etaples in France and John Colet in England called for a return to the austere Christianity of the early church. Both men stressed the importance of sound preaching of the Scriptures.

In Holland, beginning in the late fourteenth century, a group of pious laymen and laywomen called the Brethren of the Common Life lived in stark simplicity while daily carrying out the Gospel teaching of feeding the hungry, clothing the naked, and visiting the sick. The Brethren also established schools for the education of the young, their most famous pupil being Erasmus of Rotterdam. The spirituality of the Brethren of the Common Life found its finest expression in the classic *The Imitation of Christ* by Thomas à Kempis. As its title suggests, *The Imitation of Christ* urges ordinary Christians to take Christ as their model and to seek perfection in a simple way of life. The movement, which spread to Germany, France, and Italy, was a real religious revival.

So too were the activities of the Oratories of Divine Love in Italy. The oratories were groups of priests living in communities who worked to revive the church through prayer and preaching. They did not withdraw from the world as medieval monks had done, but devoted themselves to pastoral and charitable activities such as founding hospitals and orphanages. Oratorians served God in an active ministry.

If external religious observances are a measure of depth of heartfelt conviction, Europeans in the early sixteenth century remained deeply pious and loyal to the Roman Catholic church. Villagers participated in processions honoring the local saints. Middle-class people made pilgrimages to the great national shrines, as the enormous wealth of Saint Thomas Becket's tomb at Canterbury in England and the shrine of Saint James de Compostella in Spain testify. The upper classes continued to remember the church in their wills. In England, for example, between 1480 and 1490 almost £30,000, a prodigious sum in those days, was bequeathed to religious foundations. People of all social classes devoted an enormous amount of their time and

GRUNEWALD: CRUCIFIXION *The bloodless hands, tortured face, and lacerated body reveal profound sorrow for Christ's physical agony and suggest the intense piety of northern Europe. Grunewald, court* *painter to Albert of Brandenburg, shows in this painting (ca 1510) his strong attraction to Luther's ideas. (National Gallery of Art, Washington, D.C. Samual H. Kress Collection)*

income to religious causes and foundations. Sixteenth-century society remained deeply religious; all across Europe people sincerely yearned for salvation.

The papacy also expressed concern for reform. Pope Julius II summoned an ecumenical (universal) council, which met in the church of St. John Lateran in Rome from 1512 to 1517. Since most of the bishops were Italian and did not represent a broad cross-section of international opinion, the term *ecumenical* is not appropriate. Nevertheless, the bishops and theologians present strove earnestly to reform the church. They criticized the ignorance of priests, lamenting that only 2 percent of the clergy could understand the Latin of the liturgical books. The Lateran Council also condemned superstitions believed by many of the laity. The council recommended higher standards for education of the clergy and instruction of the common people. The bishops placed the responsibility for eliminating bureaucratic corruption squarely on the papacy and suggested significant doctrinal reforms. But many obstacles stood in the way of ecclesiastical change. Nor did the actions of an obscure German friar immediately force the issue.

MARTIN LUTHER AND THE BIRTH OF PROTESTANTISM

As the result of a personal religious struggle, a German Augustinian friar, Martin Luther (1483-1546), launched the Protestant Reformation of the sixteenth century. Luther was not a typical person of his time; miners' sons who become professors of theology are never typical. But Luther is representative of his time in the sense that he articulated the widespread desire for reform of the Christian church and the deep yearning for salvation. In the sense that concern for salvation motivated Luther and other reformers, the sixteenth-century Reformation was in part a continuation of the medieval religious search.

LUTHER'S EARLY YEARS

Martin Luther was born at Eisleben in Saxony, the second son of a hardworking and ambitious copper miner. At considerable sacrifice, his father sent him to school and then to the University of Erfurt, where Martin earned a master's degree with distinction at the young age of twenty-one. Hans Luther intended his son to proceed to the study of law and a legal career, which had since Roman times been the steppingstone to public office and material success. Badly frightened during a thunderstorm, however, Martin Luther vowed to become a friar. Without consulting his father, he entered the monastery of the Augustinian friars at Erfurt in 1505. Luther was ordained a priest in 1507, and after additional study earned the doctorate of theology. From 1511 until his death in 1546, he served as professor of Scripture at the new University of Wittenberg.

Martin Luther was exceedingly scrupulous in his monastic observances and devoted to prayer, penances, and fasting; nevertheless, the young friar's conscience troubled him constantly. The doubts and conflicts felt by any sensitive young person who has just taken a grave step were especially intense in young Luther. He had terrible anxieties about sin and worried continually about his salvation. Luther intensified his monastic observances but still found no peace of mind.

A recent psychological interpretation of Luther's early life suggests that he underwent a severe inner crisis in the years 1505-1515. Luther had disobeyed his father, thus viola-

YOUNG LUTHER Lucas Cranach, court painter to Elector Frederick of Saxony and a friend of Luther's, captured the piety, the strength, and the intense struggle of the young friar. (Photo: Caroline Buckler)

ting one of the Ten Commandments, and serious conflict persisted between them. The religious life seemed to provide no answers to his mental and spiritual difficulties. Three fits that he suffered in the monastic choir during those years may have been outward signs of his struggle.[3] Luther was grappling, as had thousands of medieval people before him, with the problem of salvation and thus the meaning of life. He was also searching for his life's work.

Luther's wise and kindly confessor, Staupitz, directed him to the study of Saint Paul's letters. Gradually, Luther arrived at a new understanding of the Pauline letters and of all Christian doctrine. He came to believe that salvation comes not through external observances and penances but through a simple faith in Christ. Faith is the means by which God sends humanity his grace, and faith is a free gift that cannot be earned. Thus Martin Luther discovered himself, God's work for him, and the centrality of faith in the Christian life.

THE NINETY-FIVE THESES

An incident illustrative of the condition of the church in the early sixteenth century propelled Martin Luther onto the stage of history and brought about the Reformation in Germany. The University of Wittenberg lay within the ecclesiastical jurisdiction of the archdiocese of Magdeburg. The twenty-seven-year-old archbishop of Magdeburg, Albert, was also administrator of the see of Halberstadt and had been appointed archbishop of Mainz. To hold all three offices simultaneously – blatant pluralism – required papal dispensation. At that moment Pope Leo X was anxious to continue the construction of St. Peter's Basilica, but was hard pressed for funds. Archbishop Albert borrowed money from the Fuggers, a wealthy banking family of Augsburg, to pay for the papal dispensation allowing him to hold the several episcopal benefices. Only a few powerful financiers and churchmen knew the details of the arrangement, but Leo X authorized Archbishop Albert to sell indulgences, or pardons, in Germany. With the proceeds the archbishop could repay the Fuggers.

Wittenberg was in the political jurisdiction of Frederick of Saxony, one of the seven electors of the Holy Roman Empire. When Frederick forbade the sale of indulgences within his duchy, people of Wittenberg, including some of Professor Luther's students, streamed across the border from Saxony into Jüteborg in Thuringia to buy indulgences.

What was an indulgence? According to Catholic theology, individuals who sin alienate themselves from God and his love. In order to be reconciled to God, the sinner must confess his or her sins to a priest and do the penance assigned. For example, the man who steals must first return the stolen goods and then perform the penance given by the priest, usually certain prayers or good works. This is known as the temporal (or earthly) penance, since no one knows what penance God will ultimately require.

The doctrine of indulgence rested on three principles. First, God is merciful, but he is also just. Second, Christ and the saints, through their infinite virtue, established a "treasury of merits," which the church, through its special relationship with Christ and the saints, can draw upon. Third, the church has the authority to grant to sinners the spiritual benefits of those merits. Originally, an indulgence was a remission of the temporal (priest-imposed) penalties for sin. Beginning in the twelfth century, the papacy and bishops had given Crusaders such indulgences. By the later Middle Ages people widely believed that an indulgence secured total remission of penalties for sin – on earth or in purgatory – and assured swift entry into heaven.

Archbishop Albert hired the Dominican friar John Tetzel to sell the indulgences. Tetzel mounted a blitz advertising campaign. One of his slogans – "As soon as coin in coffer rings, the soul from purgatory springs" – brought phenomenal success. Men and women could buy indulgences not only for themselves but for deceased parents, relatives, or friends. Tetzel even drew up a chart with specific prices for the forgiveness of particular sins. The

massive amounts of junk that "sophisticated" Americans buy today should make one cautious in condemning the gullibility of sixteenth-century German peasants. Who wouldn't want a spiritual insurance policy?

Luther was severely troubled that ignorant people believed that they had no further need for repentance once they had purchased an indulgence. Accordingly, in the academic tradition of the times, on the eve of All Saints' Day (October 31) 1517, he attached to the door of the church at Wittenberg castle a list of ninety-five theses (or propositions) on indulgences. By this act Luther intended only to start a theological discussion of the subject and to defend the theses publicly.

Some of the theses challenged the pope's power to grant indulgences, and others criticized papal wealth: "Why does not the Pope, whose riches are at this day more ample than those of the wealthiest of the wealthy, build the one Basilica of St. Peter's with his own money, rather than with that of poor believers . . . ?"[4] Luther at first insisted that the pope had not known about the traffic in indulgences, for if he had known, he would have put a stop to it.

The theses were soon printed and read by Germans all over the empire. Immediately, broad theological issues were raised. When questioned, Luther insisted that Scripture persuaded him of the invalidity of indulgences. He rested his fundamental argument on the principle that there was no biblical basis for indulgences. But, replied Luther's opponents, to deny the legality of indulgences was to deny the authority of the pope who had authorized them. The issue was drawn: where did authority lie in the Christian church?

Through 1518 and 1519, Luther studied the history of the papacy. Gradually, he gained the conviction, like Marsiglio and Hus before him (pages 408–409), that ultimate authority in the church belonged not to the papacy but to a general council. Then, in 1519, in a large public disputation with the Catholic debater John Eck at Leipzig, Luther denied both the authority of the pope and the infallibility of a general council. The Council of Constance, he said, had erred when it condemned John Hus in 1415.

The papacy responded with a letter condemning some of Luther's propositions, ordering that his books be burned, and giving him two months to recant or be excommunicated. Luther retaliated by publicly burning the letter. Shortly afterward – January 3, 1521 – his excommunication became final. By this time the controversy involved more than theological issues. The papal legate wrote, "All Germany is in revolution. Nine-tenths shout 'Luther' as their war-cry; and the other tenth cares nothing about Luther, and cries 'Death to the court of Rome.' "[5]

In this highly charged atmosphere the twenty-one-year-old emperor Charles V held his first diet (assembly of the Estates of the empire) at Worms and summoned Luther to appear before it. When ordered to recant, Luther replied in language that rang all over Europe:

Unless I am convinced by the evidence of Scripture or by plain reason – for I do not accept the authority of the Pope or the councils alone, since it is established that they have often erred and contradicted themselves – I am bound by the Scriptures I have cited and my conscience is captive to the Word of God. I cannot and will not recant anything, for it is neither safe nor right to go against conscience. God help me. Amen.[6]

Luther was declared an outlaw of the empire, which meant that he was denied legal protection.

Between 1520 and 1530, Luther worked out the basic theological tenets that became the articles of faith for his new church and subsequently for all Protestant groups. The word *Protestant* derives from the protest drawn up by a small group of reforming German princes at the Diet of Speyer in 1529. The princes "protested" the decisions of the Catholic majority. At first Protestant meant Lutheran, but with the appearance of many protesting sects it became a general term applied to all non-Catholic Christians. Lutheran Protestant thought was officially formulated in the Confession of Augsburg in 1530.

Ernst Troeltsch, a German student of the sociology of religion, has defined Protestantism as a "modification of Catholicism, in which the Catholic formulation of questions was retained, while a different answer was given to them." Luther provided new answers to four old, basic theological issues.

First, how is a person to be saved? Traditional Catholic teaching held that salvation was achieved by both faith *and* good works. Luther held that salvation comes by *faith alone*. Women and men are saved, said Luther, by the arbitrary decision of God, irrespective of good works or the sacraments.

Second, where does religious authority reside? Christian doctrine had long maintained that authority rests both in the Bible and in the traditional teaching of the church. Luther maintained that authority rests in the Word of God as revealed in the Bible alone and as interpreted by an individual's conscience. He urged that each person read and reflect upon the Scriptures.

Third, what is the church? Luther reemphasized the Catholic teaching that the church consists of the entire community of

Christian believers. The medieval church had tended to identify the church with the clergy. Luther insisted upon the priesthood of all believers.

Finally, what is the highest form of Christian life? The medieval church had stressed the superiority of the monastic and religious life over the secular. Luther argued that all vocations have equal merit, whether ecclesiastical or secular, and that every person should serve God in his or her individual calling.[7] Protestantism, in sum, represented a reformulation of the Christian heritage.

THE SOCIAL IMPACT OF LUTHER'S BELIEFS

In the sixteenth century, religion infused many aspects of life, and theological issues had broad social implications. The Lutheran movement started a religious revolution, which soon led to social revolt. As early as 1521, Luther had a vast following. Every encounter with ecclesiastical or political authorities attracted attention to him. Pulpits and printing presses spread his message all over Germany. By the time of his death, people of all social classes had become "Lutheran."

What was the immense appeal of Luther's religious ideas? Historians have puzzled over this question for centuries. It is always difficult to distinguish between spiritual and altruistic motives and materialistic, self-serving ones. The attraction of the German peasants to Lutheran beliefs was logical and almost predictable. Luther himself came from a peasant background, and he knew their ceaseless toil. The peasants must have admired Luther's defiance of the authority of the church. Moreover, they thrilled to the words Luther used in his treatise *On Christian Liberty* (1520): "A Christian man is the most free lord of all and subject to none." Taken by themselves, these words easily contributed to social unrest.

In the early sixteenth century, the economic condition of the peasantry varied from place to place, but was generally worse than it had been in the fifteenth century and was continuing to deteriorate. Although the lords did not attempt to reimpose or increase servile obligations that had been set aside after the Black Death, nevertheless rising prices hurt people living on fixed incomes. A huge number of beggars swelled the populations of the towns. At Hamburg, for example, perhaps 20 percent of the people were paupers.

The upper classes viewed the peasants and their wretched conditions with contempt. Nobles looked upon peasants as little more than animals, "the ox without horns." Luther's fellow professor and colleague in reform at Wittenberg, Philip Melanchthon, enjoyed a great reputation as a Christian humanist, yet dismissed the peasants with the words "the ass *will* have blows and the people *will* be ruled by force."

In June 1524, a massive revolt broke out near the Swiss frontier and swept into the Rhineland, Swabia, Franconia, and Saxony. As many townspeople as farm laborers participated. Urban proletariat and agricultural laborers poured their grievances into the *Twelve Articles,* published in 1525. The peasants wanted complete abolition of serfdom, an end to oppressive taxes and tithes, reform of the clergy, confiscation of church property, and such basic privileges as the right to cut wood in the lords' forests. The slogans of the crowds that swept across Germany came directly from Luther's writings. "God's righteousness" and "the Word of God" were invoked in the effort to secure social and economic justice.[8]

The poor who expected Luther's support

THE PEASANTS' REVOLT *The peasants were attracted to Luther's faith because it seemed to give religious support to their economic grievances. Carrying the banner of the Peasants' League and armed with pitchforks and axes, a group of peasants surround a knight. (Photo: Caroline Buckler)*

were soon disillusioned. Background, education, and monastic observance all inclined him toward obedience to political authority and respect for social superiors. Luther had written of the "freedom" of the Christian, but he had meant the freedom to obey the Word of God, for in sin men and women lose their freedom and break their relationship with God. Freedom for Luther meant independence from the authority of the Roman church; it did *not* mean opposition to legally established secular powers. Accordingly he tossed off a tract, *Against the Murderous, Thieving Hordes of the Peasants,* calling upon the nobility to

put down the unlawful revolt. The German nobility crushed it with ferocity. Historians have estimated that as many as a hundred thousand peasants were slaughtered.

Luther took literally these words of Saint Paul's letter to the Romans: "Let every soul be subject to the higher powers. For there is no power but of God: the powers that be are established by God. Whosoever resists the power, resists the ordinance of God: and they that resist shall receive to themselves damnation."[9] As it developed, Lutheran theology exalted the state, subordinated the church to the state, and everywhere championed "the powers that be." The consequences for German society were profound and have redounded into the twentieth century. After the revolt, the condition of the working classes worsened, and their religion taught complete obedience to divinely appointed authority, the state.

Scholars in many disciplines have attributed Luther's fame and success to the new invention of the printing press, which rapidly reproduced and made known his ideas. Equally important is Luther's incredible skill with language. Some thinkers have lavished praise on the Wittenberg reformer; others have bitterly condemned him. But, in the words of psychologist Erik Erikson:

The one matter on which professor and priest, psychiatrist and sociologist, agree is Luther's immense gift for language: his receptivity for the written word; his memory for the significant phrase; and his range of verbal expression (lyrical, biblical, satirical, and vulgar) which in English is paralleled only by Shakespeare.[10]

Language proved to be the weapon with which this peasant's son changed the world.

Educated people and humanists, like the peasants, were much attracted by Luther's words. He advocated a simpler, personalized religion based on faith, a return to the spirit of the early church, the centrality of the Scriptures in the liturgy and in the Christian life, the abolition of elaborate ceremonial — precisely the reforms the nothern Christian humanists had been calling for. Ulrich Zwingli (1483–1531), for example, a humanist of Zurich, was strongly influenced by Luther's writings; they stimulated Zwingli's reforms in that Swiss city. The nobleman Ulrich von Hutton (1488–1523), who had published several humanistic tracts, in 1519 dedicated his life to the advancement of Luther's reformation. And as we shall see, the

Frenchman John Calvin (1509–1564), often called the organizer of Protestantism, owed a great deal to Luther's thought.

The publication of Luther's German translation of the New Testament in 1523 democratized religion. His insistence that everyone should read and reflect upon the Scriptures attracted the literate and thoughtful middle classes partly because Luther appealed to their intelligence. Moreover, the business classes, preoccupied with making money, envied the church's wealth, disapproved of the luxurious lifestyle of some churchmen, and resented tithes and ecclesiastical taxation. Luther's doctrines of salvation by faith and the priesthood of all believers not only raised the religious status of the commercial classes but protected their pocketbooks as well.

Martin Luther's attitude toward women became the standard for German and Protestant women for centuries. Luther believed that marriage was a woman's career. A student recorded Luther as saying, early in his public ministry, "Let them bear children until they are dead of it; that is what they are for." A happy marriage to the ex-nun Katharine von Bora mellowed him, and another student later quoted him as saying, "Next to God's Word there is no more precious treasure than holy matrimony. God's highest gift on earth is a pious, cheerful, God-fearing, home-keeping wife, with whom you may live peacefully, to whom you may entrust your goods, and body and life."[11] Although Luther deeply loved his "dear Katie," he believed that women's concerns revolved exclusively around the children, the kitchen, and the church. A happy woman was a patient wife, an efficient manager, and a good mother.

Luther's viewpoint reflected contemporary values: German women were no more oppressed than Italian, Spanish, or even French ones. But few men considered women intelligent enough to handle a profession outside the home.

GERMANY AND THE PROTESTANT REFORMATION

The history of the Holy Roman Empire in the later Middle Ages is a story of dissension, disintegration, and debility. Unlike Spain, France, and England, the empire lacked a strong central power. The Golden Bull of 1356 created government by an aristocratic federation. Each of seven electors – the archbishops of Mainz, Trier, and Cologne, the margrave of Brandenburg, the duke of Saxony, the count palatine of the Rhine, and the king of Bohemia – gained virtual sovereignty in his own territory. The agreement ended disputed elections in the empire; it also reduced the central authority of the emperor. Thereafter, Germany was characterized by weak borders, localism, and chronic disorder. The nobility strengthened their territories, while imperial power declined.

Against this background of decentralization and strong local power, Martin Luther had launched a movement to reform the church. Two years after Luther posted the Ninety-Five Theses, the electors chose as emperor a nineteen-year-old Habsburg prince, who ruled as Charles V. How did the goals and interests of the emperor influence the course of the Reformation in Germany? What impact did the upheaval in the Christian church have on the political condition in Germany?

THE RISE OF THE HABSBURG DYNASTY

The marriage in 1477 of Maximilian I of the house of Habsburg and Mary of Burgundy was a decisive event in early modern European history. Through this union with the rich and powerful duchy of Burgundy, the Austrian house of Habsburg became the strongest ruling family within the empire. Its fortunes became permanently linked to those of the empire.

In the fifteenth and sixteenth centuries, as in the Middle Ages, relations among states continued to be greatly affected by the connections of royal families. Marriage often determined the diplomatic status of states. The Habsburg-Burgundian marriage angered the French, who considered Burgundy part of French territory. Louis XI of France repeatedly ravaged parts of the Burgundian Netherlands until he was able to force Maximilian to accept French terms: the Treaty of Arras (1482) emphatically declared Burgundy a part of the kingdom of France. The Habsburgs, however, never really renounced their claim to Burgundy, and intermittent warfare over it continued between France and Maximilian. Within the empire, German principalities that resented Austria's pre-eminence began to see that they shared interests with France. The marriage of Maximilian and Mary was to inaugurate two centuries of conflict between the Austrian house of Habsburg and the Valois kings of France. And Germany was to be the chief arena of the struggle.

"Other nations wage war; you, Austria, marry." Historians dispute the origins of the adage, but no one questions its accuracy. The heir of Mary and Maximilian, Philip of Burgundy, married Joanna of Castile, daughter of Ferdinand and Isabella of Spain. Philip and Joanna's son Charles V (1500–1558) fell heir to a vast conglomeration of territories. Through a series of accidents and unexpected deaths, Charles inherited Spain from his mother, together with her possessions in the New World and the Spanish dominions in

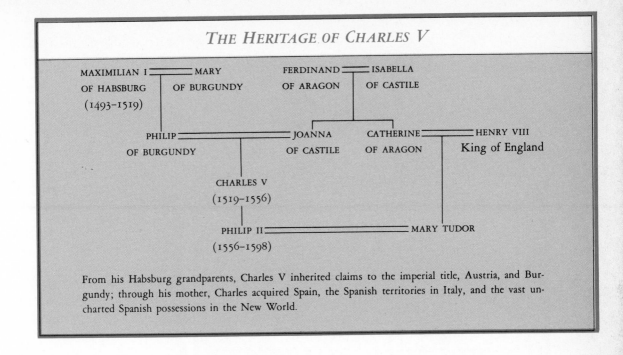

THE HERITAGE OF CHARLES V

MAXIMILIAN I ═══ MARY   FERDINAND ═══ ISABELLA
OF HABSBURG   OF BURGUNDY   OF ARAGON   OF CASTILE
(1493–1519)

PHILIP ══════════ JOANNA   CATHERINE ═══ HENRY VIII
OF BURGUNDY   OF CASTILE   OF ARAGON   King of England

CHARLES V
(1519–1556)

PHILIP II ══════════ MARY TUDOR
(1556–1598)

From his Habsburg grandparents, Charles V inherited claims to the imperial title, Austria, and Burgundy; through his mother, Charles acquired Spain, the Spanish territories in Italy, and the vast uncharted Spanish possessions in the New World.

Italy, Sicily, Sardinia, and Naples. From his father he inherited the Habsburg lands in Austria, southern Germany, the Low Countries, and Franche-Comté in east central France.

Charles's inheritance was an incredibly diverse collection of states and peoples, each governed in a different manner and held together only by the person of the emperor. Charles's Italian adviser, the grand chancellor Gattinara, told the young ruler: "God has set you on the path towards world monarchy." Charles not only believed this; he was convinced that it was his duty to maintain the political and religious unity of Western Christendom. In this respect Charles V was the last medieval emperor.

Charles needed and in 1519 secured the imperial title. Forward-thinking Germans proposed governmental reforms. They urged placing the administration in the hands of an imperial council whose president, the emperor's appointee, would have ultimate executive power. Reforms of the imperial finances, the army, and the judiciary were also recommended. Such ideas did not interest the young emperor at all. When he finally arrived in Germany from Spain and opened his first diet at Worms in January 1521, he naively announced that "the empire from of old has had not many masters, but one, and it is our intention to be that one." Charles went on to say that he was to be treated as of greater account than his predecessors because he was more powerful than they had been. In view of the long history of aristocratic power, Charles's notions were pure fantasy.

Charles continued the Burgundian policy of his grandfather Maximilian. That is, German revenues and German troops were subordinated to the needs of other parts of the empire, first Burgundy and then Spain. Habs-

EMPEROR CHARLES V   Sometimes called a second Charlemagne, Charles V unsuccessfully tried to unite millions of people divided by geography, custom, language, and centuries of historical development under his family rule. The full beard partially conceals the long jutting jaw, a Habsburg family trait. (Photo: Caroline Buckler)

burg international interests came before the need for reform in Germany.

THE POLITICAL IMPACT OF LUTHER'S BELIEFS

In the sixteenth century, the practice of religion remained a public matter. Everyone participated in the religious life of the community, just as almost everyone shared in the local agricultural work. Whatever spiritual convictions individuals held in the privacy of their consciences, the emperor, king, prince, magistrate, or other civil authority determined the official form of religious practice within his jurisdiction. Religion had too many social implications to be left to individual judgment. Almost everyone believed that the presence of a faith different from that of the majority represented a political threat to the security of the state. Only a tiny minority, and certainly none of the princes, believed in religious liberty.

Against this background, the religious storm launched by Martin Luther swept across northern and central Germany. Several elements in his religious reformation stirred patriotic feelings. Anti-Roman sentiment ran high. Humanists lent eloquent intellectual support. And Luther's translation of the New Testament into German evoked national pride. Lutheranism contributed to the development of German nationalism.

For decades devout laymen and churchmen had called on the German princes to reform the church. In 1520, Luther took up the cry in his *Appeal to the Christian Nobility of the German Nation.* Unless the princes destroyed papal power in Germany, Luther argued, reform was impossible. He urged the princes to confiscate ecclesiastical wealth and to abolish indulgences, dispensations, pardons, and clerical celibacy. He told them that it was their public duty to bring about the moral reform of the church. Luther based his argument in part on the papacy's financial exploitation of Germany:

Now that Italy is sucked dry, they come into Germany, and begin, oh so gently. But let us beware, or Germany will soon become like Italy. Already we have some cardinals; what the Romans seek by that the "drunken Germans" are not to understand until we have not a bishopric, a monastery, a living, a benefice, a mite or a penny left. . . . They skim the cream off the bishoprics, monasteries, and benefices, and because they do not yet venture to turn them all to shameful use, as they have done in Italy, they only practice for the present the sa-

cred trickery of coupling together ten or twenty prelacies and taking a yearly portion from each of them so as to make a tidy sum after all. The priory of Würzburg yields a thousand gulden; that of Bamberg, something; Mainz, Trier, and the others, something more; and so . . . that a cardinal might live at Rome like a rich king.

How comes it that we Germans must put up with such robbery and such extortion of our property at the hands of the pope? If the Kingdom of France has prevented it, why do we Germans let them make such fools and apes of us? It would all be more bearable if in this way they only stole our property; but they lay waste the churches and rob Christ's sheep of their pious shepherds, and destroy the worship and the Word of God. Even if there were not a single cardinal, the Church would not go under. As it is they do nothing for the good of Christendom; they only wrangle about the incomes of bishoprics and prelacies, and that any robber could do. . . .

Since we here come to the heart of the matter, we will pause a little, and let it be seen that the Germans are not quite such gross fools as not to note or understand the sharp practices of the Romans. I do not now complain that at Rome God's command and Christian law are despised; for such is the state of Christendom, and particularly of Rome, that we may not now complain of such high matters. Nor do I complain that natural or temporal law and reason count for nothing. The case is worse even than that. I complain that they do not keep their own self-devised canon law, though it is, to be sure, mere tyranny, avarice, and temporal splendor, rather than law. . . .[12]

These words fell on welcome ears and itchy fingers. Luther's appeal to German patriotism gained him strong support, and national feeling influenced many princes otherwise confused by or indifferent to the complexities of the religious issues.

The church in Germany possessed great

wealth. And, unlike other countries, Germany had no strong central government to check the flow of gold to Rome. Rejection of Roman Catholicism and adoption of Protestantism would mean the legal confiscation of lush farmlands, rich monasteries, and wealthy shrines. Some German princes, such as the prince-archbishop of Cologne, Hermann von Wied, were sincerely attracted to Lutheranism, but many civil authorities realized that they had a great deal to gain by embracing the new faith. A steady stream of duchies, margraviates, free cities, and bishoprics secularized church property, accepted Lutheran theological doctrines, and adopted simpler services conducted in German. The decision reached at Worms in 1521 to condemn Luther and his teaching was not enforced because the German princes did not want to enforce it.

Charles V was a vigorous defender of Catholicism, and contemporary social and political theory denied the possibility of two religions coexisting peacefully in one territory. Thus, many princes used the religious issue to extend their financial and political independence. When doctrinal differences became linked to political ambitions and financial receipts, the results proved unfortunate for the improvement of German government. The Protestant movement ultimately proved a political disaster for Germany.

Charles V must share blame with the German princes for the disintegration of imperial authority in the empire. He neither understood nor took an interest in the constitutional problems of Germany, and he lacked the material resources to oppose Protestantism effectively there. Throughout his reign he was preoccupied with his Flemish, Spanish, Italian, and American territories.

Five times between 1521 and 1555, Charles V went to war with the Valois kings of France. The issue each time was the Habsburg lands acquired by the marriage of Maximilian and Mary of Burgundy. Much of the fighting occurred in Germany. The cornerstone of French foreign policy in the sixteenth and seventeenth centuries was the desire to keep the German states divided. Thus Europe witnessed the paradox of the Catholic king of France supporting the Lutheran princes in their challenge to his fellow Catholic, Charles V. French policy was successful. The long dynastic struggle commonly called the Habsburg-Valois wars advanced the cause of Protestantism and promoted the political fragmentation of the German empire.

Charles's efforts to crush the Lutheran states were unsuccessful. Finally in 1555 he agreed to the Peace of Augsburg, which, in accepting the status quo, officially recognized Protestantism. Each prince was permitted to determine the religion of his territory. Most of northern and central Germany became Lutheran, while the south remained Roman Catholic. There was no freedom of religion, however. Princes or town councils established state churches to which all subjects of the area had to belong. Dissidents, whether Lutheran or Catholic, had to convert or leave. The political difficulties Germany inherited from the Middle Ages had been compounded by the religious crisis of the sixteenth century.

THE GROWTH OF THE PROTESTANT REFORMATION

The printing press publicized Luther's defiance of the Roman church and spread his theological ideas all over Europe. Working people discovered in Luther's ideas the economic theories they wanted to find. Christian humanists believed initially that Luther supported their own educational and intellectual goals. Princes steadily read in Luther's theories an expansion of state power and authority. What began as one man's religious search in a small corner of Germany soon became associated with many groups' interests and aspirations.

By 1555, much of northern Europe had broken with the Roman Catholic church. All of Scandinavia, England, Scotland, and such self-governing cities as Geneva and Zurich in Switzerland and Strasbourg in eastern France had rejected the religious authority of Rome and adopted new faiths. In that a common religious faith had been the one element uniting all of Europe for almost a thousand years, the fragmentation of belief led to profound changes in European life and society. The most significant new form of Protestantism was Calvinism, of which the Peace of Augsburg had made no mention at all.

JOHN CALVIN *The lean, ascetic face with the strong jaw reflects the iron will and determination of the organizer of Protestantism. The fur collar represents his training in law. (Photo: Caroline Buckler)*

CALVINISM

In 1509, while Luther was studying for the doctorate at Wittenberg, John Calvin (1509–1564) was born in Noyon in northwestern France. Luther inadvertently launched the Protestant Reformation. Calvin, however, had the greater impact on future generations. His theological writings profoundly influenced the social thought and attitudes of Europeans and English-speaking peoples all over the world, especially in Canada and the United States. Although he had originally intended to have an ecclesiastical career, Calvin studied law, which had a decisive impact on his mind and later thought. In 1533, he experienced a religious crisis, as a result of which he converted to Protestantism.

Calvin believed that God had delegated him to reform the church. Accordingly, he accepted an invitation to assist in the reformation of the Swiss city of Geneva. There, beginning in 1541, Calvin established a theocracy, which was, according to contemporary theory, a society ruled by God through reformed ministers and civil magistrates. Geneva, "a city that was a Church," became the model of a Christian community for sixteenth-century Protestant reformers.

To understand Calvin's Geneva, it is necessary to understand Calvin's ideas. These he embodied in *The Institutes of the Christian Re-*

ligion, first published in 1536 and definitively issued in 1559. The cornerstone of Calvin's theology was his belief in the absolute sovereignty and omnipotence of God and the total weakness of humanity. Before the infinite power of God, he asserted, men and women are as insignificant as grains of sand:

Our souls are but faint flickerings over against the infinite brilliance which is God. We are created, he is without beginning. We are subject to ignorance and shame. God in his infinite majesty is the summation of all virtues. Whenever we think of him we should be ravished with adoration and astonishment.... The chief end of man is to enjoy the fellowship of God and the chief duty of man is to glorify God.... [13]

Calvin did not grant free will to human beings, because that would detract from the sovereignty of God. Men and women cannot actively work to achieve salvation; rather, God in his infinite wisdom decided at the beginning of time who would be saved and who damned. This viewpoint constitutes the theological principle called predestination:

Predestination we call the eternal decree of God, by which he has determined in himself, what he would have become of every individual of mankind. For they are not all created with a similar destiny; but eternal life is foreordained for some, and eternal damnation for others....

In conformity, therefore, to the clear doctrine of the Scripture, we assert, that by an eternal and immutable counsel, God has once for all determined, both whom he would admit to salvation, and whom he would condemn to destruction. We affirm that this counsel, as far as concerns the elect, is founded on his gratuitous mercy, totally irrespective of human merit; but that to those whom he devotes to condemnation, the gate of life is closed by a just and irreprehensible, but incomprehensible, judgment.

How exceedingly presumptuous it is only to inquire into the causes of the Divine will; which is in fact, and is justly entitled to be, the cause of everything that exists.... For the will of God is the highest justice; so that what he wills must be considered just, for this very reason, because he wills it. [14]

Many people have found this a pessimistic view of the nature of God, who revealed himself in the Old and New Testaments as merciful as well as just. Calvin's response was that although individuals cannot know whether they will be saved — and the probability is that they will be damned — still, good works are a "sign" of election. In any case, people should concentrate on worshiping God and doing his work and not waste time worrying about salvation.

While Luther subordinated the church to the state, Calvin made the state subordinate to the church, and he succeeded in arousing Genevans to a high standard of public and private behavior. For Calvin, God was perpetually active, vigilant, and busy, and he selected certain individuals to do his work. Calvin, convinced that he was one of those individuals, worked tirelessly to transform Geneva into the perfect Christian community. Those who denied predestination were banished.

Austere living, religious instruction for all, public fasting, and evening curfew became the order of the day. Dancing, card playing, fashionable clothes, and heavy drinking were absolutely prohibited. The ministers investigated the private morals of citizens but were unwilling to punish the town prostitutes as severely as Calvin would have preferred.

Calvin reserved his harshest condemnation for religious dissenters. He declared:

If anybody slanders a mortal man he is punished and shall we permit a blasphemer of the living God to go unscathed? If a prince is injured, death appears to be insufficient for vengeance. And now when God, the sovereign Emperor, is reviled by a word, is nothing to be done? God's glory and our salvation are so conjoined that a traitor to God is also an enemy to the human race and worse than a murderer because he brings souls to perdition. Some object that since the offense consists only in words, there is no need for severity. But we muzzle dogs, and shall we leave men free to open their mouths as they please? Those who object are dogs and swine. They murmur that they will go to America where nobody will bother them.

God makes plain that the false prophet is to be stoned without mercy. We are to crush beneath our heel all affections of nature when His honor is concerned. The father should not spare his child, nor brother his brother, nor husband his own wife or the friend who is dearer to him than life. No human relationship is more than animal unless it be grounded in God[15]

Calvin translated his words into action. In the 1550s, the Spanish humanist Michael Servetus had gained international notoriety for his publications denying the Christian dogma of the Trinity, which holds that God is three divine persons, Father, Son, and Holy Spirit. Servetus had been arrested by the Spanish Inquisition, but escaped to Geneva, where he hoped for support. He was promptly rearrested. At his trial he not only held to his belief that there is no scriptural basis for the Trinity but rejected child baptism and insisted that a person under twenty cannot commit a mortal sin. The city fathers considered this last idea dangerous to public morality, "especially in these days when the young are so corrupted." Although Servetus begged that he be punished by banishment, Calvin and the town council maintained that the denial of child baptism and the Trinity amounted to a threat to all society. Whispering "Jesus, Son of the eternal God, have pity on me," Servetus was burned at the stake.

To many sixteenth-century Europeans, Calvin's Geneva seemed "the most perfect school of Christ since the days of the Apostles." Religious refugees from France, England, Spain, Scotland, and Italy poured into the city. Subsequently, Calvin's church served as the model for the Presbyterian church in Scotland, the Huguenot church in France, and Puritan churches in England and New England.

Calvinism became the compelling force in international Protestantism. The Calvinist ethic of the "calling" dignified all work with a religious aspect. Hard work, well done, was pleasing to God. This doctrine encouraged an aggressive, vigorous social activism. In the *Institutes* Calvin provided a systematic theology for Protestantism. The reformed church of Calvin had a strong and well-organized machinery of government. These factors, together with the social and economic applications of Calvin's theology, made Calvinism the most dynamic force in sixteenth- and seventeenth-century Protestantism.

THE ANABAPTISTS

The name *Anabaptist* derives from a Greek word meaning "to baptize again." The Anabaptists, sometimes described as "the left wing of the Reformation," believed that only adults could make a free choice about religious faith, baptism, and entry into the Christian community. Thus they considered the practice of baptizing infants and children preposterous and claimed there was no scriptural basis for it. They wanted to rebaptize believers who had been baptized as children.

Anabaptists took the Gospel and, at first, Luther's teachings absolutely literally and favored a return to the kind of church that had existed among the earliest Christians – a voluntary association of believers who had experienced an inner light.

Anabaptists maintained that only a few people would receive the inner light. This position meant that the Christian community and the Christian state were not identical. In other words, Anabaptists believed in the separation of church and state and in religious tolerance. They almost never tried to force their values on others. In an age that believed in the necessity of state-established churches, Anabaptist views on religious liberty were far ahead of their time.

Each Anabaptist community or church was entirely independent; it selected its own ministers and ran its own affairs. In 1534 the community at Münster in Germany, for example, established a legal code that decreed the death penalty for insubordinate wives. Moreover, the Münster community also practiced polygamy and forced all women under a certain age to marry or face expulsion or execution.

Anabaptist attitudes toward women were sexist and discriminatory, although Anabaptists admitted women to the priesthood. They shared goods as the early Christians had done, refused all public offices, and would not serve in the armed forces. In fact, they laid great stress on pacifism. A favorite Anabaptist scriptural quotation was "By their fruits you shall know them," meaning that if Christianity was a religion of peace, the Christian should not fight. Good deeds were the sign of Christian faith, and to be a Christian meant to imitate the meekness and mercy of Christ. With such beliefs Anabaptists were inevitably a minority. Anabaptism attracted the poor,

the unemployed, the uneducated. Geographically, Anabaptists drew their members from depressed urban areas – from among the followers of Zwingli in Zurich, and from Basel, Augsburg, and Nuremberg.

Ideas such as absolute pacifism and the distinction between the Christian community and the state brought down upon these unfortunate people fanatical hatred and bitter persecution. Zwingli, Luther, Calvin, and Catholics all saw – quite correctly – the separation of church and state as leading ultimately to the complete secularization of society. The powerful rulers of Swiss and German society immediately saw the connection between religious heresy and economic dislocation. Civil authorities feared that the combination of religious differences and economic grievances would lead to civil disturbances. In Saxony, in Strasbourg, and in the Swiss cities, Anabaptists were either banished or cruelly executed by burning, beating, or drowning. Their ideas, however, survived.

Later, the Quakers with their gentle pacifism; the Baptists with their emphasis on an inner spiritual light, the Congregationalists with their democratic church organization; and, in 1789, the authors of the United States Constitution with their concern for the separation of church and state – all these trace their origins in part to the Anabaptists of the sixteenth century.

THE ENGLISH REFORMATION

As on the Continent, the Reformation in England had social and economic causes as well as religious ones. As elsewhere, too, Christian humanists had for decades been calling for the purification of the church. When the political matter of the divorce of King Henry VIII (1509–1547) became enmeshed with other issues, a complete break with Rome resulted.

Demands for ecclesiastical reform dated back to the fourteenth century. The Lollards (pages 409–410) had been driven underground in the fifteenth century, but survived in parts of London, East Anglia, west Kent, and southern England. Working-class people, especially cloth workers, were attracted to their ideas. The Lollards stressed the individual's reading and interpretation of the Bible, which they considered the only standard of Christian faith and holiness. Consequently, they put no stock in the value of the sacraments and were vigorously anticlerical. Lollards opposed ecclesiastical wealth, the veneration of the saints, prayers for the dead, and all war. Although they had no notion of justification by faith, like Luther they insisted upon the individual soul's direct responsibility to God.

The work of the English humanist William Tyndale (ca 1494–1536) stimulated cries for reform. Tyndale visited Luther at Wittenberg in 1524, and a year later at Antwerp he began printing an English translation of the New Testament. From Antwerp merchants carried the New Testament into England, where it was distributed by Lollards. Fortified with copies of Tyndale's English Bible and some of Luther's ideas, the Lollards represented the ideal of "a personal, scriptural, non-sacramental, and lay-dominated religion."[16] Thus, in this manner, doctrines that would later be called Protestant flourished underground in England before any official or state-approved changes.

In the early sixteenth century the ignorance of much of the parish clergy, and the sexual misbehavior of some, compared unfavorably with the education and piety of lay people. In 1510 Dr. William Melton, an official of York Cathedral, exhorted the newly ordained priests of the diocese:

... from this darkness of ignorance ... arises that great and deplorable evil throughout the whole Church of God, that everywhere throughout town and countryside there exists a crop of oafish and boorish priests, some of whom are engaged in ignoble and servile tasks, while others abandon themselves to tavern haunting, swilling and drunkenness. Some cannot get along without their wenches; others pursue their amusement in dice and gambling and other such trifling all day long.... This is inevitable, for since they are completely ignorant of good literature, how can they obtain improvement or enjoyment in reading and study. Nay rather, they throw aside their books in contempt and everywhere they return to the wretched and unlovely life I have mentioned.... We must avoid and keep far from ourselves that grasping, deadly plague of avarice for which practically every priest is accused and held in disrepute before the people, when it is said that we are greedy for rich promotions, or harsh and grasping in retaining and amassing money....[17]

Even more than the ignorance and lechery of the lower clergy, the wealth of the English church fostered resentment and anticlericalism. The church controlled perhaps 20 percent of the land, and also received an annual tithe of the produce of lay people's estates. Since the church had jurisdiction over wills, the clergy also received mortuary fees, revenues paid by the deceased's relatives. Mortuary fees led to frequent lawsuits, since the common lawyers nursed a deep jealousy of the ecclesiastical courts.

The career of Thomas Wolsey (1474?–1530) provides an extreme example of pluralism in the English church in the early sixteenth century. The son of a butcher, Wolsey became a priest and in 1507 secured an

HENRY VIII'S "VICTORY" *This cartoon shows Henry VIII, assisted by Cromwell and Cranmer, triumphing over Pope Clement VII. Although completely removed from the historical facts, such illustrations were effectively used to promote antipapal feeling in late sixteenth-century England. (Photo: Caroline Buckler)*

appointment as chaplain to Henry VII. In 1509 Henry VIII made Wolsey a privy councillor, where his remarkable ability and energy won him rapid advancement. In 1515 he became a cardinal and lord chancellor, and in 1518 papal legate. As chancellor, Wolsey dominated domestic and foreign policy, prosecuted the rich in the royal courts, and attacked the nobility in Parliament. As papal legate he ruled the English church, with final authority in all matters relating to marriage, wills, the clergy, and ecclesiastical appointments. Wolsey had more power than any previous royal minister, and he used that power to amass a large number of church offices, including the archbishopric of York, the rich bishoprics of Winchester and Lincoln, and the abbacy of St. Albans. He displayed the vast wealth these positions brought him with ostentation and arrogance, which in turn fanned the embers of anticlericalism. The divorce of Henry VIII ignited all these glowing coals.

Having fallen in love with Anne Boleyn, sister of his cast-off mistress Mary Boleyn, Henry wanted to divorce his wife Catherine of Aragon. Legal, diplomatic, and theological problems stood in his way, however. Catherine had first been married to Henry's brother Arthur. Contemporaries doubted that Arthur's union with Catherine had been consumated during the short time Arthur lived, and theologians therefore believed that no true marriage existed between them. When Henry married Catherine in 1509, he boasted that she was a virgin. According to custom, and in order to eliminate all doubts and legal technicalities about Catherine's marriage to Arthur, Henry secured a dispensation from Pope Julius II. For eighteen years Catherine and Henry lived together in what contemporaries thought a happy marriage. Catherine produced six children, but only the princess Mary survived childhood.

Precisely when Henry lost interest in his wife as a woman is unknown, but around 1527 he began to quote from a passage in the Old Testament Book of Leviticus: "You must not uncover the nakedness of your brother's wife; for it is your brother's nakedness. . . . The man who takes to wife the wife of his brother: that is impurity; he has uncovered his brother's nakedness, and they shall be childless."[18] Henry insisted that God was denying him a male heir to punish him for marrying his brother's widow. Henry claimed that he wanted to spare England the dangers of a disputed succession. The anarchy and disorders of the Wars of the Roses would surely be repeated if a woman, the princess Mary, inherited the throne. Although Henry contended that the succession was the paramount issue in his mind, his behavior suggests otherwise.

Henry went about the business of insuring a peaceful succession in a most extraordinary manner. He petitioned Pope Clement VII for an annulment of his marriage to Catherine. Henry wanted the pope to declare that a legal marriage with Catherine had never existed, in which case Princess Mary was illegitimate and thus ineligible to succeed to the throne. The pope was an indecisive man whose attention at the time was focused on the Lutheran revolt in Germany and the Habsburg-Valois struggle for control of Italy. Clement delayed acting on Henry's request. The capture and sack of Rome in 1527 by the emperor Charles V, Queen Catherine's nephew, thoroughly tied the pope's hands. Charles could hardly allow the pope to grant the annulment, thereby acknowledging that Charles's aunt, the queen of England, was a loose woman who had lived in sin with Henry VIII.

Accordingly, Henry determined to get his divorce in England. The convenient death of the archbishop of Canterbury allowed Henry to appoint a new archbishop, Thomas Cranmer (1489–1556). Cranmer heard the case in his archiepiscopal court, granted the annulment, and thereby paved the way for Henry's marriage to Anne Boleyn. English public opinion was against this marriage and strongly favored Queen Catherine as a woman much wronged. By rejecting Catherine, Henry ran serious political risks, and all for a woman whom contemporaries found neither very intelligent nor very attractive. The only distinguishing feature they noticed was a sixth finger on her right hand. The marriage between Henry and Anne was publicly announced on May 28, 1533. In September the princess Elizabeth was born.

Since Rome had refused to support Henry's matrimonial plans, he decided to remove the English church from papal jurisdiction. Henry used Parliament to legalize the Reformation in England. The Act in Restraint of Appeals (1533) declared that:

Where, by divers sundry old authentic histories and chronicles, it is manifestly declared and expressed that this realm of England is an empire, and so hath been accepted in the world, governed by one supreme head and king having the dignity and royal estate of the imperial crown of the same (he being also institute and furnished by the goodness and sufferance of Almighty God with plenary, whole, and entire power, pre-eminence, authority, prerogative, and jurisdiction to render and yield justice and final determination to all manner of folk residents or subjects within this his realm, in all causes, matters, debates, and contentions happening to occur, insurge, or begin within the limits thereof, without restraint or provocation to any foreign princes or potentates of the world....).[19]

The act went on to forbid all judicial appeals to the papacy, thus establishing the Crown as the highest legal authority in the land. In effect, the Act in Restraint of Appeals placed sovereign power in the king. The Act for the Submission of the Clergy (1534) required churchmen to submit to the king and forbade the publication of all ecclesiastical laws without royal permission. The Supremacy Act of 1534 declared the king the supreme head of the Church of England.

Englishmen had long criticized ecclesiastical abuses. Sentiment for reform was strong, and a minority of people held distinctly Protestant doctrinal views. Still, it is difficult to gauge the degree of popular support for Henry's break with Rome. Scholars have pointed out that the king had to bribe, threaten, and intimidate the House of Commons to get his legislation passed. Some opposed the king. John Fisher, the bishop of Rochester, a distinguished scholar and humanist who had preached the oration at the funeral of Henry VII, lashed the clergy with scorn for their cowardice. Another humanist, Thomas More, resigned the chancellorship to protest the passage of the Act for the Submission of the Clergy and would not take an oath recognizing Anne's heir. Fisher, More, and other dissenters were beheaded.

When Anne Boleyn failed in her second attempt to produce a male child, Henry VIII charged her with adulterous incest and in 1536 had her beheaded. Parliament promptly proclaimed the princess Elizabeth illegitimate and, with the royal succession thoroughly confused, left the throne to whomever Henry chose. His third wife, Jane Seymour, gave Henry the desired son, Edward, and then died in childbirth. Henry went on to three more wives. Before he passed to his reward in 1547, he got Parliament to reverse the decision of 1536, relegitimating Mary and Elizabeth and fixing the succession first in his son and then in his daughters.

Between 1535 and 1539, under the influence of his chief minister, Thomas Cromwell, Henry decided to dissolve the English monasteries because, he charged, they were economically mismanaged and morally corrupt. Actually, he wanted their wealth. Justices of the peace and other local officials who visited religious houses throughout the land found the contrary. Ignoring their reports, the king ended nine hundred years of English monastic life, dispersed the monks and nuns, and confiscated their lands. Hundreds of properties were later sold to the middle and upper classes and the proceeds spent on war. The dissolution of the monasteries did not achieve a more equitable distribution of land and wealth or advance the cause of social justice. Rather, the "bare ruined choirs where late the

HOLBEIN: SIR THOMAS MORE *This powerful portrait (1527), revealing More's strong character and humane sensitivity, shows Holbein's complete mastery of detail—down to the stubble on More's chin. The chain was an emblem of More's service to Henry VIII. (© The Frick Collection, New York)*

sweet birds sang" – as Shakespeare described the desolate religious houses – testified to the loss of a valuable esthetic and cultural force in English life.

The English Reformation under Henry VIII was primarily a matter of political, social, and economic issues, rather than religious ones. In fact, the Henrician Reformation retained such traditional Catholic practices and doctrines as confession to a priest, clerical celibacy, and transubstantiation (the doctrine of the real presence of Christ in the bread and wine of the Eucharist). On the other hand, Protestant literature circulated, Protestant doctrines captured increasing numbers of people, and Henry approved the selection of men with known Protestant sympathies as tutors for his son. Until late in the century the religious situation remained fluid.

The nationalization of the church and the dissolution of the monasteries led to important changes in governmental administration. Vast tracts of land came temporarily under the Crown's jurisdiction, and new bureaucratic machinery had to be developed to manage those properties. New departments had to be coordinated with old ones. Medieval government had been household government: all branches of the state were associated with the person and personality of the monarch. In finances, for example, no distinction was made between the king's personal income and state revenues. Each branch of government was supported with funds from a specific source; if the source had a bad year, that agency suffered while other branches of government were well in the black. Massive confusion and overlapping of responsibilities existed.

Thomas Cromwell reformed and centralized the king's household, the council, the secretariats, and the Exchequer. New departments of state were set up. Surplus funds from all departments went into a liquid fund to be applied to areas where there were deficits. This balancing resulted in greater efficiency and economy. In Henry VIII's reign can be seen the growth of the modern centralized bureaucratic state.

For several decades after Henry's death in 1547, the English church shifted left and right. In the short reign of Henry's sickly son Edward VI (1547–1553), the strongly Protestant ideas of Archbishop Thomas Cranmer exerted a significant influence on the religious life of the country. Cranmer drastically simplified the liturgy, invited Protestant theologians to England, and prepared the first *Book of Common Prayer* (1549). In stately and dignified English, the *Book of Common Prayer* included, together with the Psalter, the order for all services of the Church of England.

The equally brief reign of Mary Tudor (1553–1558) witnessed a sharp move back to Catholicism. The devoutly Catholic daughter of Catherine of Aragon, Mary rescinded the Reformation legislation of her father's reign and fully restored Roman Catholicism. Mary's marriage to her cousin Philip of Spain, son of the emperor Charles V, proved highly unpopular in England, and her persecution and execution of several hundred Protestants further alienated her subjects. During her reign many Protestants fled to the Continent. Mary's death raised to the throne her sister Elizabeth (1558–1603) and inaugurated the beginnings of religious stability.

For a long time, Elizabeth's position as queen was insecure. Although the populace cheered her accession, many questioned her legitimacy. On the one hand, Catholics wanted a Roman Catholic ruler. On the other hand, a vocal number of returned English exiles wanted all Catholic elements in the Church of England destroyed. The latter, because they wanted to "purify" the church, were called Puritans.

Elizabeth had been raised a Protestant, but if she had genuine religious convictions she kept them to herself. Probably one of the shrewdest politicians in English history, Elizabeth chose a middle course between Catholic and Puritan extremes. She insisted upon dignity in church services and political order in the land. She did not care what people believed as long as they kept quiet about it. Avoiding precise doctrinal definitions, Elizabeth had herself styled "Supreme Governor of the Church of England, Etc.," and left it to her subjects to decide what the "Etc." meant.

The parliamentary legislation of the early years of Elizabeth's reign — laws sometimes labeled the "Elizabethan Settlement" — required outward conformity to the Church of England and uniformity in all ceremonies. Everyone had to attend Church of England services; those who refused were fined. In 1563, a convocation of bishops approved the Thirty-Nine Articles, a summary in thirty-nine short statements of the basic tenets of the Church of England. During Elizabeth's reign, the Anglican church (for the Latin *Ecclesia Anglicana*), as the Church of England was called, moved in a moderately Protestant direction. Services were conducted in English, monasteries were not re-established, and the clergy were allowed to marry. But the bishops remained as church officials, and apart from language, the services were quite traditional.

THE ESTABLISHMENT OF THE CHURCH OF SCOTLAND

Reform of the church in Scotland did not follow the English model. In the early sixteenth century, the church in Scotland presented an extreme case of clerical abuse and corruption, and Lutheranism initially attracted sympathetic support. In Scotland as elsewhere, political authority was the decisive influence in reform. The monarchy was very weak, and factions of virtually independent nobles competed for power. King James V and his daughter Mary, Queen of Scots (1560–1567), staunch Catholics and close allies of Catholic France, opposed reform. The Scottish nobles supported it. One man, John Knox (1505?–1572) dominated the movement for reform in Scotland.

In 1559, Knox, a dour, narrow-minded, and fearless man with a reputation as a passionate preacher, set to work reforming the church. He had studied and worked with Calvin in Geneva, and was determined to structure the Scottish church after the model of Calvin's Geneva. In 1560, Knox persuaded the Scottish parliament, which was dominated by reform-minded barons, to enact legislation ending papal authority. The mass was abolished and attendance at it forbidden under penalty of death. Knox then established the Presbyterian Church of Scotland, so named because presbyters, or ministers — not bishops — governed it. The Church of Scotland was strictly Calvinist in doctrine, adopted a simple and dignified service of worship, and laid great emphasis on preaching. Knox's *Book of Common Order* (1564) became the liturgical directory for the church. The Presbyterian Church of Scotland was a national, or state, church, and many of its members maintained close relations with English Puritans.

PROTESTANTISM IN IRELAND

To the ancient Irish hatred of English political and commercial exploitation, the Reformation added the bitter antagonism of religion. Henry VIII wanted to "reduce that realm to the knowledge of God and obedience to us." English rulers in the sixteenth century regarded the Irish as barbarians, and a policy of complete extermination was rejected only because "to enterprise [attempt] the whole ex-tirpation and total destruction of all the Irishmen in the land would be a marvelous sumptious charge and great difficulty."[20] In other words, it would have cost too much.

In 1536, on orders from London, the Irish parliament, which represented only the English landlords and the people of the Pale (the area around Dublin), approved the English laws severing the church from Rome and making the English king sovereign over ecclesiastical organization and practice. The Church of Ireland was established on the English pattern, and the (English) ruling class adopted the new reformed faith. Most of the Irish, probably for political reasons, defiantly remained Roman Catholic. Monasteries were secularized. Catholic property was confiscated and sold, and the profits shipped to England. With the Roman church driven underground, the Catholic clergy acted as national as well as religious leaders.

LUTHERANISM IN SWEDEN, NORWAY, AND DENMARK

In Sweden, Norway, and Denmark the monarchy took the initiative in the religious reformation. The resulting institutions were Lutheran state churches. Since the late fourteenth century, the Danish kings had ruled Sweden and Norway as well as Denmark. In 1520, the Swedish nobleman Gustavus Vasa led a successful revolt against Denmark, and Sweden became independent. As king, Gustavus Vasa seized church lands and required the bishops' loyalty to the Swedish crown. The Wittenberg-educated Swedish reformer Olaus Petri (1493–1552) translated the New Testament into Swedish and, with the full support of Gustavus Vasa, organized the church along strict Lutheran lines. This consolidation of the Swedish monarchy in the

MAP 14.1 *THE PROTESTANT AND THE CATH-OLIC REFORMATIONS The reformations shattered the religious unity of Western Christendom. What common cultural traits predominated in regions where a particular branch of the Christian faith was maintained or took root?*

sixteenth century was to have a profound effect on Germany in the seventeenth century.

In Denmark, King Christian III (1534–1559) secularized church property and set up a Lutheran church. Norway, which was governed by Denmark until 1814, became Lutheran under Danish influence.

THE CATHOLIC AND THE COUNTER REFORMATIONS

Between 1517 and 1547, the reformed versions of Christianity known as Protestantism made remarkable advances. All of England, Scotland, Scandinavia, half of Germany, and sizable parts of France and Switzerland adopted the creeds of Luther, Calvin, and other reformers. Still, the Roman Catholic church made a significant comeback. After about 1540, no new large areas of Europe, except for the Netherlands, accepted Protestant beliefs (see Map. 14.1).

Historians distinguish between two types of reform within the Catholic church in the sixteenth and seventeenth centuries. The Catholic Reformation began before 1517 and sought renewal basically through the stimulation of a new spiritual fervor. The Counter Reformation started in the 1530s as a reaction to the rise and spread of Protestantism. The Counter Reformation involved Catholic efforts to convince dissidents or heretics to return to the church lest they corrupt the entire community of Catholic believers. Fear of the "infection" of all Christian society by the religious dissident was a standard sixteenth-

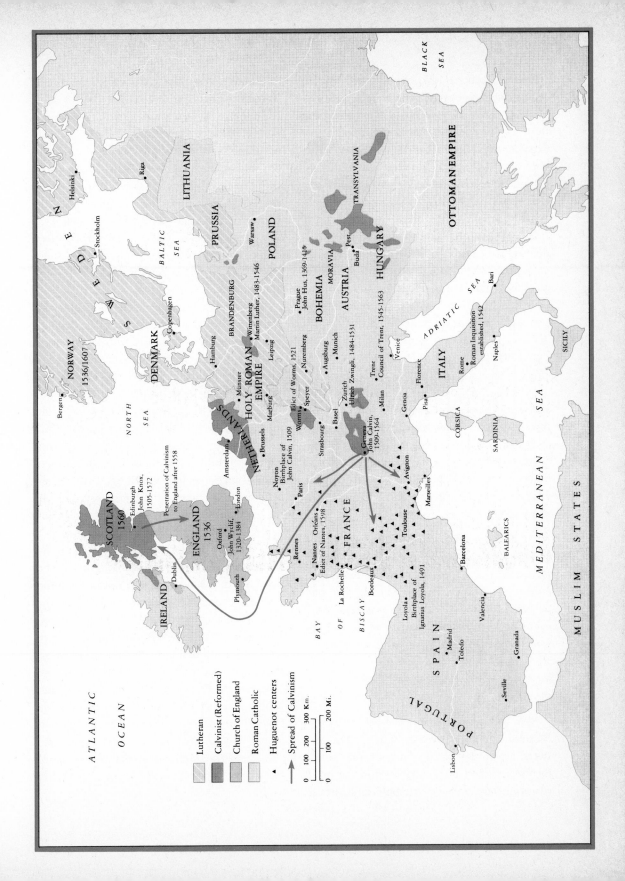

BLACK SEA

OTTOMAN EMPIRE

Riga

Helsinki

LITHUANIA

D E N

Stockholm

BALTIC SEA

PRUSSIA

Warsaw

POLAND

TRANSYLVANIA

NORWAY
1536/1607

Copenhagen

DENMARK

Hamburg

BRANDENBURG

Münster

Leipzig

Wittenberg
Martin Luther, 1483-1546

Nuremberg

Augsburg

Munich

Prague
John Hus, 1369-1415

BOHEMIA

MORAVIA

AUSTRIA

Pest
Buda

HUNGARY

ADRIATIC SEA

Bari

Bergen

NORTH SEA

HOLY ROMAN
EMPIRE

Marburg

Worms

Edict of Worms, 1521

Speyer

Basel

Zurich
Ulrich Zwingli, 1484-1531

Trent
Council of Trent, 1545-1563

Venice

Milan

Genoa

ITALY

Rome

Roman Inquisition
established, 1542

Naples

SICILY

NETHERLANDS

Brussels

Amsterdam

Strasbourg

Geneva
John Calvin,
1509-1564

Florence

Pisa

CORSICA

SARDINIA

ADRIATIC SEA

SCOTLAND
1560

Edinburgh
John Knox,
1505-1572

Penetration of Calvinism
to England after 1558

ENGLAND
1536

Oxford

John Wyclif,
1320-1384

London

Noyon
Birthplace of
John Calvin, 1509

Paris

Avignon

Marseilles

MEDITERRANEAN SEA

IRELAND

Dublin

Plymouth

Rennes

Nantes

Orléans
Edict of Nantes, 1598

FRANCE

Toulouse

Barcelona

BALEARICS

M U S L I M   S T A T E S

BAY

OF

BISCAY

La Rochelle

Bordeaux

Loyola
Birthplace of
Ignatius Loyola, 1491

Valencia

SPAIN

Madrid

Toledo

Granada

PORTUGAL

Seville

Lisbon

ATLANTIC

OCEAN

Lutheran

Calvinist (Reformed)

Church of England

Roman Catholic

◀ Huguenot centers

⬆ Spread of Calvinism

100 200 300 Km.

100   200 Mi.

0

0

century attitude. If the heretic could not be persuaded to reconvert, counter-reformers believed it necessary to call upon temporal authorities to defend Christian society by expelling or eliminating the dissident. The Catholic Reformation and the Counter Reformation were not mutually exclusive; in fact, after about 1540 they progressed simultaneously.

What factors influenced the attitudes and policies of the papacy? Why did church leaders wait so long before dealing with the issues of schism and reform? How did the Catholic church succeed in reforming itself and in stemming the tide of Protestantism?

THE SLOWNESS OF INSTITUTIONAL REFORM

The Renaissance princes who sat on the throne of Saint Peter were not blind to the evils that existed. Modest reform efforts had begun with the Lateran Council called in 1512 by Pope Julius II. The Dutch pope Adrian VI (1522–1523) had instructed his legate in Germany to

say that we frankly confess that God permits this [Lutheran] persecution of his church on account of the sins of men, especially those of the priests and prelates. . . . We know that in this Holy See now for some years there have been many abominations, abuses in spiritual things, excesses in things commanded, in short that all has become perverted. . . . We have all turned aside in our ways, nor was there, for a long time, any who did right – no, not one.[21]

Why did the popes, spiritual leaders of the Western church, move so slowly? The answers lie in the personalities of the popes themselves, their preoccupation with political affairs in Italy, and the awesome difficulty of

reforming so complicated a bureaucracy as the Roman curia.

Pope Leo X (1513–1521), who opened his pontificate with the words "Now that God has given us the papacy, let us enjoy it," typified the attitude of the Renaissance papacy. Leo concerned himself with artistic beauty and sensual pleasures. He first dismissed the Lutheran revolution as "a monkish quarrel," and by the time he finally acted with a letter condemning Luther, much of northern Germany had already rallied around the sincere Augustinian.

Adrian VI tried desperately to reform the church and to check the spread of Protestantism. His reign lasted only thirteen months, however, and the austerity of his life and his Dutch nationality provoked the hostility of pleasure-loving Italian curial bureaucrats.

Clement VII, a true Medicean, was far more interested in elegant tapestries and Michelangelo's painting of the Last Judgment than in theological disputes in barbaric Germany. Indecisive and vacillating, Pope Clement must bear much of the responsibility for the great spread of Protestantism. While Emperor Charles V and the French king Francis I competed for the domination of divided Italy, the papacy worried about the security of the Papal States. Clement tried to follow a middle course, backing first the emperor and then the French ruler. At the battle of Pavia in 1525, Francis I suffered a severe defeat and was captured. In a reshuffling of diplomatic alliances, the pope switched from Charles and the Spaniards to Francis I. The emperor was victorious once again, however, and in 1527 his Spanish and German mercenaries sacked and looted Rome and captured the pope. Obviously, papal concern about Italian affairs and the Papal States diverted attention from reform.

The idea of reform was closely linked to the idea of a general council representing the entire church. Early in the sixteenth century, Ferdinand of Spain appointed a committee of Spanish bishops to draft materials for conciliar reform of the church. In France, the University of Paris also pressed for a council. (French monarchs subsequently used this academic demand to support their military intervention in Italy.) The emperor Charles V, increasingly disturbed by the Lutheran threat, called for "a free Christian council in German lands." German Catholic bishops drew up lists of "oppressive disorders" that needed reform. A strong contingent of countries from beyond the Alps – from Spain, Germany, and France – wanted to reform the vast bureaucracy of Latin officials, reducing offices, men, and revenues.

Popes from Julius II to Clement VII, remembering fifteenth-century conciliar attempts to limit papal authority, resisted calls for a council. The papal bureaucrats who were the popes' intimates warned the popes against a council, fearing loss of power and prestige. Five centuries before, Saint Bernard of Clairvaux had anticipated the situation: "The most grievous danger of any Pope lies in the fact that, encompassed as he is by flatterers, he never hears the truth about his own person and ends by not wishing to hear it."[22]

THE COUNCIL OF TRENT

In the papal conclave that followed the death of Clement VII, Cardinal Alexander Farnese promised two German cardinals that if he were elected pope he would summon a council. He won the election and ruled as Pope Paul III (1534–1549). This Roman aristocrat, humanist, and astrologer, who immediately made his teenage grandsons cardinals, seemed an unlikely person to undertake serious reform. Yet Paul III appointed as cardinals several learned churchmen, such as Caraffa (later Pope Paul IV), established the Inquisition in the Papal States and – true to his word – called a council, which finally met at Trent in northern Italy.

The Council of Trent met intermittently from 1545 to 1563. It was called not only to reform the church but to secure reconciliation with the Protestants. Lutherans and Calvinists were invited to participate, but their insistence that the Scriptures be the sole basis for discussion made reconciliation impossible. Other problems bedeviled all the sessions of the council. International politics repeatedly cast a shadow over the theological debates. Charles V opposed discussions on any matter that might further alienate his Lutheran subjects, fearing the loss of additional imperial territory to Lutheran princes. Meanwhile, the French kings worked against the reconciliation of Roman Catholicism and Lutheranism: as long as religious issues divided the German states, the empire would be weakened, and a weak and divided empire meant a stronger France.

Trent had been selected as the site for the council because of its proximity to Germany. The city's climate, small size, and poor accommodations, the advanced age of many bishops, the difficulties of travel in the sixteenth century, and the refusal of Charles V and Henry II of France to allow their national bishops to attend certain sessions – these factors drastically reduced attendance. Portugal, Poland, Hungary, and Ireland sent representatives, but very few German bishops attended.

Another problem was the persistence of the conciliar theory of church government. Some bishops wanted a concrete statement asserting the supremacy of a church council over the

THE COUNCIL of TRENT

The Representation of the Fathers assembled in the Council of Trent: begun about the end of the year 1545. Concluded towards the end of 1563, under ye Pontificate of Paul III. Iulius III. Marcel II. Paul IV. and Pius IV. There were XXV. Sessions, in which were present VII. Cardinals V. whereof were the Popes Legates. XVI. Ambassadours from Kings, Princes & Republicks. CCL. Patriarchs, Archbishops, Bishops. Abbots and Generals of Orders. All Divines and Doctours of the Civil and Canon Law.

THE COUNCIL OF TRENT This seventeenth-century engraving depicts one of the early and sparsely attended sessions of the Council of Trent. The tridentine sessions of 1562–63 drew many more bishops and laymen, but there were never many representatives from northern Europe. (Photo: Caroline Buckler)

papacy. The adoption of the conciliar principle could have led to a divided church. The bishops had a provincial and national outlook; only the papacy possessed an international perspective. Fortunately, the centralizing tenet was established that all acts of the council required papal approval.

In spite of the obstacles, the achievements of the Council of Trent are impressive. It dealt with both doctrinal and disciplinary matters. The council gave equal validity to the Scriptures and to tradition as sources of religious truth and authority in the church. It reaffirmed the seven sacraments and the traditional Catholic teaching on transubstantiation – the belief in the conversion of the bread and wine used in the Mass into the actual body and blood of Christ. Thus, Lutheran and Calvinist positions were rejected.

The council tackled the problems arising from ancient abuses by strengthening ecclesiastical discipline. Tridentine (from *Tridentum,* the Latin word for Trent) decrees required bishops to reside in their own dioceses, suppressed pluralism and simony, and forbade the sale of indulgences. Clerics who kept concubines were to be warned to give them up and, if they refused, stripped of all ecclesiastical income. The jurisdiction of bishops over all the clergy of their dioceses was made almost absolute, and bishops were ordered to visit every religious house within the diocese at least once every two years. In a highly original canon, the council required every diocese to establish a seminary for the education and training of the clergy; the council even prescribed the curriculum and insisted that preference for admission be given to sons of the poor. Finally, great emphasis was laid on preaching and instructing the laity, especially the uneducated.

The Council of Trent did not meet everyone's expectations. Reconciliation with Protestantism was not achieved, nor was reform brought about immediately. Nevertheless, the Tridentine decrees laid a solid basis for the spiritual renewal of the church and for the enforcement of correction. For four centuries the doctrinal and disciplinary legislation of Trent served as the basis for Roman Catholic faith, organization, and practice.

NEW RELIGIOUS ORDERS

The establishment of new religious orders within the church reveals a central feature of the Catholic Reformation. These new orders developed in response to one crying need: to raise the moral and intellectual level of the clergy. Education was a major goal of them all.

The Ursuline order of nuns founded by Angela Merici (1474-1540) attained enormous prestige for the education of women. The daughter of a country gentleman, Angela Merici worked for many years among the poor, sick, and uneducated around her native Brescia in northern Italy. In 1535 she established the Ursuline order to combat heresy through Christian education. The first religious order concentrating exclusively on teaching young girls, the Ursulines sought to re-Christianize society by training future wives and mothers. Approved as a religious community by Paul III in 1544, the Ursulines rapidly grew and spread to France and the New World. Their schools in North America, stretching from Quebec to New Orleans, provided superior education for young women and inculcated the spiritual ideals of the Catholic Reformation.

The Society of Jesus, founded by Ignatius Loyola (1491-1556), a former Spanish soldier, played a powerful international role in resisting the spread of Protestantism, converting Asians and Latin American Indians to Catholicism, and spreading Christian education all over Europe. While recuperating from a severe battle wound in his legs, Loyola studied a life of Christ and other religious books and decided to give up his military career and become a soldier of Christ. During a year spent in seclusion, prayer, and personal mortification, he gained the religious insights that went into his great classic, *Spiritual Exercises.* This work, intended for study during a four-week period of retreat, directed the individual imagination and will to the reform of life and a new spiritual piety.

Loyola was apparently a man of considerable personal magnetism. After study at the universities in Salamanca and Paris, he gathered a group of six companions and in 1540 secured papal approval of the new Society of Jesus, whose members were called Jesuits. Their goals were the reform of the church primarily through education, preaching the Gospel to pagan peoples, and fighting Protestant heresy. Within a short time, the Jesuits had attracted many recruits.

The Society of Jesus was a highly centralized, tightly knit organization. Candidates underwent a two-year novitiate, in contrast to the usual one-year probation. Although new members took the traditional vows of poverty, chastity, and obedience, the emphasis was on obedience. Carefully selected members made a fourth vow of obedience to the pope and the governing members of the society. As faith was the cornerstone of Luther's life, so obedience became the bedrock of the Jesuit tradition.

The Jesuits had a modern, quasi-military quality; a sort of ecclesiastical Green Berets, they achieved phenomenal success for the papacy and the reformed church. Jesuit schools adopted modern teaching methods, and while they first concentrated on the children of the poor, they were soon educating the sons of the nobility. As confessors and spiritual directors to kings, Jesuits exerted great political influence. Operating on the principle that the end sometimes justifies the means, they were not above spying. Indifferent to physical comfort and personal safety, they carried Christianity to the Moluccan Islands, Ceylon, and Japan before 1550, to Brazil and the Congo in the seventeenth century. Within Europe, the Jesuits brought southern Germany and much of eastern Europe back to Catholicism.

THE SACRED CONGREGATION OF THE HOLY OFFICE

In 1542, Pope Paul III established the Sacred Congregation of the Holy Office with jurisdiction over the Roman Inquisition, which became a powerful instrument of the Counter Reformation. The Inquisition was a committee of six cardinals with judicial authority over all Catholics and with the power to arrest, imprison, and execute. Under the direction of the fanatical Cardinal Caraffa, it vigorously attacked heresy.

The Roman Inquisition operated under the principles of Roman law. It accepted hearsay evidence, was not obliged to inform accused people of the charges against them, and sometimes applied torture. Echoing one of Calvin's remarks about heresy, Cardinal Caraffa wrote, "No man is to lower himself by showing toleration towards any sort of heretic, least of all a Calvinist."[23] The Holy Office published the *Index of Prohibited Books,* a catalog of forbidden reading that included the publications of many printers.

Within the Papal States in central Italy, the Inquisition effectively destroyed heresy (and many heretics). Outside the papal territories, however, its influence was slight. Governments had their own judicial systems for the suppression of treasonable activities, as religious heresy was then considered. The republic of Venice is a good case in point.

In the sixteenth century, Venice was one of the great publishing centers of Europe. The Inquisition and the Index could have badly damaged the Venetian book trade. Authorities there cooperated with the Holy Office only when heresy became a great threat to the security of the republic. The Index had no influence on scholarly research in nonreligious areas, such as law, classical literature, and mathematics. Venetians and Italians, as a result of the Inquisition, were not cut off from the main currents of European learning.[24]

———◆———

The age of the Reformation presents very real paradoxes. The break with Rome and the rise of Lutheran, Anglican, Calvinist, and other faiths destroyed the unity of Europe as an organic Christian society. Saint Paul's exhortation, "There should be no schism in the body [of the church]. . . . You are all one in Christ,"[25] was gradually ignored. On the other hand, religious belief remained tremendously strong. In fact, the strength of religious convictions caused political fragmentation. In the later sixteenth century and through most of the seventeenth, religion and religious issues continued to play a major role in the lives of individuals and in the policies and actions of governments. Religion, whether Protestant or Catholic, decisively influenced the growth of national states.

For almost a thousand years, the church had taught Europeans "to believe in order that you may know." In the seventh through ninth centuries, European peoples had been led in massive numbers to the waters of Christian baptism. The Christian faith and Christian practices, however, meant little to the pagan barbarians of the early Middle Ages.

Many centuries passed before the church had a significantly Christianizing impact on those peoples. Therein lies another paradox. At the moment when literature, sermons, and especially art were expressing the widespread desire for individual and emotional experience within a common spiritual framework, the schism brought confusion, divisiveness, and destruction. The Reformation was, ironically, a tribute to the successful educational work of the medieval church.

Finally, scholars have maintained that the sixteenth century witnessed the beginnings of the modern world. They are both right and wrong. The sixteenth-century revolt from the church paved the way for the eighteenth-century revolt from the Christian God, one of the strongest supports of life in Western culture. In this respect, the Reformation marked the beginning of the modern world, with its secularism and rootlessness. At the same time, it can equally be argued that the sixteenth century represented the culmination of the Middle Ages. Martin Luther's anxieties about salvation show him to be very much a medieval man. His concerns had deeply troubled serious individuals since the time of Saint Augustine. Modern people tend to be less troubled by this issue. The sixteenth century was a definite watershed.

NOTES

1. Romans 12:2–3.

2. Quoted by J. Burckhardt, *The Civilization of the Renaissance in Italy,* Phaidon Books, London, 1951, p. 262.

3. See E. Erickson, *Young Man Luther: A Study in Psychoanalysis and History,* W. W. Norton, New York, 1962, passim.

4. T. C. Mendenhall et al., eds., *Ideas and Institu-*

tions in European History: 800–1715, Henry Holt, New York, 1948, p. 220.

5. Quoted by O. Chadwick, *The Reformation,* Penguin Books, Baltimore, 1976, p. 55.

6. Quoted by E. H. Harbison, *The Age of Reformation,* Cornell University Press, Ithaca, N.Y., 1963, p. 52.

7. I have leaned heavily here on Harbison, pp. 52–55.

8. H. Hillerbrand, *Men and Ideas in the Sixteenth Century,* Rand McNally, Chicago, 1969, p. 28.

9. Romans 13:1–2.

10. Erickson, p. 47.

11. Quoted by J. Atkinson, *Martin Luther and the Birth of Protestantism,* Penguin Books, Baltimore, 1968, pp. 247–248.

12. *Martin Luther: Three Treatises,* Muhlenberg Press, Philadelphia, 1947, pp. 28–31.

13. Quoted by R. Bainton, *The Travail of Religious Liberty,* Harper & Brothers, New York, 1958, p. 65.

14. J. Allen, trans., *John Calvin: The Institutes of the Christian Religion,* Westminster Press, Philadelphia, 1930, book 3, chap. 21, paras. 5, 7.

15. Quoted by Bainton, pp. 69–70.

16. A. G. Dickens, *The English Reformation,* Schocken Books, New York, 1964, p. 36.

17. A. G. Dickens and Dorothy Carr, eds., *The Reformation in England to the Accession of Elizabeth I,* Edward Arnold, London, 1969, pp. 15–16.

18. Leviticus 18:16, 20, 21.

19. C. Stephenson and G. F. Marcham, *Sources of English Constitutional History,* Harper & Row, New York, 1937, p. 304.

20. Quoted by P. Smith, *The Age of the Reformation,* rev. ed., Henry Holt, New York, 1951, p. 346.

21. Ibid., p. 84.

22. Quoted by H. Jedin, *A History of the Council of Trent,* Nelson & Sons, London, 1957, 1.126.

23. Quoted by Chadwick, p. 270.

24. See P. Grendler, *The Roman Inquisition and the Venetian Press,* 1540–1605, Princeton University Press, Princeton, N.J., 1977.

25. I Corinthians 1:25, 27.

SUGGESTED READING

There are many lucidly written and easily accessible studies of the religious reformations of the sixteenth century. O. Chadwick, *The Reformation* (1976); E. H. Harbison, *The Age of Reformation* (1963); R. Bainton, *The Reformation of the Sixteenth Century* (1961); and H. Hillerbrand, *Men and Ideas in the Sixteenth Century* (1969), are all good general introductions. P. Smith's *The Age of the Reformation,* rev. ed. (1951) is an older but comprehensive and often amusing treatment. The recent work of Steven Ozment, *The Age of Reform, 1250–1550: An Intellectual and Religious History of Late Medieval and Reformation Europe* (1980), provides a sophisticated survey of the ideas of the period.

Students who wish to explore aspects of Luther's life and work in greater detail should see, in addition to the titles in the Notes, R. Bainton, *Here I Stand* (1960); J. Atkinson, *Martin Luther and the Birth of Protestantism* (1968); and the sensitively scholarly work of H. Boehmer, *Martin Luther: Road to Reformation* (1960), a well-balanced book by a distinguished Protestant theologian. The perceptive study of H. G. Haile, *Luther: An Experiment in Biography* (1980), focuses on the character of the mature and aging reformer. The pioneering work of Gerald Strauss, *Luther's House of Learning: The Indoctrination of the Young in the German Reformation* (1978), describes how plain people were imbued with Reformation ideas and behavior. The best biography of the central political figure in the period of the German Reformation remains K. Brandi, *Charles V* (1954), while G. Barraclough, *The Origins of Modern Germany* (1952), gives a closet Marxist treatment.

The best introduction to Calvin as a man and theologian is probably the balanced account of F. Wendel, *Calvin: The Origins and Development of His Thought,* trans. P. Mairet (1963). J. T. McNeill, *History and Character of Calvinism* (1954), presents useful and previously inaccessible information. W. E. Monter, *Calvin's Geneva* (1967), is an excellent account of the impact of Calvinism on the social and economic life of that Swiss city. R. T. Kendall,

Calvinism and English Calvinism to 1649 (1981), treats English conditions, while Robert M. Mitchell, *Calvin and the Puritan's View of the Protestant Ethic* (1979), provides a good interpretation of the socioeconomic implications of Calvin's thought. Students interested in the left wing of the Reformation should see the profound work of G. H. Williams, *The Radical Reformers* (1962).

For England, in addition to the fundamental works by Dickens cited in the Notes, see S. T. Bindoff, *Tudor England* (1959), a good short synthesis. The marital trials of Henry VIII are treated in both the sympathetic study of G. Mattingly, *Catherine of Aragon* (1949), and H. A. Kelly, *The Matrimonial Trials of Henry VIII* (1975). A persuasive treatment of Henry VIII's possible syphilis and its effects on his children is given in F. S. Cartwright, *Disease and History* (1972). The legal implications of Henry VIII's divorces have been thoroughly analyzed by J. J. Scarisbrick, *Henry VIII* (1968), an almost definitive biography. On the dissolution of the English monasteries, see D. Knowles, *The Religious Orders in England,* vol. 3 (1959), one of the finest examples of historical prose in English written in the twentieth century. Knowles's *Bare Ruined Choirs* (1976) is an attractively illustrated abridgement of *Religious Orders.* G. R. Elton, *The Tudor Revolution in Government* (1959), discusses the modernization of English government under Thomas Cromwell.

P. Janelle, *The Catholic Reformation* (1951), is a fine comprehensive treatment of the Catholic reformation from a Catholic point of view, and A. G. Dickens, *The Counter Reformation* (1969), gives the Protestant standpoint in a beautifully illustrated book. The definitive study of the Council of Trent was written by H. Jedin, *A History of the Council of Trent,* 3 vols. (1957-1961).

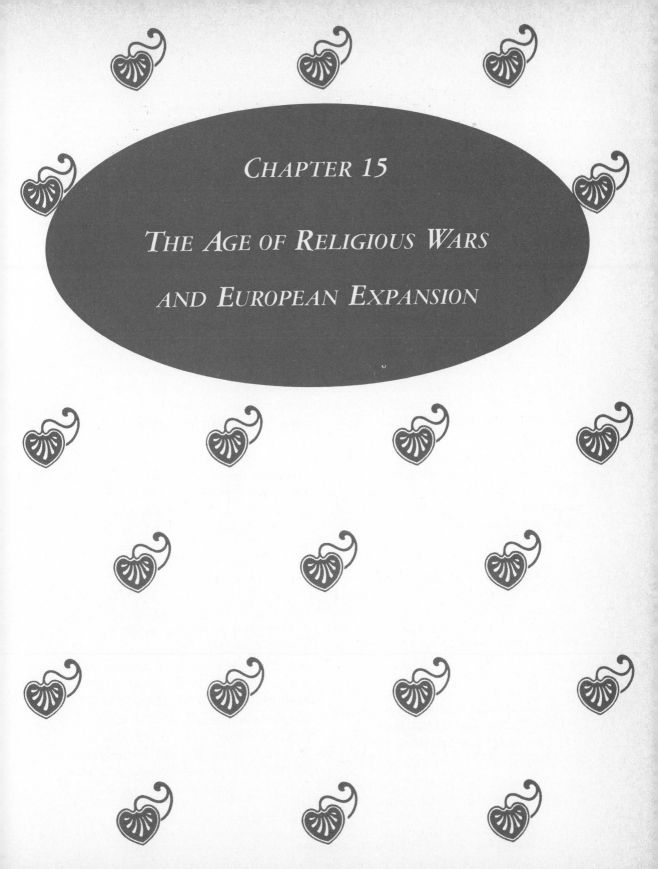

CHAPTER 15

THE AGE OF RELIGIOUS WARS
AND EUROPEAN EXPANSION

THE RENAISSANCE and the reformations of the fifteenth and sixteenth centuries drastically altered intellectual, political, religious, and social life in Europe. But even before Martin Luther initiated the movement to reform the church, European peoples had been involved in overseas activities that had profound consequences for the domestic life of Europe and for the rest of the world. In the middle of the fifteenth century, Europeans began to confront ancient civilizations in Africa, Asia, and the Americas. These confrontations led first to conquest, then to exploitation, and finally to significant changes in both Europe and the conquered territories. European expansion took place amidst domestic and international conflict.

For much of the period 1560-1648, war and religious issues dominated the politics of European states. Wars were fought for power and territorial expansion, although religion was commonly used to rationalize those wars. Meanwhile Europeans carried their political, religious, and social attitudes to the new continents they subdued. This chapter seeks to explore the following questions. Why, in the sixteenth and seventeenth centuries, did European peoples expand overseas? How were a relatively small number of people living on the edge of the Eurasian landmass able to gain control of the major sea-lanes of the world and establish economic and political hegemony on distant continents far from home? What effect did overseas expansion have on Europe and on conquered societies?

DISCOVERY, RECONNAISSANCE, AND EXPANSION

Historians have variously called the period 1450-1650 "The Age of Discovery," "The

WORLD MAP OF VESCONTE MAGGIOLI, 1511 Renaissance geographers still accepted the Greco-Egyptian Ptolemy's theory (second century A.D.) that the earth was one continuous land mass. Cartographers could not subscribe to the idea of a new, separate continent. Thus, this map, inaccurate when it was drawn, shows America as an extension of Asia. (John Carter Brown Library, Brown University, Providence)

Age of Reconnaissance," and "The Age of Expansion." All three labels are appropriate. "The Age of Discovery" refers to the era's phenomenal advances in geographical knowledge and in technology, often achieved through trial and error. In 1350, it took as long to sail from the eastern end of the Mediterranean to the western end as it had taken a thousand years earlier, in 350. Even in the fifteenth century, Europeans knew little more about the earth's surface than the Romans had known. By 1650, however, Europeans had made an extensive reconnaissance – or preliminary exploration – and had sketched fairly accurately the physical outline of the whole earth. Much of the geographical information they had gathered was tentative and not fully understood – hence the appropriateness of the term "The Age of Reconnaissance."

The designation of the era as "The Age of Expansion" refers to the migration of Europeans to other parts of the world. This colonization resulted in political control of much of South America and North America, coastal regions of Africa, India, China, Japan, and many Pacific islands. Political hegemony was accompanied by economic exploitation, religious domination, and the introduction of European patterns of social and intellectual life. The sixteenth-century expansion of European society launched a new age in world history.

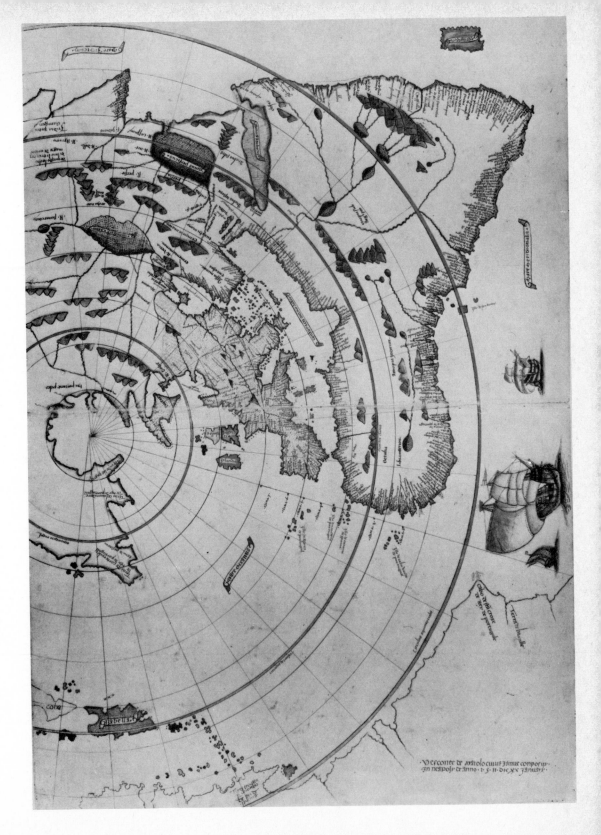

The outward expansion of Europe began with the Viking voyages across the Atlantic in the tenth and eleventh centuries. Under Eric the Red and Leif Ericson, the Vikings discovered Greenland and the eastern coast of North America. They may even have traveled down the New England coast as far south as Boston. The Crusades of the eleventh through thirteenth centuries were another phase in Europe's attempt to explore, Christianize, and exploit territories and peoples on the periphery of the Continent. But these early thrusts outward resulted in no permanent settlements. The Vikings made only quick raids in search of booty. Lacking stable political institutions in Scandinavia, they had no workable forms of government to impose on distant continents. In the twelfth and thirteenth centuries, the lack of a strong territorial base, weak support from the West, and sheer misrule combined to make the medieval Crusader kingdoms short-lived. Even in the mid-fifteenth century, Europe seemed ill-prepared for international ventures. By 1450, a grave new threat had appeared in the East — the Ottoman Turks.

Combining excellent military strategy with efficient administration of their conquered territories, the Turks had subdued most of Asia Minor and begun to settle on the Western side of the Bosporus. The Ottoman Turks under Sultan Mohammed II (1451–1481) captured Constantinople in 1453, pressed southwest into the Balkans, and by the early sixteenth century controlled the eastern Mediterranean. The Turkish menace badly frightened Europeans. In France in the fifteenth and sixteenth centuries, twice as many books were printed about the Turkish threat as about the American discoveries. The Turks imposed a military blockade on eastern Europe, thus forcing Europeans' attention westward. Yet the fifteenth and sixteenth centuries witnessed a fantastic continuation, on a global scale, of European expansion: great discoveries led to overseas empires.

Political centralization in Spain, France, and England helps to explain those countries' outward push. In the fifteenth century, Isabella and Ferdinand had consolidated their several kingdoms to achieve a united Spain. The Catholic rulers slashed the powers of the nobility, revamped the Spanish bureaucracy, and humbled dissident elements, notably the Muslims and the Jews. The Spanish monarchy was stronger than ever before, and in a position to support foreign ventures; it could bear the costs and dangers of exploration. But Portugal, situated on the extreme southwestern edge of the European continent, got the start on the rest of Europe.

Portugal's taking of Ceuta, an Arab city in northern Morocco, in 1415 marked the beginning of European exploration and control of overseas territory. The objectives of Portuguese policy included the historic Iberian crusade to Christianize Muslims, and the search for gold, for an overseas route to the spice markets of India, and for the mythical Christian ruler of Ethiopia, Prester John.

In the early phases of Portuguese exploration, Prince Henry (1394–1460), called "the Navigator" because of the annual expeditions he sent down the western coast of Africa, played the leading role. In the fifteenth century, most of the gold that reached Europe came from the Sudan in West Africa and from Ashanti blacks living near the gold coast. Muslim caravans brought the gold from the African cities of Niani and Timbuktu and carried it north across the Sahara to Mediterranean ports. Then the Portuguese muscled in on this commerce in gold. Prince Henry's carefully planned expeditions succeeded in reaching Guinea, and under King John II (1481–1495), the Portuguese established trading posts and forts on the Guinea coast and penetrated into the continent all the way to Timbuktu (see Map 15.1). Portuguese ships transported gold to Lisbon, and by 1500 Portugal controlled the flow of gold to Europe. The golden century of Portuguese prosperity had begun.

Still the Portuguese pushed farther south down the west coast of Africa. In 1487, Bartholomew Diaz rounded the Cape of Good Hope at the southern tip, but storms and a threatened mutiny forced him to turn back. On a second expedition (1497–1499), the Portuguese mariner Vasco da Gama reached India and returned to Lisbon loaded with samples of Indian wares (see Map 15.1). King Manuel (1495–1521) promptly dispatched thirteen ships under the command of Pedro Alvares Cabral, assisted by Diaz, to set up trading posts in India. On April 22, 1500, the coast of Brazil in South America was sighted and claimed for the crown of Portugal. Cabral then proceeded south and east around the Cape of Good Hope and reached India. Half the fleet was lost on the return voyage, but the six spice-laden vessels that dropped anchor in Lisbon harbor in July 1501 more than paid for the entire expedition. Thereafter, convoys were sent out every March. Lisbon became the entrance port for Asian goods into Europe — but not without a fight.

For centuries the Muslims had controlled the rich spice trade of the Indian Ocean, and they did not surrender it willingly. Portuguese commercial activities were accompanied by the destruction or seizure of strategic Muslim coastal forts, which later served Portugal as both trading posts and military bases.

Alfonso de Albuquerque, whom the Portuguese crown appointed as governor of India (1509–1515), decided that these bases and not inland territories should control the Indian Ocean. Accordingly, his cannon blasted open the ports of Calicut, Ormuz, Goa, and Malacca, the vital centers of Arab domination of south Asian trade. This bombardment laid the foundation for Portuguese imperialism in the sixteenth and seventeenth centuries: a strange way to bring Christianity to "those who were in darkness." As one scholar wrote about the opening of China to the West, "while Buddha came to China on white elephants, Christ was borne on cannon balls."[1]

In March 1493, between the first and second voyages of Vasco da Gama, Spanish ships entered Lisbon harbor bearing a triumphant Italian explorer in the service of the Spanish monarchy. Christopher Columbus (1451–1506), a Genose mariner, had secured Spanish support for an expedition to the East. He sailed from Palos, Spain, to the Canary Islands and crossed the Atlantic to the Bahamas, landing in October 1492 on an island that he named San Salvador and believed to be the coast of India.

Columbus explained the motives for his expedition in the journal of his voyage, entitled *Book of the First Navigation and Discovery of the Indies:*

And Your Highnesses, as Catholic Christians and Princes devoted to the Holy Christian Faith and the propagators thereof, and enemies of the sect of Mahomet and of all idolatries and heresies, resolved to send me Christopher Columbus to the said regions of India, to see the said princes and peoples and lands and [to observe] the disposition of them and of all, and the manner in which may be undertaken their conversion to our Holy Faith, and ordained that I should not go by land (the usual

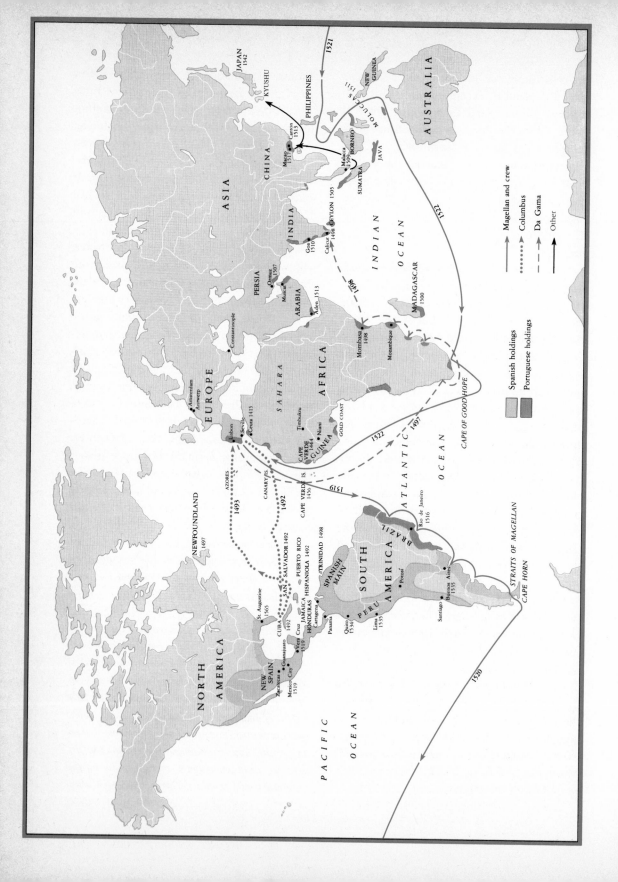

MAP 15.1 OVERSEAS EXPLORATION AND CON-
QUEST, FIFTEENTH AND SIXTEENTH CEN-
TURIES *The voyages of discovery marked another
phase in the centuries-old migrations of European
peoples. Consider the major contemporary significance
of each of the three voyages depicted on the map.*

*way) to the Orient, but by the route of the Oc-
cident, by which no one to this day knows for sure
that anyone has gone.*[2]

Like most people of his day, Christopher Columbus was a deeply religious man. The crew
of his flagship, *Santa Maria,* recited vespers
every night and sang a hymn to the Virgin,
the "Salve Regina," before going to bed.
Nevertheless, the Spanish fleet, sailing westward to find the East, sought wealth as well as
souls to convert to Christianity.

Between 1492 and 1502, Columbus made
four voyages to America, discovering all the
major islands of the Caribbean – Haiti
(which he called Dominica and the Spanish
named Hispaniola), San Salvador, Puerto
Rico, Jamaica, Cuba, Trinidad – and Hon-
duras in Central America. Columbus believed
until he died that the islands he found were
off the coast of India. In fact, he had opened
up for the rulers of Spain a whole new world.
The Caribbean islands – the West Indies –
represented to Spanish missionary zeal millions of Indian natives for conversion to
Christianity. Hispaniola, Cuba, and Puerto
Rico also offered gold.

Forced labor, disease, and starvation in the
Spaniards' gold mines rapidly killed off the
Indians of Hispaniola. When Columbus arrived in 1493, the population had been approximately 100,000; in 1570, 300 people
survived. Indian slaves from the Bahamas and
black Africans from Guinea were then imported to do the mining.

The search for precious metals determined

the direction of Spanish exploration and expansion into South America. When it became
apparent that placer mining in the Caribbean
islands was slow and the rewards slim, new
routes to the East and new sources of gold
and silver were sought.

In 1519, the Spanish ruler Charles V commissioned Ferdinand Magellan (1480-1521)
to find a direct route to the Moluccan Islands
off the southeast coast of Asia. Magellan sailed
southwest across the Atlantic to Brazil, and
proceeded south around Cape Horn into the
Pacific Ocean (see Map 15.1). He crossed the
Pacific, sailing west, to the Malay Archipel-
ago, which he called the Western Isles. (These
islands were conquered in the 1560s and
named the Philippines for Philip II of Spain.)

Although Magellan was killed, the expedition continued, returning to Spain in 1522
from the east by way of the Indian Ocean, the
Cape of Good Hope, and the Atlantic. Terrible storms, mutiny, starvation, and disease
haunted this voyage. Nevertheless, it verified
Columbus's theory that the earth was round
and brought information about the vastness
of the Pacific. Magellan also proved that the
earth was much larger than Columbus and
others had believed.

In the West Indies, the slow recovery of
gold, the shortage of a healthy labor force,
and sheer restlessness speeded up Spain's
search for wealth. In 1519, the year Magellan
departed on his worldwide expedition, a brash
and determined Spanish adventurer Hernando
Cortez (1485-1547), crossed from Hispaniola
to mainland Mexico with six hundred men,
seventeen horses, and ten canon. Within three
years, Cortez had conquered the fabulously
rich Aztec empire, taken captive the Aztec
emperor Montezuma, and founded Mexico
City as the capital of New Spain. The subjugation of northern Mexico took longer, but
between 1531 and 1550 the Spanish gained

COLUMBUS LANDS ON SAN SALVADOR *The printed page and illustrations, such as this German woodcut, spread reports of Columbus's voyage all over Europe. According to Columbus, a group of naked Indians greeted the Spaniards' arrival. Pictures of the Indians as "primitive" and "uncivilized" instilled prejudices which centuries have not erased. (Photo: Caroline Buckler)*

control of Zacatecas and Guanajuato, where rich silver veins were soon tapped.

Another Spanish conquistador, Francisco Pizzaro (1470–1541), repeated Cortez's feat in Peru. Between 1531 and 1536, with even fewer resources, Pizzaro crushed the Inca empire in northern South America and established the Spanish viceroyalty of Peru with its center at Lima. In 1545, Pizzaro opened at Potosí in the Peruvian highlands what became the richest silver mines in the New World.

Between 1525 and 1575, the riches of the Americas poured into the Spanish port of Seville and the Portuguese capital of Lisbon. For all their new wealth, however, Lisbon and Seville did not become important trading centers. It was the Flemish city of Antwerp, although controlled by the Spanish Habsburgs, that developed into the great entrepôt for overseas bullion and Portuguese spices and served as the commercial and financial capital of the entire European world.

Since the time of the great medieval fairs, cities of the Low Countries – so called because much of the land lies below sea level – had been important sites for the exchange of products from the Baltic and Italy. Antwerp, ideally situated on the Scheldt River at the intersection of many trading routes, steadily expanded as the chief intermediary for international commerce and finance. English woolens, Baltic wheat, fur, and timber, Portuguese spices, German iron and copper, Spanish fruit, French wines and dyestuffs, Italian silks, marbles, and mirrors, together with vast amounts of cash, were exchanged at Antwerp. The city's harbor could dock 2,500 vessels at once, and 5,000 merchants from many nations gathered daily in the bourse (or exchange). Spanish silver was drained to the Netherlands to pay for food and luxury goods. Even so, the desire for complete economic independence from Spain was to play a major role in the Netherlands' revolt in the late sixteenth century.

By the end of the century, Amsterdam had overtaken Antwerp as the financial capital of Europe. The Dutch had also embarked on foreign exploration and conquest. The Dutch East India Company, founded in 1602, became the major organ of Dutch imperialism and within a few decades expelled the Portuguese from Ceylon and other East Indian islands. By 1650, the Dutch West India Company had successfully horned in on the Spanish possessions in America and gained control of much of the African and American trade.

English and French explorations lacked the immediate and sensational results of the Spanish and Portuguese. In 1497 John Cabot, a Genoese merchant living in London, sailed for Brazil but discovered Newfoundland. The next year he returned and explored the New England coast and perhaps as far south as Delaware. Since these expeditions found no spices or gold, the English king Henry VII lost interest in exploration. Between 1534 and 1541, the Frenchman Jacques Cartier made several voyages and explored the St. Lawrence region of Canada, but the first permanent French settlement, at Quebec, was not founded until 1608.

COLONIAL ADMINISTRATION

Columbus, Cortez, and Pizzaro claimed the lands they had "discovered" for the crown of Spain. How were they to be governed? According to the Spanish theory of absolutism, the Crown was entitled to exercise full authority over all imperial lands. In the sixteenth century the Crown divided its New World territories into four viceroyalties or administrative divisions: New Spain, which consisted of Mexico, Central America, and present-day California, Arizona, New Mexico, and Texas, with the capital at Mexico City; Peru, originally all the lands in continental South America, later reduced to the territory of modern Peru, Chile, Bolivia, and Equador, with the viceregal seat at Lima; New Granada, including present-day Venezuela, Colombia, Panama, and after 1739 Ecuador, with Bogata as its administrative center; and La Plata, consisting of Argentina, Uruguay, and Paraguay,

with Buenos Aires as the capital. Within each territory, the viceroy or imperial governor exercised broad military and civil authority as the direct representative of the sovereign in Madrid. The viceroy presided over the *audiencia,* a board of twelve to fifteen judges, which served as his advisory council and the highest judicial body. The enlightened Spanish king Charles III (1716–1788) introduced the system of intendants. These royal officials possessed broad military, administrative, and financial authority within their intendancy, and were responsible not to the viceroy but to the Crown in Madrid.

From the early sixteenth century to the beginning of the nineteenth, the Spanish monarchy acted on the mercantilist principle that the colonies existed for the financial benefit of the mother country. The mining of gold and silver was always the most important industry in the colonies. The Crown claimed the *quinto,* one-fifth of all precious metals mined in South America. Gold and silver yielded the Spanish monarchy 25 percent of its total income. In return, it shipped manufactured goods to America and discouraged the development of native industries.

The Portuguese governed their colony of Brazil in a similar manner. After the union of the crowns of Portugal and Spain in 1580, Spanish administrative forms were introduced. Local officials called *corregidores* held judicial and military powers. Mercantilist policies placed severe restrictions on Brazilian industries that might compete with those of Portugal. In the seventeenth century the use of black slave labor made possible the cultivation of coffee and cotton, and in the eighteenth century Brazil led the world in the production of sugar. The unique feature of colonial Brazil's culture and society was its thoroughgoing intermixture of Indians, whites, and blacks.

THE ECONOMIC EFFECTS OF SPAIN'S DISCOVERIES IN THE NEW WORLD

The sixteenth century has often been called the golden century of Spain. The influence of Spanish armies, Spanish Catholicism, and Spanish wealth was felt all over Europe. This greatness rested largely upon the influx of precious metals from the New World.

The mines at Zacatecas and Guanajuato in Mexico and Potosí in Peru poured out huge quantities of precious metals. To protect this treasure from French and English pirates, armed convoys transported it each year to Spain. Between 1503 and 1650, 16 million kilograms of silver and 185,000 kilograms of gold entered the port of Seville. Scholars have long debated the impact of all this bullion on the economies of Spain and Europe as a whole. Spanish predominance, however, proved temporary.

In the sixteenth century, Spain experienced a steady population increase, creating a sharp rise in the demand for food and goods. Spanish colonies in the Americas also represented a demand for products – olive oil, wine, wool, steel cutlery, and a variety of luxury goods. Since Spain had expelled some of the best farmers and businessmen, the Muslims and the conversos, in the fifteenth century, the Spanish economy was already suffering and could not meet the new demands. Prices rose. Because the costs of manufacturing cloth and other goods increased, Spanish products could not compete in the international market with cheaper products made elsewhere. The textile industry was badly hurt. Prices spiraled upward, faster than the government could levy taxes to dampen the economy. (Higher taxes would have cut the public's buying power; with fewer goods sold, prices would have come down.)

Several times between 1557 and 1647, Philip II and his successors were forced to repudiate the state debt, which in turn undermined confidence in the government. The enormous flow of silver and gold from the Americas thus contributed to the destruction of Spanish agriculture and industry. When the flow declined in the seventeenth century, the economy was in a shambles.

As Philip II paid his armies and foreign debts with silver bullion, the Spanish inflation was transmitted to the rest of Europe. Between 1560 and 1600, much of Europe experienced large price increases. Prices doubled and in some cases quadrupled. Spain suffered most severely, but all European countries were affected. People who lived on fixed incomes, such as the continental nobles, were badly hurt because their money bought less. Those who owed fixed sums of money, such as the middle class, prospered: in a time of rising prices, debts had less value each year. Food costs rose most sharply, and the poor fared worst of all.

TECHNOLOGICAL STIMULI TO EXPLORATION

Technological developments were the key to Europe's remarkable outreach. By 1350, cannon – iron or bronze guns that fired iron or stone balls – had been fully developed in western Europe. These pieces of artillery emitted frightening noises and great flashes of fire and could batter down fortresses and even city walls. Sultan Mohammed II's siege of Constantinople in 1453 provides a classic illustration of the effectiveness of cannon fire.

Constantinople had the strongest walled fortifications in the West. The sultan secured the services of a Western technician who built fifty-six small cannon and a gigantic gun that could hurl stone balls weighing about eight hundred pounds. The gun could be moved only by several hundred oxen, and loaded and fired only by about a hundred men working together. Reloading took two hours. This awkward but powerful weapon breached the walls of Constantinople before it cracked on the second day of the bombardment. Lesser cannon finished the job.

Early cannon posed serious technical difficulties. Iron cannon were cheaper than bronze to construct, but they were difficult to cast effectively and were liable to crack and injure the artillerymen. Bronze guns, made of copper and tin, were less subject than iron to corrosion, but they were very expensive. All cannon were extraordinarily difficult to move, required considerable time for reloading, and were highly inaccurate. They thus proved inefficient for land warfare. However, they could be used at sea.

The mounting of cannon on ships and improved techniques of shipbuilding gave impetus to European expansion.[3] Since ancient times, most seagoing vessels had been narrow open boats called galleys, propelled by manpower. Slaves or convicts who had been sentenced to the galleys manned the oars of the ships that sailed the Mediterranean, and both cargo and warships carried soldiers for defense. Although well suited to the placid and thoroughly explored waters of the Mediterranean, galleys could not withstand the rough winds and uncharted shoals of the Atlantic. The need for sturdier craft, as well as population losses caused by the Black Death, forced the development of a new style of ship that would not require soldiers for defense.

In the course of the fifteenth century, the Portuguese developed the caravel, a small, light, three-masted sailing ship. Although somewhat slower than the galley, the caravel held more cargo and was highly maneuverable. When fitted with cannon, it could dominate larger vessels, such as the round ships commonly used as merchantmen. The substitution of windpower for manpower, and artillery fire for soldiers, signaled a great technological advance and gave Europeans navigational and fighting ascendancy over the rest of the world.[4]

Other fifteenth-century developments in navigation helped make possible the conquest of the Atlantic. The magnetic compass enabled sailors to determine their direction and position at sea. The astrolabe, an instrument used to determine the altitude of the sun and other celestial bodies, permitted mariners to plot their latitude, or position north or south of the equator. Steadily improved maps and sea charts provided information about distance, sea depths, and general geography.

THE EXPLORERS' MOTIVES

The expansion of Europe was not motivated by demographic pressures. The Black Death had caused serious population losses from which Europe had not recovered in 1500. Few Europeans emigrated to North or South America in the sixteenth century. Half of those who did sail to begin a new life in America died en route; half of those who reached the New World eventually returned to their homeland. Why, then, did explorers brave the Atlantic and Pacific oceans, risking their lives to discover new continents and spread European culture?

The reasons are varied and complex. People of the sixteenth century were still basically medieval, in the sense that their attitudes and values were shaped by religion and expressed in religious terms. In the late fifteenth century, crusading fervor remained a basic part of the Portuguese and Spanish national ideal. The desire to Christianize Muslims and pagan peoples played a central role in European expansion. Queen Isabella of Spain, for example, showed a fanatical zeal for converting the Muslims to Christianity, but she concentrated her efforts on the Arabs in Granada. After the abortive crusading attempts of the thirteenth century, Isabella and other rulers realized full well that they lacked the material resources to mount the full-scale assault on Islam necessary for victory. Crusading impulses thus shifted from the Muslims to the pagan peoples of Africa and the Americas.

Government sponsorship and encouragement of exploration also help to account for the results of the various voyages. Mariners and explorers could not afford, as private individuals, the massive sums needed to explore mysterious oceans and to control remote continents. The strong financial support of Prince Henry the Navigator led to Portugal's phenomenal success in the spice trade. Even the grudging and modest assistance of Isabella and Ferdinand eventually brought untold riches – and complicated problems – to Spain. The Dutch in the seventeenth century, through such government-sponsored trading companies as the Dutch East India Company, reaped enormous wealth, and although the Netherlands was a small country in size, it dominated the European economy in 1650. In England, by contrast, Henry VII's lack of interest in exploration delayed English expansion for a century.

Scholars have frequently described the European discoveries as a manifestation of Renaissance curiosity about the physical universe, the desire to know more about the geography and peoples of the world. There is truth to this explanation. Cosmography, natural history, and geography aroused enormous interest among educated people in the fifteenth and sixteenth centuries. Just as science fiction and speculation about life on other planets excite readers today, quasi-scientific literature about Africa, Asia, and the Americas captured the imaginations of literate Europeans. Oviedo's *General History of the Indies,* a detailed eyewitness account of plants, animals, and peoples, was widely read.

Spices were another important incentive to undertake voyages of discovery. Introduced into western Europe by the Crusaders in the twelfth century, nutmeg, mace, ginger, cinnamon, and pepper added flavor and variety to the monotonous diet of Europeans. Spices were also used in the preparation of medicinal drugs and in the manufacture of incense for religious ceremonies. In the late thirteenth century, the Venetian Marco Polo (1254?–1324?), the greatest of the medieval travelers, had visited the court of the Chinese emperor. The widely publicized account of his travels in the *Book of Various Experiences* stimulated a rich trade in spices between Asia and Italy. The Venetians came to hold a monopoly of the spice trade in western Europe.

Spices were grown in India and China, shipped across the Indian Ocean to ports on the Persian Gulf, and then transported by Arabs across the Arabian Desert to Mediterranean ports. But the rise of the Ming dynasty in China in the late fourteenth century resulted in the expulsion of foreigners. And the steady penetration of the Ottoman Turks into the eastern Mediterranean and of hostile Muslims across North Africa forced Europeans to seek a new route to the Asian spice markets.

The basic reason for European exploration and expansion, however, was the quest for material profit. Mariners and explorers frankly admitted this. As Bartholomew Diaz put it, his motives were "to serve God and His Majesty, to give light to those who were in darkness and to grow rich as all men desire to do." When Vasco da Gama reached the port of Calicut, India, in 1498, a native asked what the Portuguese wanted. Da Gama replied, "Christians and spices."[5] The bluntest of the Spanish conquistadors, Hernando Cortez, announced as he prepared to conquer Mexico, "I have come to win gold, not to plow the fields like a peasant."[6]

Spanish and Portuguese explorers carried the fervent Catholicism and missionary zeal of the Iberian Peninsula to the New World, and once in America they urged home governments to send clerics "to bring light to those who were in darkness." At bottom, however, wealth was the driving motivation. A sixteenth-century diplomat, Ogier Gheselin de Busbecq, summed up this paradoxical attitude well: in expeditions to the Indies and the Antipodes, he said, "religion supplies the pretext and gold the motive."[7] The mariners, explorers, and conquistadors were religious and "medieval" in justifying their actions, materialistic and "modern" in their behavior.

POLITICS, RELIGION, AND WAR

In 1559, France and Spain signed the Treaty of Cateau-Cambrésis, which ended the long conflict known as the Habsburg-Valois wars. This event marks a decisive watershed in early modern European history. Spain was the victor. France, exhausted by the struggle, had to acknowledge Spanish dominance in Italy, where much of the war had been fought. Spanish governors ruled in Sicily, Naples, and Milan, and Spanish influence was strong in the Papal States and Tuscany.

The emperor Charles V had divided his attention between the Holy Roman Empire and Spain. Under his son Philip II (1556–1598), however, the center of the Habsburg empire and the political center of gravity for all of Europe shifted westward to Spain. Before 1559, Spain and France had fought bitterly for control of Italy; after 1559, the two Catholic powers aimed their guns at Protestantism. The Treaty of Cateau-Cambrésis ended an era of dynastic wars and initiated a period of conflicts in which religion played a dominant role.

Because a variety of issues were stewing, it is not easy to generalize about the wars of the late sixteenth century. Some were continuations of struggles between the centralizing goals of monarchies and the feudal reactions of nobilities. Some were crusading battles between Catholics and Protestants. Some were struggles for national independence or for international expansion.

These wars differed considerably from earlier wars. Sixteenth- and seventeenth-century armies were bigger than medieval ones; some forces numbered as many as fifty thousand men. Because large armies were expensive, governments had to reorganize their administrations to finance them. The use of gunpowder altered both the nature of war and popular attitudes toward it. Guns and cannon killed and wounded from a distance, indiscriminately. Writers scorned gunpowder as a coward's weapon that allowed a common soldier to kill a gentleman. The Italian poet Ariosto lamented:

Through thee is martial glory lost, through
Thee the trade of arms becomes a worthless art:
And at such ebb are worth and chivalry that
The base often plays the better part.[8]

Gunpowder destroyed the notion, common during the Hundred Years' War, that warfare was an ennobling experience. Governments had to utilize propaganda, pulpits, and the printing press to arouse public opinion to support war.[9]

Late-sixteenth-century conflicts fundamentally tested the medieval ideal of a unified Christian society governed by one political ruler, the emperor, to whom all rulers were theoretically subordinate, and one church, to which all people belonged. The Protestant Reformation had killed this ideal, but few people recognized it as dead. Catholics continued to believe that Calvinists and Lutherans could be reconverted; Protestants persisted in thinking that the Roman church should be destroyed. Catholics and Protestants alike feared people of the other faith living in their midst. The settlement finally achieved in 1648, known as the Peace of Westphalia, signaled the end of the medieval ideal.

THE ORIGINS OF DIFFICULTIES IN FRANCE (1515–1559)

In the first half of the sixteenth century, France continued the recovery begun under Louis XI (page 457). The population losses caused by the plague and the disorders accompanying the Hundred Years' War had created such a labor shortage that serfdom virtually disappeared. Cash rents replaced feudal rents and servile obligations. This development clearly benefited the peasantry. Meanwhile, the declining buying power of money hurt the nobility. The steadily increasing French population brought new lands under cultivation, but the division of property among sons meant that most peasant holdings were very small. Domestic and foreign trade picked up; mercantile centers such as Rouen and Lyons expanded; and in 1517 a new port city was founded at Le Havre.

ROSSO AND PRIMATICCIO: THE GALLERY OF FRANCES I *Flat paintings alternating with rich sculpture provide a rhythm that directs the eye down the long gallery at Fontainebleau, the construction of which occupied much of Francis I's attention from 1530 to 1540. He sought to re-create in France the elegant Renaissance lifestyle he had discovered in Italy. (Giraudon)*

The charming and cultivated Francis I (1515–1547) and his athletic, emotional son Henry II (1547–1559) governed through a small, efficient council. Great nobles held titular authority in the provinces as governors, but Paris-appointed officials, the baillis and seneschals, continued to exercise actual fiscal and judicial responsibility (pages 353–354). In 1539, Francis issued an ordinance that placed all France under the jurisdiction of the royal law courts and made French the language of those courts. This act had a powerful centralizing impact. The taille, a tax on land, provided such strength as the monarchy had and supported a strong standing army. Unfortunately, the tax base was too narrow for France's extravagant promotion of the arts and ambitious foreign policy.

Deliberately imitating the Italian Renaissance princes, the Valois monarchs lavished money on a magnificent court and vast building program, and on Italian artists. Francis I commissioned the Paris architect Pierre Lescot to rebuild the palace of the Louvre. Francis secured the services of Michelangelo's star pupil, Il Rosso, who decorated the wing of the Fontainebleau chateau, subsequently called the Gallery Francis I, with rich scenes of classical and mythological literature. After acquiring Leonardo da Vinci's Mona Lisa, Francis brought Leonardo himself to France, where he soon died. Henry II built a castle at Dreux for his mistress, Diana de Poitiers, and a palace in Paris, the Tuileries, for his wife, Catherine de' Medici. Art historians credit

Francis I and Henry II with importing Italian Renaissance art and architecture to France. Whatever praise these monarchs deserve for their cultural achievement, they spent far more than they could afford.

The Habsburg-Valois wars, waged intermittently through the first half of the sixteenth century, also cost more than the government could afford. Financing the war posed problems. In addition to the time-honored practices of increasing taxes and heavy borrowing, Francis I tried two new devices to raise revenue: the sale of public offices and a treaty with the papacy. The former proved to be only a temporary source of money. The offices sold tended to become hereditary within a family, and once a man bought an office he and his heirs were tax-exempt. The sale of public offices thus created a tax-exempt class called the nobility of the robe, which held positions beyond the jurisdiction of the Crown.

The treaty with the papacy was the Concordat of Bologna (page 457), in which Francis agreed to recognize the supremacy of the papacy over a universal council. In return, the French crown gained the right to appoint all French bishops and abbots. This understanding gave the monarchy a rich supplement of money and offices and a power over the church that lasted until the Revolution of 1789. The Concordat of Bologna helps to explain why France did not later become Protestant: it in effect established Catholicism as the national religion. Because they possessed control over appointments and had a vested financial interest in Catholicism, French rulers had no need to revolt from Rome.

However, the Concordat of Bologna perpetuated disorders within the French church. Ecclesiastical offices were used primarily to pay and reward civil servants. Churchmen in France, as elsewhere, were promoted to the hierarchy not for any special spiritual qualifications but because of their services to the state. Such bishops were unlikely to work to elevate the intellectual and moral standards of the parish clergy. Few of the many priests in France devoted scrupulous attention to the needs of their parishioners. The teachings of Luther and Calvin, as the presses disseminated them, found a receptive audience.

Luther's tracts first appeared in France in 1518, and his ideas attracted some attention. After the publication of Calvin's *Institutes* in 1536, sizable numbers of French people were attracted to the "reformed religion," as Calvinism was called. Because Calvin wrote in French, rather than Latin, his ideas gained wide circulation. Initially, Calvinism drew converts from among reform-minded members of the Catholic clergy, the industrious middle classes, and from artisan groups. Most Calvinists lived in major cities, such as Paris, Lyons, Meaux, and Grenoble.

In spite of condemnation by the universities, government bans, and massive burnings at the stake, the numbers of Protestants grew steadily. When Henry II died in 1559, there were 40 well-organized and 2,150 mission churches in France. Perhaps one-sixth of the population had become Calvinist.

RELIGIOUS RIOTS AND CIVIL WAR IN FRANCE (1559–1589)

For thirty years, from 1559 to 1589, violence and civil war divided and shattered France. The feebleness of the monarchy was the seed from which the weeds of civil violence germinated. The three weak sons of Henry II who occupied the throne could not provide the necessary leadership. Francis II (1559–1560) died after seventeen months. Charles IX (1560–1574) succeeded at the age of ten and was thoroughly dominated by his opportunis-

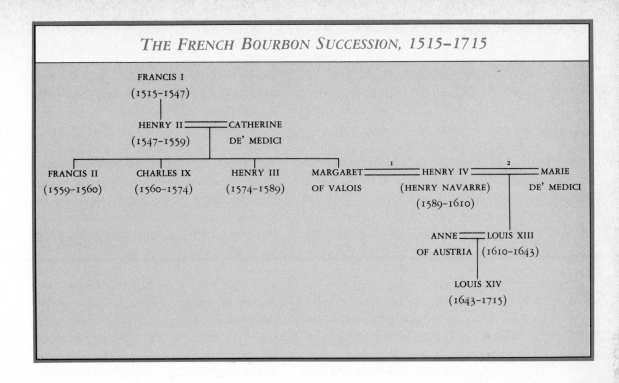

THE FRENCH BOURBON SUCCESSION, 1515–1715

FRANCIS I
(1515–1547)

HENRY II ══════ CATHERINE
(1547–1559)   DE' MEDICI

FRANCIS II   CHARLES IX   HENRY III   MARGARET ══════¹══════ HENRY IV ══════²══════ MARIE
(1559–1560)   (1560–1574)   (1574–1589)   OF VALOIS   (HENRY NAVARRE)   DE' MEDICI
                                                                              (1589–1610)

                                                                              ANNE ══════ LOUIS XIII
                                                                              OF AUSTRIA │ (1610–1643)

                                                                              LOUIS XIV
                                                                              (1643–1715)

tic mother, Catherine de' Medici, who would support any party or position to maintain her influence. The intelligent and cultivated Henry III (1574–1589) divided his attention between debaucheries with his male lovers and frantic acts of repentance.

The French nobility took advantage of this monarchial weakness. In the second half of the sixteenth century, between two-fifths and half of the nobility at one time or another became Calvinist. Just as German princes in the Holy Roman Empire had adopted Lutheranism as a means of opposition to the emperor Charles V, so French nobles frequently adopted the "reformed religion" as a religious cloak for their independence. No one believed that peoples of different faiths could coexist peacefully within the same territory. The Reformation thus led to a resurgence of feudal disorder. Armed clashes between Catholic royalist lords and Calvinist antimonarchial lords occurred in many parts of France.

Among the upper classes the Catholic-Calvinist conflict was the surface issue, but the fundamental object of the struggle was power. Working-class crowds composed of skilled craftsmen and the poor wreaked terrible violence on people and property. Both Calvinists and Catholics believed that the others' books, services, and ministers polluted the community. Preachers incited violence, and ceremonies like baptisms, marriages, and funerals triggered it. Protestant pastors encouraged their followers to destroy statues and liturgical objects in Catholic churches. Catholic priests urged their flocks to shed the blood of the Calvinist heretics.

In 1561 in the Paris church of St.-Médard, a Protestant crowd cornered a baker guarding a box containing the consecrated Eucharistic bread. Taunting "Does your God of paste protect you now from the pains of death?"[10] the mob proceeded to kill the poor man. Calvinists believed that the Catholic emphasis on symbols in their ritual desecrated what was truly sacred and promoted the worship of images. In scores of attacks on Catholic churches religious statues were knocked down, stained-glass windows smashed, and sacred vestments, vessels, and Eucharistic elements defiled. In 1561, a Catholic crowd charged a group of just-released Protestant prisoners, killed them, and burned their bodies in the street. Hundreds of Huguenots, as French Calvinists were called, were tortured, had their tongues or throats slit, were maimed or murdered.

In the fourteenth and fifteenth centuries, crowd action — attacks on great nobles and rich prelates — had expressed economic grievances. Religious rioters of the sixteenth century believed that they could assume the power of public magistrates and rid the community of corruption. Municipal officials criticized the crowds' actions, but the participation of pastors and priests in these demonstrations lent riots a sort of legitimacy.[11]

A savage Catholic attack on Calvinists in Paris on August 24, 1572 (Saint Bartholomew's Day) followed the usual pattern. The occasion was a religious ceremony, the marriage of the king's sister Margaret of Valois to the Protestant Henry of Navarre. Among the many Calvinists present for the wedding festivies was the admiral de Coligny, head of one of the great noble families of France and leader of the Huguenot party. Coligny had recently replaced Catherine in influence over the young king Charles IX. When, the night before the wedding, the leader of the Catholic aristocracy, Henry of Guise, had Coligny murdered, rioting and slaughter followed. The Huguenot gentry in Paris were massacred, and religious violence spread to the provinces. Between August 25 and October 3, perhaps twelve thousand Huguenots perished at Meaux, Lyons, Orléans, and Paris. The contradictory orders of the unstable Charles IX worsened the situation.

The Saint Bartholomew's Day massacre launched the War of the Three Henrys, a civil conflict among factions led by the Catholic Henry of Guise, the Protestant Henry of Navarre, and King Henry III, who succeeded the tubercular Charles IX in 1574. Although he remained Catholic, King Henry realized that the Catholic Guise group represented his greatest danger. The Guises wanted, through an alliance of Catholic nobles called the Holy League, not only to destroy Calvinism but also to replace Henry III as king with a member of the Guise family. Violence continued. France suffered fifteen more years of religious rioting and domestic anarchy. Agriculture in many areas was destroyed; commercial life declined severely; starvation and death haunted the land.

What ultimately saved France was a small group of Catholic moderates called *politiques* who believed that only the restoration of strong monarchy could reverse the trend toward collapse. No religious creed was worth the incessant disorder and destruction. Therefore the *politiques* supported religious toleration. The death of Catherine de' Medici, followed by the assassinations of Henry of Guise and King Henry III, paved the way for the accession of Henry of Navarre, who became Henry IV (1589–1610).

This glamorous prince, "who knew how to fight, to make love and to drink," as a contemporary remarked, wanted above all a strong and united France. He knew too that the majority of the French were Roman Catholics. Declaring "Paris is worth a mass," Henry knelt before the archbishop of Bourges and was received into the Roman Catholic church. Henry's willingness to sacrifice religious principles to political necessity saved France. The Edict of Nantes, which Henry published in 1598, granted to Huguenots liberty of conscience and liberty of worship in certain specified towns, such as La Rochelle. The reign of Henry IV and the Edict of Nantes prepared the way for French absolutism in the seventeenth century by helping to restore internal peace in France.

THE NETHERLANDS UNDER CHARLES V

In the last quarter of the sixteenth century, the political stability of England, the international prestige of Spain, and the moral influence of the Roman papacy all became mixed up with the religious crisis in the Low Countries. The Netherlands was the pivot around which European money, diplomacy, and war revolved. What began as a movement for the reformation of the church developed into a struggle for Dutch independence.

The emperor Charles V (1519–1556) had inherited the seventeen provinces that compose present-day Belgium and Holland (pages 480–481). Ideally situated for commerce between the Rhine and Scheldt rivers, the great towns of Bruges, Ghent, Brussels, Arras, and Amsterdam made their living by trade and industry. The French-speaking southern towns produced fine linens and woolens, while the wealth of the Dutch-speaking northern cities rested on fishing, shipping, and international banking. The city of Antwerp was the largest port and the greatest money market in Europe. In the cities of the Low Countries trade and commerce had produced a vibrant cosmopolitan atmosphere, which was well personified by the urbane Erasmus of Rotterdam.

Each of the seventeen provinces of the Netherlands possessed historic liberties: each was self-governing and enjoyed the right to make its own laws and collect its own taxes. Only the recognition of a common ruler in the person of the emperor Charles V united the provinces. Delegates from each province met together in the Estates General, but important decisions had to be referred back to each province for approval. In the middle of the sixteenth century, the seventeen provinces had a limited sense of federation.

In the Low Countries as elsewhere, corruption in the Roman church and the critical spirit of the Renaissance provoked pressure for reform. Lutheran tracts and Dutch translations of the Bible flooded the seventeen provinces in the 1520s and 1530s, attracting many people to Protestantism. Charles V's government responded with condemnation and mild repression. This policy was not particularly effective, however, because ideas circulated freely in the cosmopolitan atmosphere of the commercial centers. But Charles's personality checked the spread of Lutheranism. Charles had been born in Ghent and raised in the Netherlands; he was Flemish in language and culture. He identified with the Flemish and they with him.

In 1556, however, Charles V abdicated, dividing his territories between his brother Ferdinand, who received Austria and the Holy Roman Empire, and his son Philip, who inherited Spain, the Low Countries, and the Spanish possessions in America. Charles delivered his abdication speech before the Estates General at Brussels. The emperor was then fifty-five years old, white-haired, and so crippled in the legs that he had to lean for support on the young Prince William of Orange. According to one account:

His under lip, a Burgundian inheritance, as faithfully transmitted as the duchy and county, was heavy and hanging, the lower jaw protruding so far beyond the upper that it was impossible for him to bring together the few fragments of teeth which still remained, or to speak a whole sentence in an intelligible voice.[12]

Charles spoke in Flemish. His small, shy, and sepulchral son Philip responded in Spanish; he could speak neither French nor Flemish. The Netherlanders had always felt Charles one of themselves. They were never to forget that Philip was a Spaniard.

THE REVOLT OF THE NETHERLANDS (1556–1587)

By the 1560s, there was a strong, militant minority of Calvinists in most of the cities of the Netherlands. The seventeen provinces possessed a large middle-class population, and the "reformed religion," as a contemporary remarked, had a powerful appeal "to those who had grown rich by trade and were therefore ready for revolution."[13] Calvinism appealed to the middle classes because of its intellectual seriousness, moral gravity, and emphasis on any form of labor well done. It took deep root among the merchants and financiers in Amsterdam and the northern provinces. Working-class people were also converted, partly because their employers would hire only fellow Calvinists. Well-organized and with the backing of rich merchants, Calvinists quickly gained a wide following. Lutherans taught respect for the powers that be; the "reformed religion," however, tended to encourage opposition to "illegal" civil authorities.

In 1559, Philip II appointed his half-sister Margaret as regent of the Netherlands (1559–1567). A proud, energetic, and strong-willed woman who once had Ignatius Loyola as her confessor, Margaret pushed Philip's orders to wipe out Protestantism. She introduced the Inquisition. Her more immediate problem, however, was revenue to finance the government of the provinces. Charles V had steadily increased taxes in the Low Countries. When Margaret appealed to the Estates General, they claimed that the Low Countries were more heavily taxed than Spain. Nevertheless, Margaret raised taxes. In so doing, she quickly succeeded in uniting the opposition to the government's fiscal policy with the opposition to official repression of Calvinism.

In August 1566, fanatical Calvinists, primarily of the poorest classes, embarked upon a rampage of frightful destruction. As in France, Calvinist destruction in the Low Countries was incited by popular preaching, and attacks were aimed at religious images as symbols of false doctrines, not at people. The Cathedral of Notre Dame at Antwerp was the first target. Begun in 1124 and finished only in 1518, this church stood as a monument to the commercial prosperity of Flanders, the piety of the business classes, and the artistic genius of centuries. On six successive summer evenings, crowds swept through the nave. While the town harlots held tapers to the greatest concentration of art works in northern Europe, people armed with axes and sledgehammers smashed altars, statues, paintings, books, tombs, ecclesiastical vestments, missals, manuscripts, ornaments, stained-glass windows, and sculptures. Before the havoc was over, thirty more churches had been sacked and irreplaceable libraries burned. From Antwerp the destruction spread to Brussels and Ghent and north to the provinces of Holland and Zeeland.

From Madrid, Philip II sent twenty thousand Spanish troops under the duke of Alva to pacify the Low Countries. Alva interpreted

To Purify the Church *The destruction of pictures and statues representing biblical events, Christian doctrine, or sacred figures was a central feature of the Protestant Reformation. Here Dutch Protestant soldiers destroy what they consider idols in the belief that they are purifying the church. (Fotomas Index)*

"pacification" to mean the ruthless extermination of religious and political dissidents. On top of the Inquisition he opened his own tribunal, soon called the Council of Blood. On March 3, 1568, fifteen hundred men were executed. Even Margaret was sickened and resigned her regency. Alva resolved the financial crisis by levying a 10 percent sales tax on every transaction, which in a commercial society caused widespread hardship and confusion.

For ten years, between 1568 and 1578, civil war raged in the Netherlands between Catholics and Protestants and between the seventeen provinces and Spain. A series of Spanish generals could not halt the fighting. In 1576, the seventeen provinces united under the leadership of Prince William of Orange, called "the Silent" because of his remarkable discretion. In 1578, Philip II sent his nephew Alexander Farnese, duke of Parma, to crush the revolt once and for all. A general with a superb sense of timing, an excellent knowledge of the geography of the Low Countries, and a perfect plan, Farnese arrived with an army of German mercenaries. Avoiding pitched battles, he fought by patient sieges. One by one the cities of the south fell – Maastricht, Tournai, Bruges, Ghent, and finally the financial capital of northern Europe, Antwerp. Calvinism was forbidden in these territories, and Protestants were compelled to convert or leave. The collapse of Antwerp marked the farthest extent of Spanish jurisdiction and the political division of the Netherlands.

The ten southern provinces, the Spanish Netherlands (the future Belgium), remained under the control of the Spanish Habsburgs. The seven northern provinces, led by Holland, formed the Union of Utrecht, and in 1581 declared their independence from Spain. Thus was born the United Provinces of the Netherlands (see Map 15.2).

Geography, language and sociopolitical structure differentiated the two countries. The northern provinces were ribboned with sluices and canals and therefore were highly defensible. Several times the Dutch had broken the dikes and flooded the countryside to halt the advancing Farnese. In the southern provinces the Ardennes mountains interrupt the otherwise flat terrain. The Dutch spoken in the north was akin to German, while the Flemish spoken in the south was close to French. In the north the commercial aristocracy possessed the predominant power; in the south the landed nobility had the greater influence. The north was Protestant; the south remained Catholic.

Philip II and Alexander Farnese did not accept this geographical division, and the struggle continued after 1581. The United Provinces repeatedly begged the Protestant Queen Elizabeth of England for assistance.

The crown on the head of Elizabeth I (pages 494-495) did not rest easily. She had steered a moderately Protestant course between the Puritans, who sought the total elimination of Roman Catholic elements in the English church, and the Roman Catholics, who wanted full restoration of the old religion. Elizabeth survived a massive uprising by the Catholic north in 1569-1570. She survived two serious plots against her life. In the 1570s, the presence in England of Mary, Queen of Scots, a Roman Catholic and the legal heir to the English throne, produced a very embarrassing situation. Mary was the rallying point of all opposition to Elizabeth, yet the English sovereign hesitated to set the terrible example of regicide by ordering Mary executed.

Elizabeth faced a grave dilemma. If she responded favorably to Dutch pleas for military support against the Spanish, she would antagonize Philip II. The Spanish king had the steady flow of silver from the Americas at his disposal, and Elizabeth, lacking such treasure, wanted to avoid war. But if she did not help the Protestant Netherlands and they were crushed by Farnese, the likelihood was that the Spanish would invade England.

Three developments forced Elizabeth's hand. First, the wars in the Low Countries – the chief market for English woolens – badly hurt the English economy. When wool was not exported, the Crown lost valuable customs revenues. Second, the murder of William the Silent in July 1584 eliminated not only a great Protestant leader but the chief military check on the Farnese advance. Third, the collapse of Antwerp appeared to signal a

Catholic sweep throughout the Netherlands. The next step, the English feared, would be a Spanish invasion of their island. For these reasons, Elizabeth pumped £250,000 and two thousand troops into the Protestant cause in the Low Countries between 1585 and 1587. Increasingly fearful of the plots of Mary, Queen of Scots, Elizabeth finally signed her death warrant. Mary was beheaded on February 18, 1587. Sometime between March 24 and 30, the news of Mary's death reached Philip II.

PHILIP II AND THE SPANISH ARMADA

Philip pondered the Dutch and English developments at the Escorial northwest of Madrid. Begun in 1563 and completed under the king's personal supervision in 1584, the Monastery of Saint Lawrence of the Escorial served as a monastery for Jeromite monks, a tomb for the king's Habsburg ancestors, and a royal palace for Philip and his family. The vast buildings resemble a gridiron, the instrument on which Saint Lawrence (d. 258) had supposedly been roasted alive. The royal apartments were in the center of the Italian Renaissance building complex. King Philip's tiny bedchamber possessed a concealed sliding window that opened directly onto the high altar of the monastery church so he could watch the services and pray along with the monks. In this somber atmosphere, surrounded by a community of monks and close to the bones of his ancestors, the Catholic ruler of Spain and of much of the globe passed his days.

Philip of Spain considered himself the international defender of Catholicism and the heir to the medieval imperial power. Hoping to keep England within the Catholic church when his wife Mary Tudor died, Philip had asked Elizabeth to marry him; she had em-

MAP 15.2 THE NETHERLANDS, 1578–1609
Although small in geographical size, the Netherlands held a strategic position in the religious struggles of the sixteenth century. Why?

phatically refused. Several popes had urged him to move against England. When Pope Sixtus V (1585–1590) heard of the death of the queen of Scots, he promised to pay Philip 1 million gold ducats the moment Spanish troops landed in England. Alexander Farnese had repeatedly warned that to subdue the Dutch, he would have to conquer England and cut off the source of Dutch support. Philip worried that the vast amounts of South American silver he was pouring into the conquest of the Netherlands seemed to be going down a bottomless pit. Two plans for an expedition were considered. Philip's naval adviser recommended that a fleet of 150 ships sail from Lisbon, attack the English navy in the Channel, and invade England. In Antwerp, Farnese urged Philip to assemble a collection of barges and troops in Flanders to stage a cross-Channel assault. With the "inevitable" support of English Catholics, Spain would achieve a great victory.

Philip compromised. He prepared a vast armada to sail from Lisbon to Flanders, fight off Elizabeth's navy *if* it attacked, rendezvous with Farnese, and escort his barges across the English Channel. The expedition's purpose was to transport the Flemish army.

On May 9, 1588, *la felicissima armada* – "the most fortunate fleet," as it was ironically called in official documents – sailed from Lisbon harbor on the last medieval crusade. The Spanish fleet of 130 vessels carried 123,790 cannon balls and perhaps 30,000 men, every one of whom had confessed his sins and received the Eucharist. An English fleet of about 150 ships met the Spanish in the Channel. It was composed of smaller, faster, more maneuverable ships, many of which had greater firing power. A combination of storms and squalls, spoiled food and rank water, inadequate Spanish ammunition, and, to a lesser extent, English fire ships that caused the Spanish to panic and scatter, gave England the victory. Many Spanish ships went to the bottom of the ocean; perhaps 65 managed to crawl home by way of the North Sea.

The battle in the Channel has frequently been described as one of the decisive battles in the history of the world. In fact, it had mixed consequences. Spain soon rebuilt its navy, and after 1588 the quality of the Spanish fleet improved. The destruction of the Armada did not halt the flow of silver from the New World. More silver reached Spain between 1588 and 1603 than in any other fifteen-year period. The war between England and Spain dragged on for years.

The defeat of the Spanish Armada was decisive, however, in the sense that it prevented Philip II from reimposing unity on western Europe by force. He did not conquer England, and Elizabeth continued her financial and military support of the Dutch. In the Netherlands, however, neither side gained significant territory. The borders of 1581 tended to become permanent. In 1609, Philip III of Spain (1598–1621) agreed to a truce, in effect recognizing the independence of the United Provinces.

THE THIRTY YEARS' WAR (1618–1648)

While Philip II dreamed of building a second armada and Henry IV began the reconstruction of France, the political-religious situation in central Europe deteriorated. An uneasy truce had prevailed in the Holy Roman Empire since the Peace of Augsburg of 1555 (page 484). The Augsburg settlement, in recognizing the independent power of the German princes, had destroyed the authority of the central government. The Habsburg ruler in Vienna enjoyed the title of emperor but had no power.

According to the Augsburg settlement, the faith of the prince determined the religion of his subjects. Later in the century, though, Catholics grew alarmed because Lutherans, in violation of the Peace of Augsburg, were steadily acquiring north German bishoprics. The spread of Calvinism further confused the issue. The Augsburg settlement had pertained only to Lutheranism and Catholicism, but Calvinists ignored it and converted several princes. Lutherans feared that the Augsburg principles would be totally undermined by

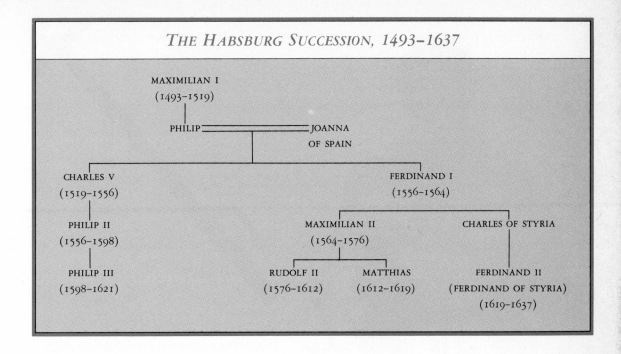

THE HABSBURG SUCCESSION, 1493–1637

MAXIMILIAN I
(1493–1519)

PHILIP ══════════ JOANNA
OF SPAIN

CHARLES V
(1519–1556)

FERDINAND I
(1556–1564)

PHILIP II
(1556–1598)

MAXIMILIAN II
(1564–1576)

CHARLES OF STYRIA

PHILIP III
(1598–1621)

RUDOLF II
(1576–1612)

MATTHIAS
(1612–1619)

FERDINAND II
(FERDINAND OF STYRIA)
(1619–1637)

Catholic and Calvinist gains. Also, the militantly active Jesuits had reconverted several Lutheran princes to Catholicism. In an increasingly tense situation, Lutheran princes formed the Protestant Union (1608) and Catholics retaliated with the Catholic League (1609). Each alliance was determined that the other should make no religious (that is, territorial) advance. The empire was composed of two armed camps.

Dynastic interests were also involved in the German situation. When Charles V abdicated in 1556, he had divided his possessions between his son Philip II and his brother Ferdinand I. This partition began the Austrian and Spanish branches of the Habsburg family. Ferdinand inherited the imperial title and the Habsburg lands in central Europe, including Austria, Bohemia, and Hungary. Ferdinand's

grandson, Matthias, had no direct heirs and promoted the candidacy of his fanatically Catholic cousin, Ferdinand of Styria. The Spanish Habsburgs strongly supported the goals of their Austrian relatives: the unity of the empire and the preservation of Catholicism within it.

In 1617, Ferdinand of Styria secured election as king of Bohemia, a title that gave him jurisdiction over Silesia and Moravia as well as Bohemia. The Bohemians were Czech and German in nationality, and Lutheran, Calvinist, Catholic, and Hussite in religion; all these faiths enjoyed a fair degree of religious freedom. When Ferdinand proceeded to close some Protestant churches, the heavily Protestant Estates of Bohemia protested. On May 23, 1618, Protestants hurled two of Ferdinand's officials from a castle window in

SIXTEENTH-CENTURY GERMAN BATTLE HAM-
MER *Held in the hand with the leather thong secured around the wrist, a powerful blow from this
battle hammer could instantly crush a skull or smash
a rib cage. (Photo: Caroline Buckler)*

SEVENTEENTH-CENTURY BATTLE ARMOR *Ar-
mor remained a symbol of the noble's high social status
and military profession, although armor gave much
less protection after the invention of gun powder. The
maker had a sense of humor. (Photo: Caroline
Buckler)*

Prague. They fell seventy feet but survived: Catholics claimed that angels had caught them; Protestants said the officials fell on a heap of soft horse manure. Called "the defenestration of Prague," this event marked the beginning of the Thirty Years' War.

Historians traditionally divide the war into four phases. The first or Bohemian phase (1618-1625) was characterized by civil war in Bohemia between the Catholic League, led by Ferdinand, and the Protestant Union, headed by Prince Frederick of the Palatinate. The Bohemians fought for religious liberty and independence from Habsburg rule. In 1618, the Bohemian Estates deposed Ferdinand and gave the crown of Bohemia to Frederick, thus uniting the interests of German Protestants with those of the international enemies of the Habsburgs. Frederick wore his crown only a few months. In 1620, he was totally defeated by Catholic forces at the battle of the White Mountain. Ferdinand, who had recently been elected Holy Roman emperor as Ferdinand II, followed up his victories by wiping out Protestantism in Bohemia through forcible conversions and the activities of militant Jesuit missionaries. Within ten years, Bohemia was completely Catholic.

The second or Danish phase of the war (1625-1629) – so called because of the participation of King Christian IV of Denmark (1588-1648), the ineffective leader of the Protestant cause – witnessed additional Catholic victories. The Catholic imperial army led by Albert of Wallenstein scored smashing victories. It swept through Silesia, north through Schleswig and Jutland to the Baltic, and east into Pomerania. Wallenstein had made himself indispensable to the emperor Ferdinand, but he was an unscrupulous opportunist who used his vast riches to build an army loyal only to himself. The general seemed interested more in carving out an empire for himself than in aiding the Catholic cause. He quarreled with the Catholic League, and soon the Catholic forces were badly divided. Religion was eclipsed as a basic issue of the war.

The year 1629 marked the peak of Habsburg power. The Jesuits persuaded the emperor to issue the Edict of Restitution, whereby all Catholic properties lost to Protestantism since 1552 were to be restored and only Catholics and Lutherans (*not* Calvinists, Hussites, or other sects) were to be allowed to practice their faiths. Ferdinand appeared to be embarked on a policy to unify the empire. When Wallenstein began ruthless enforcement of the edict, Protestants throughout Europe feared a complete collapse of the balance of power in north central Europe.

The third or Swedish phase of the war (1630-1635) began with the arrival in Germany of the Swedish king Gustavus Adolphus (1594-1632). The ablest administrator of his day and a devout Lutheran, Gustavus Adolphus intervened to support the oppressed Protestants within the empire and to assist his relatives, the exiled dukes of Mecklenburg. Cardinal Richelieu, the chief minister of King Louis XIII of France (1610-1643) subsidized the Swedes, hoping to weaken Habsburg power in Europe. In 1631, with a small but well-disciplined army equipped with superior muskets and warm uniforms, Gustavus Adolphus won a brilliant victory at Breitenfeld. Again in 1632, he was victorious at Lützen, although he was fatally wounded in the battle.

The participation of the Swedes in the Thirty Years' War proved decisive for the future of Protestantism and of later German history. When Gustavus Adolphus landed on German soil, he had already brought Denmark, Poland, Finland, and the smaller Baltic states under Swedish influence. The Swedish victories ended the Habsburg ambition of uniting all the German states under imperial authority.

The death of Gustavus Adolphus, followed by the defeat of the Swedes at the battle of Nördlingen in 1634, prompted the French to enter the war on the side of the Protestants. Thus began the French, or international, phase of the Thirty Years' War (1635–1648). For almost a century French foreign policy had been based on opposition to the Habsburgs, because a weak empire divided into scores of independent principalities enhanced France's international stature. In 1622, when the Dutch had resumed the war against Spain, the French had supported Holland. Now, in 1635, Cardinal Richelieu declared war on Spain and again sent financial and military assistance to the Swedes and the German Protestant princes. The war dragged on. French, Dutch, and Swedes, supported by Scots, Finns, and German mercenaries, burned, looted, and destroyed German agriculture and commerce. The Thirty Years' War lasted so long because neither side had the resources to win a quick, decisive victory. Finally, in October 1648, peace was achieved.

The treaties signed at Münster and Osnabrück, commonly called the Peace of Westphalia, mark a turning point in European political, religious, and social history. The treaties recognized the sovereign independent authority of the German princes. Each ruler could govern his particular territory and make war and peace as well. With power in the hands of more than three hundred princes, with no central government, courts, or means of controlling unruly rulers, the Holy Roman Empire as a real state was effectively destroyed (see Map 15.3).

The independence of the United Provinces of the Netherlands was acknowledged. The

MAP 15.3 EUROPE IN 1648 *Which country emerged from the Thirty Years War as the strongest European power? What dynastic house was that country's major rival in the early modern period?*

international stature of France and Sweden was also greatly improved by the Peace of Westphalia. The political divisions within the empire, the weak German frontiers, and the acquisition of the province of Alsace increased France's size and prestige. The treaties allowed France to intervene at will in German affairs. Sweden received a large cash indemnity and jurisdiction over German territories along the Baltic Sea. The powerful Swedish presence in northeastern Germany subsequently posed a major threat to the future kingdom of Brandenburg-Prussia. The treaties also denied the papacy the right to participate in German religious affairs – a restriction symbolizing the reduced role of the Roman Catholic church in European politics.

In religion the Westphalian treaties stipulated that the Augsburg agreement of 1555 should stand permanently. The sole modification was that Calvinism, along with Catholicism and Lutheranism, would become a legally permissible creed. In practice the north German states remained Protestant, the south German states Catholic. The war settled little. Both sides had wanted peace, and with remarkable illogic they fought for thirty years to get it.

GERMANY AFTER THE THIRTY YEARS' WAR

The Thirty Years' War was a disaster for the German economy and society, probably the most destructive event in German history before the twentieth century. Population losses were frightful. Perhaps one-third of the urban residents and two-fifths of the inhabitants of

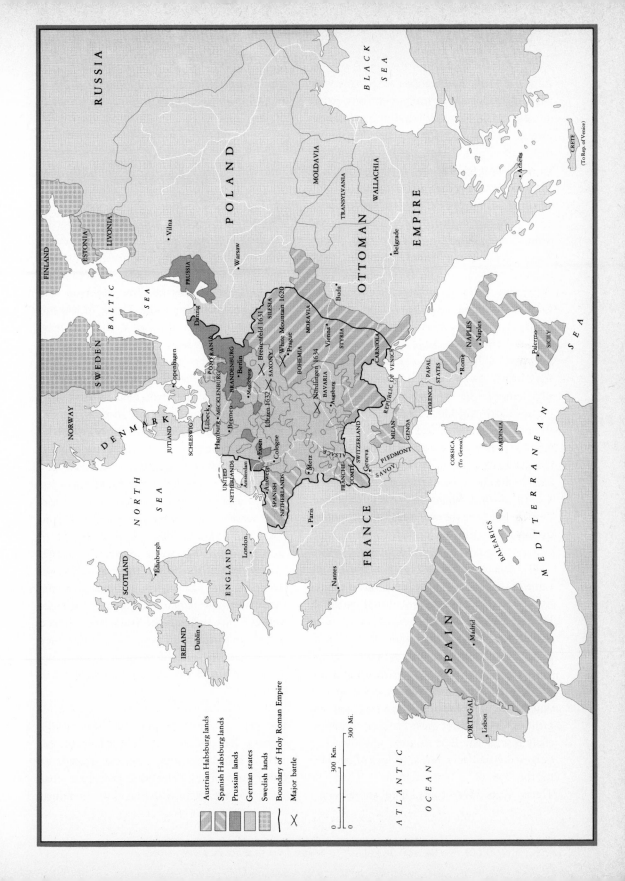

RUSSIA

FINLAND

ESTONIA

LIVONIA

• Vilna

BALTIC SEA

SWEDEN

NORWAY

DENMARK

JUTLAND

SCHLESWIG

NORTH SEA

SCOTLAND

• Edinburgh

ENGLAND

• London

IRELAND

• Dublin

ATLANTIC OCEAN

• Nantes

FRANCE

• Paris

POLAND

• Warsaw

PRUSSIA

• Danzig

POMERANIA

MECKLENBURG

BRANDENBURG

• Berlin

• Lübeck

• Hamburg

• Bremen

• Magdeburg

SILESIA

Breitenfeld 1631

SAXONY

White Mountain 1620

• Prague

BOHEMIA

Lützen 1632

MORAVIA

Nördlingen 1634

• Vienna

STYRIA

BAVARIA

• Augsburg

• Essen

• Cologne

UNITED NETHERLANDS

• Amsterdam

• Antwerp

SPANISH NETHERLANDS

FRANCHE-COMTÉ

• Metz

ALSACE

SWITZERLAND

• Geneva

SAVOY

PIEDMONT

MILAN

GENOA

CARNIOLA

REPUBLIC OF VENICE

MOLDAVIA

WALLACHIA

TRANSYLVANIA

• Belgrade

OTTOMAN EMPIRE

• Buda

BLACK SEA

FLORENCE

PAPAL STATES

• Rome

NAPLES

• Naples

CORSICA
(To Genoa)

SARDINIA

BALEARICS

SPAIN

• Madrid

PORTUGAL

• Lisbon

SICILY

• Palermo

MEDITERRANEAN SEA

CRETE
(To Rep. of Venice)

• Athens

Austrian Habsburg lands
Spanish Habsburg lands
Prussian lands
German states
Swedish lands
Boundary of Holy Roman Empire
Major battle

300 Mi.

300 Km.

0

0

rural areas died. Entire areas of Germany were depopulated, partly by military actions, partly by disease – typhus, dysentery, bubonic plague, and syphilis accompanied the movements of armies – and partly by the thousands of refugees who fled to safer areas.

In the late sixteenth and early seventeenth centuries, all Europe experienced an economic crisis primarily caused by the influx of silver from South America. Because the Thirty Years' War was fought on German soil, these economic difficulties were badly aggravated in the empire. Scholars still cannot estimate the value of losses in agricultural land and livestock, in trade and commerce. The trade of southern cities like Augsburg, already hard hit by the shift in transportation routes from the Mediterranean to the Atlantic, was virtually destroyed by the fighting in the south. Meanwhile, towns like Lübeck, Hamburg, and Bremen in the north and Essen in the Ruhr actually prospered because of the many refugees they attracted. The destruction of land and foodstuffs, compounded by the flood of Spanish silver, brought on a severe price rise. During and after the war, inflation was worse in Germany than anywhere else in Europe.

Agricultural areas suffered catastrophically. The population decline caused a rise in the value of the labor, and owners of great estates had to pay more for agricultural workers. Farmers who needed only small amounts of capital to restore their lands started over again. Many small farmers, however, lacked the revenue to rework their holdings and had to become day laborers. Nobles and landlords bought up many small holdings and acquired great estates. In some parts of Germany, especially east of the Elbe in areas like Mecklenburg and Pomerania, peasants' loss of land led to the rise of a new serfdom.[14] Thus the Thirty Years' War contributed to the legal and economic decline of the largest segment of German society.

THE GREAT EUROPEAN WITCH-HUNT

The period of the religious wars witnessed a startling increase in the phenomenon of witch-hunting, whose prior history was long but sporadic. "A witch," according to Chief Justice Coke of England, "was a person who hath conference with the Devil to consult with him or to do some act." This definition by the highest legal authority in England demonstrates that educated people, as well as the ignorant, believed in witches. Belief in witches – individuals who could mysteriously injure other people, for instance by causing them to become blind or impotent, and who could harm animals, for example by preventing cows from giving milk – dates back to the dawn of time. For centuries tales had circulated about old women who made nocturnal travels on greased broomsticks to "sabbats," or assemblies of witches, where they participated in sexual orgies and feasted on the flesh of infants. In the popular imagination witches had definite characteristics: the vast majority were married women or widows between fifty and seventy years old, crippled or bent with age, with pockmarked skin; they often practiced midwifery or folk medicine, and most had sharp tongues and were quick to scold.

In the sixteenth century religious reformers' extreme notions of the devil's powers, and the insecurity created by the religious wars, contributed to the growth of belief in witches. The idea developed that witches made pacts with the devil in return for the power to work mischief on their enemies. Since pacts with the devil meant the renunciation of God, witchcraft was considered heresy, and all religions persecuted it.

Fear of witches took a terrible toll of innocent lives in parts of Europe. In southwestern Germany 3,229 witches were executed between 1561 and 1670, most by burning. The communities of the Swiss Confederation tried 8,888 persons between 1470 and 1700 and executed 5,417 of them as witches. In all the centuries before 1500 witches in England had been suspected of causing perhaps "three deaths, a broken leg, several destructive storms and some bewitched genitals." Yet between 1559 and 1736 witches were thought to have caused thousands of deaths, and in that period almost 1,000 witches were executed in England.[15]

Historians and anthropologists have offered a variety of explanations for the great European witch-hunt. Some scholars maintain that charges of witchcraft were a means of accounting for inexplicable misfortunes. Just as the English in the fifteenth century had blamed their military failures in France on Joan of Arc's sorcery, so in the seventeenth century the English Royal College of Physicians attributed undiagnosable illnesses to witchcraft. Some scholars hold that in small communities, which typically insisted on strict social conformity, charges of witchcraft were a means of attacking and eliminating the nonconformist; witches, in other words, served the collective need for scapegoats. The evidence of witches' trials, some writers suggest, shows that women were not accused because they harmed or threatened their neighbors; rather, their communities believed such women worshiped the devil, engaged in wild sexual activities with him, and ate infants. Other scholars argue the exact opposite:

that people were tried and executed as witches because their neighbors feared their evil powers. Finally, there is the theory that the unbridled sexuality of which witches were accused was a psychological projection on the part of their accusers, resulting from Christianity's repression of sexuality. The reasons for the persecution of witches probably varied from place to place. Perhaps witches, symbolizing unacceptable ideas or practices, were "victims of society's constant pressure towards intellectual conformity."[16]

SEXISM, RACISM, AND SKEPTICISM

The age of religious wars revealed extreme and violent contrasts. It was a deeply religious period in which men fought passionately for their beliefs; seventy percent of the books printed dealt with religious subjects. Yet the times saw the beginnings of religious skepticism. Europeans explored new continents, partly with the missionary aim of Christianizing the peoples they encountered. Yet the Spanish, Portuguese, Dutch, and English proceeded to enslave the Indians and blacks they encountered. While Europeans indulged in gross sensuality, the social status of women declined. Sexism, racism, and skepticism had all originated in ancient times. But late in the sixteenth century they began to take on their familiar modern forms.

THE STATUS OF WOMEN

The decades between 1560 and 1648 witnessed another decline in the status of women in European society. The Reformation did not help women. The early reformers had urged study of the Bible as the means of improving human conduct. Scriptural study, however, tended to revive Saint Paul's notion that women are the source of sin and vice in the world. Also, the violence and upheaval of the religious wars was followed by a period of reaction and retrenchment. While early humanists such as Erasmus and Zwingli had allowed divorce on grounds of insanity and extreme cruelty, by 1600 all faiths firmly opposed divorce on any grounds. In England, for example, only an act of Parliament could dissolve a marriage.

Although private opinions and public laws relating to the social position of women varied widely, the weight of evidence from the sixteenth and seventeenth centuries indicates that women were considered to be decidedly inferior beings. Their social value rested on their ability to produce heirs. A few women, of course, had power and influence. Margaret of Austria, Charles V's aunt, and Louise of Savoy, Francis I's mother – they cannot be identified apart from their male relatives – conducted the diplomatic negotiations that in 1529 led to the Peace of Cambrai and the end of the second phase of the Habsburg-Valois wars. Jeanne d'Albret, the mother of Henry of Navarre (later Henry IV of France), legalized Calvinism in her domain and aided its spread through France; she was known as "the Saint of the Reform." Likewise, Mary Tudor reestablished Catholicism in England. All these women, however, were of royal blood.

The great majority of women were treated either as grown-up children to be teasingly indulged or as hopelessly irrational. The attitude of John Knox, the Calvinist reformer of the Scottish church, was not atypical: "Nature doth paint them forth to be weak, frail, impatient, feeble and foolish, and experience hath declared them to be unconstant, variable, cruel, and void of the spirit of council and regiment." (Knox had in mind the Catholic

VERONESE: MARS AND VENUS UNITED BY LOVE Taking a theme from classical mythology, the Venetian painter Veronese celebrates in clothing, architecture, and landscape the luxurious wealth of the aristocracy (painted ca 1580). The lush and curvaceous Venus and the muscular and powerfully built Mars suggest the anticipated pleasures of sexual activity and the frank sensuality of the age. (Metropolitan Museum of Art, New York, Kennedy Fund, 1910)

Mary, Queen of Scots, whom he had good political reasons for fearing.) In 1595, the professors at Wittenberg University solemnly debated whether or not women are human beings. Humanists repeated the ancient story of woman the temptress and cause of sin in the world.

Artists' drawings of plump, voluptuous women and massive, muscular men reveal the contemporary standards of physical beauty. It was a sensual age that gloried in the delights of the flesh. Some people, such as the humanist-poet Aretino, found sexual satisfaction with both sexes. Reformers and public officials simultaneously condemned and condoned sexual "sins." The oldest profession had many practitioners, and when in 1566 Pope Pius IV expelled all the prostitutes from Rome, so many people left and the city suffered such a loss of revenue that in less than a month the pope was forced to rescind the order. Scholars debated Saint Augustine's notion that whores serve a useful social function by preventing worse sins. Prostitution was common, because desperate poverty forced women and young men into it. The general public took it for granted. Consequently, civil authorities in both Catholic and Protestant countries licensed houses of public prostitution. These establishments were intended for the convenience of single men, and some Protestant cities, such as Geneva and Zurich, installed officials in the brothels with the ex-

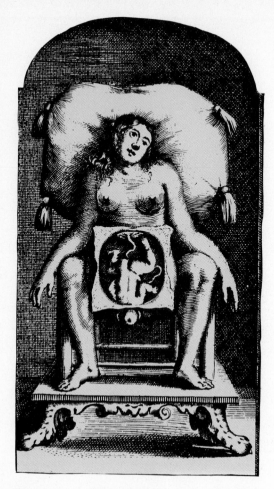

WOMAN IN LABOR *The production of male heirs was women's major social responsibility. Long into modern times a sitting or squatting position for the delivery of babies was common, because it allowed the mother to push. The calm and wistful look on the mother's face suggests a remarkably easy delivery; it is the artist's misconception of the process. (Photo: Caroline Buckler)*

press purpose of preventing married men from patronizing them.

Marriage for all social classes remained a serious business, entered into primarily to advance the economic interests of the parties. There are some remarkable success stories. Elizabeth Hardwick, the orphaned daughter of an obscure English country squire, made four careful marriages, each of which brought her more property and carried her higher up the social ladder. She managed her estates, amounting to more than a hundred thousand acres, with a degree of business sense rare in any age. The two great mansions she built, Chatsworth and Hardwick, stand today as monuments to her acumen. As countess of Shrewsbury, "Bess of Hardwick" so thoroughly enjoyed the trust of Queen Elizabeth that Elizabeth appointed her jailer of Mary, Queen of Scots. Having established several aristocratic dynasties, the countess of Shrewsbury died in 1608, past her eightieth year, one of the richest people in England.[17]

While the Catholic church held up the ideal of celibacy and the religious life as the highest form of Christian life, Protestantism exalted the dignity of marriage. Luther insisted that absolute celibacy was impossible. In the Middle Ages, and later in Catholic countries, the religious life provided a career option for women who did not choose or could not afford to marry. For Protestant women, marriage became the only professional possibility. Protestant marriages took on the form of a contract, whereby each partner promised the other support, understanding, and sharing of material goods. Within marriage many women certainly controlled their own destinies, but there was no question of social or legal equality: wives were subordinate to their husbands.

If some nuns in the later Middle Ages

lacked a religious vocation, and if some religious houses witnessed moral laxness and financial mismanagement, nevertheless convents provided the only scope for the literary, artistic, and administrative talents of unmarried women. In abolishing the religious houses, Protestantism threw out the baby with the bathwater. Marriage became virtually the only occupation for Protestant women, which helps to explain why Anglicans, Calvinists, and Lutherans established communities of religious women in the eighteenth and nineteenth centuries.

Many sixteenth-century reformers, including Luther, Erasmus, and several popes, believed polygamy less of an evil than divorce. (By polygamy they meant a man having several wives at the same time, not a woman having more than one husband.) Theologians found scriptural justification for their position on polygamy. Except among the Anabaptists, however, polygamy was rarely practiced.

If the partners to a monogamous marriage found themselves unsuited, there was virtually no socially acceptable way out. In Catholic countries as well as Protestant ones, a woman could not secure a divorce on grounds of extreme cruelty, desertion, adultery, or complete incompatibility. Women's social and legal position became steadily more confined, and, apart from the upper classes, that position would not change much before the nineteenth century. Death alone dissolved a legitimate marriage. When a spouse died, the great majority of survivors remarried.[18]

ORIGINS OF NORTH AMERICAN RACISM: THE AFRICAN SLAVE TRADE

The Age of Discovery opened up vast new continents for European exploration and exploitation. Once across the Atlantic, the major problem European settlers faced was a shortage of labor. As early as 1495, the Spanish solved the problem by enslaving the native Indians. In the sixteenth and seventeenth centuries, the Portuguese, the Dutch, and the English followed suit.

Unaccustomed to any form of manual labor, and certainly to panning gold for more than twelve hours a day in the broiling sun, the Indians died "like fish in a bucket," as one Spanish settler reported.[19] In 1515, a Spanish missionary, Bartholomé de Las Casas (1474–1566), who had seen the evils of Indian slavery, urged Emperor Charles V to end Indian slavery in his American dominions. Las Casas recommended the importation of blacks from Africa, both because church law did not strictly forbid black slavery and because blacks could better survive under South American conditions. The emperor agreed, and in 1518 the African slave trade began.

Several European nations participated in the African slave trade. Spain brought the first slaves to Brazil; by 1600, 44,000 were being imported annually. Between 1619 and 1623, the Dutch West India Company, with the full support of the government of the United Provinces, transported 15,430 Africans to Brazil. Only in the late seventeenth century, with the chartering of the Royal African Company, did the English get involved. Thereafter, large numbers of African blacks poured into the North American colonies. In 1790, there were 757,181 Negroes in a total United States population of 3,929,625. When the first census was taken in Brazil in 1798, Negroes numbered about 2 million in a total population of 3.25 million.

Almost all peoples in the world have engaged in slavery at some time in their histories. Since ancient times, victors in battle had enslaved conquered peoples. European slavers found slavery widespread in Africa when they arrived in the sixteenth and seventeenth centuries, and they had no difficulty finding Africans willing to sell their captured tribal enemies for cloth, jewelry, guns and whiskey. In seeking slaves in Africa, Europeans encouraged more slave hunting.

Almost as soon as the institution of black slavery was introduced into the New World, controversy arose about it. Las Casas and others soon became disgusted with the Spanish treatment of blacks, and criticized black slavery on the same grounds as Indian slavery: it was inhumane. By the late seventeenth century, abolitionist movements existed in both South and North America.

European settlers brought to the New World the racial attitudes they had absorbed in Europe. North American attitudes derive basically from England. On the eve of the Age of Discovery, the English were overwhelmingly a rural people. Tough, sober, accustomed to unending hard work relieved by few physical comforts, a quarrelsome but rarely violent people, they accepted life with stoical patience. The age was cruel, and the English were not compassionate. The public execution of criminals and the stoning of wretches tied up in the village stocks were major occasions for public entertainment. When a good workman fell from a ladder and was permanently disabled, his community was more concerned that he would become a public charge than about his misfortune.[20]

Early Christian writers in the fourth and fifth centuries had identified blackness with sin and corruption. This notion had become deep-rooted over the centuries. Thus in 1550, when the first black Africans appeared on the streets of London, the concept of blackness was already loaded with emotional meaning. Black meant "deeply stained with dirt, soiled,

THE SPANISH IN AMERICA *The Spanish used barbaric methods to frighten and subdue the Indians. Based on the eyewitness accounts of the Spanish missionary Bartholomew de las Casas, illustrations of Spanish cruelties satisfied Europeans' curiosity about the New World, gratified appetites for bizarre tortures, and promoted anti-Spanish and anti-Catholic feelings. (Photo: Caroline Buckler)*

dirty, foul . . . malignant, having dark or deadly purposes."[21] White, on the other hand, connoted purity and virginity, goodness and cleanliness. Physical beauty to the English meant an almost alabaster white skin tinged with pink. The Negro's black skin, "disfigured" facial features, and curled hair seemed the exact opposite of the physical ideal.

Art and literature had already given English people some acquaintance with "Ethiopians," as black Africans had been called since Roman times. In the sixteenth and seventeenth centuries, the English were still extremely curious about Africans' lives and customs, and slavers' accounts were extraordinarily popular. Travel literature depicted Africans as savages because of their eating habits, morals, clothing, and social customs; as barbarians because of their language and methods of war; and as heathens because they were not Christian. English people saw similarities between apes and Africans; thus, the terms "bestial" and "beastly" were frequently applied to Africans. Africans were believed to possess a potent sexuality and to be extremely lustful. One seventeenth-century observer considered Africans "very lustful and impudent, .. (for a Negroes hiding his members, their extraordinary greatness) is a token of their lust." African women were considered sexually aggressive and "possessed of a temper hot and lascivious."[22]

The English used the heathenism of the Africans as a justification for enslaving them.

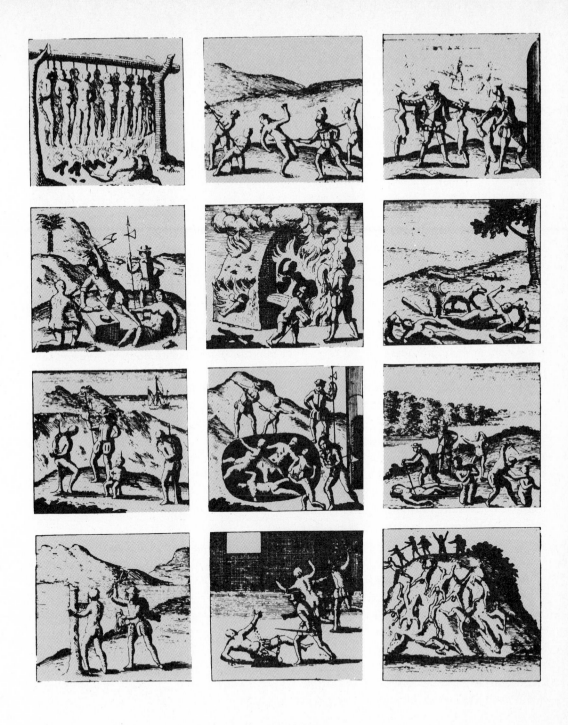

Africans appeared to suit the agricultural needs of the underpopulated continent of North America. Unlike the North American Indians, who were armed, however primitively, and had the psychological support of their tribes, the Africans, stripped of their languages and tribal cultures, were powerless in the New World. Moreover, in spite of the dangers of the trade in Africa and the frightful loss of life among both traders and slaves, the profits in slavery were enormous.

In the seventeenth and eighteenth centuries, English colonists· in North America continued to believe in these supposed social characteristics of Africans. Gradually they became part of the American mental furniture. The myths of black savagery, barbarism, and lechery became the classic stereotypes of modern American racial attitudes.

The Origin of Modern Skepticism: Michel de Montaigne

The decades of religious fanaticism, bringing in their wake death, famine, and civil anarchy, caused both Catholics and Protestants to doubt that any one faith contained absolute truth. The late sixteenth and early seventeenth centuries witnessed the beginnings of modern skepticism. Skepticism is a school of thought founded on doubt that total certainty or definitive knowledge is ever attainable. The skeptic is cautious and critical, and suspends judgment. Perhaps the finest representative of early modern skepticism is the Frenchman Michel de Montaigne (1533–1592).

Montaigne came from a bourgeois family that had made a fortune selling salted herring and in 1477 had purchased the title and property of Montaigne in Gascony. Montaigne received a classical education before studying law and securing a judicial appointment in 1554. Although a member of the nobility, in

embarking on a judicial career he identified with the new nobility of the robe. He condemned the ancient nobility of the sword for being more concerned with war and sports than with the cultivation of the mind.

At the age of thirty-eight, Montaigne resigned his judicial post, retired to his estate, and devoted the rest of his life to study, contemplation, and the effort to understand himself. Like the Greeks, he believed that the object of life was to "know thyself," for self-knowledge teaches men and women how to live in accordance with nature and God. Montaigne developed a new literary genre, the essay – from the French *essayer,* meaning to test or try – to express his thoughts and ideas.

Montaigne's *Essays* provide insight into the mind of a remarkably humane, tolerant, and civilized man. He was a humanist; he loved the Greek and Roman writers and was always eager to learn from them. In his essay "On Solitude," he quoted the Roman poet Horace:

Reason and sense remove anxiety,
Not villas that look out upon the sea

Ambition, avarice, irresolution, fear, and lust do not leave us when we change our country.

Some said to Socrates that a certain man had grown no better by his travels. "I should think not," he said; "he took himself along with him. . . ."
We should have wife, children, goods, and above all health, if we can; but we must not bind ourselves to them so strongly that our happiness depends on them. We must reserve a back shop all our own, entirely free, in which to establish our real liberty and our principal retreat and solitude. . . .[23]

From the ancient authors, especially the Roman stoic Seneca, Montaigne acquired a sense of calm, inner peace, and patience. The ancient authors also inculcated in him a tolerance and broad-mindedness. Montaigne had grown up during the French civil wars, perhaps the worst kind of war. Religious ideology had set family against family, even brother against brother. He wrote:

In this controversy . . . France is at present agitated by civil wars, the best and soundest side is undoubtedly that which maintains both the old religion and the old government of the country. However, among the good men who follow that side (for I speak not of those who use it as a pretext either to wreak their private vengeances, or to supply their avarice, or to pursue the favor of princes; but of those who follow it out of true zeal toward their religion and a holy concern for maintaining the peace and the status of their fatherland) — of these, I say, we see many whom passion drives outside the bounds of reason, and makes them sometimes adopt unjust, violent, and even reckless courses. . . .[24]

Although he remained a Catholic, Montaigne possessed a detachment, an independence, an openness of mind, and a willingness to look at all sides of a question. As he wrote, "I listen with attention to the judgment of all men; but so far as I can remember, I have followed none but my own. Though I set little value upon my own opinion, I set no more on the opinions of others."

In a violent and cruel age, Montaigne was a gentle and sensitive man. In his famous essay "On Cruelty," he said:

Among other vices, I cruelly hate cruelty, both by nature and by judgment, as the extreme of all vices. . . .

I live in a time when we abound in incredible examples of this vice, through the license of our civil wars; and we see in the ancient histories nothing more extreme than what we experience of

this every day. But that has not reconciled me to it at all.[25]

In the book-lined tower where Montaigne passed his days, he became a deeply learned man. Yet he was not ignorant of the world of affairs, and he criticized scholars and bookworms who ignored the life around them. Montaigne's essay "On Cannibals" reflects the impact of overseas discoveries on Europeans' consciousness. His tolerant mind rejected the notion that one culture is superior to another:

I long had a man in my house that lived ten or twelve years in the New World, discovered in these latter days, and in that part of it where Villegaignon landed [Brazil]. . . .

I find that there is nothing barbarous and savage in [that] nation, by anything that I can gather, excepting, that every one gives the title of barbarism to everything that is not in use in his own country. As, indeed, we have no other level of truth and reason, than the example and idea of the opinions and customs of the place wherein we live: there is always the perfect religion, there is perfect government, there the most exact and accomplished usage of all things. . . .[26]

In his belief in the nobility of human beings in the state of nature, uncorrupted by organized society, and in his cosmopolitan attitude toward different civilizations, Montaigne anticipated many eighteenth-century thinkers.

The thought of Michel de Montaigne marks a sharp break with the past. Faith and religious certainty had characterized the intellectual attitudes of Western society for a millennium. Montaigne's rejection of any kind of dogmatism, his secularism, and his skepticism thus represent a basic change. In his own time, and throughout the seventeenth century, few would have agreed with him. The publication of his ideas, however, anticipated a basic shift in attitudes. Montaigne inaugurated an era of doubt. "Wonder," he said, "is the foundation of all philosophy, research is the means of all learning, and ignorance is the end."[27]

ELIZABETHAN AND JACOBEAN LITERATURE

The age of the religious wars and European expansion also experienced an extraordinary degree of intellectual ferment. In addition to the development of the essay as a distinct literary genre, the late sixteenth and early seventeenth centuries fostered remarkable creativity in other branches of literature. England, especially, in the latter part of Elizabeth's reign and the first years of her successor James I (1603–1625), witnessed unparalleled brilliance. The terms *Elizabethan* and *Jacobean* (referring to the reign of James) are used to designate the English music, poetry, prose, and drama of this period. The poetry of Sir Philip Sidney (1554–1586), such as *Astrophel and Stella*, strongly influenced later poetic writing. *The Faerie Queene* of Edmund Spenser (1552–1599) endures as one of the greatest moral epics in any language. The rare poetic beauty of the plays of Christopher Marlowe (1564–1593), such as *Tamburlaine* and *The Jew of Malta*, paved the way for the work of Shakespeare. Above all, the immortal dramas of Shakespeare and the stately prose of the Authorized or King James Bible mark the Elizabethan and Jacobean periods as the golden age of English literature.

William Shakespeare (1564–1616), the son of a successful glove manufacturer who rose to the highest municipal office in the Warwickshire town of Stratford-on-Avon, chose a career on the London stage. By 1592 he had gained recognition as an actor and playwright.

Between 1599 and 1603 Shakespeare performed in the Lord Chamberlain's Company and became co-owner of the Globe Theater, which after 1603 presented his plays.

Shakespeare's genius lies in the originality of his characterizations, the diversity of his plots, his understanding of human psychology, and his unexcelled gift for language. Shakespeare was a Renaissance man in his deep appreciation for classical culture, individualism, and humanism. Such plays as *Julius Caesar, Pericles,* and *Antony and Cleopatra* deal with classical subjects and figures. Several of his comedies have Italian Renaissance settings. The nine history plays, including *Richard II, Richard III,* and *Henry IV,* enjoyed the greatest popularity among Shakespeare's contemporaries. Written during the decade after the defeat of the Spanish Armada, the history plays express English national consciousness; lines such as these from *Richard II* reflect this sense of national greatness with unparalleled eloquence:

This royal Throne of Kings, this scepter'd Isle,
This earth of Majesty, this seat of Mars,
This other Eden, demi-paradise,
This fortress built by Nature for herself,
Against infection and the hand of war:
This happy breed of men, this little world,
This precious stone, set in the silver sea,
Which serves it in the office of a wall,
Or as a moat defensive to a house,
Against the envy of less happier Lands,
This blessed plot, this earth, this Realm, this
     England. . .

Shakespeare's later plays, above all the tragedies *Hamlet, Othello,* and *Macbeth,* explore an enormous range of human problems and are capable of an almost infinite variety of interpretations. *Othello,* which the nineteenth-century historian Thomas Macaulay called "perhaps the greatest work in the world,"

A ROYAL PICNIC *The English court imitated the Italian Renaissance devotion to nature. (See Bellini's* Feast of the Gods — *in first color section.) In this pastoral atmosphere suggestive of classical mythology, Queen Elizabeth interrupts the day's hunt for a picnic in the forest. The meal seems to consist of fowl, bread, wine, and perhaps pastries. (The Huntington Library, San Marino, California)*

portrays an honorable man destroyed by a flaw in his own character and the satanic evil of his supposed friend Iago. *Macbeth's* central theme is exorbitant ambition. Shakespeare analyzes the psychology of sin in the figures of Macbeth and Lady Macbeth whose mutual love under the pressure of ambition leads to their destruction. The central figure in *Hamlet,* a play suffused with individuality, wrestles with moral problems connected with revenge and with man's relationship to life and death. The soliloquy in which Hamlet debates suicide is perhaps the most widely quoted passage in English literature:

To be, or not to be: that is the question:
Whether 'tis nobler in the mind to suffer
The slings and arrows of outrageous fortune,
Or to take arms against a sea of troubles,
And by opposing end them? To die: to sleep;
No more; and by a sleep to say we end
The heart-ache and the thousand natural shocks
That flesh is heir to, 'tis a consummation
Devoutly to be wish'd.

Hamlet's sad cry, "There is nothing either good or bad but thinking makes it so," expresses the anguish and uncertainty of modern man. *Hamlet* has always enjoyed great popularity, because in his many-faceted personality people have seen an aspect of themselves.

Shakespeare's dynamic language bespeaks his extreme sensitivity to the sounds and meanings of words. Perhaps no phrase better summarizes the reason for his immortality than this line, slightly modified, from *Antony and Cleopatra:* "Age cannot wither [him], nor custom stale/[his] infinite variety."

The other great masterpiece of the Jacobean period was the *Authorized Bible.* At a theological conference in 1604, a group of Puritans urged James I to support a new translation of the Bible. The king in turn assigned the task to a committee of scholars, who published their efforts in 1611. Based on the best scriptural research of the time and divided into chapters and verses, the Authorized Version is actually a revision of earlier Bibles more than an original work. Yet it provides a superb expression of the mature English vernacular in the early seventeenth century. Thus, Psalm 37:

Fret not thy selfe because of evill doers, neither bee thou envious against the workers of iniquitie.
For they shall soone be cut downe like the grasse; and wither as the greene herbe.
Trust in the Lord, and do good, so shalt thou dwell in the land, and verely thou shalt be fed.
Delight thy selfe also in the Lord; and he shall give thee the desires of thine heart.
Commit thy way unto the Lord: trust also in him, and he shall bring it to passe.
And he shall bring forth thy righteousness as the light, and thy judgement as the noone day.

The Authorized Version, so-called because it was produced under royal sponsorship – it had no official ecclesiastical endorsement – represented the Anglican and Puritan desire to encourage lay people to read the Scriptures. It quickly achieved great popularity and displaced all earlier versions. British settlers carried this Bible to the North American colonies, where it became known as the *King*

James Bible. For centuries the *King James Bible* has had a profound influence on the language and lives of English-speaking peoples.

———◆———

In the sixteenth and seventeenth centuries, Europeans explored and for the first time gained access to large parts of the globe. European peoples had the intellectual curiosity, the driving ambition, and the scientific technology to attempt feats that were as difficult and expensive then as is going to the moon in our own time. Exploration and exploitation contributed to a more sophisticated standard of living, in the form of spices and Asian luxury goods, and to a terrible international inflation resulting from the influx of South American silver and gold. Governments, the upper classes, and the peasantry were badly hurt by the inflation. Meanwhile the middle class of bankers, shippers, financiers, and manufacturers prospered for much of the seventeenth century.

European expansion and colonization took place against a background of religious conflict and budding national consciousness. The seventeenth century was by no means a secular period. Although the medieval religious framework had broken down, people still thought largely in religious terms. Europeans explained what they did politically and economically in terms of religious doctrine. Religious ideology served as a justification for a variety of goals: the French nobles' opposition to the Crown, the Dutch struggle for political and economic independence from Spain. In Germany religious pluralism and foreign ambitions added to political difficulties. After 1648, the divisions between Protestant and Catholic tended to become permanent. Religious skepticism and racial attitudes were harbingers of developments to come.

NOTES

1. Quoted by C. M. Cipolla, *Guns, Sails, and Empires: Technological Innovation and the Early Phases of European Expansion, 1400–1700,* Minerva Press, New York, 1965, pp. 115–116.

2. Quoted by S. E. Morison, *Admiral of the Ocean Sea: A Life of Christopher Columbus,* Little, Brown, Boston, 1946, p. 154.

3. Cipolla, pp. 90–131.

4. J. H. Parry, *The Age of Reconnaissance,* Mentor Books, New York, 1963, chaps. 3 and 5.

5. Quoted by Cipolla, p. 132.

6. Quoted by F. H. Littell, *The Macmillan Atlas History of Christianity,* Macmillan, New York, 1976, p. 75.

7. Quoted by Cipolla, p. 133.

8. Quoted by J. Hale, "War and Public Opinion in the Fifteenth and Sixteenth Centuries," *Past and Present* 22 (July 1962):29.

9. See ibid., pp. 18–32.

10. Quoted by N. Z. Davis, "The Rites of Violence: Religious Riot in Sixteenth Century France," *Past and Present* 59 (May 1973):59.

11. See ibid., pp. 51–91.

12. Quoted by J. L. Motley, *The Rise of the Dutch Republic,* David McKay, Philadelphia, 1898, 1.109.

13. Quoted by P. Smith, *The Age of the Reformation,* Henry Holt, New York, 1951, p. 248.

14. H. Kamen, "The Economic and Social Consequences of the Thirty Years' War," *Past and Present* 39 (April 1968):44–61.

15. Norman Cohn, *Europe's Inner Demons: An Enquiry Inspired by the Great Witch-Hunt,* Basic Books, New York, 1975, pp. 253–254; Keith Thomas, *Religion and the Decline of Magic,* Charles Scribner's Sons, New York, 1971, pp. 450–455.

16. See Keith Thomas, op. cit., pp. 435–446; Cohn, op. cit., pp. 258–263.

17. See D. Durant, *Bess of Hardwick: Portrait of an Elizabethan Dynast,* Weidenfeld & Nicolson, London, 1977.

18. S. M. Wyntjes, "Women in the Reformation Era," in *Becoming Visible: Women in European History,* ed. R. Bridenthal and C. Koonz, Houghton Mifflin, Boston, 1977, p. 187.

19. Quoted by D. P. Mannix, *Black Cargoes: A History of the Atlantic Slave Trade,* Viking, New York, 1968, p. 5.

20. W. Notestein, *The English People on the Eve of Colonization,* Harper & Brothers, New York, 1954, p. 14.

21. Quoted by W. D. Jordan, *The White Man's Burden: Historical Origins of Racism in the United States,* Oxford University Press, New York, 1974, p. 6.

22. Ibid., p. 19.

23. Quoted by D. M. Frame, trans., *The Complete Works of Montaigne,* Stanford University Press, Stanford, Calif., 1958, pp. 175–176.

24. Ibid., p. 177.

25. Ibid., p. 306.

26. Quoted by C. Cotton, trans., *The Essays of Michel de Montaigne,* A. L. Burt, New York, 1893, pp. 207, 210.

27. Ibid., p. 523.

SUGGESTED READING

Perhaps the best starting point for the study of European society in the age of exploration is J. H. Parry, *The Age of Reconnaissance* (1963), which treats the causes and consequences of the voyages of discovery. Parry's splendidly illustrated *The Discovery of South America* (1979) examines Europeans' reactions to the maritime discoveries and treats the entire concept of new *discoveries.* The urbane studies of C. M. Cipolla present fascinating material on technological and sociological developments written in a lucid style: *Guns, Sails, and Empires: Technological Innovation and the Early Phases of European Expansion, 1400–1700* (1965); *Clocks and Culture, 1300–1700* (1967); *Cristofano and the Plague: A Study in the History of Public Health in the Age of Galileo* (1973); and *Public Health and the Medical Profession in the Renaissance* (1976). S. E. Morison, *Admiral of the Ocean Sea: A Life of Christopher Columbus* (1946), is the standard biography of the great discoverer.

For the religious wars, in addition to the references in the Suggested Reading for Chapter 14 and in the Notes to this chapter, see J. H. M. Salmon, *Society in Crisis: France in the Sixteenth Century* (1975), which traces the fate of French institutions during the civil wars. A. N. Galpern, *The Religions of the People in Sixteenth-Century Champagne* (1976), is a useful case study in religious anthropology, and William A. Christian, Jr., *Local Religion in Sixteenth Century Spain* (1981) traces the attitudes and practices of ordinary people.

A beautifully illustrated introduction to Holland is K. H. D. Kaley, *The Dutch in the Seventeenth Century* (1972). The best comprehensive treatment of the religious strife and civil wars in the Low Countries remains that of J. L. Motley, *The Rise of the Dutch Republic,* 3 vols. (1898). The student who reads French will find a wealth of material in H. Hauser, *La prépondérance espagnole, 1559–1660* (1948).

Of the many biographies of Elizabeth of England, Wallace T. MacCaffrey, *Queen Elizabeth and the Making of Policy, 1572–1588* (1981), examines the problems posed by the Reformation and how Elizabeth solved them. J. E. Neale, *Queen Elizabeth I* (1957), remains valuable, and L. B. Smith, *The Elizabethan Epic* (1966), is a splendid evocation of the age of Shakespeare with Elizabeth at the center.

Nineteenth- and early twentieth-century historians described the defeat of the Spanish Armada as a great victory for Protestantism, democracy, and capitalism, which those scholars tended to link together. Recent historians have treated the event in terms of its contemporary significance. G. Mattingly, *The Armada* (1959), combines superb readability with the highest scholarly standards: this is history at its best. M. Lewis, *The Spanish Armada* (1972), tells a good story from the English perspective; David Howarth, *The Voyage of the Armada: the Spanish Story* (1981), presents the other side in an exciting narrative. C. V. Wedgwood, *The*

Thirty Years' War (1961), must be qualified in light of recent research on the social and economic effects of the war, but it is still a good (if detailed) starting point on a difficult period. A variety of opinions on the causes and results of the war are given in T. K. Rabb's anthology, *The Thirty Years' War* (1981). The following articles, all of which appear in the scholarly journal *Past and Present,* provide some of the latest important findings: H. Kamen, "The Economic and Social Consequences of the Thirty Years' War," no. 39 (1968); J. Hale, "War and Public Opinion in the Fifteenth and Sixteenth Centuries," no. 22 (1962); J. V. Polišenský, "The Thirty Years' War and the Crises and Revolutions of Sixteenth Century Europe," no. 39 (1968); and for the overall significance of Sweden, M. Roberts, "Queen Christina and the General Crisis of the Seventeenth Century," no. 22 (1962).

As background to the intellectual changes instigated by the Reformation, D. C. Wilcox, ed., *In Search of God and Self: Renaissance and Reformation Thought* (1975), contains perceptive articles, and T. Ashton, ed., *Crisis in Europe, 1560–1660* (1967), is fundamental. On witches and witchcraft, see, in addition to the titles by Norman Cohn and Keith Thomas in the Notes, Jeffrey B. Russell, *Witchcraft in the Middle Ages* (1976); Montague Summers, *The History of Witchcraft and Demonology* (1973); and H. R. Trevor-Roper, *The European Witch-Craze of the Sixteenth and Seventeenth Centuries* (1967), a brilliant collection of essays. Among the fascinating studies on North American racism, the interested student should consult W. D. Jordan, *The White Man's Burden: Historical Origins of Racism in the United States* (1974), and D. P. Mannix in collaboration with M. Cowley, *Black Cargoes: A History of the Atlantic Slave Trade* (1968), a hideously fascinating account. South American conditions may be contrasted in C. R. Boxer, *Four Centuries of Portuguese Expansion* (1969). The leading authority on Montaigne is D. M. Frame. See his *Montaigne's Discovery of Man* (1955), and his translation, *The Complete Works of Montaigne* (1958).

CHAPTER 16

ABSOLUTISM AND CONSTITUTIONALISM

IN WESTERN EUROPE (CA 1589–1715)

THE SEVENTEENTH CENTURY was a period of revolutionary transformation. Some of its most profound developments were political: the seventeenth century has been called the century when government became modern. The sixteenth century had witnessed the emergence of the nation-state. The long series of wars fought in the name of religion – but actually contests between royal authority and aristocratic power – brought social dislocation and agricultural and commercial disaster. Increasingly, strong national monarchy seemed the only solution. Spanish and French monarchs gained control of the major competing institution in their domains, the Roman Catholic church. In England and some of the German principalities, where rulers could not completely regulate the church, they set up national churches. In the German Empire the Treaty of Westphalia placed territorial sovereignty in the hands of the princes. The kings of France, England, and Spain claimed the basic loyalty of their subjects. Monarchs made laws, to which everyone within their borders was subject. These powers added up to something close to sovereignty.

A nation may be termed sovereign when it possesses a monopoly over the instruments of justice and the use of force within clearly defined boundaries. In a sovereign state no system of courts, such as ecclesiastical tribunals, competes with state courts in the dispensation of justice; and private armies, such as those of feudal lords, present no threat to royal authority because the national army is stronger. Royal law touches all persons within the country. Sovereignty had been evolving in the late sixteenth century. Seventeenth-century governments now faced the problem of *which* authority within the state would possess sovereignty – the Crown or the nobility.

In the period between roughly 1589 and 1715, two basic patterns of government emerged in Europe: absolute monarchy and the constitutional state. Almost all subsequent governments have been modeled on one or the other of these patterns. How were these forms of government "modern"? How did they differ from the feudal and dynastic monarchies of earlier centuries? Which countries best represent the new patterns of political organization? This chapter will be concerned with these political questions.

ABSOLUTISM

In the absolutist state, sovereignty is embodied in the person of the ruler. The ruler is not restrained by any legal authority. Absolute kings claimed to rule by divine right, meaning that they were responsible to God alone. (Medieval kings had governed "by the grace of God," but invariably they acknowledged that they had to respect and obey the law.) Absolute monarchs in the seventeenth and eighteenth centuries were not checked by national assemblies. Estates general and parliaments met at the wish and in response to the needs of kings. Because these meetings provided opportunities for opposition to the Crown to coalesce, absolute monarchs eventually stopped summoning them.

Absolute rulers effectively controlled all competing jurisdictions, all institutions or interest groups within their territories. They regulated religious sects. They abolished the liberties (privileges) long held by certain areas, groups, or provinces. Absolute kings also secured mastery over the one class that historically had posed the greatest threat to monarchy, the nobility. Medieval governments had been able to do none of these things. They had been restrained by the church, by the feudal nobility, and by their own financial limitations.

In some respects the key to the power and success of absolute monarchs lay in how they solved their financial problems. The solution was the creation of new state bureaucracies, which directed the economic life of the country in the interests of the king, raising ever higher taxes or devising other methods of raising revenue.

Bureaucracies were composed of career officials, appointed by and solely accountable to the king. The backgrounds of these civil servants varied. Absolute monarchs sometimes drew on the middle class, as in France, or utilized members of the nobility, as in Spain and eastern Europe. Where there was no middle class or an insignificant one, as in Austria, Prussia, Spain, and Russia, the government of the absolutist state consisted of an interlocking elite of monarchy, aristocracy, and bureaucracy.

Royal agents in medieval kingdoms had used their public offices and positions to benefit themselves and their families. In England, for example, Crown servants from Thomas Becket to Thomas Wolsey had treated their high offices as their personal private property, and reaped considerable profit from the positions they held. The most striking difference between seventeenth-century bureaucracies and their medieval predecessors was that seventeenth-century civil servants served the state as represented by the king. Bureaucrats recognized that the offices they held were public, or state, positions. The state paid them salaries to handle revenues that belonged to the Crown, and they were not supposed to use their official positions for private gain. Bureaucrats gradually came to distinguish between public duties and private property.

Absolute monarchs also maintained permanent standing armies. Medieval armies had been raised by feudal lords for particular wars or campaigns, after which the troops were disbanded. In the seventeenth century, monarchs alone recruited and maintained armies – in peacetime as well as during war. Kings deployed their troops both inside and outside the country in the interests of the monarchy. Armies became basic features of absolutist, and modern, states. Absolute rulers also invented new methods of compulsion. They concerned themselves with the private lives of potentially troublesome subjects, often through the use of secret police.

Thus rule of absolute monarchs was not all-embracing because they lacked the financial and military resources and the technology to make it so. Thus the absolutist state was not the same as a totalitarian state. Totalitarianism is a twentieth-century phenomenon; it seeks to direct all facets of a state's culture – art, education, religion, the economy, and politics – in the interests of the state. By definition totalitarian rule is *total* regulation. By twentieth-century standards, the ambitions of an absolute monarch were quite limited: he sought the exaltation of himself as the embodiment of the state. When King Louis XIV of France declared, "L'état, c'est moi!" ("I am the state!"), he meant that he personally was the incarnation of France. Yet the absolutist state did foreshadow recent totalitarian regimes in two fundamental respects: in the glorification of the state over all other aspects of the national culture, and in the use of war and an expansionist foreign policy to divert attention from domestic ills.

All of this is best illustrated by the experience of France, aptly known as the model of absolute monarchy.

THE FOUNDATIONS OF ABSOLUTISM IN FRANCE: HENRY IV AND SULLY

The ingenious Huguenot-turned-Catholic, Henry IV (pages 524–525), ended the French religious wars with the Edict of Nantes. The first of the Bourbon dynasty, and probably the first French ruler since Louis IX in the thirteenth century genuinely to care about the French people, Henry IV and his great minister Sully (1560–1641) laid the foundations of later French absolutism. Henry denied influence on the royal council to the nobility, which had harassed the countryside for half a century. Maintaining that "if we are without compassion for the people, they must succumb and we all perish with them," Henry also lowered the severe taxes on the overburdened peasantry.

Sully proved himself a financial genius. He not only reduced the crushing royal debt but began to build up the treasury. He levied an annual tax, the *paulette,* on people who had purchased financial and judicial offices and had consequently been exempt from royal taxation. One of the first French officials to appreciate the significance of overseas trade, Sully subsidized the Company for Trade with the Indies. He started a countrywide highway system and even dreamed of an international organization for the maintenance of peace.

In twelve short years Henry IV and Sully restored public order in France and laid the foundations for economic prosperity. By late-sixteenth-century standards, Henry IV's government was both progressive and promising. His murder in 1610 by a crazed fanatic plunged the country into civil war and threatened to undo his work.

THE CORNERSTONE OF FRENCH ABSOLUTISM: LOUIS XIII AND RICHELIEU

After the death of Henry IV, the queen-regent Marie de' Medici led the government for the child-king Louis XIII (1610–1643), but in fact feudal nobles and princes of the blood dominated the political scene. In 1624, Marie de' Medici secured the appointment of Armand Jean du Plessis – Cardinal Richelieu (1585–

1642) – to the council of ministers. It was a remarkable appointment. The next year Richelieu became president of the council, and after 1628 he was first minister of the French crown and the actual ruler of France. Richelieu used his strong influence over King Louis XIII to exalt the French monarchy as the embodiment of the French state. One of the greatest servants of the French state, Richelieu set in place the cornerstone of French absolutism, and his work served as the basis for France's cultural domination of Europe in the later seventeenth century.

Richelieu's policy was the total subordination of all groups and institutions to the French monarchy. The French nobility, with its selfish and independent interests, had long constituted the foremost threat to the centralizing goals of the Crown and to a strong national state. Therefore, Richelieu broke the power of the nobility. He leveled castles, long the symbol of feudal independence. He crushed aristocratic conspiracies with quick executions. For example, when the duke de Montmorency, the first peer of France and the godson of Henry IV, became involved in a revolt in 1632, he was summarily put to death. Richelieu abolished the great medieval military dignities that had exalted the prestige and local power of some great nobles. He banned dueling. He prevented the great lords from sitting in the king's council.

The constructive genius of Cardinal Richelieu is best reflected in the administrative system he established. He extended the use of royal commissioners called intendants. France was divided into thirty-two *généralités* (districts), in each of which a royal intendant had complete responsibility for justice, police, and finances. The intendants were authorized "to decide, order and execute all that they see good to do." Usually members of the upper middle class or minor nobility, the intendants were appointed directly by the monarch, to whom they were solely responsible. They had complete power in their districts and were to use that power for two related purposes: to enforce royal orders in the *généralités* of their jurisdiction and to weaken the power and influence of the regional nobility. The system of government by intendants derived from Philip Augustus's baillis and seneschals, and ultimately from Charlemagne's *missi dominici.* As the intendants' power grew during Richelieu's administration, so did the power of the centralized state.

Although Richelieu succeeded in building a rational and centralized political machine in the intendant system, he was not the effective financial administrator Sully had been. France lacked a sound system of taxation, a method of raising sufficient revenue to meet the needs of the state. Richelieu reverted to the old device of selling offices. He increased the number of sinecures, tax exemptions, and benefices that were purchasable and inheritable. In 1624, this device brought in almost 40 percent of royal revenues.

The rising cost of foreign and domestic policies led to the auctioning of tax farms, the system whereby a man bought the right to collect taxes. Tax farmers kept a very large part of the receipts they collected. The sale of offices and this antiquated system of tax collection were improvisations that promoted confusion and corruption. Even worse, state offices, once purchased, were passed on to heirs, which meant that a family that held a state office was eternally exempt from taxation. Richelieu's inadequate and temporary solutions created grave financial problems for the future.

The cardinal perceived that Protestantism all too often served as a cloak for the political intrigues of ambitious lords. When the Huguenots revolted in 1625, under the duke de Rohan, Richelieu personally supervised the siege of their walled city, La Rochelle, and forced it to surrender. Thereafter, fortified places of security were abolished. Huguenots were allowed to practice their faith, but they no longer possessed armed strongholds or the means to be an independent party in the state. Another aristocratic prop was knocked down.

French foreign policy under Richelieu was aimed at the destruction of the fence of Habsburg territories that surrounded France. Consequently, Richelieu supported the Habsburgs' enemies. In 1631, he signed a treaty with the Lutheran king Gustavus Adolphus promising French support against the Catholic Habsburgs in what has been called the Swedish phase of the Thirty Years' War (page 533). French influence became an important factor in the political future of the German empire. Richelieu added Alsace in the east (1639) and Arras in the north (1640) to French territory.

Richelieu's efforts at centralization extended even to literature. In 1635 he gave official recognition to a group of philologists who were interested in grammar and rhetoric. Thus was born the French Academy. With Richelieu's encouragement, the Academy began the preparation of a *dictionary* to standardize the French language; it was completed in 1694. The French Academy survives as a prestigious learned society, whose membership has been broadened to include people outside the field of literature.

Richelieu personified the increasingly secular spirit of the seventeenth century. Although a bishop of the Roman Catholic church, he gave his first loyalty to the French state. Although a Roman Catholic cardinal, he gave strong support to the Protestant Lutherans of Germany. The portrait of Richelieu by Philippe de Champaigne – with its penetrating eyes, expression of haughty and imperturbable cynicism, and dramatic sweep of rich red robes — reveals the authority, grandeur, and power the cardinal wanted to convey as first minister of France. Just before Richelieu died in 1642, worn out with work and ulcers, the curé of St.-Eustache asked him to forgive his enemies. Richelieu replied, characteristically, that he had no enemies save those of the king and the state.

Richelieu had persuaded Louis XIII to appoint his protegé Jules Mazarin (1602-1661) as his successor. An Italian diplomat of great charm, Mazarin served on the Council of State under Richelieu, acquiring considerable political experience. He became a cardinal in 1641 and a French citizen in 1643. When Louis XIII followed Richelieu to the grave in 1643 and a regency headed by Queen Anne of Austria governed for the child-king Louis XIV, Mazarin became the dominant power in the government. He continued the antifeudal and centralizing policies of Richelieu, but his attempts to increase royal revenues led to the civil wars known as the Fronde.

The word *fronde* means slingshot or catapult, and a *frondeur* was originally a street urchin who threw mud at the passing carriages of the rich. The term came to be used for anyone who opposed the policies of the government. Richelieu had stirred up the bitter resentment of the aristocracy, who felt its constitutional status and ancient privileges threatened. He also bequeathed to the Crown a staggering debt, and when Mazarin tried to impose financial reforms the monarchy incurred the enmity of the middle classes. Both groups plotted against Anne and Mazarin. Most historians see the Fronde as the last serious effort by the French nobility to oppose the monarchy by force. When in 1648 Mazarin proposed new methods for raising income, bitter civil war ensued between the monarchy on the one side and the frondeurs

(the nobility and the upper-middle classes) on the other. Riots and public turmoil wracked Paris and the nation. The violence continued intermittently for almost twelve years. Factional disputes among the nobles led to their ultimate defeat.

The conflicts of the Fronde had two significant results for the future: a badly disruptive effect on the French economy and a traumatic impact on the young Louis XIV. The king and his mother were frequently threatened and sometimes treated as prisoners by aristocratic factions. On one occasion a mob broke into the royal bedchamber to make sure the king was actually there; it succeeded in giving him a bad fright. Louis never forgot such humiliations. The period of the Fronde formed the cornerstone of his political education and of his unalterable conviction that the sole alternative to anarchy was absolute monarchy.

THE ABSOLUTE MONARCHY OF LOUIS XIV

According to the court theologian Bossuet, the clergy at the coronation of Louis XIV in Reims Cathedral asked God to cause the splendors of the French court to fill all who beheld it with awe. God subsequently granted that prayer. In the reign of Louis XIV (1643–1715), the longest in European history, the French monarchy reached the peak of absolutist development. In the magnificence of his court, in his absolute power, in the brilliance of the culture over which he presided and which permeated all of Europe, and in his remarkably long life, Louis XIV dominated his age. No wonder scholars have characterized the second half of the seventeenth century as "The Grand Century," "The Age of Magnificence," and, echoing the eighteenth-century philosopher Voltaire, "The Age of Louis XIV."

Who was this phenomenon of whom it was said that when Louis sneezed, all Europe caught cold? Born in 1638, king at the age of five, he entered into personal, or independent, rule in 1661. One of his first recorded remarks reveals the astonishing sense of self that was to awe French people and foreigners alike. Taken as a child to his father's deathbed, he identified himself as "Louis Quatorze" ("Louis the fourteenth").

In old age Louis claimed that he had grown up learning very little, and many historians have agreed. He knew little Latin and only the rudiments of arithmetic, and was thus by Renaissance standards not well educated. On the other hand, he learned to speak Italian and Spanish fluently; he knew some French history, and more European geography than the ambassadors accredited to his court. He imbibed the devout Catholicism of his mother Anne of Austria, and throughout his long life scrupulously performed his religious duties. Religion, Anne, and Mazarin all taught Louis that God had established kings as His rulers on earth. The royal coronation consecrated him to God's service, and he was certain – to use Shakespeare's phrase – that there was a divinity that doth hedge a king. Although kings were a race apart, they could not do as they pleased: they must obey God's laws and rule for the good of the people.

Louis's education was more practical than formal. Under Mazarin's instruction he studied state papers as they arrived, and he attended council meetings and sessions at which French ambassadors were dispatched abroad and foreign ambassadors received. He learned by direct experience and gained professional training in the work of government. Above all, the misery he suffered during the Fronde gave Louis an eternal distrust of the nobility and a profound sense of his own isolation. Accordingly, silence, caution, and secrecy became political tools for the achievement of his goals. His characteristic answer to requests of all kinds became the enigmatic "Je verrai" ("I shall see").

Louis grew up with an absolute sense of his royal dignity. Tall and distinguished in appearance, he was inclined to fatness because of the gargantuan meals in which he indulged. Seduced by one of his mother's maids when he was sixteen, the king matured into a highly sensual man easily aroused by an attractive female face and figure. It is to his credit, however, that neither his wife, Queen Maria Theresa, whom he married as the result of a diplomatic agreement with Spain, nor his mistresses ever possessed any political influence. Extraordinarily selfish, Louis doted on flattery, which he interpreted as glory.

Whatever his negative qualities, Louis XIV worked extremely hard and succeeded in being "every moment and every inch a king." Because he so thoroughly relished the role of king, historians have had difficulty distinguishing the man from the monarch. Louis XIV was a consummate actor, and his "terrifying majesty" awed all who saw him.

The reign of Louis XIV witnessed great innovations in style but few in substance; Louis extended and intensified earlier practices and trends. The most significant development was his acquisition of absolute control over the French nobility. Indeed, it is often said that Louis achieved the complete "domestication" of the nobility.

Louis XIV turned the royal court into a fixed institution. In the past the king of France and the royal court had traveled constantly, visiting the king's properties, the great noblemen, and his *bonnes villes* or good towns. Since the time of Louis IX, or even Charlemagne, rulers had traveled to maintain order in distant parts of the realm, to impress humbler subjects with the royal dignity and

AERIAL VIEW OF VERSAILLES *Awe-inspiring, monumental, and over a quarter of a mile long, Versailles is the supreme example of classical baroque architecture in the service of absolute monarchy. The vast formal gardens with their geometric regularity pro-* *vided the outdoor setting for Louis XIV's festivities, while the three avenues radiating from the palace symbolize the king as source of all power. (French Government Tourist Office)*

magnificence, and in so doing to bind the country together through loyalty to the king. Since the early Middle Ages, the king's court had consisted of his family, trusted advisers and councilors, a few favorites, and servants. Except for the very highest officials of the state, members of the council had changed constantly.

Louis XIV installed the court at Versailles, a small town ten miles from Paris. He required all the great nobility of France, at the peril of social, political, and sometimes economic disaster, to come live at Versailles for at least part of the year. Today, Versailles stands as the best surviving museum of a vanished society on earth. In the seventeenth century, it became a model of rational order, the center of France and thus the center of Western civilization, the perfect symbol of the king's absolute power.

Louis XIII had begun Versailles as a hunting lodge, a retreat from a queen he did not

HALL OF MIRRORS AT VERSAILLES *This long and magnificently impressive room takes up much of the central block of Versailles. The hundreds of mirrors, which give the illusion of width, reflected the court spectacles and the king's glory. The splendor of this hall and many other adjacent palace rooms was a far cry, however, from the cramped conditions that many nobles were forced to live with at the royal court. (French Government Tourist Office)*

like. His son's architects, Le Nôtre and Le Vau, turned what Saint-Simon called "the most dismal and thankless of sights" into a veritable paradise. Wings were added to the original building to make the palace U-shaped. Everywhere at Versailles the viewer has a sense of grandeur, vastness, and incredible elegance. Enormous state rooms became display galleries for inlaid tables, Italian marble statuary, Gobelin tapestries woven at the state factory in Paris, silver ewers, and beautiful (if uncomfortable) furniture. If genius means attention to detail, Louis XIV and his designers had it: the décor was perfected down to the last doorknob and keyhole. In the gigantic Hall of Mirrors, which was later to reflect so much of German as well as French history, hundreds of candles illuminated the domed ceiling, where allegorical paintings celebrated the king's victories.

The Ambassador's Staircase is of brilliantly colored marble, with part of the railing gold-plated. The staircase is dominated by a great bust of the king, which when completed so overwhelmed a courtier that he exclaimed to the sculptor Bernini, "Don't do anything more to it, it's so good I'm afraid you might spoil it." The statue, like the staircase – and the entire palace – succeeded from the start in its purpose: it awed.

The formal, carefully ordered, and perfectly landscaped gardens at Versailles express at a glance the spirit of the age of Louis XIV. Every tree, every bush, every foot of grass, every fountain, pool, and piece of statuary within three miles is perfectly laid out. The vista is of the world made rational and absolutely controlled. Nature itself was subdued to enhance the greatness of the king.

Under the vast terrace stands one of the great architectural splendors of France, the Orangerie. Designed to house the king's twelve hundred potted palms and orange trees, the Orangerie is a huge vaulted space, so large that when it was completed in 1686 several operas could be performed there simultaneously without inconvenience. The Siamese ambassador is reputed to have said that the magnificence of Louis XIV must indeed be great, since he had raised so superb a palace simply for his orange trees.

Against this background of magnificent splendor, as the great aristocrat Saint-Simon describes, Louis XIV

reduced everyone to subjection, and brought to his court those very persons he cared least about. Whoever was old enough to serve did not dare demur. It was still another device to ruin the nobles by accustoming them to equality and forcing them to mingle with everyone indiscriminately....

... To keep everyone assiduous and attentive, the King personally named the guests for each festivity, each stroll through Versailles, and each trip. These were his rewards and punishments. He

knew there was little else he could distribute to keep everyone in line. He substituted idle rewards for real ones and these operated through jealousy, the petty preferences he showed many times a day, and his artfulness in showing them. No one was more ingenious than him in nourishing the hopes and satisfactions to which these petty preferences and distinctions gave birth....

... Upon rising, at bedtime, during meals, in his apartments, in the gardens of Versailles, everywhere the courtiers had a right to follow, he would glance right and left to see who was there; he saw and noted everyone; he missed no one, even those who were hoping they would not be seen.... For the most distinguished persons, it was a demerit not to put in a regular appearance at court. It was just as bad for those of lesser rank to come but rarely, and certain disgrace for those who never, or almost never, came....

... Louis XIV took great pains to inform himself on what was happening everywhere, in public places, private homes, and even on the international scene.... Spies and informers of all kinds were numberless....

... But the King's most vicious method of securing information was opening letters....[1]

Through ritual and ceremony the king turned the proud and ancient nobility into a pack of trained seals. He destroyed their ancient right to advise and counsel the monarch. Operas, fetes, and balls occupied the nobles' time and attention. They become solely instruments of the king's pleasure. Louis XIV may have had limited native intelligence, but through painstaking attention to detail and precisely calculated showmanship, he emasculated the major threat to his absolute power. He separated power from grandeur: the nobility enjoyed the grandeur in which they lived; the king alone enjoyed the power.

The art and architecture of Versailles served as fundamental tools of state policy under

Louis XIV. Architecture was the device the king used to overawe his subjects and foreign visitors. Versailles was seen as a reflection of French genius. Thus the Russian czar Peter the Great imitated Versailles in the construction of his palace, Peterhof, as did the Prussian emperor Frederick the Great in his palace at Potsdam outside Berlin.

As in architecture, so too in language. Beginning in the reign of Louis XIV, French became the language of polite society and the vehicle of diplomatic exchange. French also gradually replaced Latin as the language of international scholarship and learning. The wish of other kings to ape the courtly style of Louis XIV and the imitation of French intellectuals and artists spread the French language all over Europe. The royal courts of Sweden, Russia, Poland, and Germany all spoke French. In the eighteenth century, the great Russian aristocrats were more fluent in French than in Russian. In England the First Hanoverian king, George I, spoke French but no English. France inspired a cosmopolitan European culture in the late seventeenth century, and that culture was inspired by the king. That is what Voltaire meant when he called the period "The Age of Louis XIV."

Louis dominated the court, and the court was the center of France. In the king's scheme of things, the court was more significant than the government. Louix XIV made no innovations in the government of France. He continued the system of the intendants, appointing them entirely from the middle class. By curbing the power of the local aristocracy and gentry, the intendants advanced royal sovereignty in the provinces. Members of the royal councils — such as the Council of State, which dealt with diplomacy, war, and peace — were drawn from the class Saint-Simon called "the bookkeepers," the middle class.

Louis feared and distrusted the nobility, and so he eliminated them from government. Throughout his long reign, and in spite of increasing financial problems, he never called the French nobility together in a meeting of the Estates General. The nobility, therefore, had no means of united expression or action. Nor did Louis have a first minister, freeing him from worry about the inordinate power of a Richelieu. Louis's use of terror — a secret police force, a system of informers, and the practice of opening private letters — foreshadowed some of the devices of the modern state. French government remained highly structured, bureaucratic, centered in Paris, and responsible to Louis XIV.

ECONOMIC MANAGEMENT UNDER LOUIS XIV: COLBERT AND MERCANTILISM

As controller-general of finances, the king named Jean Baptiste Colbert. The son of a draper of Reims, Colbert (1619–1683) came to manage the entire royal administration and proved himself a financial genius. Colbert's central principle was that the economy and the wealth of France should serve the state. He did not invent the economic system or program called mercantilism, but he rigorously applied it to France.

Mercantilism is a system for the regulation of economic activities, especially commercial activities, by and for the state. In seventeenth- and eighteenth-century economic theory, a nation's international power was thought to be based on its wealth, specifically its gold supply. To accumulate gold, a country should always sell abroad more than it bought. Colbert believed that a successful economic policy meant more than a favorable balance of trade. He insisted that the French sell abroad and buy *nothing* back. France should be self-sufficient, able to produce within its borders everything the subjects of the French king needed. Consequently, the outflow of gold would be halted and the power and prestige of the state enhanced.

Colbert attempted to accomplish self-sufficiency through state support for both old industries and newly created ones. He subsidized the established cloth industries at Abbeville, St.-Quentin, and Carcassonne. He granted special royal privileges to the rug and tapestry industries at Paris, Gobelin, and Beauvais. New factories at St.-Antoine in Paris manufactured mirrors to replace Venetian imports. Looms at Chantilly and Alençon competed with English lacemaking, and foundries at St.-Etienne made steel and firearms that cut Swedish imports. To insure a high-quality finished product, Colbert set up a system of state inspection and regulation. To insure order within every industry he compelled all craftsmen to organize into guilds, and within every guild he gave the masters absolute power over their workers. Colbert encouraged skilled foreign craftsmen and manufacturers to immigrate to France, and he gave them special privileges. To protect French products, Colbert enacted high tariffs, which prevented foreign goods from competing with French ones.

Colbert's most important work was the creation of a powerful merchant marine to transport French goods. He gave bonuses to French shipowners and builders, and established a method of maritime conscription, arsenals, and academies for the training of sailors. In 1661, France possessed 18 unseaworthy vessels; by 1681, France had 276 frigates, galleys, and ships of the line. Colbert tried to organize and regulate the entire French economy for the glory of the French state as embodied in the king.

Colbert hoped to make Canada — rich in untapped minerals and some of the best agricultural land in the world — part of a vast French empire. He gathered four thousand peasants from western France and shipped them to Canada, where they peopled the province of Quebec. (In 1608, one year after the English arrived at Jamestown, Virginia, Sully had established the city of Quebec, which became the capital of French Canada.) Subsequently, the Jesuit Marquette and the merchant Joliet sailed down the Mississippi River and took possession of the land on both sides as far south as present-day Arkansas. In 1684, the French explorer La Salle continued down the Mississippi to its mouth and claimed vast territories and the rich delta for Louis XIV. The area was called, naturally, Louisiana.

Nothing did more to destroy Colbert's system of commercial and colonial regulation than the revocation of the Edict of Nantes — an event that, on the surface at least, had little to do with economic life. For almost a century the edict had granted equal political and some religious rights to the Huguenots of France. Scholars have debated at length the reasons for Louis XIV's revocation of it in 1685. Was the revocation due to the powerful influence of the king's Catholic wife, Madame de Maintenon? Was it the result of pressure from Catholic business interests who resented the competition of the clever Huguenots? Did Louis abolish freedom of religion because of his pride and religious intolerance, which could not countenance the existence in France of a sizable group with a faith different from his own? Or was it sheer ignorance of the large numbers of his Calvinist subjects and their social and economic importance to the state, an ignorance attributable to the isolation of the court? Whatever the exact causes of the revocation, its consequences proved disastrous.

Perhaps 300,000 French citizens chose to emigrate rather than convert. Some of the best craftsmen, businessmen, soldiers, and sailors fled to England, Holland, and Prussia. They left their goods behind but carried their skills and hatred of Louis XIV with them. The loss of so many experts and the taxes they represented — on top of Louis's chronic need for money — severely aggravated the national financial situation. After 1685, the French government had to resort again to the expediency of creating offices and selling them on a broad scale. This stopgap measure paid for the present by mortgaging the future, since officeholders and their descendants paid no taxes.

Most catastrophic of all, the revocation of the Edict of Nantes provoked domestic turmoil within France and fear and hatred abroad. Calvinist peasants in Languedoc revolted, for example, and Louis was ultimately forced to back down. The Protestant states of northern Europe — Holland, Brandenburg, and Sweden — united against Louis XIV, and from 1688 until his death France was almost continually at war. With some justification, historians have called the revocation of the Edict of Nantes the greatest error the Bourbon dynasty committed.

FRENCH CLASSICISM

Scholars characterize the art and literature of the age of Louis XIV as French Classicism. By this they mean that the artists and writers of the late seventeenth century deliberately imitated the subject matter and style of classical antiquity; that their work resembles that of Renaissance Italy; and that French art possessed the classical qualities of discipline, balance, and restraint. Classicism was the official style of Louis's court. In painting, however, French classicism had already reached its peak before 1661, the beginning of the king's personal government.

Nicholas Poussin (1593–1665) is generally considered the finest example of French classicist painting. Poussin spent all but eighteen months of his creative life in Rome because he found the atmosphere in Paris uncongenial. Deeply attached to classical antiquity, he believed that the highest aim of painting was to represent noble actions in a logical and orderly, but not realistic, way. His masterpiece, "The Rape of the Sabine Women," exhibits these qualities. Its subject is an incident in Roman history; the figures of people and horses are ideal representations, and the emotions expressed are studied, not spontaneous. Even the buildings are exact architectural models of ancient Roman structures.

While Poussin selected grand and "noble" themes, Louis Le Nain (1593–1648) painted genre scenes of peasant life. At a time when artists favored Biblical and classical allegories, Le Nain's paintings are unique for their depiction of peasants. The highly realistic group assembled in "The Peasant Family" have great human dignity. The painting itself is reminiscent of portrayals of peasants by seventeenth-century Dutch painters.

Le Nain and Poussin, whose paintings still had individualistic features, did their work before 1661. After Louis's accession to power, the principles of absolutism molded the ideals of French classicism. Individualism was not allowed, and artists' efforts were directed to the glorification of the state as personified by the king. Precise rules governed all aspects of culture, with the goal of formal and restrained perfection.

Contemporaries said that Louis XIV never

ceased playing the role of grand monarch on the stage of his court. If the king never fully relaxed from the pressures and intrigues of government, he did enjoy music and theater and used them as a backdrop for court ceremonial. Louis favored Jean-Baptiste Lully (1632–1687), whose orchestral works combine lively animation with the restrained austerity typical of French classicism. Lully also composed court ballets, and his operatic productions achieved a powerful influence throughout Europe. Louis supported Francois Couperin (1668–1733), whose harpsicord and organ works possess the regal grandeur the king loved, and Marc-Antoine Charpentier (1634–1704), whose solemn religious music entertained him at meals. Charpentier received a pension for the *Te Deums,* hymns of thanksgiving he composed to celebrate French military victories.

Louis XIV loved the stage, and in the plays of Molière and Racine his court witnessed the finest achievements in the history of the French theater. When Jean-Baptiste Poquelin (1622–1673), the son of a prosperous tapestry maker, refused to join his father's business and entered the theater, he took the stage name Molière. As playwright, stage manager, director, and actor, Molière produced comedies that exposed the hypocrisies and follies of society though brilliant caricature. *Tartuffe* satirized the religious hypocrite, *Le Bourgeois Gentilhomme (The Would-Be Gentleman)* attacked the social parvenu, and *Les Femmes savantes (The Learned Women)* mocked the fashionable pseudo-intellectuals of the day. In structure Molière's plays followed classical models, but they were based on careful social observation. Molière made the bourgeoisie the butt of his ridicule; he stopped short of criticizing the nobility, thus reflecting the policy of his royal patron.

While Molière dissected social mores, his

POUSSIN: THE RAPE OF THE SABINE WOMEN *Considered the greatest French painter of the seventeenth century, Poussin in this dramatic work (ca 1636) shows his complete devotion to the ideals of classicism. The heroic figures are superb physical specimens, but hardly life-like. (Metropolitan Museum of Art, New York [Dick Fund, 1946])*

contemporary Jean Racine (1639–1699) analyzed the power of love. Racine based his tragic dramas on Greek and Roman legends, and his persistent theme is the conflict of good and evil. Several plays – *Andromache, Berenice, Iphigenie,* and *Phedre* – bear the names of women and deal with the power of passion in women. Louis preferred *Mithridates* and *Brittanicus* because of the "grandeur" of their themes. For simplicity of language, symmetrical structure, and calm restraint, the plays of Racine represent the finest examples of French classicism. His tragedies and Molière's comedies are still produced today.

LOUIS XIV'S WARS

Just as the architecture and court life at Versailles served to reflect the king's glory, and as the economy of the state under Colbert was managed to advance the king's prestige, so did Louis XIV use war to exalt himself above the other rulers and nations of Europe. He visualized himself as a great military hero. "The character of a conqueror," he remarked, "is regarded as the noblest and highest of titles." Military glory was his aim. In 1666, Louis appointed François le Tellier (later Marquis de Louvois) as secretary of war. Louvois created a professional army, which was modern in the sense that the French state, rather than private nobles, employed the soldiers.

Because of the justifiable fear that an army of native French soldiers would turn on their oppressors, the army of Louis XIV was re-

cruited heavily from Swiss, German, and Irish mercenaries. Officers were French, the ranks largely foreign. A foreign mercenary army could more easily be employed against rebellious peasants whose language they did not speak. It is one of the ironies of Louis' wars that a French army of Protestant Swiss and German troops was sent against the Protestant Dutch.

A commissariat was established to feed the troops, in place of the ancient practice of living off the countryside. An ambulance corps was designed to look after the wounded. Uniforms and weapons were standardized. Finally, a rational system of recruitment, training, discipline, and promotion was imposed. With this new military machine, for the first time in Europe's history one national state, France, was able to dominate the politics of Europe.

Louis continued on a broader scale the expansionist policy begun by Cardinal Richelieu. In 1667, using a dynastic excuse, he invaded Flanders, part of the Spanish Netherlands, and Franche-Comté in the east. In consequence he acquired twelve towns, including the important commercial centers of Lille and Tournai (see Map 16.1). Five years later, Louis personally led an army of over a hundred thousand men into Holland, and the Dutch ultimately saved themselves only by opening the dikes and flooding the countryside. This war, which lasted six years and eventually involved the German empire and Spain, was concluded by the Treaty of Nijmegen (1678). Louis gained additional Flemish towns and the whole of Franche-Comté.

Encouraged by his successes, by the weakness of the German empire, and by divisions among the other European powers, Louis continued his aggression. In 1684 he seized the city of Trier, and the province of Lorraine was permanently occupied by France. At that moment, the king seemed invincible.

In fact, Louis had reached the limit of his expansion at Nijmegen. The wars of the 1680s and 1690s brought him no additional territories. In 1689, the Dutch prince William of Orange, a bitter foe of Louis XIV, became king of England. William joined the League of Augsburg – which included the German emperor, the kings of Spain and Sweden, and the electors of Bavaria, Saxony, and the Palatinate – adding British resources and men to the alliance. Neither the French nor the league won any decisive victories. The alliance served instead as preparation for the long-expected conflict known as the War of the Spanish Succession.

This struggle (1701–1713), provoked by the territorial disputes of the past century, also involved the dynastic question of the succession to the Spanish throne. It was an open secret in Europe that the king of Spain, Charles II (1665–1700), was mentally defective and sexually impotent. In his will Charles left his territories to his grandnephew, Philip of Anjou, who was also Louis XIV's grandson. When Charles died on November 1, 1700, the line of the Spanish Habsburgs ended. Immediately, Louis claimed the Spanish throne on behalf of his grandson.

The union of the French and Spanish crowns would have totally upset the European balance of power, and Louis's declaration that "the Pyrenees no longer exist" provoked the long-anticipated crisis. In May 1702 England, Holland, and the Holy Roman Empire declared war on France. They claimed that they were fighting to prevent France from becoming too strong in Europe, but during the previous half-century overseas maritime rivalry among France, Holland, and England had created serious international tension. The secondary motive of the Allied Powers was to check France's expanding commercial power in North America, Asia, and Africa. In the

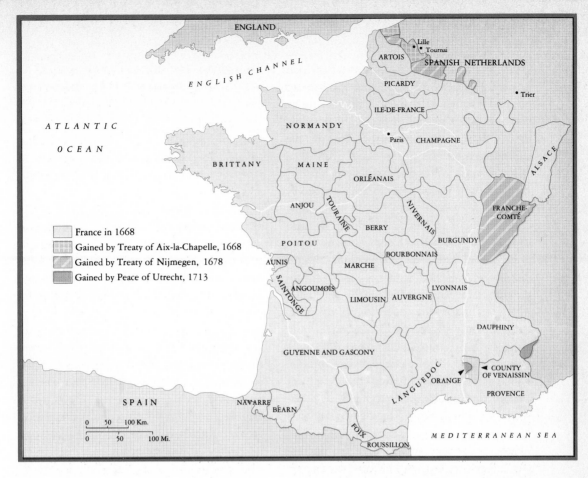

Legend:
- France in 1668
- Gained by Treaty of Aix-la-Chapelle, 1668
- Gained by Treaty of Nijmegen, 1678
- Gained by Peace of Utrecht, 1713

MAP 16.1   THE ACQUISITIONS OF LOUIS XIV, 1668–1713   *The desire for glory and the weakness of his German neighbors encouraged Louis' expansionist policy. But he paid a high price for his acquisitions.*

ensuing series of conflicts, two great soldiers dominated the alliance against France: Eugene, prince of Savoy, representing the Holy Roman Empire, and the Englishman John Churchill, subsequently duke of Marlborough. Eugene and Churchill inflicted a crushing defeat on Louis in 1704 at Blenheim in Bavaria. Marlborough followed with another victory at Romilles near Namur in Brabant.

The war was finally concluded at Utrecht in 1713, where the principle of partition was applied. Louis's grandson Philip became the first Bourbon king of Spain on the understanding that the French and Spanish crowns would never be united. France surrendered Newfoundland, Nova Scotia, and the Hudson Bay territory to England, which also acquired Gibraltar, Minorca, and the *asiento,* or control of the African slave trade from Spain. The Dutch received little because the former Spanish Netherlands was given to Austria.

The Peace of Utrecht had important international consequences. It represented the balance-of-power principle in operation, setting limits on the extent to which any one power, in this case France, could expand. The treaty completed the decline of Spain as a great power. It vastly expanded the British Empire. Finally, Utrecht gave European powers experience in international cooperation and thus prepared them for the great alliances against France at the end of the eighteenth century.

For Louis XIV, Utrecht was a severe defeat. He had waged his wars in the quest for glory. He had gained little (see Map 16.1). Utrecht marked the end of French expansion. To raise revenue for the wars, forty thousand additional offices had been sold, thus increasing the number of families exempt from future taxation. Constant war had disrupted trade, which meant the state could not tax the profits of trade. Widespread starvation in the provinces provoked peasant revolts, especially in Brittany. In 1714, France hovered on the brink of financial bankruptcy. Louis had exhausted the country without much compensation. It is no wonder that when he died on September 1, 1715, Saint-Simon wrote, "Those . . . wearied by the heavy and oppressive rule of the King and his ministers, felt a delighted freedom. . . . Paris . . . found relief in the hope of liberation. . . . The provinces . . . quivered with delight . . . [and] the people, ruined, abused, despairing, now thanked God for a deliverance which answered their most ardent desires."[2]

THE DECLINE OF ABSOLUTIST SPAIN IN THE SEVENTEENTH CENTURY

Spanish absolutism and greatness had preceded that of the French. In the sixteenth century, Spain had developed the standard features of absolute monarchy: a permanent bureaucracy staffed by professionals employed in the various councils of state, a standing army, and national taxes, the *servicios,* which fell most heavily on the poor.

France depended upon financial and admin-

VELAZQUEZ: THE MAIDS OF HONOR The Infanta Margarita painted in 1656 with her maids and playmates has invaded the artist's studio, while her parents' image is reflected in the mirror on the back wall. Velazquez (extreme left), who powerfully influenced nineteenth-century impressionist painters, imbued all of his subjects, including the pathetic dwarf (right, in black) with a sense of dignity. (Giraudon)

istrative unification within its national borders; Spain had developed an international absolutism on the basis of silver bullion from Peru. Spanish gold and silver, Spanish armies, and Spanish glory had dominated the continent of Europe for most of the sixteenth century, but by the 1590s the seeds of disaster were sprouting. While France in the seventeenth century represented the classic model of the modern absolute state, Spain was experiencing steady decline and decay. Fiscal disorder, political incompetence, population decline, intellectual isolation, and psychological malaise – all combined to reduce Spain, by 1715, to the rank of a second-rate power.

The fabulous and seemingly inexhaustible flow of silver from Mexico and Peru had led Philip II (page 529) to assume the role of defender of Roman Catholicism in Europe. In order to humble the Protestant Dutch and to control the Spanish Netherlands, Philip believed that England, the Netherlands' greatest supporter, had to be crushed. He poured millions of Spanish ducats and all of Spanish hopes into the vast fleet that sailed in 1588. When the "Invincible Armada" went down in the North Sea, a century of Spanish pride and power went with it. After 1590, a spirit of defeatism and disillusionment crippled almost all efforts at reform.

Philip II's Catholic crusade had been financed by the revenues of the Spanish-Atlantic economy. These included, in addition to silver and gold bullion, the sale of cloth,

grain, oil, and wine to the colonies. In the early seventeenth century, the Dutch and English began to trade with the Spanish colonies, cutting into the revenues that had gone to Spain. Mexico and Peru themselves developed local industries, further lessening their need to buy from Spain. Between 1610 and 1650, Spanish trade with the colonies fell 60 percent.

At the same time the native Indians and African slaves, who worked the South American silver mines under conditions that would have disgraced the ancient Egyptian pharaohs, suffered frightful epidemics of disease. Moreover, the lodes started to run dry. Consequently, the quantity of metal produced for Spain steadily declined. Nevertheless, in Madrid royal expenditures constantly exceeded income. The remedies applied in the face of a mountainous state debt and declining revenues were devaluation of the coinage and declarations of bankruptcy. In 1596, 1607, 1627, 1647, and 1680 Spanish kings found no solution to the problem of an empty treasury other than cancellation of the national debt. Naturally, public confidence in the state deteriorated.

Spain, in contrast to the other countries of western Europe, had only a tiny middle class. Disdain for money, in a century of increasing commercialism and bourgeois attitudes, reveals a significant facet of the Spanish national character. Public opinion, taking its cue from the aristocracy, condemned moneymaking as vulgar and undignified. Those with influence or connections sought titles of nobility and social prestige. Thousands entered economically unproductive professions and became priests, monks, and nuns: there were said to be nine thousand monasteries in the province of Castile alone. The flood of gold and silver had produced severe inflation, pushing the

costs of production in the textile industry higher and higher, to the point that Castilian cloth could not compete in colonial and international markets. Many manufacturers and businessmen found so many obstacles in the way of profitable enterprise that they simply gave up.[3]

Spanish aristocrats, attempting to maintain an extravagant lifestyle they could no longer afford, increased the rents on their estates. High rents and heavy taxes in turn drove the peasants from the land. Agricultural production suffered and the peasants departed for the large cities, where they swelled the ranks of unemployed beggars.

Their most Catholic majesties, the kings of Spain, had no solutions to these dire problems. The portraits of Philip III (1598-1622), Philip IV (1622-1665), and Charles II hanging in the Prado, the Spanish national museum in Madrid, reflect the increasing weakness of the dynasty. Their faces — the small beady eyes, the long noses, the jutting Habsburg jaws, the constipated and pathetically stupid expressions — tell a story of excessive inbreeding and decaying monarchy. These Spanish kings all lacked force of character. Philip III, a pallid, melancholy, and deeply pious man "whose only virtue appeared to reside in a total absence of vice," handed the government over to the lazy duke of Lerma, who used it to advance his personal and familial wealth. Philip IV left the management of his several kingdoms to Count Olivares.

Olivares was an able administrator. He did not lack energy and ideas; he devised new sources of revenue. But he clung to the grandiose belief that the solution to Spain's difficulties rested in a return to the imperial tradition. Unfortunately, the imperial tradition demanded the revival of war with the Dutch at the expiration of a twelve-year truce in 1622 and a long war with France over Mantua (1628–1659). These conflicts on top of an empty treasury brought disaster.

In 1640, Spain faced serious revolts in Naples and Portugal, and in 1643 the French inflicted a crushing defeat on a Spanish army in Belgium. By the Treaty of the Pyrenees of 1659, which ended the French-Spanish wars, Spain was compelled to surrender extensive territories to France. This treaty marked the end of Spain as a great power.

Seventeenth-century Spain was the victim of its past. It could not forget the grandeur of the sixteenth century and look to the future. The bureaucratic councils of state continued to function as symbols of the absolute Spanish monarchy. But because those councils were staffed by aristocrats, it was the aristocracy that held the real power. Spanish absolutism had been built largely on slave-produced gold and silver. When the supply of bullion decreased, the power and standing of the Spanish state declined.

The most cherished Spanish ideals were military glory and strong Roman Catholic faith. In the seventeenth century, Spain lacked the finances and the manpower to fight the expensive wars in which it foolishly got involved. Spain also ignored the new mercantile ideas and scientific methods, because they came from heretical nations, Holland and England. The incredible wealth of South America destroyed the tiny Spanish middle class and created contempt for business and manual labor.

The decadence of the Habsburg dynasty and the lack of effective royal councilors also contributed to Spanish failure. Spanish leaders seemed to lack the will to reform. Pessimism and fatalism permeated national life. In the reign of Philip IV, a royal council was appointed to plan the construction of a canal linking the Tagus and Manzanares rivers in Spain. After interminable debate, the committee decided that "if God had intended the rivers to be navigable, He would have made them so."

In the novel *Don Quixote,* the Spanish writer Cervantes (1547–1616) produced one of the great masterpieces of world literature. The main character, Don Quixote, lives in a world of dreams, traveling about the countryside seeking military glory. From the title of this book English has borrowed the word *quixotic.* Meaning idealistic but impractical, it characterizes seventeenth-century Spain.

CONSTITUTIONALISM

The seventeenth century, which witnessed the development of absolute monarchy, also saw the appearance of the constitutional state. While France and later Prussia, Russia, and Austria solved the question of sovereignty with the absolutist state, England and Holland evolved toward the constitutional state. What is constitutionalism? Is it the same as democracy?

Constitutionalism is the limitation of government by law. Constitutionalism also implies a balance between the authority and power of the government on the one hand, and the rights and liberties of the subjects on the other. The balance is often very delicate.

A nation's constitution may be written or unwritten. In may be embodied in one basic document, occasionally revised by amendment or judicial decision, like the Constitution of the United States. Or a constitution may be partly written and partly unwritten and include parliamentary statutes, judicial decisions, and a body of traditional procedures and practices, like the English and Canadian constitutions. Whether written or unwritten, a constitution gets its binding force from the government's acknowledgment that it must respect that constitution – that is, that the state must govern according to the laws. Likewise, in a constitutional state, the people look upon the law and the constitution as the protectors of their rights, liberties, and property.

Modern constitutional governments may take either a republican or a monarchial form. In a constitutional republic, the sovereign power resides in the electorate and is exercised by the electorate's representatives. In a constitutional monarchy, a king or queen serves as the head of state and possesses some residual political authority, but again the ultimate or sovereign power rests in the electorate.

A constitutional government is not, however, quite the same as a democratic government. In a complete democracy, *all* the people have the right to participate either directly, or indirectly through their elected representatives, in the government of the state. Democratic government, therefore, is intimately tied up with the franchise (the vote). Most men could not vote until the late nineteenth century. Even then, women – probably the majority in Western societies – lacked the franchise; they gained the right to vote only in the twentieth century. Consequently, although constitutionalism developed in the seventeenth century, full democracy was achieved only in very recent times.

THE DECLINE OF ROYAL ABSOLUTISM IN ENGLAND (1603–1649)

In the late sixteenth century the French monarchy was powerless; a century later the king's power was absolute. In 1588, Queen Elizabeth I of England exercised very great personal power; by 1689, the English monarchy was severely circumscribed and limited. Change in England was anything but orderly: England in the seventeenth century displayed as much political stability as some African states in the twentieth. They executed one king, experienced a bloody civil war, experimented with military dictatorship, then restored the son of the murdered king, and finally, after a bloodless revolution, established a constitutional monarchy. Political stability came only in the 1690s. How do we account for the fact that after such a violent and tumultuous century, England laid the foundations for a constitutional monarchy? What combination of political, socioeconomic, and religious factors brought on first a civil war in 1642–1649 and then the constitutional settlement of 1688–1689?

The extraordinary success of Elizabeth I had rested on her political shrewdness and flexibility, her careful management of finances, her wise selection of ministers, her clever manipulation of Parliament, and her sense of royal dignity and devotion to hard work. The aging queen had always refused to discuss the succession. After her Scottish cousin James Stuart succeeded her as James I (1603–1625), Elizabeth's strengths seemed even greater than they actually had been. The Stuarts lacked every quality Elizabeth had possessed.

King James was well educated and learned but lacking in common sense – he was once called "the wisest fool in Christendom." He also lacked the common touch. Urged to wave at the crowds who waited to greet their new ruler, James complained that he was tired, and threatened to drop his breeches "so they can cheer at my arse." Having left barbarous and violent Scotland for rich and prosperous England, James believed he had entered "the Promised Land." As soon as he got to London, the new English king went to see the Crown jewels.

Abysmally ignorant of English law and of the English Parliament, but sublimely arrogant, James was devoted to the theory of the divine right of kings. He expressed his ideas about divine right in his essay "The Trew Law of Free Monarchy." According to James I, a monarch has a divine (or God-given) right to his authority, and is responsible only to God. Rebellion is the worst of political crimes. If a king orders something evil, the subject should respond with passive disobedience but should be prepared to accept any penalty for non-compliance.

James substituted political theorizing and talk for real work. He lectured the House of Commons: "There are no privileges and immunities which can stand against a divinely appointed King." This notion, implying total royal jurisdiction over the liberties, persons, and properties of English men and women, formed the basis of the Stuart concept of absolutism. Such a view ran directly counter to the long-standing English idea that a person's property could not be taken away without due process of law. James's expression of such views before the English House of Commons constituted a grave political mistake.

The House of Commons guarded the pocketbook of the nation, and James and later Stuart kings badly needed to open that pocketbook. Elizabeth had bequeathed to James a sizable royal debt. Through prudent management the debt could have been gradually reduced, but James I looked upon all revenues as a happy windfall to be squandered on a lavish court and favorite courtiers. In fact, the extravagance and licentiousness of James' court, and the public flaunting of his male lovers, weakened respect for the monarchy.

Elizabeth had also left to her Stuart successors a House of Commons that appreciated its

THE LAMENTABLE COMPLAINTS OF NICK FROTH the Tapster, and RVLEROST the Cooke. Concerning the restraint lately set forth, against drinking, potting, and piping on the Sabbath day, and against selling meate.

Printed in the yeare, 1641.

PURITAN IDEALS OPPOSED The Puritans preached sober living and abstention from alcoholic drink, rich food, and dancing. This pamphlet reflects the common man's hostility to such restraints. "Potting" refers to tankards of beer; "piping" means making music. (The British Museum)

own financial strength and intended to use that strength to acquire a greater say in the government of the state. The knights and burgesses who sat at Westminster in the early seventeenth century wanted to discuss royal expenditures, religious reform, and foreign affairs. In short, the Commons wanted what amounted to sovereignty.

Profound social changes had occurred since the sixteenth century. The English House of Commons during the reigns of James I and his son Charles I (1625-1649) was very different from the assembly Henry VIII had terrorized into passing his Reformation legislation. A social revolution had brought about the change. The dissolution of the monasteries and the sale of monastic land had enriched many people. Agricultural techniques like the draining of wasteland and the application of fertilizers improved the land and its yield. Old manorial common land had been enclosed and turned into sheep runs; breeding was carefully supervised, and the size of the flocks increased. In these activities, as well as in renting and leasing parcels of land, precise accounts were kept.

Many men invested in commercial ventures at home, such as the expanding cloth industry, and in partnerships and joint stock companies engaged in foreign enterprises. They made prudent marriages. All these developments led to a great deal of social mobility. Both in commerce and in agriculture, the English in the late sixteenth and early seventeenth centuries were capitalists, investing their profits to make more money. Although the international inflation of the period hit everywhere, in England commercial and agricultural income rose faster than prices. Wealthy country gentry, rich city merchants, and financiers invested abroad.

The typical pattern was for the commercially successfully to set themselves up as country gentry, thus creating an elite group that possessed a far greater proportion of land and of the national wealth in 1640 than had been the case in 1540. Small wonder that in 1640 someone could declare in the House of Commons, probably accurately, "We could buy the House of Lords three times over." Increased wealth had also produced a better-educated and more articulate House of Commons. Many members had acquired at least a

smattering of legal knowledge, and they used that knowledge to search for medieval precedents from which to argue against the king. The class that dominated the Commons wanted political power corresponding to its economic strength.

In England, unlike France, there was no social stigma attached to paying taxes. Members of the House of Commons were willing to tax themselves provided they had some say in the expenditure of those taxes and in the formulation of state policies. The Stuart kings, however, considered such ambitions intolerable presumption and a threat to their divine-right prerogative. Consequently, at every Parliament between 1603 and 1640 bitter squabbles erupted between the Crown and the wealthy, articulate, and legal-minded Commons. Charles I's attempt to govern without Parliament (1629-1640), and to finance his government by arbitrary nonparliamentary levies, brought the country to a crisis.

An issue graver than royal extravagance and Parliament's desire to make the law also disturbed the English and embittered relations between the king and the House of Commons. That problem was religion. In the early seventeenth century, increasing numbers of English men and women felt dissatisfied with the Church of England established by Henry VIII and reformed by Elizabeth. Many believed the Reformation had not gone far enough. They wanted to "purify" the Anglican church of Roman Catholic elements — elaborate vestments and ceremonial, the position of the altar at the east end of the church, even the giving and wearing of wedding rings. These people were called Puritans.

It is very difficult to establish what proportion of the English population was Puritan. It is clear, however, that many English men and women were attracted by the socioeconomic implications of John Calvin's theology. Calvinism emphasized hard work, sobriety, thrift, competition, and postponement of pleasure, and tended to link sin and poverty with weakness and moral corruption. These attitudes fit in precisely with the economic approaches and practices of many (successful) businessmen and farmers. These values have frequently been called the Protestant, or middle-class, or capitalist, ethic. While it is hazardous to identify capitalism and progress with Protestantism – there were many successful Catholic capitalists – the "Protestant virtues" represented the prevailing values of the great majority of members of the House of Commons.

James I and Charles I both gave the impression of being highly sympathetic to Roman Catholicism. Charles supported the policies of William Laud, archbishop of Canterbury (1573-1645), who tried to impose elaborate ritual and rich ceremonial on all churches. Laud insisted on complete uniformity of church services, and enforced that uniformity through an ecclesiastical court called High Commission. People believed the country was being led back to Roman Catholicism. When in 1639 Laud attempted to impose a new prayer book, modeled on the Anglican Book of Common Prayer, on the Presbyterian Scots, the Scots revolted. In order to finance an army to put down the Scots, King Charles was compelled to summon Parliament in November 1640.

For eleven years Charles I had ruled without Parliament, financing his government through extraordinary stopgap levies, considered illegal by most English people. For example, the king revived a medieval law requiring coastal districts to help pay the cost of ships for defense, but levied the tax, called ship money, on inland as well as coastal counties. When the issue was tested in the courts, the judges, having been suborned, decided in the king's favor.

Most members of Parliament believed that such taxation without consent amounted to arbitrary and absolute despotism. Consequently, they were not willing to trust the king with an army. Accordingly, this Parliament, commonly called the Long Parliament because it sat from 1640 to 1660, proceeded to enact legislation that limited the power of the monarch and made arbitrary government impossible.

In 1641, the Commons passed the Triennial Act, which compelled the king to summon Parliament every three years. The Commons impeached Archbishop Laud and abolished the House of Lords and the Court of High Commission. It went further and threatened to abolish the institution of episcopacy. King Charles, fearful of a Scottish invasion – the original reason for summoning Parliament – accepted these measures. Understanding and peace were not achieved, however, partly because radical members of the Commons pushed increasingly revolutionary propositions, partly because Charles maneuvered to rescind those he had already approved. An uprising in Ireland precipitated civil war.

Ever since Henry II had conquered Ireland in 1171, English governors had mercilessly ruled the Irish, and English landlords had ruthlessly exploited them. The English Reformation had made a bad situation worse: because the Irish remained Catholic, religious differences became united with economic and political oppression. Without an army, Charles I could neither come to terms with the Scots nor put down the Irish rebellion, and the Long Parliament remained unwilling to place an army under a king it did not trust.

Charles thus instigated military action against parliamentary forces. He recruited an army drawn from the nobility and their cavalry staff, the rural gentry, and mercenaries. The Parliamentary army was composed of the militia of the City of London, country squires with business connections, and men with a firm belief in the spiritual duty of serving.

The English Civil War (1642-1646) tested whether sovereignty in England was to reside in the king or in Parliament. The Civil War did not resolve that problem, although it ended in 1649 with the execution of King Charles on the charge of high treason – a severe blow to royal power. The period between 1649 and 1660, called the Interregnum because it separated two monarchial periods, saw England's one experience of military dictatorship.

PURITANICAL ABSOLUTISM IN ENGLAND: CROMWELL AND THE PROTECTORATE

The problem of sovereignty was vigorously debated in the middle years of the seventeenth century. In *Leviathan,* the English philosopher and political theorist Thomas Hobbes (1588-1679) maintained that sovereignty is ultimately derived from the people, who transfer it to the monarchy by implicit contract. The power of the ruler is absolute, but kings do not hold their power by divine right. This view pleased no one in the seventeenth century.

When Charles I was beheaded on January 30, 1649, the kingship was abolished. A commonwealth, or republican form of government, was proclaimed. Theoretically, legislative power rested in the surviving members of Parliament and executive power in a council of state. In fact, the army that had defeated the royal forces controlled the government, and Oliver Cromwell controlled the army.

Although called the Protectorate, the rule of Cromwell (1653-1658) constituted military dictatorship.

Oliver Cromwell (1599-1658) came from the country gentry, the class that dominated the House of Commons in the early seventeenth century. He himself had sat in the Long Parliament. Cromwell rose in the parliamentary army, and achieved nationwide fame by infusing the army with his Puritan convictions and molding it into the highly effective military machine, called the New Model Army, that defeated the royalist forces.

Parliament had written a constitution, the Instrument of Government (1653), that invested executive power in a lord protector (Cromwell) and a council of state. The Instrument provided for triennial parliaments and gave Parliament the sole power to raise taxes. But after repeated disputes Cromwell tore the document up. He continued the standing army and proclaimed quasi-martial law. He divided England into twelve military districts, each governed by a major general. On the issue of religion Cromwell favored broad toleration, and the Instrument of Government gave all Christians, except Roman Catholics, the right to practice their faith. Toleration meant state protection of many different Protestant sects, and most English people had no enthusiasm for such a notion; the idea was far ahead of its time. Cromwell identified Irish Catholicism with sedition. In 1649 he crushed rebellion there with merciless savagery, leaving a legacy of Irish hatred for England that has not yet subsided. The state rigorously censored the press, forbade sports, and kept the theaters closed.

Cromwell's regulation of the nation's economy had features typical of seventeenth-century absolutism. The lord protector's policies were mercantilist, similar to those Colbert established in France. Cromwell enforced a navigation act requiring that English goods be transported on English ships. The navigation act was a great boost to the development of an English merchant marine, and brought about a short but successful war with the commercially threatened Dutch. Cromwell also welcomed the immigration of Jews, because of their skills, and they began to return to England in larger numbers after four centuries of absence.

Absolute government collapsed when Cromwell died in 1658. Absolutism failed because the English got fed up with military rule. They longed for a return to civilian government, restoration of the common law, and social stability. Moreover, the strain of creating a community of puritanical saints proved too psychologically exhausting. Government by military dictatorship was an unfortunate experiment that English men and women never forgot and never repeated. By 1660, they were ready to restore the monarchy.

THE RESTORATION OF THE ENGLISH MONARCHY

The Restoration of 1660 re-established the monarchy in the person of Charles II (1660–1685), eldest son of Charles I. At the same time both houses of Parliament were restored, together with the established Anglican church, the courts of law, and the system of local government through justices of the peace. The Restoration failed to resolve two serious problems. What was to be the attitude of the state toward Puritans, Catholics, and dissenters from the established church? And what was to be the constitutional position of the king – that is, what was to be relationship between the king and Parliament?

About the first of these issues, Charles II, a relaxed, easygoing, and sensual man, was basically indifferent. He was not interested in

THE HOUSE OF COMMONS   *This seal of the Commonwealth shows the small House of Commons in session with the speaker presiding; the legend "in the third year of freedom" refers to 1651, three years after the abolition of the monarchy. In 1653, however, Cromwell abolished this "Rump Parliament" — so-called because it consisted of the few surviving members elected before the Civil War — and he and the army governed the land. (The British Museum)*

doctrinal issues. Parliamentarians were, and they proceeded to enact a body of laws that sought to compel religious uniformity. Those who refused to receive the sacrament of the Church of England could not vote, hold public office, preach, teach, attend the universities, or even assemble for meetings, according to the Test Act of 1673. These restrictions could not be enforced. When the Quaker William Penn held a meeting of his friends and was arrested, the jury refused to convict him.

In politics, Charles II was determined "not to set out in his travels again," which meant that he intended to get along with Parliament. Charles II's solution to the problem of the relationship between the king and the House of Commons had profound importance for later constitutional development. Generally good rapport existed between the king and the strongly royalist Parliament that had restored him. This rapport was due largely to the king's appointment of a council of five men who served both as his major advisers and as members of Parliament, thus acting as liaison agents between the executive and the legislature. This body – known as the Cabal from the names of its five members (Clifford, Arlington, Buckingham, Ashley-Cooper and Lauderdale) – was an ancestor of the later cabinet system. It gradually came to be accepted that the Cabal was answerable in Parliament for the decisions of the king. This development gave rise to the concept of ministerial responsibility: royal ministers must answer to the Commons.

Harmony between the Crown and Parliament rested on the understanding that Charles would summon frequent parliaments and that Parliament would vote him sufficient revenues. However, although Parliament believed Charles had a virtual divine right to govern, it did not grant him an adequate income. Accordingly, Charles entered into a secret agreement with Louis XIV. The French king would give Charles £200,000 annually, and in return Charles would relax the laws against Catholics, gradually re-Catholicize England, and support French policy against the Dutch.

When the details of this secret treaty leaked out, a great wave of anti-Catholic fear swept England. This fear was compounded by a crucial fact: although Charles had produced several bastards, he had no legitimate children. It therefore appeared that his brother and heir, James, Duke of York, who had publicly acknowledged his Catholicism, would inaugu-

rate a Catholic dynasty. The combination of hatred for the French absolutism embodied in Louis XIV, hostility to Roman Catholicism, and fear of a permanent Catholic dynasty produced virtual hysteria. The Commons passed an exclusion bill denying the succession to a Roman Catholic, but Charles quickly dissolved Parliament and the bill never became law.

James II (1685–1688) did succeed his brother, and almost at once the worst English anti-Catholic fears were realized. In direct violation of the Test Act, James appointed Roman Catholics to positions in the army, the universities, and local government. When these actions were tested in the courts, the judges, whom James had appointed, decided for the king. The king was suspending the law at will, and appeared to be reviving the absolutism of his father and grandfather. He went further. Attempting to broaden his base of support with Protestant dissenters and nonconformists, James issued a declaration of indulgence granting religious freedom to all.

Two events gave the signals for revolution. First, seven bishops of the Church of England petitioned the king that they not be forced to read the declaration of indulgence because of their belief it was an illegal act. They were imprisoned in the Tower of London but subsequently acquitted amid great public enthusiasm. Second, in June 1688, James's queen produced a male heir. A Catholic dynasty seemed assured. The fear of a Roman Catholic monarchy, supported by France and ruling outside the law, prompted a group of eminent persons to offer the English throne to James's Protestant daughter Mary and her Dutch husband, Prince William of Orange. In November 1688, James II, his queen, and infant son fled to France and became pensioners of Louis XIV.

The English call the events of 1688 the Glorious Revolution. The revolution was indeed glorious in the sense that it replaced one king with another with a minimum of bloodshed. It also represented the destruction, once and for all, of the idea of divine-right monarchy. William and Mary accepted the English throne from Parliament, and in so doing explicitly recognized the supremacy of Parliament. The revolution of 1688 established the principle that sovereignty, the ultimate power in the state, rested in Parliament, and that the king ruled with the consent of the governed.

The men who had brought about the revolution quickly framed their intentions in the Bill of Rights, which is the cornerstone of the modern British constitution. The basic principles of the Bill of Rights were formulated in direct response to Stuart absolutism. Law was to be made in Parliament; once made, the law could not be suspended by the Crown. Parliament had to be called at least every three years. Both elections to and debate in Parliament were to be free in the sense that the Crown was not to interfere in them; this aspect of the Bill was widely disregarded in the eighteenth century. Judges would hold their offices "during good behavior," which assured the independence of the judiciary. No longer could the Crown get the judicial decisions it wanted by threats of removal. There was to be no standing army in peacetime – a limitation designed to prevent the repetition of either Stuart or Cromwellian military government. The Bill of Rights granted "that the subjects which are Protestants may have arms for their defense suitable to their conditions and as al-

lowed by law,"[4] meaning that Catholics could not possess firearms because the Protestant majority feared them. Additional parliamentary legislation granted freedom of worship to Protestant dissenters and nonconformists and required that the English monarch always be Protestant in faith.

The Glorious Revolution found its best defense in the political philosopher John Locke's "Second Treatise on Civil Government" (1690). A spokesman for the great land-owning class that had brought about the revolution, Locke (1632-1704) maintained that men set up civil governments in order to defend property. Thus the purpose of government is to protect life, liberty, and property. Locke's ideas, though not profound, had great influence throughout the eighteenth century.

However glorious, the events of 1688-1690 did not constitute a *democratic* revolution. The revolution placed sovereignty in Parliament, and Parliament represented the upper classes. The great majority of English people acquired no say in their government. The English revolution established a constitutional monarchy; it also inaugurated an age of aristocratic government, which lasted at least until 1832 and probably until 1914.

In the course of the eighteenth century, the cabinet system of government evolved. The term *cabinet* refers to the small private room in which English rulers consulted their chief ministers. In a cabinet system the leading ministers, who must have seats in and the support of a majority of the House of Commons, formulate common policy and conduct the business of the country. During the administration of one royal minister, Sir Robert Walpole (1721-1742), the idea developed that the cabinet was responsible to the House of Commons. The king normally presided at cabinet meetings, but because the Hanoverian king George I (1714-1727) did not understand enough English to follow the discussions, he stopped attending cabinet sessions. George II (1727-1760) followed that precedent. The influence of the Crown in decision making accordingly declined. Walpole enjoyed the favor of the monarchy and of the House of Commons, and came to be called the king's first, or prime, minister. In the English cabinet system both legislative and executive power are held by the leading ministers, who form the government.

THE DUTCH REPUBLIC IN THE SEVENTEENTH CENTURY

The seventeenth century witnessed an unparalled flowering of Dutch scientific, artistic, and literary achievement. In this period, often called "the golden age of the Netherlands," Dutch ideas and attitudes played a profound role in shaping a new and modern worldview. At the same time the Republic of the United Provinces of the Netherlands represents another model of the development of the modern state.

In the late sixteenth century, the seven northern provinces of the Netherlands, of which Holland and Zeeland were the most prosperous, succeeded in throwing off Spanish domination. This success was based on their geographical lines of defense, the wealth of the cities, the brilliant military strategy of William the Silent, the preoccupation of Philip II of Spain with so many other concerns, and the northern provinces' vigorous Calvinism. In 1581 the seven provinces of the Union of Utrecht had formed the United Provinces (page 528). Philip II continued to try to crush the Dutch with the Armada but in 1609 his son Philip III agreed to a truce that implicitly recognized the independence of the United Provinces. At the time neither side

expected the peace to be permanent. The Peace of Westphalia in 1648, however, confirmed the Dutch republic's independence.

Within each province an oligarchy of wealthy merchants called regents handled domestic affairs in the local Estates. The provincial Estates held virtually all the power. A federal assembly, or States General, handled matters of foreign affairs, such as war. But the States General did not possess sovereign authority, since all issues had to be referred back to the local Estates for approval. The States General appointed a representative, the stadholder, in each province. As the highest executive there, the stadholder carried out ceremonial functions and was responsible for defense and good order. The sons of William the Silent, Maurice and William Louis, held the office of stadholder in all seven provinces. The regents in each province jealously guarded local independence and resisted efforts at centralization. Nevertheless, Holland, which had the largest navy and the most wealth, dominated the republic and the States General. Significantly, the Estates assembled at Holland's capital, The Hague.

The government of the United Provinces fits none of the standard categories of seventeenth-century political organization. The Dutch were not monarchial, but fiercely republican. The government was controlled by wealthy merchants and financiers. Although rich, their values were not aristocratic but strongly middle-class, emphasizing thrift, hard work, and simplicity in living. The Dutch republic was not a strong federation but a confederation – that is, a weak union of strong provinces. The provinces were a temptation to powerful neighbors, yet the Dutch resisted the long Spanish effort at reconquest and withstood both French and English attacks in the second half of the century. Louis XIV's hatred of the Dutch was proverbial. They

MODEL OF A SEVENTEENTH-CENTURY FLUYT
The Dutch surpassed all nations in the design of fast-sailing ships. The fluyt or fluteship was cheap to construct, carried a large cargo, and required only a small crew. It gave the Dutch a great advantage, resulting in their notable commercial success. (Photo: Caroline Buckler)

represented all that he despised — middle-class values, religious toleration, and political independence.

The political success of the Dutch rested on the phenomenal commercial prosperity of the Netherlands. The moral and ethical bases of that commercial wealth were thrift, frugality, and religious toleration. John Calvin had written, "From where do the merchant's profits come except from his own diligence and industry"; this attitude undoubtedly encouraged a sturdy people who had waged a centuries-old struggle against the sea.

Alone of all European peoples in the seventeenth century, the Dutch practiced religious toleration. Peoples of all faiths were welcome within their borders. It is a striking testimony to the urbanity of Dutch society that in a century when patriotism was closely identified with religious uniformity, the Calvinist province of Holland allowed its highest official, Jan van Oldenbarneveldt, to continue to practice his Roman Catholic faith. As long as a businessman conducted his religion in private, the government did not interfere with him.

Toleration also paid off: it attracted a great deal of foreign capital and investment. Deposits at the Bank of Amsterdam were guaranteed by the city council, and in the middle years of the century the bank became Europe's best source of cheap credit and commercial intelligence, and the main clearinghouse for bills of exchange. Men of all races and creeds traded in Amsterdam, at whose docks on the Amstel River five thousand ships, half the merchant marine of the United Provinces, were berthed. Joost van den Vondel, the poet of Dutch imperialism, exulted:

God, God, the Lord of Amstel cried, hold every conscience free;
And Liberty ride, on Holland's tide, with billowing sails to sea,
And run our Amstel out and in; let freedom gird the bold,
And merchant in his counting house stand elbow deep in gold.[5]

The fishing industry was the cornerstone of the Dutch economy. For half the year, from June to December, fishing fleets combed the dangerous English coast and the North Sea, raking in tiny herring. Profits from herring stimulated shipbuilding, and even before 1600 the Dutch were offering the lowest shipping rates in Europe. Although Dutch cities became famous for their exports – diamonds, linen from Haarlem, pottery from Delft – Dutch wealth depended less on exports than on transport. The merchant marine was the largest in Europe.

In 1602, a group of the regents of Holland formed the Dutch East India Company, a joint stock company. Each investor received a percentage of the profits proportional to the amount of money he had put in. Within half a century, the Dutch East India Company had cut heavily into Portuguese trading in the Far East. The Dutch seized the Cape of Good

VERMEER: WOMEN WEIGHING GOLD *Vermeer painted pictures of middle-class women involved in ordinary activities in the quiet interiors of their homes. Unrivaled among Dutch masters for his superb control of light, in this painting (ca 1657) Vermeer illuminates the pregnant woman weighing gold on her scales, as Christ in the painting on the wall weighs the saved and the damned. (National Gallery of Art, Washington, D.C. Widener Collection)*

Hope, Ceylon, and Malacca, and established trading posts in each place. In the 1630s, the Dutch East India Company was paying its investors about 35 percent return annually on their investments. The Dutch West India Company, founded in 1621, traded extensively with Latin America and Africa.

Although the initial purpose of both companies was commercial – the import of spices and silks to Europe – the Dutch found themselves involved in the imperialistic exploitation of large parts of the Pacific and Latin America. Amsterdam, the center of a worldwide Dutch empire, became the commercial and financial capital of Europe. During the seventeenth century the Dutch translated their commercial acumen and flexibility into political and imperialist terms with striking success. But war with France and England in the 1670s hurt the United Provinces. The long War of the Spanish Succession, in which the Dutch supported England against France, was a costly drain on Dutch manpower and financial resources. The peace signed in 1715 to end the war marked the beginning of Dutch economic decline.

———◆———

According to Thomas Hobbes, the central drive in every man is "a perpetual and restless desire of Power, after Power, that ceaseth only in Death." The seventeenth century solved the problem of *sovereign power* in two fundamental

ways, absolutism and constitutionalism. The France of Louis XIV witnessed the emergence of the fully absolutist state. The king commanded all the powers of the state: judicial, military, political, and to a great extent ecclesiastical. France developed a centralized bureaucracy, a professional army, a state-directed economy, all of which Louis personally supervised. For the first time in history all the institutions and powers of the national state were effectively controlled by a single person. The king saw himself as the representative of God on earth, and it has been said that "to the seventeenth century imagination God was a sort of image of Louis XIV."[6]

As Louis XIV personifies absolutism, so Stuart England exemplifies the evolution of the first modern constitutional state. The conflicts between Parliament and the first two Stuart rulers, James I and Charles I, tested where sovereign power would rest in the state. The resulting Civil War did not solve the problem. The Instrument of Government, the document produced in 1653 by the victorious parliamentary army, provided for a balance of governmental authority and recognition of popular rights; as such, the Instrument has been called the first modern constitution. Unfortunately, it lacked public support. James II's absolutist tendencies brought on the Revolution of 1688, and the people who made that revolution settled three basic issues. Sovereign power was divided between king and parliament, with parliament enjoying the greater share. Government was to be based on the rule of law. And the liberties of English people were made explicit in written form, in the Bill of Rights. The framers of the English constitution left to later generations the task of making constitutional government work.

The models of governmental power established by seventeenth-century England and France strongly influenced other states then and ever since. As the Mississippi novelist William Faulkner wrote, "The past isn't dead; it's not even past."

NOTES

1. S. de Gramont, ed., *The Age of Magnificence: Memoirs of the Court of Louis XIV by the Duc de Saint-Simon,* Capricorn Books, New York, 1964, pp. 141–145.

2. Ibid., p. 183.

3. S. H. Elliott, *Imperial Spain, 1469–1716,* Mentor Books, New York, 1963, pp. 306–308.

4. C. Stephenson and G. F. Marcham, *Sources of English Constitutional History,* Harper & Row, New York, 1937, p. 601.

5. Quoted by D. Maland, *Europe in the Seventeenth Century,* Macmillan, New York, 1967, pp. 198–199.

6. Quoted by Carl J. Friedrich and Charles Blitzer, *The Age of Power,* Cornell University Press, Ithaca, New York, 1957, p. 112.

SUGGESTED READING

Students who wish to explore the problems presented in this chapter in greater depth will easily find a rich and exciting literature with many titles available in paperback editions. Geoffrey Parker, *Europe in Crisis, 1598–1618* (1980), provides a readable introduction to the religious, social, and economic tensions of the period. C. Friedrich, *The Age of the Baroque, 1610–1660* (1962), is a good survey. Perhaps the best recent study of absolutism is P. Anderson, *Lineages of the Absolutist State* (1974), a Marxist interpretation of absolutism in western and eastern Europe. The short study of M. Beloff, *The Age of Absolutism* (1967), concentrates on the social forces that underlay administrative change. H. Rosenberg, "Absolute Monarchy and Its Legacy," in *Early Modern Europe, 1450–1650* (1967), ed. N. F. Cantor and S. Werthman, is a seminal study. T. Aston, ed., *Crisis in Europe, 1560–1660* (1967), contains stimulating essays by leading authorities. The classic treatment of constitutionalism remains that of C. H. McIlwain, *Constitutionalism: Ancient and Modern* (1940), written by a great scholar during the rise of German fascism. S. B. Crimes, *English Constitutional History* (1967), is an excellent survey with valuable chapters on the sixteenth through eighteenth centuries.

Louis XIV and his age have seduced the attention of many scholars. The best contemporary biography is J. Wolf, *Louis XIV* (1968), which stresses Louis' contribution to the development of the modern bureaucratic state. For a variety of opinions about Louis, see William F. Church, ed., *Louis XIV in Historical Thought* (1978). Two works of W. H. Lewis, *The Splendid Century* (1957) and *The Sunset of the Splendid Century* (1963), make delightful reading and contain useful material on social history. R. Hatton, *Europe in the Age of Louis XIV* (1979), is a splendidly illustrated survey of many aspects of European culture in the seventeenth century. O. Ranum, *Paris in the Age of Absolutism* (1968), describes the geographical, political, economic, and architectural significance of the cultural capital of Europe. R. Mousnier, *Peasant Uprisings in Seventeenth-Century France, Russia, and China* (1970), an important study in comparative history, treats agrarian relationships and social stratification. V. L. Tapie, *The Age of Grandeur: Baroque Art and Architecture* (1960), is a magnificently illustrated book that emphasizes the relationship between art and politics. Part 4 of L. Romier, *A History of France,* trans. A. L. Rowse (1962), offers an intelligible and nationalistic narrative. For Spain, J. H. Elliott, *Imperial Spain, 1469–1716,* rev. ed. (1977), is a sensitively written and authoritative study.

G. M. Trevelyan, *England Under the Stuarts* (1960), is a good starting point for English social and political history. Brief accounts of many facets of English culture are contained in M. Ashley, *England in the Seventeenth Century* (1961), and J. H. Plumb, *England in the Eighteenth Century* (1961). M. Weber, *The Protestant Ethic and the Spirit of Capitalism* (1958), traces the relationship between Protestantism and socioeconomic developments. W. Haller, *The Rise of Puritanism* (1957), is the best treatment of English Puritanism, but it is for the advanced student. For the background to the Civil War and the war itself, see C. V. Wedgwood, *The King's Peace* (1969) and *The King's War* (1959), both highly readable; the old but scholarly biography of Cromwell by C. Firth, *Oliver Cromwell* (1956); and the recent popular study by A. Fraser, *Cromwell* (1975). C. Brinton, *The Anatomy of Revolution* (1952), contains an interesting analysis of the English Civil War and contrasts it with the French and Russian revolutions. L. Stone, *The Crisis of the Aristocracy, 1558–1641* (1967), is broader in scope than the title implies and in fact treats many aspects of English social history. Stone is a leading authority on English family history.

On Holland, the best introduction to the relationship between commercial development and the growth of democratic ideas and institutions remains Henri Pirenne, *Early Democracies in the Low Countries* (1963), especially chapters X and XI. C. R. Boxer, *The Dutch Seaborne Empire* (1980), and the appropriate chapters of D. Maland, *Europe in the Seventeenth Century* (1967), are useful for Dutch overseas expansion and the reasons for Dutch prosperity. K. H. D. Haley, *The Dutch in the Seventeenth Century* (1972), is a splendidly illustrated appreciation of Dutch commercial and artistic achievements. No recent work has replaced the well-written, thorough narrative of J. L. Motley, *The Rise of the Dutch Republic,* 3 vols., (1898).

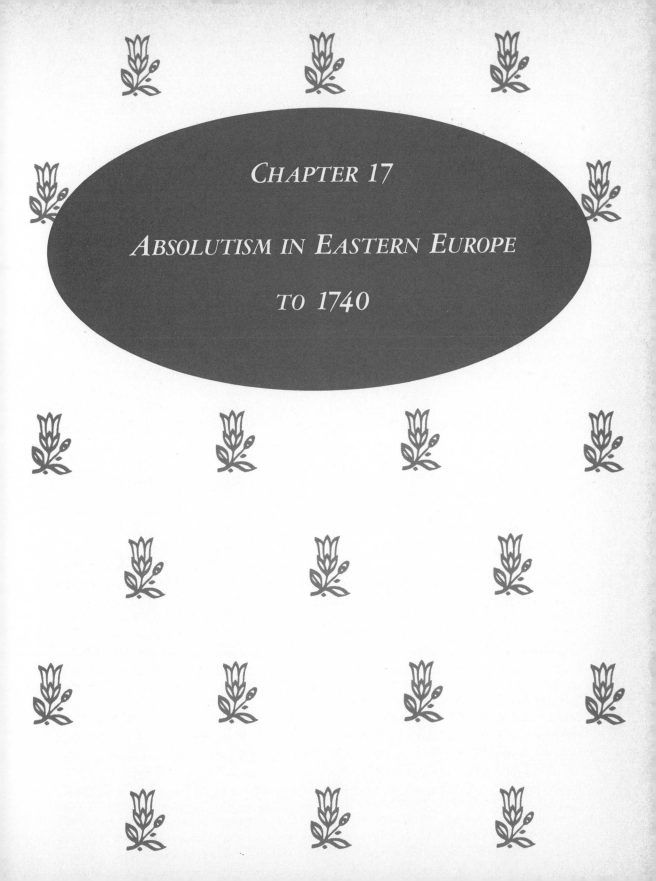

CHAPTER 17

ABSOLUTISM IN EASTERN EUROPE

TO 1740

THE SEVENTEENTH CENTURY witnessed a struggle between constitutionalism and absolutism in eastern Europe. With the notable exception of the kingdom of Poland, monarchial absolutism was everywhere triumphant in eastern Europe; constitutionalism was decisively defeated. Absolute monarchies emerged in Austria, Prussia, and Russia. This was a development of great significance: these three monarchies exercised enormous influence until 1918, and they created a strong authoritarian tradition that is still dominant in eastern Europe.

Although the monarchs of eastern Europe were greatly impressed by Louis XIV and his model of royal absolutism, their states differed in several important ways from their French counterpart. Louis XIV built French absolutism on the heritage of a well-developed medieval monarchy and a strong royal bureaucracy. And when Louis XIV came to the throne the powers of the nobility were already somewhat limited, the French middle class was relatively strong, and the peasants were generally free from serfdom. Eastern absolutism rested upon a very different social reality: a powerful nobility, a weak middle class, and an oppressed peasantry condemned to serfdom.

These differences in social conditions raise three major questions. First, why did the basic structure of society in eastern Europe move away from that of western Europe in the early modern period? Second, how and why, in their different social environments, did the rulers of Austria, Prussia, and Russia manage to build powerful absolute monarchies, which proved more durable than that of Louis XIV? Finally, how did the absolute monarchs' interaction with artists and architects contribute to the splendid achievements of baroque culture? These are the questions this chapter seeks to answer.

LORDS AND PEASANTS IN EASTERN EUROPE

When absolute monarchy took shape in eastern Europe in the seventeenth century, it built on social and economic foundations laid between roughly 1400 and 1650. In those years the princes and the landed nobility of eastern Europe rolled back the gains made by the peasantry during the High Middle Ages and reimposed a harsh serfdom on the rural masses. The nobility also reduced the importance of the towns and the middle classes. This process differed profoundly from developments in western Europe at the same time. In the west peasants won greater freedom and the urban capitalistic middle class continued its rise. Thus, the east that emerged contrasted sharply with the west – another aspect of the shattered unity of medieval Latin Christendom.

THE MEDIEVAL BACKGROUND

Between roughly 1400 and 1650, nobles and rulers re-established serfdom in the eastern lands of Bohemia, Silesia, Hungary, eastern Germany, Poland, Lithuania, and Russia. The east – the land east of the Elbe River in Germany, which historians often call "East Elbia" – gained a certain social and economic unity in the process. But eastern peasants lost their rights and freedoms. They became bound first to the land they worked and then, by degrading obligations, to the lords they served.

This development was a tragic reversal of trends in the High Middle Ages. The period from roughly 1050 to 1300 had been a time of general economic expansion characterized by the growth of trade, towns, and population. Expansion also meant clearing the forests and colonizing the frontier beyond the Elbe River. Anxious to attract German settlers to their sparsely populated lands, the rulers and nobles of eastern Europe had offered potential newcomers attractive economic and legal incentives. Large numbers of incoming settlers obtained land on excellent terms and gained much greater personal freedom. These benefits were also gradually extended to the local Slavic populations, even those of central Russia. Thus by 1300 there had occurred a very general improvement in peasant conditions in eastern Europe. Serfdom all but disappeared. Peasants bargained freely with their landlords and moved about as they pleased. Opportunities and improvements east of the Elbe had a positive impact on western Europe, where the weight of serfdom was also reduced between 1100 and 1300.

After about 1300, however, as Europe's population and economy both declined grievously, mainly because of the Black Death, the east and the west went in different directions. In both east and west there occurred a many-sided landlord reaction, as lords sought to solve their tough economic problems by more heavily exploiting the peasantry. Yet this reaction generally failed in the west. In many western areas by 1500 almost all of the peasants were completely free, and in the rest of western Europe serf obligations had declined greatly. East of the Elbe, however, the landlords won. By 1500, eastern peasants were well on their way to becoming serfs again.

Throughout eastern Europe, as in western Europe, the drop in population and prices in the fourteenth and fifteenth centuries caused severe labor shortages and hard times for the nobles. Yet rather than offer better economic and legal terms to keep old peasants and attract new ones, eastern landlords used their political and police power to turn the tables on the peasants. They did this in two ways.

First, the lords made their kings and princes issue laws that restricted or eliminated the peasants' precious, time-honored right of free movement. Thus, a peasant could no longer leave to take advantage of better opportunities elsewhere without the lord's permission, and the lord had no reason to make such concessions. In Prussian territories by 1500, the law required that runaway peasants be hunted down and returned to their lords; a runaway servant was to be nailed to a post by one ear and given a knife to cut himself loose. Until the middle of the fifteenth century, medieval Russian peasants had been free to move wherever they wished and seek the best landlord. Thereafter this freedom was gradually curtailed, so that by 1497 a Russian peasant had the right to move only during a two-week period after the fall harvest. Eastern peasants were losing their status as free and independent men and women.

Second, lords steadily took more and more of their peasants' land and imposed heavier and heavier labor obligations. Instead of being independent farmers paying reasonable, freely negotiated rents, peasants tended to become forced laborers on the lords' estates. By the early 1500s, lords in many territories could command their peasants to work for them without pay as many as six days a week. A German writer of the mid-sixteenth century described peasants in eastern Prussia who "do not possess the heritage of their holdings and have to serve their master whenever he wants them."[1]

The gradual erosion of the peasantry's economic position was bound up with manipulation of the oppressive legal system. The local lord was also the local prosecutor, judge, and jailer. As a matter of course, he ruled in his own favor in disputes with his peasants. There were no independent royal officials to provide justice or uphold the common law.

THE CONSOLIDATION OF SERFDOM

Between 1500 and 1650, the social, legal, and economic conditions of peasants in eastern Europe continued to decline. Free peasants lost their freedom and became serfs. In Poland, for example, nobles gained complete control over their peasants in 1574, after which they could legally inflict the death penalty on their serfs whenever they wished. In Prussia a long series of oppressive measures reached their culmination in 1653. Not only were all the old privileges of the lords reaffirmed, but peasants were assumed to be in "hereditary subjugation" to their lords unless they could prove the contrary in the lords' courts, which was practically impossible. Prussian peasants were serfs tied to their lords as well as to the land.

In Russia the right of peasants to move from a given estate was "temporarily" suspended in the 1590s and permanently abolished in 1603. In 1649, a new law code completed the process. At the insistence of the lower nobility, the Russian tsar lifted the nine-year time limit on the recovery of runaways. Henceforth, runaway peasants were to be returned to their lords whenever they were caught, as long as they lived. The last small hope of escaping serfdom was gone. Control of serfs was strictly the lords' own business, for the new law code set no limits on the lords' authority over their peasants. Although the political development of the various eastern states differed, the legal re-establishment of permanent hereditary serfdom was the common fate of peasants in the east by the middle of the seventeenth century.

The consolidation of serfdom between 1500 and 1650 was accompanied by the growth of estate agriculture, particularly in Poland and eastern Germany. In the sixteenth century European economic expansion and population growth resumed after the great declines of the late Middle Ages. Prices for agricultural commodities also rose sharply as gold and silver flowed in from the New World. Thus, Polish and German lords had powerful economic incentives to increase the production of their estates. And they did.

Lords seized more and more peasant land for their own estates and then demanded and received ever more unpaid serf labor on those enlarged estates. Even when the estates were inefficient and technically backward, as they generally were, the great Polish nobles and middle-rank German lords squeezed sizable, cheap, and thus very profitable surpluses out of their impoverished peasants. These surpluses in wheat and timber were easily sold to big foreign merchants, who exported them to the growing cities of the west. The poor east helped feed the much wealthier west.

The re-emergence of serfdom in eastern Europe in the early modern period was clearly a momentous human development, and historians have advanced a variety of explanations for it. As always, some scholars have stressed the economic interpretation. Agricultural depression and population decline in the fourteenth and fifteenth centuries led to a severe labor shortage, they have argued, and thus eastern landlords naturally tied their precious peasants to the land. With the return of prosperity and the development of export markets in the sixteenth century, the landlords finished the job, grabbing the peasants' land and making them work as unpaid serfs on the enlarged estates. This argument by itself is not very convincing, for almost identical economic developments "caused" the opposite result in the west. Indeed, some historians have maintained that labor shortage and subsequent renewed expansion were key factors in the virtual disappearance of serfdom in western Europe.

PUNISHING SERFS *This seventeenth-century illus-*
tration from Olearius's famous Travels to Moscovy
suggests what eastern serfdom really meant. The scene
is eastern Poland. There, according to Olearius, a
common command of the lord was, "Beat him till the
skin falls from the flesh." (Photo: Caroline Buckler)

It seems fairly clear, therefore, that political rather than economic factors were crucial in the simultaneous rise of serfdom in the east and decline of serfdom in the west. Specifically, eastern lords enjoyed much greater political power than their western counterparts. In the late Middle Ages, when much of eastern Europe experienced innumerable wars and general political chaos, the noble landlord class greatly increased its political power at the expense of the ruling monarchs. There were, for example, many disputed royal successions, so that weak kings were forced to grant political favors to win the support of the nobility. Thus while strong "new monarchs" were rising in Spain, France, and England and providing effective central government, kings were generally losing power in the east. Such weak kings could not resist the demands of the lords regarding their peasants.

Moreover, most eastern monarchs did not want to resist even if they could. The typical king was only "first among equals" in the noble class. He too thought mainly in "private" rather than "public" terms. He too wanted to squeeze as much as he could out of *his* peasants and enlarge *his* estates. The western concept and reality of sovereignty, as embodied in a king who protected the interests of all his people, was not well developed in eastern Europe before 1650.

The political power of the peasants was also weaker in eastern Europe, and declined steadily after about 1400. Although there were occasional bloody peasant uprisings against the oppression of the landlords, they never succeeded. Nor did eastern peasants effectively resist day-by-day infringements on their liberties by their landlords. Part of the reason was that the lords, rather than the kings, ran the courts – one of the important concessions nobles extorted from weak monarchs. It has also been suggested that peasant solidarity was weaker in the east, possibly reflecting the lack of long-established village communities on the eastern frontier.

Finally, with the approval of weak kings, the landlords systematically undermined the medieval privileges of the towns and the power of the urban classes. Instead of selling their products to local merchants in the towns, as required in the Middle Ages, the landlords sold directly to big foreign capitalists. For example, Dutch ships sailed up the rivers of Poland and eastern Germany to the loading docks of the great estates, completely short-circuiting the local towns. Moreover, "town air" no longer "made people free," for the eastern towns lost their medieval right of refuge and were compelled to return runaways to their lords. The population of the towns and the importance of the urban middle classes declined greatly. This development both reflected and promoted the supremacy of noble landlords in most of eastern Europe in the sixteenth century.

THE RISE OF AUSTRIA AND PRUSSIA

In spite of the strength of the nobility and the weakness of many monarchs before 1600,

strong kings did begin to emerge in many lands in the course of the seventeenth century. War and the threat of war aided rulers greatly in their attempts to build absolute monarchies. There was an endless struggle for power, as eastern rulers not only fought each other but also battled with hordes of Asiatic invaders. In this atmosphere of continuous wartime emergency, monarchs reduced the political power of the landlord nobility. Cautiously leaving the nobles the unchallenged masters of their peasants, the absolutist monarchs of eastern Europe gradually gained and monopolized political power in three key areas. They imposed and collected permanent taxes without consent. They maintained permanent standing armies, which policed their subjects in addition to fighting abroad. And they conducted relations with other states as they pleased.

As with all general historical developments, there were important variations on the absolutist theme in eastern Europe. The royal absolutism created in Prussia was stronger and more effective than that established in Austria. This advantage gave Prussia a thin edge over Austria in the struggle for power in east-central Europe in the eighteenth century. That edge had enormous long-term political significance, for it was a rising Prussia that unified the German people in the nineteenth century and imposed upon them a fateful Prussian stamp.

AUSTRIA AND THE OTTOMAN TURKS

Like all the peoples and rulers of central Europe, the Habsburgs of Austria emerged from the Thirty Years' War (pages 530–536) impoverished and exhausted. The effort to root out Protestantism in the German lands had failed utterly, and the authority of the Holy Roman Empire and its Habsburg em-

THE OTTOMAN SLAVE TAX   *This contemporary drawing shows Ottoman officials rounding up male Christian children in the Balkans. The children became part of a special slave corps, which served the* *sultan for life as soldiers and administrators. The slave tax and the slave corps were of great importance to the Ottoman Turks in the struggle with Austria. (The British Museum)*

perors had declined almost to the vanishing point. Yet defeat in central Europe also opened new vistas. The Habsburg monarchs were forced to turn inward and eastward in the attempt to fuse their diverse holdings into a strong unified state.

An important step in this direction had actually been taken in Bohemia during the Thirty Years' War. Protestantism had been strong among the Czechs of Bohemia, and in 1618 the Czech nobles who controlled the Bohemian Estates – the semiparliamentary body of Bohemia – had risen up against their Habsburg king. Not only was this revolt crushed, but the old Czech nobility was wiped out as well. Those Czech nobles who did not die in 1620 at the battle of the White Mountain (page 533), a momentous turning point in Czech history, had their estates confiscated. The Habsburg king, Ferdinand II (1619–1637), then redistributed the Czech lands to a motley band of aristocratic soldiers of fortune from all over Europe.

In fact, after 1650, 80 to 90 percent of the Bohemian nobility was of recent foreign origin and owed everything to the Habsburgs.

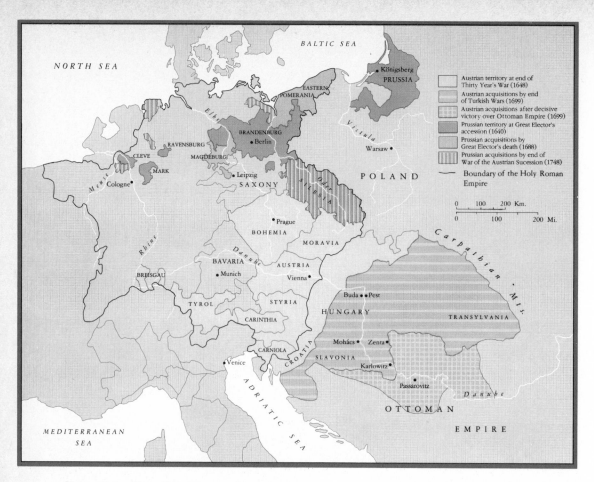

MAP 17.1 *THE GROWTH OF AUSTRIA AND BRANDENBURG-PRUSSIA TO 1748* Austria expanded to the southwest into Hungary and Transylvania at the expense of the Ottoman Empire. But it was unable to hold the rich German province of Silesia, which was conquered by Brandenburg-Prussia.

With the help of this new nobility, the Habsburgs established strong direct rule over reconquered Bohemia. The condition of the enserfed peasantry worsened: three days per week of unpaid labor – the *robot* – became the norm, and a quarter of the serfs worked for their lords every day but Sundays and religious holidays. Serfs also paid the taxes, which further strengthened the alliance between the Habsburg monarch and the Bohemian nobility. Protestantism was also stamped out, in the course of which a growing unity of religion was brought about. The reorgani-

zation of Bohemia was a giant step toward absolutism.

After the Thirty Years' War, Ferdinand III centralized the government in the old hereditary provinces of Austria proper, the second part of the Habsburg holdings (see Map 17.1). For the first time he created a permanent standing army, which stood ready to put down any internal opposition. The Habsburg monarchy was then ready to turn toward the vast plains of Hungary, which it claimed as the third and largest part of its dominion, in opposition to the Ottoman Turks.

The Ottomans came out of the Anatolia, in present-day Turkey, and they created one of history's greatest military empires. At their peak in the middle of the sixteenth century under Suleiman the Magnificent (1520–1566), they ruled the most powerful empire in the world, bar none. Their possessions stretched from western Persia across North Africa and up into the heart of central Europe. Apostles of Islam, the Ottoman Turks were old and determined foes of the Catholic Habsburgs. Their armies had almost captured Vienna in 1529, and for more than 150 years thereafter they ruled all of the Balkans, almost all of Hungary, and part of southern Russia.

The Ottoman Empire was originally built on a fascinating and very non-European conception of state and society. There was an almost complete absence of private landed property. All the agricultural land of the empire was the personal hereditary property of the sultan, who exploited the land as he saw fit according to Ottoman political theory. There was, therefore, no security of landholding and no hereditary nobility. Everyone was dependent upon the sultan and virtually his slave.

Indeed, the top ranks of the bureaucracy were staffed by the sultan's slave corps. Every year the sultan levied a "tax" of one to three thousand male children upon the conquered Christian populations in the Balkans. These and other slaves were raised in Turkey as Muslims, and trained to fight and to administer. The most talented slaves rose to the top of the bureaucracy; the less fortunate formed the brave and skillful core of the sultan's army, the so-called janissary corps.

As long as the Ottoman Empire expanded, the system worked well. As the sultan won more territory, he could impose his slave tax on larger populations. Moreover, he could amply reward loyal and effective servants by letting them draw a carefully defined income from conquered Christian peasants on a strictly temporary basis. For a long time Christian peasants in eastern Europe were economically exploited less by the Muslim Turks than by Christian nobles, and they were not forced to convert to Islam. After about 1570, however, the powerful, centralized Ottoman system slowly began to disintegrate as the Turks' western advance was stopped. Temporary landholders became hard-to-control permanent oppressors. Weak sultans left the glory of the battlefield for the delights of the harem, and the army lost its dedication and failed to keep up with European military advances.

Yet in the late seventeenth century, under vigorous reforming leadership, the Ottoman Empire succeeded in marshaling its forces for one last mighty blow at Christian Europe. After wresting territory from Poland, fighting a long inconclusive war with Russia, and establishing an alliance with Louis XIV of France, the Turks turned again on Austria. A huge Turkish army surrounded Vienna and laid siege to it in 1683. But after holding out against great odds for two months, the city was relieved by a mixed force of Habsburg, Saxon, Bavarian, and Polish troops, and the Ottomans were forced to retreat. Soon the retreat became a rout. As their Russian and Venetian allies attacked on other fronts, the Habsburgs conquered all of Hungary and Transylvania (part of present-day Rumania) by 1699.

The Turkish wars and this great expansion strengthened the Habsburg army and promoted some sense of unity in the Habsburg lands. The Habsburgs moved to centralize their power and make it as absolute as possible. These efforts to create a fully developed, highly centralized, absolutist state were only partly successful.

The Habsburg state was composed of three separate and distinct territories – the old "hereditary provinces" of Austria, the kingdom of Bohemia, and the kingdom of Hungary. These three parts were tied together primarily by their common ruler – the Habsburg monarch. Each part had its own laws and political life, for the three noble-dominated Estates continued to exist, though with reduced powers. The Habsburgs themselves were well aware of the fragility of the union they had forged. In 1713, Charles VI (1711–1740) proclaimed the so-called Pragmatic Sanction, which stated that the Habsburg possessions were never to be divided and were always to be passed intact to a single heir, who might be female since Charles had no sons. Charles spent much of his reign trying to get this principle accepted by the various branches of the Habsburg family, by the three different Estates of the realm, and by the states of Europe. His fears turned out to be well founded.

The Hungarian nobility, despite its reduced strength, effectively thwarted the full development of Habsburg absolutism. Time and again throughout the seventeenth century, Hungarian nobles – the most numerous in Europe, making up from 5 to 7 percent of the Hungarian population – rose in revolt against the attempts of Vienna to impose absolute rule. They never triumphed decisively, but neither were they ever crushed and replaced as the Czech nobility had been in 1620.

Hungarians resisted because many of them were Protestants, especially in the area long ruled by the more tolerant Turks, and they hated the heavy-handed attempts of the conquering Habsburgs to re-Catholicize everyone. Moreover, the lords of Hungary often found a powerful military ally in Turkey. Finally, the Hungarian nobility, and even part of the peasantry, had become attached to a national ideal long before most of the peoples of Europe. They were determined to maintain as much independence and local control as possible. Thus when the Habsburgs were bogged down in the War of the Spanish Succession (page 570), the Hungarians rose in one last patriotic rebellion under Prince Francis Rakoczy in 1703. Rakoczy and his forces were eventually defeated, but this time the Habsburgs had to accept a definitive compromise. Charles VI restored many of the traditional privileges of the Hungarian aristocracy in return for Hungarian acceptance of hereditary Habsburg rule. Thus Hungary, unlike Austria or Bohemia, never came close to being fully integrated into a centralized, absolute Habsburg state.

PRUSSIA IN THE SEVENTEENTH CENTURY

After 1400, the status of east German peasants declined steadily; their serfdom was formally spelled out in the early seventeenth century. While the local princes lost political power and influence, a revitalized landed nobility became the undisputed ruling class. The Hohenzollern family, which ruled through its senior and junior branches as the electors of Brandenburg and the dukes of Prussia, had little real princely power. The Hohenzollern rulers were nothing more than the "first among equals," the largest landowners in a landlord society.

Nothing suggested that the Hohenzollerns and their territories would ever play an important role in European or even German affairs. The elector of Brandenburg's right to help choose the Holy Roman emperor with six other electors was of little practical value, and the elector had no military strength whatsoever. The territory of his cousin, the duke of Prussia, was actually part of the kingdom of Poland. Moreover, geography conspired against the Hohenzollerns. Brandenburg, their power base, was completely cut off from the sea (see Map 17.1). A tiny part of the vast north European plain that stretches from France to Russia, Brandenburg lacked natural frontiers and lay open to attack from all directions. The land was poor, a combination of sand and swamp. Contemporaries contemptuously called Brandenburg "the sand-box of the Holy Roman Empire."[2]

Brandenburg was a helpless spectator in the Thirty Years' War, its territory alternately ravaged by Swedish and by Habsburg armies. Population fell drastically, and many villages disappeared. The power of the Hohenzollerns reached its lowest point. Yet the devastation of the country prepared the way for Hohenzollern absolutism, because foreign armies dramatically weakened the political power of the Estates — the representative assemblies of the realm. This weakening of the Estates helped the very talented young elector Frederick William (1640–1688), later known as the Great Elector, to ride roughshod over traditional parliamentary liberties and to take a giant step toward royal absolutism. This constitutional struggle, often unjustly neglected by historians, was the most crucial in Prussian history for hundreds of years, until that of the 1860s.

When he came to power in 1640, the twenty-year-old Great Elector was determined to unify his three quite separate provinces and to add to them by diplomacy and war. These provinces were historic Brandenburg, the area around Berlin; Prussia, inherited in 1618 when the junior branch of the Hohenzollern family died out; and completely separate, scattered holdings along the Rhine in western Germany, inherited in 1614 (see Map 17.1). Each of the three provinces was inhabited by Germans; but each had its own Estates, whose power had increased until about 1600 as the power of the rulers declined. Although the Estates had not met regularly during the chaotic Thirty Years' War, they still had the

power of the purse in their respective provinces. Taxes could not be levied without their consent. The Estates of Brandenburg and Prussia were dominated by the nobility and the landowning classes, known as the Junkers. But it must be remembered that this was also true of the English Parliament before and after the Civil War. Had the Estates successfully resisted the absolutist demands of the Great Elector, they too might have evolved toward more broadly based constitutionalism.

The struggle between the Great Elector and the provincial Estates was long, complicated, and intense. After the Thirty Years' War, the representatives of the nobility zealously reasserted the right of the Estates to vote taxes, a right the Swedish armies of occupation had simply ignored. Yet first in Brandenburg in 1653, and then in Prussia between 1661 and 1663, the Great Elector eventually had his way.

To pay for the permanent standing army he first established in 1660, Frederick William forced the Estates to accept the introduction of permanent taxation without consent. Moreover, the soldiers doubled as tax collectors and policemen, becoming the core of the rapidly expanding state bureaucracy. The power of the Estates declined rapidly thereafter, for the Great Elector had both financial independence and superior force. He turned the screws of taxation: the state's total revenue tripled during his reign. The size of the army leaped about tenfold. In 1688, a population of one million was supporting a peacetime standing army of thirty thousand. Many of the soldiers were French Huguenot immigrants, whom the Great Elector welcomed as the talented, hardworking citizens they were.

In accounting for the Great Elector's fateful triumph, two factors appear central. As in the formation of every absolutist state, war was a decisive factor. The ongoing struggle between Sweden and Poland for control of the

Baltic after 1648 and the wars of Louis XIV in western Europe created an atmosphere of permanent crisis. The wild Tartars of southern Russia swept through Prussia in the winter of 1656–1657, killing and carrying off as slaves more than fifty thousand people, according to an old estimate. This invasion softened up the Estates and strengthened the urgency of the elector's demands for more money for more soldiers. It was no accident that, except for commercially minded Holland, constitutionalism won out only in England, the only major country to escape devastating foreign invasions in the seventeenth century.

Second, the nobility had long dominated the government through the Estates, but only for its own narrow self-interest. When the crunch came, the Prussian nobles proved unwilling to join the representatives of the towns in a consistent common front against royal pretensions. The nobility was all too concerned with its own rights and privileges, especially its freedom from taxation and its unlimited control over the peasants. When, therefore, the Great Elector reconfirmed these privileges in 1653 and after, even while reducing the political power of the Estates, the nobility growled but did not bite. It accepted a compromise whereby the bulk of the new taxes fell upon towns, and royal authority stopped at the landlords' gates. The elector could and did use naked force to break the liberties of the towns. The main leader of the urban opposition in the key city of Königsberg, for example, was simply arrested and imprisoned for life without trial.

THE CONSOLIDATION OF PRUSSIAN ABSOLUTISM

By the time of his death in 1688, the Great Elector had created a single state out of scattered principalities. But his new creation was still small and fragile. All the leading states of Europe had many more people – France with 20 million was fully twenty times as populous – and strong monarchy was still a novelty. Moreover, the Great Elector's successor, Elector Frederick III, "the Ostentatious" (1688–1713), was weak of body and mind.

Like so many of the small princes of Germany and Italy at the time, Frederick III imitated Louis XIV in every possible way. He built his own very expensive version of Versailles. He surrounded himself with cultivated artists and musicians and basked in the praise of toadies and sycophants. His only real political accomplishment was to gain the title of king from the Holy Roman emperor, a Habsburg, in return for military aid in the War of the Spanish Succession, and in 1701 he was crowned King Frederick I.

This tendency toward luxury-loving, happy, and harmless petty tyranny was completely reversed by Frederick William I (1713–1740), "the Soldiers' King." A crude, dangerous psychoneurotic, Frederick William I was nevertheless the most talented reformer ever produced by the Hohenzollern family. It was he who truly established Prussian absolutism and gave it its unique character. It was he who created the best army in Europe, for its size, and who infused military values into a whole society. In the words of a leading historian of Prussia:

For a whole generation, the Hohenzollern subjects were victimized by a royal bully, imbued with an obsessive bent for military organization and military scales of value. This left a deep mark upon the institutions of Prussiandom and upon the molding of the "Prussian spirit."[3]

Frederick William's passion for the army and military life was intensely emotional. He had, for example, a bizarre, almost pathological love for tall soldiers, whom he credited

THE "TOBACCO PARLIAMENT" In absolutist
Prussia the informal discussion of politics by the king
and his friends over a pipe after dinner was the only
parliament. (Historical Picture Service, Chicago)

with superior strength and endurance. Austere and always faithful to his wife, he confided to the French ambassador: "The most beautiful girl or woman in the world would be a matter of indifference to me, but tall soldiers — they are my weakness." Like some fanatical modern-day basketball coach in search of a championship team, he sent his agents throughout both Prussia and all of Europe, tricking, buying, and kidnapping top recruits. Neighboring princes sent him their giants as gifts to win his gratitude. Prussian mothers told their sons: "Stop growing or the recruiting agents will get you."[4]

Profoundly military in temperament, Frederick William always wore an army uniform, and he lived the highly disciplined life of the professional soldier. He began his work by five or six in the morning; at ten he almost always went to the parade ground to drill or inspect his troops. A man of violent temper, Frederick William personally punished the

*MOLDING THE PRUSSIAN SPIRIT Discipline was
strict and punishment brutal in the Prussian army.
This scene, intended to instruct school children, shows
one soldier being flogged while another is being beaten
with canes as he walks between rows of troops. (Photo:
Caroline Buckler)*

most minor infractions on the spot: a missing
button off a soldier's coat quickly provoked a
savage beating with his heavy walking stick.

Frederick William's love of the army was
also based on a hardheaded conception of the
struggle for power and a dog-eat-dog view of
international politics. Even before ascending
the throne he bitterly criticized his father's
ministers: "They say that they will obtain
land and power for the king with the pen; but
I say it can be done only with the sword."
Years later he summed up his life's philosophy in his instructions to his son: "A formidable army and a war chest large enough to
make this army mobile in times of need can
create great respect for you in the world, so
that you can speak a word like the other
powers."[5] This unshakable belief that the welfare of king and state depended upon the
army above all else reinforced Frederick William's personal passion for playing soldier.

The cult of military power provided the rationale for a great expansion of royal absolutism. As the king himself put it with his

characteristic ruthlessness: "I must be served with life and limb, with house and wealth, with honour and conscience, everything must be committed except eternal salvation – that belongs to God, but all else is mine."[6] To make good these extraordinary demands, Frederick William created a strong centralized bureaucracy. More commoners probably rose to top positions in the civil government than at any other time in Prussia's history. The last traces of the parliamentary Estates and local self-government vanished.

The king's grab for power brought him into considerable conflict with the noble landowners, the Junkers. In his early years, he even threatened to destroy them; yet, in the end, the Prussian nobility was not destroyed but enlisted – into the army. Responding to a combination of threats and opportunities, the Junkers became the officer caste. By 1739, all but 5 of 245 officers with the rank of major or above were aristocrats, and most of them were native Prussians. A new compromise had been worked out, whereby the proud nobility imperiously commanded the peasantry in the army as well as on its estates.

Coarse and crude, penny-pinching and hardworking, Frederick William achieved results. Above all, he built a first-rate army on the basis of third-rate resources. The standing army increased from 38,000 to 83,000 during his reign. Prussia, twelfth in Europe in population, had the fourth largest army by 1740. Only the much more populous states of France, Russia, and Austria had larger forces, and even France's army was only twice as large as Prussia's. Moreover, soldier for soldier, the Prussian army became the best in Europe, astonishing foreign observers with its precision, skill, and discipline. For the next two hundred years, Prussia and then Prussianized Germany would almost always win the crucial military battles.

Frederick William and his ministers also built an exceptionally honest and conscientious bureaucracy, which not only administered the country but tried with some success to develop it economically. Finally, like the miser he was, living very frugally off the income of his own landholdings, the king loved his "blue boys" so much that he hated to "spend" them. This most militaristic of kings was, paradoxically, almost always at peace.

Nevertheless, the Prussian people paid a heavy and lasting price for the obsessions of the royal drillmaster. Civil society became rigid and highly disciplined. Prussia became "the Sparta of the North"; unquestioning obedience was the highest virtue. As a Prussian minister later summed it up, "To keep quiet is the first civic duty."[7] Thus, the policies of Frederick William I combined with harsh peasant bondage and Junker tyranny to lay the foundations for what later evolved into probably the most militaristic country of modern times.

Frederick II (1740–1786), also known as Frederick the Great, built masterfully upon his father's work. This was somewhat surprising, for like many children with tyrannical (or kindly) parents, he rebelled against his parents' wishes in his early years. Rejecting the crude life of the barracks, Frederick embraced culture and literature, even writing poetry and fine prose in French, a language his father detested. He threw off his father's dour Calvinism and dabbled with atheism. After trying, unsuccessfully, to run away at age eighteen in 1730, he was virtually imprisoned and even compelled to watch his companion in flight beheaded at his father's command. Yet, like many other rebellious youths, Frederick eventually reached a reconciliation with his father, and by the time he came to the throne ten years later he was determined to follow in his father's footsteps.

When, therefore, the emperor of Austria, Charles VI, also died in 1740 and his young and beautiful daughter, Maria Theresa, became queen of the Habsburg dominions, Frederick suddenly and without warning invaded her rich all-German province of Silesia. This action defied solemn Prussian promises to respect the Pragmatic Sanction, which guaranteed Maria Theresa's succession, but no matter. For Frederick, it was the opportunity of a lifetime to expand the size and power of Prussia. Although Maria Theresa succeeded in dramatically rallying the normally quarrelsome Hungarian nobility, her multinational army was no match for Prussian precision. In 1742, as other greedy powers were falling upon her lands in the general European War of the Austrian Succession (1740–1748), she was forced to cede all of Silesia to Prussia. In one stroke Prussia doubled its population to 6 million people. Now Prussia unquestionably towered above all the other German states and stood as a European Great Power.

Frederick had to spend much of his reign fighting against great odds not only to hold onto his initial gains but to save Prussia from total destruction. In the end he succeeded, worthy heir of "the Soldiers' King" he sought to please. In 1760, at the very height of his struggle against invading armies on all sides, Frederick recounted a dream in which he met his father with his favorite general at the palace. "Have I done well?" he asked. "Very well," Frederick William replied. "That pleases me greatly," said Frederick. "Your approval means more to me than that of the whole world."[8]

THE DEVELOPMENT OF RUSSIA

One of the favorite parlor games of nineteenth-century Russian (and non-Russian) intellectuals was debating whether Russia was a part of western European civilization or was a "nonwestern," "Asiatic" civilization. This question was particularly fascinating because it was unanswerable. A good case could be made for either position. To this day Russia differs fundamentally from the West in some basic ways, though Russian history has paralleled that of the West in other ways. Thus the hypnotic attraction of Russian history.

The differences between Russia and the West were particularly striking before 1700, when Russia's overall development began to draw progressively closer to that of its western neighbors. These early differences and Russia's long isolation from Europe explain why little has so far been said here about Russia. Yet it is impossible to understand how Russia has increasingly influenced and been influenced by western European civilization since roughly the late seventeenth century without looking at the course of early Russian history. Such a brief survey will also help explain how, when absolute monarchy finally and decisively triumphed under the rough guidance of Peter the Great in the early eighteenth century, it was a quite different type of absolute monarchy from that of France or even Prussia.

THE VIKINGS AND THE KIEVAN PRINCIPALITY

In antiquity the Slavs lived as a single people in central Europe. With the start of the mass migrations of the late Roman Empire, the Slavs moved in different directions and split into three groups. Between the fifth and ninth centuries the eastern Slavs, from whom the Ukrainians, the Russians, and the White Russians descend, moved into the vast and practically uninhabited area of present-day European Russia (see Map 17.2).

This enormous area consisted of an immense virgin forest to the north, where most of the eastern Slavs settled, and an endless prairie grassland to the south. Probably organized as tribal communities, the eastern Slavs, like many North American pioneers much later, lived off the great abundance of wild game and a crude "slash and burn" agriculture. After clearing a piece of the forest to build log cabins, they burned the stumps and brush. The ashes left a rich deposit of potash and lime, and the land gave several good crops before it was exhausted. The people then moved on to another untouched area and repeated the process.

In the ninth century the Vikings, those fearless warriors from Scandinavia, appeared in the lands of the eastern Slavs. Called Varangians in the old Russian chronicles, the Vikings were interested primarily in international trade, and the opportunities were good, since the Muslim conquests of the eighth century had greatly reduced Christian trade in the Mediterranean. Moving up and down the rivers, the Vikings soon linked Scandinavia and northern Europe with the Black Sea and the Byzantine Empire with its capital at Constantinople. They built a few strategic forts along the rivers, from which they raided the neighboring Slavic tribes and collected tribute. Slaves were the most important article of tribute, and the word *Slav* even became the word for slave in several European languages.

In order to increase and protect their international commerce, the Vikings declared themselves the rulers of the eastern Slavs. According to tradition, the semilegendary chieftain Ruirik founded the princely dynasty about 860. In any event, the Varangian ruler Oleg (878–912) established his residence at Kiev. He and his successors ruled over a loosely united confederation of Slavic territories – the Kievan state – until 1054. The Viking prince and his clansmen quickly became assimilated into the Slavic population,

taking local wives and emerging as the noble class.

Assimilation and loss of Scandinavian ethnic identity was speeded up by the conversion of the Vikings to Eastern Orthodox Christianity by missionaries from the Byzantine Empire. The written language of these missionaries, Slavic – Church Slavonic – was subsequently used in all religious and nonreligious documents in the Kievan principality. Thus the rapidly Slavified Vikings left two important legacies for the future. They created a loose unification of Slavic territories under a single ruling prince and a single ruling dynasty. And they imposed a basic religious unity by accepting Orthodox Christianity, as opposed to Roman Catholicism, for themselves and the eastern Slavs.

Even at its height under Great Prince Iaroslav the Wise (1019–1054), the unity of the Kievan principality was extremely tenuous. Trade, rather than government, was the main concern of the rulers. Moreover, the Slavified Vikings failed to find a way of peacefully transferring power from one generation to the next. In medieval western Europe this fundamental problem of government was increasingly resolved by resort to the principle of primogeniture: the king's eldest son received the crown as his rightful inheritance when his father died. Civil war was thus averted; order was preserved. In early Kiev, however, there were apparently no fixed rules and much strife accompanied each succession.

Possibly to avoid such chaos, before his death in 1054 Great Prince Iaroslav divided the Kievan principality among his five sons, who in turn divided their properties when they died. Between 1054 and 1237, Kiev disintegrated into more and more competing units, each ruled by a prince claiming to be a descendant of Ruirik. Even when only one prince was claiming to be the great prince, the whole situation was very unsettled.

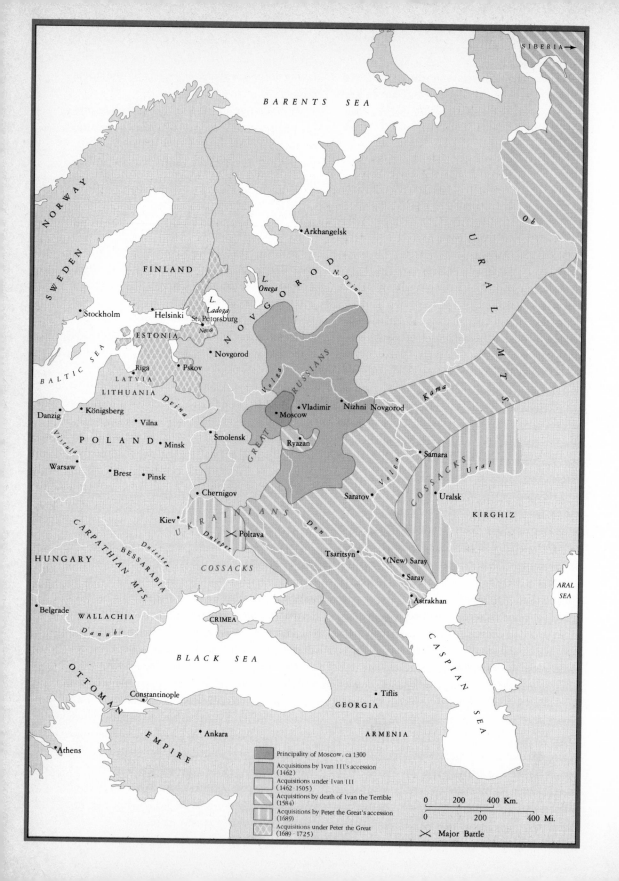

SIBERIA →

BARENTS SEA

NORWAY

SWEDEN

FINLAND

• Stockholm

• Helsinki

L. Onega

L. Ladoga

St. Petersburg

Neva

ESTONIA

BALTIC SEA

• Riga

LATVIA

LITHUANIA

Dvina

N O V G O R O D

• Arkhangelsk

N. Dvina

• Pskov

• Novgorod

Volga

GREAT

RUSSIANS

Ob

U R A L   M T S.

Kama

Danzig

• Königsberg

• Vilna

POLAND

• Minsk

Vistula

• Warsaw

• Brest

• Pinsk

• Smolensk

GREAT

• Vladimir

• Moscow

• Ryazan

• Nizhni Novgorod

Volga

Samara

Ural

COSSACKS

• Uralsk

KIRGHIZ

Don

• Saratov

• Chernigov

Kiev •

U K R A I N I A N S

Dnieper

✕ Poltava

Dniester

CARPATHIAN MTS.

BESSARABIA

HUNGARY

COSSACKS

• Belgrade

WALLACHIA

Danube

CRIMEA

BLACK SEA

• Tsaritsyn

• (New) Saray

• Saray

• Astrakhan

ARAL SEA

CASPIAN SEA

OTTOMAN

• Constantinople

• Tiflis

GEORGIA

EMPIRE

• Ankara

ARMENIA

• Athens

Principality of Moscow, ca 1300

Acquisitions by Ivan III's accession (1462)

Acquisitions under Ivan III (1462-1505)

Acquisitions by death of Ivan the Terrible (1584)

Acquisitions by Peter the Great's accession (1689)

Acquisitions under Peter the Great (1689-1725)

0   200   400 Km.

0   200   400 Mi.

✕ Major Battle

MAP 17.2 THE EXPANSION OF RUSSIA TO 1725 After the disintegration of the Kievan state and the Mongol conquest, the princes of Moscow and their descendants gradually extended their rule over an enormous territory.

The princes divided their land like private property because they thought of it as private property. A given prince owned a certain number of farms or landed estates, and had them worked directly by his people, mainly slaves, called *kholops* in Russian. Outside of these estates, which constituted the princely domain, the prince exercised only very limited authority in his principality. Excluding the clergy, two kinds of people lived there: the noble boyars and the commoner peasants.

The boyars were the descendants of the original Viking warriors, and they also held their lands as free and clear private property. And although the boyars normally fought in princely armies, the customary law declared they could serve any prince they wished. The ordinary peasants were also truly free. The peasants could move at will wherever opportunities were greatest. In the touching phrase of the times, theirs was "a clean road, without boundaries."[9] In short, fragmented princely power, private property, and personal freedom all went together.

THE MONGOL YOKE AND THE RISE OF MOSCOW

The eastern Slavs, like the Germans and the Italians, might have emerged from the Middle Ages weak and politically divided, had it not been for a development of extraordinary importance – the Mongol conquest of the Kievan state. Wild nomadic tribes from present-day Mongolia, the Mongols were temporarily unified in the thirteenth century by Jenghiz Khan (1162–1227), one of history's greatest conquerors. In five years his armies subdued all of China. His successors then wheeled westward, smashing everything in their path and reaching the plains of Hungary victoriously before they pulled back in 1242. The Mongol army – the Golden Horde – was savage in the extreme, often slaughtering the entire population of cities before burning them to the ground. On route to Mongolia, Archbishop John of Plano Carpini, the famous papal ambassador to Mongolia, passed through Kiev in southern Russia in 1245–1246 and wrote an unforgettable eyewitness account:

The Mongols went against Russia and enacted a great massacre in the Russian land. They destroyed towns and fortresses and killed people. They besieged Kiev which had been the capital of Russia, and after a long siege they took it and killed the inhabitants of the city. For this reason, when we passed through that land, we found lying in the field countless heads and bones of dead people; for this city had been extremely large and very populous, whereas now it has been reduced to nothing: barely two hundred houses stand there, and those people are held in the harshest slavery.[10]

Having devastated and conquered, the Mongols ruled the eastern Slavs for more than two hundred years. They built their capital of Saray on the lower Volga (see Map 17.2). They forced all the bickering Slavic princes to submit to their rule and to give them tribute and slaves. If the conquered peoples rebelled, the Mongols were quick to punish with death and destruction. Thus, the Mongols unified the eastern Slavs, for the Mongol khan was acknowledged by all as the supreme ruler.

The Mongol unification completely changed the internal political situation. Although the Mongols conquered, they were quite willing to use local princes as their obedient servants and tax collectors. Therefore they did not abolish the title of great prince, bestowing it instead upon the prince who served them best and paid them most handsomely.

Beginning with Alexander Nevsky in 1252, the previously insignificant princes of Moscow became particularly adept at serving the Mongols. They loyally put down popular uprisings and collected the khan's harsh taxes. By way of reward the princes of Moscow emerged as hereditary great princes. Eventually the Muscovite princes were able to destroy their princely rivals and even to replace the khan as supreme ruler. In this complex process, two princes of Moscow after Alexander Nevsky – Ivan I and Ivan III – were especially noteworthy.

Ivan I (1328–1341) was popularly known as Ivan the Moneybag. A bit like Frederick William of Prussia, he was extremely stingy and built up a large personal fortune. This enabled him to buy more property and to increase his influence by loaning money to less frugal princes to pay their Mongol taxes. Ivan's most serious rival was the prince of Tver, whom the Mongols at one point appointed as great prince.

In 1327, the population of Tver revolted against Mongol oppression, and the prince of Tver joined his people. Ivan immediately went to the Mongol capital of Saray, where he was appointed commander of a large Russian-Mongol army, which then laid waste to Tver and its lands. For this proof of devotion, the Mongols made Ivan the general tax collector for all the Slavic lands they had subjugated and named him great prince. Ivan also convinced the metropolitan of Kiev, the leading churchman of all eastern Slavs, to settle in Moscow; Ivan I thus gained greater prestige, while the church gained a powerful advocate before the khan.

In the next hundred-odd years, in the course of innumerable wars and intrigues, the great princes of Moscow significantly increased their holdings. Then, in the reign of Ivan III (1462–1505), the long process was largely completed. After purchasing Rostov, Ivan conquered and annexed other principalities, of which Novgorod with its lands extending as far as the Baltic Sea was most crucial (see Map 17.2). Thus, more than four hundred years after Iaroslav the Wise had divided the embryonic Kievan state, the princes of Moscow defeated all the rival branches of the house of Ruirik and became the unique holder of princely power.

Another dimension to princely power developed. Not only were the princes of Moscow the *unique* rulers, they were the *absolute* rulers, the autocrat, the *tsar* – the Slavic contraction for caesar, with all its connotations. This imperious conception of absolute power is expressed in a famous letter from the aging Ivan III to the Holy Roman emperor Frederick III (1440–1493). Frederick had offered Ivan the title of king in conjunction with the marriage of his daughter to Ivan's nephew. Ivan proudly refused:

We by the grace of God have been sovereigns over our domains from the beginning, from our first forebears, and our right we hold from God, as did our forebears. . . . As in the past we have never needed appointment from anyone, so now do we not desire it.[11]

The Muscovite idea of absolute authority was powerfully reinforced by two developments. First, about 1480 Ivan III stopped acknowledging the khan as his supreme ruler. There is good evidence to suggest that Ivan and his successors saw themselves as khans. Certainly they assimilated the Mongol concept of kingship as the exercise of unrestrained and unpredictable power.

Second, after the fall of Constantinople to the Turks in 1453, the tsars saw themselves as the heirs of both the caesars and Orthodox Christianity, the one true faith. All the other kings of Europe were heretics: only the tsars were rightful and holy rulers. This idea was promoted by Orthodox churchmen, who spoke of "holy Russia" and "the Third Rome." As the metropolitan Zosima stated in 1492: "Two Romes have fallen, the third Rome will be Moscow and a fourth is not to be."[12] Ivan's marriage to Sofia, the daughter of the last Byzantine emperor, further enhanced the aura of an eastern imperial inheritance for Moscow. Worthy successor to the mighty khan and the true Christian emperor, the Muscovite tsar was a king above all others.

TSAR AND PEOPLE TO 1689

By 1505, the great prince of Moscow – the tsar – had emerged as the single hereditary ruler of "all the Russias" – of all the lands of the eastern Slavs – and he was claiming unrestricted power as his God-given right. In effect, the tsar was demanding the same kind of total authority over all his subjects that the princely descendants of Ruirik had long exercised over their slaves on their own landed estates. This was an extremely radical demand.

While peasants had begun losing their freedom of movement in the fifteenth century, so had the noble boyars begun to lose power and influence. Ivan III pioneered in this regard, as in so many others. When Ivan conquered the principality of Novgorod in the 1480s, he confiscated fully 80 percent of the land, executing the previous owners or resettling them nearer Moscow. He then kept more than half of the confiscated land for himself, and distributed the remainder to members of a new emerging service nobility. The boyars had previously held their land as hereditary private property and been free to serve the prince of their choosing. The new service nobility held the tsar's land on the explicit condition that they serve in the tsar's

ST. BASIL'S CATHEDRAL in Moscow, with its steeply sloping roofs and proliferation of multicolored onion-shaped domes, was a striking example of powerful Byzantine influences on Russian culture. According to tradition, an enchanted Ivan the Terrible blinded the cathedral's architects, to insure they would never duplicate their fantastic achievement. (The New York Public Library)

army. Moreover, Ivan III began to require boyars outside of Novgorod to serve him if they wished to retain their lands. Since there were no competing princes left to turn to, the boyars had to yield.

The rise of the new service nobility accelerated under Ivan IV (1533–1584), the famous Ivan the Terrible. Having ascended the throne at age three, Ivan had suffered insults and neglect at the hands of the haughty boyars after his mother mysteriously died, possibly poisoned, when he was just eight. At age sixteen he suddenly pushed aside his hated boyar advisers. In an awe-inspiring ceremony complete with gold coins pouring down upon his head, he majestically crowned himself and officially took the august title of tsar for the first time.

Selecting the beautiful and kind Anastasia of the popular Romanov family for his wife and queen, the young tsar soon declared war on the remnants of Mongol power. He defeated the faltering khanates of Kazan and Astrakhan between 1552 and 1556, adding vast new territories to Russia. In the course of these wars Ivan virtually abolished the old distinction between hereditary boyar private property and land granted temporarily for service. All nobles, old and new, had to serve the tsar in order to hold any land.

The process of transforming the entire nobility into a service nobility was completed in the second part of Ivan the Terrible's reign. In 1557, Ivan turned westward, and for the next twenty-five years Muscovy waged an exhausting, unsuccessful war primarily with the large Polish-Lithuanian state, which controlled not only Poland but much of the Ukraine in the sixteenth century. Quarreling with the boyars over the war and blaming them for the sudden death of his beloved Anastasia in 1560, the increasingly cruel and demented Ivan turned to strike down all who stood in his way.

Above all, he struck down the ancient Muscovite boyars with a reign of terror. Leading boyars, their relatives, and even their peasants and servants were executed en masse by a special corps of unquestioning servants. Dressed in black and riding black horses, they were the forerunners of the modern dictator's secret police. Large estates were confiscated, broken up, and reapportioned to the lower service nobility. The great boyar families were

severely reduced. The newer, poorer, more nearly equal service nobility, which was still less than .5 percent of the total population, was totally dependent upon the autocrat.

Ivan also took giant strides toward making all commoners servants of the tsar. His endless wars and demonic purges left much of central Russia depopulated. It grew increasingly difficult for the lower service nobility to squeeze a living for themselves out of the peasants left on their landholdings. As the service nobles demanded more from the remaining peasants, more and more peasants fled toward the wild, recently conquered territories to the east and south. There they formed free groups and outlaw armies known as Cossacks. The Cossacks maintained a precarious independence beyond the reach of the oppressive landholders and the tsar's hated officials. The solution to this problem was to complete the tying of the peasants to the land, to make them serfs perpetually bound to serve the noble landholders, who were bound in turn to serve the tsar.

In the time of Ivan the Terrible urban traders and artisans were also bound to their towns and jobs, so that the tsar could tax them more heavily. Ivan assumed that the tsar owned Russia's trade and industry, just as he owned all the land. In the course of the sixteenth and seventeenth centuries, the tsars therefore took over the mines and industries and monopolized the country's important commercial activities. The urban classes had no security in their work or property, and even the wealthiest merchants were basically dependent agents of the tsar. If a new commercial activity became profitable, it was often taken over by the tsar and made a royal monopoly. This royal monopolization was in sharp contrast to developments in western Europe, where the capitalist middle classes were gaining strength and security in their private property. The tsar's service obligations checked the growth of the Russian middle classes, just as they led to the decline of the boyars, the rise of the lower nobility, and the final enserfment of the peasants.

Ivan the Terrible's system of autocracy and compulsory service struck foreign observers forcibly. Sigismund Herberstein, a German traveler to Russia, wrote in 1571: "All the people consider themselves to be *kholops,* that is slaves of their Prince." At the same time Jean Bodin, the French thinker who did so much to develop the modern concept of sovereignty, concluded that Russia's political system was fundamentally different from those of all other European monarchies and comparable only to that of the Turkish empire. In both Turkey and Russia, as in other parts of Asia and Africa, "the prince is become lord of the goods and persons of his subjects . . . governing them as a master of a family does his slaves."[13] The Mongol inheritance weighed heavily upon Russia.

As has so often been the case in Russian history, the death of an iron-fisted tyrant – in this case Ivan the Terrible in 1584 – ushered in an era of confusion and violent struggles for power. Events were particularly chaotic after Ivan's son Theodore died in 1598 without an heir. The years from 1598 to 1613 are aptly called the Time of Troubles.

The close relatives of the deceased tsar intrigued against and murdered each other, alternately fighting and welcoming the invading Swedes and Poles, who even occupied Moscow. Most serious for the cause of autocracy, there was a great social upheaval as Cossack bands marched northward, rallying peasants and slaughtering nobles and officials. The mass of Cossacks and peasants called for the "true tsar," who would restore their freedom of movement and allow them to farm for whomever they pleased, who would reduce their heavy taxes and lighten the yoke imposed by the landlords.

This social explosion from below, which combined with a belated surge of patriotic opposition to Polish invaders, brought the nobles, big and small, to their senses. In 1613, they elected Ivan's sixteen-year-old grand-nephew, Michael Romanov, the new hereditary tsar. Then they rallied around him in the face of common internal and external threats. Michael's election was a real restoration, and his reign saw the gradual re-establishment of tsarist autocracy. Michael was understandably more kindly disposed toward the supportive nobility than toward the sullen peasants. Thus while peasants were completely enserfed in 1649, Ivan's heavy military obligations upon the nobility were relaxed considerably. In the long reign of Michael's successor, the pious Alexis (1645–1676), this asymmetry of obligations was accentuated. The nobility gained more exemptions from military service, while the peasants were further ground down.

The result was a second round of mass upheaval and protest. In the later seventeenth century the unity of the Russian Orthodox church was torn apart by a great split. The surface question was the religious reforms introduced in 1652 by the patriarch Nikon, a dogmatic purist who wished to bring "corrupted" Russian practices of worship into line with the Greek Orthodox model. The self-serving church hierarchy quickly went along, but the intensely religious common people resisted. They saw Nikon as the anti-Christ, who was stripping them of the only thing they had – the true religion of "holy Russia."

Great numbers left the church and formed illegal communities of Old Believers, who were hunted down and persecuted. As many as twenty thousand people burned themselves alive, singing the "halleluyah" in their chants three times rather than twice as Nikon had demanded and crossing themselves in the old style, with two rather than three fingers, as they went down in flames. After the great split the Russian masses were alienated from the established church, which became totally dependent upon the state for its authority.

Again the Cossacks revolted against the state, which was doggedly trying to catch up with them on the frontiers and reduce them to serfdom. Under Stenka Razin they moved up the Volga River in 1670–1671, attracting a great undisciplined army of peasants, murdering landlords and high church officials, and proclaiming freedom from oppression. This rebellion to overthrow the established order was finally defeated by the government. In response the thoroughly scared upper classes tightened the screws of serfdom even further. Holding down the peasants, and thereby maintaining the tsar, became almost the principal obligation of the nobility until 1689.

THE REFORMS OF PETER THE GREAT

It is now possible to understand the reforms of Peter the Great (1689–1725) and his kind of monarchial absolutism. Contrary to some historians' assertions, Peter was interested primarily in military power and not in some grandiose westernization plan. A gigantic, seven-foot-tall man of enormous energy and will power, Peter was determined to redress the defeats the tsar's armies had occasionally suffered in their wars with Poland and Sweden since the time of Ivan the Terrible.

To be sure, these western foes had never seriously threatened the existence of the tsar's vast kingdom, except perhaps when they had added to the confusion of civil war and domestic social upheaval in the Time of Troubles. Russia had even gained a large mass of the Ukraine from the kingdom of Poland in 1667 (see Map 17.2). And tsarist forces had completed the conquest of the primitive tribes of all Siberia in the seventeenth century. Muscovy, which had been as large as all the rest

of Europe combined in 1600, was three times as large as the rest of Europe in 1689 and by far the largest kingdom on earth. But territorial expansion was the soul of tsardom, and it was natural that Peter would seek further gains. The thirty-six years of his reign knew only one year of peace.

When Peter came to the throne, the heart of his army still consisted of cavalry made up of boyars and service nobility. Foot soldiers played a secondary role, and the whole army served on a part-time basis. The Russian army was lagging behind the professional standing armies being formed in Europe in the seventeenth century. The core of such armies was a highly disciplined infantry – an infantry that fired and refired rifles as it fearlessly advanced, until it charged with bayonets fixed. Such a large permanent army was enormously expensive and could be created only at the cost of great sacrifice. Given the desire to conquer more territory, Peter's military problem was serious.

Peter's solution was, in essence, to tighten up Muscovy's old service system and really make it work. He put the nobility back in harness, with a vengeance. Every nobleman, great or small, was once again required to serve in the army or in the civil administration – for life. Since a more modern army and government required skilled technicians and experts, Peter created schools and even universities. One of his most hated reforms required five years of compulsory education away from home for every young nobleman. Peter established an interlocking military-civilian bureaucracy with fourteen ranks, and he decreed that all must start at the bottom and work toward the top. More people of non-noble origins rose to high positions in the embryonic meritocracy. Peter searched out talented foreigners – twice in his reign he went abroad to study and observe – and placed them in his service. These measures combined to make the army and government more powerful and more efficient.

Peter also greatly increased the service requirements of the commoners. He established a regular standing army of more than 200,000 soldiers, made up mainly of peasants commanded by officers from the nobility. In addition, special forces of Cossacks and foreigners numbered more than 100,000. The departure of a drafted peasant boy was celebrated by his family and village almost like a funeral, as indeed it was, since the recruit was drafted for life. The peasantry also served with its taxes, which increased threefold during Peter's reign, as people – "souls" – replaced land as the primary unit of taxation. Serfs were also arbitrarily assigned to work in the growing number of factories and mines. Most of these industrial enterprises were directly or indirectly owned by the state, and they were worked almost exclusively for the military. In general, Russian serfdom became more oppressive under the reforming tsar.

The constant warfare of Peter's reign consumed 80 or 85 percent of all revenues but brought only modest territorial expansion. Yet the Great Northern War with Sweden, which lasted from 1700 to 1721, was crowned in the end by Russian victory. After initial losses, Peter's new war machine crushed the smaller army of Sweden's Charles XII in southern Russia at Poltava in 1709, one of the most significant battles in Russian history. Sweden never really regained the offensive, and Russia eventually annexed Estonia and much of present-day Latvia (see Map 17.2), lands that had never before been under Russian rule. Russia became the dominant power on the Baltic Sea and very much a European Great Power. If victory or defeat is the ultimate criterion for historical judgment, Peter's reforms were a success.

REFORMING THE NOBILITY *After a military revolt in 1698 Peter took revenge by decreeing that all nobles adopt Western manners and dress. This contemporary cartoon shows a gigantic Peter personally cutting off the long beard of a noble, thereby humiliating him and symbolically imposing more modern values. (The New York Public Library)*

There were other important consequences of Peter's reign. Because of his feverish desire to use modern technology to strengthen the army, many westerners and western ideas flowed into Russia for the first time. A new class of educated Russians began to emerge. At the same time vast numbers of Russians, especially among the poor and weak, hated Peter's massive changes. The split between the enserfed peasantry and the educated nobility thus widened, even though all were caught up in the endless demands of the sovereign.

A new idea of state interest, as distinct from the tsar's personal interests, began to take hold. Peter himself fostered this conception of the public interest by claiming time and again to be serving the common good. For the first time a Russian tsar attached explanations to his decrees in an attempt to gain the confidence and more enthusiastic support of the populace. Yet, as before, the tsar alone decided what the common good was. Here was a source of future tension between tsar and people.

In sum, Peter built on the service obligations of old Muscovy. His monarchial absolutism was truly the culmination of the long development of a unique Russian civilization. Yet the creation of a more modern army and state introduced much that was new and western to that civilization. This development paved the way for Russia to move much closer to the European mainstream in its thought and institutions during the Enlightenment, especially under that famous administrative and sexual lioness, Catherine the Great.

ABSOLUTISM AND THE BAROQUE

The rise of royal absolutism in eastern Europe had many consequences. Nobles served their powerful rulers in new ways while the great inferiority of the urban middle classes and the peasants was reconfirmed. Armies became larger and more professional, while taxes rose and authoritarian traditions were strengthened. Nor was this all. Royal absolutism also interacted with baroque culture and art, baroque music and literature. Inspired in part by Louis XIV of France, the great and not-so-great rulers called upon the artistic talent of the age to glorify their power and magnifi-

cence. This exaltation of despotic rule was particularly striking in architecture, whose lavish masterpieces reflected and reinforced the spirit of absolutism.

BAROQUE ART AND MUSIC

Throughout European history, the cultural tastes of one age have often seemed quite unsatisfactory to the next. So it was with the baroque. The term *baroque* itself may have come from the Portuguese word for an "odd-shaped, imperfect pearl," and was commonly used by late-eighteenth-century art critics as an expression of scorn for what they considered an overblown, unbalanced style. The hostility of these critics, who also scorned the Gothic style of medieval cathedrals in favor of a classicism inspired by antiquity and the Renaissance, has long since passed. Specialists agree that the triumphs of the baroque marked one of the high points in the entire history of Western culture.

The early development of the baroque is complex, but most scholars stress the influence of Rome and the revitalized Catholic church of the later sixteenth century. The papacy and the Jesuits encouraged the growth of an intensely emotional, exuberant art. These patrons wanted artists to go beyond the Renaissance focus on pleasing a small, wealthy cultural elite. They wanted artists to appeal to the senses, and thereby touch the souls and kindle the faith of ordinary churchgoers, while proclaiming the power and confidence of the reformed Catholic church. In addition to this underlying religious emotionalism, the baroque drew its sense of drama, motion, and ceaseless striving from the Catholic Reformation. The interior of the famous Jesuit Church of Jesus in Rome – the Gesù – combined all these characteristics in its lavish, shimmering, wildly active decorations and frescoes.

Taking definite shape in Italy after 1600, the baroque style in the visual arts developed with exceptional vigor in Catholic countries – in Spain and Latin America, Austria, southern Germany, and Poland. Yet baroque art was more than just "Catholic art" in the seventeenth century and the first half of the eighteenth. True, neither Protestant England nor the Netherlands ever came fully under the spell of the baroque, but neither did Catholic France. And Protestants accounted for some of the finest examples of baroque style, especially in music. The baroque style spread partly because its tension and bombast spoke to an agitated age, which was experiencing great violence and controversy in politics and religion.

In painting, the baroque reached maturity early with Peter Paul Rubens (1577–1640), the most outstanding and representative of baroque painters. Studying in his native Flanders and in Italy, where he was influenced by the masters of the High Renaissance such as Michelangelo, Rubens developed his own rich, sensuous, colorful style, which was characterized by animated figures, melodramatic contrasts, and monumental size. Although Rubens excelled in glorifying monarchs, like queen mother Marie de' Medici of France, he was also a devout Catholic. Nearly half of his pictures treat Christian subjects. Yet one of Rubens' trademarks was fleshy, sensual nudes, who populate his canvasses as Roman goddesses, water nymphs, and remarkably voluptuous saints and angels.

Rubens was enormously successful. To meet the demand for his work, he established a large studio and hired many assistants to execute his rough sketches and gigantic murals. Sometimes the master artist added only the finishing touches. Rubens' wealth and position – on occasion he was given special diplomatic assignments by the Habsburgs – attest that distinguished artists continued to enjoy the high social status they had won in the Renaissance.

In music the baroque style reached its culminating point almost a century later in the dynamic, searching, soaring lines of the endlessly inventive Johann Sebastian Bach (1685–1750), one of the greatest composers the Western world has ever produced. Organist and choirmaster of several Lutheran churches across Germany, Bach was equally at home writing secular concertos and sublime religious cantatas. Bach's organ music, the greatest ever written, combined with unsurpassed mastery the baroque spirit of invention, tension, and emotion in an unforgettable striving toward the infinite. Unlike Rubens, Bach was not fully appreciated in his lifetime, but since the early nineteenth century his reputation has grown steadily.

PALACES AND POWER

As soaring Gothic cathedrals expressed the idealized spirit of the High Middle Ages, so dramatic baroque palaces symbolized the age of absolutist power. By 1700, palace building had become a veritable obsession with the rulers of central and eastern Europe. These baroque palaces were clearly intended to overawe the people with the monarch's strength. The great palaces were also visual declarations of equality with Louis XIV, Europe's most awesome ruler, and were therefore modeled after Versailles to a greater or lesser extent. One such palace was Schönbrunn, an enormous Viennese Versailles, begun in 1695 by Emperor Leopold to celebrate Austrian military victories and Habsburg might. Charles XI of Sweden, having reduced the power of the aristocracy, ordered the construction in 1693 of his Royal Palace, which dominates the center of Stockholm to this day. Frederick I of Prussia began his imposing new royal residence in Berlin in 1701, a year after he attained the title of king.

Petty princes also contributed mightily to the palace-building mania. Frederick the Great of Prussia noted that every descendant of a princely family "imagines himself to be something like Louis XIV. He builds his Versailles, has his mistresses, and maintains his army."[14] The not very important elector-archbishop of Mainz, the ruling prince of that city, confessed apologetically that "building is a craze which costs much, but every fool likes his own hat."[15] The archbishop of Mainz's own "hat" was an architectural gem, like that of another churchly ruler, the prince-bishop of Würzburg. So too was the Zwinger palace of Dresden, built by Augustus the Strong of Saxony, who managed to get himself elected king of Poland and unsuccessfully challenged Prussia for leadership among the German states.

In central and eastern Europe the favorite noble servants of royalty became extremely rich and powerful, and they too built grandiose palaces in the capital cities. These palaces were in part an extension of the monarch, for they surpassed the buildings of less favored nobles and showed all with eyes to see the high road to fame and fortune. Take, for example, the palaces of Prince Eugene of Savoy. A French nobleman by birth and education, Prince Eugene entered the service of Leopold I with the relief of besieged Vienna in 1683, and he became Austria's most outstanding military hero. It was he who reorganized the Austrian army, smashed the Turks, fought Louis XIV to a standstill, and generally guided the triumph of absolutism in Austria. Rewarded with great wealth by his grateful royal employer, Eugene called upon the leading architects of the day, J. B. Fischer von Erlach and Johann Lukas von Hildebrandt, to consecrate his glory in stone and fresco. Fischer built Eugene's Winter (or Town) Palace in Vienna, and he and Hildebrandt collaborated on the prince's Summer Palace on the city's outskirts.

The Summer Palace was actually two enormous buildings, the Lower Belvedere and the Upper Belvedere, completed in 1713 and 1722 respectively, and joined by one of the most exquisite gardens in Europe. The Upper Belvedere, Hildebrandt's masterpiece, stood gracefully, even playfully, behind a great sheet of water. One entered through magnificent iron gates into a fantastic hall where sculptured giants crouched as pillars, and then moved on to a great staircase of dazzling whiteness and luscious ornamentation. Even today the emotional impact of this building is great: here, indeed, art and beauty create a sense of immense power and wealth.

Palaces like the Upper Belvedere were magnificent examples of the baroque style. They expressed the baroque delight in bold, sweeping statements, which were intended to provide a dramatic emotional experience. To create this experience baroque masters dissolved the traditional artistic frontiers: the architect permitted the painter and the artisan to cover his undulating surfaces with wildly colorful paintings, graceful sculptures, and fanciful carvings. Space was used in a highly original way, to blend everything together in a total environment. These techniques shone in all their glory in the churches of southern Germany and in the colossal entrance halls of palaces like that of the prince-bishop of Würzburg. Artistic achievement and political statement reinforced each other.

ROYAL CITIES

Absolute monarchs and baroque architects were not content with fashioning ostentatious

THE WÜRZBURG RESIDENCE *This palace was a masterpiece of German baroque architecture. Here, in the Hall of the Kaiser, painter, sculptor, and architect have combined to create a dramatic visual experience. (AMA/Adelmann/EPA)*

palaces. They remodeled existing capital cities, or even built new ones, to reflect royal magnificence and the centralization of political power. Karlsruhe, founded in 1715 as the capital city of a small German principality, is only an extreme example. There, broad, straight avenues radiated out from the palace, so that all roads – like all power – were focused upon the ruler. More typically, the monarch's architects added new urban areas alongside the old city; these areas then became the real heart of the expanding capital.

The distinctive features of these new additions were their broad avenues, their imposing government buildings, and their rigorous mathematical layout. Along these major thoroughfares the nobles built elaborate baroque townhouses; stables and servants' quarters were built on the alleys behind. Wide avenues also facilitated the rapid movement of soldiers through the city to quell any disturbance (the king's planners had the needs of the military constantly in mind). Under the arcades along the avenues appeared smart and very expensive shops, the first department stores, with plateglass windows and fancy displays.

The new avenues brought reckless speed to the European city. Whereas everyone had walked through the narrow, twisting streets of the medieval town, the high and mighty raced down the broad boulevards in their elegant carriages. A social gap opened up between the wealthy riders and the ordinary, gaping, dodging pedestrians. "Mind the carriages!" wrote one eighteenth-century observer in Paris:

Here comes the black-coated physician in his chariot, the dancing master in his coach, the fencing master in his surrey – and the Prince behind six horses at the gallop as if he were in the open country.... The threatening wheels of the overbearing rich drive as rapidly as ever over stones stained with the blood of their unhappy victims.[16]

Speeding carriages on broad avenues, an endless parade of power and position: here was the symbol and substance of the baroque city.

THE GROWTH OF ST. PETERSBURG

No city illustrated better than St. Petersburg the close ties among politics, architecture, and urban development in this period. In 1700, when the Great Northern War between Russia and Sweden began, the city did not exist. There was only a small Swedish fortress on one of the water-logged islands at the mouth of the Neva River, where it flows into the Baltic Sea. In 1702, Peter the Great's armies seized this desolate outpost. Within a year the reforming tsar had decided to build a new city there and to make it, rather than ancient Moscow, his capital.

Since the first step was to secure the Baltic coast, military construction was the main concern for the next eight years. A mighty fortress was built on Peter Island, and a port and shipyards were built across the river on the mainland, as a Russian navy came into being. The land was swampy and uninhabited, the climate damp and unpleasant. But Peter cared not at all: for him, the inhospitable northern marshland was a future metropolis, gloriously bearing his name.

After the decisive Russian victory at Poltava in 1709 greatly reduced the threat of Swedish armies, Peter moved into high gear. In one imperious decree after another, he ordered his people to build a city that would equal any in the world. Such a city had to be western and baroque, just as Peter's army had to be western and permanent. From such a new city, his "window on Europe," Peter also believed it would be easier to reform the country militarily and administratively. The hand of tradition would rest lightly on the banks of the Neva.

These general political goals matched Peter's architectural ideas, which had been influenced by his travels in western Europe. First, Peter wanted a comfortable, "modern" city. Modernity meant broad, straight, stone-paved avenues, houses built in a uniform line and not haphazardly set back from the street, large parks, canals for drainage, stone bridges, and street lighting. Second, all building had to conform strictly to detailed architectural regulations set down by the government. Finally, each social group – the nobility, the merchants, the artisans, and so on – was to live in a certain section of town. In short, the city and its population were to conform to a

ST. PETERSBURG, CA 1760   Rastrelli's remodeled Winter Palace is on the left and the Navy Office with its famous spire is on the right. Russia became a naval power and St. Petersburg became a great port. (From G. H. Hamilton, Art and Architecture in Russia, *Penguin Books, 1954)*

carefully defined urban plan of the baroque type.

Peter used the traditional but reinforced methods of Russian autocracy to build his modern capital. The creation of St. Petersburg was just one of the heavy obligations he dictatorially imposed on all social groups in Russia. The peasants bore the heaviest burdens. Just as the government drafted peasants for the army, it also drafted twenty-five to forty thousand men each summer to labor in St. Petersburg for three months, without pay. Every ten to fifteen peasant households had to furnish one such worker each summer, and then pay a special tax in order to feed that worker in St. Petersburg.

Peasants hated this forced labor in the capital, and each year a fourth to a third of those sent risked brutal punishments and ran away. Many peasant construction workers died each summer from hunger, sickness, and accidents. Many also died because peasant villages tended to elect old men or young boys to labor in St. Petersburg, since strong and able-bodied men were desperately needed on the farm in the busy summer months. Thus beautiful St. Petersburg was built on the shoveling, carting, and paving of a mass of conscripted serfs.

Peter also drafted more privileged groups to his city, but on a permanent basis. Nobles were summarily ordered to build costly stone houses and palaces in St. Petersburg and to live in them most of the year. The more serfs a noble possessed, the bigger his dwelling had to be. Merchants and artisans were also commanded to settle and build in St. Petersburg. These nobles and merchants were then required to pay for the city's avenues, parks, canals, embankments, pilings, and bridges, all of which were very costly in terms of both money and lives because they were built upon a swamp. The building of St. Petersburg was, in truth, an enormous direct tax levied on the wealthy, who in turn forced the peasantry to do most of the work. The only real beneficiaries were the indispensable foreign architects and urban planners, whose often-princely salaries added to the tax burden. No wonder so many Russians hated Peter's new city.

Yet the tsar had his way. By the time of his death in 1725 there were at least six thousand houses and numerous impressive government buildings in St. Petersburg. Under the remarkable women who ruled Russia throughout most of the eighteenth century, St. Petersburg blossomed fully as a majestic and well-organized city, at least in its wealthy showpiece sections. Peter's youngest daughter, the quick-witted, sensual beauty Elizabeth (1741–1762), named as her chief architect Bartolomeo Rastrelli, who had come to Russia from Italy as a boy of fifteen in 1715. Combining Italian and Russian traditions into a unique, wildly colorful St. Petersburg style, Rastrelli built many palaces for the nobility and all the larger government buildings erected during Elizabeth's reign. He also rebuilt the Winter Palace as an enormous,

aqua-colored royal residence, now the Hermitage Museum. There Elizabeth established a flashy, luxury-loving, and slightly crude court, which Catherine in turn made truly imperial. All the while St. Petersburg grew rapidly, and its almost 300,000 inhabitants in 1782 made it one of the world's largest cities. Peter and his successors had created out of nothing a magnificent and harmonious royal city, which unmistakably proclaimed the power and grandeur of Russia's rulers.

———◆———

From about 1400 to 1650 social and economic developments in eastern Europe increasingly diverged from those in western Europe. In the east peasants and townspeople lost precious freedoms, while the nobility increased its power and prestige. It was within this framework of resurgent serfdom and entrenched nobility that Austrian and Prussian monarchs fashioned absolutist states in the seventeenth and early eighteenth centuries. Thus monarchs won absolutist control over standing armies, permanent taxes, and legislative bodies. But they did not question the underlying social and economic relationships. Indeed, they enhanced the privileges of the nobility, which furnished the leading servitors for enlarged armies and growing state bureaucracies.

In Russia the social and economic trends were similar but the timing of political absolutism was different. Mongol conquest and rule was a crucial experience, and a harsh indigenous tsarist autocracy was firmly in place by the reign of Ivan the Terrible in the sixteenth century. More than a century later Peter the Great succeeded in tightening up Russia's traditional absolutism and modernizing it by reforming the army, the bureaucracy, and the defense industry. In Russia and throughout eastern Europe, war and the needs of war weighed heavily in the triumph of absolutism.

Triumphant absolutism interacted spectacularly with the arts. Baroque art, which had grown out of the Catholic Reformation's desire to move the faithful and exalt the true faith, admirably suited the secular aspirations of eastern rulers. They built grandiose baroque palaces, monumental public squares, and even whole cities to glorify their power and majesty. Thus baroque art attained magnificent heights in eastern Europe, symbolizing the ideal and harmonizing with the reality of imperious royal absolutism.

NOTES

1. Quoted by F. L. Carsten, *The Origins of Prussia,* Clarendon Press, Oxford, 1954, p. 152.

2. Ibid., p. 175.

3. H. Rosenberg, *Bureaucracy, Aristocracy, and Autocracy: The Prussian Experience, 1660–1815,* Beacon Press, Boston, 1966, p. 38.

4. Quoted by R. Ergang, *The Potsdam Führer: Frederick William I, Father of Prussian Militarism,* Octagon Books, New York, 1972, pp. 85, 87.

5. Ibid. pp. 6–7, 43.

6. Quoted by R. A. Dorwart, *The Administrative Reforms of Frederick William I of Prussia,* Harvard University Press, Cambridge, Mass., 1953, p. 226.

7. Quoted by Rosenberg, p. 40.

8. Quoted by Ergang, p. 253.

9. Quoted by R. Pipes, *Russia Under the Old Regime,* Charles Scribner's Sons, New York, 1974, p. 48.

10. Quoted by N. V. Riasanovsky, *A History of Russia,* Oxford University Press, New York, 1963, p. 79.

11. Quoted by I. Grey, *Ivan III and the Unification of Russia,* Collier Books, New York, 1967, p. 39.

12. Quoted by R. Mousnier, *Peasant Uprisings in Seventeenth-Century France, Russia, and China,* Harper & Row, New York, 1970, p. 154.

13. Both quoted by Pipes, pp. 65, 85.

14. Quoted by Ergang, p. 13.

15. Quoted by J. Summerson, in *The Eighteenth Century: Europe in the Age of Enlightenment,* ed. A. Cobban, McGraw-Hill, New York, 1969, p. 80.

16. Quoted by L. Mumford, *The Culture of Cities,* Harcourt Brace Jovanovich, New York, 1938, p. 97.

SUGGESTED READING

All of the books cited in the Notes are highly recommended. F. L. Carsten's *The Origins of Prussia* (1954) is the best study on early Prussian history, and H. Rosenberg, *Bureaucracy, Aristocracy, and Autocracy: The Prussian Experience, 1660–1815* (1966), is a masterful analysis of the social context of Prussian absolutism. In addition to R. Ergang's exciting and critical biography of ramrod Frederick William I, *The Potsdam Führer* (1972), there is G. Ritter, *Frederick the Great* (1968), a more sympathetic study of the talented son by one of Germany's leading conservative historians. G. Craig, *The Politics of the Prussian Army, 1640–1945* (1964), expertly traces the great influence of the military on the Prussian state over three hundred years. R. J. Evans, *The Making of the Habsburg Empire, 1550–1770* (1979), and R. A. Kahn, *A History of the Habsburg Empire, 1526–1918* (1974), analyze the development of absolutism in Austria, as does A. Wandruszka, *The House of Habsburg* (1964). J. Stoye, *The Siege of Vienna* (1964), is a fascinating account of the last great Ottoman offensive, which is also treated in the interesting study by P. Coles, *The Ottoman Impact on Europe, 1350–1699* (1968). The Austro-Ottoman conflict is also a theme of L. S. Stavrianos, *The Balkans Since 1453* (1958), and D. McKay's fine biography, *Prince Eugene of Savoy* (1978).

On eastern peasants and serfdom, J. Blum, "The Rise of Serfdom in Eastern Europe," *American His-*

torical Review 62 (July 1957):807–836, is a good point of departure, while R. Mousnier, *Peasant Uprisings in Seventeenth-Century France, Russia, and China* (1970), is an engrossing comparative study. J. Blum, *Lord and Peasant in Russia from the Ninth to the Nineteenth Century* (1961), provides a good look at conditions in rural Russia, and P. Avrich, *Russian Rebels, 1600–1800* (1972), treats some of the violent peasant upheavals those conditions produced. R. Hellie, *Enserfment and Military Change in Muscovy,* (1971), is outstanding, as is Alexander Yanov's provocative *Origins of Autocracy: Ivan the Terrible in Russian History* (1981). In addition to the fine surveys by Pipes and Riasanovsky cited in the Notes, J. Billington, *The Icon and the Axe* (1970), is a stimulating history of early Russian intellectual and cultural developments, such as the great split in the church. M. Raeff, *Origins of the Russian Intelligentsia* (1966), skillfully probes the mind of the Russian nobility in the eighteenth century. B. H. Sumner, *Peter the Great and the Emergence of Russia* (1962), is a fine brief introduction, which may be compared with the brilliant biography by Russia's greatest prerevolutionary historian, Vasili Klyuchevsky, *Peter the Great* (trans. 1958), and with R. Massie, *Peter the Great* (1980). G. Vernadsky and R. Fisher, eds., *A Source Book for Russian History from Early Times to 1917,* 3 vols. (1972), is an invaluable, highly recommended collection of documents and contemporary writings.

Three good books on art and architecture are E. Hempel, *Baroque Art and Architecture in Central Europe* (1965); G. Hamilton, *The Art and Architecture of Russia* (1954); and N. Pevsner, *An Outline of European Architecture,* 6th ed. (1960). Bach, Handel, and other composers are discussed intelligently by M. Bufkozer, *Music in the Baroque Era* (1947).

NOTES ON THE ILLUSTRATIONS

Page 20 The stone pillar containing the law code of Hammurabi is in the collection of the Louvre in Paris.

Page 34 The Hittite Atarluhas from Carchemish is in the British Museum.

Page 50 Mosaic floor of the ancient Beth Alpha Synagogue in Israel.

Page 52 The relief of Assurbanipal feasting, from Nineveh, is now in the British Museum.

Page 64 Shown here is the east stairway of the apadana (audience hall) of Darius and Xerxes, with Darius' palace in the background. Achaemenid period.

Page 77 This figure is 6½ inches high, made of gold and ivory about 1600–1500 B.C.

Page 78 The Melian relief, depicting the return of Odysseus, was made of terracotta in the fifth century B.C. Greek.

Page 103 Young warrior making libation before departure. Attic red figure technique, c. 500 B.C.

Page 127 Dieties of Palmyrene in bas-relief, gypsum. Selukos Nikator crowning the Tyche of Dura.

Page 160 Relief shows a school in Trier on the northern frontier of the Roman empire, about the third century A.D.

Page 169 This helmet, found in Lancashire, is now in the British Museum. The crown is embossed with combat scenes and a visor in the form of a face.

Page 204 Roman mosaic from the Bardo Museum, Tunis, illustrating a great estate.

Page 215 Vandal landowner, in a mosaic from Carthage, sixth century, in the British Museum.

Page 218 From *Vie de Saint Denis*, MS. Nov. Acq. Fr. 1098, fol. 50, in the Bibliothèque Nationale, Paris.

Page 235 Detail from Madonna enthroned with saints and angels, c. 1380–1390 by Agnolo Gaddi, a Florentine active 1369–1396. Wood.

Page 237 Emperor Justinian and his court, A.D. 546–548, in mosaic at San Vitale, Ravenna, Italy.

Page 242 *Above*. Samson destroying the temple of the Philistines, miniature from Rashid-ad-Zdin's *Universal History* (1306–1314). *Below*. Muhammed and follower fleeing from Mecca to Medina, watched by Christ, miniature from thirteenth-century Arabic manuscript. Both in the Edinburgh University Library.

Page 248 The Dome of the Rock, built in 691 by the Caliph Omar on the site of King Solomon's and Herod's temples in Jerusalem.

Page 267 The scribe Ezra rewriting the sacred records. Early eighth century, from the Codex Amiatinus (fol. 5r), Biblioteca Laurenziana, Florence.

Page 269 Upper cover of the binding of the Lindau Gospels, c. 870.

Page 271 Conant took this design from some of Walter Horn's early studies on the plan of St. Gall.

Page 273 Illustration from the North Italian Coden Paneth, MS. 28, in the Medical Library at Yale University.

Page 288 Woodcut from the Nuremberg Chronicle, 1493.

Page 294 From *Gouvernment des princes*, MS. 5062, fol. 149.

Page 296 This house stands on the corner of Edmund Street in Exeter, Devon, having been moved in one piece in 1961 from its original site in the city.

Page 301 From a late fifteenth-century Flemish MS.., Douce 208, fol. 120v, The Bodleian Library, Oxford.

Page 303 Benedictine Abbey of Mont-Saint-Michel, founded in 708 in the Department of the Manche in northwestern France, a mile off the French coast in the English Channel and formerly an island at high tide. Heavily fortified.

Page 306 Pope Leo IX (left) with Warinus, Abbot of St. Arnulf of Metz, from the Bern Cod. 292, fol. 73, in the Burgerbibliothek Bern, Switzerland.

Page 317 From MS. Sloane 2435, fol. 85, in The British Library.

Page 322 From *Piers Plowman*, MS. R.3, fol. 3v, in the Trinity College Library, Cambridge.

Page 324 Miniature from *Hours of the Virgin*, MS. ADD. 17012, fol. 6r, in The British Library.

Page 326 Detail of miniature from *Speculum Virginum* of Konrad von Hirschau, C. Inv. No. 15326, in Rheinisches Landesmuseum, Bonn.

Page 332 From MS. 93, fol. 102, Pseudo-Apuleius, Herbarium C 111, 2.

Page 337 Miniature from Jean de Wavrin's *Chronique d'Angleterre*, siege of the castle of Mortagne. Flemish, late fifteenth century. MS. Roy. 14. E.IV, fol. 23r, in The British Library.

Page 339 Miniature from *Psalter of Henry VI*. French c. 1430. MS. Cotton Dom. A. XVII, fol. 122v, in The British Library.

Page 341 From St. Gregory's *Moralia in Job*. French (Citeaux), 1111 MS. 170, fol. 59r, in the Bibliothèque Publique de Dijon, France.

Page 342 Frontispiece of Moralized Bible, thirteenth century.

Page 345 From Kenneth John Conant, *Cluny: Les églises et la maison du chef d'ordre*. The Medaeival Academy of America Publication No. 77. Cambridge, Mass., 1968.

Page 351 Presumed to be the work of Matilda, queen of William the Conqueror, the original tapestry (c. 1100) can be seen in the city of Bayeux, France. A replica is in the Victoria and Albert Museum, London.

Page 359 Aquamanile. German, twelfth or thirteenth century.

Page 362 From thirteenth-century psalter.

Page 370 Painting by Lorenzo Voltolini, eighteenth-century Veronese painter.

Page 373 Lancets with stained glass from Évron. French, fourteenth century.

Page 376 Detail of the statue of the Queen of Sheba (c. 1230) on the right portal of the north transept of Chartres Cathedral.

Page 377 Flemish. Story of Jehu, Jezebel, and the sons of Ahab, II Kings 9-10.

Page 382 Fourteenth century. From MS. Fr. 352, fol. 52v, in Bibliothèque Nationale, Paris.

Page 391 *St. Sebastian Interceding for the Plague-Stricken* by Josse Lieferinxe, in the Walters Art Gallery, Baltimore, Maryland.

Page 392 From MS. of Gilles le Msisis, *Annales,* Bibliothèque Royale 13076/7, fol. 16v, in the Bibliothèque Royale Albert I, Brussels.

Page 399 Episode from the battle of Crècy from Froissart's *Chronicle,* as reproduced in *Larousse Ancient and Medieval History,* p. 363.

Page 405 Florentine school, sixteenth century (c. 1530). Allegorical portrait of Dante on wood, 50 by 47¼ inches.

Page 412 From Froissart's *Chronicles,* MS. Fr. 2643, fol. 125, in Bibliothèque Nationale, Paris.

Page 416 Miniature from *Roman de Fauvel,* MS. Fr. 146, fol. 34, in Bibliothèque Nationale, Paris.

Page 418 *The Four Horsemen of the Apocalypse,* woodcut c. 1498, by Albrecht Dürer, German painter and engraver (1471-1528) regarded as leader of the German Renaissance school of painting.

Page 423 Sixteenth-century woodcut.

Page 425 Banquet scene from Boccaccio's *Decameron* by Sandro Botticelli, Italian painter (1444?-1510).

Page 430 The original painting can be found in the Uffizi Gallery, Florence.

Page 432 Hans Memling (real name Mimmelinghe, also spelled Memline and Hemmelinck), active c. 1465-d. 1494. Tommaso Portinari (ca. 1432-1501), tempera and oil on wood, 17⅜ inches high by 13¼ wide. Maria Portinari (b. 1456), tempera and oil on wood, 17⅜ inches high by 13⅜ wide.

Page 434 Terracotta, School of Luca della Robbia, late fifteenth century. Della Robbia's invention of the process of making polychrome glazed terracottas led contemporaries to consider him one of the great artistic innovators. The warm humanity of this roundel (circular panel) is characteristic of della Robbia's art.

Page 438 Engraving by Johannes Stradanus (J. van der Straet), Belgian painter (1523-1605).

Page 441 Tiziano Vecellio, Italian painter, 1477-1576.

Page 442 *The Adoration,* 1507, by Hans Baldung (also called Hans Grien or Grün), German painter, engraver, and designer of woodcuts and glass painting (1476?-1545).

Page 450 Hieronymus Bosch (Hieronymus van Aeken), Dutch painter (c. 1450-1516).

Page 454 Paolo Uccello, Florentine painter (1397-1475).

Page 456 Fifteenth-century miniature from *Ethique d'Aristotle*, MS. I.2, fol. 145, in Bibliothèque Municipale, Rouen, France.

Page 472 *The Small Crucifixion*, c. 1510, by Matthias Grünewald, German painter (c. 1465-1528). Wood.

Page 493 *Sir Thomas More* (1478-1535), painted in 1527 by Hans Holbein the Younger, German painter (1497?-1543) and court painter to Henry VIII.

Page 509 World chart by Vesconte Maggiolo, 1511, showing North America as a promontory of Asia.

Page 521 Long the site of a royal residence and hunting lodge, Fontainebleau was expanded and transformed by Francis I in 1530-1540. Il Rosso (Giovanni Battista de'Rossi, 1494-1540), Florentine painter; Francesco Primaticcio, Italian painter and architect (1504-1570); and Sebastiano Serlio, Italian architect and writer on art (1475-1554) were called by Francis I from Italy to build and decorate the palace. The gallery of Francis I set a fashion in decoration imitated throughout Europe.

Page 527 *Iconoclasts in The Netherlands*, 1583.

Page 539 *Mars and Venus United by Love*, c. 1580, by Paolo Veronese, Italian painter (1528-1588).

Page 547 From George Turberville, *The Noble Art of Venery* (1575).

Page 548 *Portrait of Juan de Paraja*, c. 1650, by Diego Rodriguez de Silva y Velasquez, Spanish painter (1599-1660). Oil.

Page 562 On the left side of the palace are the Parterres du Nord, on the right the Parterres du Midi (South of France). In the middle distance are the water gardens and Fountain de Latone, and in the foreground, the beginning of the Green Carpet. The Orangérie (hot house) extends to the lower right of the palace. Construction of Versailles was begun in the mid-seventeenth century under the direction of the French architect Louis Le Vau (1612-1670); after his death, Jules Hardouin-Mansart (1646-1708), Louis XIV's building superintendent and architect, completed the palace. Charles Le Brun (1619-1690), first painter to the king, worked for eighteen years on decoration of the palace. André Le Nôtre (1613-1700), French landscape architect and director of royal gardens, designed the famous gardens.

Page 569 *The Rape of the Sabine Women*, c. 1636-1637, by Nicolas Poussin, French painter (1594-1665). Oil on canvas.

Page 573 *Las Menimas* (The Maids of Honor), 1656, by Diego Rodriguez de Silva y Velasquez (1599-1660), leading painter of the Spanish school.

Page 577 Title page of *The Lamentable Complaints of Nick Froth the Tapster and Rulerost the Cooke*, 1641, in The British Library.

Page 581 Second Great Seal of the Commonwealth, 1651.

Page 587 *A Woman Weighing Gold*, by Jan Vermeer, Dutch genre, landscape, and portrait painter (1632-1675). Canvas.

Page 597 From A. Thevet, *Cosmographie universelle*, 1575.

Page 611 Feast of the Trinity at St. Basil's, Moscow.

Page 619 The episcopal residence, built 1720-1744, was designed by the German architect Balthasar Neumann (1687-1753), master of the German Baroque school. The Venetian Giovanni Battista Tiepolo (1696-1770) came to Würzburg to paint the ceilings in 1750, accompanied by his sons, Giovanni Domenico (1727-1804) and Lorenzo (1736-1776). Damaged by bombing in World War II, the palace was restored in the 1950s.

Page 621 The Winter Palace *(left)*, designed for Peter the Great by Domenico Trezzini and refurbished for Elizabeth by Bartolomeo Rastrelli (1700-1771), and *(right)* the Old Admiralty, St. Petersburg, from an engraving by M. I. Makhaev, 1761.

INDEX

Babylonian Captivity (of Jews), 51
Babylonian Captivity (papal court in France), 383, 407-408
Bach, Johann Sebastian, 617
Bactria, 111, 112
Baghdad flood, 12
Ball, John, 412
Baroque arts, 616-622
Baths, Roman, 165, 166 (illus.)
Beaumont, Sir Henry, 410
Becket, Thomas, 327, 361-362, 471
Bede, 222, 266-267, 427
Bedouins, 242, 244
Belgium, in Roman era, 197. *See also* Netherlands
Beloch, K. J., 70
Benedictines, *see* Monasteries
Beowulf, 267-268
Bernard (at Cîteaux), 305
Bernard of Clairvaux, 427, 499
Bernini, 564
Berno, abbot of Cluny, 304
Bessarion, John, 426
"Bess of Hardwick," *see* Hardwick, Elizabeth
Bible: Mesopotamian influence on, 15, 18-19; Old Testament, 43, 44, 45-47, 48, 50; New Testament, 226-227; Mohammed's familiarity with, 246; Wycliff's reliance on, 409; Luther's translation, 479; Tyndale's, 489; King James Version, 549-550
Bill of Rights, English, 583
Black Death, *see* Bubonic plague
Blacks, in Renaissance, 441-443. *See also* Slavery
Blenheim, battle of, 571
Blood, Council of, 526-527
Boccaccio, Giovanni, 336, 392, 428-429
Bodin, Jean, 613
Boeotia, 72, 73, 77-78, 104
Boghazköy, 33
Bohemia, 531-532, 533, 597-598
Boleyn, Anne, *see* Anne Boleyn
Bologna, Concordat of, 522
Bologna, University of, 365
Bonhomme, Jacques, 411
Boniface, *see* St. Boniface
Boniface VIII, pope, 381-383
Book of Common Order (Knox), 495
Book of Common Prayer (Cranmer), 494
Book of the First Navigation and Discovery of the Indies (Columbus), 511
Books, first printing from movable type, 437-439
Borgia, Cesare, 452
Borgia, Rodrigo, *see* Alexander VI, pope
Borgia family, 471
Bosch, Jerome, 450
Bossuet, Jacques, 560
Botany, beginnings in Hellenistic period, 136
Botticelli, 430
"Bourgeois," meaning of word, 289
Bourges, Pragmatic Sanction of, 456, 600
Boutham, England, 295
Boyars, 609, 611-613
Brandenburg, elector of, 600-602
Breast-feeding, *see* Nursing of babies
Breitenfeld, battle of, 533

Brethren of the Common Life, 471
Britain, *see* England
Britons, conquest by Germanic tribes, 185-186
Bronze Age, 28-29, 75-78
Brunelleschi, Filippo, 431, 433, 441
Bruni, Leonardo, 427
Bubonic plague (Black Death): spread of in 14th century, 388, 389; pathology of, 389-393; consequences of, 393
Bulgaria, in time of Rome, 181
Burckhardt, Jacob, 88
"Burgher," meaning of word, 289
Burgundians, 217, 455
Bury St. Edmunds, 342
Bussy, Sir William, 410
Byblos, 40-41, 42
Byzantine Empire: 200, 237-242; compared with Germanic West, 238-239; Justinian's law codes, 239-240; intellectual life, 240-242
Byzantium, 206, 238

Cabal, 582
Cabinet system, 583-584
Cabot, John, 515
Cabral, Pedro Alvares, 511
Caesar, Julius, 164, 167, 170, 171-172, 179
Calais, 402
Calendar, 161
Caligula, 185, 188
Callisthenes, 110
Calvin, John: debt to Luther, 479; life and ideas, 485-487; influence on Knox, 495; quoted, 585
Calvinism: tenets of, 485-487; in France, 522, 523-524; in Netherlands, 526; in Germany, 530-531, 534; and Puritanism, 578-579; and the Dutch, 585
Cambridge University, 367, 371
Cambyses, 62
Campania, 144, 149
Canaan, 43
Canada, 515; developed by Colbert for French Empire, 566
Cannae, battle of, 155
Cannon, 516-517
Canon law, 223
Canossa, 309
Canterbury Cathedral, 375, 471
Canterbury Tales, 404, 468
Canton, foreign merchants in, 917
Canute, 285, 351
Capitalism, medieval, 300-301
Capitoline Hill, 146
Caracalla, 197
Caraffa, Cardinal, 499, 502
Caravels, 517
Cardinals, 307. *See also* Papacy
Caribbean islands, 513
Carolingian dynasty: rise of, 257-260; chart of, 259; Charlemagne's empire, 260-262; government of, 262-264; Charlemagne becomes Holy Roman emperor, 264-265; cultural revival of, 265-266, 269-274; collapse of, 274-276
Carthage, 42, 154-157
Cartier, Jacques, 515
Cassian, John, 234

Cassiodorus, 234–235, 236
Castiglione, Baldassare, 433, 435, 439–440
Castile, 459
Çatal Hüyük, 9
Catapult, 134
Cateau-Cambrésis, Treaty of, 519
Cathedrals: as centers of bishops' authority, 224; as origin of towns, 289; and medieval schools, 365, 366; building and uses of, 371–378
Catherine II (the Great), empress of Russia, 616, 622
Catherine de' Medici, 520, 522–523, 524
Catherine of Aragon, queen of England, 458, 491, 494
Catherine of Siena, 407
Catholic church, *see* Roman Catholic church
Catholicism, *see* Roman Catholic church
Catholic League, 533
Catholic Reformation, 496–503
Cato, Marcus, 159
Causes of Plants (Theophrastus), 136–163
Cave paintings, 6
Celibacy, of clergy, 305–306, 469
Cellini, Benvenuto, 426–427, 433
Celts: invade Italy, sack Rome, 148–149; as native Britons, 221; to Wales, 222; Christianity of, compared to Roman, 222
Census, Roman, 179
Cervantes, 575
Chaeronea, 104 (illus.), 105
Champaigne, Philippe de, 559
Chariot racing, Roman, 194–195
Charlemagne: described, 260–261; as warrior/expansionist, 261–262; style of governing, 262–263; crowned Holy Roman emperor, 264–265; stimulates learning, 265–274; dies, empire collapses, 274–276
Charles II (the Bald), Holy Roman emperor, 275, 276
Charles V, Holy Roman emperor: and Titian, 432; wars with Italy, 455; vast patrimony, 462; outlaws Luther, 476; and ideas of empire, 480–482; and German reaction to Luther, 484; and war over Italy, 498; and Council of Trent, 499; commissions exploration, 513; and the Netherlands, 525–526; and slave trade, 541
Charles VI, Holy Roman emperor, 600
Charles I, king of England, 578–580
Charles II, king of England, 581–582
Charles III (the Simple), king of France, 284
Charles IV, king of France, 395
Charles V, king of France, 408
Charles VI, king of France, 403
Charles VII, king of France, 400–401, 403, 455–456
Charles VIII, king of France, 455
Charles IX, king of France, 522–523, 524
Charles II, king of Spain, 570, 574
Charles III, king of Spain, 515
Charles XI, king of Sweden, 617
Charles XII, king of Sweden, 615
Charles the Bold, duke of Burgundy, 457
Charpentier, Marc-Antoine, 568
Chartres Cathedral, 365, 375, 377
Chaucer, Geoffrey, 336, 404
Childbirth: in Hebrew society, 49; in Middle Ages, 331–333
Child rearing, *see* Children; Family

Children: Hebrew, 49–50; Spartan, 85–86; Roman, 159, 160–161; in medieval Europe, 325, 326–327, 333–334, 340–341; on Crusades, 380. *See also* Family
Children's Crusade, 380
Chivalry, 330, 397–398
Christ, *see* Jesus Christ
Christian III, king of Denmark, 496
Christian IV, king of Denmark, 533
Christian church, *see* Christianity; Roman Catholic church
Christian humanism, 444–450, 468, 469
Christianity: Hebrew influence on, 45, 47; Hellenism, paves way for, 129; Roman rituals' influence on, 163; Judaism and rise of, 184–188; Paul's contribution to, 186–187; appeal to Roman world, 187–188; ascendancy in Rome, 204–206; reasons for pagan's distrust of early, 205; acceptance by Germanic tribes, 220; early survival and growth of, 222–234; Roman emperors, church vs. state debate, 223–224; church leadership, 224–225; early missionary activity, 225–227; ideals of, 226–227; conversion, assimilation of pagans, 227–229; penitential system, 229; and Greco-Roman culture, 230–232; St. Augustine and impact on, 232–233; and monasticism, 234–237; schism between Roman Catholic, Greek Orthodox churches, 238–239; and 10th-, 11th-century peace moves, 286; revival, reform in High Middle Ages, 302–312; as center of medieval life, 327–330; and medieval cathedrals, 371–378; and Crusades, 378–381; decline in prestige, Great Schism in church, 407–410; in Renaissance, 429; reform, renewal in church, 468–504; church's condition from 1400 to 1517, 468–473; Protestant Reformation, 473–496; Catholic and Counter Reformations, 496–503; Vikings in Russia convert to Eastern Orthodox church, 607
Chrysoloras, Manuel, 425–426
Church of England: and Henry VIII, 494; under Elizabeth I, 495; Puritans' wish to reform, 578
Churchill, John (duke of Marlborough), 571
Cicero, 167, 170–171
Cincinnatus, 147, 170
Circumcision, Hebraic, 49
Cistercians, 302, 304–305, 343–344
Cîteaux, Cistercian Monastery at, 304–305
Cities: in Mesopotamia, 12; in Greece, 72–75; Hellenistic, 114–117; Rome's growth as, 164; in Roman Empire, 196–197; rise of, Middle Ages, 287–297; designed to express royal power, 618–622; building of St. Petersburg, 620–622. *See also* Towns
Citizenship, Roman, 149, 152–154
City of God (St. Augustine), 233, 261
City-states: Greek polis, 72–75, 114, 115; Italian, 452–455
Classicism, Renaissance revival of, 427–428
Claudius, 183, 188, 189
Cleisthenes, 87
Clement V, pope, 383
Clement VII, pope, 408, 491, 498
Cleomenes, 132
Cleopatra, 172, 184
Clergy, *see* Christianity; Roman Catholic church
Climate: influence on Greek life, 74; of Italy, 142; clemency of 11th century, 287
Clovis, 217, 218 (illus.), 219
Cluny monastery, 304, 342, 344–345
Code (Justinian), 240

Lech River, battle of, 285
Leech Book of Bald, The, 343
Lefèvre d'Etaples, Jacques, 445
Legnano, battle of, 357
Le Havre, founded, 520
Leisure, *see* Recreation
Le Nain, Louis, 567
Le Nôtre, André, 563
Leo I, pope, 225
Leo III, pope, 264–265
Leo IX, pope, 306, 307
Leo X, pope, 429, 455, 457, 471, 474, 498
Leonardo da Vinci, *see* da Vinci, Leonardo
Leopold II (of Austria), Holy Roman emperor, 617
Lepidus, 172
Leprosy, 287
Lérins, 234
Lesbos, 83
Lescot, Pierre, 520
Le Tellier, François, 568
Leuctra, 104
Le Vau, Louis, 563
Leviathan (Hobbes), 580
Libation Bearers, The (Aeschylus), 95
Libyans, 41
Licinian-Sextian rogations, 152
Licinius, 152
Life of the Emperor Augustus (Suetonius), 261
Lisbon, and Portuguese commerce, 511, 514
Literacy: in ancient Israel, 49; among Hellenistic women, 133; under Charlemagne, 270; in Middle Ages, 334, 365
Literature: Roman, 165, 181–184; Byzantine, 240–241; Bede, *Beowulf,* 267–269; development of vernacular, 404–406; writings of Northern Renaissance, 445–450; Montaigne, 544–546; Elizabeth, Jacobean, 546–550; French, encouraged by Richelieu, 559; French classicism, 567–568
Lithuania, 612
Livy, 146, 151, 159, 183
Locke, John, 583
Loftus, W. K., 11
Lollards, 409, 489
Lombard, Peter, 369
Lombards, 217; invasion of Rome, 225; defeated by Carolingians, 260, 262
London, 12th-century, described, 295–297
Long Parliament, 579
Lords, House of, *see* Parliament, English
Lorenzo the Magnificent, 429
Lot, Ferdinand, 208–209
Lothair, Carolingian ruler, 275
Louis VI, king of France, 352–353, 372–373
Louis VII, king of France, 372–373
Louis VIII, king of France, 353, 358
Louis IX, king of France, 353, 358, 360, 380
Louis XI, king of France, 451, 457, 480
Louis XII, king of France, 455, 469
Louis XIII, king of France, 558, 560
Louis the German, 275–276
Louis the Pious, 274–275, 276
Louise of Savoy, 538
Louvre, 520
Low Countries, *see* Netherlands

Loyola, Ignatius, 501–502
Lucretia, 159–160
Lully, Jean-Baptiste, 568
Lupercalia, 228–229
Luther, Martin: and printing, 439; use of Lefèvre's texts, 445; early years, 473–474; launches Protestant Reformation, 474–476; his theology, 476–477, 478–479; and impact of his beliefs, 477–479, 482–484
Lutheranism: in Scandinavia, 496; in France, 522; in Germany, 530–531, 534; supported by Richelieu, 559
Lützen, battle of, 533
Lycurgan regimen, 85–86
Lydia, 60
Lyons, 197

Macbeth (Shakespeare), 546, 549
Macaulay, Thomas, 546
Macedonia: victory over Greeks, 104–105; conquests under Alexander, 110–111; after Alexander's death, 111–112; Roman conquest of, 157
Machiavelli, Niccoló: Livy's influence on, 183; despised masses, 433; life, work, 436–437; and Renaissance kings, 451–452; Borgia hero of *The Prince,* 452; on the church, 468
Magellan, Ferdinand, 513
Magic "cures," 137
Magna Carta, 363
Magnetic compass, 517
Magyars, 277, 279, 285
Maintenon, Madame de, 566
Malaria, 287
Manetho, 28
Manicheanism, 62
Manorial system, 257, 319–321
Manuel, king of Portugal, 511
Manufacturing, *see* Industry
Maps, improvements in, 517
Marathon, battle of, 88
Marcus Aurelius, 190
Marduk (Babylonian god), 16, 18–19
Margaret, regent of the Netherlands, 526
Margaret of Austria, 538
Margaret of Valois, 524
Maria Theresa, queen of France, 561
Maritain, Jacques, 996
Marius, 167
Markets: medieval, 293–294
Marquette, Jacques, 566
Marriage: under Hammurabi's Code, 22–23; in ancient Israel, 47–49; in ancient Athens, 100; Roman, 159–160; Muslim, 245–246; Charlemagne decrees on, 258; in Middle Ages, 335–336; in 14th century, 413–415; in 16th, 17th centuries, 540. *See also* Family; Women
Marseilles, bubonic plague in, 389
Marshal, William, 335
Marsiglio of Padua, 408–409, 476
Martel, Charles, 248, 254, 256, 258
Martin V, pope, 409
Mary, queen of Scots, 495, 528, 529, 538
Mary I, queen of England, 491, 492, 494, 539
Mary II (William and Mary), queen of England, 582, 583
Mary, Virgin, 329

Versailles, Louis XIV builds, 562–565
Vespasian, 188–189
Vienna: Turks' siege of, 599; palaces in, 617
Vikings, 215, 276–279, 510, 607–609
Villeins, 318–319
Villon, François, 404
Vincent of Beauvais, 333
Virgil, 181, 182–183, 184, 210
Visconti, Gian Galeazzo, 424
Visigoths, 215, 216, 217, 221, 247
Vitry, Jacques de, 411
Vivarium, 234
Vivisection, 136–137
Völkerwanderungen, 214
Volsci, 147
Voltaire (François Marie Arouet), quoted on Louis XIV, 565
Vulgate, 232

Wagner, Richard, 258
Wales, 222
Walpole, Robert, 583–584
Walsingham, 403
Walter of Henley, 323
Warfare: weapons in Early Egyptian, 29; under Assyrians, 51–54; in feudal Europe, 286
War of the Spanish Succession, 570–571, 586, 600
War of the Three Henrys, 524
Wars of the Roses, 457, 459
Wen-Amon, 40, 42
Wergeld, 219
West Indies, 513
Westphalia, Peace of, 534, 584
Wet nursing, *see* Nursing of Babies
Whitby, Synod of, 226, 266
White Mountain, battle of, 533, 597
White Russians, 606
William I (the Conqueror), King of England: as duke of Normandy, 284; and church peace movement, 286; and lay investiture, 308, 310; mentioned, 340, 343; and governing of England, 351–352; sets penalty for rape, 440
William II (Rufus), king of England, 310
William III (Prince William of Orange), king of England, 570, 582, 583
William of Newburgh, 295
William of Sens, 373
William the Pious, duke of Aquitaine, 304
William the Silent (first Prince William of Orange), 525, 527, 528

Willibrord, 258
Winter Palace (Vienna), 610
Witan, 285
Witches, 20, 401–402, 537
Wittenberg, University of, 473, 474–475, 538
Wolsey, Thomas, 469, 489–491
Women: Paleolithic, 5–6, under Hammurabi's Code, 22–23; Hebrew, 47–49; in Greek polis, 75; in Athens, 88, 89–99, 100; Hellenistic, 131–133; Roman, 159–161, 165, 194; as nuns, 236; Muslim, 245–246; in feudal society, 256; physicians in Middle Ages, 274; and Viking, Magyar raids, 277; in medieval Europe, 292, 324, 327, 331–333, 335–336, 338–339; in 14th century, 413, 414; in Renaissance, 439–440; Luther's views on, 479–480; accused of witchcraft, 536, 537; in 16th, 17th centuries, 537–541
Wool industry: English, 298–300; after Hundred Years' War, 403; 14th-century Italian, 423, 424; and influence on Elizabeth I, 528
Workers, *see* Peasantry
Works and Days (Hesiod), 80–81
Worms, conferences of, 309, 310
Worms, Diet of, 476, 481, 484
Writ, 352
Writers, *see* Literature
Writing: Neolithic roots of, 7; in Mesopotamia, 16–17; Egyptian, used by Kush, 41
Würzburg palace, 618
Wycliff, John, 409
Wynfrith, *see* St. Boniface

Xenophon, 11, 56
Xerxes, 61, 62 (illus.), 88, 92, 110

Yahweh, 43, 45–46, 185, 186
Year of the Four Emperors (Rome), 188
York, House of, 457

Zama, 157
Zarathustra, 62
Zealots, 185
Zeeland, 584
Zeno, 131, 135
Zeus, 74
Ziggurat, 13
Zoroastrianism, 62
Zosima, 611
Zwinger, palace, 618
Zwingli, Ulrich, 479